T0189214

Lecture Notes in Computer Science   **14758**

Founding Editors

Gerhard Goos
Juris Hartmanis

Editorial Board Members

Elisa Bertino, *Purdue University, West Lafayette, IN, USA*
Wen Gao, *Peking University, Beijing, China*
Bernhard Steffen ⓘ, *TU Dortmund University, Dortmund, Germany*
Moti Yung ⓘ, *Columbia University, New York, NY, USA*

The series Lecture Notes in Computer Science (LNCS), including its subseries Lecture Notes in Artificial Intelligence (LNAI) and Lecture Notes in Bioinformatics (LNBI), has established itself as a medium for the publication of new developments in computer science and information technology research, teaching, and education.

LNCS enjoys close cooperation with the computer science R & D community, the series counts many renowned academics among its volume editors and paper authors, and collaborates with prestigious societies. Its mission is to serve this international community by providing an invaluable service, mainly focused on the publication of conference and workshop proceedings and postproceedings. LNCS commenced publication in 1973.

Jian Ma
Editor

Research in Computational Molecular Biology

28th Annual International Conference, RECOMB 2024
Cambridge, MA, USA, April 29 – May 2, 2024
Proceedings

 Springer

Editor
Jian Ma (ID)
Carnegie Mellon University
Pittsburgh, PA, USA

ISSN 0302-9743   ISSN 1611-3349 (electronic)
Lecture Notes in Computer Science
ISBN 978-1-0716-3988-7   ISBN 978-1-0716-3989-4 (eBook)
https://doi.org/10.1007/978-1-0716-3989-4

Preface

This volume includes 18 full papers and 39 short papers, totaling 57 proceedings papers presented at the 28th International Conference on Research in Computational Molecular Biology (RECOMB 2024). The conference was organized by the MIT Computer Science & Artificial Intelligence Laboratory (CSAIL), MIT Mathematics Department, and Tufts University and held in Cambridge, MA, USA, from April 29 to May 2, 2024. These 57 proceedings papers were selected through a rigorous peer-review process from 352 full submissions. Each submission was reviewed by at least three members of the Program Committee (PC) or their designated sub-reviewers. Following the initial review process, all submissions were discussed by their reviewers and the Program Chair through the EasyChair Conference Management System, with final decisions made to ensure both high quality and a broad coverage of topics in computational biology.

RECOMB 2024 allowed authors the option to publish full papers in the proceedings or to publish short four-page versions in the proceedings while pursuing publication of the journal versions elsewhere. Authors of a subset of accepted papers were invited to submit revised manuscripts for consideration in two partner journals, Genome Research and Cell Systems. All papers in the proceedings were invited for submission to the RECOMB 2024 special issue in the Journal of Computational Biology. The conference also had highlight talks of papers published in journals within 16 months prior to the conference, from which five of 62 submissions were selected for oral presentation at RECOMB.

RECOMB 2024 featured five invited keynote talks given by distinguished scientists:

- James J. Collins (Massachusetts Institute of Technology, USA)
- Shafi Goldwasser (Simons Institute, UC Berkeley, USA & Massachusetts Institute of Technology, USA)
- Robert S. Langer (Massachusetts Institute of Technology, USA)
- Xihong Lin (Harvard University, USA)
- Steven Salzberg (Johns Hopkins University, USA)

In addition, five RECOMB satellite conferences held in parallel directly preceded the main RECOMB meeting, including:

- RECOMB-Seq 2024: The 14th RECOMB Satellite Conference on Biological Sequence Analysis, co-chaired by Mingfu Shao (Pennsylvania State University, USA) and Ritambhara Singh (Brown University, USA).
- RECOMB-CCB 2024: The 14th RECOMB Satellite Conference on Computational Cancer Biology, co-chaired by Mohammed El-Kebir (University of Illinois at Urbana-Champaign, USA) and Kamila Naxerova (Harvard Medical School, USA).
- RECOMB-CG 2024: The 21st RECOMB Satellite Conference on Comparative Genomics, co-chaired by Maribel Hernández Rosales (Center for Research and Advanced Studies, Mexico) and Celine Scornavacca (University of Montpellier, France).

- RECOMB-Genetics 2024: The 12th RECOMB Satellite Conference on Computational Methods in Genetics, chaired by Bogdan Pasaniuc (University of California, Los Angeles, USA).
- RECOMB-PRIEQ 2024: The 1st RECOMB Satellite Conference on Biomedical Data Privacy and Equity, co-chaired by Ercüment Çiçek (Bilkent University, Turkey), Gamze Gürsoy (Columbia University, USA), and Mona Singh (Princeton University, USA).

The conference's organization was made possible by the dedication of many colleagues, who contributed their time, effort, and expertise. Special thanks to the Organizing Committee, particularly co-chairs Bonnie Berger (Massachusetts Institute of Technology, USA) and Lenore Cowen (Tufts University, USA), and member Ezgi Ebren (Skygen Bioinformatics Solutions, Turkey) for her exceptional support in making RECOMB happen. Appreciation is also extended to: Industry chair Iman Hajirasouliha (Weill Cornell Medicine, USA); Travel Fellowship co-chairs, Gürkan Bebek (Case Western Reserve University, USA) and Pawel Przytycki (Boston University, USA); Poster chair, Joshua Welch (University of Michigan, USA); Highlights chair, Michal Linial (Hebrew University of Jerusalem, Israel); along with all those who helped ensure a high-quality program. I am grateful to Haixu Tang (Indiana University Bloomington, USA) and Can Alkan (Bilkent University, Turkey) for sharing their experience from RECOMB 2023, and to Jose (Pepe) Abola for all his support at MIT. My thanks also goes to the RECOMB Steering Committee for their wisdom and advice.

I extend my deep gratitude to all Program Committee members and sub-reviewers for dedicating time from their busy schedules to meticulously review and discuss submissions within a tight timeframe. Additionally, I thank the authors of the proceedings papers, the highlights, and the posters for their valuable contributions to the meeting and for their participation at the conference.

Much gratitude is expressed to our conference sponsors, including BioTuring, Akamai Technologies, The Black Women in Computational Biology Network, 10X Genomics, Vevo Therapeutics, and the sponsors of our student travel awards: the US National Science Foundation (NSF) and the International Society for Computational Biology (ISCB).

RECOMB 2024 maintains the tradition of emphasizing the importance of computational methodological contributions. It values both theoretical and foundational algorithm contributions and more applied directions that engage with new technologies and intriguing biological questions. The significant number of submissions highlights the field's enthusiasm. Given the rapid advancements in computational techniques and high-throughput data acquisition in biomedical research, it is an exhilarating time for RECOMB. As the Program Chair for RECOMB 2024, I am honored to contribute to the RECOMB community.

April 2024   Jian Ma

Organization

Organizing Committee Co-chairs

Bonnie Berger   Massachusetts Institute of Technology, USA
Lenore Cowen   Tufts University, USA

Program Chair

Jian Ma   Carnegie Mellon University, USA

Steering Committee

Vineet Bafna   University of California, San Diego, USA
Bonnie Berger (Chair)   Massachusetts Institute of Technology, USA
Eleazar Eskin   University of California, Los Angeles, USA
Teresa Przytycka   National Institutes of Health, USA
Cenk Sahinalp   National Institutes of Health, USA
Roded Sharan   Tel Aviv University, Israel
Martin Vingron   Max Planck Institute for Molecular Genetics, Germany

Program Committee

Can Alkan   Bilkent University, Turkey
Srinivas Aluru   Georgia Institute of Technology, USA
Kin-Fai Au   University of Michigan, USA
Ferhat Ay   La Jolla Institute for Immunology, USA
Vineet Bafna   University of California, San Diego, USA
Serafim Batzoglou   Seer Inc., USA
Bonnie Berger   Massachusetts Institute of Technology, USA
Mathieu Blanchette   McGill University, Canada
Karsten Borgwardt   Max Planck Institute of Biochemistry, Germany
Christina Boucher   University of Florida, USA
Phil Bradley   Fred Hutchinson Cancer Center, USA
Maria Brbic   École Polytechnique Fédérale de Lausanne (EPFL), Switzerland
Sebastian Böcker   Friedrich Schiller University Jena, Germany
Mark Chaisson   University of Southern California, USA

Cedric Chauve	Simon Fraser University, Canada
Ken Chen	MD Anderson Cancer Center, USA
Rayan Chikhi	Institut Pasteur & CNRS, France
Maria Chikina	University of Pittsburgh, USA
Hyunghoon Cho	Yale University, USA
Ercument Cicek	Bilkent University, Turkey
Lenore Cowen	Tufts University, USA
Bianca Dumitrascu	Columbia University, USA
Mohammed El-Kebir	University of Illinois at Urbana-Champaign, USA
Nadia El-Mabrouk	University of Montreal, Canada
Anthony Gitter	University of Wisconsin-Madison, USA
Gamze Gursoy	Columbia University, USA
Faraz Hach	University of British Columbia, Canada
Iman Hajirasouliha	Weill Cornell Medicine, USA
Bjarni Halldorsson	Reykjavik University, Iceland
Stephanie Hicks	Johns Hopkins University, USA
Brian Hie	Stanford University, USA
Farhad Hormozdiari	Google Health, USA
Fereydoun Hormozdiari	University of California, Davis, USA
Chirag Jain	Indian Institute of Science, India
Sunduz Keles	University of Wisconsin-Madison, USA
Daisuke Kihara	Purdue University, USA
Carl Kingsford	Carnegie Mellon University, USA
Gunnar Klau	Heinrich Heine University Düsseldorf, Germany
Mikhail Kolmogorov	National Cancer Institute, USA
Peter Koo	Cold Spring Harbor Laboratory, USA
David Koslicki	Pennsylvania State University, USA
Mehmet Koyutürk	Case Western Reserve University, USA
Smita Krishnaswamy	Yale University, USA
Anshul Kundaje	Stanford University, USA
Benjamin Langmead	Johns Hopkins University, USA
Christina Leslie	Memorial Sloan-Kettering Cancer Center, USA
Heng Li	Dana-Farber Cancer Institute & Harvard Medical School, USA
Wei Vivian Li	University of California, Riverside, USA
Jingyi Jessica Li	University of California, Los Angeles, USA
Mohammad Lotfollahi	Wellcome Sanger Institute, UK
Yunan Luo	Georgia Institute of Technology, USA
Jianzhu Ma	Tsinghua University, China
Ahmed Mahfouz	Leiden University Medical Center, Netherlands
Salem Malikic	National Institutes of Health, USA
Paul Medvedev	Pennsylvania State University, USA

Siavash Mirarab	University of California, San Diego, USA
Erin Molloy	University of Maryland, USA
Sara Mostafavi	University of Washington, USA
Veli Mäkinen	University of Helsinki, Finland
Luay Nakhleh	Rice University, USA
William Stafford Noble	University of Washington, USA
Ibrahim Numanagic	University of Victoria, Canada
Yaron Orenstein	Bar-Ilan University, Israel
Julia Palacios	Stanford University, USA
Robert Patro	University of Maryland, USA
Yann Ponty	CNRS & Ecole Polytechnique, France
Shyam Prabhakar	Genome Institute of Singapore, Singapore
Yuri Pritykin	Princeton University, USA
Teresa Przytycka	National Institutes of Health, USA
Pawel Przytycki	Boston University, USA
Ben Raphael	Princeton University, USA
Knut Reinert	Freie Universität Berlin, Germany
Sushmita Roy	University of Wisconsin-Madison, USA
Cenk Sahinalp	National Institutes of Health, USA
Kristoffer Sahlin	Stockholm University, Sweden
Sriram Sankararaman	University of California, Los Angeles, USA
Michael Schatz	Johns Hopkins University, USA
Alexander Schoenhuth	Bielefeld University, Germany
Russell Schwartz	Carnegie Mellon University, USA
Manu Setty	Fred Hutchinson Cancer Center, USA
Ron Shamir	Tel Aviv University, Israel
Mingfu Shao	Pennsylvania State University, USA
Roded Sharan	Tel Aviv University, Israel
Mona Singh	Princeton University, USA
Rohit Singh	Duke University, USA
Ritambhara Singh	Brown University, USA
Sagi Snir	University of Haifa, Israel
Martin Steinegger	Seoul National University, Korea
Jens Stoye	Bielefeld University, Germany
Fengzhu Sun	University of Southern California, USA
Jonathan Terhorst	University of Michigan, USA
Alexandru Tomescu	University of Helsinki, Finland
Tamir Tuller	Tel Aviv University, Israel
David van Dijk	Yale University, USA
David Van Valen	California Institute of Technology, USA
Fabio Vandin	University of Padova, Italy

Martin Vingron	Max Planck Institute for Molecular Genetics, Germany
Jerome Waldispuhl	McGill University, Canada
Sheng Wang	University of Washington, USA
Xiaowo Wang	Tsinghua University, China
Yijie Wang	Indiana University Bloomington, USA
Bo Wang	University of Toronto, Canada
Tandy Warnow	University of Illinois at Urbana-Champaign, USA
Joshua Welch	University of Michigan, USA
Yufeng Wu	University of Connecticut, USA
Min Xu	Carnegie Mellon University, USA
Vicky Yao	Rice University, USA
Yuzhen Ye	Indiana University Bloomington, USA
Kevin Yip	Sanford Burnham Prebys, USA
Yun William Yu	Carnegie Mellon University, USA
Jianyang Zeng	Westlake University, China
Louxin Zhang	National University of Singapore, Singapore
Martin Zhang	Carnegie Mellon University, USA
Nancy R. Zhang	University of Pennsylvania, USA
Ruochi Zhang	Broad Institute of MIT and Harvard, USA
Sai Zhang	University of Florida, USA
Shaojie Zhang	University of Central Florida, USA
Xiuwei Zhang	Georgia Institute of Technology, USA
Jie Zheng	ShanghaiTech University, China
Degui Zhi	UT Health Science Center at Houston, USA
Jian Zhou	UT Southwestern Medical Center, USA

Additional Reviewers

Evelin Aasna	Dmitry Antipov
Mohamed Abuelanin	Erick Armingol
Piyush Agarwal	Isabel Armour-Garb
Omar Ahmed	Hossein Asghari
Shahul Alam	Mahdi Asmae
Michael Altenbuchinger	Thomas Atkins
Umut Berkay Altintas	Pavel Avdeyev
Javed Aman	Mahmud Sami Aydın
Bayarbaatar Amgalan	Tamjeed Azad
Ulzee An	Mihir Bafna
Francesco Andreace	Audrey Baguette
Virgile Andreani	Tavor Baharav
Sandro Andreotti	Ali Balapour

Ali Tugrul Balci
Mukul S. Bansal
Sina Barazandeh
Brittany Baur
Gurkan Bebek
Harmon Bhasin
Sourya Bhattacharyya
Kirti Biharie
Wout Bittremieux
Jacob Blindenbach
Leonard Bohnenkämper
Cristian Boldrin
Dante Bolzan
Richard Border
Gerard Bouland
Broňa Brejová
Hardy Bright Jr
Nishat Bristy
Anton Bushuiev
Christopher J. F. Cameron
Kai Cao
Qin Cao
Abhijit Chakraborty
Adelaide Chambers
Mohammed Charrout
Dexiong Chen
Kathy Chen
Ke Chen
Nae-Chyun Chen
Qingyu Chen
Siqi Chen
Tong Chen
Yanjin Chen
Wenduo Cheng
Yuqi Cheng
Jennifer Chiang
Uthsav Chitra
Yoolim Choi
Savio Chow
Charles Christoffer
Kelly Cochran
Andrea Cracco
Alessandro Crnjar
Manuel Cáceres
Junyan Dai

Shadi Darvish Shafighi
Arun Das
Dan DeBlasio
Mattéo Delabre
Yifan Deng
Luca Denti
John Desmarais
Kapil Devkota
Kerr Ding
Meleshko Dmitrii
Natnatee Dokmai
Gabriel Dolsten
Chris Dong
Shiyi Du
Yuxuan Du
Jingqi Duan
Kseniia Dudnyk
Yoann Dufresne
Dannie Durand
Kai Dührkop
Mark Maher Makram Ebeid-Ataullah
Shane Elder
Ahmed Elhussein
Mostafa Eltager
Mahsa Faizrahnemoon
Tangqi Fang
Bin Feng
Yimiao Feng
Mohsen Ferdosi
James Fife
Connor Finkbeiner
Can Firtina
David Fischer
Michael Ford
Alireza Fotuhi Siahpirani
David Froelicher
Boyang Fu
Yilin Gao
Yuan Gao
Mathieu Gascon
Sam Gelman
Ali Ghaffaari
Parham Ghasemloo Gheidari
Daniel Gibney
Cameron Gilchrist

Madalina Giurgiu
Ameya Gokhale
Michal Golovanevsky
Purnachandra Aditya Gorla
Ilan Gronau
Yichen Gu
Jiaqi Guan
Mustafa Guler
Ruihan Guo
Revant Gupta
Ellie Haber
Mohammad Mohsen Hajari Taheri
Spencer Halberg
Peter Halmos
Yunheng Han
Ananth Hari
Arif Harmanci
Philip Hartout
Suvojit Hazra
Dongze He
Jianping He
Xuan He
Michael Heinzinger
Ralf Herwig
Mary Hirsch
Quang Minh Hoang
Jan Hoinka
Man-Hou Hong
Seungwan Hong
Kangcheng Hou
Borislav Hristov
Mengying Hu
Jiawei Huang
Kexin Huang
Yin Huang
Wolfgang Huber
Linh Huynh
Hyeyeon Hwang
Nabil Ibtehaz
Eliel Ingervo
Sheikh Muhammad Saiful Islam
Stefan Ivanovic
Shani Jacobson
Elham Jafari
Atishay Jain

Katharine Jenike
Moonseong Jeong
Anupama Jha
Kanchan Jha
Chengfeng Jiang
Xilin Jiang
Yueyu Jiang
Junru Jin
Bowen Jing
Anoushka Joglekar
Bryce Johnson
Georgios Kalantzis
Onur Karakaslar
Fatih Karaoglanoglu
Alireza Karbalayghareh
Matthew Karikomi
Ryan Kassab
Gun Kaynar
Birte Kehr
Ziynet Nesibe Kesimoglu
Jamshed Khan
Nabila Shahnaz Khan
Yasir Ali Khan
Bryce Kille
Chanwoo Kim
Hyunbin Kim
Jaebeom Kim
Junbum Kim
Mirae Sunny Kim
Vitalii Kleshchevnikov
Kassian Kobert
Can Kockan
Clemens Kohl
Tim Kosfeld
Sam Kovaka
Thomas Krannich
Fleming Kretschmer
Spencer Krieger
Tim Kucera
Yael Kupershmidt
Halil Ibrahim Kuru
Lukas Käll
Zlatko-Salko Lagumdzija
Qiliang Lai
Max Land

Christy Lee
Wei-Hao Lee
Chen Li
Dongshunyi Li
Gang Li
Han Li
Hechen Li
Hui Li
Jiaqi Li
Kelly Yichen Li
Lechuan Li
Pengyong Li
Qinyao Li
Qiuhui Li
Shuya Li
Xiang Li
Xingjian Li
Xuan Li
Yu Li
Huan Liang
Shaoheng Liang
Chris Lin
Jiacheng Lin
Jialin Liu
Ruishan Liu
Shaopeng Liu
Shengchao Liu
Shichao Liu
Xianggen Liu
Xin Liu
Xinhao Liu
Yifeng Liu
Yuda Liu
Yuelin Liu
Zequn Liu
Zhengtong Liu
Zixuan Liu
Sebastian Lobentanzer
Kaiser Loell
Yang Lu
Dillon Lue
Xiao Luo
Maksym Lupei
Cong Ma
Ying Ma

Christopher Magnano
Salil Maharjan
Uyen Mai
Lauren Mak
Aniket Mane
Qirong Mao
Weiguang Mao
Cemil Can Marandi
Lennart Martens
Guillaume Marçais
Tomas Matteson
Zachary McCaw
Daniel McNeela
Svenja Mehringer
Lucas Miranda
Milot Mirdita
Sneha Mitra
Intae Moon
Niema Moshiri
Justin Moy
Ghulam Murtaza
Harun Mustafa
Surag Nair
Anupama Nandi
Sourena Naser Moghaddasi
Ardalan Naseri
Rami Nasser
Rahul Nihalani
Kirill Nikitin
Naman Nimbale
Claudio Novella Rausell
Carlos Oliver
Baraa Orabi
Dominik Otto
Sinan Ozbay
Xinhai Pan
Aditya Parekh
Kwangmoon Park
Sukhwan Park
Tyler Park
Luca Parmigiani
Ananya Pavuluri
Daniel Paysan
Leonardo Pellegrina
Paolo Pellizzoni

Alexander Petri
Rebecca Katharina Pfeil
Tuan Pham
William Phu
Luna Pianesi
Giulio Ermanno Pibiri
Masoud Poorghaffar Aghdam
Victoria Popic
Andrey D. Prjibelski
Mattia Prosperi
Yuanyuan Qi
Wei Qiu
Yutong Qiu
Du Qixiu
Thomas Rachman
Md Mahfuzur Rahaman
Javad Rahimikollu
Elior Rahmani
Sven Rahmann
René Rahn
Félix Raimundo
Suraj Rajendran
Chandana Rajesh
Srividya Ramakrishnan
Farid Rashidi Mehrabadi
Eeshaan Rehani
Vladimir Reinharz
Andreas Rempel
Lucas Robidou
Mrinmoy Saha Roddur
Judith Rodriguez
Jiazhen Rong
Yusuf Roohani
Yanay Rosen
Sölvi Rögnvaldsson
Wouter Saelens
Daniela Salgado
Justin Sanders
Kris Sankaran
Nicolae Sapoval
Hirak Sarkar
Roman Sarrazin-Gendron
Palash Sashittal
Johannes Schlüter
Sebastian Schmidt

Sven Schrinner
Till Schulz
Tizian Schulz
Remy Schwab
Enrico Seiler
Pramesh Shakya
Gaurav Sharma
Nitesh Kumar Sharma
Titus Sharman
Jim Shaw
Chengze Shen
Siqi Shen
Yihang Shen
Yilun Sheng
Christina Shi
Qian Shi
Peter Shor
Rahul Siddharthan
Lorenzo Federico Signorini
Brynja Sigurpálsdóttir
Gagandeep Singh
Noor Pratap Singh
Aditya Sinha
Samuel Sledzieski
Whitney Sloneker
Donna Slonim
Haris Smajlović
Susie Song
Zhenqiao Song
Arda Soylev
Avi Srivastava
Arjun Srivatsa
Tina Subic
Amanda Sun
Yanni Sun
Zhigang Sun
Yasamin Tabatabaee
Yukun Tan
Bingjing Tang
Haixu Tang
Wei Tang
Ziqi Tang
Siyu Tao
Sharma V. Thankachan
Matthew The

Ivan Tolstoganov
Shushan Toneyan
Xinming Tu
David van Bruggen
Aarthi Venkat
Giorgio Venturin
Kevin Vizhalil
Ramon Viñas
Max von Kleist
Conor Walker
Fangping Wan
Austin Wang
Brendan Wang
Haochen Wang
Qingyang Wang
Rui Wang
Shike Wang
Weijian Wang
Xiao Wang
Yang Wang
Ye Wang
Ying Wang
Ziye Wang
Leah Weber
Eleanor Wedell
Yuan Wei
Zheng Wei
Shuo Wen
J. White Bear
Maciej Wiatrak
Roland Wittler
Wilfred Wong
Alexander Po-Yen Wu
Chih Wu
Chih Hao Wu
Wenxu Wu
Yue Wu
Ziqian Xie
Peng Xiong
Chenling Xu
Hanwen Xu
Junyan Xu
Guan'Ao Yan
Qianming Yan
Junwei Yang
Muyu Yang

Rui Yang
Yang Yang
Hua-Ting Yao
Grace Yeo
Jingi Yeo
Mehmet Alper Yilmaz
Melih Yilmaz
Jiale Yu
Tingyang Yu
Xin Yuan
Serhan Yılmaz
Tasfia Zahin
Xiaofei Zang
Zahra Zare Jousheghani
Zhiqian Zhai
Chao Zhang
Haotian Zhang
Haowen Zhang
Jiaqi Zhang
Jing Zhang
Julie Zhang
Qimin Zhang
Ran Zhang
Shilu Zhang
Xinyi Zhang
Yanlin Zhang
Yiming Zhang
Yuqi Zhang
Zhaojun Zhang
Zhenghao Zhang
Zijun Zhang
Ziqi Zhang
Ziting Zhang
Hongyu Zheng
Ye Zheng
Cuncong Zhong
Hao Zhou
Jingtian Zhou
Qinghui Zhou
Tianming Zhou
Yuchen Zhou
Kaiyuan Zhu
Shanfeng Zhu
Yuehua Zhu
Wenxuan Zuo

Contents

Fast Approximate IsoRank for Scalable Global Alignment of Biological Networks

Kapil Devkota[1,2] , Anselm Blumer[2] , Xiaozhe Hu[3] ,
and Lenore Cowen[2(✉)]

[1] Duke University, Durham, NC, USA
kapil.devkota@duke.edu
[2] Department of Computer Science, Tufts University, Medford, MA, USA
cowen@cs.tufts.edu
[3] Department of Mathematiccs, Tufts University, Medford, MA, USA

Abstract. The pioneering and still popular IsoRank method of Singh, Xu, and Berger for global alignment of two protein-protein interaction networks across species was introduced at Recomb in 2007, and was awarded the Recomb test of time award in 2019. However, with the availability of increasing amounts of experimental data the number of edges in the networks to align has grown considerably, making running IsoRank unfeasible on these networks without access to substantial computational resources. In this paper, we develop a new IsoRank approximation that exploits the mathematical properties of IsoRank's linear system to solve the problem in quadratic time with respect to the maximum size of the two PPI networks. We further propose a refinement to this initial approximation so that the updated result is even closer to the original IsoRank formulation while remaining computationally inexpensive. In experiments on synthetic and real PPI networks with various proposed metrics to measure alignment quality, we find the results of our approximate IsoRank are nearly as accurate as the original IsoRank. In fact, for functional enrichment-based measures of global network alignment quality we find our approximation performs better than exact IsoRank, doubtless because it is more robust to the noise of missing or incorrect edges. It also performs competitively against two more recent global network alignment algorithms.

Keywords: Network Alignment · Biological Networks · IsoRank

1 Introduction

The first spectral method designed by computational biologists for the *global network alignment problem* (the problem of aligning protein-protein interaction networks across species), was the IsoRank method of Singh, Xu and Berger [16]. This method for global biological network alignment is still used today. With access to 15 more years of experimental data since IsoRank was first suggested,

© The Author(s), under exclusive license to Springer Nature Switzerland AG 2024
J. Ma (Ed.): RECOMB 2024, LNCS 14758, pp. 1–16, 2024.
https://doi.org/10.1007/978-1-0716-3989-4_1

the size of the networks available to match has grown considerably, making running IsoRank on the desktop unfeasible on these networks, and instead requiring access to high-performance computing resources. In this paper, we develop a new IsoRank approximation that exploits the eigenproperties of IsoRank's linear system to solve the problem in quadratic time with respect to the maximum size of the two PPI networks. This is in contrast to the original IsoRank, whose performance in theory had no polynomial bound in the general case, and whose performance in practice scaled cubically. Approximate IsoRank is fast enough to be run on a desktop computer, provided there is sufficient RAM.

We further propose a computational refinement to this initial approximation so that the updated result is even closer to the original IsoRank formulation while still remaining computationally affordable.

We demonstrate the quality of our approximation in two different settings. First, in synthetic experiments, we create random graphs using the Erdős-Rényi [7] and Barabási-Albert models [1], and ask IsoRank to recover the graph isomorphism between our graphs and a random node permutation.

In this setting, we add various levels of noise to the node similarities, E, (which scale from 0 to 1, where 1 indicates random node permutation). We measure the quality of our IsoRank approximation for three ranges of the noise level: a low-error regime where IsoRank itself will recover the matching of the true isomorphism, an intermediate E where IsoRank only gets 80%–90% of the true matching, and a noisy E where IsoRank gets only 70%–75% of the true matching. In each case, we show how close approximate IsoRank comes, as well as demonstrating the considerable savings in CPU time. Next, we return to the biological domain, and consider real-world networks from 5 species: mouse (*Mus musculus*), rat (*Rattus norvegicus*), fly (*Drosophila melanogaster*), baker's yeast (*Sacharomyces cerevisiae*) and human (*Homo sapiens*). In this case, the more distant species can be seen as having a noisier E value, since the sequence similarity diverges over evolutionary time (i.e. it is much easier to align mouse and rat than human and fly). However, in addition to increasing amounts of noise in the node similarity E (measured by BLAST [2]) in the real networks, we don't have the same number of nodes in each PPI network because of gene duplication and loss. There will also be increasing network rewiring as evolutionary distance increases, resulting in inserted and deleted edges in each PPI network. Finally, the networks differ because we have only a noisy and incomplete sample of the true PPI networks. Because we of course do not have a ground truth alignment in this setting as we do for the synthetic data, we instead adopt the most commonly-reported measures of alignment quality, namely the purely graph theoretic EC, LCCS measures [8], as well as the AFS measure [8] which measures how often aligned proteins are known to be involved in similar biological functions across the two species (see Sect. 3.2 below for definitions). While these are the quality measures we adopt here, we note that alternative ways of measuring quality of biological network alignment appear in [6,12,13,19].

We additionally compare exact and approximate IsoRank to Hubalign [8] and FINAL [20], where these alternative alignment methods were chosen because 1) they are both in the set of recent well-performing competing network alignment algorithms, and 2) from this set, they are the ones we found that can also be successfully run on a desktop computer (with sufficient memory). While Approximate IsoRank is consistently slightly worse than exact IsoRank on the graph theoretic measures, when compared to Hubalign and FINAL, Approximate IsoRank is often better, and when not, usually a close second. Most interestingly, across the board, we find that Approximate IsoRank performs better than exact IsoRank according to the AFS measure of functional enrichment, and has better AFS in the majority of experiments than the competing alignment methods.

2 Algorithm

2.1 IsoRank

Let us first recall the IsoRank algorithm [16] and some basic techniques from linear algebra [18]. The key observation is that IsoRank looks at the *tensor product* of two graphs, which is essential for developing our approximation algorithm. The relation to tensor product was also previously observed by Zhang et al. [10,20,21].

Consider two simply connected, undirected, and possibly weighted graphs $\mathcal{G}_1 = (\mathcal{V}_1, \mathcal{E}_1)$ and $\mathcal{G}_2 = (\mathcal{V}_2, \mathcal{E}_2)$. Their adjacency matrices are A_1 and A_2, respectively, and weighted degree matrices are $D_1 := \mathrm{diag}(\boldsymbol{d}_1)$, $\boldsymbol{d}_1 := A_1 \mathbf{1}_{|\mathcal{V}_1|}$, and $D_2 := \mathrm{diag}(\boldsymbol{d}_2)$, $\boldsymbol{d}_2 := A_2 \mathbf{1}_{|\mathcal{V}_2|}$, respectively. Thus, the corresponding transition matrices are

$$P_1 = A_1 D_1^{-1} \in \mathbb{R}^{|\mathcal{V}_1| \times |\mathcal{V}_1|} \quad \text{and} \quad P_2 = A_2 D_2^{-1} \in \mathbb{R}^{|\mathcal{V}_2| \times |\mathcal{V}_2|},$$

which are both column stochastic, i.e., $\mathbf{1}_{|\mathcal{V}_1|}^T P_1 = \mathbf{1}_{|\mathcal{V}_1|}^T$ and $\mathbf{1}_{|\mathcal{V}_2|}^T P_2 = \mathbf{1}_{|\mathcal{V}_2|}^T$. P_1 and P_2 can be viewed as transition matrices defining the random walk in the PageRank algorithm that underlies the IsoRank algorithm.

Next we consider the tensor product of the two graphs, which is a graph with $|\mathcal{V}_1||\mathcal{V}_2|$ nodes and its adjacency matrix is defined as

$$A = A_1 \otimes A_2 \in \mathbb{R}^{|\mathcal{V}_1||\mathcal{V}_2| \times |\mathcal{V}_1||\mathcal{V}_2|},$$

where $\otimes$ denotes the Kronecker product [14]. Similarly, the transition matrix of the tensor product graph is

$$\begin{aligned} P = P_1 \otimes P_2 &= (A_1 D_1^{-1}) \otimes (A_2 D_2^{-1}) \\ &= (A_1 \otimes A_2)(D_1^{-1} \otimes D_2^{-1}) = (A_1 \otimes A_2)(D_1 \otimes D_2)^{-1} \\ &= AD^{-1} \in \mathbb{R}^{|\mathcal{V}_1||\mathcal{V}_2| \times |\mathcal{V}_1||\mathcal{V}_2|}. \end{aligned}$$

where $D = D_1 \otimes D_2 \in \mathbb{R}^{|\mathcal{V}_1||\mathcal{V}_2| \times |\mathcal{V}_1||\mathcal{V}_2|}$ is the degree matrix of the tensor product graph. This is because

$$\begin{aligned} \boldsymbol{d} := A\mathbf{1} &= (A_1 \otimes A_2)\mathbf{1}_{|\mathcal{V}_1||\mathcal{V}_2|} \\ &= (A_1 \otimes A_2)(\mathbf{1}_{|\mathcal{V}_1|} \otimes \mathbf{1}_{|\mathcal{V}_2|}) = (A_1 \mathbf{1}_{|\mathcal{V}_1|}) \otimes (A_2 \mathbf{1}_{|\mathcal{V}_2|}) \\ &= \boldsymbol{d}_1 \otimes \boldsymbol{d}_2, \end{aligned}$$

and

$$D := \operatorname{diag}(\boldsymbol{d}) = \operatorname{diag}(\boldsymbol{d}_1 \otimes \boldsymbol{d}_2) = \operatorname{diag}(\boldsymbol{d}_1) \otimes \operatorname{diag}(\boldsymbol{d}_2)$$
$$= D_1 \otimes D_2.$$

As suggested in [16], the basic version of IsoRank tries to find $\boldsymbol{R} \in \mathbb{R}^{|\mathcal{V}_1||\mathcal{V}_2|}$, $\|\boldsymbol{R}\|_1 = 1$, such that

$$\boldsymbol{R} = P\boldsymbol{R}. \tag{1}$$

This is done by the power method, which is the following iterative procedure, for $k = 0, 1, 2, \cdots$

$$\overline{\boldsymbol{R}}^{k+1} = P\boldsymbol{R}^k, \quad \boldsymbol{R}^{k+1} = \frac{\overline{\boldsymbol{R}}^{k+1}}{\|\overline{\boldsymbol{R}}^{k+1}\|_1}.$$

The initial value $\boldsymbol{R}^0$ should be chosen based on data.

A modified version of IsoRank tries to find $\boldsymbol{R}$, $\|\boldsymbol{R}\|_1 = 1$, such that, for $0 \le \alpha \le 1$

$$\boldsymbol{R} = (1 - \alpha)P\boldsymbol{R} + \alpha\boldsymbol{E}, \tag{2}$$

where $\boldsymbol{E} \in \mathbb{R}^{|\mathcal{V}_1||\mathcal{V}_2|}$, $\|\boldsymbol{E}\|_1 = 1$ which typically contains domain specific information to improve the graph alignment result. For example, in the original IsoRank paper [16], besides the two PPI networks of the species, additional sequence similarity data, which is presented by $E \in \mathbb{R}^{|\mathcal{V}_1| \times |\mathcal{V}_2|}$, is required in order to perform the graph matching. Here E_{ij} denotes how similar the amino acid sequence of the ith protein of $\mathcal{G}_1$ is to that of the jth protein of $\mathcal{G}_2$. This sequence similarity information is obtained using the standard BLAST sequence alignment [2]. Since we use the tensor product notation in our paper, we have transformed E to $\operatorname{vec}(E) \in \mathbb{R}^{|\mathcal{V}_1||\mathcal{V}_2|}$, where $\operatorname{vec}(\cdot)$ converts a matrix to a vector.

As suggested in [16], (2) is again solved iteratively as follows, for $k = 0, 1, 2, \cdots$

$$\overline{\boldsymbol{R}}^{k+1} = (1 - \alpha)P\boldsymbol{R}^k + \alpha\boldsymbol{E}, \quad \boldsymbol{R}^{k+1} = \frac{\overline{\boldsymbol{R}}^{k+1}}{\|\overline{\boldsymbol{R}}^{k+1}\|_1}. \tag{3}$$

Other approximation methods can also be used to solve (2), e.g., [10].

Remark 1. Note that, in both iterative procedures, the normalization step is not needed if we have $\boldsymbol{R}^0 \ge 0$, $\|\boldsymbol{R}^0\|_1 = 1$, $\boldsymbol{E} \ge 0$, and $\|\boldsymbol{E}\|_1 = 1$. This is because

$$\begin{aligned}
\|\overline{\boldsymbol{R}}^{k+1}\|_1 &= \mathbf{1}_{|\mathcal{V}_1||\mathcal{V}_2|}^T \overline{\boldsymbol{R}}^{k+1} = \mathbf{1}_{|\mathcal{V}_1||\mathcal{V}_2|}^T \left((1 - \alpha)P\boldsymbol{R}^k + \alpha\boldsymbol{E} \right) \\
&= (1 - \alpha)\mathbf{1}_{|\mathcal{V}_1||\mathcal{V}_2|}^T P\boldsymbol{R}^k + \alpha\mathbf{1}_{|\mathcal{V}_1||\mathcal{V}_2|}^T \boldsymbol{E} \\
&= (1 - \alpha)\mathbf{1}_{|\mathcal{V}_1||\mathcal{V}_2|}^T \boldsymbol{R}^k + \alpha\mathbf{1}_{|\mathcal{V}_1||\mathcal{V}_2|}^T \boldsymbol{E} \\
&= (1 - \alpha)\|\boldsymbol{R}^k\|_1 + \alpha\|\boldsymbol{E}\|_1 = 1.
\end{aligned}$$

2.2 Approximate IsoRank

Let us first consider the basic version of IsoRank (1) and the key here is to notice that IsoRank is actually working on a tensor product graph of the original two graphs. Therefore, based on the Perron-Frobenius theorem [17], the basic IsoRank (1) tries to find the right eigenvector of the transition matrix P that corresponds to the unique eigenvalue 1. Therefore, $\boldsymbol{R}$ is nothing but the steady state distribution (SSD) $\boldsymbol{\pi}$ of the tensor product graph, which can be computed directly without using the power method at all since IsoRank works on a tensor product graph. Using the properties of the transition matrix P of a simply connected, undirected, and possibly weighted graph, the SSD can be obtained without any iterative procedure as follows,

$$\boldsymbol{\pi} := \frac{\boldsymbol{d}}{d_{\text{total}}}, \tag{4}$$

where $\boldsymbol{d} = D\mathbf{1}_{|\mathcal{V}_1||\mathcal{V}_2|}$ and $d_{\text{total}} = \boldsymbol{d}^T \mathbf{1}_{|\mathcal{V}_1||\mathcal{V}_2|}$ (which is the weighted total degree). This means, for the basic version IsoRank (1), we have $\boldsymbol{R} := \boldsymbol{\pi}$ directly and there is no need of the power method or any iterative procedure which involves matrix vector multiplications.

Now let us consider the modified version of IsoRank (2), which is preferred in practice due to the incorporation of the extra information. Note that when $\alpha = 0$, (2) reduces to (1) and, therefore, $\boldsymbol{R} = \boldsymbol{\pi}$. On the other hand, when $\alpha = 1$, we have $\boldsymbol{R} = \boldsymbol{E}$. Thus, for $0 \le \alpha \le 1$, we can use the following convex combination to get an approximation

$$\boldsymbol{R}^0 = (1 - \alpha)\boldsymbol{\pi} + \alpha\boldsymbol{E}. \tag{5}$$

Again, there is no iterative procedure and no matrix-vector multiplications at all. The reason we call this approximation $\boldsymbol{R}^0$ is that it can be used either directly, or as the initial guess of an iterative procedure for solving (2).

According to (2) and (5), we have

$$\begin{aligned}
\boldsymbol{R} - \boldsymbol{R}^0 &= (1 - \alpha)P\boldsymbol{R} + \alpha\boldsymbol{E} - (1 - \alpha)\boldsymbol{\pi} - \alpha\boldsymbol{E} \\
&= (1 - \alpha)(P\boldsymbol{R} - \boldsymbol{\pi}) = (1 - \alpha)(P\boldsymbol{R} - P\boldsymbol{\pi}) \\
&= (1 - \alpha)P(\boldsymbol{R} - \boldsymbol{\pi}).
\end{aligned}$$

Let us introduce $\widetilde{\boldsymbol{R}} = D^{-\frac{1}{2}}\boldsymbol{R}$, $\widetilde{\boldsymbol{\pi}} = D^{-\frac{1}{2}}\boldsymbol{\pi}$, $\widetilde{\boldsymbol{E}} = D^{-\frac{1}{2}}\boldsymbol{E}$, and $\widetilde{A} = D^{-\frac{1}{2}}AD^{-\frac{1}{2}}$. Then we have

$$\begin{aligned}
\widetilde{\boldsymbol{R}} - \widetilde{\boldsymbol{R}}^0 &= D^{-\frac{1}{2}}\left(\boldsymbol{R} - \boldsymbol{R}^0\right) \\
&= (1 - \alpha)D^{-\frac{1}{2}}P(\boldsymbol{R} - \boldsymbol{\pi}) \\
&= (1 - \alpha)\widetilde{A}(\widetilde{\boldsymbol{R}} - \widetilde{\boldsymbol{\pi}}).
\end{aligned}$$

On the other hand, multiplying $D^{-\frac{1}{2}}$ on the left of both sides of (2), we obtain

$$\widetilde{\boldsymbol{R}} = (1 - \alpha)\widetilde{A}\widetilde{\boldsymbol{R}} + \alpha\widetilde{\boldsymbol{E}}.$$

This implies

$$\widetilde{R} = \alpha \left[I - (1-\alpha)\widetilde{A} \right]^{-1} \widetilde{E} \tag{6}$$

Since $\widetilde{A}$ is symmetric and its largest eigenvalue is 1, its eigenvalues are $1 = \lambda_1 > \lambda_2 \geq \lambda_3 \geq \cdots \geq \lambda_n$, $n = |\mathcal{V}_1||\mathcal{V}_2|$. The corresponding eigenvectors are denoted by v_i, $i = 1, \cdots, n$, with $\|v_i\| = 1$ and $v_i^T v_j = 0$, $i \neq j$. It is easy to check that $v_1 = \sqrt{d_{\text{total}}}\, \widetilde{\pi}$. Since $\widetilde{A}$ is symmetric, v_i, $i = 1, \cdots, n$, form an orthonormal basis and, thus $\widetilde{E} = \sum_{i=1}^n \mu_i v_i$ with $\mu_i = v_i^T \widetilde{E}$. Note that,

$$\mu_1 = v_1^T \widetilde{E} = \sqrt{d_{\text{total}}} \left[D^{-\frac{1}{2}} \frac{D\mathbf{1}_n}{d_{\text{total}}} \right]^T D^{-\frac{1}{2}} E = \frac{1}{\sqrt{d_{\text{total}}}}.$$

Now we are ready to present the following theorem which measures the approximation error of R^0.

Theorem 1. *Let R^0 be defined as (5), for $0 < \alpha \leq 1$, we have*

$$\|R - R^0\|_{D^{-1}}^2 \leq \alpha^2 \left(1 - \frac{1}{d_{\text{total}}} \right) \left[\frac{(1-\alpha)\lambda_2}{1 - (1-\alpha)\lambda_2} \right]^2.$$

where $\|x\|_{D^{-1}}^2 := \sqrt{x^T D^{-1} x}$.

Proof. Based on (6), for $0 < \alpha \leq 1$,

$$\widetilde{R} = \alpha \left[I - (1-\alpha)\widetilde{A} \right]^{-1} \left[\sum_{i=1}^n \mu_i v_i \right]$$

$$= \sum_{i=1}^n \frac{\alpha \mu_i}{1 - (1-\alpha)\lambda_i} v_i$$

$$= \mu_1 v_1 + \sum_{i=2}^n \frac{\alpha \mu_i}{1 - (1-\alpha)\lambda_i} v_i$$

$$= \widetilde{\pi} + \sum_{i=2}^n \frac{\alpha \mu_i}{1 - (1-\alpha)\lambda_i} v_i.$$

This means,

$$\widetilde{R} - \widetilde{R}^0 = (1-\alpha)\widetilde{A}(\widetilde{R} - \widetilde{\pi})$$

$$= (1-\alpha)\widetilde{A} \left[\sum_{i=2}^n \frac{\alpha \mu_i}{1 - (1-\alpha)\lambda_i} v_i \right]$$

$$= \alpha \sum_{i=2}^n \frac{(1-\alpha)\lambda_i}{1 - (1-\alpha)\lambda_i} \mu_i v_i.$$

Therefore,

$$\|\boldsymbol{R} - \boldsymbol{R}^0\|_{D^{-1}}^2 = \|\widetilde{\boldsymbol{R}} - \widetilde{\boldsymbol{R}}^0\|^2$$

$$= \alpha^2 \sum_{i=2}^{n} \left[\frac{(1-\alpha)\lambda_i}{1-(1-\alpha)\lambda_i} \right]^2 \mu_i^2$$

$$\leq \alpha^2 \left[\frac{(1-\alpha)\lambda_2}{1-(1-\alpha)\lambda_2} \right]^2 \sum_{i=2}^{n} \mu_i^2$$

$$= \alpha^2 \left[\frac{(1-\alpha)\lambda_2}{1-(1-\alpha)\lambda_2} \right]^2 (1 - \mu_1^2).$$

This completes the proof.

As we mentioned, if we are not satisfied with $\boldsymbol{R}^0$ (5), we can use it as an initial guess and perform power iterations. In practice, since it provides a good initial guess, we found that usually only one step of power iteration is needed which provides another approximation $\boldsymbol{R}^1$ as follows,

$$\boldsymbol{R}^1 = (1-\alpha)P\boldsymbol{R}^0 + \alpha\boldsymbol{E}. \tag{7}$$

Note that, due to the fact that $P = P_1 \otimes P_2$, the matrix-vector multiplication step $\boldsymbol{y} = P\boldsymbol{x}$ can be computed without explicitly forming P. We can use the following equivalent expression to compute $\boldsymbol{y}$

$$\boldsymbol{y} \leftarrow \mathrm{vec}(P_2 \, \mathrm{vec}^{-1}(\boldsymbol{x}) \, P_1^T).$$

where $\mathrm{vec}^{-1}(\cdot)$ is the inverse operation of $\mathrm{vec}(\cdot)$.

2.3 Computational Complexity

As we can see, the computational cost of using the iterative method (3) to solve IsoRank (2), our approximation (5), and (7) mainly depends on the matrix-vector multiplication for computing $P\boldsymbol{x}$ in the iteration (if the implementation uses the tensor product, then this step becomes matrix-matrix multiplication) and vector addition for computing $a\boldsymbol{x} + b\boldsymbol{y}$, $a, b \in \mathbb{R}$. Let us assume the complexity for matrix-vector multiplication (or matrix-matrix multiplication in the tensor product implementation) is t_1 and the complexity for vector addition is t_2. Then the complexity of using the iterative method (3) to solve IsoRank (2) is $k(t_1 + t_2)$, where k is the number of iterations used in the implementation. Using the standard convergence analysis of (3), at least $k \geq \dfrac{\log \varepsilon}{\log(1-\alpha)\lambda_2}$ steps are requires to reach a given relative error tolerance ε (measured in $\|\cdot\|_{D^{-1}}$ norm). Here λ_2 is the second largest eigenvalue of P, which happens to be the second largest eigenvalue of $\widetilde{A}$ since P and $\widetilde{A}$ are similar.

For our approximation $\boldsymbol{R}^0$, since we only use vector addition once, the complexity is t_2. Finally, the approximation $\boldsymbol{R}^1$ does one step of iteration using $\boldsymbol{R}^0$ as the initial guess. Thus, its computational cost is $t_2 + (t_1 + t_2) = t_1 + 2t_2$.

As we can see, our approximation's main computational advantage is that there is no need for iterations. Consider the worst case that $\lambda_2 \approx 1$, let us choose $\alpha = 0.6$ as used in our experiments. The iterative method (3) needs about $k = 30$ iterations to achieve $\varepsilon = 10^{-12}$. This implies that our approximations are about 30 times faster than iterating to convergence here. Of course, the computational saving will depend on specific implementations and computers.

3   Experiments

3.1   Synthetic Networks

Our first set of experiments uses the Erdős-Rényi (ER) random graphs [7] and the Barabási-Albert (BA) random graphs [1]. For the ER graphs, to ensure with high probability that the resulting random graphs are simply connected, we set the probability of using an edge to connect any two nodes to be $\frac{4 \log n}{n}$. For the BA graphs, we use a tree graph consisting of 5 nodes and edge set $\{(1, 2), (1, 5), (2, 4), (3, 4)\}$ as the seed graph. Each new node is connected to 5 existing nodes with a probability proportional to the number of edges the existing nodes already have.

To apply and test the IsoRank algorithm (2) and our two approximation algorithms, i.e., (5) and (7), we first generate a simply-connected random graph and then randomly permute the nodes to obtain another random graph. As suggested in [16], we choose $\alpha = 0.6$ in (2) and all the tests. In addition, we generate different E by adding a different level of random noise to the edge weights of the correct random permutation. Starting with the correct random permutation, whose values are either 0 or 1, for a "good" E, we add random noise between $[-0.5, 0.5]$. For a "bad" E, we add random noise between $[-0.7, 0.7]$. When we add random noise between $[-0.6, 0.6]$, we refer to the resulting E as "intermediate". Once the random noise is added, we take the absolute value component-wise and then normalize to ensure that $\|E\|_1 = 1$ and all the components are non-negative. Intuitively, the "good" E provides more information about the correct alignment, resulting in better accuracy than other choices of E. Finally, since IsoRank(2) is solved by an iterative procedure, we stop the iteration when the Frobenius norm (denoted by $\|\cdot\|_F$, and equal to the square root of the summed squares of absolute values of the elements of A) of the difference between two successive iterations is less than 10^{-12} or the maximal number of iterations, which is set to be 100, is reached. In all our experiments, it took less than 20 iterations to converge.

We report the accuracy, CPU time, $\|\cdot\|$ error, and $\|\cdot\|_{D^{-1}}$ error. The accuracy of the alignment is measured in terms of how many pairs of nodes between the original network and permuted network are predicted correctly (in percentage). Since we implement all the algorithms in Matlab, the CPU time is measured in seconds using the Matlab built-in functions tic and toc. Finally, we use the standard $\|\cdot\|$ norm to measure the error between the IsoRank result and its approximations. To verify the theory, we also look at the error using the weighted $\|\cdot\|_{D^{-1}}$ norm. The numerical results are reported in Tables 1 and 2.

Table 1. Erdős-Rényi Graphs: by equation #s: $R = (2)$; $R^0 = (5)$; $R^1 = (7)$

	good E				intermediate E				bad E			
	Acc	CPU	$\|\cdot\|^{(err)}$	$\|\cdot\|^{(err)}_{D-1}$	Acc	CPU	$\|\cdot\|^{(err)}$	$\|\cdot\|^{(err)}_{D-1}$	Acc	CPU	$\|\cdot\|^{(err)}$	$\|\cdot\|^{(err)}_{D-1}$
	$|V|=2,500, |E|=39,053$				$|V|=2,500, |E|=38,802$				$|V|=2,500, |E|=39,424$			
R	100%	1.44	–	–	83.9%	1.41	–	–	71.6%	1.53	–	–
R^0	100%	0.19	4.92e–6	1.55e–7	83.3%	0.19	4.90e–6	1.56e–7	71.1%	0.20	5.05e–6	1.57e–7
R^1	100%	0.31	4.54e–7	1.45e–8	83.8%	0.29	4.58e–7	1.46e–8	71.6%	0.32	4.66e–7	1.47e–8
	$|V|=5,000, |E|=85,630$				$|V|=5,000, |E|=84,850$				$|V|=5,000, |E|=85,248$			
R	100%	8.21	–	–	83.6%	7.88	–	–	71.2%	8.36	–	–
R^0	100%	0.83	2.25e–6	6.49e–8	83.0%	0.83	2.31e–6	6.70e–8	70.7%	0.84	2.29e–6	6.63e–8
R^1	100%	1.45	1.99e–7	5.80e–9	83.6%	1.43	2.08e–7	6.08e–9	71.2%	1.45	2.05e–7	5.97e–9
	$|V|=10,000, |E|=184,460$				$|V|=10,000, |E|=183,929$				$|V|=10,000, |E|=184,265$			
R	100%	42.56	–	–	83.1%	45.66	–	–	71.7%	44.26	–	–
R^0	100%	2.98	1.04e–6	2.78e–8	82.4%	3.27	1.05e–6	2.82e–8	71.1%	3.12	1.03e–6	2.77e–8
R^1	100%	6.33	8.81e–8	2.38e–9	83.1%	6.62	8.97e–8	2.43e–9	71.7%	6.47	8.78e–8	2.37e–9

Table 2. Barabási-Albert Graphs: by equation #: $R = (2)$; $R^0 = (5)$; $R^1 = (7)$

	good E				intermediate E				bad E			
	Acc	CPU	$\|\cdot\|^{(err)}$	$\|\cdot\|^{(err)}_{D-1}$	Acc	CPU	$\|\cdot\|^{(err)}$	$\|\cdot\|^{(err)}_{D-1}$	Acc	CPU	$\|\cdot\|^{(err)}$	$\|\cdot\|^{(err)}_{D-1}$
	$|V|=2,500, |E|=12,473$				$|V|=2,500, |E|=12,465$				$|V|=2,500, |E|=12,475$			
R	100%	3.37	–	–	87.3%	3.22	–	–	75.3%	3.27	–	–
R^0	100%	0.21	4.69e–5	2.66e–6	84.9%	0.19	4.41e–5	2.57e–6	73.2%	0.22	4.40e–5	2.63e–6
R^1	100%	0.38	1.19e–5	4.28e–7	87.2%	0.35	1.14e–5	4.04e–7	75.3%	0.40	1.07e–5	4.18e–7
	$|V|=5,000, |E|=24,975$				$|V|=5,000, |E|=24,976$				$|V|=5,000, |E|=24,974$			
R	100%	13.81	–	–	86.9%	14.03	–	–	72.9%	14.27	–	–
R^0	100%	0.84	2.41e–5	1.32e–6	83.9%	0.83	2.37e–5	1.33e–6	71.0%	0.94	2.27e–5	1.31e–6
R^1	100%	1.57	6.77e–6	2.10e–7	86.8%	1.57	6.39e–6	2.11e–7	73.0%	1.81	6.09e–6	2.08e–7
	$|V|=10,000, |E|=49,974$				$|V|=10,000, |E|=49,972$				$|V|=10,000, |E|=49,973$			
R	100%	38.85	–	–	86.6%	37.43	–	–	73.2%	38.62	–	–
R^0	100%	3.15	1.21e–5	6.60e–7	84.1%	3.08	1.22e–5	6.55e–7	71.1%	3.15	1.30e–5	6.63e–7
R^1	100%	5.18	3.62e–6	1.05e–7	86.5%	5.11	3.48e–6	1.04e–7	73.0%	5.17	3.72e–6	1.06e–7

3.2 Biological Networks

We also tested the IsoRank approximations on real PPI networks. We extracted networks from the IntAct database [9]; these networks are constructed using all physical interactions detected using Coimmunoprecipitation (Co-IP) [3] and Yeast 2-Hybrid (Y2H) [11] experiments. We generated the networks for five species: S = { *Homo sapiens, Mus musculus, Rattus norvegicus, Drosophila melanogaster,* and *Saccharomyces cerevisiae* }. We obtain pairwise node similarity scores from the blastp sequence similarity bit scores (assigning a 0 percent similarity if blastp does not align the sequences), and as above and as recommended by [16], set the α parameter that trades off between network and node similarity to be 0.6 The graph properties of these constructed PPI networks are provided in Table 3.

Table 3. Graph properties of IntAct networks. Table includes information regarding the number of nodes, number of edges, average node degree and average clustering coefficient for human, fly, mouse, rat and yeast networks.

network	#nodes	#edges	avg degree	avg cc
human	32431	301529	18.595	0.069
fly	11247	42555	7.567	0.027
mouse	13967	36541	5.232	0.051
rat	10792	23315	4.320	0.075
yeast	6478	70638	21.808	0.285

For the 10 distinct pairwise combinations of these 5 species, for each pair of corresponding PPI networks, we performed experiments using the true IsoRank similarity matrix R, and its two approximations R^0 and R^1. Finally, for each obtained similarity matrix R, R^0 and R^1, we used the greedy matching algorithm to find the top 2000 protein mappings M, M_0 and M_1 respectively.

To measure the biological properties of the mappings obtained from Iso-Rank and its approximations, we used three metrics: Edge Correctness (EC), Largest Common Connected Subgraph (LCCS) and Average Functional Similarity (AFS) [8]. A detailed description of these metrics is provided next.

Edge Correctness (EC): Let $(\mathcal{V}_1, \mathcal{E}_1)$ and $(\mathcal{V}_2, \mathcal{E}_2)$ represent two networks, with $|\mathcal{V}_1| \leq |\mathcal{V}_2|$ and let $g : \mathcal{V}_1 \to \mathcal{V}_2$ be a one-to-one mapping between the vertices of the two networks. For an edge $(u, v) \in \mathcal{E}_1$, we call $(g(u), g(v)) \in \mathcal{V}_2 \times \mathcal{V}_2$ to be a translation of (u, v) from $\mathcal{G}_1$ to $\mathcal{G}_2$. Then, the metric EC, which measures the percentage of the edge-translation of edges in $\mathcal{E}_1$ that is an actual edge in $\mathcal{E}_2$, is mathematically described as

$$EC = \frac{|(u, v) \in \mathcal{E}_1 : (g(u), g(v)) \in \mathcal{E}_2|}{|\mathcal{E}_1|} \qquad (8)$$

Since the PPI connections are (weakly) preserved during evolution, higher EC values imply better protein pairings.

Largest Common Connected Subgraph (LCCS): Given two graphs, $\mathcal{G}_1 = (\mathcal{V}_1, \mathcal{E}_1), \mathcal{G}_2 = (\mathcal{V}_2, \mathcal{E}_2)$, with $|\mathcal{V}_1| \leq |\mathcal{V}_2|$, and a one-to-one mapping $g : \mathcal{V}_1 \to \mathcal{V}_2$, let E denote the set of edges of $\mathcal{E}_1$ that map to edges in $\mathcal{E}_2$ using g. Then $LCCS(g; \mathcal{G}_1, \mathcal{G}_2)$ denotes the number of edges in the largest connected component of E. Like EC, LCCS also measures the number of edges that are preserved across the species by the mapping g.

Average Functional Similarity: The two previous metrics calculate how well the protein mapping preserves the structural features of the PPI networks. Since important biological functional pathways are also broadly preserved during evolution, we also expect a good mapping to strongly preserve protein function across species. Following [8] we also measure the *Average Functional Similarity* across species, measuring the similarity of sets of Gene Ontology [4] (GO) terms assigned to matched nodes. For each protein mapping $(p, g(p))$ we use Schlicker's similarity (i.e. $s_c(p, g(p)), c \in \{MF, BP, CC\}$) [8,15] to find the similarity of GO-Terms of p with that of $g(p)$. So, the Average Functional Similarity (AFS_c) is computed as

$$AFS_c = \frac{1}{|g|} \sum_{u \in dom(g)} s_c(u, g(u)) \qquad (9)$$

where $|g|$ represents the size of one-to-one protein mappings in g (If the alignment is global, $|g| = \max(|\mathcal{V}_1|, |\mathcal{V}_2|)$). Mappings with higher AFS based on the known functional labels are preferred. We depart from [8] to match recommended best practice in the field [5], and enforce some specificity of protein function by including only the GO labels whose shortest distance from a root is ≥ 5 in our computation of the AFS measure.

Approximation Loss, Matching Similarity and EC/LCCS Scores. In order to see how the IsoRank approximations compare with the exact Iso-Rank mappings, we performed a similar analysis to that done in Sect. 3.1. For a given pair of species $(A, B), A \neq B$, let $R(\alpha; A, B)$ be the true IsoRank similarity matrix, and let $R^0(\alpha; A, B)$ and $R^1(\alpha; A, B)$ be the approximations described in (5) and (7) respectively, for a given α-value. After using the greedy matching algorithm on $R(\alpha; A, B)$, $R^0(\alpha; A, B)$ and $R^1(\alpha; A, B)$, let $M(\alpha; A, B)$, $M_0(\alpha; A, B)$ and $M_1(\alpha; A, B)$ be the corresponding list of 2000 top one-to-one cross-species protein matches for the species pair (A, B). We generated results for each $\alpha \in \{0.2, 0.4, 0.6, 0.8\}$ and $A, B \in S$; results were remarkably stable across different α values but for space reasons present only the results with recommended $\alpha = 0.6$ [16]. We also computed the EC and LCCS scores for the matchings. Results appear in Table 4.

Functional Similarity Results. We used the Average Functional Similarity (AFS) measure, described above, to measure how functionally similar the protein-pairs mapped by IsoRank and its approximations are. The AFS results are provided in Table 5. Since the AFS result was not sensitive to α-values (fixing GO-category, species-pairs and type of IsoRank, the expected s.d. obtained by setting $\alpha = \{0.2, 0.4, 0.6, 0.8\}$ was ≈ 0.0015), we report $\alpha = 0.6$ in Table 5 and present the obtained AFS scores across all GO-categories and species-pairs.

The results are in stark contrast to the results obtained from the graph-theoretic measures. Unlike EC and LCCS outputs, the mapping obtained from the R^0 approximation gave the highest AFS scores in the majority of cases across all GO categories (though in most cases by a slight margin). So, for the biological function measures, it seems that the approximate IsoRank is superior to exact

IsoRank. Even in cases where it didn't produce the highest-scoring one-to-one mapping, it closely followed the best scoring algorithm.

3.3   Competing Methods

We further evaluated the R^0 approximation by comparing its EC, LCCS, and AFS scores against the results from two recent network alignment methods: Fast Attributed Network Alignment (FINAL) [20] and Hubalign [8]. These methods were chosen among the many competing global network alignment methods because they both have been shown to produce good alignments, plus they are relatively fast. The results appear in Tables 6 and 7. FINAL takes in two networks (and optional edge/node attributes, where we use the node pairwise similarity matrix as in the competing methods), and finds an inter-network pairwise alignment matrix that solves a topology-sensitive optimization problem. It generates the one-to-one mappings by performing greedy alignment on this optimized matrix. For our experiments, we generated the top 2000 FINAL 1-1 node alignments.

Hubalign operates by running a minimum degree heuristic algorithm to estimate topological and functional importance of proteins and comparing it with proteins from the another network to form alignments. Similar to FINAL and R^0, we wanted to obtain the top 2000 one-to-one Hublign mappings, but their current C++ implementation can only return the complete global alignment as output. To solve this issue, we re-implemented the Hubalign code from scratch. Furthermore, we made an additional change to the alignment implementation, where we postponed the selection of relatively "weak" alignment between single degree nodes by greedily selecting the stronger node mappings first. We made this change primarily to make the Hubalign results computationally feasible, but we tested our alternative Hubalign with this postponement against original Hubalign on the smallest two networks (aligning fly and yeast), and, as expected, since we are preferring stronger node mappings, all 3 reported metrics: EC, LCCS and AFS got substantially better with our change. Python source code of our Hubalign implementation is freely available in our Github repository.

4   Discussion

4.1   Synthetic Networks

As shown in Table 1 and 2, for both ER and BA random graphs, when "good" E is used, the accuracy for all three algorithms is 100%, i.e., all the algorithms can recover the network alignments perfectly, and the errors, measured in both norms, are very small. However, the original IsoRank R (2) is much slower than the two approximation algorithms. Approximate IsoRank R^0 (5) is about 7.6–14.3 times faster, and approximate IsoRank R^1 (7) is about 4.7–6.7 times faster. Since they all recover the perfect alignment, when E contains accurate information about the alignment, we suggest using approximate IsoRank R^0 (5). When

Table 4. L2 approximation loss, matching similarity, EC and LCCS results obtained from the IsoRank approximations R^0 and R^1, for $\alpha = 0.6$.

Orgs		Norms		Matching Sim		Edge Sim.			LCCS		
N1	N2	$\|R - R^0\|_2$	$\|R - R^1\|_2$	$Sim(R, R^0)$	$Sim(R, R^1)$	R^0	R^1	R	R^0	R^1	R
F	B	0.000947	0.000088	0.507	0.810	0.074	0.178	0.185	695	825	808
F	M	0.001208	0.000121	0.810	0.941	0.028	0.073	0.072	15	23	23
F	R	0.003482	0.000335	0.378	0.516	0.015	0.037	0.051	53	42	77
H	B	0.000371	0.000032	0.976	0.991	0.213	0.216	0.216	1174	1207	1202
H	F	0.000483	0.000032	0.973	0.994	0.063	0.065	0.064	21	132	134
H	M	0.000571	0.000059	0.986	0.998	0.086	0.093	0.093	158	264	264
H	R	0.001522	0.000158	0.903	0.982	0.018	0.040	0.041	76	408	388
M	B	0.001115	0.000178	0.780	0.941	0.089	0.193	0.191	389	586	581
M	R	0.005213	0.000599	0.779	0.940	0.041	0.129	0.128	57	373	363
R	B	0.004086	0.000525	0.353	0.469	0.107	0.135	0.393	426	679	1135

Table 5. AFS values for top 2000 matching-obtained approximations (R^0 and R^1) and true IsoRank (R) matrices. for all GO hierarchies, with $\alpha = 0.6$. The columns "N1" and "N2" represent IntAct networks for the different pairs of organisms: Human (H), Mouse (M), Rat (R), Fly (F) and Baker's yeast (B).

		MF			BP			CC		
N1	N2	R^0	R^1	R	R^0	R^1	R	R^0	R^1	R
F	B	0.513	0.515	**0.517**	0.261	0.266	**0.268**	0.539	0.547	**0.550**
F	M	**0.574**	0.573	0.570	0.268	**0.270**	0.269	0.579	**0.586**	0.583
F	R	**0.495**	0.429	0.391	**0.190**	0.170	0.154	**0.429**	0.399	0.369
H	B	**0.595**	0.594	0.595	**0.362**	0.362	0.361	0.503	**0.503**	0.502
H	F	**0.630**	0.627	0.628	**0.335**	0.332	0.332	**0.585**	0.582	0.581
H	M	**0.661**	0.659	0.659	**0.348**	0.346	0.345	**0.575**	0.574	0.573
H	R	**0.622**	0.621	0.621	**0.308**	0.308	0.308	**0.464**	0.464	0.464
M	B	0.515	**0.523**	0.521	0.265	0.273	**0.274**	0.526	**0.530**	0.529
M	R	**0.613**	0.600	0.600	**0.297**	0.293	0.292	**0.536**	0.530	0.530
R	B	**0.477**	0.426	0.360	**0.216**	0.188	0.159	**0.409**	0.377	0.345

"in-between" E is used, although the error between the original IsoRank and approximations are still small, the accuracy for all three algorithms decreases. As we can see, Approximate IsoRank R^0 (5) is the fastest among the three, but its accuracy is slightly worse than the original IsoRank R (2). Approximate IsoRank R^1 (7) is slightly slower than approximate IsoRank R^0 (5) but achieves roughly the same accuracy as the original IsoRank R (2). But approximate Iso-Rank (7) is still much faster than original IsoRank (2) and, therefore, balancing the accuracy and CPU time, we would suggest using approximate IsoRank (7) in this case. Finally, when E is "bad", we observe the same results as the case

Table 6. (a) EC and (b) LCCS results for top 2000 matching obtained from approximate IsoRank (R^0, $\alpha = 0.6$) and and two competing methods (FINAL and Hubalign), for all GO hierarchies. The columns "N1" and "N2" represent IntAct networks for organisms: Human (H), Mouse (M), Rat (R), Fly (F) and Baker's yeast (B).

N1	N2	R^0	FINAL	Hubalign
F	B	0.0740	**0.0996**	0.0301
F	M	0.0284	**0.0450**	0.0166
F	R	**0.0150**	0.0062	0.0033
H	B	**0.2137**	0.0969	0.0408
H	F	**0.0638**	0.0197	0.0061
H	M	**0.0862**	0.0292	0.0194
H	R	**0.0189**	0.0101	0.0037
M	B	0.0896	**0.1256**	0.0443
M	R	0.0413	**0.0658**	0.0352
R	B	**0.1077**	0.0514	0.0156

(a) Edge Correctness (EC)

N1	N2	R^0	FINAL	Hubalign
F	B	**695**	14	38
F	M	**15**	6	5
F	R	**53**	3	1
H	B	1174	1155	**1481**
H	F	21	27	**35**
H	M	158	401	**836**
H	R	**76**	29	26
M	B	**389**	31	51
M	R	**57**	**57**	55
R	B	**426**	22	23

(b) LCCS

Table 7. Average Functional Similarity (AFS) results for top 2000 matching obtained from approximate IsoRank (R^0, $\alpha = 0.6$) and and two competing methods (FINAL and Hubalign). for MF, BP and CC GO hierarchies. The columns "N1" and "N2" represent IntAct networks for the different pairs of organisms: Human (H), Mouse (M), Rat (R), Fly (F) and Baker's yeast (B).

N1	N2	MF			BP			CC		
		R^0	FINAL	Hub.	R^0	FINAL	Hub.	R^0	FINAL	Hub
F	B	0.513	**0.537**	0.521	0.261	**0.287**	0.277	0.539	**0.545**	0.538
F	M	0.574	**0.593**	0.536	0.268	**0.279**	0.246	0.579	**0.598**	0.557
F	R	**0.495**	0.482	0.478	**0.190**	0.185	0.186	**0.429**	0.419	0.420
H	B	**0.595**	0.557	0.521	**0.362**	0.329	0.295	**0.503**	0.486	0.464
H	F	**0.631**	0.606	0.513	**0.334**	0.318	0.248	**0.585**	0.562	0.487
H	M	**0.661**	0.647	0.614	**0.348**	0.344	0.308	0.575	**0.581**	0.546
H	R	**0.622**	0.588	0.579	**0.308**	0.282	0.271	**0.464**	0.436	0.437
M	B	0.515	**0.552**	0.520	0.265	**0.288**	0.269	0.526	**0.542**	0.523
M	R	0.613	0.614	**0.614**	0.297	0.298	**0.301**	0.537	0.536	**0.539**
R	B	**0.477**	0.472	0.463	**0.216**	0.209	0.207	**0.409**	0.402	0.400

E is "in-between". In particular, approximate IsoRank (5) is the fastest, but its accuracy is the worst (but not by much, still close to the accuracy of the original IsoRank (2). Approximate IsoRank R^1 (7) seems to achieve the best balance between the accuracy and CPU time, and we would suggest using it in this case as well. However, if the CPU time is the priority, then we recommend approximation IsoRank R^0 (5) since it is the fastest. Finally, from the numerical experiments, we observe that both our approximation algorithms achieve optimal computational complexity $\mathcal{O}(N^2)$, where $N = \max\{|\mathcal{V}_1|, |\mathcal{V}_2|\}$, as expected since the synthetic networks considered here are sparse (namely $|E|/|V|$ in the range 15.4–18.5 in Table 1 and approximately 5.0 in Table 2) and $t_1 = t_2 = \mathcal{O}(N^2)$ in our implementation.

4.2 Biological Networks

Interestingly, we found the R^0 approximation to IsoRank to be more robust and produce better predictions of protein functional roles across the board than even exact IsoRank. Since inferring the function of unknown proteins across species is one of the main applications of the Global Alignment of Biological Networks, perhaps given the fact that the networks aren't actually isomorphic plus we have an imperfect sample of the true edges, means that somehow our approximation to IsoRank is more robust to noise, and therefore works better than producing the best isomorphism as measured by purely graph-theoretic measures. This requires further investigation.

Acknowledgements. We thank the National Science Foundation for support under NSF grants CCF-1934553 and NSF CC* grant 2018149.

Code and Data availability. The implementation of approximate IsoRank is available at https://github.com/kap-devkota/approximate_ISORANK Gene Ontology files are from the official GO website (http://geneontology.org/ OBO data version: releases/2022-12-04, GAF version: 2.2) The biological networks used in the experiments can be downloaded from the IntAct FTP link at https://www.ebi.ac.uk/intact/download/ftp.

Disclosure of Interests. The authors have no competing interests to declare that are relevant to the content of this article.

References

1. Albert, R., Barabási, A.-L.: Statistical mechanics of complex networks. Rev. Mod. Phys. **74**(1), 47 (2002)
2. Altschul, S.F., Gish, W., Miller, W., Myers, E.W., Lipman, D.J.: Basic local alignment search tool. J. Mol. Biol. **215**(3), 403–410 (1990)
3. Anderson, N.G.: Co-immunoprecipitation. In: Clegg, R.A. (ed.) Protein Targeting Protocols, pp. 35–45. Humana Press, Totowa (1998)
4. G. O. Consortium: The Gene Ontology (GO) database and informatics resource. Nucleic Acids Res. **32**(suppl-1), D258–D261 (2004)
5. Devkota, K., Schmidt, H., Werenski, M., Murphy, J.M., Erden, M., Arsenescu, V., Cowen, L.J.: Glider: function prediction from glide-based neighborhoods. Bioinformatics **38**(13), 3395–3406 (2022)

6. El-Kebir, M., Heringa, J., Klau, G.W.: Natalie 2.0: sparse global network alignment as a special case of quadratic assignment. Algorithms **8**(4), 1035–1051 (2015)
7. Erdős, P., Rényi, A.: On the evolution of random graphs. Publ. Math. Inst. Hung. Acad. Sci **5**(1), 17–60 (1960)
8. Hashemifar, S., Xu, J.: Hubalign: an accurate and efficient method for global alignment of protein-protein interaction networks. Bioinformatics **30**(17), i438–i444 (2014)
9. Hermjakob, H., et al.: Intact: an open source molecular interaction database. Nucleic Acids Res. **32**(suppl-1), D452–D455 (2004)
10. Kazemi, E., Grossglauser, M.: On the structure and efficient computation of Isorank node similarities. arXiv preprint arXiv:1602.00668 (2016)
11. X Kohalmi, M., Reader, L.J.V., Samach, A., Nowak, J., Haughn, G.W., Crosby, W.L.: Identification and characterization of protein interactions using the yeast 2-hybrid system. In: Gelvin, S.B., Schilperoort, R.A. (eds.) Plant Molecular Biology Manual, pp. 95–124. Springer, Dordrecht (1998). https://doi.org/10.1007/978-94-011-5242-6_6
12. Mamano, N., Hayes, W.B.: SANA: simulated annealing far outperforms many other search algorithms for biological network alignment. Bioinformatics **33**(14), 2156–2164 (2017)
13. Neyshabur, B., Khadem, A., Hashemifar, S., Arab, S.S.: Netal: a new graph-based method for global alignment of protein-protein interaction networks. Bioinformatics **29**(13), 1654–1662 (2013)
14. Schafer, R.D.: An Introduction to Nonassociative Algebras. Courier Dover Publications, Mineola (2017)
15. Schlicker, A., Domingues, F.S., Rahnenführer, J., Lengauer, T.: A new measure for functional similarity of gene products based on gene ontology. BMC Bioinf. **7**(1), 1–16 (2006)
16. Singh, R., Xu, J., Berger, B.: Global alignment of multiple protein interaction networks with application to functional orthology detection. Proc. Natl. Acad. Sci. **105**(35), 12763–12768 (2008)
17. Smyth, M.: A spectral theoretic proof of perron-frobenius. In: Mathematical Proceedings of the Royal Irish Academy, pp. 29–35. JSTOR (2002)
18. Strang, G.: Introduction to Linear Algebra, 3rd edn. Wellesley-Cambridge Press, Wellesley (2003)
19. Vijayan, V., Saraph, V., Milenković, T.: MAGNA++: maximizing accuracy in global network alignment via both node and edge conservation. Bioinformatics **31**(14), 2409–2411 (2015)
20. Zhang, S., Tong, H.: FINAL: Fast attributed network alignment. In: Proceedings of the 22nd ACM SIGKDD International Conference on Knowledge Discovery and Data Mining, pp. 1345–1354 (2016)
21. Zhang, S., Tong, H., Tang, J., Xu, J., Fan, W.: iNEAT: incomplete network alignment. In: 2017 IEEE International Conference on Data Mining (ICDM), pp. 1189–1194. IEEE (2017)

Sequential Optimal Experimental Design of Perturbation Screens Guided by Multi-modal Priors

Kexin Huang[1,2(✉)], Romain Lopez[1,3], Jan-Christian Hütter[1], Takamasa Kudo[1], Antonio Rios[1], and Aviv Regev[1]

[1] Research and Early Development, Genentech, South San Francisco, USA
kexinh@cs.stanford.edu, regev.aviv@gene.com
[2] Department of Computer Science, Stanford University, Stanford, USA
[3] Department of Genetics, Stanford University, Stanford, USA

Abstract. Understanding a cell's expression response to genetic perturbations helps to address important challenges in biology and medicine. This includes the inference of gene circuits, the discovery of therapeutic targets and the reprogramming and engineering of cells. In recent years, Perturb-seq, pooled genetic screens with single cell RNA-seq (scRNA-seq) readouts, has emerged as a common method to collect such data. Despite technological advancements, the unpredictable, non-additive effects of gene perturbation combinations imply that the number of experimental configurations far exceeds what is experimentally feasible. In some cases, this may even surpass the number of available cells for research. While recent machine learning models, trained on existing Perturb-seq datasets, can predict perturbation outcomes with some degree of accuracy, they are currently limited by sub-optimal training set selection and the small number of cell contexts of training data. This leads to poor predictions for unexplored parts of perturbation space. As biologists deploy Perturb-seq across diverse biological systems, there is a significant need for algorithms to design iterative experiments. These tools are essential for exploring the large space of possible perturbations and their combinations. Here, we propose a sequential approach for designing Perturb-seq experiments that uses the model to strategically select the most informative perturbations at each step for subsequent experiments. This enables a significantly more efficient exploration of the perturbation space, while predicting the effect of the rest of the unseen perturbations with high-fidelity. Analysis of a previous large-scale Perturb-seq experiment reveals that our setting is severely restricted by the number of examples and rounds, falling into a non-conventional active learning regime called "active learning on a budget". Motivated by this insight, we develop ITERPERT, a novel active learning method that exploits rich and multi-modal prior knowledge in order to efficiently guide the selection of subsequent perturbations. Using prior knowledge for this task is novel, and crucial for successful active learning on a budget. We validate ITERPERT using in-silico benchmarking of active learning, constructed from a large-scale CRISPRi Perturb-seq dataset. We find that ITERPERT outperforms other active learning strategies by reaching comparable accuracy at only a third of the number of perturbations profiled as the next best method. Overall, our results demonstrate the potential of sequentially designing perturbation screens through ITERPERT.

J. Ma (Ed.): RECOMB 2024, LNCS 14758, pp. 17–37, 2024.
https://doi.org/10.1007/978-1-0716-3989-4_2

Keywords: Perturb-seq · Active Learning · Experimental Design

1 Introduction

The expression response of a cell to a genetic perturbation reveals fundamental insights into cell and gene function [1]. Perturb-seq is a relatively recent technology for pooled genetic screens with a single-cell RNA seq (scRNA-seq) readout of the expression response to a perturbation [2–4]. Perturb-seq provides insights into gene regulatory machinery [5], helps identify target genes for therapeutic intervention [6], and can facilitate the engineering cells with a specific target state [7, 8]. Recent technical advances have enhanced the scope, scale and efficiency of Perturb-seq [4, 9, 10]. However, because of the plethora of biological contexts, across cell types, states and stimuli, and the need to test combinations of perturbations (due to the possibility of non-additive genetic interactions), the number of required experiments explodes combinatorially. With trillions of potential experimental configurations or more, it becomes unrealistic to conduct all of them directly [8, 11].

Recently, researchers proposed machine learning models to predict perturbation outcomes [12–14]. Such models are trained on existing Perturb-seq datasets [2, 8, 10, 11] and then predict expression outcomes of unseen single-gene or multi-gene perturbations. While promising, these models suffer from a selection bias caused by the design of the original experiment used for training, in terms of selected perturbations and biological conditions. In particular, the training data are often profiled to answer a specific biological question, but not to maximize the predictive accuracy of the machine learning model across a large pool of unprofiled perturbations.

In this work, we present a novel paradigm for exploring a perturbation space by executing a sequence of Perturb-seq experiments. At the core of this paradigm lies a sequential optimal design procedure that interleaves the machine learning model and the wet-lab, where the Perturb-seq assay is performed. At each step of the sequence, we acquire data and use it to re-train the machine learning model. Then, we apply an optimal design strategy to select a batch of perturbation experiments that will most benefit the model to predict all of the unprofiled perturbations. The key idea is to sample the perturbation space intelligently by considering perturbations that are most informative and representative to the model, while accounting for diversity. Using this strategy, we can run as few perturbation experiments as possible, while obtaining a model that has sufficiently explored the perturbation space.

This idea is well-studied in the machine learning literature and is the topic of active learning [15]. Active learning has been used in practice across many domains, such as document classification [16], medical imaging [17] and speech recognition [18]. However, we noticed that effective active learning approaches necessitate a substantial initial set of labeled examples (i.e., in our case, profiled perturbations), complemented by numerous batches that collectively result in tens of thousands of labeled data points [19, 20]. In contrast, the constraints of iterative Perturb-seq in the lab make such conditions unattainable, both in terms of cost and time (as shown in our economic analysis in Sect. 3.1). In this "budgeted" regime, it has been reported that random selection outperforms most active learning strategies [21–23].

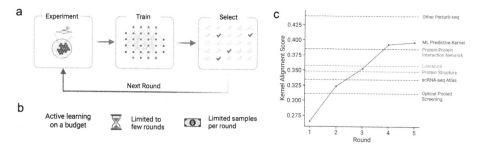

Fig. 1. Sequential design of Perturb-seq experiments. a. Illustration of the iterative Perturb-seq procedure. In each round, a batch of perturbations is selected and the corresponding experiments are conducted. Then, a machine learning model is updated with these newly-profiled perturbations. An active learning strategy uses the model's predictions to select the set of perturbations for the next round. Through this iteration, the goal is to reach high accuracy with a minimal number of experiments. **b.** Illustration of "active learning on a budget". Active learning for Perturb-seq is highly restricted to much fewer profiled perturbations (i.e., labeled examples) compared to a conventional active learning setting. This motivates the development of a specialized method for this setting. **c.** Exploratory data analysis shows that the model kernel suffers from poor representation when few perturbations have been profiled (low budget). However, other data sources, described in Sect. 3.3, contain rich and complementary information that can be potentially transferred to the model kernel, motivating ITERPERT.

We therefore propose a new strategy called ITERPERT (ITERative PERTurb-seq) that tackles the active learning on a budget setting for Perturb-seq data. Motivated by a data-driven analysis, our key observation is that when on a budget, it may be beneficial to combine the evidence from the data with publicly available sources of prior-knowledge, especially in the first few rounds. Such examples of prior knowledge include Perturb-seq data from related systems, large scale genetic screens with other modalities, such as genome-scale optical pooled screens [24,25], and data on physical molecular interactions, such as protein complexes [26,27]. This prior information spans multiple modalities such as networks, text, image, and 3D structure, which may be challenging to exploit during active learning. We overcome this by defining reproducing kernel Hilbert spaces on each of the modalities, and applying a kernel fusion strategy [28] to combine information from multiple sources.

To compare ITERPERT against other commonly used methods, we conducted an extensive empirical study using a large-scale single-gene CRISPRi Perturb-seq dataset collected in a cancer cell line (K562 cells) [11] and benchmarked 8 recent active learning strategies. ITERPERT achieved similar accuracy as the best active learning strategy but with three times fewer perturbations profiled as the training data. ITERPERT also showed robust performance in both essential genes screens and genome-scale screens, and when considering batch effects across iterations.

To summarize, our contributions are (1) proposing a sequential experimental design approach to Perturb-seq profiling for efficient exploration of a perturbation space; (2) identifying the algorithmic problem of active learning on a budget in this setting; (3) proposing a new active learning strategy that incorporates prior information and obtains a speedup of more than three times over the best baseline strategy.

2   Background

Perturb-Seq Prediction Model. We consider a predictive model f_θ with parameters θ that maps a set of perturbations $\mathcal{P} = (P_1, \cdots, P_M)$ to the post-perturbed expression outcome $\hat{\mathbf{y}} \in \mathbb{R}^L$, where L denotes the number of genes with measured expression levels. We denote the set of available Perturb-seq training data as $\mathcal{D}_{\text{train}} = \mathcal{X}_{\text{train}} \times \mathcal{Y}_{\text{train}}$, where $\mathcal{X}_{\text{train}} = \{\mathcal{P}_i\}_{i=1}^{N_{\text{train}}}$ and $\mathcal{Y}_{\text{train}} = \{\mathbf{y}_i\}_{i=1}^{N_{\text{train}}}$, respectively.

Several models have been designed for this specific task [12,13,29,30], and our proposed framework can be adapted for any of those (refer to Sect. 5). However, in the remainder of this paper we focus on adopting the current state-of-the-art model GEARS [12] as the prediction model for active learning. GEARS is a deep learning model customized for perturbation prediction that uses graph neural networks (GNN) to incorporate gene ontology and gene co-expression graphs to learn perturbation embeddings from data. GEARS uses a focal loss as the objective function during training in order to assign higher weight to differentially expressed genes: $\mathcal{L} = \frac{1}{|\mathcal{D}|} \sum_{u=1}^{|\mathcal{D}|} \frac{1}{L} \sum_{v=1}^{L} (\mathbf{y}_v^u - \hat{\mathbf{y}}_v^u)^{2+\gamma}$, where $\gamma = 2$ and $\hat{\mathbf{y}}_v^u, \mathbf{y}_v^u$ are the predicted and true expression level of gene v after perturbation u, respectively.

Batch-Mode Pool-Based Active Learning. Except for the specific low-budget setting, the active learning problem we are interested in has been well-studied in the literature [15] and corresponds to batch-mode pool-based active learning. It can be formulated as follows: We consider an initial labeled training set $\mathcal{D}_{\text{train}}^{(0)}$ and an unlabeled pool set $\mathcal{X}_{\text{pool}}^{(0)}$. In each subsequent round i, we first train a model f_θ on $\mathcal{D}_{\text{train}}^{(i-1)}$. Then, an active learning selection strategy g takes in (1) a pre-specified batch size N_{batch}, (2) the training set $\mathcal{D}_{\text{train}}^{(i-1)}$, (3) the unlabeled pool set $\mathcal{X}_{\text{pool}}^{(i-1)}$, and (4) the model f_θ and selects a batch $\mathcal{X}_{\text{batch}} \subset \mathcal{X}_{\text{pool}}^{(i-1)}$. We then acquire the labels $\mathcal{Y}_{\text{batch}}$ for $\mathcal{X}_{\text{batch}}$ (i.e., for our biological setting, we run the perturbation experiment). Finally, we update the labeled set $\mathcal{D}_{\text{train}}^{(i)} = \mathcal{D}_{\text{train}}^{(i-1)} \cup \mathcal{X}_{\text{batch}}$ and pooled set $\mathcal{X}_{\text{pool}}^{(i)} = \mathcal{X}_{\text{pool}}^{(i-1)} \setminus \mathcal{X}_{\text{batch}}$. We proceed with the next round until a total of R rounds is reached.

Recently, the algorithmic framework by Holzmüller et al. [31] unified a large number of existing methods for this task. Their approach relies on reproducing kernel Hilbert spaces (RKHS), and computations on kernel matrices. Specifically, it consists of three steps. (1) *Base kernel calculation.* We construct a positive semi-definite kernel $k : \mathcal{X} \times \mathcal{X} \to \mathbb{R}$ to capture how the predictions from f_θ change with respect to $\mathcal{X}$. A common choice is to build a finite-dimensional feature map $\phi : \mathcal{X} \to \mathbb{R}^d$ with $k(x, x') = \phi(x)^\top \phi(x')$. Typical examples are the full gradient kernel, obtained for $\phi_{\text{grad}}(x) = \nabla_\theta f_\theta(x)$, as well as the last layer kernel $\phi_{\text{ll}}(x) = \nabla_{\mathbf{W}^{(L)}} f_\theta(x)$, where $\mathbf{W}^{(L)}$ is denoted as the last layer parameter of the model f_θ. We note that because there are L gene expression levels to predict for each perturbation, we are interested in a multi-task prediction problem. Yet, we may still operate within this framework. Indeed, even though the gradient vector $\nabla_\theta f_\theta$ becomes a Jacobian matrix $\text{Jac} f_\theta(\theta)$, we may just identify the matrix space to a finite-dimensional vector space. (2) *Kernel transformation.* While the base kernel defines the relation among inputs, it often requires an additional kernel transformation step for better performance, such as min-max normalization. (3) *Selection rule.* Lastly, given the transformed kernel, a selection method is invoked. The overall principle is to select informative and representative points that account for diversity. Since our proposed strategy modifies neither the kernel transformation nor the selection rules, we refer the readers to [31] for a more detailed review.

3   Method

3.1   Sequential Design of Perturb-Seq Experiment

We now describe the unique challenges that may arise while designing an active learning strategy for the sequential design of Perturb-seq experiments.

Problem Definition. We consider an initial Perturb-seq readout $\mathcal{D}_{\text{train}}^{(0)}$ and a pool of unperturbed genes $\mathcal{X}_{\text{pool}}^{(0)}$. In each round i, we train a perturbation prediction model f_θ using available data $\mathcal{D}_{\text{train}}^{(i-1)}$. Then, an active learning selection strategy g selects a batch $\mathcal{X}_{\text{batch}} \in \mathcal{X}_{\text{pool}}^{(i-1)}$. We then conduct a wet-lab Perturb-seq experiment on these selected perturbations and obtain a batch of new readouts $\mathcal{Y}_{\text{batch}}$, and proceed with the next round. The goal is find a selection strategy g that minimizes the model's prediction error $\mathcal{L}^{(i)}$ on all the perturbations. For evaluation purposes, we evaluate the performance on a hold-out set of perturbations $\mathcal{D}_{\text{test}}$ at each round i.

Experimental Setup. We focus on a CRISPRi Perturb-seq screen on cells from the K562 cell line undergoing 2,058 single-gene perturbations (essential genes as defined in [11]). We construct a benchmark to simulate the real-world active learning loop. First, we randomly select a hold out set of 205 perturbations for evaluation. This randomly selected hold out set gauges a model's capacity to predict the entire perturbation space. Next, we set the number of rounds $R = 5$ and the number of perturbations that can be performed in each round $N_{\text{batch}} = 100$. For the sake of a fair comparison, we fix a random initial set of 100 perturbations for all methods. We measure the error at round i using the GEARS training loss at the hold out test set.

Economic Analysis Reveals Active Learning on a Budget Setting. Our problem is drastically different from the conventional active learning setting in several ways. First, previous works focus on single-output classification/regression tasks [31, 32], while the outcome of a Perturb-seq experiment is high-dimensional. This means that the predictive model may be harder to learn and thus may require more data.

Second, in a typical setting, the initial labeled set $|\mathcal{D}_{\text{train}}|$ is large enough for model training [32], followed by a large number of labels queried per round. However, this large number of labeled data is unattainable for Perturb-seq data, because each perturbation is associated with a high cost. Perturb-seq's cost (currently dominated by the cost of scRNA-seq) for one perturbation can be estimated as the price of processing and sequencing a cell (which varies across techniques, but for droplet-based microfluidics, is approximately \$0.5 [33]) times the number of guides per perturbation ($\sim$2) times the number of cells per guide ($\sim$30) in addition to the pro-rated cost of labor, instruments, and quality control. Thus, a single perturbation is currently estimated to cost more than \$30, making the number of perturbations intrinsically limited per round.

Indeed, most Perturb-seq experiments reported to date are in the order of hundreds of perturbations [2,8,10,34], largely driven by cost, as the experiment scales readily to genome-scale in the lab.

Third, previous works assume that many rounds of data acquisition can be performed. For example, the recent GeneDisco active learning challenge uses up to 40 rounds [35]. In contrast, each round of a Perturb-seq experiment is time-consuming. With some variation due to differences in the experimental platform, on average, each round of Perturb-seq takes at least a month (1 week for oligonucleotides synthesis, 1 week for library cloning, 1 week for titering, and 1 week for experiments). Thus, the number of rounds R should be small since the total time grows linearly with R for sequential Perturb-seq design. 40 rounds correspond to more than 3 years of implementation and is thus not realistic with current assay capabilities. This is why in our setting, we use $R = 5$.

Overall, we are operating in a different regime that we summarize as active learning on a budget [32]. We demonstrate below that this has significant impact on the design of the active learning strategy.

3.2 Data-Driven Motivation for Incorporating Prior Knowledge

We hypothesize that the setting of active learning on a budget will affect the performance of any active learning strategy significantly because of the estimation of the kernel matrix, and therefore also the estimated relationships between perturbations, may be highly biased. We next present an analysis to support this hypothesis.

Testing Alignment of Kernels. We develop a simple test to gauge the quality of any kernel for downstream utilization in an active learning strategy. Since we have access to ground truth data (i.e., the outcome of all perturbations), we construct a ground truth kernel k_{truth} with $\phi_{\text{truth}}(x) = \mathbf{y}$, where $\mathbf{y}$ denotes the experimental result. We expect the kernel matrix $\tilde{\mathbf{K}}$ to reflect pairwise perturbation relationships, up to experimental noise. Therefore, the kernel matrix $\mathbf{K}$ derived from the predictive model f_θ should ideally be aligned as closely to the ground truth kernel as possible. To measure the alignment between the query kernel $\mathbf{K}$ and the ground truth kernel $\tilde{\mathbf{K}}$, we use the kernel alignment score $\text{KA}(\mathbf{K}, \tilde{\mathbf{K}})$ [36] defined as the cosine similarity between the two matrices (using the inner product canonically induced by Frobenius norm).

Poor Alignment of the Predictive Model Kernel When on a Budget. We apply a baseline active learning algorithm for five rounds, where, at each round, we randomly query 100 new perturbations (random selection rule). At each of these five rounds, we also retrieve the perturbation prediction model, compute the kernel matrices and calculate the alignment score with ground truth. To make these kernel matrices comparable across rounds, we calculate them on the list of perturbations in the pool set of the last round. We observe that as the number of profiled perturbations increases, the model kernel alignment score also increases (Fig. 1c). However, the alignment scores are low during the first few rounds, suggesting that the kernel matrix does not accurately represent the similarities between perturbations. This will lead to suboptimal selections since selection rules solely rely on the kernel to make selections.

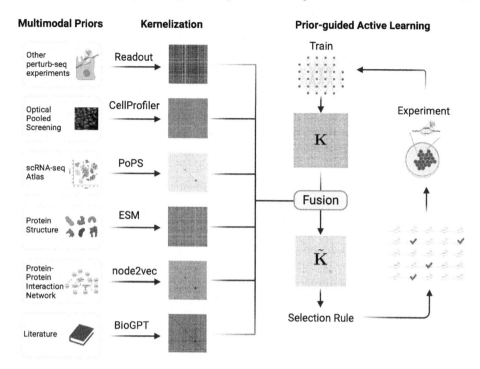

Fig. 2. Illustration of ITERPERT. Driven by the exploratory data analysis in Sect. 3.2, we introduce ITERPERT, an active learning selection approach that integrates a wide range of multi-modal prior knowledge to tackle the problem of active learning on a budget for Perturb-seq data. Our primary technique involves enhancing the model kernel when faced with budget constraints. We achieve this by transforming each source of multi-modal prior knowledge into a reproducing kernel Hilbert space through diverse featurization methods for each modality, explained in Sect. 3.3 These kernels are then fused to refine the model kernel, ensuring a more precise characterization of perturbation relations. We then apply standard selection rules to this enhanced kernel, giving rise to ITERPERT.

Prior Knowledge Contains Auxiliary Information of Perturbation Relationships. To tackle the insufficiency of the model kernel, we hypothesize that we can leverage abundant information about perturbation relationships stored in other sources of prior knowledge. To support this hypothesis, we collect a list of such sources and derive kernels that represent perturbation similarities (details about the sources and kernel derivations appear in Sect. 3.3). Using the same kernel alignment metric (Fig. 1c), we observe that kernels derived from prior information have better alignment with the ground truth kernel compared to the model predictive kernel, especially in the first 2 rounds, suggesting rich information that could be complementary to the model kernel. This motivates us to design a method that integrates prior knowledge into active learning strategies (Fig. 2).

3.3 ITERPERT: A Multi-modal Prior-Guided Active Learning Strategy

Overview. Motivated by the exploratory analysis in Sect. 3.2, we propose ITERPERT, an active learning strategy that incorporates diverse sources of prior knowledge to complement the model kernel when on a budget. The key step of our method consists in defining a kernel on each source of prior knowledge and combining those kernels with the model kernel to capture the relations between perturbations more accurately. This new prior-fused kernel is then followed by standard selection rules to form an active learning strategy.

Kernelized Multi-modal Prior Information. Prior knowledge may come from diverse modalities, such as images, texts, and networks; therefore, how to employ these sources of prior knowledge for active learning is not straightforward. The information needed for active learning is not the raw prior knowledge, but the relations between the perturbed genes captured in the prior knowledge (e.g., using a kernel matrix). Thus, we propose to define a kernel $k(x, x') = \phi_{\text{prior}}(x)^\top \phi_{\text{prior}}(x')$ for each source of prior knowledge. Here, we introduce 6 distinct categories of prior knowledge, explain how to engineer a feature map ϕ, and provide insight on why each one should intuitively help map the perturbation space. The detailed preprocessing for each source can be found in Appendix A.

(1) Additional Perturb-seq data. Multiple Perturb-seq experiments have been conducted across several cell contexts [34]. Perturb-seq data from other cell contexts or experiments contain useful prior information since certain relations between perturbations might be either context-agnostic or at least transferable to the cell context of interest. For each perturbation x, $\phi(x)$ is defined as the mean of pseudo-bulk expression change from the non-targeting control cells from the Perturb-seq readouts.

(2) Optical pooled screens (OPS). OPS [24,25] data consists of cell morphological images associated with a genetic perturbation in each individual cell in a pool. Intuitively, perturbations that elicit similar morphological phenotypes could also have similar expression phenotypes. For each perturbation x, $\phi(x)$ is the imaging features from CellProfiler [37], an image processing software that extracts morphology profiles.

(3) scRNA-seq atlas. Genes that are co-expressed together likely belong to similar pathways, and perturbations in the same pathway tend to have similar expression effects. Thus, gene co-expression data could be useful for the prediction task. For each perturbation x, $\phi(x)$ is the list of normalized gene expression measurements for gene x across a collection of scRNA-seq experiments [38]. The kernel matrix derived from this feature map corresponds to the co-expression matrix.

(4) Protein structures. If the proteins encoded by the perturbed genes have similar structures, they are more likely to have similar functions, and similar perturbation outcomes [26]. For each perturbation x, we obtain its protein coding sequence, and then feed it into a recent protein language model (15B ESM model [27]) to obtain structural features $\phi(x)$.

(5) Protein-protein interaction network (PPI). A PPI network connects proteins that physically interact with each other [39]. Intuitively, a physical interaction between two proteins suggest that they might participate in a shared biomolecular pathway or complex. Thus, perturbations of genes coding for physically interacting proteins might lead

to similar effects [40]. For each perturbation x, $\phi(x)$ is a node embedding of x in the PPI network, such as node2vec [41].

(6) Literature. Perturbations that are mentioned in similar contexts in the literature are more likely to have similar functions and phenotypes. To encode this, for each perturbation x, $\phi(x)$, we feed the corresponding gene name to a recent large language model that is fine-tuned on biological literature (e.g. BioGPT [42]) and use the text embedding as the feature map.

Kernel fusion. The kernelization step enables integration across kernels with diverse modalities, since it converts different modalities into one — a kernel matrix of the same size. Now, we study how to fuse all the prior kernels with the model kernel. Given the set of prior kernels $\{k_1, \cdots, k_m\}$ and their kernel matrices $\{\mathbf{K}_1, \cdots, \mathbf{K}_m\}$, we update the model kernel matrix $\mathbf{K}$ at each round to obtain the kernel matrix $\hat{\mathbf{K}}$ for our active learning procedure as follows:

$$\hat{\mathbf{K}} = \text{FUSION}(\mathbf{K}, \mathbf{K}_1, \cdots, \mathbf{K}_m)$$

Since the different prior kernels have different feature map dimensions, and the kernel corresponds to taking the dot product between feature maps, the scale differs significantly across kernels. Thus, to avoid one kernel with a large scale overriding the others, we apply a min-max scale normalization to each kernel.

We experiment with multiple strategies for the FUSION operator, including element-wise operators, such as mean, max, and product, and adaptive kernel aggregation methods, such as the kernel alignment weighted operator and the kernel regression operator. A discussion and performance study of these fusion operator appears in Appendix B. Interestingly, the mean operator $\hat{\mathbf{K}} = \frac{1}{m+1}(\mathbf{K} + \mathbf{K}_1 + \cdots + \mathbf{K}_m)$ has the best empirical performance. Additionally, this approach has the theoretical advantage of guaranteeing that the fused kernel is positive and semi-definite (PSD), which is a required property for several downstream selection rules [31]. Note that the mean operator also has an interpretation in the feature maps space, where it is equivalent to the concatenation of all the feature maps.

Selection Rule. ITERPERT only modifies the base kernel and is agnostic to the selection rule. For the sake of simplicity, in our experiments, we apply ITERPERT with only one popular rule called greedy distance maximization. This method greedily select points with maximum distance to all previously selected points [43]. Particularly, given the prior-fused kernel $\hat{k}$, for a perturbation u in the pool set and any point v in the selected set, it first calculates the distance $d_{uv} = \sqrt{\hat{k}(x_u, x_u) + \hat{k}(x_v, x_v) - 2\hat{k}(x_u, x_v)}$. This is equivalent to taking the squared distance in the feature map space. Next, it selects point u^* greedily as

$$u^* = \text{argmax}_{u \in \mathcal{X}_{\text{rem}}} \min_{v \in \mathcal{X}_{\text{sel}}} d_{uv}, \tag{1}$$

where $\mathcal{X}_{\text{sel}}$ is the union of the training set and the points already selected, and $\mathcal{X}_{\text{rem}}$ is the pool set excluding the already selected points.

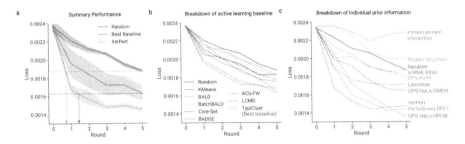

Fig. 3. a. ITERPERT achieves significant speedup of model learning compared to the best baseline and random selection. Focal loss (training objective of the base model, y axis) across active learning rounds (x axis). We conduct 10 random runs where the solid line is the average and the error bar is the 95% confidence interval of the mean. **b.** Detailed breakdown of state-of-the-art active learning baselines. The best baseline is TypiClust [32]. Plot as in panel a, with the solid line denoting the average across 10 runs. **c.** Detailed breakdown of individual prior-augmented active learning. The solid line is the average across 5 runs. Error bars are not visualized in panels b and c for visual clarity and can be found in Appendix C.

4   Experiment

We conduct experiments to demonstrate ITERPERT's advantage over state-of-the-art active learning strategies in efficiently designing Perturb-seq experiments. We also conduct systematic ablation studies to delineate the contribution of each prior information source. We evaluate the performance of our benchmarked methods in various settings, including an extension to a larger pool size by leveraging a genome-scale Perturb-seq screen and also accounting for batch effects across rounds.

Benchmarking State-of-the-Art Active Learning Methods. We first benchmark the set of active learning methods (Fig. 3b) available from the open-source repository released by Holzmüller et al. [31]. We observed that all active learning methods have better performance than uniform/random sampling. The best-performing method was TypiClust [32], which is a recent active learning on a budget method that prioritizes typical examples instead of uncertain examples and shows significant improvement over random selection. This corroborates our hypothesis that the problem of sequential Perturb-seq experimental design corresponds to the setting of active learning on a budget.

ITERPERT Achieves Significant Improvement Over the Best Baseline. We report the performance of ITERPERT against the best active learning baseline and random sampling in Fig. 3a. Importantly, ITERPERT uses roughly one round to reach the same accuracy as five rounds of uniform sampling, reflecting a greater than 5-fold speedup. Similarly, ITERPERT uses roughly 1.5 rounds (through linear extrapolation) to reach the same accuracy as five rounds of uniform sampling, reflecting a more than 3-fold speedup. We also observe similar improvements in other biologically meaningful metrics, such as the mean squared error (MSE) of predicted expression profiles calculated

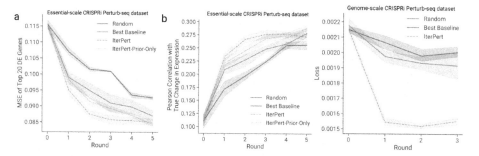

Fig. 4. Biologically meaningful metrics as used in [12]. Metrics (y axis) across active learning rounds (x axis). Each method is averaged across 10 runs and error bar is the 95% CI of the mean. **a.** MSE of top 20 differentially expressed genes per perturbation. **b.** Pearson correlation coefficient between the predicted and true expression changes (centered on non-targeting controls). ITERPERT-Prior-Only is an ablation of ITERPERT where we remove the model kernel. Best baseline is TypiClust [32].

Fig. 5. Performance for genome-scale K562 CRISPRi screen. Focal loss (y axis) across active learning rounds (x axis). Solid line: mean over 10 runs, error bar: 95% CI of the mean. Best baseline is TypiClust [32]. Results for other baselines can be found in Appendix D.

on the top 20 differentially expressed genes in each perturbation (Fig. 4a) and the Pearson correlation coefficient over changes in gene expression (Fig. 4b). This showcases that ITERPERT is an efficient method for designing Perturb-seq experiments. Moreover, the first round had the steepest increase of accuracy for ITERPERT, confirming our data analysis in Sect. 3.2 on the usefulness of prior knowledge.

Dissecting ITERPERT Performance Across Multi-modal Priors. To further understand the origin of the performance improvement of ITERPERT, we conduct several ablations. First, we report performance when using a single prior kernel, so that we may understand which prior source contributes most to the performance of the method (Fig. 3c). Aggregation of all priors outperformed any individual prior alone. This showcases synergies across the diverse sources of prior knowledge. Comparing across priors, the best-performing prior is the Perturb-seq data in RPE1 cells, highlighting that there is transferable information across Perturb-seq experiments, even from different cell contexts. Optical pooled screens were also strongly informative, demonstrating that cell morphology carries shared information with Perturb-seq outcomes. Notably, different cell contexts and treatment/phenotypes of OPS lead to different improvement levels. The HeLa cell line seems to have a larger contribution to model performance increase than an OPS in the A549 cell line. Other prior knowledge sources, such as literature and a scRNA-seq atlas, also show an improvement, while PPI has limited contribution, maybe due to noise. Overall, perturbation-specific priors have richer signals compared to general gene-based priors. We also conduct an ablation where we remove the model kernel (Fig. 4a,b). We observe a performance degradation, highlighting the synergy between prior knowledge and the model kernel.

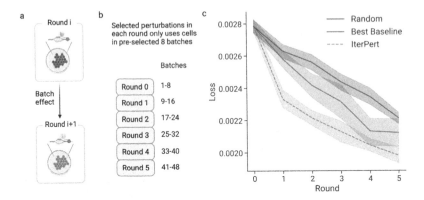

Fig. 6. a. Batch effects exist across active learning rounds, which could bias model training and selection. **b.** Illustration of simulation evaluation settings where we restrict the cells from the selected perturbations in each round to certain batches (lanes) such that different rounds use cells from different batches. **c.** Active learning performance in the batch effect setting. Each method is averaged across 10 runs and error bar is 95% CI. Best baseline is TypiClust [32].

Extension to Genome-Scale Experiment. The pool set of the essential genes in K562 dataset is relatively small (<2,000 perturbations). For many real-world applications of Perturb-seq, one may want to select from a larger pool set size, for example, in genome-scale screens or in combinatorial screens. To gauge the improvement in larger setups, we conducted another experiment by leveraging the genome-scale K562 CRISPRi perturb-seq screen from [11]. This dataset has 9,748 single-gene perturbations and thus corresponds to a much larger pool of possible perturbations. We set $N_{batch} = 300$ and performed $R = 3$ rounds in total. We report the performance in Fig. 5. We find that ITERPERT consistently displays a significant efficiency improvement over both the random and best active learning baselines, especially in the first round.

Accounting for Batch Effects Across Rounds. One important consideration when developing an active learning strategy for Perturb-seq data is that there are batch effects across rounds (Fig. 6a), which could bias the predictive model and selection strategy. To evaluate the our method's robustness to this, we simulate batch effects by leveraging the batch information in the dataset, which consists of 48 batches (lanes) (Fig. 6b). In particular, we restrict the cells for $\mathcal{X}_{batch}$ in each round to come from different batches (8 batches for each round), to ensure that the model experiences some batch effects. We conduct the same experiment and report the performance in Fig. 6c. We observe that the absolute value of the loss is worse than in the previously explored settings without batch effects. This may mainly be due to the fact that 6 times fewer cells are available for training. In this challenging setting, we still observe that ITERPERT has a more efficient selection strategy compared to the best baseline and uniform sampling.

5   Related Works

Active Learning. We highlight recent advancements that we consider as baselines and refer the readers to surveys [15, 31, 44] for a more comprehensive overview. BALD [45] selects instances where the model's predictions exhibit the most disagreement across possible parameter configurations, focusing on uncertainty. BatchBALD [46] is an extension of BALD and it selects batches of data points to maximize joint information and reduce redundancy in batch selection. Core-Set [43] identifies a subset of data that summarizes the entire dataset, aiming for comparable performance with fewer training examples. BADGE [47] chooses data points based on diverse gradient embeddings, capturing instances that offer varied learning experiences. ACS-FW [48] uses the Frank-Wolfe optimization algorithm to select instances from the pool set whose conic combinations best represent the entire set to promote representativeness. LCMD [31] first finds the largest cluster for representativeness and then enforces diversity by picking the maximum distance point within this cluster.

Active Learning on a Budget. Active learning on a budget has been studied in [21–23]. They showed that in this setting, random selection outperforms most deep active learning strategies. This phenomenon is often explained by the poor ability of neural models to capture uncertainty on a small budget. The recently proposed method Typi-Clust [32] prioritizes typical examples instead of uncertain examples and shows significant improvement over random selection. We consider it as our baseline. Note that with ITERPERT, we do not propose a new selection rule but instead use prior information to adjust the estimation of the perturbation space. We show that ITERPERT has significant improvement over TypiClust, but we leave the problem of integrating ITERPERT with TypiClust as future work.

Perturbation Prediction Models. CellOracle [29] relies on gene regulatory network inference and conducts linear network propagation of perturbation signals to make predictions. CPA [30] uses a non-linear compositional autoencoder to predict effects but it is restricted to predicting seen perturbations. GEARS [12] is a deep learning model customized for perturbation prediction. It is based on a GNN perturbation and cell encoder with a deep composition layer that simulates multi-gene perturbations on cells, and it features a loss function focusing on differentially expressed genes. Recently, single-cell foundation models have gained popularity and claim to excel at perturbation outcome prediction. Notably, scGPT [13] uses a generative pre-training objective over a massive scRNA-seq atlas and is finetuned on perturbation prediction tasks. However, it requires the perturbed genes to be detected in the scRNA-seq experiment, which is not the case for many perturbations in our dataset. Although we use GEARS in this work, the approach is general and applicable to other models.

Active Learning for Genomics Experimental Design. Sequential optimal design is increasingly popular in high throughput genomics assays. The main task is to identify genes that maximize an endpoint such as cell proliferation [49, 50]. Note that this setting is highly different from ours, because there, the goal is to identify a data point in the data distribution with the highest response (Bayesian optimization). In contrast, we are interested in selecting points that enable a machine learning model to reduce the overall loss across the data distribution (active learning). The more related work GeneDisco [35] is a benchmark for the sequential design of genetic perturbation experiments, proposing both Bayesian optimization and active learning tasks. The key difference in our work is that we focus on active learning for expensive Perturb-seq, where the response is high-dimensional expression profiles, while GeneDisco focuses on functional genomics CRISPR assays with a single scalar readout. This leads to different base prediction models and a different active learning setting than the one discussed in Sect. 3.1. Also note that we have included the active learning methods benchmarked in GeneDisco (BADGE, KMeans, BALD) in our baselines, and in this study, our proposed method ITERPERT has significantly better performance.

6   Discussion

We introduced an iterative Perturb-seq procedure for efficient design of perturbation experiments. We highlighted the challenges of active learning on a budget constraints and evaluated current active learning techniques. Motivated by an initial data analysis, we presented ITERPERT, a new active learning strategy that incorporates multi-modal priors, achieving over three times the speed of the best baseline.

While ITERPERT shows promise in designing efficient Perturb-seq experiments, it still faces limitations, and further work is necessary for its practical implementation. For instance, while we strive to simulate a realistic setting *in-silico*, several points of divergence could occur in practice. One such divergence is experimental batch effects, which could be more significant than those considered in our setting. Moreover, while our method is very useful for mapping genome-scale single-gene perturbations, further work is needed to extend this approach to multi-gene (combinatorial) perturbations that are currently intractable to experimentally interrogate in an exhaustive way. Extending the framework to multi-gene perturbations requires higher-order kernels or the use of tensor product spaces, which presents an interesting methodological challenge that we leave for future work. Similarly, extensions to chemical perturbations or optical readouts are also exciting future avenues. More specific to our prior-guided strategy, while our empirical study finds that mean fusion works the best, it is not context-specific. Ideally, different combinations of prior information could be automatically picked in different cell contexts. Lastly, with the increasing interest in models to predict the outcome of perturbations, we expect more base prediction models to become available. While our proposed active learning strategy is compatible with any of these, future work remains to investigate ITERPERT performance with these methods.

Overall, we believe that the sequential design of Perturb-seq could drastically reduce the experimental cost of understanding a complex space of perturbations, thanks to its sample efficiency, and could help answer central biological questions, such as the effect of multi-gene perturbations.

Acknowledgements and Funding Information. We thank Xinming Tu, Jerry Wang, and Rebecca Boiarsky for feedback throughout the duration of this project that greatly improved this work. We warmly thank Jure Leskovec for valuable discussions and feedback for improving the manuscript. We also thank members of the Regev Lab and the Biological Research — AI development (BRAID) department at Genentech for providing constructive feedback on earlier versions of the results presented in this work.

Romain Lopez, Jan-Christian Hütter, Takamasa Kudo, Antonio Rios, and Aviv Regev are employees of Genentech, and may have equity in Roche. Aviv Regev is a co-founder and equity holder of Celsius Therapeutics and an equity holder in Immunitas. She was an SAB member of Thermo Fisher Scientific, Syros Pharmaceuticals, Neogene Therapeutics, and Asimov until July 31st, 2020.

Code Availability. The raw source code is available at https://github.com/Genentech/iterative-perturb-seq and is released under the Apache 2.0 license. The notebooks to reproduce each figure are provided in https://github.com/Genentech/iterative-perturb-seq/tree/master/reproduce_repo. The python package is available at iterpert. We implemented the source code in PyTorch. The base machine learning model is adapted from https://github.com/snap-stanford/GEARS. The active learning strategy framework is adapted from https://github.com/dholzmueller/bmdal_reg.

Appendix

In Appendix A, we describe pre-processing steps for each prior source we leverage. In Appendix B, we describe different fusion operators to fuse across prior kernels and report their empirical performance. In Appendix C, we further provide plots of the main experiments that include all error bars since they are withheld for the sake of visibility in the main text. In Appendix D, we discuss the experiments on the genome-scale Perturb-seq data and report the obtained performance metrics.

A   Data Processing on Multi-modal Priors

1. Additional Perturb-seq data: we use the essential-wide RPE1 cell line CRISPRi dataset from the same paper [11] as the K562 dataset. Particularly, for each perturbation, we obtain the NTC centered pseudobulk expression profile and use that as the feature embedding. For genome-scale experiment, since we do not have another cell line with genome-scale perturbations, we remove this prior source.
2. Optical pooled screens: [25] conducts a genome-wide optical pooled screen and calculated CellProfiler features for each perturbation. We retrieve each perturbation embedding from https://github.com/broadinstitute/2022_PERISCOPE# downloading-profiles. Notably, we use the median aggregation version. For A549, we used 20200805_A549_WG_Screen_guide_normalized_median_merged_ALLBATCHES_ALLWELLS.csv.gz. For HeLa, we used both DMEM 20210422_6W_CP257_guide_normalized_median_merged_ALLBATCHES__DMEM__ALLWELLS.csv and HPLM 20210422_6W_CP257_guide_normalized_median_merged_ALLBATCHES__HPLM__ALLWELLS.csv.
3. scRNA-seq atlas: we used processed scRNA profiles aggregated from multiple scRNA-seq experiments in [38] (https://github.com/FinucaneLab/pops).

4. Protein structures: we retrieve the protein coding sequence of the corresponding gene perturbation from uniprot and then feed each into ESM-2 15 billion parameter model(https://huggingface.co/facebook/esm2_t48_15B_UR50D) and the output [CLS] token embedding is used as the protein embedding.
5. Protein-protein interaction network: we used the PPI knowledge network from https://arxiv.org/abs/2306.04766, and apply node2vec (https://github.com/eliorc/node2vec) to obtain each gene embedding.
6. Literature: we feed the gene name of each perturbation into BioGPT (https://huggingface.co/microsoft/BioGPT-Large) and we use the [CLS] token embedding as the gene embedding.

B Fusion Operator

We experiment with multiple strategies for the FUSION operator, including element-wise operators:

1. Mean operator: $\hat{\mathbf{K}} = \frac{1}{m+1}(\mathbf{K} + \mathbf{K}_1 + \cdots + \mathbf{K}_m)$
2. Max operator: $\hat{\mathbf{K}} = \mathrm{MAX}(\mathbf{K}, \mathbf{K}_1, \cdots, \mathbf{K}_m)$
3. Product operator: $\hat{\mathbf{K}} = \mathbf{K} \times \mathbf{K}_1 \times \cdots \times \mathbf{K}_m$

We also experiment with adaptive kernel aggregation methods. Given the subset of kernel matrix with ground truth at round i called $\mathbf{K}^{(i)}_{\mathrm{truth}}$, we can estimate the kernel alignment scores $KA(\mathbf{K}, \mathbf{K}^{(i)}_{\mathrm{truth}})$, where KA [36] is defined as the cosine similarity between the two matrices (using the inner product canonically induced by Frobenius norm). The *kernel alignment weighted operator* is then defined as

$$\hat{\mathbf{K}} = KA(\mathbf{K}, \mathbf{K}^{(i)}_{\mathrm{truth}}) * \mathbf{K} + KA(\mathbf{K}_1, \mathbf{K}^{(i)}_{\mathrm{truth}}) * \mathbf{K}_1 + \cdots + KA(\mathbf{K}_m, \mathbf{K}^{(i)}_{\mathrm{truth}}) * \mathbf{K}_m.$$

Another learnable operator is to estimate the weights $\alpha, \alpha_1, \cdots, \alpha_m$ by solving a linear regression problem to fit the ground truth sub-kernel from prior sub-kernel using validation dataset at each round i:

$$\mathbf{K}^{(i)}_{\mathrm{truth}} \approx \alpha * \mathbf{K}^{(i)} + \alpha_1 * \mathbf{K}^{(i)}_1 + \cdots + \alpha_m * \mathbf{K}^{(i)}_m,$$

and then use the weights to update the entire kernel

$$\hat{\mathbf{K}} = \alpha * \mathbf{K} + \alpha_1 * \mathbf{K}_1 + \cdots + \alpha_m * \mathbf{K}_m.$$

We report performance comparisons of these different operators in Fig. 7. We observe that the mean operator has the best empirical performance. We hypothesize that the reason for this that while the learnable operators can capture context-specific relations among the kernels, their estimation is biased due to the limited size of available data for each round. We also experimented with non-linear integration of kernels, but they easily led to overfitting. In the end, we adopt the mean fusion operator.

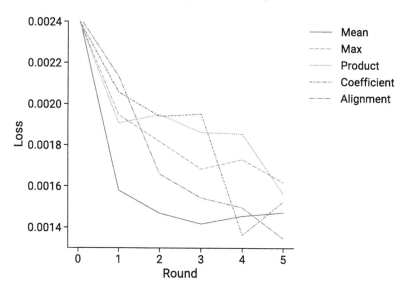

Fig. 7. Performance comparison on a seed different from the main experiments across different fusion operators. Mean operator has the best empirical performance.

C   Error Bars for Baselines

Error bars are omitted in Figs. 3b and 3c in the main paper to make the plots easier to read. We here report the error bar for Fig. 3b (breakdown of active learning baselines) in Fig. 8 and the error bar for Fig. 3c (breakdown of individual prior information) in Fig. 9.

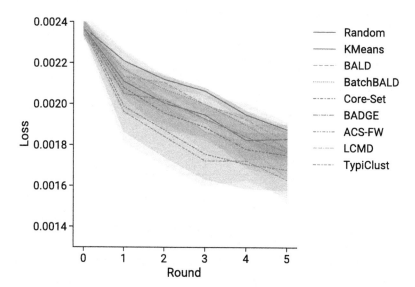

Fig. 8. Performance comparison across different baselines with error bar corresponding to 95% confidence interval.

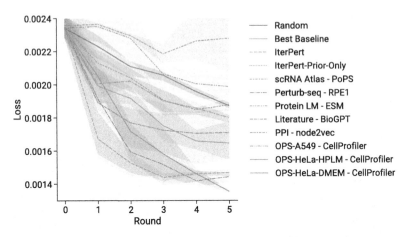

Fig. 9. Performance comparison across different prior information with error bar corresponding to 95% confidence interval.

D   Baseline Performance for Genome-Scale Perturbation Screen

In Fig. 10, we report the performance of all the baseline state-of-the-art active learning strategies on the genome-scale perturbation screen that were omitted in Fig. 5.

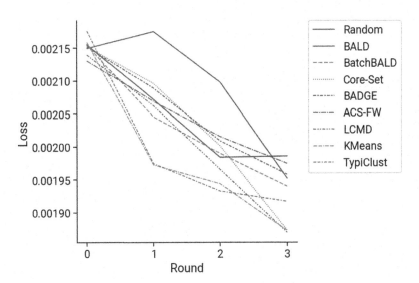

Fig. 10. Performance comparison across baseline methods for genome-scale K562 screens with error bar corresponding to 95% confidence interval.

References

1. Kitano, H.: Systems biology: a brief overview. Science **295**(5560), 1662–1664 (2002)
2. Dixit, A., et al.: Perturb-seq: dissecting molecular circuits with scalable single-cell rna profiling of pooled genetic screens. Cell **167**(7), 1853–1866 (2016)
3. Schraivogel, D., et al.: Targeted perturb-seq enables genome-scale genetic screens in single cells. Nat. Methods **17**(6), 629–635 (2020)
4. Ursu, O., et al.: Massively parallel phenotyping of coding variants in cancer with perturb-seq. Nat. Biotechnol. **40**(6), 896–905 (2022)
5. Schnitzler, G.R., et al.: Mapping the convergence of genes for coronary artery disease onto endothelial cell programs. In: bioRxiv, pp. 2022–11 (2022)
6. Nelson, M.R., et al.: The support of human genetic evidence for approved drug indications. Nat. Genet. **47**(8), 856–860 (2015)
7. Buganim, Y., Faddah, D.A., Jaenisch, R.: Mechanisms and models of somatic cell reprogramming. Nat. Rev. Genet. **14**(6), 427–439 (2013)
8. Norman, T.M., et al.: Exploring genetic interaction manifolds constructed from rich single-cell phenotypes. Science **365**(6455), 786–793 (2019)
9. Yao, D., et al.: Compressed perturb-seq: highly efficient screens for regulatory circuits using random composite perturbations. In: bioRxiv, pp. 2023–01 (2023)
10. Adamson, B., et al.: A multiplexed single-cell CRISPR screening platform enables systematic dissection of the unfolded protein response. Cell **167**(7), 1867–1882 (2016)
11. Replogle, J.M., et al.: Mapping information-rich genotype-phenotype landscapes with genome-scale perturb-seq. Cell **185**(14), 2559–2575 (2022)
12. Roohani, Y., Huang, K., Leskovec, J.: Predicting transcriptional outcomes of novel multigene perturbations with gears. Nat. Biotechnol. 1–9 (2023)
13. Cui, H., Wang, C., Maan, H., Pang, K., Luo, F., Wang, B.: scGPT: Towards building a foundation model for single-cell multi-omics using generative AI. In: bioRxiv, pp. 2023–04 (2023)
14. Gong, J., et al.: xTrimoGene: an efficient and scalable representation learner for single-cell RNA-seq data. In: bioRxiv, pp. 2023–03 (2023)
15. Settles, B.: Active Learning Literature Survey. Department of Computer Sciences, University of Wisconsin-Madison (2009)
16. Schohn, G., Cohn, D.: Less is more: active learning with support vector machines. In: International Conference on Machine Learning (2000)
17. Nath, V., Yang, D., Landman, B.A., Xu, D., Roth, H.R.: Diminishing uncertainty within the training pool: active learning for medical image segmentation. IEEE Trans. Med. Imaging **40**(10), 2534–2547 (2020)
18. Riccardi, G., Hakkani-Tur, D.: Active learning: theory and applications to automatic speech recognition. IEEE Trans. Speech Audio Process. **13**(4), 504–511 (2005)
19. Sinha, S., Ebrahimi, S., Darrell, T.: Variational adversarial active learning. In: Proceedings of the IEEE/CVF International Conference on Computer Vision, pp. 5972–5981 (2019)
20. Beluch, W.H., Genewein, T., Nürnberger, A., Köhler, J.M.: The power of ensembles for active learning in image classification. In: Proceedings of the IEEE Conference on Computer Vision and Pattern Recognition, pp. 9368–9377 (2018)
21. Zhu, Yu., et al.: Addressing the item cold-start problem by attribute-driven active learning. IEEE Trans. Knowl. Data Eng. **32**(4), 631–644 (2019)
22. Siméoni, O., Budnik, M., Avrithis, Y., Gravier, G.: Rethinking deep active learning: Using unlabeled data at model training. In: 2020 25th International Conference on Pattern Recognition, pp. 1220–1227. IEEE (2021)
23. Mittal, S., Tatarchenko, M., Çiçek, Ö., Brox, T.: Parting with illusions about deep active learning. arXiv:1912.05361 (2019)

24. Feldman, D., et al.: Optical pooled screens in human cells. Cell **179**(3), 787–799 (2019)
25. Ramezani, M., et al.: A genome-wide atlas of human cell morphology. In: bioRxiv (2023)
26. Giurgiu, M., et al.: Corum: the comprehensive resource of mammalian protein complexes-2019. Nucleic Acids Res. **47**(D1), D559–D563 (2019)
27. Rives, A., et al.: Biological structure and function emerge from scaling unsupervised learning to 250 million protein sequences. Proc. Natl. Acad. Sci. **118**(15), e2016239118 (2021)
28. Lanckriet, G.R., Deng, M., Cristianini, N., Jordan, M.I., Noble, W.S.: Kernel-based data fusion and its application to protein function prediction in yeast. In: Biocomputing, pp. 300–311. World Scientific (2003)
29. Kamimoto, K., Stringa, B., Hoffmann, C.M., Jindal, K., Solnica-Krezel, L., Morris, S.A.: Dissecting cell identity via network inference and in silico gene perturbation. Nature **614**(7949), 742–751 (2023)
30. Lotfollahi, M., et al.: Predicting cellular responses to complex perturbations in high-throughput screens. Molec. Syst. Biol. e11517 (2023)
31. Holzmüller, D., Zaverkin, V., Kästner, J., Steinwart, I.: A framework and benchmark for deep batch active learning for regression. J. Mach. Learn. Res. **24**(164), 1–81 (2023)
32. Hacohen, G., Dekel, A., Weinshall, D.: Active learning on a budget: opposite strategies suit high and low budgets. In: International Conference on Machine Learning (2022)
33. Huang, D., et al.: Advances in single-cell RNA sequencing and its applications in cancer research. J. Hematol. Oncol. **16**(1), 1–48 (2023)
34. Green, T.D., et al.: scPerturb: Information resource for harmonized single-cell perturbation data. In: Advances in Neural Information Processing Systems Workshop on Learning Meaningful Representations of Life (2022)
35. Mehrjou, A., et al.: Genedisco: a benchmark for experimental design in drug discovery. In: International Conference on Learning Representations (2022)
36. Kornblith, S., Norouzi, M., Lee, H., Hinton, G.: Similarity of neural network representations revisited. In: International Conference on Machine Learning (2019)
37. Carpenter, A.E., et al.: Cell Profiler: image analysis software for identifying and quantifying cell phenotypes. Genome Biol. **7**, 1–11 (2006)
38. Weeks, E.M., et al.: Leveraging polygenic enrichments of gene features to predict genes underlying complex traits and diseases. Nat. Genet. **55**(8), 1267–1276 (2023)
39. von Mering, C., Huynen, M., Jaeggi, D., Schmidt, S., Bork, P., Snel, B.: String: a database of predicted functional associations between proteins. Nucleic Acids Res. **31**(1), 258–261 (2003)
40. Geiger-Schuller, K.R., et al.: Systematically characterizing the roles of E3-ligase family members in inflammatory responses with massively parallel perturb-seq. In: bioRxiv, pp. 2023–01 (2023)
41. Grover, A., Leskovec, J.: node2vec: scalable feature learning for networks. In: In: Proceedings of the 22nd ACM SIGKDD International Conference on Knowledge Discovery and Data Mining, pp. 855–864 (2016)
42. Luo, R., et al.: BioGPT: generative pre-trained transformer for biomedical text generation and mining. Brief. Bioinf. **23**(6), bbac409 (2022)
43. Sener, O., Savarese, S.: Active learning for convolutional neural networks: a core-set approach. In: International Conference on Learning Representations (2018)
44. Ren, P., et al.: A survey of deep active learning. ACM Comput. Surv. **54**(9), 1–40 (2021)
45. Houlsby, N., Huszár, F., Ghahramani, Z., Lengyel, M.: Bayesian active learning for classification and preference learning. arXiv:1112.5745 (2011)
46. Kirsch, A., Van Amersfoort, J., Gal, Y.: Batchbald: efficient and diverse batch acquisition for deep Bayesian active learning. Adv. Neural Inf. Process. Syst. **32** (2019)

47. Ash, J.T., Zhang, C., Krishnamurthy, A., Langford, J., Agarwal, A.: Deep batch active learning by diverse, uncertain gradient lower bounds. In: International Conference on Learning Representations (2020)
48. Pinsler, R., Gordon, J., Nalisnick, E., Hernández-Lobato, J.M.: Bayesian batch active learning as sparse subset approximation. Adv. Neural Inf. Process. Syst. **32** (2019)
49. Pacchiano, A., Wulsin, D., Barton, R.A., Voloch, L.: Neural design for genetic perturbation experiments. In: International Conference on Learning Representations (2023)
50. Lyle, C., et al.: DiscoBAX: discovery of optimal intervention sets in genomic experiment design. In: International Conference on Machine Learning (2023)

Efficient Analysis of Annotation Colocalization Accounting for Genomic Contexts

Askar Gafurov[1], Tomáš Vinař[2], Paul Medvedev[3,4,5], and Broňa Brejová[1(✉)]

[1] Department of Computer Science, Faculty of Mathematics,
Physics and Informatics, Comenius University in Bratislava, Bratislava, Slovakia
brejova@fmph.uniba.sk
[2] Department of Applied Informatics, Faculty of Mathematics,
Physics and Informatics, Comenius University in Bratislava, Bratislava, Slovakia
[3] Department of Computer Science and Engineering,
The Pennsylvania State University, State College, USA
[4] Huck Institutes of the Life Sciences, The Pennsylvania State University,
State College, USA
[5] Department of Biochemistry and Molecular Biology,
The Pennsylvania State University, State College, USA

Abstract. An annotation is a set of genomic intervals sharing a particular function or property. Examples include genes, conserved elements, and epigenetic modifications. A common task is to compare two annotations to determine if one is enriched or depleted in the regions covered by the other. We study the problem of assigning statistical significance to such a comparison based on a null model representing two random unrelated annotations. To incorporate more background information into such analyses and avoid biased results, we propose a new null model based on a Markov chain which differentiates among several genomic contexts. These contexts can capture various confounding factors, such as GC content or sequencing gaps. We then develop a new algorithm for estimating p-values by computing the exact expectation and variance of the test statistic and then estimating the p-value using a normal approximation. Compared to the previous algorithm by Gafurov et al., the new algorithm provides three advances: (1) the running time is improved from quadratic to linear or quasi-linear, (2) the algorithm can handle two different test statistics, and (3) the algorithm can handle both simple and context-dependent Markov chain null models.

We demonstrate the efficiency and accuracy of our algorithm on synthetic and real data sets, including the recent human telomere-to-telomere assembly. In particular, our algorithm computed p-values for 450 pairs of human genome annotations using 24 threads in under three hours. The use of genomic contexts to correct for GC-bias also resulted in the reversal of some previously published findings.

Availability. The software is freely available at https://github.com/fmfi-compbio/mcdp2 under the MIT licence. All data for repro-

© The Author(s), under exclusive license to Springer Nature Switzerland AG 2024
J. Ma (Ed.): RECOMB 2024, LNCS 14758, pp. 38–53, 2024.
https://doi.org/10.1007/978-1-0716-3989-4_3

ducibility are available at https://github.com/fmfi-compbio/mcdp2 -reproducibility.

Keywords: genome annotation · colocalization · Markov chains

1   Introduction

Recent years have brought rapid growth in the number of different assays that can extract genome-scale functional information. This has led to growing collections of genome annotations; for example in the UCSC Genome browser, the GRCh38 human genome assembly currently features 136 different annotation tracks, many of which have multiple subtracks. In this work, we provide new models and algorithms for annotation colocalization analysis, where the goal is to determine if one input annotation is significantly colocated with regions covered by another annotation. Such analyses may hint at possible connections between biological processes governing individual annotations (e.g. histone modification H3K4me3 sites are colocated with promoter regions, and H3K4me3 indeed plays a role in gene transcription regulation [10]).

Mathematically, we view a genome annotation as a set of non-overlapping chromosomal intervals. Given two annotations, query Q and reference R, we consider two widely-used colocalization statistics. The *overlap statistic* is the number of intervals in R that intersect with at least one interval in Q. The *shared bases statistic* is the number of positions in the genome covered by both R and Q. However, even randomly generated annotations will share bases or have overlapping intervals by chance. In order to ascertain statistical significance of the observed statistic, its p-value needs to be computed under a suitable null hypothesis. Until very recently, all the methods [3,6,11,17–19] were limited by having a null hypothesis that either does not properly model the data or its p-value computation does not scale to annotations of human-sized genomes.

Recently, Gafurov et al. [5] proposed an alternative null hypothesis in which the annotation is produced by a two-state Markov chain. The algorithm, called MCDP, was a substantial improvement in time and memory over previous approaches. However, it is quadratic in the number of reference intervals and still takes several hours for the human exon reference annotation. It thus remains time-prohibitive to compare many pairs of annotations against each other.

Another limitation of MCDP as well as other approaches is that two unrelated annotations may appear to be colocalized because they are each colocalized with another genomic feature [12]. For example, two annotations may appear colocalized simply due to their prevalence in high-GC regions, even though they are not related. More generally, different regions of the genome can be thought of as providing different background to the null model, and we think of these various backgrounds as partitioning the genome into *contexts*. Accounting for contexts in calculating p-values is important to limit false associations, yet this capability is limited or absent in existing tools.

In this paper, we propose a model and an algorithm to overcome these scalability and accuracy barriers. Our first contribution is a new algorithm MCDP2 for estimating p-values, which is linear in the number of reference intervals. To demonstrate the scalability of our algorithm, we considered 10 reference annotations, corresponding to different types of repeats in the human genome, and 45 query annotations, corresponding to epigenetic modifications in different cell lines. MCDP2 computed p-values for all 450 pairs using 24 threads in under 2 hours for the number of overlaps and 3 hours for the number of shared bases.

Our second contribution expands the modeling capability of the Markov chain null hypothesis so that it takes into account genomic context and thus captures various confounding factors influencing annotation colocalization. Unlike previous approaches [11], our model is able to handle annotation intervals that span class boundaries. We demonstrate the importance of modeling the genomic context by re-analyzing colocalization of copy number deletions with various gene classes [21] and find that adding a genome context in fact reverses some of the previous conclusions. In one striking example, the set of all exons appears enriched for overlap with copy number losses but enrichment turns into depletion after taking into account gaps and GC content. We also compare the colocalization of epigenetic marks with subtelomeric repeats on the new human telomere-to-telomere assembly [8], using a genome context to compare enrichment between two classes of repeats.

Related Work. Several null hypotheses for colocalization statistics have been considered prior to the Markov chain model [5]. Some lend themselves to fast and simple statistical tests (e.g. Fisher's exact test) but do not capture relevant properties of the data. For example, one can assume that all positions in the query annotation are chosen uniformly at random [3,19]. However, this does not capture either the integrity of intervals or their length distribution. A more faithful option is the permutational null hypothesis (also called gold null hypothesis [5]), which reshuffles the query intervals while maintaining their lengths [6,11,17]. Computing the exact p-values for the overlap statistic in this model is NP-hard [5], and the only known efficient algorithms are either inaccurate or impractical for human-sized annotations [18]. Sampling approaches can be used, but their accuracy is directly proportional to the number of samples, making it difficult to estimate small p-values. With these limitations, it was impossible to compute small p-values for human-sized genomes while having a null hypothesis that is faithful to the data.

Accounting for genomic contexts has also been considered but most previous approaches [3,6,15,19] are only able to account for contexts which are completely inadmissible to annotations (e.g. assembly gaps, which are unassembled regions of the genome). A notable exception is GAT [11], which splits a genome into multiple contexts and analyzes colocalization in each context independently. However, this approach does not satisfactorily handle intervals that span context boundaries, which become prevalent when the contexts are short.

2 Methods

In this section, we define our context-aware Markov chain null model ($\mathcal{H}_0^{\text{context}}$) and provide an overview of our algorithm for efficient estimation of p-values under this model. We first present our results on a single chromosome; an extension to multiple chromosomes is discussed in Sect. 2.5.

We will denote the chromosome length as L and use 0-based coordinates. An *annotation* is a set of intervals contained in $[0, L)$ so that each two intervals are disjoint and separated by at least one base. By $|Q|$ we denote the number of intervals in annotation Q. We will represent an annotation either as a list of half-open intervals ordered from left to right $Q = ([b_1, e_1), \ldots, [b_{|Q|}, e_{|Q|}))$, or as a binary sequence $Q = (Q_0, Q_1, \ldots, Q_{L-1})$, where Q_i is 1 if position i is covered by one of the intervals and 0 otherwise.

Let R and Q be two annotations, denoted as the reference and the query, respectively. In this setting, a test statistic is a function that measures the extent to which R and Q are colocalized. We will consider two concrete test statistics. One is the number of overlaps $K(R, Q)$, which is defined as the number of intervals in R that overlap some interval in Q. The other is the number of shared bases $B(R, Q)$, which is defined as the number of bases in the genome covered by both R and Q. Let F be the distribution of the query annotation under the null hypothesis of the query being generated independently of the reference annotation. Given some test statistic $A(R, Q)$, we are interested in computing the p-value measuring the statistical significance of enrichment of Q with respect to R, that is, probability $\Pr_{Q' \sim F}[A(R, Q') \geq A(R, Q)]$.

Our algorithm is based on the observation that the distribution of the test statistics is in most realistic scenarios well approximated by the normal distribution (see Sects. 3 and 4). Therefore, instead of computing the full probability mass function (PMF), we compute only its exact mean and variance and use them as the parameters of the normal distribution. This means that we calculate the p-value by first computing the *Z-score*, which is the number of standard deviations that $A(R, Q)$ is above the expected value, under the null. Formally,

$$Z_A(R, Q) = \frac{A(R, Q) - \mathrm{E}_{Q' \sim F}[A(R, Q')]}{\sqrt{\mathrm{Var}_{Q' \sim F}[A(R, Q')]}}.$$

Under the assumption that the statistic is normally distributed, the desired p-value is then simply $1 - \Phi(Z_A(R, Q))$, where Φ is the cumulative distribution function of the standard normal distribution. Analogously, the p-value for the statistical significance of depletion is computed as $\Phi(Z_A(R, Q))$.

In Sect. 2.1, we describe our context-aware Markov chain model for generating random annotations and then use it to formally define the $\mathcal{H}_0^{\mathrm{context}}$ null model in Sect. 2.2. In Sects. 2.3 and 2.4, we outline our algorithm for computing the mean and variance of the overlap and shared bases test statistics. Finally, we describe how our model naturally extends to multiple chromosomes (Sect. 2.5).

2.1   A Generative Model

An annotation of a chromosome of length L can be generated by running a two-state Markov chain for L steps. The state at step i indicates whether the annotation includes position i on the chromosome. The lengths of the generated intervals and of the gaps between them are known to be geometrically distributed in this model, and the transition probabilities of the Markov chain dictate the expected values of these two distributions [13]. The Markov chain generative model makes many properties easy to derive and fast to compute [5], and so we build upon it in this work.

We want to use such a generative model to test if a given query annotation Q behaves as if it was "randomly shuffled" on the chromosome. To this end, we set the parameters of the Markov chain so that the expected interval lengths and gaps between them match what is observed in the query Q. However, this does not allow us to incorporate background knowledge of the chromosome; i.e., some regions of the genome may be *a priori* more likely to generate an interval.

We therefore introduce the notion of genome contexts. Given a finite set of class labels Λ, a *genome context* is a mapping $\phi : \{0, \ldots, L-1\} \longrightarrow \Lambda$ of each position on the genome onto a class label (e.g. $\Lambda = \{\text{gap}, \text{non-gap}\}$). This mapping partitions the genome into several segments with the same class assigned. We will refer to the positions where the class differs from the class label at the previous position as to *class boundaries*. We assume throughout the paper that a context is represented as a sequence of class boundary positions with the corresponding class labels, sorted in an increasing order by positions.

Our generative model allows each context class to have its own Markov chain, i.e. its own distribution of interval lengths and gaps. An annotation is then generated by iterating over the genome positions from left to right, and at each position i transitioning to the next state of the Markov chain according to the transition probabilities of the class at position i (see Fig. 1). A similar model was proposed by Burge and Karlin [1] for gene finding; their hidden Markov model uses different transition and emission probabilities based on GC content in the current window of the genome.

Definition 1. *A* context-aware Markov chain *is a pair* $(\phi, \mathbf{T})$, *where* ϕ *is a genome context and* $\mathbf{T} : \Lambda \to \mathbb{R}^{2 \times 2}$ *is a mapping that provides a transition probability matrix for each context class. The context-aware Markov chain* $(\phi, \mathbf{T})$ *generates a sequence of states* $(s_{-1}, s_0, \ldots, s_{L-1}) \in \{0,1\}^{L+1}$ *with probability*

$$\Pr[(S_{-1}, S_0, \ldots, S_{L-1}) = (s_{-1}, s_0, \ldots, s_{L-1})] = \vec{\pi}_{s_{-1}} \cdot \prod_{i=0}^{L-1} \mathbf{T}(\phi(i))_{s_{i-1}, s_i},$$

where $\mathbf{T}(\phi(i))_{s,s'}$ *is the probability of transition from state* s *to state* s' *in context class* $\phi(i)$, *and* $\vec{\pi}_s$ *is the probability of state* s *in the stationary distribution of the Markov chain with transition probabilities* $\mathbf{T}(\phi(0))$. *Namely,*

$$\vec{\pi} = \left(\frac{\mathbf{T}(\phi(0))_{1,0}}{1 - \mathbf{T}(\phi(0))_{0,0} + \mathbf{T}(\phi(0))_{1,0}} \quad \frac{1 - \mathbf{T}(\phi(0))_{0,0}}{1 - \mathbf{T}(\phi(0))_{0,0} + \mathbf{T}(\phi(0))_{1,0}} \right)$$

Note that we are indexing vectors and matrices starting from 0 in order to make the formulas more readable. The produced binary sequence of states $(s_0, \ldots, s_{L-1})$ can be viewed as an annotation of a genome of size L. State s_{-1}

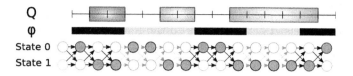

Fig. 1. An example of a query annotation $Q = \{[1,3), [5,7), [9,14)\}$ and the corresponding sequence of states of the context-aware Markov chain that induces the annotation. Genome context ϕ is shown with black and gray colors corresponding to two distinct class labels. The same colors are also used on transition arrows between successive states of the Markov chain, as the transition probabilities depend on the genome context.

is added to the start for notational convenience, as we will often refer to the state preceding the start of an interval. The distribution of the random vector of generated states $(S_{-1}, S_0, \ldots, S_{L-1})$ will be denoted as $C(\phi, \mathbf{T})$. We will use the same notation to denote the distribution of the induced annotation.

2.2   The Context-Aware Markov Chain Null Model

The generative model above serves as a basis for our null model, which we call $\mathcal{H}_0^{\text{context}}$. Given a context ϕ and a query annotation $Q = (Q_0, \ldots, Q_{L-1})$, we first need to find the transition probabilities $\mathbf{T}_Q$ that would maximize the probability of the context-aware Markov chain $(\phi, \mathbf{T}_Q)$ generating Q. This is achieved through the standard approach of training Markov chains by counting transition frequencies [4]. In particular, for each class, we count the number of times each possible state transition occurs in Q. Formally,

$$n_{\lambda,s,s'} = 1 + \sum_{i=1}^{L-1} \mathbb{1}((\phi(i) = \lambda) \text{ and } (s = Q_{i-1}) \text{ and } (s' = Q_i)),$$

where $\mathbb{1}$ is the indicator function which evaluates to 1 if the logical expression inside is true and 0 otherwise. A pseudocount 1 is added to avoid zero probabilities [4]. The transition matrix is then defined from these counts as

$$\mathbf{T}_Q(\lambda) = \begin{pmatrix} \dfrac{n_{\lambda,0,0}}{n_{\lambda,0,0} + n_{\lambda,0,1}} & \dfrac{n_{\lambda,0,1}}{n_{\lambda,0,0} + n_{\lambda,0,1}} \\ \dfrac{n_{\lambda,1,0}}{n_{\lambda,1,0} + n_{\lambda,1,1}} & \dfrac{n_{\lambda,1,1}}{n_{\lambda,1,0} + n_{\lambda,1,1}} \end{pmatrix}.$$

The mapping $\mathbf{T}_Q$ is computable in time $\mathcal{O}(|Q| + c)$ and space $\mathcal{O}(|\Lambda|)$, where c is the number of class boundaries. We can now formally define the context-aware Markov chain null hypothesis.

Definition 2. *The context-aware Markov chain null hypothesis ($\mathcal{H}_0^{\text{context}}$) for query annotation Q and context $\phi : \{0, \ldots, L-1\} \to \Lambda$ is that the query annotation Q is generated by the context-aware Markov chain $(\phi, \mathbf{T}_Q)$.*

Note that under context ϕ with a single class, the context-aware Markov chain null hypothesis $\mathcal{H}_0^{\text{context}}$ reduces to the Markov chain null hypothesis by Gafurov et al. [5], with a small difference that the initial state distribution $\vec{\pi}$ is set to the stationary distribution at position -1 instead of always starting in state 0 at position 0.

When there is just one context class, $\mathcal{H}_0^{\text{context}}$ can be viewed as an approximation to the permutational null, i.e. shuffling the query intervals around in a random fashion [5]. In the case of multiple classes, $\mathcal{H}_0^{\text{context}}$ can be thought of as an approximation to shuffling the query intervals around separately within each class. However, $\mathcal{H}_0^{\text{context}}$ also transparently handles intervals spanning one or even multiple class boundaries.

2.3 Computing the Mean and Variance of the Overlap and Shared Bases Test Statistics

Here, we state our main algorithmic result: fast computation of the mean and variance of $K(R,Q)$ and $B(R,Q)$ statistics under $\mathcal{H}_0^{\text{context}}$. The mean and variance are then used to compute the p-values using the normal approximation.

Theorem 1. *Let R and Q be two annotations and let ϕ be a genome context with c class boundaries. Let A be either the number of overlaps test statistic K or the number of shared bases test statistic B. It is possible to compute the mean $E_{Q' \sim C(\phi, \mathbf{T}_Q)}[A(R, Q')]$ and variance $\text{Var}_{Q' \sim C(\phi, \mathbf{T}_Q)}[A(R, Q')]$ in space $\mathcal{O}(|R|+c)$ and in time*

- $\mathcal{O}(|R| + |Q| + c)$ *when A is the overlap test statistic,*
- $\mathcal{O}(|Q| + (|R| + c)\log t)$ *when A is the shared bases test statistic; here, t is the length of the longest stretch of positions within a single reference interval with the same context class in R.*

Under the assumption that the test statistic is approximately normally distributed, this algorithm can be used to obtain the full probability mass function of its distribution under the null, i.e. values $\text{Pr}_{Q' \sim C(\phi, \mathbf{T}_Q)}[A(R, Q') = x]$ for all values of x. Note that the previous MCDP algorithm for this problem only works with a single context, only works for the overlap statistic K, and runs in $\mathcal{O}(|R|^2 + |Q|)$ time [5]. However, it makes no assumption about normality.

In the next section, we provide a high-level description of the algorithm for computing expectation and variance. The details and proof of correctness were omitted due to space constraints.

2.4 Mean and Variance of Any Separable Statistic

We call a statistic *separable* if it can be expressed as a sum of contributions from each reference interval and each contribution depends only on the part of the query annotation inside this reference interval. For example, the contribution of each reference interval in the overlap statistic K is 1 or 0, depending on whether there is an overlap with some query interval. In the shared bases statistic B, the contribution is the number of bases that a particular reference interval shares with the query intervals.

Thanks to linearity of expectation, the expected value of any separable statistic can be computed for every reference interval separately and then summed together. The simplest case is the shared bases statistic B, which can be expressed as the sum of indicator variables for each base covered by R, and in the case of single-class null model, the expectation can be computed simply as the number of bases covered by R multiplied by the stationary probability of state 1 of the Markov chain. Context-aware models complicate the situation, as each base of the genome has its unique marginal distribution over states, depending on the sequence of class labels preceding it.

Computing variance is more complicated, as the values of the statistic in individual intervals of R are dependent, and therefore the overall variance is not a simple sum of individual variances. However, in a sequence of Markov chain states $(S_0, \ldots, S_{L-1})$, states S_i and S_j are conditionally independent given $S_k = s$ for $i \leq k \leq j$. Therefore, if random variable X is a function of $S_i, \ldots, S_{k-1}$ and random variable Y is a function of $S_k, \ldots, S_{j-1}$, then $\mathrm{Var}[X + Y \mid S_k = s] = \mathrm{Var}[X \mid S_k = s] + \mathrm{Var}[Y \mid S_k = s]$.

Our algorithm computes conditional variance in individual intervals of R conditioning on states at both interval boundaries, and then combines them using this formula. In order to remove conditioning on the boundary states, we use the law of total variance, which for binary variable S_k can be written as $\mathrm{Var}(X) = \sum_{s=0}^{1} \mathrm{Var}[X \mid S_k = s] \Pr[S_k = s] + \sum_{s=0}^{1} E[X \mid S_k = s]^2 \Pr[S_k = s](1 - \Pr[S_k = s]) - 2\prod_{s=0}^{1} E[X \mid S_k = s]^2 \Pr[S_k = s]$.

The key data structure in our algorithm is a $\mathcal{O}(1)$-sized vector called a *two-sided plumbus* defined below. It contains the quantities that we need to compute for every interval of R, conditioning on states at interval boundaries. In the definition, function v expresses the contribution of a reference interval to the separable test statistic.

Definition 3. *Let $(\phi, \mathbf{T})$ be a context-aware Markov chain with state sequence $S_{-1}, S_0, \ldots S_{|L|-1}$, let $[i, j)$ be a subinterval of $[0, L)$, and let v be a function on a binary sequence of length $j - i$. We define the* two-sided plumbus *for interval $[i, j)$ as the collection of values*

$$\mu_v(i, j \mid x, y) := E[v(S_i, \ldots, S_{j-1}) \mid S_{i-1} = x, S_{j-1} = y]$$

$$\sigma_v^2(i, j \mid x, y) := \mathrm{Var}[v(S_i, \ldots, S_{j-1}) \mid S_{i-1} = x, S_{j-1} = y]$$

$$\Psi(x \overset{i-1, j-1}{\to} y) := \Pr[S_{j-1} = y \mid S_{i-1} = x]$$

for all combinations of (x, y) in $\{0, 1\}^2$.

The two-sided plumbuses computed for individual intervals of R and gaps between them are then combined to plumbuses for successively longer intervals, until we cover the whole chromosome and obtain the overall variance and expected value of the statistic of interest (see Fig. 2).

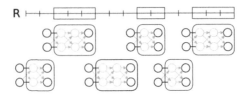

Fig. 2. Two-sided plumbuses for a reference annotation R. The plumbuses in the first row correspond to the reference intervals, and the plumbuses in the second row correspond to the gaps between the intervals. We highlight in black the boundary states on which we condition the values in each plumbus. Note that the conditional means μ_v and variances σ_v^2 in the gap plumbuses are constant zeroes, since gaps do not contribute to the total test statistic.

In the algorithm, we compute $\Pr[S_j = y \mid S_i = x]$ and $\Pr[S_i = S_{i+1} = \cdots = S_j = 0]$ in constant time, provided that interval $[i, j]$ is labeled by the same context class. This leads to a linear-time algorithm for $K(R, Q)$ statistic. For $B(R, Q)$ statistic, we split an interval of R into subintervals of size 1, compute plumbuses for them, and combine them in a similar manner, as we combine plumbuses in the overall algorithm. However, within a single context class, corresponding plumbus depends only on the interval length, and thus we can compute plumbuses for interval sizes which are powers of two and combine them to obtain a plumbus for any interval length within a single context in logarithmic time.

2.5   Multiple Chromosomes

Both our model and our algorithm can be extended to genomes with multiple chromosomes in a straightforward way. We assume that the query annotation is generated independently for each chromosome. The training of the context-aware Markov chain is accomplished simply by counting transition frequencies on all chromosomes. The test statistic for the whole genome is defined as the sum of test statistic values for the individual chromosomes. This, in turn, allows to compute the mean and variance of the total statistic by summing the means and variances, respectively, for the individual chromosomes. Note that this simple computation works for the variance thanks to the chromosome independence assumption. Therefore, the time and space complexity of our algorithm remains the same for the case of multiple chromosomes.

3   Experiments

The Normal Distribution Yields an Accurate p-value Approximation. Our MCDP2 algorithm computes the exact expectation and variance of the null distribution and uses them to approximate the null distribution by the normal distribution. Here, we first compare the accuracy of this approximation for the $K(R, Q)$ statistic with the exact distribution computed by the previous MCDP algorithm [5]. The comparison was performed on synthetic data sets with genome

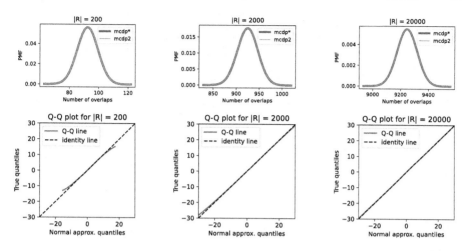

Fig. 3. The comparison of the exact probability mass functions (PMFs) for the number of overlaps K statistic (MCDP*) with its normal approximation (MCDP2) on synthetic data sets. Each column represents a different number of reference intervals ($|R| \in \{200, 2000, 20000\}$). The bottom plots show the quantile-quantile plot (Q-Q plot) between the two distributions.

length $L = 10^8$ bp, query annotations with 50 000 randomly generated intervals of length 500 bp each and reference annotations with up to 20 000 intervals of length 500 bp each. To understand the influence of the number of reference intervals on the accuracy, we vary $|R|$ from 200 to 20 000.

Figure 3 shows that the exact PMF in general agrees well with the normal approximation. The approximation approach allows to estimate even very low p-values accurately with the growing number of reference intervals. However, for $|R| = 200$ the differences in the extreme tail of the distribution lead to overly conservative p-values. Therefore, for small values of $|R|$ we recommend the use of the exact MCDP algorithm, which is not time-prohibitive. The new MCDP2 tool includes a reimplementation of the exact computation of the PMF and its extension to multiple context classes, and we use it in these experiments under the label MCDP*. We have also conducted similar experiments for the shared bases statistic $B(R, Q)$ with similar results (results not shown due to space constraints).

MCDP2 is Fast and Memory Efficient. The speed of our algorithm enables us to apply our tools to large-scale comparisons, such as the data from a recent study of ENCODE epigenetic modification enrichment for different repeat types in the human genome [8], employing the Telomere-to-Telomere (T2T) human genome assembly [14]. We use a context with two classes, one corresponding to all repeats and one to the rest of the genome, leading to over 4 million class boundaries. We use one of the 10 repeat types as the reference and one of the 45 available combinations of an epigenetic modification and a cell line as the

Table 1. Data set sizes and average running times for comparison of repeat types (R) with epigenetic modifications (Q), using all repeats as context. Averages are computed across 45 different query annotations, each representing a specific epigenetic modification in a specific cell line. Note that the running time grows with $|R| + c$, and in this experiment, c is large even for inputs with small $|R|$.

Repeat type	$|R|$	time (s)	
		$K(R,Q)$	$B(R,Q)$
RNA	11 139	220	160
Other	8 835	220	157
Unknown	11 229	226	159
Satellite	47 041	229	202
Low-complexity	102 521	244	223
DNA	505 896	343	588
LTR	660 823	387	769
Simple	708 565	398	637
LINE	1 440 792	578	1 477
SINE	1 672 984	640	1 637

query. Using 24 CPU threads, MCDP2 computed p-values for all 450 pairs in approx. 2 hours (wall clock) for the number of overlaps and approx. 3 hours for the number of shared bases, using at most 4.2 Gb (2.3 Gb) memory per comparison for overlaps (shared bases) statistic (see Table 1).

We compare the running time of MCDP2 to the quadratic-time MCDP* algorithm on the synthetic data sets used for Fig. 3, with 20 pairs of R and Q generated for each setting (Fig. 4). Note that MCDP* is faster than the original MCDP implementation [5], thanks to more extensive use of numpy library and reimplementation of part of the algorithm in C++. For the overlaps statistic, the MCDP* needs more than 1 000 seconds for 20 000 reference intervals, while our new approach MCDP2 only takes approximately 8 seconds on the same inputs. Computation for the number of shared bases is slightly slower (23 seconds for $|R| = 20 000$), which is consistent with its quasi-linear time complexity (in contrast to purely linear for the number of overlaps).

Genome Contexts Enable More Detailed Analysis of Colocalization of Copy Number Loss with Different Gene Groups. To illustrate the power of our context-aware null model, we have reanalyzed the colocalization of exons of different gene groups with copy number loss regions, originally performed by Zarrei et al. [21]. Figure 5 shows the Z-scores for both K and B test statistics and for three types of contexts. The first context function only uses a single class. The second context function creates two classes by masking regions that are assembly gaps; this is motivated by the fact that both copy number losses and exons are annotated exclusively outside the gaps and, therefore, may appear colocated

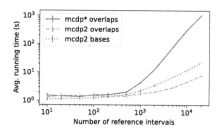

Fig. 4. Average running time on synthetic data for overlaps (MCDP2, MCDP*) statistic and shared bases (MCDP2) statistic. The vertical bars represent the standard deviation over 20 samples. Both axes are in log scale. The calculations were performed on a single thread on Intel(R) Xeon(R) Gold 6248R CPU.

even if they were independent (previously also studied by Domanska et al. [2]). The third context function uses six classes: one for gaps and the other five for discretization of the GC content in 1 kbp windows; this is motivated by the fact that GC content is known to be a significant confounding factor in many genomic analyses [1,7].

Figure 5 illustrates the importance of having a class in the context dedicated to gaps. In one jarring scenario, the set of all exons is enriched for overlaps with copy number losses (also observed by Zarrei et al.), but after accounting for gaps, the exons become depleted. More generally, across all studied gene groups, the Z-score decreases when the gaps are taken into account. This is expected as neither exons nor copy number losses occur in gaps, and thus ignoring gaps in the analysis may create spurious enrichments or lower the degree of observed depletion compared with analysis that takes gaps into account.

The GC-aware context also proves crucial for an accurate analysis. For example, the depletion of all exons for overlaps with copy number losses becomes much more pronounced in the GC-aware context. In another striking example, genes with no known phenotype appear enriched for overlap with losses (also in agreement with Zarrei et al.) when using the gap-aware context, but enrichment turns into slight depletion after taking GC content into account.

Other observations from Fig. 5 are generally consistent with biological expectations. Protein-coding genes are only slightly depleted in the single-class context but become significantly depleted when using gap-aware or GC-aware contexts. This depletion is consistent with the expectation that protein-coding exons are mostly evolutionarily conserved. Interestingly, the set of non-coding genes is strongly enriched for copy number losses under all three context functions, and the enrichment was also observed by Zarrei et al.

Differential Analysis of Non-telomeric and Telomeric TAR Elements. Completion of the previously inaccessible parts of the human genome [14] has allowed Gershman et al. [8] to study telomere-associated repeats (TARs) and their colocalization with epigenetic modifications. While TARs located in subtelomeric regions are presumed to be important for telomere length regulation,

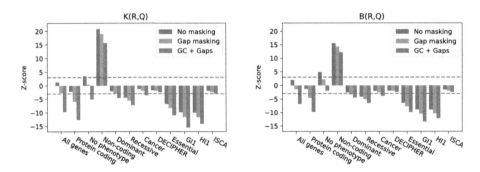

Fig. 5. Z-scores for colocalization of exons of various gene groups (R, x-axis) with copy number losses (Q) under three different null models: single-class context, gap-aware context, and GC–aware context. Left: overlap statistic K; Right: shared bases statistic B. The green and red dashed lines stand for Z-score +3 and –3 respectively, corresponding to p-value 0.00135 for enrichment/depletion. (Color figure online)

TAR copies have also been dispersed to other parts of the genome. Differences between these two groups may further clarify mechanisms and functions of TARs in subtelomeric regions. While Gershman et al. observe differences in enrichment of some epigenetic marks, they do not assign statistical significance to their findings.

We adapted our context-aware Markov chain model to perform such differential analysis of enrichment between two annotations. In general, consider two references $R_1 \subseteq R_2$. In our case, R_1 are non-telomeric TARs, R_2 are all TARs, and Q are regions with a particular epigenetic mark. One could compare the enrichment p-value of Q in R_1 with the enrichment p-value of Q in R_2; however, this is not statistically sound [9,20]. Instead, we create a context ϕ_{rel} with two class labels {outside, inside}, where positions covered by R_2 are labeled "inside" and all other positions are labeled "outside." We then use a test statistic to measure the significance of enrichment of Q in reference R_1 with context ϕ_{rel}. This context ensures that within R_1 the null model uses the parameters estimated from intervals of Q that overlap R_2, thus comparing colocalization of Q in R_1 relative to colocalization of Q in the whole R_2. Note that the query intervals can occur also outside of R_2, and their properties are summarized in the parameters of the Markov chain for the "outside" class. These outside areas then influence the distribution of the test statistic under the null only by influencing the initial state distribution at the start of each interval of R_1.

Figure 6 shows the result of this analysis. Similarly to Gershman et al. [8] we observe relative enrichment of activating marks *H3K27ac* and *H3K4me3* in non-telomeric TARs using both K and B statistics. We can also see enrichment of *CTCF*, which is significant only under the shared bases statistic, perhaps due to the small number of intervals in R_1. Gershman et al. were not able to observe relative enrichment for *CTCF* on non-telomeric TARs, although they do observe that *CTCF* is strongly enriched in both TAR classes compared to

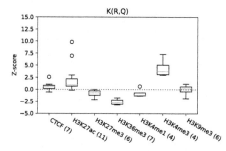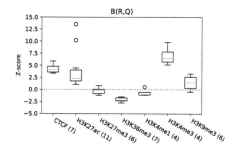

Fig. 6. Relative enrichment of telomere-associated repeats (TARs) located further than 20 kbp from chromosome ends (R_1) with epigenetic modifications (Q) in comparison to all TARs (R_2), using both the number of overlaps statistic K (left) and the number of shared bases statistic B (right). The numbers in the parentheses denote the number of cell lines available for each modification.

the background. This highlights usefulness of our context model in scenarios requiring relative analysis of two reference annotations.

4   Discussion

We have introduced a novel model for annotation colocalization analysis, which uses genomic contexts to capture confounding factors that may lead to false significance results. Taking advantage of the Markovian properties of our model, we have provided a general framework to compute the exact mean and variance of a broad class of colocalization test statistics (which we named *separable*). Using this framework, we were able to obtain linear and quasi-linear algorithms to compute the Z-scores for the number of overlaps and the number of shared bases. We have then proposed to convert the exact Z-score to approximate p-values using the normal distribution.

Our algorithm computes the Z-score in $\mathcal{O}(|Q| + |R| + c)$ time for the overlap number statistic and in $\mathcal{O}(|Q| + (|R| + c)\log t)$ time for the shared bases statistic, where $|Q|$ and $|R|$ are the number of intervals in the query and reference, respectively, c is the number of context class switches, and t is an upper bound on the reference interval length. This is in contrast to the previous best algorithm, which did not account for genome contexts and took $\mathcal{O}(|R|^2 + |Q|)$ time to compute the probability mass function of the p-values [5].

In our experiments, we have demonstrated that our algorithm is sufficiently fast to allow large-scale studies comparing many pairs of annotations with large reference sets and frequent context class boundaries. We have reanalyzed data sets from two large-scale studies [8,21], and thanks to our new context-aware model, we were able to further illuminate the nature of colocalizations discovered in these works, in some cases reversing previously published findings.

We have experimentally shown that the normal approximation of the distribution of the number of overlaps under $\mathcal{H}_0^{\text{context}}$ yields accurate p-values, and the approximation gets tighter with increasing number of reference annotation intervals. This behaviour intuitively follows from the representation of a separable statistic as a sum of contributions for individual reference intervals. If those contributions were independent, their sum would converge to a normal distribution with a growing number of reference intervals under the classical central limit theorem. Though the contributions of individual intervals are dependent in our case, the fact that the dependencies stem from a Markov chain makes it possible that the sum converges under some extensions of the central limit theorem. In future, we hope to characterize sufficient conditions for such convergence. Additionally, we would like to explore the possibility of providing lower and upper bounds on the precision of the p-value estimation, possibly by applying the Stein's method [16].

On a more practical side, in our future research, we would like to explore the possibility of using quantitative contexts, with numeric values such as GC content, epigenetic mark density, sequence conservation etc. Some work in this direction has already been done, particularly in HyperBrowser [17]. In MCDP2 this could be achieved for example by parameterizing the weights of the underlying Markov chains with the context value at each position. The challenge would be to keep the running time efficient for large genomes.

Another challenge is to provide statistical significance for statistics comparing colocalization of query Q with respect to two different references R_1 and R_2, such as $B(R_1, Q)/B(R_2, Q)$. This may in some situations be preferable to our approach of comparing such colocalization through contexts, which we used for the analysis of TAR elements.

Funding Information. This material is based upon work supported by the National Science Foundation under Grant No. DBI-2138585. Research reported in this publication was supported by the National Institute Of General Medical Sciences of the National Institutes of Health under Award Number R01GM146462. The content is solely the responsibility of the authors and does not necessarily represent the official views of the National Institutes of Health. This work was also supported by a grant from the European Union Horizon 2020 research and innovation program No. 872539 (PANGAIA); and grants from the Slovak Research and Development Agency APVV-22-0144 and the Scientific Grant Agency VEGA 1/0538/22.

References

1. Burge, C., Karlin, S.: Prediction of complete gene structures in human genomic DNA. J. Mol. Biol. **268**(1), 78–94 (1997)
2. Domanska, D., Kanduri, C., Simovski, B., Sandve, G.K.: Mind the gaps: overlooking inaccessible regions confounds statistical testing in genome analysis. BMC Bioinf. **19**(1), 481 (2018). https://doi.org/10.1186/s12859-018-2438-1
3. Dozmorov, M.G., Cara, L.R., Giles, C.B., Wren, J.D.: GenomeRunner web server: regulatory similarity and differences define the functional impact of SNP sets. Bioinformatics **32**(15), 2256–2263 (2016)

4. Durbin, R., Eddy, S.R., Krogh, A., Mitchison, G.: Biological Sequence Analysis: Probabilistic Models of Proteins and Nucleic Acids. Cambridge University Press, Cambridge (1998). https://doi.org/10.1017/CBO9780511790492

5. Gafurov, A., Brejová, B., Medvedev, P.: Markov chains improve the significance computation of overlapping genome annotations. Bioinformatics **38**(Supplement-1), i203–i211 (2022). https://doi.org/10.1093/bioinformatics/btac255

6. Gel, B., Diez-Villanueva, A., Serra, E., Buschbeck, M., Peinado, M.A., Malinverni, R.: regioneR: an R/Bioconductor package for the association analysis of genomic regions based on permutation tests. Bioinformatics **32**(2), 289–291 (2016)

7. Gelfman, S., Ast, G.: When epigenetics meets alternative splicing: the roles of DNA methylation and GC architecture. Epigenomics **5**(4), 351–353 (2013)

8. Gershman, A., et al.: Epigenetic patterns in a complete human genome. Science **376**(6588) (2022). https://doi.org/10.1126/science.abj5089

9. Goodman, S.: A dirty dozen: twelve p-value misconceptions. Semin. Hematol. **45**(3), 135–140 (2008). https://doi.org/10.1053/j.seminhematol.2008.04.003

10. Guenther, M.G., Levine, S.S., Boyer, L.A., Jaenisch, R., Young, R.A.: A chromatin landmark and transcription initiation at most promoters in human cells. Cell **130**(1), 77–88 (2007). https://doi.org/10.1016/j.cell.2007.05.042

11. Heger, A., Webber, C., Goodson, M., Ponting, C.P., Lunter, G.: GAT: a simulation framework for testing the association of genomic intervals. Bioinformatics **29**(16), 2046–2048 (2013). https://doi.org/10.1093/bioinformatics/btt343

12. Kanduri, C., Bock, C., Gundersen, S., Hovig, E., Sandve, G.K.: Colocalization analyses of genomic elements: approaches, recommendations and challenges. Bioinformatics **35**(9), 1615–1624 (2019). https://doi.org/10.1093/bioinformatics/bty835

13. Koller, D., Friedman, N.: Probabilistic Graphical Models: Principles and Techniques. MIT press, Cambridge (2009)

14. Nurk, S., et al.: The complete sequence of a human genome. Science **376**(6588), 44–53 (2022). https://doi.org/10.1126/science.abj6987

15. Quinlan, A.R., Hall, I.M.: BEDTools: a flexible suite of utilities for comparing genomic features. Bioinformatics **26**(6), 841–842 (2010). https://doi.org/10.1093/bioinformatics/btq033

16. Ross, N.: Fundamentals of Stein's method. Probab. Surv. **8**(1), 210–293 (2011). https://doi.org/10.1214/11-PS182

17. Sandve, G.K., et al.: The genomic hyperbrowser: inferential genomics at the sequence level. Genome Biol. **11**(12) (2010). https://doi.org/10.1186/gb-2010-11-12-r121

18. Sarmashghi, S., Bafna, V.: Computing the statistical significance of overlap between genome annotations with ISTAT. Cell Syst. **8**(6), 523–529 (2019). https://doi.org/10.1016/j.cels.2019.05.006

19. Sheffield, N.C., Bock, C.: LOLA: enrichment analysis for genomic region sets and regulatory elements in R and Bioconductor. Bioinformatics **32**(4), 587–589 (2016). https://doi.org/10.1093/bioinformatics/btv612

20. Sullivan, G.M., Feinn, R.: Using effect size-or why the P value is not enough. J. Grad. Med. Educ. **4**(3), 279–282 (2012)

21. Zarrei, M., MacDonald, J.R., Merico, D., Scherer, S.W.: A copy number variation map of the human genome. Nat. Rev. Genet. **16**(3), 172–183 (2015). https://doi.org/10.1038/nrg3871

Secure Federated Boolean Count Queries Using Fully-Homomorphic Cryptography

Alexander T. Leighton[1,2] and Yun William Yu[3,4(✉)]

[1] Harvard Medical School, Boston, MA 02115, USA
[2] Brandeis University, Waltham, MA 02453, USA
[3] University of Toronto Scarborough, Toronto, ON M1C 1A4, Canada
[4] Carnegie Mellon University, Pittsburgh, PA 15213, USA
ywyu@cmu.edu

Abstract. Biomedical data is often distributed between a network of custodians, causing challenges for researchers wishing to securely compute aggregate statistics on those data without centralizing everything—the prototypical 'count query' asks how many patients match some multifaceted set of conditions across a network of hospitals. Difficulty arises from two sources: (1) the need to deduplicate patients who may be present in the records of multiple hospitals and (2) the need to unify partial records for the same patient which may be split across hospitals. Although cryptographic tools for secure computation promise to enable collaborative studies with formal privacy guarantees, existing approaches either are computationally impractical or support only simplified analysis pipelines. To the best of our knowledge, no existing practical secure method addresses both of these difficulties simultaneously.

Here, we introduce secure federated Boolean count queries using a novel 2-stage probabilistic sketching and sampling protocol that can be efficiently implemented in off-the-shelf federated homomorphic encryption libraries (Palisade and Lattigo), provably ensuring data security. To this end, we needed several key technological innovations, including re-encoding the LogLog union-cardinality sketch and designing an appropriate sampling for intersection cardinalities. Our benchmarking shows that we can answer federated Boolean count queries in less than 2 CPU-minutes with absolute errors in the range of 6% of the total number of touched records, while revealing only the final answer and the total number of touched records. With modern core-parallelism, we can thus answer queries on the order of seconds. Our study demonstrates that by computing on compressed and encrypted data, it is possible to securely answer federated Boolean count queries in real-time.

Keywords: Federated count-query · Probabilistic sketch · Homomorphic encryption

1 Introduction

The federated Boolean count query asks how many unique patients in a network match a given set of criteria [22]. Computing a cardinality is algorithmi-

J. Ma (Ed.): RECOMB 2024, LNCS 14758, pp. 54–67, 2024.
https://doi.org/10.1007/978-1-0716-3989-4_4

cally straight-forward; however, as patient information is confidential, ideally statistics should be computed privately, protected even from other hospitals in the network. Since arbitrary statistical on a distributed database can be easily computed from federated boolean queries, there is significant motivation in constructing these secure primitives.

Two major problems arise when trying to compute aggregate statistics without revealing information about individuals: (1) it is difficult to resolve duplicate patients across institutions, and (2) it is difficult to combine partial information about the same patient across institutions. To illustrate, suppose we are interested in the question of how many patients at Beth Israel Deaconess Medical Center (BIDMC) and at Massachusetts General Hospital (MGH) have both hypertension and diabetes. If a patient Alice has records for hypertension and diabetes at both BIDMC and MGH, she may be double-counted. On the other hand, a patient Bob who is recorded at BIDMC only for hypertension and at MGH only for diabetes may not be counted at all, unless those records can be combined.

Note that because any Boolean query can be written in conjunctive normal form (an "AND of ORs"), we can rewrite any Boolean count as an intersection of unions. Thus, more precisely, given n parties and n_c conditions, let $A_{i,j}$ be the records at party i matching condition j. Then, it is sufficient to be able to compute

$$\bigcap_{j=1}^{n_c} \bigcup_{i=1}^{n} A_{i,j}.$$

For example, if we want to know all patients who broke their legs and either have hypertension or diabetes (or both), we can rewrite that query as the union of hypertension and diabetes patients, intersected with the set of patients who broke their legs.

A growing body of work seeks to address this issue, but all practical approaches we have seen either rely on a trusted third party or reveal some private information. It is possible to control this data leakage with data use agreements, financial penalties, etc., but those are legal controls, not technical ones [20]. In prior work, we showed that probabilistic cardinality estimators (such as HyperLogLog [10]) can be used to trade off accuracy for privacy [23], as measured by the metric of k-anonymity [18]. Intuitively, probabilistic sketches and other lossy compression algorithms inherently add noise to the system, which may decrease the ability of an adversary to pinpoint an individual. Unfortunately, Desfontaines et al. [7] proved that an adversary with access to all intermediate HyperLogLog probabilistic sketch representations during computation can reconstruct a large fraction of records. Furthermore, even a weaker adversary with only access to the partial sketches each hospital sends to a central party can reveal substantial amounts of information [19]. Stronger privacy guarantees can be had by combining sketching with differential privacy [9] on the intermediate sketches [16], but the noise-based mechanisms do still leak a quantifiable amount of private information, and furthermore decrease the accuracy of the aggregate statistics.

Modern cryptographic tools can in theory resolve these shortcomings through fully homomorphic encryption (FHE) [13]. All sensitive computations are run on ciphertext (encrypted data) and only the final answer is revealed, removing the need of adding noise to the data all together; this is in many ways both simpler and more secure than the noise-based mechanisms when properly implemented—no data is leaked by intermediate computation. The typical Achilles heel of secure multi-party computation (MPC) is its speed—to compare, even the fast secure MPC GWAS protocols require hours of total single-threaded compute [3,11], perhaps reducible to tens of minutes using parallelization. While suitable for complex analyses, such runtimes exceed reasonable expectations in the workflow of clinical query systems, such as i2b2 or Shrine, which are expected to return queries on the order of only a few minutes at most. The recent MPC-FM [15] and DP-DICE [21] algorithms fully solve what they call the secure distributed cardinality estimation problem, the latter on the order of minutes, which is very nearly fast enough. However, the secure distributed cardinality estimation task only resolves duplicate records across data custodians, and does not allow for combining partial information about the same patient, so those do not solve the federated Boolean count query problem we pose—in the notation above, these methods only solve the union half of the problem, but not the intersection portion. Indeed, to our knowledge, there are no efficient protocols for the full federated Boolean count query problem.

In this work, we introduce secure federated Boolean count queries using a novel 2-stage probabilistic sketching and sampling protocol implemented using fully-homomorphic ring-learning with errors cryptography. In particular, we use the residue number system (RNS) variant of BFV encryption [14], as implemented in the Palisade [17] and Lattigo [1] software libraries. Our algorithm works by first computing an approximate count query of all "touched records" from encrypted LogLog [8] sketches; one key conceptual advance is in determining that unlike other sketches, a unary encoding of the LogLog sketches can be manipulated efficiently in ciphertext. This provides a very fast resolution to the secure distributed cardinality estimation problem (also solved by MPC-FM and DP-DICE). Then, we use the results of that count-query to determine the density at which to perform a blind coordinated random subsampling of the touched records at each hospital to estimate an intersection cardinality.

2 Methods

The maturity of fully homomorphic cryptographic libraries means that it is now feasible to treat them as black-box alternate computation platforms. A webdesigner need not understand the intricacies behind the HTTPS protocol, but can simply specify the security/computation tradeoff they want. A data scientist using GPU-acceleration needs only know that matrix multiplication and vectorized operations are faster, but conditionals are much slower. Similarly, with Palisade and Lattigo, algorithms designers can choose relevant parameters, and then are given a set of primitives around which to design algorithms, abstracting away the underlying cryptography.

In particular, our methodology relies on primitives of secure multiparty encryption and decryption, as well as secure addition and multiplication of encrypted numerics. Our methods, roughly speaking, use Palisade and Lattigo as black boxes to construct secure union cardinality estimates E. Then, by statistical sampling we construct secure intersection cardinality estimates from secure unions. From these simple primitives, it is rather straightforward to construct more complex statistical queries.

2.1 Background

Most work tackling privacy-preserving multiset cardinality estimation relies on the LogLog-family of cardinality estimators [8, 10]. The basic idea behind these estimators is that given n uniformly random numbers between 0 and 1, the expected minimum of these numbers of $\frac{1}{n+1}$. Thus, one naive way to estimate cardinality is to hash elements in an arbitrary set to uniformly random numbers, and then take the inverse of the minimum such value. Assuming we are consistent with our choice of hash function, we automatically get de-duplication because duplicate elements hash to the same value.

The LogLog family of algorithms reformulates the procedure to reduce both space-complexity and variance. First, instead of storing the minimum hash value exactly, one only needs to store the order-of-magnitude of the minimum hash values, which are likewise already logarithmic in the size of the set through binary encoding. Importantly, the double logarithmic space compression allows us to later use an exponential blow-up through a unary encoding of the bit vectors while still maintaining reasonable logarithmic space.

Another key idea from the literature is that keeping track of multiple minimum hash values for a set of buckets reduces variance; these buckets are purely an algorithmic feature unrelated to any clinical queries. In the LogLog algorithm, a fixed number of buckets, m, is picked. Then, elements are assigned a random hash value and bucket. We keep track of the minimum for each bucket, taking the combined minimum per bucket when merging into an aggregate approximation. Much of the rich historic work in the development of the LogLog family has aimed to construct lower-variance estimators. The original LogLog estimator uses an arithmetic mean of bucket values, and had a standard error of around $\frac{1.30}{\sqrt{m}}$. SuperLogLog improves upon LogLog by truncating extreme data, getting an effective error of around $\frac{1.05}{\sqrt{m}}$. The most popular today, HyperLogLog, replaces the arithmetic mean of LogLog with a harmonic mean, with standard error $\frac{1.04}{\sqrt{m}}$. Unfortunately, neither conditional truncation nor harmonic means are efficient on the platform of modern homomorphic encryption, which really only efficiently supports addition and a few multiplications. As such, we realized we needed to switch to the older LogLog, which is less efficient on normal CPUs, but more efficient on ciphertext.

In the following section the **parties** are hospitals in the network. And the **cloud** is an untrusted central server (or servers) performing some given computation in ciphertext.

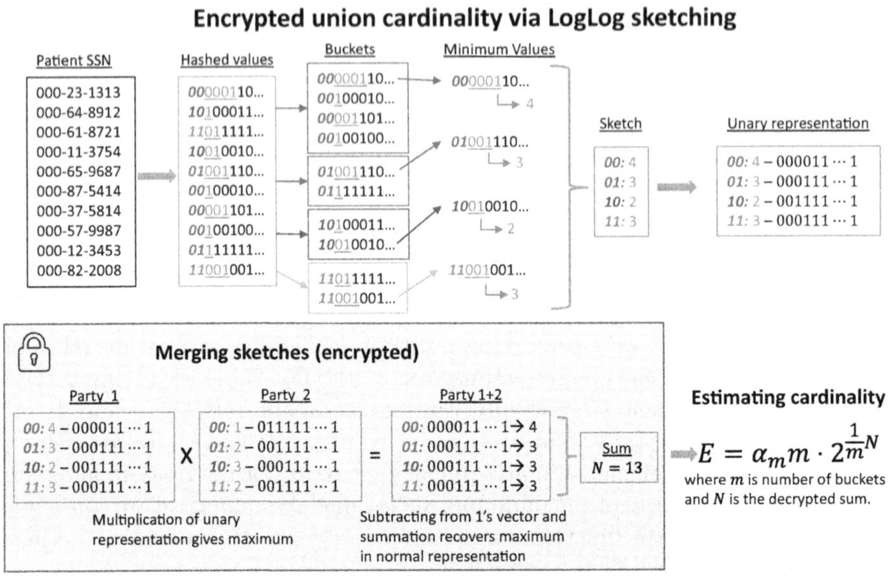

Encrypted union cardinality via LogLog sketching

Fig. 1. The encrypted union cardinality task can be solved via LogLog sketching and a unary encoding to allow for easy ciphertext maximums. Each party computes a ciphertext unary-encoded LogLog sketch, which is then sent an homomorphically merged to get just the raw value N, which can be used in conjunction with the number of buckets m to estimate union cardinality.

2.2   Union Cardinality

We begin by giving our implementation of secure union cardinality. Although existing work like MPC-FM [15] and DP-DICE [21] also solve this problem, that work was concurrent to ours, and ours is both easy to implement and fairly efficient (Fig. 1).

Our algorithm takes as input the query and each hospital returns m unary vectors representing a party's sketches of the query. These sketches are encrypted using a multiparty public key, so that all of the hospitals have to coordinate in order to decrypt anything—more precisely, we use threshold FHE [2] where each party can freely encrypt, but decryption requires all parties; thus, every party can ensure that only the aggregate statistic at the end of the protocol is decrypted. Importantly, the hash values for LogLog are integers between 0 and 31 (the LogLog estimators allow access to cardinalities exponential in the hash value, so a max value of 31 is sufficient for datasets as large as 2 billion patients), so we encode 0 as a vector of 32 ciphertext 1's, 1 as a vector with a single 0 and then 31 1's, and so on. Although the homomorphic operation operates at a vector level, in this first stage, we restrict ourselves to a bit-vector, getting effectively bitwise operations. If 5 is encoded as $0000011\cdots$, and 2 is encoded as $0011111\cdots$ (counting the number of initial 0's), then $(5, 2) = 0000011\cdots \times 0011111\cdots = 0000011\cdots$, which correctly encodes 5. This multiplication is the key to homomorphically merging LogLog sketches from different hospitals, as this operation lets us compute the maximum value in a particular bucket across sketches using $\log(n)$ multiplications, where n is the number of hospitals.

Once all the sketches are merged, the unary encoding has served its purpose. Then, we switch to a more standard ciphertext encoding of integers. To do that conversion, we just need to count the number of 0's in the sketch vector, which we do by subtracting component-wise from a vector of all 1's, and summing across the vector. We can thus sum up the total value in all merged buckets (recall that we have m total buckets), all while remaining in ciphertext and only using a small number of additions and multiplications. At the end of the protocol, we decrypt the sum of all bucket values N and we estimate the cardinality using the regular LogLog estimation in plaintext [8]:

$$E = a_m m 2^{\frac{33m-N}{m}},$$

where

$$a_m = \left(\Gamma \left(-\frac{1}{m} \right) \frac{1 - 2^{1/m}}{\ln 2} \right)^{-m}, \text{ and } \Gamma(s) = \frac{1}{s} \int_0^\infty e^t t^2 dt.$$

Since the number of buckets m is known and must be agreed upon to enact the protocol, the only sensitive information in that formula is N, the sum of all the bucket values. The information revealed by the estimate E is thus exactly equivalent to the information revealed by N. Hence, this entire computation reveals no information other than the answer to the query, and because it is precisely the LogLog algorithm shifted into ciphertext, the standard relative error is still $\frac{1.30}{\sqrt{m}}$.

2.3   Intersections Through Sampling

Private set intersection cardinality (PSI-CA), where parties want to jointly compute the intersection size between their sets without revealing anything else, has been extensively studied in the literature [5,6], including the multiparty variant [12]. However, unlike in prior work, we are not taking an intersection of sets belonging entirely to separate parties, but instead taking an intersection of sets that are themselves unions of the original data. Although it is possible to compute union sketches entirely in ciphertext, applying an intersection to them without decrypting is unfortunately not easy, even if we apply highly compressed intersection sketches [24], and we did not directly come up with a method of doing so.

Instead, we took an orthogonal approach based on sampling (Fig. 2). Consider first taking an intersection of unions over a small population of total size N, where we have n hospitals collaborating. We can resolve this by simply using a bitvector of length n. Each hospital can then generate a bitvector $A_{i,j}$ for hospital i and condition j, where $A_{i,j}[k] = 1$ if and only if patient k has condition j at hospital i. Then we can create merged condition bitvectors $C_j = A_{1,j} \lor$

Encrypted intersection sampling

Conditions A and B. Let $E \approx |A \cup B|$ across all parties. Want $|A \cap B|$. Use bitvectors of length m.

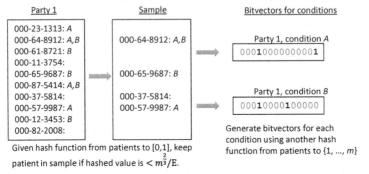

Party 1   Sample   Bitvectors for conditions

000-23-1313: A
000-64-8912: A,B   000-64-8912: A,B
000-61-8721: B   Party 1, condition A
000-11-3754:   00010000000001
000-65-9687: B   000-65-9687: B
000-87-5414: A,B
000-37-5814:   000-37-5814:   Party 1, condition B
000-57-9987: A   000-57-9987: A   00010000100000
000-12-3453: B
000-82-2008:   Generate bitvectors for each
                                                  condition using another hash
Given hash function from patients to [0,1], keep   function from patients to {1, ..., m}
patient in sample if hashed value is $< m^{\frac{2}{3}}/E$.

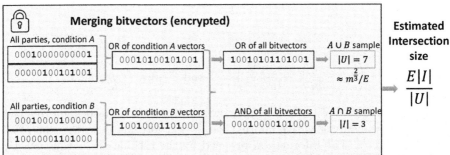

Merging bitvectors (encrypted)   **Estimated**

All parties, condition A   **Intersection**
00010000000001   OR of condition A vectors   OR of all bitvectors $A \cup B$ sample   **size**
00000100101001   00010100101001   10010101101001 $|U| = 7$
                                                                        $\approx m^{\frac{2}{3}}/E$ $\dfrac{E|I|}{|U|}$

All parties, condition B
00010000100000   OR of condition B vectors   AND of all bitvectors $A \cap B$ sample
10000001101000   10010001101000   00010000101000 $|I| = 3$

Fig. 2. Given knowledge of an approximate size for the union of multiple conditions, we can use coordinated random sampling at a specified density to estimate the size of the intersection of those conditions. See Theorem 1 for the proof of a near-optimal sampling rate. Note that one of the inputs is E, the union cardinality of all patients that match at least one of the conditions of interest.

$A_{2,j} \vee \cdots \vee A_{n,j}$, where $C_j[k] = 1$ if and only if patient k has condition j anywhere. The $\vee$ (OR) operator can be implemented by $X \vee Y = 1 - (1 - X) \times (1 - Y)$ in homomorphic subtraction and multiplication. Afterwards, we can compute the intersection of the condition bitvectors by $I = C_1 \wedge \cdots \wedge C_{n_c}$, where the $\wedge$ (AND) operator can be implemented by $A \wedge B = A \times B$. Then, $I[k] = 1$ if and only if patient k has all of the conditions anywhere across the hospital system. After, we can do an internal sum of all set bits in the I vector to get the number of such patients. We can also easily generate a U vector by replacing the AND with an OR, to recover $|U|$ the number of patients with any of the conditions.

Unfortunately, the universe of possible patients is too large for this to be currently feasible—because the hospitals do not want to reveal their patient populations, the bitvector would need length nearly 8 billion for the population of the planet (potentially less if geographically constrained, but still in the tens to hundreds of millions in many areas). If we could subsample, we might be able to use the bitvector technique on a smaller sample of patients, but we'd of course have to ensure that we sample the same sets of patients at each hospital. Another issue is that if we simply randomly sample patients, we might spend a large portion of our sample on patients that have nothing at all to do with the conditions we are interested in, especially if we are interested in looking at rare diseases.

Here, we make use of the union cardinality estimate E from the prior section, which we assume to be available in plaintext. Although no hospital knows the full list of patients that contributed to the union cardinality, notice that only patients who contributed to the union are potentially in the intersection. We can thus use E to compute a sampling rate S/E. Given a random hash function h_1 (shared among the hospitals) mapping patient IDs to the unit interval $[0, 1]$, we sample an ID if its hash function is less than the sampling rate. In expectation, we will then get a sample of S patients from the union, some fraction of which will be in the intersection. We then use some other random hash function h_2 from patient IDs to $[m]$. For each condition j, hospital i creates a bitvector $A_{i,j}$ of size m, and uses h_2 to set bits for the appropriate sampled patients. That is, $A_{i,j}[k] = 1$ if for some patient x, $h_1(x) < S/E$ and $h_2(x) = k$. Afterwards, all of the $A_{i,j}$ vectors can be merged as above, returning a count $|I|$ of sampled patients in the intersection of all conditions and a count $|U|$ of sampled patients in the union of all conditions. We then return $\frac{E|I|}{|U|}$ as the estimate of the total number of patients across the hospital network with all conditions.

Theorem 1. *Consider a bitvector of length m as described above. Then choosing an expected sample size $S = (m)^{2/3}$ minimizes the total expected error from hash collisions and sampling variance.*

The expected standard error is approximately $\frac{3}{2}m^{1/3}$.

Proof. There are two major sources of error in the returned count $|I|$ of sampled patients in the intersection: (1) sampling variation and (2) errors due to hash collisions. Hash collisions are a problem because multiple patients may end up in the same bit within the bitvector, resulting in undercounting if both are in the intersection or overcounting if neither is in the intersection but between the two of them, they have all of the conditions. One solution would be to choose $m = O(S^2)$ large enough to avoid collisions entirely, but this is inefficient. Instead, we will strive to jointly minimize both types of errors.

First, note that the standard absolute error from sampling S items can be approximated by $\sqrt{S}$. Second, we can upper bound the number of bins with multiple patients by simply the number of hash collisions. The expected number of hash collisions is $\binom{S}{2} \cdot \frac{1}{m} = \frac{S(S-1)}{2m}$ because the collision probability for any pair of hashes is $\frac{1}{m}$, and we use linearity of expectation over all pairs. Thus, absolute error $e(S) \leq \sqrt{S} + \frac{S(S-1)}{2m}$, given fixed m.

Minimizing absolute error gives $S = 0$, which is not helpful, so instead we will minimize relative error $f(S) \leq \frac{1}{\sqrt{S}} + \frac{S-1}{2m}$ given fixed bitvector length m

$$f(S) = \leq \frac{1}{\sqrt{S}} + \frac{S-1}{2m}$$
$$\text{Then } f'(\hat{S}) = -\frac{1}{2}\hat{S}^{-\frac{3}{2}} + \frac{1}{2m} = 0$$
$$\implies \hat{S} = m^{2/3}$$

Furthermore, substituting this value back in gives an expected absolute error of

$$e(\hat{S}) \approx \frac{3}{2}m^{1/3}$$

3   Results

The typical Achilles heel of secure multi-party computation (MPC) is its speed, but we show that our methods return queries on the order of only a few minutes at most with reasonable accuracy while maintaining secure.

3.1   Runtime Benchmarks

We wrote benchmarking code (https://github.com/atleighton/rlwe-hll for union cardinality and https://github.com/yunwilliamyu/federated-approx-boolean for intersection sampling) to determine the single-threaded runtimes of the cryptographic steps within our protocol, using a 128-bit security parameter and varying the number of buckets and parties—in Palisade, using HEStd_128_classic (plaintext modulus=65537) for the scheme parameters, and in Lattigo, using bfv.PN15QP827pq (logN=15, logQP=827, plaintext modulus=65537) for the scheme parameters. We measure the total computation across all computing parties, referring to the central server as the "cloud" (Fig. 3).

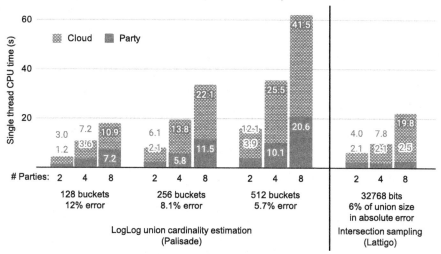

Fig. 3. Single-thread runtime of ciphertext operations. (left) The LogLog union cardinality estimation implemented in Palisade increases linearly in runtime with number of buckets, and also number of buckets, for both the cloud and for all other parties (total). (right) The intersection sampling implemented in Lattigo empirically increases in runtime linearly to the number of parties; note that the party runtimes seems to be going up sublinearly as the number of parties increases, but we think this is simply a result of a large constant factor overhead in our implementation.

We implemented the LogLog union cardinality estimation in the Palisade C++ library. Even simulating up to 8 parties on a single CPU thread takes only just over one minute to return an estimate using 512 buckets (and commensurately less time for fewer buckets). With parallelization across cores on modern 32-core servers, ignoring network communication time, it is thus feasible to return queries in much less than a minute, on the order of seconds, making the method feasible for interactive query systems.

We also implemented intersection sampling using the Lattigo Golang library. To fully utilize the bit parallelism in the cryptosystem, we used a 32768 bit bitvector. For 8 parties on a single CPU-thread, this operation takes less than 25 s without parallelism. Per Theorem 1, we downsample the density such that the union of all conditions should set roughly 1024 bits

3.2 Accuracy Analysis

Our encrypted protocol for computing the union cardinality using a LogLog sketch exactly matches the unencrypted equivalent, and therefore has the same accuracy. The standard error of **LogLog** sketches is $\approx \frac{1.30}{\sqrt{\#\text{buckets}}}$, which is somewhat less efficient than e.g. the standard error of **HyperLogLog** approximations at $\approx \frac{1.04}{\sqrt{\#\text{buckets}}}$. However, it follows simply we are able to achieve similar accuracy, regardless of our choice of sketching algorithms. In the **LogLog** case we increase the number of buckets by a factor of $\left(\frac{1.30}{1.04}\right)^2 = 1.56$. For the 512 bucket example, we end up with a 5.7% standard relative error in the union cardinality.

For the intersection sampling, we choose the sampling rate according to Theorem 1. Given a $2^{15} = 32768$ bit vector, we therefore had in expectation 1024 bits set by the union of all conditions, and 48 incorrectly set bits, so $\leq 5\%$ of the bits. This 5% error is of course scaled up by the density parameter through multiplying by the union cardinality estimate, so the total absolute final intersection error is roughly 5.985%$\approx$ 6% of the union cardinality.

3.3   Security Analysis

The security of our protocol in the semi-honest setting follows from the security of the well-known BFVrns homomorphic encryption scheme, and satisfies a threshold MPC condition, necessitating at least one party be honest. For additional details, we refer readers to Theorem 1 in Appendix B of"Multiparty Homomorphic Encryption from Ring-Learning-with-Errors" [4], implemented in Lattigo, which we use as a black box. Outside of this box, only three plaintext quantities are revealed: the bucket sum for the union cardinality LogLog sketch, the number of bits set from the subsampled union, and the number of bits set from the subsampled intersection. Together, these are used to compute the query outputs of the union and intersection cardinalities of the conditions that went into the query.

Importantly, in our protocol we do not seek to protect the outputs of the query from the adversary, only the underlying patient medical records. Thus, we are allowed to reveal the union and intersection cardinalities, as those are the answers to the queries. The union and intersection cardinalities correspond to the first and third quantities described above (after rescaling), so those quantities do not leak any information beyond the outputs of the queries. Also, the second quantity, the number of bits set from the subsampled union, will be a distribution centered around the expected sample size of $m^{2/3}$. How far off the quantity is from the expected value may leak some small amount of information about which patients were subsampled by the hash function, but the set of potentially sampled patients is of course also fully revealed by the choice of hash function, which is public knowledge, so this leakage is minimal. Overall, this is just a restatement of the thesis of homomorphic encryption, which is that only the outputs of the algorithm are leaked in plaintext.

4   Discussion

A growing body of work aims to securely and efficiently compute statistics on medical data. Prior work has only addressed the federated union cardinality count query, but cannot be used for arbitrary Boolean queries including both ANDs and ORs (intersections and unions). We are the first to build a protocol capable of answering arbitrary Boolean queries across many computing parties, while having all the strong security guarantees of homomorphic encryption, revealing only three statistics, one of which is the query answer. Furthermore, our protocol is very fast, able to answer queries in a couple minutes without parallelism, and seconds with parallelism; these answers have error on the order of 6% of the union cardinality of all conditions considered, but that can of course be decreased with additional sampling in the standard fashion.

Beyond just prototyping a new system, our work demonstrates that modern homomorphic encryption libraries are sufficiently fast to be used in interactive federated queries, not just off-line analysis, resolving an open question about practically approximating federated Boolean count with almost no leakage of information. Furthermore, this manuscript shows that, provided that the correct algorithms and data representations are chosen, we can solve federated private Boolean count-queries that at first glance are not amenable to modern FHE based MPC frameworks.

Ultimately, we believe that the approach in this manuscript will become increasingly necessary as problems relating to the security and privacy of biomedical data grow in prevalence. Our work demonstrates that privacy trade-offs can be turned into computational power trade-offs. As computers become faster, we envision a future where patient privacy can be guaranteed even while aggregating their data for clinical research.

Acknowledgments. We thank Dr. Griffin Weber for introducing us to the federated count-query problem in addition to his guidance. We thank Dr. Isaac Kohane for his guidance and encouragement to think outside the box. Lastly, we thank Adam Sealfon for fruitful discussions.

Funding Information. Work supported by Natural Sciences and Engineering Research Council of Canada (NSERC) grant RGPIN-2022-03074.

References

1. Lattigo v4 (2022). https://github.com/tuneinsight/lattigo. ePFL-LDS, Tune Insight SA
2. Asharov, G., Jain, A., López-Alt, A., Tromer, E., Vaikuntanathan, V., Wichs, D.: Multiparty computation with low communication, computation and interaction via threshold fhe. In: Advances in Cryptology–EUROCRYPT 2012: 31st Annual International Conference on the Theory and Applications of Cryptographic Techniques, Cambridge, UK, 15–19 April 2012. Proceedings, vol. 31, pp. 483–501. Springer, Heidelberg (2012). https://doi.org/10.1007/978-3-642-29011-4_29
3. Blatt, M., Gusev, A., Polyakov, Y., Goldwasser, S.: Secure large-scale genome-wide association studies using homomorphic encryption. PNAS **117**(21), 11608–11613 (2020)
4. Christian, Mouchet, J., Troncoso-Pastoriza, J.P., Bossuat, J.P., Hubaux: multiparty homomorphic encryption from ring-learning-with-errors. In: Proceedings on Privacy Enhancing Technologies, pp. 291—311. Sciendo (2021)

5. De Cristofaro, E., Gasti, P., Tsudik, G.: Fast and private computation of cardinality of set intersection and union. In: Pieprzyk, J., Sadeghi, AR., Manulis, M. (eds.) International Conference on Cryptology and Network Security, pp. 218–231. Springer, Heidelberg (2012). https://doi.org/10.1007/978-3-642-35404-5_17

6. Debnath, S.K., Dutta, R.: Secure and efficient private set intersection cardinality using bloom filter. In: Lopez, J., Mitchell, C. (eds.) International Conference on Information Security, pp. 209–226. Springer, Heidelberg (2015). https://doi.org/10.1007/978-3-319-23318-5_12

7. Desfontaines, D., Lochbihler, A., Basin, D.: Cardinality estimators do not preserve privacy. arXiv preprint arXiv:1808.05879 (2018)

8. Durand, M., Flajolet, P.: Loglog counting of large cardinalities. In: Di Battista, G., Zwick, U. (eds.) Algorithms-ESA 2003: 11th Annual European Symposium, Budapest, Hungary, 16–19 September 2003. Proceedings, vol. 11, pp. 605–617. Springer, Heidelberg (2003). https://doi.org/10.1007/978-3-540-39658-1_55

9. Dwork, C., Roth, A.: The algorithmic foundations of differential privacy. Found. Trends Theor. Comput. Sci. **9**(3–4), 211–407 (2014). https://doi.org/10.1561/0400000042

10. Flajolet, P., Fusy, É., Gandouet, O., Meunier, F.: Hyperloglog: the analysis of a near-optimal cardinality estimation algorithm. In: Discrete Mathematics and Theoretical Computer Science, pp. 137–156 (2007)

11. Froelicher, D., et al.: Truly privacy-preserving federated analytics for precision medicine with multiparty homomorphic encryption. Nat. Commun. **12**(1), 5910 (2021). https://doi.org/10.1038/s41467-021-25972-y

12. Gao, J., Trieu, N., Yanai, A.: Multiparty private set intersection cardinality and its applications. Cryptology ePrint Archive (2022)

13. Gentry, C.: A fully homomorphic encryption scheme (2009). http://crypto.stanford.edu/craig

14. Halevi, S., Polyakov, Y., Shoup, V.: An improved rns variant of the bfv homomorphic encryption scheme. In: Matsui, M. (ed.) Topics in Cryptology–CT-RSA 2019: The Cryptographers' Track at the RSA Conference 2019, San Francisco, CA, USA, 4–8 March 2019, Proceedings, pp. 83–105. Springer (2019). https://doi.org/10.1007/978-3-030-12612-4_5

15. Hu, C., et al.: How to make private distributed cardinality estimation practical, and get differential privacy for free. In: 30th USENIX security symposium (USENIX Security 2021), pp. 965–982 (2021)

16. Kreuter, B., Wright, C.W., Skvortsov, E.S., Mirisola, R., Wang, Y.: Privacy-preserving secure cardinality and frequency estimation (2020)

17. Polyakov, Y., Rohloff, K., Ryan, G.W.: Palisade lattice cryptography library user manual. Cybersecurity Research Center, New Jersey Institute of Technology (NJIT). Technical Report 15 (2017)

18. Sweeney, L.: k-anonymity: a model for protecting privacy. Int. J. Uncertain. Fuzz. Knowl.-Based Syst. **10**(05), 557–570 (2002)

19. Tao, Z., Weber, G.M., Yu, Y.W.: Expected 10-anonymity of hyperloglog sketches for federated queries of clinical data repositories. Bioinformatics **37**(Supplement-1), i151–i160 (2021)

20. Wan, Z., Hazel, J.W., Clayton, E.W., Vorobeychik, Y., Kantarcioglu, M., Malin, B.A.: Sociotechnical safeguards for genomic data privacy. Nat. Rev. Genet. **23**(7), 429–445 (2022)

21. Wang, P., et al.: An effective and differentially private protocol for secure distributed cardinality estimation. Proc. ACM Manag. Data **1**(1), 1–24 (2023)

22. Weber, G.M.: Federated queries of clinical data repositories: scaling to a national network. J. Biomed. Inf. **55**, 231–236 (2015)
23. Yu, Y.W., Weber, G.M.: Balancing accuracy and privacy in federated queries of clinical data repositories: algorithm development and validation. J. Med. Internet Res. **22**(11), e18735 (2020)
24. Yu, Y.W., Weber, G.M.: Hyperminhash: minhash in loglog space. IEEE Trans. Knowl. Data Eng. **34**(1), 328–339 (2022)

FragXsiteDTI: Revealing Responsible Segments in Drug-Target Interaction with Transformer-Driven Interpretation

Ali Khodabandeh Yalabadi, Mehdi Yazdani-Jahromi, Niloofar Yousefi, Aida Tayebi, Sina Abdidizaji, and Ozlem Ozmen Garibay[✉]

University of Central Florida, Orlando, FL 32816, USA
{yalabadi,yazdani,niloofar.yousefi,aida.tayebi,
sina.abdidizaji,ozlem}@ucf.edu

Abstract. Drug-Target Interaction (DTI) prediction is vital for drug discovery, yet challenges persist in achieving model interpretability and optimizing performance. We propose a novel transformer-based model, FragXsiteDTI, that aims to address these challenges in DTI prediction. Notably, FragXsiteDTI is the first DTI model to simultaneously leverage drug molecule fragments and protein pockets. Our information-rich representations for both proteins and drugs offer a detailed perspective on their interaction. Inspired by the Perceiver IO framework, our model features a learnable latent array, initially interacting with protein binding site embeddings using cross-attention and later refined through self-attention and used as a query to the drug fragments in the drug's cross-attention transformer block. This learnable query array serves as a mediator and enables seamless information translation, preserving critical nuances in drug-protein interactions. Our computational results on three benchmarking datasets demonstrate the superior predictive power of our model over several state-of-the-art models. We also show the interpretability of our model in terms of the critical components of both target proteins and drug molecules within drug-target pairs.

Keywords: Drug-Target Interaction · Drug Discovery · Machine Learning · Deep Learning · Interpretability · Explainable AI

1 Introduction

Drug-target interaction (DTI), representing the binding relationship between a drug and its target, is pivotal for developing new drugs and/or repurposing existing ones. While computational approaches have been present for several decades, their increased effectiveness and prominence as alternatives to High-Throughput Screening (HTS) have mainly been realized with the advancements of Machine Learning (ML) algorithms, with deep learning models offering a

---

A. Khodabandeh Yalabadi and M. Yazdani-Jahromi—These authors contributed equally.

J. Ma (Ed.): RECOMB 2024, LNCS 14758, pp. 68–85, 2024.
https://doi.org/10.1007/978-1-0716-3989-4_5

significant improvement in the accuracy of DTI predictions. Deep Learning's advantage lies in its ability to automatically capture valuable latent features, enabling it to handle intricate patterns in molecular data effectively.

However, a notable constraint in utilizing deep learning models for drug discovery lies in the inherent lack of interpretability. While these models are powerful in predicting potential drug candidates, they often fall short in providing meaningful insights into why a particular compound exhibits certain properties or behaviors [25]. This challenge pertains to understanding the intricacies of communication between proteins and drugs, each characterized by its own unique language or representation. Understanding the mechanistic basis of drug efficacy or inefficacy is critical for optimizing drug design [36], refining candidate selection [1], and anticipating potential side effects or unforeseen interactions [20], all of which are fundamental to the drug development process.

To address this challenge and further enhance the performance of deep learning models in drug discovery, we need **information-rich representations** of both proteins and drugs. These representations should encapsulate the structural, chemical, and functional aspects of each component comprehensively. For proteins, this may involve encoding details about their 3D structures, amino acid sequence, and binding sites. Similarly, it may entail capturing information about molecular fragments, chemical properties, and pharmacological characteristics of drugs. Another crucial component is a **mediator that serves as a common language**, bridging the gap between the two linguistic worlds of drug and protein. Such a common language facilitates information translation from the protein language to the drug language and vice versa. This translation process enables the model to effectively understand and interpret the interactions between proteins and drugs. This ensures that the information conveyed by proteins and drugs is not lost in translation, allowing the model to capture the nuances of their interaction, leading to improved interpretability and performance in DTI prediction tasks.

Considering these challenges and leveraging the recent advancements in transformer-based models, we present FragXsiteDTI, an innovative transformer-based model that takes a new perspective on Drug-Target Interaction (DTI) prediction. Our approach provides a promising solution to both challenges by incorporating information-rich representations for both proteins and drugs alongside the integration of a learnable mediator that seamlessly connects these two distinct domains of drugs and proteins.

Our approach hinges on utilizing molecule fragments and protein pockets as the primary inputs to the model, a paradigm shift that enhances our understanding of the intricate interplay between drugs and their target proteins. Limited prior studies in the field have predominantly focused on using either protein pockets [37] or drug fragments for their DTI prediction models. However, to our knowledge, no existing research has harnessed protein pockets and drug fragments simultaneously as inputs in the context of DTI prediction. This finer granularity allows for a more precise analysis of which parts of the drug are critical for binding to specific binding sites of the protein targets. This information is pivotal for designing and creating drugs with specific properties. Instead of designing drugs as whole molecules and hoping to achieve effective interaction with a target protein, scientists can strategically design, combine or modify these fragments to optimize their ability to interact with specific proteins. Also, this detailed perspective doesn't just predict; it explains by looking into the reasons behind cause-and-effect relationships. Fragments often represent functional groups or motifs within drugs that directly contribute to their pharmacological activity. This granular-level analysis can help answer fundamental questions, such as why particular functional groups or binding regions are critical for interaction or why some drug-protein pairs do not exhibit the desired interaction.

We introduce a transformer-based architecture inspired by the Perceiver IO framework, which facilitates the use of a mediator, enabling seamless communication between the distinct linguistic realms of proteins and drugs. This mediator is indeed a learnable latent array that undergoes a dynamic learning process. Initially, it is shaped based on the unique characteristics of proteins, allowing the model to focus on critical binding pockets of the protein. As the process unfolds, this query array undergoes adjustments influenced by the self-attention block. Then, our end-to-end learning process allows the model to fine-tune its focus, aligning the latent query with essential drug-related information. This learnable latent query array, guided by both proteins and drugs, is at the heart of our model's ability to decipher intricate drug-protein interactions effectively.

The proposed framework can be found in Fig. 1. The computational results on three datasets demonstrate the predictive power of our FragXsiteDTI compared to several state-of-the-art models and across multiple evaluation metrics. Also, our model is the first and the only one providing an information-rich interpretation of the interaction in terms of the critical parts of the target protein and drug molecule in a drug-target pair.

2   Related Works

Deep learning-based approaches have emerged as effective solutions for addressing the challenging problem of Drug-Target Interaction (DTI) prediction. These approaches exhibit variations in both their architectural design and their strategies for representing input data.

In DeepDTA [17], a Convolutional Neural Network (CNN) is employed to analyze both the raw SMILES string and the protein sequence, allowing for the extraction of local residue patterns. The primary objective is to predict binding affinity values. To transform this into a binary classification problem, a Sigmoid activation function can be introduced at the end of the model. DeepConv-DTI [11] employs CNN along with a global max-pooling layer to capture local patterns of varying lengths within the protein sequence. Additionally, it applies a fully connected layer to the drug fingerprint Extended-Connectivity Fingerprint 4 (ECFP4).

Notably, while small drug molecules can be efficiently represented in one-dimensional space, proteins, due to their larger size and intricate interactions, often necessitate more comprehensive 3D representations. Despite the limited

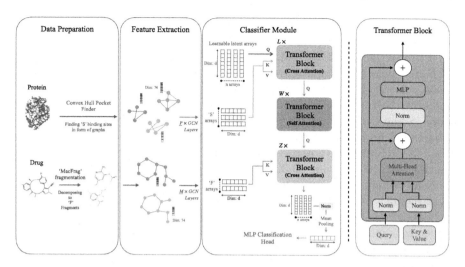

Fig. 1. Our proposed framework, FragXsiteDTI, includes three main modules: (1) Preprocessing module, which consists of finding the binding sites of proteins, decomposing drugs' molecules into smaller fragments, and passing all of them to the next module in the form of graphs; (2) Feature extraction module, where we get graph representations of drugs' fragments and proteins' binding sites, and we create two multiple-layer graph convolutional neural networks to extract learnable embeddings; (3) Classifier module, where we introduce learnable latent arrays to first, find the most probable proteins' binding site(s) for interaction in a cross-attention transformer block (TB), second, pass through a self-attention TB to be prepared for finding the most probable drugs' fragment(s) in last cross-attention TB - Transformer Block (TB) at the right shows the details of TBs in our classifier module.

availability of datasets containing 3D protein structures, recent deep learning literature has increasingly incorporated these structures into their investigations. For instance, AtomNet [31] pioneered the utilization of 3D protein structures as input for a 3D Convolutional Neural Network (CNN), enabling the prediction of drug-target binding using a binary classifier. Ragoza et al. [21] proposed a CNN scoring function that harnessed the 3D representation of protein-ligand complexes to discern critical features crucial for binding prediction, surpassing the performance of the AutoDock Vina score. Pafnucy [24], another significant advancement, employed 3D CNNs to predict binding affinity values for drug-target pairs. Their approach involved representing inputs as a 3D grid, treating both protein and ligand atoms similarly. By applying regularization techniques, their designed network focused on capturing the general properties governing interactions between proteins and ligands.

These studies face several limitations, primarily stemming from the considerable difficulty in experimentally acquiring high-quality 3D protein structures. Consequently, there is a scarcity of datasets containing 3D structural information [40]. Moreover, most studies that employ 3D structural data predominantly rely on CNNs, which exhibit sensitivity to structural orientations and are computationally demanding.

CPI-GNN [28], and GraphDTA [16] employ graph convolutional network (GCN) for molecular graph representation of drugs, and improve the prediction accuracy in the result. Some other studies [7,10] introduced the use of GCN approaches to take advantage of protein 3D structures as input for DTI prediction. Some studies have extended the application of GCNs to protein-ligand complexes. A notable example is GraphBAR [23], which stands as the pioneering 3D graph CNN utilizing a regression approach for predicting drug-target binding affinities. Instead of relying on 3D voxelized grids, GraphBAR employs graphs to represent protein-ligand complexes. These graphs manifest in the form of multiple adjacency matrices, with entries calculated based on distances and feature matrices encapsulating molecular properties of atoms. Additionally, GraphBAR augments its model with data derived from docking simulations.

Lim et al. [14] introduced a graph convolutional network model complemented by a distance-aware graph attention mechanism. This model extracts interaction features directly from the 3D structures of drug-target complexes generated through docking software. While their model demonstrated improved performance compared to both docking simulations and various deep learning-based models, it exhibited limitations, including reduced explainability and the introduction of additional docking errors into the deep learning model.

Pocket Feature, proposed as an unsupervised autoencoder model by Torng et al. [26], specializes in learning representations from binding sites within target proteins. The model employs 3D graph representations for protein pockets and 2D graph representations for drugs. It trains a GCN model to extract features from these graph representations and drug SMILEs. Notably, Pocket Feature outperforms 3D CNNs, as demonstrated in reference [21], and also surpasses docking simulation models such as AutoDock Vina [27], RF-Score [15], and NNScore [15].

Zheng et al. [40] drew attention to the inefficiency of employing direct 3D structure inputs. Instead, they adopted 2D distance maps to represent proteins. In doing so, they reformulated the DTI prediction problem as a classical visual question-answering (VQA) task. In this paradigm, given a distance map of a protein, the model determines whether a given drug interacts with the target protein. Although their model outperformed several state-of-the-art models, it was primarily tailored to classification, predicting interactions between drug-target pairs, without any interpretability.

With the emergence of Transformers and their proven power, Transformer-CPI [2] utilizes sequence representation of drugs and proteins. After a customized encoder layer, this model employs a transformer decoder to construct an interaction sequence and predict the interaction based on that. MolTrans [8] combines the transformer's capability with sub-structures of drugs and targets. This model decomposes drugs and proteins into smaller structures based on their graphs and sequences respectively. Then, an interaction module is responsible for explicable prediction.

In more recent studies, Yazdani et al. [37] exploited 3D protein binding sites along with graph attention embeddings for both drug and protein. Their model finds protein binding sites by a simple docking-based model proposed by Fathi et al. [22]. By using a self-attention module and sentence-level relation from NLP literature, this model determines the most probable candidate binding site for interaction resulting in interpretability as well as high accuracy. Furthermore, they demonstrated that the 3D structure of protein binding sites carries an immense amount of information related to binding affinity and it can improve the performance of benchmark models just by adding this information to the classifier [38].

CSDTI [18] is another model that focuses on the representation of drugs and proteins to improve interpretability and gain better performance in prediction. They employed a drug molecule aggregator and the multiscale 1D convolution-based protein encoder in order to extract the best representation and a cross-attention block to learn the relation between them. Focusing on representation, the MDL-CPI model [34] considers proteins as words and employs a hybrid network architecture based on BERT and CNN to extract the feature representations. Following this work, AMMVF-DTI [33] is a model that utilizes local and global information of proteins and ligands in the form of node-level and graph-level embeddings, respectively. This model tried to improve performance with attention mechanisms and interactive information.

3   Methodology

Our architecture is delineated into three principal modules:

1. **Data Preparation Module**: This module employs a fragmentation algorithm to dissect drugs and a simulation method to identify protein binding sites. Subsequently, a unique graph is constructed for each drug fragment and protein binding site. A comprehensive explanation is provided in Subsect. 3.1.
2. **Feature Extraction**: Within this module, we utilize message-passing neural networks (MPNNs) to extract features from fragments and sites, encapsulating them into desired-sized embeddings. Further details are expounded in Subsect. 3.2.
3. **Classifier Module**: Inspired by the Transformer and Perceiver IO architectures, our approach systematically models drug-protein interactions in a tripartite manner. Initially, a learnable query is employed to attend to protein embeddings. This query undergoes refinement and subsequently interacts with drug fragment embeddings, culminating in a holistic interaction representation. Detailed insights are presented in 3.3.

A schematic representation of the entire architecture is illustrated in Fig. 1.

3.1 Data Preparation

Extracting Fragments from the Ligand Molecule (MacFrag). Creating high-quality fragment libraries by dividing organic compounds is a crucial aspect of drug discovery. Utilizing fragments of drug molecules can result in a more information-rich representation embedding. In this regard, we chose a recent paper in this domain called MacFrag [5]. This study introduces a novel approach for efficiently fragmenting molecules. MacFrag employs an adapted version of rules for the breaking of retrosynthetically interesting chemical substructures (BRICS rules) [4] to cleave chemical bonds and introduces an efficient algorithm for swiftly extracting subgraphs, enabling rapid enumeration of the fragment space. Using this approach, the size of fragments can vary depending on the number of chosen building blocks, enabling flexibility. This method permits overlaps between fragments, ensuring that no critical information is overlooked. Moreover, based on their experiments, the fragments generated using this approach exhibit a closer adherence to the 'Rule of Three.'

Extracting Protein's Ligand-Binding Pockets. We leverage the 3D configurations of proteins derived from the Protein Data Bank (PDB) files. PDB datasets comprise experimental measurements from Nuclear Magnetic Resonance (NMR), x-ray diffraction, cryo-electron microscopy, etc. associated with proteins. To identify protein binding sites, we employ the algorithm introduced by Saberi Fathi et al. [22]. This approach stands out for its simplicity in extracting protein binding sites from their 3D configurations. It operates on a simulation-based paradigm and can be applied before feeding the data to a deep-learning architecture. It simplifies the deep-learning models because they are no longer responsible for processing large molecules of protein. The algorithm calculates bounding box coordinates for each protein binding site. These coordinates subsequently simplify the entire protein structure to a selection of peptide segments.

Graph Construction. Post the extraction of protein binding sites and ligand fragmentation, we devised a representation technique. For proteins, atoms in binding sites are nodes in distinct graphs, with edges defined by inter-atomic distances below a threshold. For ligand fragments, edges are determined by atomic bonds. Atom features, encoded via one-hot vectors, encompass atom type, degree, implicit valence, charge, radical electrons, hybridization, aromaticity, and attached hydrogen count, yielding a 1×74 vector per node. This methodology produces multiple graphs for both individual proteins and distinct ligands.

3.2 Feature Extraction

Subsequent to this Data Preparation stage, we employed message-passing neural networks (MPNNs) to encapsulate the constructed graphs into embeddings. This serves as the feature extraction component of our architecture.

MPNN Networks

Topology Adaptive Graph Convolutional Networks (TAGCN) is a graph representation learning approach that captures the local structures of a graph by applying polynomial filters to its adjacency matrix. Unlike traditional Graph Convolutional Networks (GCNs) that use a fixed neighborhood size, TAGCN considers varying neighborhood sizes by leveraging different powers of the adjacency matrix. Specifically, the method operates as demonstrated in Eq. 1.

$$H^{(l+1)} = \sigma \left(\sum_{k=0}^{K} \Theta_k^{(l)} A^k H^{(l)} \right) \tag{1}$$

where $H^{(l)}$ is the feature matrix at layer l, A is the adjacency matrix, $\Theta_k^{(l)}$ is the trainable weight matrix for the k-th power of the adjacency matrix at layer l, K is the maximum power considered, and σ is a non-linear activation function [6].

Graph Attention Networks (GAT) introduce an attention mechanism to graph neural networks, allowing nodes to weigh their neighbors differently during aggregation. Instead of uniformly aggregating information from neighbors like traditional GCNs, GAT computes attention coefficients that capture the importance of each neighbor node. The main operation in GAT is described by Eq. 2.

$$h_i^{(l+1)} = \sigma \left(\sum_{j \in \mathcal{N}(i)} \alpha_{ij}^{(l)} W^{(l)} h_j^{(l)} \right) \tag{2}$$

where $h_i^{(l)}$ is the feature of node i at layer l, $W^{(l)}$ is a weight matrix, $\alpha_{ij}^{(l)}$ is the attention coefficient between nodes i and j at layer l, and σ is a non-linear activation function. The attention coefficients are computed using a shared attention mechanism across all node pairs, making the model's capacity invariant to the graph size [30].

We combined two layers of TAGCN followed by a GAT layer; the model harnesses the strengths of both methods, potentially outperforming architectures that rely solely on TAGCN or GAT. The TAGCN layers adeptly capture varying local structures by considering different powers of the adjacency matrix, ensuring sensitivity to the graph's topology and enhancing local feature extraction [6]. Subsequently, the GAT layer introduces an attention-based pooling mechanism, allowing nodes to assign varying importance scores to their neighbors, emphasizing more relevant nodes and down-weighting less pertinent ones [30]. This selective attention mechanism leads to more discriminative graph embeddings, especially in graphs with varying node importance. Moreover, the combination ensures that the model recognizes diverse local structures while discerning node importance, offering a dual capability beneficial in complex graphs. Additionally, the GAT layer can mitigate the over-smoothing problem often seen in deep graph neural networks, ensuring distinct and informative node representations [13].

3.3   Classifier Module

We present a method to model drug-protein interactions, drawing inspiration from the Transformer architecture [29] and the Perceiver IO model [9]. Our approach is delineated into three distinct stages:

1. **Cross-Attention with Learnable Query:** We initiate with a learnable latent query array. This query attends to protein binding site embeddings through a cross-attention mechanism. The outcome of this stage is a weighted representation of protein binding sites based on the learnable query.
2. **Latent Query Processing:** The weighted representation from the first stage undergoes further refinement via a self-attention Transformer block. This processed query encapsulates the nuanced features of protein binding sites, preparing it for interaction modeling with drug fragments.
3. **Drug-Protein Interaction Modeling:** In this stage, the processed query from the preceding step acts as Q in a cross-attention Transformer block. Drug fragment embeddings serve as both K and V. This setup allows the model to focus on drug fragments that are most pertinent in relation to the protein binding sites, yielding a holistic representation of drug-protein interaction dynamics.

Our approach to modeling drug-protein interactions, while bearing foundational similarities with the Perceiver IO architecture [9], diverges in its handling of the latent queries and the source of keys and values for attention. Both methodologies employ learnable latent queries to attend to input data, facilitating the extraction of intricate patterns without the need for domain-specific architectures. However, in our method, we introduce a unique twist after the initial cross-attention between the latent query and protein binding site embeddings and subsequent latent query processing. Instead of relying on another set of learnable queries or expert-generated ones for outputs, as in Perceiver IO, we source the keys and values directly from the drug fragment space. This processed query then interacts with the drug fragment embeddings in a cross-attention Transformer block, with the query as Q and the drug fragment embeddings serving as both K and V. This design choice tailors our approach to more effectively capture the nuances of drug-protein interactions.

Self-Attention Mechanism assigns weights to different segments of an input sequence when formulating an output sequence. Defined as Eq. 3.

$$\text{Attention}(Q, K, V) = \text{softmax}\left(\frac{QK^{T}}{\sqrt{d_k}}\right) V \qquad (3)$$

where Q, K, and V are the query, key, and value matrices, respectively, and d_k is their dimensionality. This mechanism adeptly captures long-range dependencies without the constraints of recurrent layers.

Cross-Attention Mechanism the queries come from one sequence (or representation), while the keys and values come from another. This allows the model to focus on relevant parts of the second sequence based on the information from the first, effectively bridging information between two distinct sources.

Transformer Block is a composite of attention layers, feed-forward networks, and normalization organized in a layered fashion (Fig. 1 - Right).

4 Experiments

4.1 Datasets

We establish the effectiveness of our proposed model through a series of comparative experiments. In these experiments, we evaluate the performance of FragXsiteDTI alongside several state-of-the-art methods. To do so, we employ three benchmark datasets that offer essential 3D structural information of target proteins, a crucial requirement for our model. All datasets were split with a ratio of 8:1:1 for the training, validation, and test.

Human, C.elegans, and DrugBank. These datasets were constructed by amalgamating a collection of exceptionally trustworthy and dependable negative drug-protein samples through a systematic in silico screening technique, which was then combined with the known positive samples from sources such as HumanBase [15] and the comprehensive DrugBank database [35]. The DrugBank dataset included 68696 positive and 67072 negative drug-protein interactions, with a total of 6641 unique drugs and 3547 unique targets, providing a robust foundation for interaction prediction models. The Human dataset comprises 3,369 positive interactions involving 1,052 distinct compounds and 852 unique proteins; the *C. elegans* dataset encompasses 4,000 positive interactions, encompassing 1,434 distinct compounds and 2,504 unique proteins.

We also, made a contribution to the enhancement of the DrugBank and *C.elegans* datasets by augmenting the PDB (Protein Data Bank) IDs of the target sequences to the datasets. This means that we have successfully extracted the three-dimensional structures of the proteins contained within these datasets. By doing so, we have enriched the datasets, paving the way for future research and applications that rely on 3D structure-based methods. To enable a direct comparison, identical train, validation, and test partitions (80%, 10%, 10%) were adopted, as in recent studies [37, 40].

4.2 Implementation and Evaluation

Experimentation. For our implementations, we utilized PyTorch 1.8.2, a longtime support version. The experimentation was conducted on an Nvidia RTX 3090 GPU with 24 GB of memory.

Evaluation Metrics. We conducted evaluations of our models using various metrics, such as the Area Under the Receiver Operating Characteristic Curve (AUC), precision, recall, and the F1 score.

4.3 Comparison on Target Datasets

aHuman. We conducted a comprehensive comparison of our model against recently developed deep learning-based approaches, including GraphDTA [16], CPI-GNN [28], DrugVQA [40], AttentionSiteDTI [37], DeepDTA [17], DeepConv-DTI [11], MolTrans [8], TransformerCPI [2], as well as CSDTI [18]. In Sect. 2, you can find a brief overview of each of these models.

The performance of these models is summarized in Table 1. Notably, our proposed model demonstrates superior prediction performance compared to all these models. It achieves competitive results with AttentionSiteDTI, which currently holds the top performance among them. Deep learning models prove to be highly effective in extracting essential features governing the intricate interactions within drug-target pairs. Building upon this foundation, our model further enhances accuracy, highlighting the quality of features extracted and learned during the end-to-end training process of fragXsiteDTI.

Table 1. Human Dataset Comparison

	AUC	Precision	Recall	F1 Score
GraphDTA	0.960	0.882	0.912	0.897
GCN	0.956	0.862	0.928	0.894
CPI-GNN	0.970	0.923	0.918	0.920
DrugVQA	0.979	0.954	0.961	0.957
DeepDTA	0.972	0.938	0.935	0.936
DeepConv-DTI	0.967	0.939	0.907	0.923
MolTrans	0.974	0.955	0.933	0.944
TransformerCPI	0.97	0.911	0.937	0.924
AttentionSiteDTI	0.991	0.951	**0.975**	0.963
CSDTI	0.982	0.937	0.946	0.941
AMMVF-DTI	0.986	0.976	0.938	0.957
FragXsiteDTI(Ours)	**0.991**	**0.977**	0.952	**0.964**

C.elegans. For this dataset, we compared our model with deep learning models that had high performance based on the selected metrics. These models include MDL-CPI [34], CPI-GNN [28], graph convolutional network (GCN), GraphDTA [16], TransformerCPI [2], and AMMVF-DTI [33]. The performance of these models is summarized in Table 2. Similar to the Human dataset, our model outperforms the existing good models in all prediction metrics.

4.4 DrugBank

For the DrugBank dataset, we benchmarked our model against a suite of advanced computational models known for their high performance according

Table 2. *C.elegans* Dataset Comparison

	AUC	Precision	Recall	F1 Score
MDL-CPI	0.975	0.943	0.923	0.933
CPI-GNN	0.978	0.938	0.929	0.933
GCN	0.975	0.921	0.927	0.924
GraphDTA	0.974	0.927	0.912	0.919
AttentionSiteDTI	0.988	**0.974**	0.932	0.953
TransformerCPI	0.988	0.952	0.953	0.952
AMMVF-DTI	0.990	0.962	0.96	0.961
FragXsiteDTI(Ours)	**0.992**	0.971	**0.971**	**0.971**

to the chosen evaluation metrics. Specifically, we compared with methods such as Random Walk with Restart (RWR) [12], DrugE-Rank [39], DeepCPI [32], DeepConv-DTI [11], and MHSADTI [3]. These methods represent a diverse range of approaches, from network-based algorithms like RWR and DrugE-Rank, which prioritize the global structure of drug-target interaction networks, to deep learning architectures such as DeepCPI and DeepConv-DTI, which leverage convolutional networks, and MHSADTI that integrates multiple heterogeneous sources for drug-target interaction prediction. The comparative performance analysis of these models is detailed in Table 3. Our results indicate that, akin to what was observed with the Human and *C.elegans* datasets, our model surpasses the aforementioned well-established models across all prediction metrics.

Table 3. Drugbank Dataset Comparison

	AUC	Precision	Recall	F1 Score
RWR	0.759	0.704	0.651	0.677
DrugE-Rank	0.759	0.707	0.629	0.666
DeepConv-DTI	0.853	0.789	0.738	0.763
DeepCPI	0.700	0.700	0.556	0.62
MHSADTI	0.863	0.771	0.792	0.781
TransformerCPI	0.865	0.774	0.821	0.797
FragXsiteDTI(Ours)	**0.901**	**0.816**	**0.842**	**0.829**

4.5   Interpretation

Protein. In this study, we leverage the attention mechanism to enhance the model's ability to predict the likelihood of specific protein binding sites interacting with a given ligand. This likelihood is quantified through the attention matrix computed within the model. The visualization of this attention mechanism can be observed in Fig. 2, where it is presented as a heatmap for the protein with PDB code of 4BHN when interacting with a drug characterized by the molecular formula of $C_{21}H_{23}Cl_2N_5O_2$. This figure also includes the projection of the heatmap onto the protein structure.

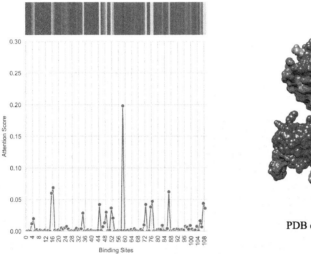

PDB code: 4BHN

Fig. 2. (Left) a heatmap and line plot that represent the cross-attention mechanism weights for every binding site with the latent array. These weights signify the likelihood of each computed binding site on the protein becoming active when interacting with the specific ligand $(C_{21}H_{23}Cl_2N_5O_2)$. (Right) a heatmap that projects the cross-attention weights onto the protein with the PDB code 4BHN (The highest weights are red atoms). This visualization illustrates our model's interpretability with respect to the proteins. The protein's visualization was generated using UCSF Chimera software [19].

Drug. We also have an attention matrix for each drug molecule that determines which fragments of that drug have the highest probabilities for interaction with the particular protein. These candidate fragments can explain the chemical properties that caused the interaction or be used for designing and generating new drugs. Figure 3 demonstrate an example of certain drug $(C_{21}H_{23}Cl_2N_5O_2)$ that binds with the target protein (4BHN).

The provided depiction of multiple interactions in Fig. 4 illustrates the structural interactions between specific drugs and their associated proteins, as determined by our advanced computational model. Central to the depicted interactions is the presence of distinct molecular fragments within each drug, highlighted by the dotted red circles. These fragments are of utmost importance as they represent the primary contact points or key residues that likely mediate the drug's binding affinity to its target protein.

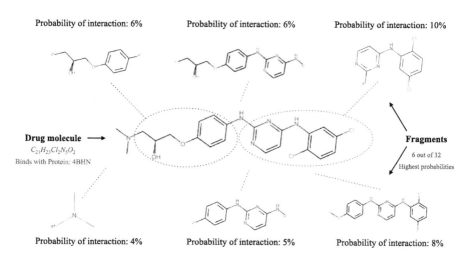

Fig. 3. This figure demonstrates the interpretability of our model regarding the drug molecules. It showcases the specific drug molecule that binds to protein 4BHN, along with its six fragments exhibiting the highest interaction probabilities among a total of 32 fragments. These probabilities are normalized, and 10% is the highest. Note that since these fragments can be repeated in other fragments, these probabilities can be summed up to higher numbers for each fragment.

For instance, for the drug associated with protein '4BHN', our model has ranked the highlighted fragment as the second most crucial component within the drug's structure for mediating protein binding. This rank is further supported by an impressive 99% confidence level in the fragment's binding model. This trend of high-ranking fragments paired with high confidence levels is consistent across the displayed drugs, such as those paired with proteins '6DAV', '4GD7', '2AZT', and '1OPL'. Specifically, the fragments in these drugs are ranked 2, 4, 4, and 2, respectively, all backed by a binding model confidence of 99%.

An intriguing observation from the visualization is the recurring appearance of the same molecular fragment across different drugs. This consistency accentuates the significance of this particular fragment in mediating drug-protein interactions, suggesting its central role in the binding process.

Such findings hold transformative implications for the realm of drug discovery. By pinpointing and understanding these pivotal molecular fragments within drug compounds, researchers are presented with a novel approach to optimize drug design. Recognizing fragments responsible for effective binding can pave the way for the design of new drugs, where these fragments can be incorporated or modified to enhance binding affinity, selectivity, or other pharmacological properties. Essentially, by targeting and modifying these "hotspots", there's potential to not only improve existing drugs but also innovate the development of next-generation therapeutics.

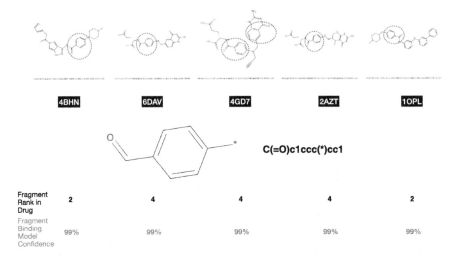

Fig. 4. Visualization of key molecular fragments within various drugs, highlighted in red dotted circles, showcasing their potential significance in mediating drug-protein interactions. Consistent appearance of the same fragment across multiple drugs underscores its pivotal role in binding. Model-derived rankings and confidences emphasize the fragment's importance (Color figure online)

However, it's imperative to highlight that these results are derived from computational analyses. While they offer insightful and potentially groundbreaking perspectives, they must be rigorously validated in laboratory settings to confirm their efficacy and accuracy. As with all computational findings, empirical evidence from experimental assays is crucial to establish the true potential of these identified drug fragments.

5   Conclusion

In this work, we introduced a groundbreaking method for modeling drug-protein interactions, drawing from the robustness of both the Transformer and Perceiver IO architectures. Our empirical evaluations on Human and *C. elegans* datasets not only underscore the superiority of our approach in terms of predictive accuracy but also highlight its unparalleled interpretability. One of the standout features of our method is its capability to pinpoint which fragment of a drug interacts with specific regions of a protein. This granularity is invaluable, offering researchers a detailed map of interaction hotspots, which can guide drug modifications and optimizations. The use of attention modules doesn't merely serve as a mechanism for improved performance; it acts as a window into the model's decision-making process. By visualizing attention scores, we can discern the importance the model assigns to different fragments, shedding light on potential pharmacologically active regions. With the insights provided by our model, drug designers can make informed decisions, potentially reducing the trial-and-error nature of drug discovery. By knowing which fragments are likely to interact with target proteins, drug modifications can be more strategic and purpose-driven. Given the model's precision in understanding drug-protein dynamics, there's potential for tailoring drug designs to individual protein structures, paving the way for more personalized therapeutic interventions in the future. While our current evaluations are on specific datasets, the foundational architecture suggests potential scalability to other organisms and broader drug-protein interaction landscapes, making it a versatile tool in the bioinformatics toolkit. As the pharmaceutical industry and medical research communities continue their quest for more effective and targeted drugs, our method stands out as a beacon, promising to play a transformative role in the future landscape of drug discovery and design.

Data Availibility Statement. All datasets and all instructions and codes for our experiments are publicly available at Github.

References

1. Baptista, D., Correia, J., Pereira, B., Rocha, M.: Evaluating molecular representations in machine learning models for drug response prediction and interpretability. J. Integr. Bioinform. **19**(3), 20220006 (2022)
2. Chen, L., et al.: TransformerCPI: improving compound-protein interaction prediction by sequence-based deep learning with self-attention mechanism and label reversal experiments. Bioinformatics **36**(16), 4406–4414 (2020)
3. Cheng, Z., Yan, C., Wu, F.X., Wang, J.: Drug-target interaction prediction using multi-head self-attention and graph attention network. IEEE/ACM Trans. Comput. Biol. Bioinf. **19**(4), 2208–2218 (2021)
4. Degen, J., Wegscheid-Gerlach, C., Zaliani, A., Rarey, M.: On the art of compiling and using 'drug-like' chemical fragment spaces. ChemMedChem Chem. Enabling Drug Discov. **3**(10), 1503–1507 (2008)
5. Diao, Y., Hu, F., Shen, Z., Li, H.: MacFrag: segmenting large-scale molecules to obtain diverse fragments with high qualities. Bioinformatics **39**(1), btad012 (2023)
6. Du, J., Zhang, S., Wu, G., Moura, J.M., Kar, S.: Topology adaptive graph convolutional networks. arXiv preprint arXiv:1710.10370 (2017)
7. Gomes, J., Ramsundar, B., Feinberg, E.N., Pande, V.S.: Atomic convolutional networks for predicting protein-ligand binding affinity. arXiv preprint arXiv:1703.10603 (2017)
8. Huang, K., Xiao, C., Glass, L.M., Sun, J.: MolTrans: molecular interaction transformer for drug-target interaction prediction. Bioinformatics **37**(6), 830–836 (2021)
9. Jaegle, A., et al.: Perceiver IO: a general architecture for structured inputs & outputs. arXiv preprint arXiv:2107.14795 (2021)
10. Karimi, M., Wu, D., Wang, Z., Shen, Y.: DeepAffinity: interpretable deep learning of compound-protein affinity through unified recurrent and convolutional neural networks. Bioinformatics **35**(18), 3329–3338 (2019)
11. Lee, I., Keum, J., Nam, H.: DeepConv-DTI: prediction of drug-target interactions via deep learning with convolution on protein sequences. PLoS Comput. Biol. **15**(6), e1007129 (2019)

12. Lee, I., Nam, H.: Identification of drug-target interaction by a random walk with restart method on an interactome network. BMC Bioinformatics **19**(8), 9–18 (2018)
13. Li, Q., Han, Z., Wu, X.M.: Deeper insights into graph convolutional networks for semi-supervised learning. In: Proceedings of the AAAI Conference on Artificial Intelligence, vol. 32 (2018)
14. Lim, J., Ryu, S., Park, K., Choe, Y.J., Ham, J., Kim, W.Y.: Predicting drug-target interaction using a novel graph neural network with 3D structure-embedded graph representation. J. Chem. Inf. Model. **59**(9), 3981–3988 (2019)
15. Liu, H., Sun, J., Guan, J., Zheng, J., Zhou, S.: Improving compound-protein interaction prediction by building up highly credible negative samples. Bioinformatics **31**(12), i221–i229 (2015). https://doi.org/10.1093/bioinformatics/btv256
16. Nguyen, T., Le, H., Quinn, T.P., Nguyen, T., Le, T.D., Venkatesh, S.: GraphDTA: predicting drug-target binding affinity with graph neural networks. Bioinformatics **37**(8), 1140–1147 (2021)
17. Öztürk, H., Özgür, A., Ozkirimli, E.: DeepDTA: deep drug-target binding affinity prediction. Bioinformatics **34**(17), i821–i829 (2018)
18. Pan, Y., Zhang, Y., Zhang, J., Lu, M.: CSDTI: an interpretable cross-attention network with GNN-based drug molecule aggregation for drug-target interaction prediction. Appl. Intell., 1–14 (2023)
19. Pettersen, E.F., et al.: UCSF Chimera-a visualization system for exploratory research and analysis. J. Comput. Chem. **25**(13), 1605–1612 (2004)
20. Preto, A.J., Matos-Filipe, P., Mourão, J., Moreira, I.S.: SYNPRED: prediction of drug combination effects in cancer using full-agreement synergy metrics and deep learning. GigaScience **11**, giac087 (2022)
21. Ragoza, M., Hochuli, J., Idrobo, E., Sunseri, J., Koes, D.R.: Protein-ligand scoring with convolutional neural networks. J. Chem. Inf. Model. **57**(4), 942–957 (2017)
22. Saberi Fathi, S.M., Tuszynski, J.A.: A simple method for finding a protein's ligand-binding pockets. BMC Struct. Biol. **14**(1), 18 (2014). https://doi.org/10.1186/1472-6807-14-18
23. Son, J., Kim, D.: Development of a graph convolutional neural network model for efficient prediction of protein-ligand binding affinities. PLoS ONE **16**(4), e0249404 (2021)
24. Stepniewska-Dziubinska, M.M., Zielenkiewicz, P., Siedlecki, P.: Development and evaluation of a deep learning model for protein-ligand binding affinity prediction. Bioinformatics **34**(21), 3666–3674 (2018)
25. Tang, Y.: Deep learning in drug discovery: applications and limitations. Frontiers Comput. Intell. Syst. **3**(2), 118–123 (2023)
26. Torng, W., Altman, R.B.: Graph convolutional neural networks for predicting drug-target interactions. J. Chem. Inf. Model. **59**(10), 4131–4149 (2019). https://doi.org/10.1021/acs.jcim.9b00628
27. Trott, O., Olson, A.J.: AutoDock vina: improving the speed and accuracy of docking with a new scoring function, efficient optimization, and multithreading. J. Comput. Chem. **31**(2), 455–461 (2010)
28. Tsubaki, M., Tomii, K., Sese, J.: Compound-protein interaction prediction with end-to-end learning of neural networks for graphs and sequences. Bioinformatics **35**(2), 309–318 (2019)
29. Vaswani, A., et al.: Attention is all you need. In: Advances in Neural Information Processing Systems, vol. 30 (2017)
30. Veličković, P., Cucurull, G., Casanova, A., Romero, A., Lio, P., Bengio, Y.: Graph attention networks. arXiv preprint arXiv:1710.10903 (2017)

31. Wallach, I., Dzamba, M., Heifets, A.: AtomNet: a deep convolutional neural network for bioactivity prediction in structure-based drug discovery. arXiv preprint arXiv:1510.02855 (2015)
32. Wan, F., et al.: DeepCPI: a deep learning-based framework for large-scale in silico drug screening. Genomics Proteomics Bioinf. **17**(5), 478–495 (2019)
33. Wang, L., Zhou, Y., Chen, Q.: AMMVF-DTI: a novel model predicting drug-target interactions based on attention mechanism and multi-view fusion. Int. J. Mol. Sci. **24**(18), 14142 (2023)
34. Wei, L., Long, W., Wei, L.: MDL-CPI: multi-view deep learning model for compound-protein interaction prediction. Methods **204**, 418–427 (2022)
35. Wishart, D.S., et al.: DrugBank: a knowledgebase for drugs, drug actions and drug targets. Nucleic Acids Res. **36**(suppl_1), D901–D906 (2008)
36. Yang, J., Li, Z., Wu, W., Yu, S., Chu, Q., Zhang, Q.: Deep learning can identify explainable reasoning paths of mechanism of drug action for drug repurposing from multilayer biological network. Briefings Bioinf. **23**(6), bbac469 (2022)
37. Yazdani-Jahromi, M., et al.: AttentionSiteDTI: an interpretable graph-based model for drug-target interaction prediction using NLP sentence-level relation classification. Briefings Bioinf. **23**(4), bbac272 (2022)
38. Yousefi, N., et al.: BindingSite-AugmentedDTA: enabling a next-generation pipeline for interpretable prediction models in drug repurposing. Briefings Bioinf. **24**(3), bbad136 (2023). https://doi.org/10.1093/bib/bbad136
39. Yuan, Q., Gao, J., Wu, D., Zhang, S., Mamitsuka, H., Zhu, S.: DrugE-Rank: improving drug-target interaction prediction of new candidate drugs or targets by ensemble learning to rank. Bioinformatics **32**(12), i18–i27 (2016)
40. Zheng, S., Li, Y., Chen, S., Xu, J., Yang, Y.: Predicting drug-protein interaction using quasi-visual question answering system. Nat. Mach. Intell. **2**(2), 134–140 (2020)

An Integer Programming Framework for Identifying Stable Components in Asynchronous Boolean Networks

Shani Jacobson and Roded Sharan[✉]

Blavatnik School of Computer Science, Tel Aviv University, 69978 Tel Aviv, Israel
roded@tauex.tau.ac.il

Abstract. Executable models of biological circuits offer the ability to simulate their behavior under different settings with important biomedical applications. In particular, Boolean network models have been a prime research focus and dozens of manually curated Boolean models are available in public databases. A key challenge in studying the dynamics of these models is determining their asymptotic behavior, that is the state-sets or attractors they converge to. This is particularly challenging for large networks, as the state space size grows exponentially. Here we introduce a novel method for identifying stable components within attractors under an asynchronous update scheme. Our method leverages the observation that the majority of cellular functions in current models can be described as linear threshold functions, facilitating an efficient integer programming formulation for the problem. We conduct simulations on both synthetic and real biological networks, demonstrating that our proposed method is highly efficient and outperforms previous methods.

Keywords: Boolean network · asynchronous update · attractor finding · quasi attractor · integer linear programming

1 Introduction

The construction of executable models of biological systems is one of the holy grails of systems biology as they allow the simulation of the modeled systems under different environmental and genetic cues [23]. Several models have been proposed to describe a system's dynamics, including those based on differential equations [3, 28, 29] and discrete models [2, 6, 22]. The most common framework, studied already 50 years ago in the pioneering work of Kauffman [12], is a Boolean network model (BN) [25]. In this model, the activity value of each node is limited to a binary choice: either it is in an ON state or an OFF state. This activity value is determined by a Boolean function of the values of the node's predecessors in the network. Despite the model's simplicity, it still captures crucial aspects of the dynamic characteristics of the systems being modeled [10].

The model's state at a specific time point can be represented as a vector containing the activity values of all nodes. At each time point, the network's state

J. Ma (Ed.): RECOMB 2024, LNCS 14758, pp. 86–98, 2024.
https://doi.org/10.1007/978-1-0716-3989-4_6

may change according to the previous network state and the Boolean functions of the nodes. Several update schemes that determine which node can update its value at each time point can be considered. The simplest update scheme is the synchronous scheme [7] where all the nodes update their values simultaneously. Under this update scheme each state can transition to only one state and the resulting dynamic behavior is deterministic. In contrast, here we focus on the asynchronous update scheme [26], where only one random node can modify its value at each time point. This update scheme is stochastic in nature, as each state may transition to multiple possible states, depending on the randomly chosen node. While the analysis of asynchronous models is more complex, they resemble better real biological processes [21].

The dynamics of the system consists of all possible trajectories in the state space. Since there is a finite number of states, each trajectory will eventually enter a state-set, called an *attractor*, from which it cannot escape. The attractors characterize asymptotic behavior of the system. From a biological perspective, different attractors represent different modes of the cell, which may indicate potential asymptotic cellular functionalities [11]. An attractor can consist of a single network state, a.k.a. a fixed point, or a group of alternating states. In a fixed-point attractor all node values remain constant, while in a complex attractor some nodes change states (oscillate) while others may remain fixed. Figure 1a presents an example of a BN, and Fig. 1b depicts its state transition graph and its attractors under an asynchronous update scheme.

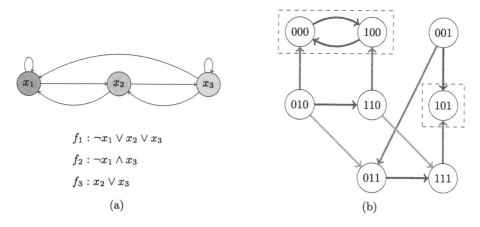

$f_1 : \neg x_1 \lor x_2 \lor x_3$

$f_2 : \neg x_1 \land x_3$

$f_3 : x_2 \lor x_3$

(a)   (b)

Fig. 1. A Boolean network (a) and its state transition graph (b). The colors of the edges in panel b indicate which node was updated. In this example, the network has two attractors, denoted by dotted boxes: a fixed point attractor and a complex attractor.

While the state space is finite, exhaustive search is not feasible in large networks because the number of states is exponential in the network's size. In the synchronous case, any trajectory that visits the same state twice is inevitably an attractor, facilitating SAT- or ILP-based approaches for their detection [4,5]. In contrast, an asynchronous update scheme may induce more complex attractor structures, calling for different solutions. Klarner et al. [14,15] and Abdallah et al. [1] used answer set programming, a declarative programming method, to search for trap sets in the state transition graph. Mizera et al. [17] proposed a strongly connected component decomposition method. Several other works were based on creating an acyclic state transition graph, identifying fixed points within it and expanding them to attractors of the original network [24,27].

A state-of-the-art approach for attractor detection in the asynchronous setting is based on reducing the effective network size, thus shrinking the search space to allow exhaustive enumeration [18,30]. This reduction is achieved by identifying nodes that have no impact on the overall network dynamics, such as nodes without outgoing edges, or identifying sets of nodes that, under specific assignments, remain fixed regardless of the values of other nodes in the network. In particular, Albert's group introduced an algorithm to identify all such stable components within an attractor, referred to as a *quasi-attractors* [20,31]. The method searches for stable motifs, which are subsets of nodes together with assigned values that do not depend on the values of the rest of the nodes, and recursively constructs quasi-attractors from them. Notably, the search for stable motifs is based on identifying minimal cycles in the Boolean network and, thus, it is less efficient for networks containing many cycles.

Here we develop a novel integer linear programming (ILP) formulation for finding quasi-attractors in Boolean networks. The ILP simultaneously identifies all nodes that stabilize in an attractor, enabling a rapid and efficient detection of all quasi-attractors. It is based on the observation that the vast majority of biological Boolean functions (96% of the functions in the Cell Collective repository [9]) can be described as linear threshold functions. This insight facilitates the formulation of constraints on the node activity states as dictated by their Boolean functions in a concise manner. Moreover, it allows us to formulate linear constraints that express the stabilization criteria for a node based on the states of other nodes in the network. We evaluate our algorithm on both synthetic and real biological networks, demonstrating that our proposed method is highly efficient and outperforms previous methods.

2   Preliminaries

2.1   Boolean Networks

A Boolean network $\mathsf{BN} = (\mathsf{G}, \mathcal{F})$ consists of a directed graph $\mathsf{G} = (\mathsf{V}, \mathsf{E})$ with N nodes, and a set $\mathcal{F} = \{f_1, f_2, ..., f_N\}$ of associated Boolean functions. For a node $v_i \in V$, define $\mathcal{P}_i = \{j \in [N] : (v_j, v_i) \in E\}$ as the set of indices of its predecessors in the network, and let $x_i \in \{0,1\}$ denote its associated binary activity value.

Let $f : \{0,1\}^k \to \{0,1\}$ be a Boolean function. We say that $f(x_1, x_2, ..., x_k)$ is *positive unate* in x_j, if for every possible assignment except x_j, marked by $x_{-j} \in \{0,1\}^{k-1}$:

$$f(\{x_{-j}, \ x_j = 0\}) \leq f(\{x_{-j}, \ x_j = 1\})$$

Similarly, we say that $f(x_1, x_2, ..., x_k)$ is *negative unate* in x_j, if for every $x_{-j} \in \{0,1\}^{k-1}$:

$$f(\{x_{-j}, \; x_j = 0\}) \geq f(\{x_{-j}, \; x_j = 1\})$$

If for every $j \in [k]$, f is either positive or negative unate in x_j, we say that f is a *unate* function.

2.2   Linear Threshold Functions

A Boolean function f is a *linear threshold function* (LTF) [19] if and only if there exist $w_1, w_2, ...w_k \in \mathbb{Z}$ and a threshold $\tau \in \mathbb{Z}$ such that for every assignment $x \in \{0,1\}^k$:

$$f(x_1, x_2, ...x_k) = 1 \iff w_1 x_1 + w_2 x_2 + ... + w_k x_k \geq \tau$$

Note that for every $j \in [k]$, if $w_j > 0$ then f is positive unate in x_j, and if $w_j < 0$ then f is negative unate in x_j. Thus, a necessary (but insufficient) condition for a Boolean function to be a LTF is that the function is unate. Figure 2 illustrates an LTF.

Consider an LTF as described above. Let y_{min} be the minimum value that the LTF can attain, and let $\{x_j^{min}\}_{j=1}^k$ be the assignment that achieves this value:

$$y_{min} = \sum_{j=1}^k w_j x_j^{min}, \quad x_j^{min} = \begin{cases} 0 & w_j > 0 \\ 1 & w_j < 0 \end{cases}$$

Note that if $y_{min} \geq \tau$ then for any possible assignment the value of f is 1. Similarly, let y_{max} be the maximum value that the LTF can attain, and let $\{x_j^{max}\}_{j=1}^k$ be the assignment that achieves this value:

$$y_{max} = \sum_{j=1}^k w_j x_j^{max}, \quad x_j^{max} = \begin{cases} 0 & w_j < 0 \\ 1 & w_j > 0 \end{cases}$$

Note that if $y_{max} \leq \tau$ then for any possible assignment the value of f is 0.

2.3   Network Dynamics

Given a BN with N nodes, a *state* of the network is an assignment of activity values to its nodes. A state $(x_1, \ldots, x_N)$ can transition to another state $(x'_1, \ldots, x'_n)$ under an asynchronous update scheme if they differ by exactly one bit at some position i and the Boolean function f of node i satisfies: $f(x_1, \ldots, x_N) = x'_i$. The corresponding *state transition graph* has 2^N nodes corresponding to all possible network states, and every two nodes s and s' are connected by a directed edge iff s can transition to s'. We say that s *reaches* s' iff $s = s'$ or there is a directed path from s to s' in the state transition graph.

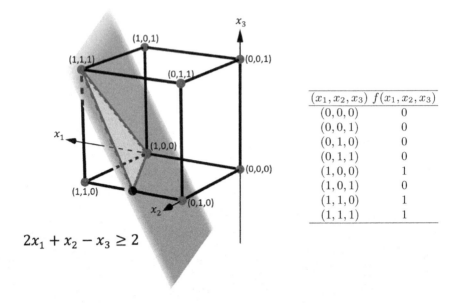

(x_1, x_2, x_3)	$f(x_1, x_2, x_3)$
$(0,0,0)$	0
$(0,0,1)$	0
$(0,1,0)$	0
$(0,1,1)$	0
$(1,0,0)$	1
$(1,0,1)$	0
$(1,1,0)$	1
$(1,1,1)$	1

Fig. 2. An illustration of the linear threshold function $f(x_1, x_2, x_3) = (x_1 \wedge x_2) \vee (x_1 \wedge \neg x_3)$. Left: 3D-Boolean cube and the plane $2x_1 + x_2 - x_3 = 2$ that defines the LTF. It can be seen that points corresponding to assignments with a value of 1 (blue) are on or to the left of the plane, while points corresponding to assignments with a value of 0 (red) are to the right of the plane. Right: the function's truth table. (Color figure online)

Let $\mathcal{A} \subseteq \{0,1\}^N$ be a set of states in a BN. We say that $\mathcal{A}$ is an *attractor* iff any state in $\mathcal{A}$ can reach any other state in $\mathcal{A}$ and no state outside $\mathcal{A}$. A *quasi-attractor* is a maximal set of nodes and their assignment, such that their values remain fixed under updates regardless of the values of all other nodes.

The definitions of an attractor and a quasi-attractor are closely related. Specifically, it can be observed that each attractor has a corresponding quasi-attractor (which could be empty): a set of nodes that stabilize within the attractor. Conversely, each quasi-attractor defines a subspace within the state space that necessarily contains at least one attractor. For example, in Fig. 1b the fixed attractor, '101', has a corresponding quasi-attractor with the same value, and the complex attractor, {'000', '100'}, has 'X00' as its corresponding quasi-attractor (v_1 oscillates).

3   ILP Framework for Finding Quasi-Attractors

In this section, we present the novel ILP framework we have designed to find quasi-attractors in a Boolean network whose functions are all LTFs. Consider a Boolean network $\mathsf{BN} = (\mathsf{G}, \mathcal{F})$ with N nodes. Define a *stable set* to be a subset of nodes $S \subseteq V$ of size k and their corresponding values $\{x_i\}_{v_i \in S}$ that satisfy the following conditions:

- if $v_i \in S$, its value remains fixed and equals to x_i, given $\{x_i\}_{v_i \in S}$, and under all possible assignments of the nodes in $V \setminus S$.
- If $v_i \notin S$, given $\{x_i\}_{v_i \in S}$, there must exist two different assignments of nodes in $V \setminus S$ that yield different values for v_i.

3.1 LTF Representation

To represent a unate Boolean function as a linear threshold function, we design an ILP formulation that learns the coefficients and threshold of the representation. While a non-integer linear program could be used instead, the integer formulation is easily solved and the resulting integer coefficients enhance the performance of the main program in Sect. 3.2. Specifically, for a given unate Boolean function f with K predecessors $\mathcal{P} = \{p_1, p_2, \ldots, p_K\}$, we introduce K integer variables $w_1, w_2, \ldots, w_K$ and an integer variable τ. For each possible assignment of the predecessors $(x_1, x_2, \ldots, x_K) \in \{0, 1\}^K$, if $f(x_1, x_2, \ldots, x_K) = 1$ we add a constraint:

$$\sum_{k=1}^{K} w_k \cdot x_k \geq \tau$$

if $f(x_1, x_2, \ldots, x_K) = 0$ we add a constraint:

$$\sum_{k=1}^{K} w_k \cdot x_k \leq \tau - 1$$

For a compact representation, our objective minimizes $\sum_{k=1}^{K} |w_k| = \sum_{k=1}^{K} s_k \cdot w_k$, where:

$$s_k = \begin{cases} 1 & \text{if } f \text{ is positive unate in } p_k \\ -1 & \text{if } f \text{ is negative unate in } p_k \end{cases}$$

The representations are learned as an initial step of the algorithm and are kept fixed throughout.

Higher Order Threshold Functions. To support a broader range of Boolean functions, we generalized our algorithm to handle Boolean functions that cannot be represented with a single LTF but with a combination of D LTFs. That is, given a Boolean function f with K predecessors, we now allow D LTFs with parameters $\{w_1^{(d)}, w_2^{(d)}, \ldots, w_K^{(d)}\}_{d=1}^{D}$ and $\{\tau^{(d)}\}_{d=1}^{D}$ such that for every possible assignment $(x_1, x_2, \ldots, x_K) \in \{0, 1\}^K$ it holds that:

$$f(x_1, x_2, \ldots, x_K) = 1 \iff \forall d \in D : \sum_{k=1}^{K} w_k^{(d)} x_k \geq \tau^{(d)}$$

We call such a function an LTF of order D. Interestingly, 94% of the unate functions in the Cell Collective repository [9] are LTFs of order 1, while the remaining functions are LTFs of order 2.

3.2 Quasi-attractor Detection

For convenience, we define two disjoint sets: $S_0 = \{v_i \in S : x_i = 0\}$ and $S_1 = \{v_i \in S : x_i = 1\}$. Note that $S_0 \cup S_1 = S$. For each $v_i \in V$ with an LTF representation: $\sum_{j \in \mathcal{P}_i} w_j^i x_j \geq \tau_i$, we introduce the following binary variables:

- x_i: A Boolean variable representing the value of node v_i.
- $\mathcal{I}_{v_i \in S}$: An indicator variable for the event $v_i \in S$.
- $\mathcal{I}_{v_i \in S_0}$: An indicator variable for the event $v_i \in S_0$.
- $\mathcal{I}_{v_i \in S_1}$: An indicator variable for the event $v_i \in S_1$.

We now define the constraints that ensure the values of these indicators.

Stable Nodes with Value 0. For the indicator $\mathcal{I}_{v_i \in S_0}$, we introduce variables $\{x_{i,j}^{max}\}_{j \in \mathcal{P}_i}$ and y_{max}^i, subject to the following constraints:

$$x_{i,j}^{max} = \begin{cases} x_j & \mathcal{I}_{v_j \in S} = 1 \\ 0 & \mathcal{I}_{v_j \in S} = 0 \text{ and } w_j^i < 0 \\ 1 & \mathcal{I}_{v_j \in S} = 0 \text{ and } w_j^i > 0 \end{cases} \qquad y_{max}^i = \sum_{j \in \mathcal{P}_i} w_j^i x_{i,j}^{max}$$

Here, y_{max}^i represents the maximum value achievable by the left side of the LTF under the assignment of the nodes in S. If $y_{max}^i < \tau_i$ (for any assignment to the nodes in $V \setminus S$), the value of v_i should be fixed at 0, implying the following constraints:

$$y_{max}^i \leq \tau_i - 1 + \Lambda \cdot (1 - \mathcal{I}_{v_i \in S_0})$$
$$y_{max}^i \geq \tau_i - \Lambda \cdot \mathcal{I}_{v_i \in S_0}$$

where $\Lambda > N \cdot \max_{i,j \in \mathcal{P}_i}\{|w_{i,j}|\} + \max_i\{|\tau_i|\}$ is some large constant. These constraints ensure that $\mathcal{I}_{v_i \in S_0} = 1 \iff y_{max}^i < \tau_i$. Finally, we add a constraint to ensure that if $\mathcal{I}_{v_i \in S_0} = 1$ then $x_i = 0$:

$$x_i \leq 1 - \mathcal{I}_{v_i \in S_0}$$

Stable Nodes with Value 1. For the indicator $\mathcal{I}_{v_i \in S_1}$, we introduce variables $\{x_{i,j}^{min}\}_{j \in \mathcal{P}_i}$ and y_{min}^i, subject to the following constraints:

$$x_{i,j}^{min} = \begin{cases} x_j & \mathcal{I}_{v_j \in S} = 1 \\ 0 & \mathcal{I}_{v_j \in S} = 0 \text{ and } w_j^i > 0 \\ 1 & \mathcal{I}_{v_j \in S} = 0 \text{ and } w_j^i < 0 \end{cases} \qquad y_{min}^i = \sum_{j \in \mathcal{P}_i} w_j^i x_{i,j}^{min}$$

Here, y_{min}^i represents the minimum value achievable by the left side of the LTF under the assignment of the nodes in S. If $y_{min}^i \geq \tau_i$ (for any assignment to the nodes in $V \setminus S$), the value of v_i is fixed at 1. Therefore, we have the following constraints:

$$y_{min}^i \leq \tau_i - 1 + \Lambda \cdot \mathcal{I}_{v_i \in S_1}$$
$$y_{min}^i \geq \tau_i - \Lambda \cdot (1 - \mathcal{I}_{v_i \in S_1})$$

These constraints ensure that $\mathcal{I}_{v_i \in S_1} = 1 \iff y^i_{min} \geq \tau_i$. Finally, we add a constraint to ensure that if $\mathcal{I}_{v_i \in S_1} = 1$ then $x_i = 1$:

$$x_i \geq \mathcal{I}_{v_i \in S_1}$$

Stable Set Identification. It is immediate to compute the indicator $\mathcal{I}_{v_i \in S}$ from $\mathcal{I}_{v_i \in S_0}$ and $\mathcal{I}_{v_i \in S_1}$. To restrict the ILP to find an assignment with $|S| = k$, we simply require: $\sum_{i \in [N]} \mathcal{I}_{v_i \in S} = k$.

In order to identify all possible solutions, we construct an ILP model for each $k \in [N]$ and run them iteratively until no new solutions are found. To prevent the ILP from finding the same solution twice, we store the stable set of each solution found and add an auxiliary indicator as follows. Let us mark by S^n, S^n_0 and S^n_1 the stable set of the nth solution. The indicator, $\mathcal{I}^n_\Delta$, specifies if the current stable set differs from the nth solution with the following constraints:

$$\sum_{v_i \in S^n_0} (1 - \mathcal{I}_{v_i \in S_0}) + \sum_{v_i \in S^n_1} (1 - \mathcal{I}_{v_i \in S_1}) + \sum_{v_i \notin S^n} \mathcal{I}_{v_i \in S} \leq N \cdot \mathcal{I}^n_\Delta$$

$$\sum_{v_i \in S^n_0} (1 - \mathcal{I}_{v_i \in S_0}) + \sum_{v_i \in S^n_1} (1 - \mathcal{I}_{v_i \in S_1}) + \sum_{v_i \notin S^n} \mathcal{I}_{v_i \in S} \geq \mathcal{I}^n_\Delta$$

3.3   External Nodes

An external node refers to an element or factor that exists outside the network but interacts with nodes within it, thereby exerting influence on their behavior or function. All other nodes are internal nodes. In the analysis of the network dynamics, we allow these external factors to take any value, but their values remain constant throughout the trajectory. To this end, we simply add to the program above binary variables representing the external node activities (one per external factor). Formally, consider a network BN with M external nodes $V_{ext} = \{v_{N+1}, v_{N+2}, \ldots, v_{N+M}\}$, where $V = V_{int} \cup V_{ext}$. As described in Sect. 3.2, the variables $\{x_i\}_{v_i \in V_{int}}$ represent the values of the internal nodes. We introduce new binary variables $\{e_m\}_{v_m \in V_{ext}}$ to represent the values of the external nodes and include these variables in the LTF formulations of the internal nodes.

One noteworthy observation in networks that include external nodes is that various assignments of these external factors can often yield identical solutions for the non-external nodes. However, exhaustively finding each of these solutions would be too costly. To address this computational challenge, we introduce a compact ILP designed to identify all potential assignments of external factors in the context of a single solution of the ILP above.

Specifically, given $\{x_i\}_{v_i \in S}$, $S \subseteq V_{int}$, we seek solutions $\{e_m\}_{v_m \in V_{ext}}$ such that:

- if $v_i \in S$, its value remains fixed at x_i for all possible assignments of the nodes in $V \setminus S$.
- If $v_i \notin S$, there must exist two different assignments of nodes in $V \setminus S$ that yield different values for v_i.

To this end, we compute maximum and minimum values for every internal node v_i disregarding the external nodes as follows:

$$y_{min}^i = \sum_{\substack{v_j \in V_{int} \\ j \in \mathcal{P}_i \cap S_1}} w_j^i + \sum_{\substack{v_j \in V_{int} \\ j \in \mathcal{P}_i \cap (V \setminus S)}} \min\{0, w_j^i\}$$

$$y_{max}^i = \sum_{\substack{v_j \in V_{int} \\ j \in \mathcal{P}_i \cap S_1}} w_j^i + \sum_{\substack{v_j \in V_{int} \\ j \in \mathcal{P}_i \cap (V \setminus S)}} \max\{0, w_j^i\}$$

Next, if any of v_i's predecessors is an external node, we add one of the following sets of constraints depending on the status of v_i:

- If $v_i \in S_0$, we make sure its value does not surpass the threshold using the constraint:

$$\sum_{\substack{v_m \in V_{ext} \\ m \in \mathcal{P}_i}} w_m^i e_m \leq \tau_i - y_{max}^i - 1$$

- If $v_i \in S_1$, we similarly add:

$$\sum_{\substack{v_m \in V_{ext} \\ m \in \mathcal{P}_i}} w_m^i e_m \geq \tau_i - y_{min}^i$$

- If $v_i \in V \setminus S$, we add the following constraints:

$$\sum_{\substack{v_m \in V_{ext} \\ m \in \mathcal{P}_i}} w_m^i e_m \geq \tau_i - y_{max}^i$$

$$\sum_{\substack{v_m \in V_{ext} \\ m \in \mathcal{P}_i}} w_m^i e_m \leq \tau_i - y_{min}^i - 1$$

3.4   Implementation Details

Our complete algorithm implementation is available on GitHub at https://github.com/shanijacobson/AttractorsILP. We utilized the Gurobi optimizer [8] as the solver for our ILP. For Stable Motif, we used the implementation in https://github.com/jcrozum/pystablemotifs. For the answer-set-programming approach, we used the implementation in https://github.com/hklarner/pyboolnet [16]. All experiments were executed on a personal MacBook Air (M1, 2020, 16 GB RAM, 512 GB SSD).

4   Results

We evaluated our algorithm on both synthetic and real biological networks and compared to previous work. The synthetic networks were generated randomly using the N-K model [13], in which each of the N nodes has K predecessors. The real networks were taken from the Cell Collective repository [9].

4.1 Synthetic Networks

We generated synthetic networks using the N-K model [13], with the constraint that their functions are unate. We varied N from 20 to 200 and set $K = 2$ or $K = 4$. These parameter choices follow the characteristics of the real networks analyzed below. For each (N, K) pair, we generated 100 synthetic networks. We applied our ILP algorithm and compared to the Stable Motif (SM) framework [20,31], limiting each algorithm to run up to one hour per network. Figure 3 shows the results for each (N, K) pair. The superiority of our method is evident, as it successfully solves all generated networks and its performance remains almost independent of K. In contrast, Stable Motif encounters growing difficulties as K and N increase along with the number of trajectories in the network.

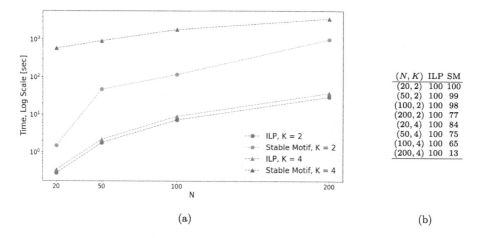

(N, K)	ILP	SM
$(20, 2)$	100	100
$(50, 2)$	100	99
$(100, 2)$	100	98
$(200, 2)$	100	77
$(20, 4)$	100	84
$(50, 4)$	100	75
$(100, 4)$	100	65
$(200, 4)$	100	13

(a)   (b)

Fig. 3. Performance results on synthetic N-K networks. a) Average running time. b) Percent of network solved within a time limit of one hour.

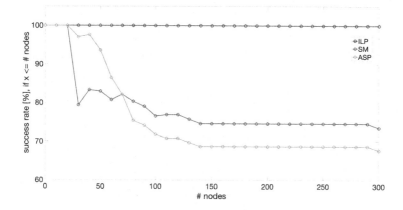

Fig. 4. Success rate of solving real networks under a time limit of 4 h as a function of the total number of nodes in the network.

Table 1. Performance evaluation on real networks with a time limit of 4 h per network.

	Network Parameters					Quasi-Attractors			Performance [sec]		
	# States	# Externals	# Edges	# 1st order LTFs	# 2nd order LTFs	Fixed	Complex	Avg Stable Nodes	ILP	ASP	SM
Cortical_Area_Development	5	0	14	5	0	2	0	5	0.05	0.15	0.2
CD4_T_cell_dynamics_-_Workshop_v2	6	10	40	6	0	10	0	6	3.72	191.7	418.57
Metabolic_Interactions_in_the_Gut_Microbiome	8	4	30	8	0	8	0	8	0.16	3.2	7.09
Mammalian_Cell_Cycle_2006	9	1	35	8	1	10	1	5.5	0.38	0.49	0.65
Regulation_of_the_Larabinose_operon_of_Escherichia_coli	9	4	22	9	0	9	0	9	0.11	1.36	1.32
Toll_Pathway_of_Drosophila_Signaling_Pathway	9	2	13	9	0	3	0	9	0.05	0.24	0.25
Cell_Cycle_Transcription_by_Coupled_CDK	9	0	19	9	0	1	0	9	0.11	0.15	0.11
Arabidopsis_thaliana_Cell_Cycle	14	0	66	10	4	0	1	0	1.68	0.29	3.19
VEGF_Pathway_of_Drosophila_Signaling_Pathway	10	8	26	10	0	5	0	10	4.64	15.55	15.23
Lac_Operon	10	3	24	10	0	4	0	10	0.15	0.92	0.8
HH_Pathway_of_Drosophila_Signaling_Pathways	11	13	45	11	0	12	0	11	3.09	938.35	997.58
SKBR3_Breast_Cell_Line_Shortterm_ErbB_Network	11	5	46	11	0	31	0	11	0.35	278.3	Failure
HCC1954_Breast_Cell_Line_Shortterm_ErbB_Network	11	5	51	11	0	17	0	11	0.4	39.25	Failure
BT474_Breast_Cell_Line_Shortterm_ErbB_Network	11	5	51	11	0	28	0	11	0.42	87.37	Time out
Wg_Pathway_of_Drosophila_Signalling_Pathways	12	14	43	12	0	10	0	12	0.33	1998.9	2552.81
Cardiac_development	13	2	39	12	1	6	0	13	0.52	0.86	1.16
TOL_Regulatory_Network	14	10	58	12	2	62	0	14	6.37	195.57	128.75
CD4+_T_Cell_Differentiation_and_Plasticity	12	6	84	12	0	24	1	11.88	8.38	29.61	Time out
Predicting_Variabilities_in_Cardiac_Gene	13	2	39	12	1	6	0	13	0.52	0.89	0.69
Body_Segmentation_in_Drosophila_2013	14	3	31	13	1	5	0	14	0.22	1.37	3.48
FGF_pathway_of_Drosophila_Signalling_Pathways	14	9	31	14	0	13	0	14	4.83	51.81	86.51
Neurotransmitter_Signaling_Pathway	14	2	22	14	0	1	1	8.5	0.17	0.98	3.23
Human_Gonadal_Sex_Determination	19	0	78	15	4	3	0	19	2.17	0.53	2.86
Budding_Yeast_Cell_Cycle_2009	18	0	57	15	3	0	1	0	0.8	Failure	55.33
B_cell_differentiation	17	5	44	17	0	58	0	17	0.42	6.24	19.5
Processing_of_Spz_Network	18	6	34	17	1	42	0	18	1.01	6.02	3.34
Aurora_Kinase_A_in_Neuroblastoma	19	4	47	17	2	2	2	15.25	0.64	12.3	6.24
TLGL_Survival_Network_2011_Reduced_Network	18	0	43	18	0	1	2	16.67	0.41	0.67	2.54
Oxidative_Stress_Pathway	18	1	32	18	0	1	0	18	0.31	0.43	54.31
Iron_acquisition_and_oxidative	20	2	40	18	2	0	1	0	0.55	2.37	2.33
HCC1954_Breast_Cell_Line_Longterm_ErbB_Network	19	6	74	19	0	212	0	19	3.15	2565.34	Failure
BT474_Breast_Cell_Line_Longterm_ErbB_Network	19	6	74	19	0	139	0	19	1.53	1721.38	Failure
Mammalian_Cell_Cycle	19	1	51	19	0	3	0	19	0.35	0.48	1.12
T_cell_differentiation	19	4	38	19	0	29	0	19	0.31	7.37	7.59
SKBR3_Breast_Cell_Line_Longterm_ErbB_Network	21	4	85	21	0	412	0	21	6.39	951.62	Failure
PTM_in_Acute_Lymphoblastic_Leukemia	24	2	80	22	2	2	1	23.33	1.28	2.95	1.78
Trichostrongylus_retortaeformis	25	1	59	24	1	6	1	23.86	0.74	9.61	2.4
FA_BRCA_pathway	28	0	122	25	3	0	1	27	2.94	11.28	**2.45**
Death_Receptor_Signaling	25	3	48	25	0	16	0	25	0.54	32.13	7.14
CD4+_T_cell_Differentiation	29	9	100	27	2	237	14	28.63	10.26	Time out	Time out
Treatment_of_Castration_Resistant_Prostate_Cancer	28	14	64	28	0	964	0	28	0.85	Time out	4100.9
Tumour_Cell_Invasion_and_Migration	30	2	158	30	0	7	0	30	15.15	97.22	141.2
Cholesterol_Regulatory_Pathway	32	2	43	32	0	3	0	32	0.74	1.87	1.17
Bordetella_bronchiseptica	33	0	79	32	1	3	0	33	1.16	7.48	4.35
TCell_Signaling_2006	37	3	56	37	0	3	0	37	1.01	21.9	2.36
Guard_Cell_Abscisic_Acid_Signaling	40	4	80	39	1	6	4	35.6	1.06	82.16	19.41
Apoptosis_Network	39	2	75	39	0	0	8	30.63	0.96	132.32	11.57
Differentiation_of_T_lymphocytes	41	9	106	39	2	1510	0	41	3.05	Time out	Failure
Virtual_chondrocyte_-GRN_layer	43	10	146	41	2	568	0	43	14.68	Time out	1164.62
Virtual_chondrocyte_-PPI_layer	44	12	109	43	1	832	64	43.41	2.38	Time out	906.28
Senescence_Associated_Secretory_Phenotype	49	2	98	48	1	14	2	47.56	2.08	6356.13	7.86
MAPK_Cancer_Cell_Fate_Network	49	4	108	49	0	6	3	46	2.02	Failure	37.67
B_bronchiseptica_and_T_retortaeformis_coinfection	52	1	136	50	2	30	0	52	3.82	Time out	Failure
Signaling_Pathway_for_Butanol_Production	53	13	150	53	0	12	76	36.53	3.53	Failure	Time out
TLGL_Survival_Network_2011	54	6	201	54	0	5	6	52.18	4.36	Time out	305.1
Glucose_Repression_Signaling_2009	55	18	114	54	1	10332	0	55	27.16	Failure	Time Out
TLGL_Survival_Network_2008	54	7	200	54	0	11	22	51.12	5.14	Time out	722.43
_Bortezomib_Responses_in_U266_Human_Myeloma_Cells	62	5	131	61	1	38	0	62	3.36	Time out	94.26
PC12_Cell_Differentiation	61	1	109	61	0	3	0	61	2.58	114.08	**2**
HGF_Signaling_in_Keratinocytes	62	6	109	62	0	13	0	62	3.04	Time Out	25.46
_IGVH_mutations_in_chronic_lymphocytic_leukemia	66	25	137	65	1	576	1392	44.95	11.05	Time out	Time out
Lymphopoiesis_Regulatory_Network	67	14	174	65	2	12280	161	66.93	47.83	Time out	Time out
Colitisassociated_colon_cancer	69	1	154	69	0	2	6	58.375	4.44	Time out	2435.06
IL6_Signaling	71	15	163	71	0	16	100	29.21	5.27	Failure	Time out
T_Cell_Receptor_Signaling	94	7	165	93	1	56	24	86.73	4.86	Time Out	43.71
IL1_Signaling	104	14	232	104	0	36	0	104	6.77	Time out	Time out
Influenza_A_Virus_Replication_Cycle	120	11	305	120	0	329	19	119.14	156.7	Time out	Time out
Signaling_in_Macrophage_Activation	268	26	552	267	1	112640	36864	329.03	286.64	Time Out	Failure

4.2   Real Biological Networks

Next, we applied our algorithm to real BNs taken from the Cell Collective repository [9], a database of Boolean representations of real biological networks. We focused on 68 networks where all functions could be expressed using LTFs. We compared our results against Stable Motif (SM) and against an answer-set programming (ASP) algorithm [14,15], which finds full attractors. We imposed a time limit of 4 hours on each method (per network).

The results are presented in Table 1. Clearly, our ILP-based method outperforms the other two algorithms in almost all tested networks, solving each network on average in 10 s and spending a maximum of 5 min. In comparison, ASP solved only 46 (68%) of the networks and Stable Motif solved only 50 (74%) of the networks under the time limit (Fig. 4). It is worth mentioning that the only one non-LTF network that could be solved by our competitors had 15 nodes and could also be solved by a simple exhaustive search approach. Additionally, in cases where ASP succeeded, we verified that for each quasi-attractor there is exactly one corresponding full attractor; moreover, for each such matching pair, all the nodes that do not stabilize in the quasi-attractor, oscillate in the full attractor. This implies that in all these cases the quasi-attractor finding could be complemented by exhaustive search to identify full attractors efficiently.

5   Conclusions

In this work, we proposed a novel ILP-based method for identifying quasi-attractors in asynchronous Boolean networks. The method leverages the representation of most Boolean functions in biological networks as linear threshold functions to construct an efficient integer program for quasi-attractor detection. Future research may use the properties of linear threshold functions to efficiently find the oscillatory parts of the corresponding attractors.

References

1. Abdallah, E.B., Folschette, M., Roux1, O., Magnin, M.: ASP-based method for the enumeration of attractors in non-deterministic synchronous and asynchronous multi-valued networks. Algorithms Mol. Biol. **12**, 20–23 (2017)
2. Albert, R., Othmer, H.G.: The topology of the regulatory interactions predicts the expression pattern of the segment polarity genes in drosophila melanogaster. J. Theor. Biol. **223**(1), 1–18 (2003)
3. Aldridge, B.B., Burke, J.M., Lauffenburger, D.A., Sorger, P.K.: Physicochemical modelling of cell signalling pathways. Nat. Cell Biol. **8**, 1195–1203 (2006)
4. Bruner, A., Sharan, R.: A robustness analysis of dynamic Boolean models of cellular circuits. J. Comput. Biol. **27**, 133–143 (2019)
5. Dubrova, E., Teslenko, M.: A sat-based algorithm for finding attractors in synchronous Boolean networks. IEEE/ACM Trans. Comput. Biol. Bioinform. **8**, 1393–1399 (2011)
6. Espinosa-Soto, C., Padilla-Longoria, P., Alvarez-Buylla, E.R.: A gene regulatory network model for cell-fate determination during Arabidopsis thaliana flower development that is robust and recovers experimental gene expression profiles. Plant Cell **16**(11), 2923–2939 (2004)
7. Fauré, A., Naldi, A., Chaouiya, C., Thieffry, D.: Dynamical analysis of a generic Boolean model for the control of the mammalian cell cycle. Bioinformatics **22**, e124–e131 (2006)
8. Gurobi Optimization, LLC: Gurobi optimizer reference manual (2023). https://www.gurobi.com

9. Helikar, T., et al.: The cell collective: toward an open and collaborative approach to systems biology. BMC Syst. Biol. **6**, 96 (2012)
10. Huang, S., Ingber, D.E.: Shape-dependent control of cell growth, differentiation, and apoptosis: switching between attractors in cell regulatory networks. Exp. Cell Res. **26**(1), 91–103 (2000)
11. de Jong, H., Page, M.: Search for steady states of piecewise-linear differential equation models of genetic regulatory networks. IEEE/ACM Trans. Comput. Biol. Bioinform. **5**(2), 208–222 (2008)
12. Kauffman, S.: Metabolic stability and epigenesis in randomly constructed genetic nets. J. Theor. Biol. **22**, 437–467 (1969)
13. Kauffman, S.: The Origins of Order: Self-Organization and Selection in Evolution. Spin Glasses and Biology, pp. 61–100. World Scientific (1992)
14. Klarner, H., Bockmayr, A., Siebert, H.: Computing maximal and minimal trap spaces of Boolean networks. Nat. Comput. **14**, 535–544 (2015)
15. Klarner, H., Siebert, H.: Approximating attractors of Boolean networks by iterative CTL model checking. Front. Bioeng. Biotechnol. **3**, #130 (2015)
16. Klarner, H., Streck, A., Siebert, H.: PyBoolNet: a Python package for the generation, analysis and visualization of Boolean networks. Bioinformatics **33**, 770–772 (2017)
17. Mizera, A., Pang, J., Qu, H., Yuan, Q.: Taming asynchrony for attractor detection in large Boolean networks. IEEE/ACM Trans. Comput. Biol. Bioinf. **16**, 31–42 (2018)
18. Naldi, A., Remy, E., Thieffry, D., Chaouiya, C.: Dynamically consistent reduction of logical regulatory graphs. Theor. Comput. Sci. **412**, 2207–2218 (2011)
19. O'Donnell, R.: Analysis of Boolean Functions, pp. 113–141. Cambridge University Press (2014)
20. Rozum, J., Zañudo, J., Gan, X., Deritei, D., Albert, R.: Parity and time reversal elucidate both decision-making in empirical models and attractor scaling in critical Boolean networks. Sci. Adv. **7**, eabf8124 (2021)
21. Saadatpour, A., Albert, I., Albert, R.: Attractor analysis of asynchronous Boolean models of signal transduction networks. J. Theor. Biol. **266**, 641–656 (2010)
22. Saez-Rodriguez, J., et al.: A logical model provides insights into t cell receptor signaling. PLoS Comput. Biol. **3**, e163 (2007)
23. Sharan, R.: Toward a role model. EMBO Rep. **14**(11), 948 (2013)
24. Skodawessely, T., Klemm, K.: Finding attractors in asynchronous Boolean dynamic. Adv. Complex Syst. **14**, 439–449 (2011)
25. Thomas, R.: Boolean formalization of genetic control circuits. J. Theor. Biol. **42**, 563–585 (1973)
26. Thomas, R.: Regulatory networks seen as asynchronous automata: a logical description. J. Theor. Biol. **153**(1), 1–23 (1991)
27. Trinh, V.G., Hiraishi, K., Benhamou, B.: Computing attractors of large-scale asynchronous Boolean networks using minimal trap spaces. In: Proceedings Bioinformatics, Computational Biology and Health (BCB), pp. 1–10 (2022)
28. Tyson, J.J., Chen, K., Novak, B.: Network dynamics and cell physiology. Nat. Rev. Mol. Cell Biol. **2**, 908–916 (2001)
29. Tyson, J.J., Chen, K., Novak, B.: Network dynamics and cell physiology. Curr. Op. Cell Biol. **15**, 221–231 (2003)
30. Veliz-Cuba, A.: Reduction of Boolean network models. Theor. Comput. Sci. **289**, 167–172 (2011)
31. Zanudo, J.G.T., Albert, R.: An effective network reduction approach to find the dynamical repertoire of discrete dynamic networks. Chaos **23**, 025111 (2013)

ImputeCC Enhances Integrative Hi-C-Based Metagenomic Binning Through Constrained Random-Walk-Based Imputation

Yuxuan Du[ID], Wenxuan Zuo, and Fengzhu Sun[✉]

Department of Quantitative and Computational Biology, University of Southern California, Los Angeles, USA
{yuxuandu,wzuo,fsun}@usc.edu

Abstract. Metagenomic Hi-C (metaHi-C) enables the recognition of relationships between contigs in terms of their physical proximity within the same cell, facilitating the reconstruction of high-quality metagenome-assembled genomes (MAGs) from complex microbial communities. However, current Hi-C-based contig binning methods solely depend on Hi-C interactions between contigs to group them, ignoring invaluable biological information, including the presence of single-copy marker genes. Here, we introduce ImputeCC, an integrative contig binning tool tailored for metaHi-C datasets. ImputeCC integrates Hi-C interactions with the inherent discriminative power of single-copy marker genes, initially clustering them as preliminary bins, and develops a new constrained random walk with restart (CRWR) algorithm to improve Hi-C connectivity among these contigs. Extensive evaluations on mock and real metaHi-C datasets from diverse environments, including the human gut, wastewater, cow rumen, and sheep gut, demonstrate that ImputeCC consistently outperforms other Hi-C-based contig binning tools. ImputeCC's genus-level analysis of the sheep gut microbiota further reveals its ability and potential to recover essential species from dominant genera such as *Bacteroides*, detect previously unrecognized genera, and shed light on the characteristics and functional roles of genera such as *Alistipes* within the sheep gut ecosystem.
Availability: ImputeCC is implemented in Python and available at https://github.com/dyxstat/ImputeCC. The Supplementary Information is available at https://doi.org/10.5281/zenodo.10776604.

Keywords: Metagenomic Hi-C · Integrative Contig Binning · MetaHi-C Contact Map Imputation · Constrained Random Walk With Restart

1 Introduction

Metagenomics is revolutionizing microbial ecology by enabling the exploration of complex microbial communities in diverse environments without the need for

J. Ma (Ed.): RECOMB 2024, LNCS 14758, pp. 99–114, 2024.
https://doi.org/10.1007/978-1-0716-3989-4_7

traditional microbial isolation or cultivation [17,18]. The recent combination of Hi-C sequencing with whole metagenomic shotgun sequencing leads to the development of the metagenomic Hi-C (metaHi-C) technique, which has provided novel perspectives on species diversity and the interactions among microorganisms within a single microbial sample [5,12,22,27]. In metaHi-C experiments, shotgun sequencing extracts genomic fragments from a microbial sample, while Hi-C sequencing conducted on the same microbial sample generates DNA-DNA proximity ligations within the same cells, resulting in millions of paired-end Hi-C short reads. These fragmented shotgun reads are assembled into longer contigs, forming the basis for aligning paired-end Hi-C reads. MetaHi-C contacts, representing the number of Hi-C read pairs linking contig pairs, reveal contig relationships based on physical proximity within the microbial community. Depending on whether the shotgun libraries in metaHi-C experiments are constructed using second-generation or third-generation sequencing technologies, metaHi-C experiments can be classified into either short-read or long-read metaHi-C datasets, respectively. Considering contigs originating from the same genome exhibit enriched Hi-C contact frequencies relative to those derived from distinct genomes, the process of Hi-C-based binning emerges and aims at grouping fragmented contigs into metagenome-assembled genomes (MAGs) [19] by leveraging Hi-C contacts between contigs [2,11,14]. The resulting MAG collections serve as fundamental prerequisites for downstream analyses, such as the elucidation of the metabolic potentials and functional roles of diverse microorganisms, as well as the exploration of virus-host interactions [8,35]. Various Hi-C-based contig binning methods have been developed, including HiCBin [14], MetaTOR [2], bin3C [11], and the MetaCC binning module (referred to as MetaCC) [15]. Compared to conventional shotgun-based binning tools reliant on sequence composition and contig coverage for contig clustering, Hi-C-based binning methods demonstrate their superior ability in MAG recovery using only one single sample [14,27].

However, existing Hi-C-based binning methods rely solely on Hi-C interactions for contig grouping, overlooking valuable biological information encapsulated within single-copy marker genes. These genes, present as single copies in the vast majority of genomes [1], hold the great potential to discriminate between contigs originating from distinct species when shared among them. This omission underscores a critical gap in current approaches, leaving ample room for enhancement and improved analyses. In response, we introduce ImputeCC, an integrative binning tool designed for metaHi-C datasets. ImputeCC manages to harness the comprehensive insights offered by both Hi-C interactions and single-copy marker genes to optimize the contig binning process. To thoroughly assess the effectiveness of ImputeCC, we conduct simulations for both short-read and long-read metaHi-C datasets. Subsequently, we demonstrate ImputeCC's performance against other publicly-available Hi-C-based binning tools using a diverse set of real short-read and long-read metaHi-C datasets including the human gut short-read [27], wastewater short-read [32], cow rumen long-read [4], and sheep gut long-read [3] metaHi-C datasets. ImputeCC's superior performance is particularly evident in the challenging sheep gut environment, where ImputeCC successfully retrieves an impressive total of 408 high-quality and 885 medium-quality

MAGs, as assessed by the latest CheckM2 [9]. To the best of our knowledge, this represents the largest number of reference-quality MAGs reported from a single microbial sample. Furthermore, ImputeCC's genus-level analyses of the sheep gut microbiota reveal ability of ImputeCC to recover essential species from dominant genera and showed its potential to detect previously unrecognized genera.

2   Results

2.1   Overview of ImputeCC

ImputeCC is an integrative Hi-C-based binner that leverages the combined power of Hi-C interactions and single-copy marker genes in the contig binning process. Figure 1 shows the outline of ImputeCC. The core concept of ImputeCC involves the preclustering of marker-gene-containing contigs guided by two fundamental principles: I) Contigs sharing the same single-copy marker gene originate from distinct species with high probability; II) Contigs without overlapping single-copy marker genes are likely from the same genome when connected by robust Hi-C signals. To address the challenge that marker-gene-containing contigs from the same genome may not be effectively linked by Hi-C contacts due to the locality characteristics of proximity ligations, we design a new constrained random walk with restart (CRWR) algorithm to impute the metaHi-C contact matrix before preclustering, with all random walks limited to start from marker-gene-containing contigs. Subsequently, by leveraging the imputed Hi-C matrix in conjunction with the aforementioned principles, ImputeCC can accurately precluster contigs with single-copy marker genes, establishing them as preliminary bins. Finally, the tool applies Leiden clustering [33] to group all assembled contigs, utilizing the information from preliminary bins to optimize the binning process.

2.2   ImputeCC Achieved Accurate Preclustering for Contigs Containing Single-Copy Marker Genes

Since ImputeCC relies on the information provided by preliminary bins for final contig clustering, the quality of these preliminary bins, as established during the preclustering step, holds a pivotal role in affecting the final binning results of ImputeCC. Mock metaHi-C datasets were created by combining simulated Hi-C reads with real shotgun sequencing data from a manually curated microbial community (see Subsect. 3.1). The shotgun data were obtained from the Illumina HiSeq 3000, ONT MinION R9, and PacBio Sequel II platforms. These datasets, named 'mock Illumina', 'mock Nanopore', and 'mock PacBio', each comprised a combination of simulated Hi-C reads and real shotgun reads corresponding to the specific sequencing platform. Since the ground truth of all contigs from the mock metaHi-C datasets were known, we could leverage the mock datasets to assess the quality of the preclustering of preliminary bins. Specifically, we calculated the Adjusted Rand Index (ARI) clustering evaluation metric (Supplementary Note 1) for preliminary bins derived from the mock Illumina, Nanopore, and PacBio

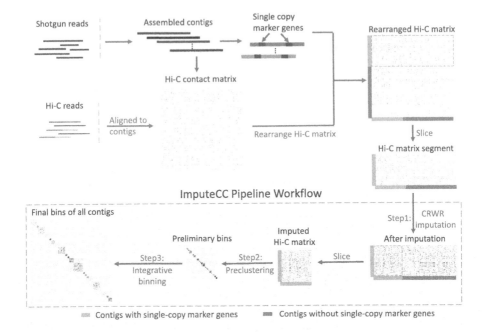

Fig. 1. Overview of the ImputeCC. Given an input of the metagenomic Hi-C contact matrix and contigs containing single-copy marker genes, ImputeCC initiates the imputation of the metaHi-C contact matrix using a new constrained random walk with restart (CRWR) algorithm, specifically limiting random walks to originate from contigs with marker genes. Subsequently, ImputeCC segregates and retains the imputed contact matrix exclusively for marker-gene-containing contigs, using it in conjunction with the characteristics of single-copy marker genes to effectively precluster these contigs as preliminary bins. Finally, ImputeCC applies the Leiden clustering method to group all assembled contigs, with insights from the preliminary bins guiding the optimization of the binning process.

datasets, resulting in values of 0.976, 0.975, and 0.988, respectively (Fig. 2a). These values indicated that ImputeCC could accomplish precise preclustering for contigs with single-copy marker genes. Furthermore, we performed preclustering directly using NormCC-normalized Hi-C contacts, omitting the imputation step. In this context, the ARI values for preliminary bins derived from the three mock datasets were decreased to 0.783, 0.903, and 0.775, respectively (Fig. 2a), underscoring the significant enhancement in the construction of preliminary bins achieved through our CRWR imputation.

2.3 ImputeCC Retrieved the Most High-Quality Genomes from the Mock metaHi-C Datasets

We first conducted a comparative evaluation of ImputeCC binning against VAMB [24], MetaTOR [2], bin3C [11], and the MetaCC binning module (referred

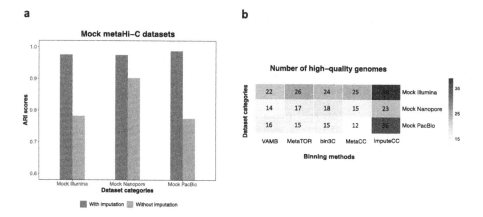

Fig. 2. Benchmarking using the three mock metaHi-C datasets. (a) Assessing the quality of preliminary bins using ARI. ImputeCC accurately grouped marker-gene-containing contigs while the CRWR imputation markedly improved the preclustering performance. (b) ImputeCC outperformed other binners on all the three mock metaHi-C datasets with respect to the number of retrieved high-quality MAGs (completeness ≥90% and contamination ≤5%). The evaluation criteria of completeness and contamination for MAGs recovered from the mock datasets are detailed in Subsect. 3.4.

to as MetaCC) [15] using the three mock metaHi-C datasets. In addition to VAMB, a popular shotgun-based binning tool that utilizes sequence composition and coverage information, three other tools in consideration are Hi-C-based. It is important to note that another publicly available Hi-C-based binner HiCBin [14] was excluded from the benchmarking study on the mock datasets due to its inability to converge when applied to the mock Nanopore and PacBio datasets. As shown in Fig. 2b, ImputeCC demonstrated a remarkable ability to reconstruct a markedly larger number of high-quality genomes (completeness ≥90% and contamination ≤5%) across all the three mock datasets. Specifically, ImputeCC outperformed the second-highest result by 46.2%, 27.8%, and 125% in terms of high-quality genome reconstruction for the mock Illumina, Nanopore, and PacBio datasets, respectively. Notably, the number of mapped Hi-C read pairs for the mock Nanopore dataset was considerably lower in comparison to the mock Illumina and PacBio datasets (Supplementary Table 1), which can be attributed to the relatively higher error rate associated with Nanopore R9 long reads. This disparity in read mapping could be one of the contributing factors for ImputeCC retrieving a comparatively lower number of high-quality genomes from the mock Nanopore dataset. Finally, we evaluated ImputeCC's stability against Hi-C sequencing depth by downsampling the Hi-C read pairs from 10 million to 5 million in the mock datasets. The recovery of high-quality MAGs slightly declined from 38 to 36 in the Illumina dataset and from 23 to 21 in the Nanopore dataset, while the PacBio dataset consistently yielded 36 MAGs.

These results highlighted ImputeCC's resilience to reduced Hi-C read counts, ensuring its reliable performance in the mock metaHi-C datasets.

2.4   ImputeCC Markedly Outperformed Existing Binners on Real metaHi-C Datasets

To validate ImputeCC on real metaHi-C data, we applied it to two short-read and two long-read metaHi-C datasets from four different environments: human gut, wastewater, cow rumen, and sheep gut. Here, we compared ImputeCC to all four publicly-available Hi-C-based binners, namely HiCBin, MetaTOR, bin3C, and MetaCC, in addition to VAMB. Given the absence of reference genomes in real-world datasets, we utilized the CheckM2 [9] to evaluate the completeness and contamination of the recovered bins (see Subsect. 3.4). The results from the two long-read metaHi-C datasets are presented in Fig. 3, while those from the two short-read metaHi-C datasets can be found in Supplementary Fig. 1. In all cases, ImputeCC recovered more high-quality (completeness $\geq 90\%$ and contamination $\leq 5\%$) and medium-quality (completeness $\geq 50\%$ and contamination $\leq 10\%$) bins than the alternatives considered. Notably, the sheep gut long-read metaHi-C dataset, owing to its high complexity, posed a greater challenge. ImputeCC binning retrieved 408 high-quality MAGs, markedly outperforming VAMB, HiCBin, MetaTOR, bin3C, and MetaCC with an increase of 235 (135.8%), 321 (369%), 279 (216.3%), 160 (64.5%), and 82 (25.2%), respectively (Fig. 3a). ImputeCC was also able to recover 125.8%, 279.8%, 91.1%, 120.1% and 23.1% more medium-quality bins than VAMB, HiCBin, MetaTOR, bin3C, and MetaCC, respectively (Fig. 3b).

Moreover, we explored the capability of different binners to capture the species diversity in microbial samples by annotating all medium-quality and high-quality bins generated by different binners on all real metaHi-C datasets using GTDB-TK [7] (see Subsect. 3.5). As shown in Fig. 3c and Supplementary Fig. 1c, medium-quality bins derived from ImputeCC represented a markedly larger taxonomic diversity at the species level on all datasets. We further conducted a detailed comparative analysis of the high-quality MAGs retrieved from the sheep gut long-read metaHi-C dataset. We employed Mash [25] to identify cases where ImputeCC binning and three other Hi-C-based binning tools (MetaTOR, bin3C, and MetaCC) retrieved identical high-quality MAGs on the sheep gut long-read metaHi-C dataset (see Subsect. 3.5). Notably, the majority of high-quality MAGs obtained through other Hi-C-based binning tools were also successfully recovered by ImputeCC (Supplementary Fig. 2a). In contrast, ImputeCC binning went beyond by reconstructing a substantial number of high-quality MAGs that remained inaccessible to the other binning tools. Further annotation analyses of the high-quality MAGs demonstrated ImputeCC recovered more distinct taxa at various taxonomic levels compared to Hi-C-based alternatives, including bin3C, MetaTOR, and MetaCC (Supplementary Fig. 2b).

Finally, ImputeCC's analysis at the genus level, leveraging its recovered high-quality MAGs, has unveiled significant insights into microbial composition of the sheep gut microbiota (Supplementary Note 2). Within this complex ecosystem, ImputeCC highlighted the dominance of the *Bacteroides* genus, known for influencing intestinal immunity [31,36], and uniquely detected critical species within it, such as *Bacteroides uniformis* and *Bacteroides vulgatus*. It was also the only tool to uncover the *Tidjanibacter* genus and extensively characterized the *Alistipes* genus, revealing species with potential roles in the sheep gut ecosystem and suggesting a broader species diversity. These capabilities demonstrate ImputeCC's unparalleled contribution to elucidating the sheep gut's microbial composition and its functional significance.

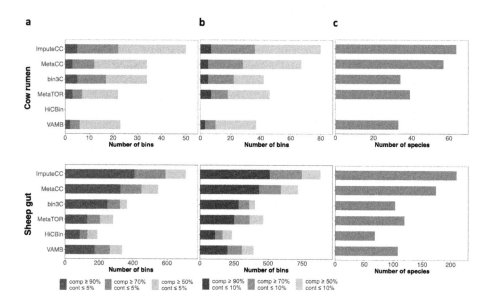

Fig. 3. Benchmarking using the real cow rumen and sheep gut long-read metaHi-C datasets. (a) The number of MAGs with varying completeness (comp) and contamination (cont) ≤5%. ImputeCC consistently outperforms other binning tools, producing a greater number of high-quality bins in both long-read metaHi-C datasets. (b) The number of MAGs with varying completeness and contamination ≤10%. ImputeCC returned more medium-quality bins when compared to alternative methods for both datasets. (c) Comparative analysis of the taxonomic diversity at the species level within medium-quality bins obtained by different binning tools. ImputeCC's binning approach stands out by capturing the broadest range of microbial species in medium-quality MAGs.

2.5 Running Time Analysis of the ImputeCC

On an Intel Xeon Processor E5-2665 with a clock speed of 2.40 GHz and 50 GB of allocated memory, the ImputeCC pipeline spent 64 min, 204 min, 25 min, and 2,115 min on the human gut short-read, wastewater short-read, cow rumen long-read, and sheep gut long-read metaHi-C datasets, respectively.

3   Materials and Methods

3.1   Datasets

Mock metaHi-C Datasets. The mock community sequencing data were downloaded from the European Nucleotide Archive under project ID PRJEB52977 [23]. The mock community comprises 71 strains representing 69 distinct species and underwent comprehensive sequencing using the Illumina HiSeq 3000, ONT MinION R9, and PacBio Sequel II platforms, generating three different shotgun libraries. The specific accession numbers and sizes of these three shotgun libraries are shown in Supplementary Table 2. After filtering the incomplete reference genomes (Supplementary Note 3), we obtained reference genomes of 66 distinct species for the following experiments. The abundances of all species were available from the supplementary data of [23]. Since the original dataset lacked Hi-C sequencing reads, we employed sim3C (v0.2) [10] to simulate metagenomic Hi-C reads based on the 66 reference genomes and their known abundances in the mock community, utilizing parameters '-n 10000000 -l 150 -e MluCI -e Sau3AI -m hic –insert-sd 20 –insert-mean 350 –insert-min 150 –linear –simple-reads'. Subsequently, we combined the same simulated Hi-C library with the three shotgun libraries, respectively, to construct three mock metaHi-C datasets. These mock Hi-C datasets were named according to the shotgun library incorporated in the mock dataset, resulting in the 'mock Illumina,' 'mock PacBio,' and 'mock Nanopore' metaHi-C datasets. Each mock dataset comprised real shotgun reads sequenced from a known mock community, along with simulated Hi-C reads.

Real metaHi-C Datasets. Four publicly-available real metaHi-C datasets were utilized in this study, comprising two short-read metaHi-C datasets and two long-read metaHi-C datasets. The specific sizes of the raw datasets are detailed in Supplementary Table 3.

The two short-read metaHi-C datasets were derived from the human gut (BioProject: PRJNA413092) [27] and wastewater (BioProject: PRJNA506462) [32] samples, respectively. Each short-read metaHi-C dataset consisted of both shotgun and Hi-C libraries originating from the same sample source. The construction of Hi-C sequencing libraries involved the use of restriction endonucleases Sau3AI and MluCI. Sequencing of both the shotgun and Hi-C libraries was carried out on Illumina platforms, producing 150-base pair reads. The two long-read metaHi-C datasets were obtained from cow rumen (BioProject: PRJNA507739) [4] and sheep gut (BioProject: PRJNA595610) [3] samples, respectively. The cow rumen long-read metaHi-C dataset comprised uncorrected PacBio long-read libraries and Hi-C libraries. The error-prone PacBio long reads were generated using both the PacBio RSII and PacBio Sequel platforms. Hi-C libraries for this dataset were prepared using the Sau3AI and MluCI restriction enzymes and subsequently sequenced on an Illumina HiSeq 2000, producing 80-base pair reads. The sheep gut long-read metaHi-C dataset consisted of PacBio circular consensus sequencing (CCS) long-read libraries and Hi-C sequencing libraries.

The PacBio CCS long reads, characterized by high accuracy with average Q scores exceeding 20, were referred to as HiFi reads. Distinct Hi-C libraries for the sheep gut long-read metaHi-C dataset were generated using the Sau3AI and MluCI restriction enzymes and sequenced at a length of 150 base pairs.

3.2   Data Preprocessing

We first conduct essential read cleaning procedures using 'bbduk' from the BBTools suite (v37.25) [6] to address issues such as adapter sequences, low-quality reads, and PCR duplication (Supplementary Note 4). For each metaHi-C dataset, reads from the shotgun library are assembled into longer contigs (Supplementary Note 5). After assembly, processed paired-end Hi-C reads are aligned to these contigs using BWA-MEM (v0.7.17) [21] with the '-5SP' parameter to prioritize the alignment with the lowest read coordinate as the primary alignment. Subsequent alignment filtering steps include the removal of unmapped reads, secondary and supplementary alignments, and alignments with low quality (nucleotide match length <30 or mapping score <30). We count Hi-C read pairs aligned to two contigs as raw Hi-C contacts between contigs and those contigs with fewer than two Hi-C contacts are excluded. Raw Hi-C contacts are normalized by NormCC [15] with default parameters to eliminate the systematic biases derived from the number of restriction sites, contig length, and coverage.

3.3   The Framework of ImputeCC Binning

Detect Assembled Contigs with Single-Copy Marker Genes. Similar to [34], we identify single-copy marker genes, which are genes typically found as single copies in the majority of genomes [1] within the assembled contigs. We accomplish this by employing FragGeneScan [30] and HMMER (v3.3.2) [16] (Supplementary Note 6).

Impute the Metagenomic Hi-C Contact Matrix for Contigs Containing Marker Genes. According to the second principle of preclustering outlined in Subsect. 2.1, the effective preclustering of contigs with single-copy marker genes partially depends on the expectation that marker-gene-containing contigs can be reliably linked through robust Hi-C interactions if they come from the same genome. However, this expectation encounters a practical limitation attributed to the localized characteristics of proximity ligations, which implies that even when two contigs share the same genomic origin, they may fail to establish Hi-C contacts if they are not in close spatial proximity within the cell, thereby contributing to the sparsity of the metagenomic Hi-C contact matrix [13]. To facilitate improved connections among marker-gene-containing contigs originating from the same genome through Hi-C interactions, we design a metagenomic Hi-C contact matrix imputation method. This involves employing a constrained random walk with restart (CRWR) technique to amplify the within-cell Hi-C signals specially for marker-gene-containing contigs. Specifically, we define m

and n as the number of contigs containing single-copy marker genes and the total number of assembled contigs, respectively. Let H denote the NormCC-normalized Hi-C contact matrix, where the entry H_{ij} represents the normalized Hi-C contacts between contig i and j. We first set all diagonal entries of H as zero and reorganize the matrix H by moving the contigs containing marker genes to the first m rows and m columns consistently and denote the reorganized matrix as H'. Then, the reorganized matrix H' is further normalized by its row sum and let M denote the matrix after the row-sum normalization, i.e.,

$$M_{ij} = \frac{H'_{ij}}{\sum_k H'_{ik}}. \tag{1}$$

We use $N^{(t)}$ to represent the matrix after the t-th iteration of random walk with restart and limit that all random walks can only start from the contigs with marker genes. Mathematically, the random walk starts from the initial matrix $N^{(0)} = \begin{bmatrix} I_{m \times m} & 0_{m \times (n-m)} \\ 0_{(n-m) \times m} & 0_{(n-m) \times (n-m)} \end{bmatrix}_{n \times n}$, and $N^{(t)}$ is computed recursively by the following:

$$N^{(t)} = (1 - p) \cdot N^{(t-1)} \cdot M + p \cdot T, \tag{2}$$

where $T = N^{(0)}$ denotes the restarting matrix, and p (default, 0.5) serves as the restarting probability used to maintain a balance between the influence of global and local network structures. Notably, since the last $n - m$ rows of all iteration matrices N are kept to be zero, the formula (2) can be simplified by omitting the last $n - m$ rows of N and T. As a result, the new RWR can be represented as

$$\tilde{N}^{(0)} = \tilde{T} = [I_{m \times m} | 0_{m \times (n-m)}]_{m \times n},$$
$$\tilde{N}^{(t)} = (1 - p) \cdot \tilde{N}^{(t-1)} \cdot M + p \cdot \tilde{T}. \tag{3}$$

To avoid the imputed matrix becoming too dense, we only retain the largest τ percent (default, 20) of non-zero entries in $\tilde{N}^{(t)}$ after each iteration, i.e.,

$$\tilde{N}^{(t)} = \tilde{N}^{(t)} \circ 1_{\{\tilde{N}^{(t)} > C_t^\tau\}}, \tag{4}$$

where C_t^τ is a $(100 - \tau)$-th percentile of all non-zero entries in $\tilde{N}^{(t)}$; 1 represents an indicator matrix and $1_{ij} = 1$ only if $\tilde{N}_{ij}^{(t)} > C_t^\tau$; $\circ$ denotes the mathematical operator of element-wise matrix multiplication.

Let $\delta_t = ||\tilde{N}^{(t)} - \tilde{N}^{(t-1)}||_2$. The iteration ends if either of the following two conditions is satisfied:

- $\delta_t < 0.01$,
- Early stop if $\delta_t - \delta_{t-1} < 0.001$ for a consecutive five times.

Let $\hat{N}$ denote the final matrix output from the imputation. Then the first m columns of $\hat{N}$, denoted by $P_{m \times m}$, can exactly represent the imputed Hi-C matrix for contigs with marker genes. Finally, we transform the matrix P to a symmetric matrix P' and further normalize P' to eliminate the contigs' coverage biases derived from the imputation using the Square Root Vanilla Coverage (sqrtVC) method [28], i.e.,

$$P' = P + P^T,$$
$$Q = D^{-\frac{1}{2}} P' D^{-\frac{1}{2}}, \tag{5}$$

where D is a diagonal matrix where each elements D_{ii} is the sum of the i-th row of P'.

Precluster Contigs with Marker Genes as Preliminary Bins. Leveraging the imputed Hi-C matrix Q as well as the characteristics of single-copy marker genes, we would like to accurately precluster contigs with marker genes as preliminary bins following the two principles outlined in Subsect. 2.1. Specifically, we first sort all categories of detected marker genes by the number of contigs containing the marker genes. If several marker genes correspond to the same number of contigs, they are further sorted by the gene length. Then, we use a greedy strategy to iteratively construct the preliminary bins as follows:

- Initialization: choose all contigs from the first marker gene and initialize preliminary bin set, denoted by $\mathcal{B}$, with each bin containing one contig.
- Iteration: in the k-th iteration, we select all contigs containing the k-th marker gene and only handle contigs that have not been assigned to any preliminary bins in $\mathcal{B}$. Let $\mathcal{C}$ denote the set of contigs to be processed in the iteration. We then define the contig-to-bin Hi-C similarity between a contig $c \in \mathcal{C}$ and a bin $B \in \mathcal{B}$ as:

$$S_{c,B} = \frac{\sum_{c_1 \in B} Q_{c,c_1}}{\#B} \tag{6}$$

where c_1 denotes the contigs in the preliminary bin B, Q_{c,c_1} is the imputed Hi-C contacts between contigs c and c_1 and $\#B$ represents the number of contigs in B. In this way, we can construct a undirected bipartite graph, where the top nodes are contigs from the set $\mathcal{C}$ and the bottom nodes are preliminary bins from the set $\mathcal{B}$. The weighted edges between top nodes and bottom nodes represent the contig-to-bin Hi-C similarity. To assign the contigs to preliminary bins, we leverage the Karp's algorithm [20] to find a maximum-weight matching between contigs and preliminary bins. For each contig in the set $\mathcal{C}$ with a matching preliminary bin, if the contig-to-bin Hi-C similarity is above the median of non-zero entries in the imputed matrix Q, we attribute the contig to its matching preliminary bin; otherwise, the contig will be discarded. Finally, we add all unmatched contigs to $\mathcal{B}$ as new preliminary bins, with each new bin containing one unmatched contig.
- Repeat the iteration step until all marker genes are processed.

Leiden Clustering for All Contigs Using the Information of Preliminary Bins. We apply the Leiden community detection algorithm [33] to the NormCC-normalized Hi-C contact matrix H to cluster all assembled contigs, using the preliminary bin set as an initial framework. The Leiden algorithm iteratively merges and refines communities to maximize modularity, a metric that quantifies the partitioning quality. To incorporate preliminary bin information, we initialize contig memberships based on preliminary bins, ensuring that contigs from the same preliminary bin are placed within the same community, while contigs not associated with any preliminary bins are initially assigned to individual communities. Throughout the Leiden iterations, these assignments for contigs from preliminary bins remain fixed. Consequently, contigs from the same preliminary bin coalesce into the same cluster, while those from different preliminary bins form distinct clusters after the Leiden clustering.

Moreover, since the Leiden algorithm is modularity-based, we select a flexible modularity function based on the Reichardt and Bornholdt's Potts model [29]. Notably, the resolution parameter r in the modularity function (Supplementary Note 7) is a hyper-parameter that determines the relative importance assigned to the configuration null part compared to the links within the communities. To ascertain the optimal resolution parameter, we conduct parallel executions of the Leiden algorithm using various resolution values and automatically select the most favorable outcome. Specifically, we identify lineage-specific genes, which act as indicators of genome quality, through the application of the CheckM (v1.1.3) [26] function 'checkm analyze'. Consequently, for any given contig bin, we employ the same evaluation strategy as CheckM to efficiently estimate its precision and recall (Supplementary Note 8). Subsequently, for each resolution parameter value, we count the number of genomic bins with precision exceeding 95% and recall surpassing 90%, 70%, and 50%, respectively. Finally, we automatically select the resolution value that maximizes the sum of three count numbers as the optimal choice.

Integrative Strategy to Obtain the Final Bins. It is essential to acknowledge that the preliminary bins may not be entirely accurate. This can occur, for instance, in cases where genome coverage is insufficient or marker genes are fragmented into several pieces. Furthermore, our clustering strategy in previous steps may exacerbate these mis-binnings arising from the preliminary bin assignments. Consequently, it is still meaningful to apply the Leiden algorithm to cluster contigs independently, without relying on the preliminary bin information. The selection of the resolution parameter follows the same methodology as previously described. We denote the resulting bin sets as $\mathcal{F}_{\text{pre}}$ and $\mathcal{F}_{\text{null}}$ for the Leiden clustering with and without preliminary bin information, respectively. We then implement an iterative greedy strategy to integrate these two bin sets. Specifically, in each iteration of this integrative procedure, we assess the quality of all existing MAGs from $\mathcal{F}_{\text{pre}}$ and $\mathcal{F}_{\text{null}}$ using the metric:

$$\text{Recall} - 2 \times (100 - \text{Precision}). \tag{7}$$

The MAG displaying the highest estimated quality across both bin sets is selected for further consideration. In situations where two or more MAGs exhibit identical estimated quality scores, ties are resolved by selecting the MAG with the greatest N50 statistic and bin size. Following the selection of a MAG, it is moved from the corresponding bin set to the final bin set, and any contigs belonging to the selected MAG are also removed from the other bin set, if present. This iterative procedure continues until the highest quality MAG identified falls below 10. Finally, we can obtain the final bin set through the integration.

3.4 Evaluating the Quality of Recovered MAGs from the Mock and Real metaHi-C Datasets

For the mock metaHi-C datasets, where all species within the mock microbial community were known, the species identity of the assembled contigs could be determined (Supplementary Note 9). Then, we can define the completeness and contamination of each MAG recovered from the mock datasets. Specifically, for each MAG, we segregated the lengths of contigs according to their respective reference genomes and attributed the MAG to the reference genome with the largest cumulative contig length, denoted as $L(q)$. The length of the corresponding reference genome was denoted as $L(r)$, and the total length of the MAG was referred to as $L(v)$. The completeness of a MAG was quantified as $\frac{L(q)}{L(r)}$, while the contamination of a MAG was defined as $\frac{L(v)-L(q)}{L(v)}$. Finally, we classified high-quality genomes obtained from the mock datasets as those MAGs with completeness $\geq 90\%$ and contamination $\leq 5\%$.

For the real metaHi-C datasets, since the actual genomes are unknown in real samples, we applied CheckM2 [9] to evaluate the completeness and contamination of retrieved MAGs. CheckM2 is an advanced machine learning-based method for assessing the quality of draft genomic bins, offering improved accuracy and computational speed compared to existing tools [9]. Based on the CheckM2 assessments of completeness and contamination, we categorized the resolved MAGs from real metaHi-C datasets as high-quality if their completeness $\geq 90\%$ and contamination $\leq 5\%$, while MAGs were designated as medium-quality if their completeness $\geq 50\%$ and contamination $\leq 10\%$.

3.5 MAG Analyses on Real metaHi-C Datasets

To assess the capacity of various binning methods in capturing taxonomic diversity within real metaHi-C datasets, we performed taxonomic annotation on all high-quality and medium-quality bins using GTDB-TK (v2.1.0, Release: R207 v2) [7] with the function 'classify_wf' to extract the taxonomic information of the MAGs recovered by different binning methods.

Furthermore, to identify overlapping high-quality bins retrieved from the sheep gut long-read metaHi-C dataset between ImputeCC binning and other Hi-C-based binning approaches, we utilized Mash (v2.2) [25] with 10,000 sketches per bin to calculate the Mash distance between high-quality bins from different bin sets. Bins with a Mash distance below 0.01 were considered MAGs originating from the same genome.

3.6   Other Binners Used in Benchmarking

All binners used for comparison, i.e., VAMB (v3.0.3) [24], HiCBin (v1.1.0) [14], MetaTOR (v1.1.4) [2], bin3C (v0.1.1) [11], and MetaCC (v1.1.0) [15] were executed with default parameters on all mock and real metaHi-C datasets.

4   Discussions

In this work, we developed ImputeCC, an integrative Hi-C-based contig binning methods. ImputeCC combines Hi-C interactions with the intrinsic discriminative potential of single-copy marker genes by preclustering marker-gene-containing contigs as preliminary bins. To enhance the Hi-C connectivity of marker-gene-containing contigs, ImputeCC introduces a constrained random walk with restart (CRWR) approach to impute the metaHi-C contact matrix. Finally, ImputeCC employs Leiden clustering to group all assembled contigs, optimizing the binning process by leveraging information from the preliminary bins. Evaluations of ImputeCC using a wide range of diverse mock/real metaHi-C datasets have demonstrated its effectiveness for retrieving reference-quality MAGs and shown its potential to unravel the structure of microbial ecosystems and their resident microorganisms. Notably, we utilized CheckM2 in assessing the binning performance for the four real metaHi-C datasets. Although CheckM2 represents the most advanced software for evaluating bin quality in real metagenomic samples, it is essential to delve further into the accuracy of this machine-learning-based validation method in reflecting the true completeness and contamination levels of the recovered MAGs. Moreover, previous research has established the efficacy of Hi-C-based binning over shotgun-based approaches [11,14]. Accordingly, our benchmarking analyses focus on Hi-C-based methods, comparing ImputeCC with similar tools and including VAMB as a reference shotgun-based method.

ImputeCC offers several promising avenues for expansion. For instance, when dealing with large MAGs characterized by high abundances, there is potential in imputing normalized Hi-C contacts for contigs within these MAGs to facilitate the scaffolding process. Moreover, exploring imputation methods that consider additional information, such as the sequence composition of contigs, could yield improved imputation results.

Acknowledgments. Y.D. and F.S. conceived the ideas and designed the study. Y.D. implemented the methods, carried out the computational analyses, and drafted the manuscript. Y.D. and W.Z. developed the software. All authors modified and finalized the paper. The research is partially funded by NSF grant EF-2125142. The authors declare no competing interests.

References

1. Albertsen, M., Hugenholtz, P., Skarshewski, A., Nielsen, K.L., Tyson, G.W., Nielsen, P.H.: Genome sequences of rare, uncultured bacteria obtained by differential coverage binning of multiple metagenomes. Nat. Biotechnol. **31**(6), 533–538 (2013)
2. Baudry, L., Foutel-Rodier, T., Thierry, A., Koszul, R., Marbouty, M.: MetaTOR: a computational pipeline to recover high-quality metagenomic bins from mammalian gut proximity-ligation (me) libraries. Front. Genet. **10**, 753 (2019)
3. Bickhart, D.M., et al.: Generating lineage-resolved, complete metagenome-assembled genomes from complex microbial communities. Nat. Biotechnol. **40**(5), 711–719 (2022)
4. Bickhart, D.M., et al.: Assignment of virus and antimicrobial resistance genes to microbial hosts in a complex microbial community by combined long-read assembly and proximity ligation. Genome Biol. **20**, 153 (2019)
5. Burton, J.N., Liachko, I., Dunham, M.J., Shendure, J.: Species-level deconvolution of metagenome assemblies with Hi-C–based contact probability maps. G3 (Bethesda) **4**(7), 1339–1346 (2014)
6. Bushnell, B.: BBMap: a fast, accurate, splice-aware aligner. Technical report, Lawrence Berkeley National Lab. (LBNL), Berkeley, CA, United States (2014)
7. Chaumeil, P.A., Mussig, A.J., Hugenholtz, P., Parks, D.H.: GTDB-Tk v2: memory friendly classification with the genome taxonomy database. Bioinformatics **38**(23), 5315–5316 (2022)
8. Chen, Y., Wang, Y., Paez-Espino, D., Polz, M.F., Zhang, T.: Prokaryotic viruses impact functional microorganisms in nutrient removal and carbon cycle in wastewater treatment plants. Nat. Commun. **12**, 5398 (2021)
9. Chklovski, A., Parks, D.H., Woodcroft, B.J., Tyson, G.W.: CheckM2: a rapid, scalable and accurate tool for assessing microbial genome quality using machine learning. Nat. Methods **20**, 1203–1212 (2023)
10. DeMaere, M.Z., Darling, A.E.: Sim3C: simulation of Hi-C and Meta3C proximity ligation sequencing technologies. GigaScience **7**(2), gix103 (2018)
11. DeMaere, M.Z., Darling, A.E.: bin3C: exploiting Hi-C sequencing data to accurately resolve metagenome-assembled genomes. Genome Biol. **20**, 46 (2019)
12. Du, Y., Fuhrman, J.A., Sun, F.: ViralCC retrieves complete viral genomes and virus-host pairs from metagenomic Hi-C data. Nat. Commun. **14**, 502 (2023)
13. Du, Y., Laperriere, S.M., Fuhrman, J., Sun, F.: Normalizing metagenomic Hi-C data and detecting spurious contacts using zero-inflated negative binomial regression. J. Comput. Biol. **29**, 106–120 (2022)
14. Du, Y., Sun, F.: HiCBin: binning metagenomic contigs and recovering metagenome-assembled genomes using Hi-C contact maps. Genome Biol. **23**, 63 (2022)
15. Du, Y., Sun, F.: MetaCC allows scalable and integrative analyses of both long-read and short-read metagenomic Hi-C data. Nat. Commun. **14**, 6231 (2023)
16. Finn, R.D., Clements, J., Eddy, S.R.: HMMER web server: interactive sequence similarity searching. Nucl. Acids Res. **39**(suppl_2), W29–W37 (2011)
17. Handelsman, J.: Metagenomics: application of genomics to uncultured microorganisms. Microbiol. Mol. Biol. Rev. **68**(4), 669–685 (2004)
18. Hugenholtz, P., Tyson, G.W.: Metagenomics. Nature **455**(7212), 481–483 (2008)
19. Hugerth, L.W., et al.: Metagenome-assembled genomes uncover a global brackish microbiome. Genome Biol. **16**, 279 (2015)

20. Karp, R.M.: An algorithm to solve the m × n assignment problem in expected time O (mn log n). Networks **10**(2), 143–152 (1980)
21. Li, H.: Aligning sequence reads, clone sequences and assembly contigs with BWA-MEM. arXiv (2013). https://doi.org/10.48550/arXiv.1303.3997
22. Marbouty, M., Cournac, A., Flot, J.F., Marie-Nelly, H., Mozziconacci, J., Koszul, R.: Metagenomic chromosome conformation capture (meta3C) unveils the diversity of chromosome organization in microorganisms. eLife **3**, e03318 (2014)
23. Meslier, V., et al.: Benchmarking second and third-generation sequencing platforms for microbial metagenomics. Sci. Data **9**(1), 694 (2022)
24. Nissen, J.N., et al.: Improved metagenome binning and assembly using deep variational autoencoders. Nat. Biotechnol. **39**, 555–560 (2021)
25. Ondov, B.D., et al.: Mash: fast genome and metagenome distance estimation using MinHash. Genome Biol. **17**, 132 (2016)
26. Parks, D.H., Imelfort, M., Skennerton, C.T., Hugenholtz, P., Tyson, G.W.: CheckM: assessing the quality of microbial genomes recovered from isolates, single cells, and metagenomes. Genome Res. **25**(7), 1043–1055 (2015)
27. Press, M.O., et al.: Hi-C deconvolution of a human gut microbiome yields high-quality draft genomes and reveals plasmid-genome interactions. bioRxiv (2017). https://doi.org/10.1101/198713
28. Rao, S.S., et al.: A 3D map of the human genome at kilobase resolution reveals principles of chromatin looping. Cell **159**(7), 1665–1680 (2014)
29. Reichardt, J., Bornholdt, S.: Statistical mechanics of community detection. Phys. Rev. E **74**(1), 016110 (2006)
30. Rho, M., Tang, H., Ye, Y.: FragGeneScan: predicting genes in short and error-prone reads. Nucl. Acids Res. **38**(20), e191–e191 (2010)
31. Routy, B., Gopalakrishnan, V., Daillère, R., Zitvogel, L., Wargo, J.A., Kroemer, G.: The gut microbiota influences anticancer immunosurveillance and general health. Nat. Rev. Clin. Oncol. **15**, 382–396 (2018)
32. Stalder, T., Press, M.O., Sullivan, S., Liachko, I., Top, E.M.: Linking the resistome and plasmidome to the microbiome. ISME J. **13**(10), 2437–2446 (2019)
33. Traag, V.A., Waltman, L., Van Eck, N.J.: From Louvain to Leiden: guaranteeing well-connected communities. Sci. Rep. **9**, 5233 (2019)
34. Wu, Y.W., Tang, Y.H., Tringe, S.G., Simmons, B.A., Singer, S.W.: MaxBin: an automated binning method to recover individual genomes from metagenomes using an expectation-maximization algorithm. Microbiome **2**(26) (2014)
35. Yaffe, E., Relman, D.A.: Tracking microbial evolution in the human gut using Hi-C reveals extensive horizontal gene transfer, persistence and adaptation. Nat. Microbiol. **5**(2), 343–353 (2020)
36. Yatsunenko, T., et al.: Human gut microbiome viewed across age and geography. Nature **486**, 222–227 (2012)

Graph-Based Genome Inference from Hi-C Data

Yihang Shen[1], Lingge Yu[1], Yutong Qiu[1], Tianyu Zhang[2],
and Carl Kingsford[1(✉)]

[1] Ray and Stephanie Lane Computational Biology Department,
Carnegie Mellon University, Pittsburgh 15213, USA
carlk@cs.cmu.edu
[2] Department of Statistics and Data Science, Carnegie Mellon University,
5000 Forbes Avenue, Pittsburgh, PA, USA

Abstract. Three-dimensional chromosome structure plays an important role in fundamental genomic functions. Hi-C, a high-throughput, sequencing-based technique, has drastically expanded our comprehension of 3D chromosome structures. The first step of Hi-C analysis pipelines involves mapping sequencing reads from Hi-C to linear reference genomes. However, the linear reference genome does not incorporate genetic variation information, which can lead to incorrect read alignments, especially when analyzing samples with substantial genomic differences from the reference such as cancer samples. Using genome graphs as the reference facilitates more accurate mapping of reads, however, new algorithms are required for inferring linear genomes from Hi-C reads mapped on genome graphs and constructing corresponding Hi-C contact matrices, which is a prerequisite for the subsequent steps of the Hi-C analysis such as identifying topologically associated domains and calling chromatin loops. We introduce the problem of genome sequence inference from Hi-C data mediated by genome graphs. We formalize this problem, show the hardness of solving this problem, and introduce a novel heuristic algorithm specifically tailored to this problem. We provide a theoretical analysis to evaluate the efficacy of our algorithm. Finally, our empirical experiments indicate that the linear genomes inferred from our method lead to the creation of improved Hi-C contact matrices, which are more effective in accurately capturing the structures of topologically associated domains.

Keywords: Hi-C · Genome Graph · Dynamic Program · NP-completeness

1 Introduction

The spatial arrangement of chromosomes plays an important role in many crucial cellular processes including gene transcription [12,32], epigenetic modification [17], and replication timing [28]. This complex structure can be discovered

---

Y. Shen, L. Yu and Y. Qiu—These authors contributed equally to this work.

J. Ma (Ed.): RECOMB 2024, LNCS 14758, pp. 115–130, 2024.
https://doi.org/10.1007/978-1-0716-3989-4_8

through Hi-C [25], a high-throughput variant of the chromosome conformation capture technique [6], which has become a prevalent tool in the study of genomic organization. The Hi-C process yields read pairs representing spatial contacts between two genomic loci. These contacts can be identified by aligning each end of a read pair to the reference genome. These aligned read pairs facilitate subsequent analyses, such as identifying topologically associated domains (TADs) [5,7,10,23,26], which are contiguous regions on chromosomes with more frequent contacts, and calling chromatin loops [33], which are pairs of genomic loci that lie far apart along the linear genome but are in close spatial proximity.

Hi-C pipelines use a linear reference genome such as Genome Reference Consortium Human Build 38 (GRCh38) as the template against which to align reads. However, these linear references do not incorporate the genetic diversity within populations. Consequently, aligning reads from genomes that diverge from the linear reference genome can result in reads either not aligning at all or being mapped to incorrect genomic locations. This issue is exacerbated when analyzing Hi-C reads from cancer samples, which frequently exhibit structural variations, including copy number variations and substantial translocations. The misalignments, arising due to structural variations, can confound the interpretation of Hi-C data, potentially producing features that may be mistaken for other biological signals, such as chromatin loops [39]. Given that read alignment is always the initial step in Hi-C analysis, errors at this stage can proliferate, leading to inaccuracies throughout the downstream analyses. To rectify the Hi-C analysis of cancer cell lines, substantial efforts have been made to develop algorithms to identify structural variations and rearrange the cancer genomes from Hi-C data, sometimes with the help of other data types such as whole genome sequencing to enhance accuracy and precision [34,39,42] of Hi-C analysis of cancer cell lines. However, these steps still rely on the linear reference genome.

The concept of pan-genome has been introduced to address the shortcomings of linear references. The pan-genome is a collection of DNA sequences that incorporates both common DNA regions and sequences unique to each individual [16,40]. These DNA sequences can be represented by genome graphs, which are graph-based data structures amalgamating the linear reference alongside genetic variations and polymorphic haplotypes [1]. Numerous computational techniques have been published in the domain of genome graphs, addressing various aspects such as efficient genome graph construction [14,15,20,27,29], graph-based genome alignment [21,30,38] and graph-based structural variation and haplotype analyses [4,9,19]. These studies have substantiated that genome graphs can enhance the analysis of genome sequencing data. Moreover, Liao et al. [24] has illustrated the potential of genome graphs in improving the analysis of various other data types, including RNA-seq, ChIP-seq, and ATAC-seq. However, there has been no research exploring the enhancement of Hi-C analyses through the use of genome graphs.

Leveraging genome graphs as the reference can enhance the accuracy of mapping Hi-C reads. However, a challenge arises from the erroneous information in the graphs post-read alignment, attributed to structural variations present in the genome graphs but absent in the actual linear genome of the Hi-C sample. Besides, these graphs are not immediately applicable for subsequent standard Hi-C analysis steps like TAD identification [10, 41] and chromatin loop calling [2], given their inherent dependence on linear genomes and the corresponding Hi-C contact matrices, the two-dimensional matrices representing chromatin interactions. A critical component to address this is to infer the appropriate, sample-specific linear genome from Hi-C reads mapped on genome graphs. These inferred genomes, which are more congruent with the Hi-C samples' unknown ground truth genomes than traditional linear reference genomes, account for polymorphisms and structural variations specific to the given sample. By using these reconstructed genomes to create Hi-C contact matrices and incorporating these matrices into subsequent analyses, we can enhance the precision of Hi-C studies. This method offers a more sample-specific genomic representation, addressing the shortcomings inherent in using standard linear reference genomes.

We investigate the problem of genome sequence inference from Hi-C data on directed acyclic genome graphs. The problem of inferring genome sequences from genome graphs and whole genome sequencing data was explored in previous work such as Ebler et al. [8]. Yet, the challenge of addressing this problem using Hi-C data remains unexplored. We propose a novel problem objective to formalize our inference problem. To infer the genome, we choose the best source-to-sink path in the directed acyclic graph that optimizes the confidence of TAD inference on the genomes. We show that optimizing this objective is NP-complete, a complexity that persists even with directed acyclic graphs. We develop a greedy heuristic for the problem and theoretically show that, under a set of relaxed assumptions, the heuristic finds the optimal path with a high probability. We test our processing pipeline and genome inference algorithms on cancer Hi-C samples K-562. Results on these samples show that compared to using the traditional linear reference genomes, the linear genomes inferred from our method create improved Hi-C contact matrices, which are more effective in accurately capturing the structures of TADs, attesting to the algorithm's potential to enhance the precision and reliability of genomic studies. The source code of our method is available at https://github.com/Kingsford-Group/graphhic. More algorithmic and experimental details are in Shen et al. [37].

2   Inferring the Sample Genome from Hi-C Data with Genome Graphs

Typical Hi-C processing pipelines, such as HiC-Pro [35], mainly consist of two steps: (i) aligning each end of raw read pairs to the linear reference genome; (ii) constructing a two-dimensional contact matrix that describes the interactions between pairs of genomic regions. A contact matrix is derived from the alignment results, wherein each entry contains the number of read pairs between two genomic bins—intervals with a fixed length such as 10 kilobases. This contact matrix is used as an input for downstream analyses, such as TAD identification. However, current Hi-C analysis pipelines are unable to process data when genome graphs are used as the reference instead of linear reference.

By using the graph-based Hi-C processing pipeline proposed in Shen et al. [36], we are able to build a genome graph and a Hi-C contact matrix M. Each dimension of this matrix represents nodes of the graphs, and each matrix entry is the number of read pairs with ends mapped to the corresponding nodes. The nodes are ordered in their topological order in the genome graph.

2.1   Problem Definition of Genome Inference

Given a directed acyclic genome graph G with a source node s and a sink node t, and the contact matrix M derived from the graph-based Hi-C pipeline [36], the objective of genome inference is to find a s-t path in G such that the concatenated DNA sequences represented by nodes in the selected path is the most similar sequence to the actual genome of the Hi-C sample. Ideally, two primary criteria should be fulfilled by this reconstructed path: (i) it should encapsulate as many mapped Hi-C read pairs as feasible, and (ii) the distribution of these mapped pairs ought to echo the distinctive spatial structures of chromosomes, especially the topologically associated domains (TADs or "domains" for brevity). Motivated by these prerequisites, our approach toward genome inference encompasses a simultaneous inference of the s-t path and the corresponding TADs from G.

Let P_{st} be the collection of all s-t paths in G, and let D_p be a set of domains along path $p \in P_{st}$. The i-th domain on path p is defined as a subpath $d_i^p = [a_i^p, b_i^p]$ that starts at node a_i^p and ends at b_i^p, where a_i^p and b_i^p are nodes on p. We require that domains of a path do not overlap with each other. Furthermore, the boundaries of two consecutive domains d_i^p and d_{i+1}^p, b_i^p and a_{i+1}^p, must be two nodes connected with an edge on path p. The first and the last domain are $d_1^p = [s, b_1^p]$ and $d_{|D_p|}^p = [a_{|D_p|}^p, t]$.

We infer the s-t path representing the actual genome from a Hi-C sample by solving the following problem:

Problem 1. We are given a directed, acyclic graph $G = (V, E)$ with a source node s and a sink node t, a pre-computed function $\mu : \mathbb{N} \to \mathbb{R}_{\geq 0}$, a real number $\gamma \geq 0$, and a cost function $c : V \times V \to \mathbb{R}_{\geq 0}$ that maps every pair of nodes to a non-negative cost. c is symmetric in a sense that $c(v, v') = c(v', v)$. The goal is to find a s-t path $p = \{v_1, v_2, \ldots, v_{|p|}\}$ over all s-t paths and a set of consecutive domains D_p on p that optimize

$$\max_{p \in P_{st}} \max_{D_p} \sum_{[a_i^p, b_i^p] \in D_p} f([a_i^p, b_i^p]), \tag{1}$$

where f is defined as:

$$f(p') := \frac{1}{|p'|^\gamma} \sum_{v_i, v_j \in p', 1 \leq i \leq j \leq |p'|} c(v_i, v_j) - \mu(|p'|). \tag{2}$$

The cost function $c(v_i, v_j)$ can be defined as the values of entries in the contact matrix $M(v_i, v_j)$ for node v_i and node v_j. f quantifies the quality of a TAD as the normalized number of interactions within the subpath p'. $\sum_{v_i,v_j \in p', 1 \leq i \leq j \leq |p'|} c(v_i, v_j)$ in Eq. (2) is the total number of interactions between nodes that are both in path p'.

The total number of interactions is normalized by two factors. First, the total number is zero-centered by a pre-computed $\mu(|p'|)$, which is the expected interaction frequency within a path with $|p'|$ nodes. Then, it is normalized by the number of nodes in p' ($|p'|$) scaled by a factor of γ. This normalization prevents the identification of TAD domains with excessively large sizes. Larger values of γ typically lead to finding smaller domains.

2.2   The Hardness of the Problem

The objective function (1) of Problem 1 is derived from that of Filippova et al. [10]. However, Filippova et al. [10] employs polynomial-time dynamic programming to infer TADs based on reads mapped to a linear reference, while our problem requires the concurrent inference of both the TAD domains (denoted as D_p) and the sample's linear genome (represented by the path p) directly from G. We show that this increased complexity results in NP-completeness of Problem 1. This hardness results motivates the development of practical heuristics for the problem.

Theorem 1. *Problem 1 is NP-complete.*

Proof. We prove Theorem 1 by reducing from the PATH AVOIDING FORBIDDEN PAIRS (PAFP) problem, which has been confirmed to be NP-complete even in directed acyclic graphs [13,22].

Problem 2 (PATH AVOIDING FORBIDDEN PAIRS [22]). Given a graph $G = (V, E)$ with two fixed vertices $s, t \in V$ and a set of pairs of vertices $F \subset V \times V$, find a path from s to t that contains at most one vertex from each pair in F, or recognize that such path does not exist.

Gabow et al. [13] prove that the path avoiding forbidden pairs problem (PAFP), introduced in Problem 2, is NP-complete in directed acyclic graphs. We now reduce PAFP on DAGs to Problem 1. Suppose we are given an instance of PAFP with a DAG $G = (V, E)$, a source node s, and a sink node t. We define a symmetric cost function c on G, such that:

$$c(v, v') = c(v', v) = \begin{cases} 0 & \text{if } (v, v') \in F \\ 1 & \text{otherwise.} \end{cases}$$

We convert G to a new DAG $G' = (V', E')$ such that every path from the source node to the sink node in the new graph has the same length (same number of nodes). We use Breadth-First-Search (BFS), starting from s to generate the new graph. We first create G' that only has a source node $\bar{s}$, i.e. $V' = \{\bar{s}\}$ and $E' = \emptyset$. Let $V_0 = \{s\}$. Given the node set V_i, via BFS on G we create a new node set V_{i+1} which are all child nodes of the nodes in V_i. For each node $v \in V_{i+1}$, we add a corresponding node $\bar{v}^{i+1}$ in G'. For each node pair (v', v) such that $v' \in V_i$ and $v \in V_{i+1}$, we add an edge from $\bar{v}'^i$ to $\bar{v}^{i+1}$ in G' if v' is a parent node of v in G. If $\bar{t}^i$ is already added in G', we add a node $\bar{t}^{i+1}$ in G' and add an edge from $\bar{t}^i$ to $\bar{t}^{i+1}$. If additionally t is in V_{i+1}, meaning that $\bar{t}^{i+1}$ is already in G', we only add an edge from $\bar{t}^i$ to $\bar{t}^{i+1}$ without adding the node $\bar{t}^{i+1}$ again. This procedure is iteratively conducted until $V_{i+1} = \{t\}$ or $V_{i+1} = \emptyset$. Figure 1 shows an example of constructing G' (Fig. 1(b)) from the original graph G (Fig. 1(a)). Since $|V_i| = O(|V|)$, we have that $|V'| = O(|V|^3)$. Therefore, the construction of G' can be accomplished within polynomial time. In addition, it is easy to see that G' is a DAG. Let $\bar{t}^n$ be the node in G' that corresponds to the sink node in G, which was added during the final iteration of the procedure. The set of s-t paths in G has a one-to-one correspondence with the set of paths from $\bar{s}$ and $\bar{t}^n$ in G'. Moreover, all the paths from $\bar{s}$ to $\bar{t}^n$ in G' maintain equal lengths $n + 1$. We define a symmetric cost function c' on G', such that:

$$c'(\bar{v}'^i, \bar{v}^j) = c'(\bar{v}^j, \bar{v}'^i) = c(v, v').$$

Therefore, the instance of PAFP is a yes-instance if only if there exists a $\bar{s} - \bar{t}^n$ path in G' such that the cost c' of any node pair in this path is 1. The DAG G', combined with the source node $\bar{s}$, the sink node $\bar{t}^n$, the cost function c', the value $\gamma = 0$ and the function $\mu(l) \equiv 0$, becomes an instance of Problem 1.

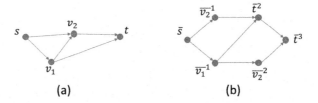

Fig. 1. An example of converting G (a) to G' (b) in the proof of Theorem 1.

We now prove that the instance of PAFP is a yes-instance if and only if there exists a solution of Problem 1 with objective value $\frac{(n+1)(n+2)}{2}$, hence Problem 1 is NP-complete.

Since $\gamma = 0$ and $\mu(l) \equiv 0$, the objective of Problem 1 becomes:

$$\max_{p \in P_{\bar{s}\bar{t}^n}} \max_{D_p} \sum_{\substack{[a_i^p, b_i^p] \in D_p}} \sum_{\substack{v_i, v_j \in [a_i^p, b_i^p] \\ 1 \le i \le j \le |[a_i^p, b_i^p]|}} c'(v_i, v_j).$$

Since the cost function is non-negative, for any given $\bar{s} - \bar{t}^n$ path, choosing the whole path as one domain leads to the maximal:

$$\max_{p \in P_{\bar{s}\bar{t}^n}} \max_{D_p} \sum_{\substack{[a_i^p, b_i^p] \in D_p}} \sum_{\substack{v_i, v_j \in [a_i^p, b_i^p] \\ 1 \le i \le j \le |[a_i^p, b_i^p]|}} c'(v_i, v_j) \le \max_{p \in P_{\bar{s}\bar{t}^n}} \sum_{\substack{v_i, v_j \in p, 1 \le i \le j \le |p|}} c'(v_i, v_j).$$

Moreover, since c' is less than or equal to 1, and each $\bar{s} - \bar{t}^n$ path has the same length $n + 1$, we have:

$$\max_{p \in P_{\bar{s}\bar{t}^n}} \sum_{v_i, v_j \in p, 1 \leq i \leq j \leq |p|} c'(v_i, v_j) \leq \frac{(n+1)(n+2)}{2}.$$

Therefore, there exists a solution of Problem 1 with objective value $\frac{(n+1)(n+2)}{2}$ if and only if there exists a $\bar{s} - \bar{t}^n$ path in G' such that the cost of any node pair in this path is 1, if and only if the instance of PAFP is a yes-instance.   □

2.3   Computation of the μ Function

Filippova et al. [10] demonstrated a method for efficiently pre-computing μ on the linear reference genome. Nevertheless, as we discuss in Shen et al. [37], calculating μ in the context of genome graphs poses a more complex challenge. Consequently, we propose a different strategy to estimate μ. Generally, samples from normal cell types bear a greater resemblance to the linear reference genome compared to those from cancer samples. Hence, we select Hi-C data from a normal sample, process it using the linear reference genome, and calculate its μ function using the same approach as Filippova et al. [10]. This function is denoted as μ_0. It is evident that the sequencing depth of the Hi-C data can influence the value of the μ function. Therefore, when analyzing new Hi-C data, we estimate its μ function as follows:

$$\hat{\mu}(l) = \mu_0(l) \frac{N_{new}}{N_{old}}. \tag{3}$$

Here, N_{old} refers to the total count of Hi-C read pairs from the original normal sample, while N_{new} indicates the total count of Hi-C read pairs from new Hi-C data.

2.4   Graph-Based Dynamic Programming Algorithm

We use a dynamic program, computed in the topological ordering of the nodes, to solve the Problem 1:

$$OPT(l) = \max_{k, P_{kl} \neq \emptyset} \left\{ \max_{v \in PA(k)} OPT(v) + q(k, l) \right\}, \tag{4}$$

where $OPT(l)$ is the optimal solution for objective (1), applied to the subgraph induced by node l along with all nodes with a topological order less than that of l within G. P_{kl} denotes the collection of all paths from node k to node l in G, and $PA(k)$ is the set of parent nodes of k. $\max_{v \in PA(k)} OPT(v) = 0$ if k has no parent node. q is a function that maximizes over all paths between k and l:

$$q(k, l) = \max_{p \in P_{kl}} f(p). \tag{5}$$

We use a standard backtracking strategy, shown in Shen et al. [37], to reconstruct the optimal path p_{opt} from the dynamic program. The reconstructed path p_{opt} is taken to be the inferred genome. We prove that $OPT(t)$ is indeed the optimal solution for Problem 1.

Proposition 1. $OPT(t) = \max_{p \in P_{st}} \max_{D_p} \sum_{[a_i^p, b_i^p] \in D_p} f([a_i^p, b_i^p])$.

The proof is in Shen et al. [37]. However, this does not provide a polynomial time algorithm. As we show in Shen et al. [37], computing the function q in (5) is NP-complete. Moreover, the NP-completeness of computing q is not attributable to the particular definition of function f as outlined in (2). We show in Shen et al. [37] that computing q remains NP-complete under various definitions of f. Therefore, it is hard to solve the dynamic programming objective shown in (4), which is consistent with the hardness conclusions in Sect. 2.2. This provides a focus for developing heuristics.

2.5   Heuristics for Computing q

We propose a novel heuristic algorithm, detailed in Algorithm 1, to compute the function $q(k, l)$ for any node pair (k, l). The central principle behind this algorithm is that a node situated between nodes k and l (in topological order) that has more interactions with other nodes is more likely to be a part of the path connecting k to l that maximizes the function f. Consequently, we sort the nodes in descending order based on their cumulative interactions with other nodes (line 6 of Algorithm 1) and progressively add nodes from the highest to the lowest interactions until a k-l path is established.

Algorithm 1. $q(k, l)$ computation

1: **Input** k,l, genome directed acyclic graph $G = (V, E)$, nodes list T that contains all nodes in G sorted by their topological order, contact matrix M, reachable matrix M_r, the function f
2: **if** $M_r[k, l] = 0$ **then**
3:     **return**
4: **end if**
5: $V_{sub} \leftarrow \{v \in V \mid T.index(v) \geq T.index(k) \text{ and } T.index(v) \leq T.index(l)\}$
6: Sort vertices v in V_{sub} according to the sum $\sum_{v' \in V_{sub}} M[v, v']$, arranging them from the highest to the lowest value to form V'_{sub}.
7: $p \leftarrow \{k, l\}$, $q \leftarrow -\infty$
8: $edges \leftarrow is\_edge(k, l)$
9: **for** $v \in V'_{sub}$ **do**
10:     $p, edges \leftarrow insert(p, M_r, T, edges, v)$
11:     **if** $edges = |p| - 1$ **then**
12:         $q \leftarrow f(p)$
13:         **return** q, p
14:     **end if**
15: **end for**

Specifically, we employ the following functions and data structures within Algorithm 1 to enhance the algorithm's efficiency:

- reachable matrix M_r, where $M_r[i, j] = 1$ if there exists a path from node i to node j in the directed acyclic genome graph G, otherwise $M_r[i, j] = 0$.
- $is\_edge(k, l)$, which returns 1 if there is an edge from k to l in G, otherwise it returns 0.
- $insert(p, M_r, T, edges, v)$, of which the pseudo-code is provided in Algorithm 2. This function contains the following steps:
  - Given a node set p which encompasses all nodes already incorporated and are topologically sorted, the function determines whether there exists a path in G that includes all nodes in $p \cup \{v\}$. Such a path may include additional nodes that are not in $p \cup \{v\}$. This step can be efficiently achieved with the help of M_r and a balanced tree structure such as AVL tree [11], of which the details are introduced in the proof of Theorem 2.
  - If the aforementioned path exists, the node v is then inserted into p according to the topological ordering (function $update$ in line 7 of Algorithm 2).
  - The function also updates an integer variable $edges$ (line 8 of Algorithm 2), which keeps track of how many neighboring nodes in p have edges in G.

The $insert$ function yields a revised node set p and an updated value for $edges$ (line 10 of Algorithm 1). A legitimate path in graph G is formed by the nodes in p if and only if the condition $edges = |p| - 1$ is met (line 11 of Algorithm 1). Once a path is established, we compute the function value $f(p)$ and use it as the value of q (line 12 of Algorithm 1). We have the following result on the time complexity of Algorithm 1:

Theorem 2. *The total time complexity for Algorithm 1 and the dynamic program using the heuristic Algorithm 1 are respectively $\mathcal{O}(|V|^2)$ and $\mathcal{O}(|V|^4)$, where $|V|$ is the number of nodes in the graph.*

The proof is in Shen et al. [37]. In practice, the time complexity is still too high for long chromosomes. To address this, as detailed in Sect. 2.7, we implement additional practical strategies to further decrease the algorithm's time complexity.

2.6   Accuracy of the Heuristic Algorithm

Let $\hat{p}$ represent the path from node k to node l as predicted by Algorithm 1, and let p_{gt} denote the "ground truth" path, defined as $p_{gt} = \arg\max_{p \in P_{kl}} f(p)$. In an ideal scenario, a heuristic algorithm would ensure that, for any specified DAG G and any interaction distribution present on G, the value $f(\hat{p})$ closely approximates $f(p_{gt})$. However, as we demonstrate in Shen et al. [37], it is possible to create an example where the discrepancy between $f(\hat{p})$ and $f(p_{gt})$ can be infinitely large, indicating that our heuristic algorithm does not offer a bounded approximation in the worst-case scenario.

Algorithm 2. *insert* function

1: **Input** node set p in which nodes are topologically sorted, matrix M_r, nodes list T that contains all nodes in G sorted by their topological order, integer variable *edges*, node v
2: Find two adjacent nodes v_1 and v_2 in p such that $T.index(v_1) \leq T.index(v) \leq T.index(v_2)$.
3: **if** $v_1 = v$ or $v_2 = v$ **then**
4:     **return** p,*edges*
5: **end if**
6: **if** $M_r[v_1, v] = 1$ and $M_r[v, v_2] = 1$ **then**
7:     $p \leftarrow update(p, v)$
8:     $edges \leftarrow edges + is\_edge(v_1, v) + is\_edge(v, v_2) - is\_edge(v_1, v_2)$
9: **end if**
10: **return** p,*edges*

However, within the scope of Hi-C analysis, the distribution of interactions on a genome graph is not arbitrary. Conceptually, each interaction, represented by a pair of nodes, stems from two primary sources: (a) The "ground truth" source. Both nodes of the interactions from this source lie on the ground truth path p_{gt}. Interactions from this source are informative when constructing $\hat{p}$. (b) The "noise" source, which accounts for interactions arising due to various systematic biases such as sequencing errors, mapping errors, etc. In this scenario, the interactions are not necessarily confined to the path p_{gt}. Under mild assumptions, we propose a theoretical framework that more accurately reflects the real-world Hi-C situation, and we demonstrate that with high probability the output path $\hat{p}$ is equivalent to p_{gt}, as long as the number of mapped read pairs is $\Omega(|p_{gt}| \log |V|)$. Although the number of total nodes $|V|$ in the graph can be large, the required number of read pairs for a successful inference is only proportional to the logarithm of it. The details of this theoretical analysis can be found in Shen et al. [37]. We observe that in practice, this criterion regarding the number of read pairs is readily met. For instance, in our experiments, the graph has approximately 5×10^5 nodes, and the total number of mapped read pairs is around 3×10^8. This result provides some theoretical justification for the choice of the heuristic in Algorithm 1.

2.7   Practical Improvements to Efficiency and Accuracy

In practice, we introduce two modifications to our heuristic algorithm to enhance its accuracy and speed. First, given that the size of TADs typically does not exceed 3 Mb [3], we implement an additional heuristic adjustment to the dynamic program. When calculating the function q, we restrict our consideration to paths where the combined length of the DNA sequences on the nodes is under 3 Mb. That is, we replace P_{kl} in Eq. (4) and (5) with $\bar{P}_{kl}$, the collection of paths from k to l that are no more than 3 Mb. Let L denote the largest length of the paths in $\bar{P}_{kl}$, where length here refers to the number of nodes; generally,

$L \sim \frac{3Mb}{k_{bin}} \ll |V|$. Now the time complexity of the dynamic program when using the heuristic algorithm for q becomes $\mathcal{O}(|E||V| + L^4)$, where $\mathcal{O}(|E||V|)$ comes from computing the reachable matrix M_r.

Second, our empirical observations suggest that for most node pairs (k, l), computing q using Algorithm 1 is quite effective. Nonetheless, this method might not adequately capture the signals of large deletions. To mitigate this, we have refined Algorithm 1, as detailed in Algorithm 3. In this adjustment, for each node pair (k, l), we initially execute a node-weighted shortest path algorithm (where each node's weight is determined by the length of its corresponding DNA sequence) to identify a path p_{base} and calculate its score (lines 5–6 of Algorithm 3). Subsequently, Algorithm 1 is applied; if the path p derived from Algorithm 1 surpasses the score of p_{base}, p is returned, otherwise p_{base} is the selected path.

The shortest path algorithm for directed graphs with nonnegative weights has a time complexity of $\mathcal{O}(|E| + |V| \log(|V|))$. Consequently, the overall time complexity for Algorithm 3 to estimate q remains $\mathcal{O}(|V|^2)$ (or $\mathcal{O}(|L|^2)$ if we use the heuristic above), equating to that of Algorithm 1. Additionally, given that the path generated by Algorithm 3 will always yield a higher score compared to that from Algorithm 1, all the theoretical results in Sect. 2.6 are applicable to Algorithm 3 as well.

Algorithm 3. $q(k, l)$ computation v.2

1: **Input** k, l, genome directed acyclic graph $G = (V, E)$, nodes list T that contains all nodes in G sorted by their topological order, contact matrix M, reachable matrix M_r, the function f
2: **if** $M_r[k, l] = 0$ **then**
3:     **return**
4: **end if**
5: $p_{base} \leftarrow$ shortest path from k to l
6: $q_{base} \leftarrow f(p_{base})$
7: $q, p \leftarrow$ Algorithm 1
8: **if** $q > q_{base}$ **then**
9:     **return** q, p
10: **else**
11:     **return** q_{base}, p_{base}
12: **end if**

---

3 Experimental Results

3.1 Construction of a Genome Graph with Hi-C Reads Mapped

We construct the genome graph with structural variations from the K-562 cancer cell line reported by Zhou et al. [43] and the linear reference genome GRCh37, against which the SVs were called. We primarily use the VG toolkit [15] to incorporate simple variants and further process the variant file and the resulting graph so that the final genome graph is a directed acyclic graph. Details on the construction of the genome graph can be found in Shen et al. [37].

We apply the graph-based Hi-C pipeline [36] to process the raw Hi-C reads of the K-562 cancer cell line from Rao et al. [31] (accession number: SRR1658693). Subsequently, we employed our graph-based heuristic dynamic programming algorithm to infer the sample genome. Finally, all raw Hi-C reads were remapped to the newly inferred linear genome to generate chromosome-specific contact matrices with bin size 10 kb. Detailed descriptions of our algorithmic implementations, including hyper-parameter configurations, are provided in Shen et al. [37].

3.2   Graph Hi-C Workflow Improves TAD Identification

Table 1. The comparisons of three metrics reflecting CTCF or SMC3 enrichments near TAD boundaries across different genomes. Linear reference: linear reference genome; Reconstruction: genome inferred by our algorithm. TADs are called by Armatus with hyper-parameter $\gamma_{Ar} = 0.5$. Hi-C sample: SRR1659693.

		Average peak	Boundary tagged ratio	Fold change
CTCF	Linear reference	0.172	0.346	0.019
	Reconstruction	**0.202**	**0.387**	**0.144**
SMC3	Linear reference	0.091	0.194	0.044
	Reconstruction	**0.115**	**0.237**	**0.249**

We assess the quality of the new contact matrices from the inferred genome by their ability to exhibit biologically sound TAD structures. We use Armatus [10] to identify TADs from these matrices. The detected TADs are then compared with those identified from contact matrices created from the linear reference using HiC-Pro. We evaluate the quality of TADs against the enrichment of regulatory elements CTCF and SMC in K-562 cell lines around detected TAD boundaries.

We measure the enrichment of CTCF and SMC3 around TAD boundaries with three metrics: average peak, boundary tagged ratio, and fold change (Table 1). Average peak measures the average occurrence frequency of peaks within 30 kb range centered on TAD boundaries. Boundary tagged ratio measures the frequency of TAD boundaries that are enriched for regulatory elements. Fold change measures the change of enrichment of regulatory elements between regions around and far away from TAD boundaries. Since the TAD boundaries identified using our method are situated along a path within the genome graph, we use Graph Peak Caller [18] for calling and comparing CTCF and SMC3 peaks on the graphs. Further details on graph peak calling and these metrics can be found in Shen et al. [37].

Both CTCF and SMC3 peaks are more concentrated around TAD boundaries identified based on the inferred genomes than linear reference. Figure 2 graphically presents these peak signals around TAD boundaries, clearly showing that the signals from the inferred linear genome are more pronounced than those from the linear reference. Table 1 shows that, relative to the linear reference, there is a higher enrichment of CTCF and SMC3 signals near the TAD boundaries identified from the new contact matrices.

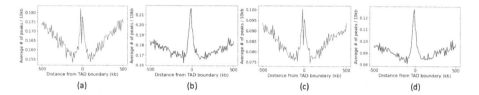

(a)   (b)   (c)   (d)

Fig. 2. (a), (b) CTCF peak signals around TAD boundaries from the linear reference genome (a) and the inferred linear genome (b). (c), (d) SMC3 peak signals around TAD boundaries from the linear reference genome (c) and the inferred linear genome (d). TADs are called by Armatus with hyper-parameter $\gamma_{Ar} = 0.5$.

4   Discussion

In this study, we establish a novel connection between Hi-C analysis and genome graphs and explore a novel application domain in pan-genomics. We develop the first algorithm that leverages genome graphs for inferring genome sequences from Hi-C reads. The experimental results demonstrate that the genomes inferred via our algorithm facilitate the creation of superior Hi-C contact matrices compared to those derived using a linear reference. These promising outcomes highlight the ability of genome graphs to enhance Hi-C analysis, especially for cancer samples that contain large-scale structural variations.

There are several avenues for future research stemming from this work. First, our dynamic programming algorithm, despite its reliance on heuristics, is not exceptionally fast. For instance, processing chromosome 1 with our algorithm requires around two days, even with some parallelism techniques applied. Accelerating our algorithm could be a fruitful area of exploration. Second, currently the normalization method for Hi-C data mapped onto graphs is lacking, which is crucial for correcting inherent biases. As a result, to ensure equitable comparisons, all contact matrices presented in the experimental section are unnormalized. Developing new methodologies for normalizing graph-based Hi-C data could be a vital and intriguing direction for future research. Third, our current approach is applicable only to DAGs. This limitation prevents us from testing these methods on more complex non-directed acyclic graphs, such as the human pangenome graphs created by Liao et al. [24]. Therefore, adapting our methodology for use with general graphs represents a significant and necessary direction for future research. Additionally, given that our algorithm is applicable not only to cancer cell lines, it would be interesting to test it on more cell types, particularly normal ones, to evaluate its performance. Finally, while there has been research like that by Wang et al. [42] focusing on identifying structural variations from Hi-C data and rearranging contact matrices accordingly, we choose not to benchmark our method against theirs. This is because our primary aim in this work is to introduce the use of genome graphs in Hi-C analysis for the first time, while the method of Wang et al., although it can create improved Hi-C contact matrices, is not able to be used on genome graphs. In the future, it would be interesting to explore the integration of these two approaches, potentially leading to even more substantial improvements in Hi-C analysis.

Acknowledgments. This work was supported in part by the US National Science Foundation [DBI-1937540, III-2232121], the US National Institutes of Health [R01HG01-2470] and by the generosity of Eric and Wendy Schmidt by recommendation of the Schmidt Futures program.

Disclosure of Interests. C.K. is a co-founder of Ocean Genomics, Inc.

References

1. Ameur, A.: Goodbye reference, hello genome graphs. Nat. Biotechnol. **37**(8), 866–868 (2019)
2. Ay, F., Bailey, T.L., Noble, W.S.: Statistical confidence estimation for Hi-C data reveals regulatory chromatin contacts. Genome Res. **24**(6), 999–1011 (2014)
3. Bonev, B., Cavalli, G.: Organization and function of the 3D genome. Nat. Rev. Genet. **17**(11), 661–678 (2016)
4. Chin, C.S., et al.: Multiscale analysis of pangenomes enables improved representation of genomic diversity for repetitive and clinically relevant genes. Nat. Methods, 1–9 (2023)
5. De Laat, W., Duboule, D.: Topology of mammalian developmental enhancers and their regulatory landscapes. Nature **502**(7472), 499–506 (2013)
6. Dekker, J., Rippe, K., Dekker, M., Kleckner, N.: Capturing chromosome conformation. Science **295**(5558), 1306–1311 (2002)
7. Dixon, J.R., et al.: Topological domains in mammalian genomes identified by analysis of chromatin interactions. Nature **485**(7398), 376–380 (2012)
8. Ebler, J., et al.: Pangenome-based genome inference allows efficient and accurate genotyping across a wide spectrum of variant classes. Nat. Genet. **54**(4), 518–525 (2022)
9. Eggertsson, H.P., et al.: GraphTyper2 enables population-scale genotyping of structural variation using pangenome graphs. Nat. Commun. **10**(1), 5402 (2019)
10. Filippova, D., Patro, R., Duggal, G., Kingsford, C.: Identification of alternative topological domains in chromatin. Algorithms Mol. Biol. **9**, 1–11 (2014)
11. Foster, C.C.: A generalization of AVL trees. Commun. ACM **16**(8), 513–517 (1973)

12. Fraser, P., Bickmore, W.: Nuclear organization of the genome and the potential for gene regulation. Nature **447**(7143), 413–417 (2007)
13. Gabow, H.N., Maheshwari, S.N., Osterweil, L.J.: On two problems in the generation of program test paths. IEEE Trans. Softw. Eng. **3**, 227–231 (1976)
14. Garrison, E., et al.: Building pangenome graphs. bioRxiv, 2023–04 (2023)
15. Garrison, E., et al.: Variation graph toolkit improves read mapping by representing genetic variation in the reference. Nat. Biotechnol. **36**(9), 875–879 (2018)
16. Gong, Y., Li, Y., Liu, X., Ma, Y., Jiang, L.: A review of the pangenome: how it affects our understanding of genomic variation, selection and breeding in domestic animals? J. Anim. Sci. Biotechnol. **14**(1), 1–19 (2023)
17. Grewal, S.I., Moazed, D.: Heterochromatin and epigenetic control of gene expression. Science **301**(5634), 798–802 (2003)
18. Grytten, I., Rand, K.D., Nederbragt, A.J., Storvik, G.O., Glad, I.K., Sandve, G.K.: Graph peak caller: calling ChIP-seq peaks on graph-based reference genomes. PLoS Comput. Biol. **15**(2), e1006731 (2019)
19. Hadi, K., et al.: Distinct classes of complex structural variation uncovered across thousands of cancer genome graphs. Cell **183**(1), 197–210 (2020)
20. Hickey, G., et al.: Pangenome graph construction from genome alignments with Minigraph-Cactus. Nat. Biotechnol., 1–11 (2023)
21. Kim, D., Paggi, J.M., Park, C., Bennett, C., Salzberg, S.L.: Graph-based genome alignment and genotyping with HISAT2 and HISAT-genotype. Nat. Biotechnol. **37**(8), 907–915 (2019)
22. Kolman, P., Pangrác, O.: On the complexity of paths avoiding forbidden pairs. Discret. Appl. Math. **157**(13), 2871–2876 (2009)
23. Li, A., et al.: Decoding topologically associating domains with ultra-low resolution Hi-C data by graph structural entropy. Nat. Commun. **9**(1), 3265 (2018)
24. Liao, W.W., et al.: A draft human pangenome reference. Nature **617**(7960), 312–324 (2023)
25. Lieberman-Aiden, E., et al.: Comprehensive mapping of long-range interactions reveals folding principles of the human genome. Science **326**(5950), 289–293 (2009)
26. Nora, E.P., et al.: Spatial partitioning of the regulatory landscape of the X-inactivation centre. Nature **485**(7398), 381–385 (2012)
27. Pandey, P., Gao, Y., Kingsford, C.: VariantStore: an index for large-scale genomic variant search. Genome Biol. **22**(1), 1–25 (2021)
28. Pope, B.D., et al.: Topologically associating domains are stable units of replication-timing regulation. Nature **515**(7527), 402–405 (2014)
29. Qiu, Y., Kingsford, C.: Constructing small genome graphs via string compression. Bioinformatics **37**(Supplement_1), i205–i213 (2021)
30. Rakocevic, G., et al.: Fast and accurate genomic analyses using genome graphs. Nat. Genet. **51**(2), 354–362 (2019)
31. Rao, S.S., et al.: A 3D map of the human genome at kilobase resolution reveals principles of chromatin looping. Cell **159**(7), 1665–1680 (2014)
32. Rennie, S., Dalby, M., van Duin, L., Andersson, R.: Transcriptional decomposition reveals active chromatin architectures and cell specific regulatory interactions. Nat. Commun. **9**(1), 487 (2018)
33. Roayaei Ardakany, A., Gezer, H.T., Lonardi, S., Ay, F.: Mustache: multi-scale detection of chromatin loops from Hi-C and Micro-C maps using scale-space representation. Genome Biol. **21**, 1–17 (2020)
34. Schöpflin, R., et al.: Integration of Hi-C with short and long-read genome sequencing reveals the structure of germline rearranged genomes. Nat. Commun. **13**(1), 6470 (2022)

35. Servant, N., et al.: HiC-Pro: an optimized and flexible pipeline for Hi-C data processing. Genome Biol. **16**(1), 1–11 (2015)
36. Shen, Y., Yu, L., Qiu, Y., Zhang, T., Kingsford, C.: Improving Hi-C contact matrices using genome graphs. bioRxiv, 2023–11 (2023)
37. Shen, Y., Yu, L., Qiu, Y., Zhang, T., Kingsford, C.: Technical report: graph-based genome inference from Hi-C data (2023). https://github.com/Kingsford-Group/graphhic/blob/main/technicalreport.pdf
38. Sirén, J., et al.: Pangenomics enables genotyping of known structural variants in 5202 diverse genomes. Science **374**(6574), abg8871 (2021)
39. Wang, S., et al.: HiNT: a computational method for detecting copy number variations and translocations from Hi-C data. Genome Biol. **21**, 1–15 (2020)
40. Wang, T., et al.: The human pangenome project: a global resource to map genomic diversity. Nature **604**(7906), 437–446 (2022)
41. Wang, X.T., Cui, W., Peng, C.: HiTAD: detecting the structural and functional hierarchies of topologically associating domains from chromatin interactions. Nucleic Acids Res. **45**(19), e163–e163 (2017)
42. Wang, X., et al.: Genome-wide detection of enhancer-hijacking events from chromatin interaction data in rearranged genomes. Nat. Methods **18**(6), 661–668 (2021)
43. Zhou, B., et al.: Comprehensive, integrated, and phased whole-genome analysis of the primary ENCODE cell line K562. Genome Res. **29**(3), 472–484 (2019)

Meta-colored Compacted de Bruijn Graphs

Giulio Ermanno Pibiri[1,2]([envelope]) [ORCID], Jason Fan[3] [ORCID], and Rob Patro[3] [ORCID]

[1] DAIS, Ca' Foscari University of Venice, Venice, Italy
giulioermanno.pibiri@unive.it
[2] ISTI-CNR, Pisa, Italy
[3] Department of Computer Science, University of Maryland,
College Park 20440, USA

Abstract. The colored compacted de Bruijn graph (c-dBG) has become a fundamental tool used across several areas of genomics and pangenomics. For example, it has been widely adopted by methods that perform read mapping or alignment, abundance estimation, and subsequent downstream analyses. These applications essentially regard the c-dBG as a map from k-mers to the set of references in which they appear. The c-dBG data structure should retrieve this set—the *color* of the k-mer—efficiently for any given k-mer, while using little memory. To aid retrieval, the colors are stored explicitly in the data structure and take considerable space for large reference collections, even when compressed. Reducing the space of the colors is therefore of utmost importance for large-scale sequence indexing.

We describe the *meta-colored* compacted de Bruijn graph (Mac-dBG)—a new colored de Bruijn graph data structure where colors are represented holistically, i.e., taking into account their redundancy across the whole collection being indexed, rather than individually as atomic integer lists. This allows the factorization and compression of common sub-patterns across colors. While optimizing the space of our data structure is NP-hard, we propose a simple heuristic algorithm that yields practically good solutions. Results show that the Mac-dBG data structure improves substantially over the best previous space/time trade-off, by providing remarkably better compression effectiveness for the same (or better) query efficiency. This improved space/time trade-off is robust across different datasets and query workloads.

Code availability. A C++17 implementation of the Mac-dBG is publicly available on GitHub at: https://github.com/jermp/fulgor.

1   Introduction

The colored compacted de Bruijn graph (c-dBG) has become a fundamental tool used across several areas of genomics and pangenomics. For example, it has been widely adopted by methods that perform read mapping or alignment, specifically

© The Author(s), under exclusive license to Springer Nature Switzerland AG 2024
J. Ma (Ed.): RECOMB 2024, LNCS 14758, pp. 131–146, 2024.
https://doi.org/10.1007/978-1-0716-3989-4_9

with respect to RNA-seq and metagenomic identification and abundance esti-mation [3,4,8,21,23,32–34]; among methods that perform homology assessment and mapping of genomes [26,27]; for a variety of different tasks in pangenome analysis [9,10,20,22,24], and for storage and compression of genomic data [31]. In most of these applications, a key requirement of the underlying representation of the c-dBG is to be able to determine—with efficiency being critical—the set of references in which an individual k-mer appears. These motivations bring us to the following problem formulation.

Problem 1 (Colored k-mer indexing). Let $\mathcal{R} = \{R_1, \ldots, R_N\}$ be a collection of references. Each reference R_i is a string over the DNA alphabet $\Sigma = \{A, C, G, T\}$. We want to build a data structure (referred to as the *index* in the following) that allows us to retrieve the set $\text{COLOR}(x) = \{i | x \in R_i\}$ as efficiently as possible for any k-mer $x \in \Sigma^k$. If the k-mer x does not occur in any reference, we say that $\text{COLOR}(x) = \varnothing$. Hereafter, we simply refer to the set $\text{COLOR}(x)$ as the *color* of the k-mer x.

Of particular importance for biological analysis is the case where $\mathcal{R}$ is a *pangenome*. Roughly speaking, a pangenome is a (large) set of genomes in a par-ticular population, species or closely-related phylogenetic group. Pangenomes have revolutionized DNA analysis by providing a more comprehensive under-standing of genetic diversity within a species [5,25]. Unlike traditional refer-ence genomes, which represent a single individual or a small set of individuals, pangenomes incorporate genetic information from multiple individuals within a species or group. This approach is particularly valuable because it captures a wide range of genetic variations, including rare and unique sequences that may be absent from any particular reference genome.

Contributions. The goal of this paper is to propose a solution to Problem 1 focusing on the specific, important, application scenario where $\mathcal{R}$ is a pangenome. (We note, however, that the approaches described herein are general, and we expect them to work well on any corpus of highly-related genomes, whether or not they formally constitute a pangenome.) To best exploit the properties of Problem 1, we capitalize on recent indexing development for c-dBGs [13]. The result is the *meta-colored* compacted de Bruijn graph (Mac-dBG)—a new data structure where colors are represented *holistically*, i.e., taking into account their redundancy across the whole collection being indexed, rather than individually as atomic integer lists.

After covering preliminary concepts in Sect. 2, we describe the Mac-dBG in Sect. 3.1 and 3.2. We present the underlying NP-hard optimization problem in Sect. 3.3 and discuss a simple framework for constructing the Mac-dBG in Sect. 3.4. Section 4 presents experimental results to demonstrate that the Mac-dBG remarkably improves the best previous space/time trade-off in the litera-ture. In fact, it essentially combines the space effectiveness of the most compact solutions with the query efficiency of the fastest solutions, at the expense of a slower construction algorithm. We conclude in Sect. 5.

A C++17 implementation of the Mac-dBG is available at: https://github.com/jermp/fulgor.

2   Preliminaries: Modular Indexing of Colored Compacted de Bruijn Graphs

In this section we provide some background information to better understand the design principles of the solution we propose in Sect. 3.

In principle, Problem 1 could be solved using a classic data structure from Information Retrieval—the *inverted index* [30]. In the context of this problem, the indexed documents are the references $\{R_1, \ldots, R_N\}$ in the collection $\mathcal{R}$ and the terms of the inverted index are all distinct k-mers of $\mathcal{R}$. Using the notation from Problem 1, it follows that $\text{COLOR}(x)$ is the inverted list of the term x. Let $\mathcal{L}$ denote the inverted index for $\mathcal{R}$. The inverted index $\mathcal{L}$ explicitly stores the ordered set $\text{COLOR}(x)$ for each k-mer $x \in \mathcal{R}$. The goal is to implement the map $x \rightarrow \text{COLOR}(x)$ as efficiently as possible in terms of both memory usage and query time. To this end, all the distinct k-mers of $\mathcal{R}$ are stored in an *associative* dictionary data structure $\mathcal{D}$. Suppose we have n distinct k-mers in $\mathcal{R}$. These k-mers are stored losslessly in $\mathcal{D}$. To implement the map $x \rightarrow \text{COLOR}(x)$, $\mathcal{D}$ is required to support the operation $\text{LOOKUP}(x)$, which returns $\bot$ if k-mer x is not found in the dictionary or a unique integer identifier in $[n] = \{1, \ldots, n\}$ if x is found. Problem 1 can then be solved using these two data structures—$\mathcal{D}$ and $\mathcal{L}$—thanks to the interplay between $\text{LOOKUP}(x)$ and $\text{COLOR}(x)$: logically, the index stores the sets $\{\text{COLOR}(x)\}_{x \in \mathcal{R}}$ in some compressed form, *sorted by* the value of $\text{LOOKUP}(x)$.

To exploit at best the potential of this modular decomposition into $\mathcal{D}$ and $\mathcal{L}$, it is essential to rely on the specific properties of Problem 1. For example, we know that consecutive k-mers share $(k-1)$-length overlaps; also, k-mers that co-occur in the same set of references have the same color. A useful, standard, formalism that captures these properties is the so-called *colored (compacted) de Bruijn graph* (c-dBG).

Let $\mathcal{K}$ be the set of all the distinct k-mers of $\mathcal{R}$. The node-centric de Bruijn graph (dBG) of $\mathcal{R}$ is a directed graph $G(\mathcal{K}, E)$ whose nodes are the k-mers in $\mathcal{K}$. There is an edge $(u, v) \in E$ if the $(k-1)$-length suffix of u equals the $(k-1)$-length prefix of v. Note that the edge set E is implicitly defined by the set of nodes, and can therefore be omitted from subsequent definitions. We refer to k-mers and nodes in a dBG interchangeably. Likewise, a path in a dBG spells the string obtained by concatenating together all the k-mers along the path, without repeating the shared $(k-1)$-length overlaps. In particular, unary paths (i.e., non-branching) can be collapsed into single nodes spelling strings that are referred to as *unitigs*. Let $\mathcal{U} = \{u_1, \ldots, u_m\}$ be the set of unitigs of the graph. The dBG arising from this compaction step is called the *compacted* dBG, and indicated with $G(\mathcal{U})$.

The *colored* compacted dBG (c-dBG) is obtained by logically annotating each k-mer x with its color, $\text{COLOR}(x)$. While different conventions have been

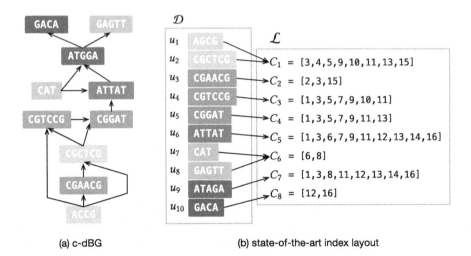

(a) c-dBG   (b) state-of-the-art index layout

Fig. 1. In panel (a), an example colored compacted de Bruijn graph (c-dBG) for $k = 3$. (In the figure, a k-mer and its reverse complement are considered as different k-mer for ease of illustration. In practice, these are considered identical.) The unitigs of the graph are colored according to the set of references they appear in. In panel (b), we schematically illustrate the state-of-the-art index layout (the Fulgor index [13]) assuming the c-dBG was built for $N = 16$ references, highlighting the modular composition of a k-mer dictionary, $\mathcal{D}$, and an inverted index, $\mathcal{L}$. Note that unitigs are stored in $\mathcal{D}$ in color order, hence allowing a very efficient mapping of k-mers to their distinct colors.

adopted in the literature, here we assume that only non-branching paths with nodes having the *same* color are collapsed into unitigs. The unitigs of the c-dBG we consider in this work have the following key properties.

1. *Unitigs spell references in $\mathcal{R}$.* Each distinct k-mer of $\mathcal{R}$ appears once, as substring of some unitig of the c-dBG. By construction, each reference $R_i \in \mathcal{R}$ can be spelled out by some *tiling* of the unitigs—an ordered sequence of unitig occurrences that, when glued together (accounting for $(k-1)$-symbol overlap and orientation), spell R_i [12]. Joining together k-mers into unitigs reduces their storage requirements and accelerates looking up k-mers in consecutive order [28].
2. *Unitigs are monochromatic.* The k-mers belonging to the same unitig u_i all have the same color. We write $x \in u_i$ to indicate that k-mer x is a sub-string of the unitig u_i. Thus, we shall use $\text{COLOR}(u_i)$ to denote the color of each k-mer $x \in u_i$.
3. *Unitigs co-occur.* Distinct unitigs often have the *same* color, i.e., they co-occur in the same set of references, because they derive from conserved sequences in indexed references that are longer than the unitigs themselves. We indicate with z the number of distinct colors $\mathcal{C} = \{C_1, \ldots, C_z\}$. Note that $z \leq m$ and that, in practice, there are almost always *many more* unitigs than there are distinct colors.

Figure 1a illustrates an example c-dBG with these properties. In the following, we refer to a compacted c-dBG as $G(\mathcal{U}, \mathcal{C})$.

State of the Art. To the best of our knowledge, the only solution that exploits *all* three properties is the recently-introduced Fulgor index [13], which we now review since it is the basis of our development in Sect. 3.

The solution implemented by Fulgor is to first map k-mers to unitigs using the dictionary $\mathcal{D}$, and then succinctly map unitigs to their colors. The colors $\mathcal{C} = \{C_1, \ldots, C_z\}$ themselves are stored in compressed form in an inverted index $\mathcal{L}$. By *composing* these mappings, Fulgor obtains an efficient map directly from k-mers to their associated colors (see also Fig. 1b). The composition is made possible by leveraging the *order-preserving* property of its dictionary data structure—SSHash [28, 29]—which explicitly stores the set of unitigs in *any* desired order. This property has some important implications. First, looking up consecutive k-mers is cache-efficient since unitigs are stored contiguously in memory as sequences of 2-bit characters. Second, if k-mer x occurs in unitig u_i, the LOOKUP(x) operation of SSHash can efficiently determine the unitig identifier i, allowing to map k-mers to unitigs. Third, if unitigs are sorted in color order, so that unitigs having the same color are consecutive, then mapping a unitig to its color can be implemented in as little as $1 + o(1)$ bits *per unitig* and in constant time via a RANK query.

3   Meta-colored Compacted de Bruijn Graphs

When indexing large pangenomes, the space taken by the (compressed) colors dominates the whole index space [2, 13, 16]. Efforts toward improving the memory usage of c-dBGs should therefore be spent in devising better compression algorithms for the colors. In this work, we focus on exploiting the following crucial property that can enable substantially better compression effectiveness: *The genomes in a pangenome are very similar* which, in turn, implies that the *colors are also very similar* (albeit distinct).

By "similar" colors we mean that they share many (potentially, very long) identical integer sub-sequences. This property is not exploited if each color C_i is compressed *individually* from the other colors. For example, if C_i shares a long sub-sequence with C_j, this sub-sequence is actually represented *twice* in the index, which wastes space. This example is instrumentally simple; yet, it suggests that the identification of such common sub-sequences across a large collection, as well as the design of an effective compression mechanism for these patterns, is not easy. A further complicating matter is that the example clearly generalizes to more than two sub-sequences, hence increasing with pangenome redundancy and aggravating the memory usage of an index that encodes them redundantly in each color.

To address this issue, we describe here the meta-colored compacted de Bruijn graph, or Mac-dBG. In the Mac-dBG, a color is represented as a sequence of references to sub-sequences that are shared with potentially many other colors. We refer to these references as *meta colors*. These common sub-sequences, which we call *partial colors*, are encoded once, rather than a number of times equal to the number of colors in which they appear. This allows reducing the required space for the index while incurring low query overhead when partial colors are sufficiently long. Indeed, we demonstrate experimentally in Sect. 4 that the Mac-dBG substantially improves over the space/time trade-off of a traditional c-dBG data structure.

Another key strength of this representation via meta/partial colors is its generality: it applies to any c-dBG data structure arising from the composition of $\mathcal{D}$ and $\mathcal{L}$ to readily improve its space and query time.

3.1 Definition

Let $G(\mathcal{U}, \mathcal{C})$ be the c-dBG built from the reference collection $\mathcal{R} = \{R_1, \ldots, R_N\}$. We recall from Sect. 2 that we indicate with $\mathcal{C} = \{C_1, \ldots, C_z\}$ the set of distinct colors of G. Let $\mathcal{N} = \{\mathcal{N}_1, \ldots, \mathcal{N}_r\}$ be a partition of $[N] = \{1, \ldots, N\}$ for some $r \geq 1$, i.e., $\mathcal{N}_i \neq \varnothing$ for all i, $\mathcal{N}_i \cap \mathcal{N}_j = \varnothing$ for all (i, j) such that $i \neq j$, and $\cup \mathcal{N}_i = [N]$. Let an order between the elements of each $\mathcal{N}_i = \{e_{i,j}\}$ be fixed (for example, by sorting the elements in increasing order). Any $\mathcal{N}$ induces a permutation $\pi : [N] \to [N]$, defined as $\pi(e_{i,j}) := j + B_{i-1}$ where $B_i = \sum_{t=1}^{i} |\mathcal{N}_t|$ for $i > 0$ and $B_0 = 0$, for $i = 1, \ldots, r$ and $j = 1, \ldots, |\mathcal{N}_i|$. We assume from now on that the N reference identifiers and the colors in $\mathcal{C}$ have been permuted according to π. After the permutation, $\mathcal{N}$ determines a partition of $\mathcal{R}$ into r disjoint sets:

$$\mathcal{R}_1 = \{R_i | 0 = B_0 < i \leq B_1\}, \ldots, \mathcal{R}_r = \{R_i | B_{r-1} < i \leq B_r = N\}.$$

Definition 1 (Partial colors). *Let $\mathcal{P}_i$ be the set*

$$\mathcal{P}_i = \Big\{ \{x - B_{i-1} | x \in C_t \cap \{B_{i-1} + 1, B_{i-1} + 2, \ldots, B_i - 1, B_i\}\} \,|\, \forall C_t \in \mathcal{C} \Big\},$$

for $i = 1, \ldots, r$. The elements $\{P_{ij}\}$ of the set $\mathcal{P}_i$ are the partial colors *induced by the partition $\mathcal{N}_i$. We indicate with $\mathcal{P} = \{\mathcal{P}_1, \ldots, \mathcal{P}_r\}$ the set of all partial color sets.*

In words, $\mathcal{P}_i$ is the set obtained by considering the distinct colors *only* for the references in the i-th partition $\mathcal{R}_i$ by noting that—by construction — they comprise integers x such that $B_{i-1} < x \leq B_i$.

The idea is that the set $\mathcal{P} = \{\mathcal{P}_1, \ldots, \mathcal{P}_r\}$ form a dictionary of sub-sequences (the partial colors) that spell the original colors $\mathcal{C} = \{C_1, \ldots, C_z\}$. Let us now formally define this spelling.

Definition 2 (Meta colors). *Let $C_t \in \mathcal{C}$ be a color. A* meta color *is an integer pair (i, j) indicating the sub-list $L := C_t[b \ldots b + |P_{ij}|]$ if there exists $0 < b \leq |C_t| - |P_{ij}|$ such that $L[l] = P_{ij}[l] + B_{i-1}$, for $l = 1, \ldots, |P_{ij}|$. It follows that C_t can be modeled as a list M_t of at most r meta colors. We indicate with $\mathcal{M} = \{M_1, \ldots, M_z\}$ the set of all meta color lists.*

Given $G(\mathcal{U}, \mathcal{C})$, the Mac-dBG is the graph $G(\mathcal{U}, \mathcal{N}, \pi, \mathcal{P}, \mathcal{M})$ where the set of nodes, $\mathcal{U}$, is the same as that of G but the colors $\mathcal{C}$ are represented with the partial colors $\mathcal{P}$ and the meta colors $\mathcal{M}$.

The Mac-dBG permits to encode the colors in $\mathcal{C}$ into smaller space compared to the original c-dBG and without compromising the efficiency of the COLOR(x) query, for the following reasons.

1. If $N_p = \sum_{i=1}^{r} |\mathcal{P}_i|$ is the total number of partial color sets, then each meta color (i, j) can be indicated with just $\log_2(N_p)$ bits. Potentially long sub-lists, shared between several color lists, are therefore encoded once in $\mathcal{P}$ and only referenced with $\log_2(N_p)$ bits instead of redundantly replicating their representation.
2. Each partial color P_{ij} can be encoded more succinctly because the permutation π guarantees that it only comprises integers lower-bounded by $B_{i-1} + 1$ and upper-bounded by B_i. Hence only $\log_2(B_i - B_{i-1})$ bits per integer are sufficient.
3. The total number of integers in $\mathcal{P}$ is *at most* that in the original $\mathcal{C}$, i.e., $\sum_{i=1}^{r} \sum_{j=1}^{|\mathcal{P}_i|} |P_{ij}| \leq \sum_{t=1}^{z} |C_t|$ because partial colors are encoded once. In practice, $\mathcal{P}$ is expected to contain a much smaller number of integers than $\mathcal{C}$.
4. It is efficient to recover the original color C_t from the meta color list M_t: for each meta color $(i, j) \in M_t$, sum B_{i-1} back to each decoded integer of P_{ij}. Hence, we decode *strictly increasing* integers. This is, again, a direct consequence of having permuted the reference identifiers with π. Observe that, in principle, the representation of the colors with meta/partial colors could be described *without* any permutation π—however, one would sacrifice space (for the reason 2. above) *and* query time since decoding a color list from meta colors would eventually need to sort the decoded integers. In conclusion, permuting the reference identifiers with π is an extra degree of freedom that we can exploit to improve index space and preserve query efficiency, noting that the correctness of the index is not compromised when reference identifiers are re-assigned globally.

Example 1. Let us consider the $z = 8$ colors from Fig. 1b, for $N = 16$. Let $r = 4$ and $\mathcal{N}_1 = \{1, 12, 13, 14, 16\}$, $\mathcal{N}_2 = \{3, 5, 9\}$, $\mathcal{N}_3 = \{7, 11\}$, $\mathcal{N}_4 = \{2, 4, 6, 8, 10, 15\}$, assuming we use the natural order between the integers to determine an order between the elements of each $\mathcal{N}_i$. Thus, we have $B_1 = 5$, $B_2 = 8$, $B_3 = 10$, and $B_4 = 16$. The induced permutation π can be visualized by concatenating the sets $\mathcal{N}_i$ from $i = 1$ to 4 and assigning "new" identifiers, from 1 to N, in this concatenated order:

$$\{ 1\ 12\ 13\ 14\ 16 \}\{ 3\ 5\ 9 \}\{ 7\ 11 \}\{ 2\ 4\ 6\ 8\ 10\ 15 \}$$
$$\textit{new identifiers} \rightarrow 1\ 2\ 3\ 4\ 5 \quad 6\ 7\ 8 \quad 9\ 10 \quad 11\ 12\ 13\ 14\ 15\ 16$$

which results in $\pi(1) = 1$, $\pi(12) = 2$, $\pi(13) = 3$, etc., that is

$$\pi = [1, 11, 6, 12, 7, 13, 9, 14, 8, 15, 10, 2, 3, 4, 16, 5].$$

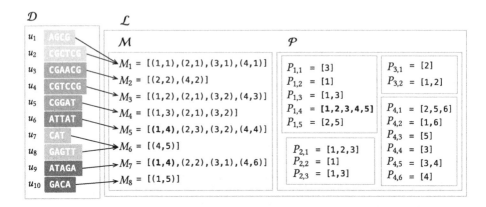

Fig. 2. Mac-dBG layout discussed in Example 1 for the colors of the c-dBG from Fig. 1. Note that the partial color $P_{1,4} = [1, 2, 3, 4, 5]$ shared between C_5 and C_7 is now represented *once* as a direct consequence of partitioning, and indicated with the pair $(1, 4)$ instead of replicating the five integers it contains in both C_5 and C_7. The same consideration applies to other shared sub-sequences.

Now we apply the permutation π to each color, obtaining the following permuted colors (vertical bars represent the partial color boundaries $B_1, \ldots, B_4$).

$$C_1 = [3|6, 7, 8|10|12, 15, 16] \qquad C_2 = [6|11, 16]$$
$$C_3 = [1|6, 7, 8|9, 10|15] \qquad C_4 = [1, 3|6, 7, 8|9, 10]$$
$$C_5 = [1, 2, 3, 4, 5|6, 8|9, 10|13] \qquad C_6 = [13, 14]$$
$$C_7 = [1, 2, 3, 4, 5|6|10|14] \qquad C_8 = [2, 5]$$

For example, color C_1, that before was $[3, 4, 5, 9, 10, 11, 13, 15]$ (see Fig. 1b), now is $[\pi(3), \pi(4), \pi(5), \pi(9), \pi(10), \pi(11), \pi(13), \pi(15)] = [6, 12, 7, 8, 15, 10, 3, 16]$ or $[3, 6, 7, 8, 10, 12, 15, 16]$ once sorted. The partial colors are the distinct sub-sequences in each partition of the permuted colors. For example, $\mathcal{P}_1$ is the set of the distinct sub-sequences in partition 1, i.e., those comprising the integers x such that $0 < x \le B_1 = 5$. Hence, we have five distinct partial colors in partition 1, and these are $[3]$, $[1]$, $[1, 3]$, $[1, 2, 3, 4, 5]$, and $[2, 5]$. Importantly, note that from the integers in partial colors from partition $i > 1$ we can subtract the lower bound B_{i-1}. For example, from the integers in the partial color $[6, 7, 8]$ from C_1 in partition 2 we can subtract $B_1 = 5$, hence obtaining $[1, 2, 3]$. Overall, we thus obtain that $\mathcal{P}$ comprises four partial color sets, as shown in Fig. 2. The figure also shows the rendering of the colors $\mathcal{C} = \{C_1, \ldots, C_8\}$ via meta color lists, i.e., how each color can be spelled by a proper concatenation of partial colors.

3.2   Data Structures Used and Two-Level Intersection Algorithm

Given a Mac-dBG $G(\mathcal{U}, \mathcal{N}, \pi, \mathcal{P}, \mathcal{M})$, a concrete implementation includes a representation for $\mathcal{U}$, $\mathcal{P}$, and $\mathcal{M}$ (plus also the sorted array $B[1..r] =$

$[0, B_1, \ldots, B_{r-1}]$). The Mac-dBG is not bound to any specific compression scheme nor any specific dictionary data structure, allowing one to obtain a spectrum of different space/time trade-offs depending on choices made. In this paper, we made the following choices: (1) we use the SSHash data structure [28, 29] to represent the set of unitigs $\mathcal{U}$; (2) we adopt the same compression methods as used in Fulgor [13] to compress the partial colors and the same mechanism to map unitigs to their colors (using a binary vector of length m, equipped with ranking capabilities); (3) we represent each meta color list as a list of $\log_2(N_p)$-bit integers.

Very importantly, note that choices (1) and (2) directly imply that our Mac-dBG implementation fully exploits the key unitig properties described in Sect. 2 as Fulgor does.

The Mac-dBG opens the possibility to achieve even faster query times than a traditional c-dBG, due to the manner in which the partitions factorize the space of references, if a two-level intersection algorithm is employed for pseudoalignment. There are several pseudoalignment algorithms (see [13, Section 4] for an overview) that standard c-dBG data structures directly support; here we focus on the *full intersection* algorithm. Given a query string Q, we consider it as a set of k-mers. Let $\mathcal{K}(Q) = \{x \in Q | \text{COLOR}(x) \neq \varnothing\}$. The full intersection method computes the intersection between the colors of all the k-mers in $\mathcal{K}(Q)$. Our two-level intersection algorithm is as follows. First, only meta colors are intersected (thus, without any need to access the partial colors) to determine the partitions in common to all colors being intersected. Then only the common partitions are considered. Two cases can happen for each partition. (1) The meta color is the same for all colors: in this case, the result of the intersection is implicit and it suffices to decode the partial color indicated by the meta color. (2) The meta color is not the same, hence we have to compute the intersection between different partial colors. This optimization is beneficial when the colors being intersected have very few partitions in common, or when they have identical meta colors.

3.3 The Optimization Problem

As evident from its definition, the effectiveness of a Mac-dBG crucially depends on the choice of the partition $\mathcal{N}$ and upon the order of the references within each partition as given by the permutation π. There is, in fact, an evident friction between the encoding costs of the partial and meta colors. Let N_m and $N_p = \sum_{i=1}^{r} |\mathcal{P}_i|$ be the number of meta and partial colors, respectively. Since each meta color can be indicated with $\log_2(N_p)$ bits, meta colors cost $N_m \log_2(N_p)$ bits overall. Instead, let $\text{COST}P_{ij}, \pi$ be the encoding cost (in bits) of the partial color P_{ij} according to some function COST. On one hand, we would like to select a large value of r so that N_p diminishes since each color is partitioned into several, small, partial colors, thereby increasing the chances that each partition has many repeated sub-sequences. This will help in reducing the encoding cost for the partial colors, i.e., the quantity $\sum_{i=1}^{r} \sum_{j=1}^{|\mathcal{P}_i|} \text{COST}P_{ij}, \pi$. On the other hand, a large value of r will yield longer meta color lists, i.e., increase N_m. This, in turn, could erode the benefit of encoding shared patterns and would require more time to decode each meta color list.

We can therefore formalize the following optimization problem that we call *minimum-cost partition arrangement* (MPA).

Problem 2 (Minimum-cost partition arrangement). Let $G(\mathcal{U}, \mathcal{C})$ be the compacted c-dBG built from the reference collection $\mathcal{R} = \{R_1, \ldots, R_N\}$. Determine the partition $\mathcal{N} = \{\mathcal{N}_1, \ldots, \mathcal{N}_r\}$ of $[N] = \{1, \ldots, N\}$ for some $r \geq 1$ and permutation $\pi : [N] \rightarrow [N]$ such that $N_m \log_2(N_p) + \sum_{i=1}^{r} \sum_{j=1}^{|\mathcal{P}_i|} \mathrm{COST} P_{ij}, \pi$ is minimum.

Depending upon the chosen encoding, smaller values of $\mathrm{COST} P_{ij}, \pi$ may be obtained when the gaps between subsequent reference identifiers are minimized. Finding the permutation π that minimizes the gaps between the identifiers over all partial colors is an instance of the bipartite minimum logarithmic arrangement problem (BIMLOGA) as introduced by Dhulipala et al. [11] for the purpose of minimizing the cost of delta-encoded lists in inverted indexes. The BIMLOGA problem is NP-hard [11]. We note that BIMLOGA is a special case of MPA: that for $r = 1$ (one partition only) and $\mathrm{COST} P_{ij}, \pi$ being the $\log_2$ of the gaps between consecutive integers. It follows that also MPA is NP-hard under these constraints. This result immediately suggests that it is unlikely that polynomial-time algorithms exist for solving the MPA problem.

3.4 The SCPO framework

In this section we propose a construction algorithm for the Mac-dBG. The algorithm is an heuristic for the MPA optimization problem defined in the previous section (Problem 2), and it is based on the intuition that *similar* references should be grouped together in the same partition so as to *increase the likeliness of having a smaller number of longer shared sub-sequences*. The algorithm therefore consists in the following four steps: (1) *Sketching*, (2) *Clustering*, (3) *Partitioning*, and (4) *Ordering* (SCPO).

1. Sketching. We argue that a reasonable way of assessing the similarity between two references is determining the number of unitigs that they have in common. Recall from Property 1 (Sect. 2) that each reference $R_i \in \mathcal{R}$ can be spelled by a proper concatenation (a "tiling") of the unitigs of the underlying compacted dBG. If these unitigs are assigned unique identifiers by SSHash, it follows that each R_i can be seen as a list of unitig identifiers. The idea is that these integer lists are much shorter and take less space than the actual DNA references. To reduce the space of a list even further, we compute a *sketch* of the list based on the fact that if two sketches are similar, then the original lists are similar as well.

2. Clustering. The sketches are fed as input of a clustering algorithm.

3. Partitioning. Once the clustering is done, each input reference R_i is labeled with the cluster label of the corresponding sketch so that the partition of $\mathcal{R}$ into $\mathcal{R}_1, \ldots, \mathcal{R}_r$ is uniquely determined.

4. Ordering. Finally, one may *order* the references in each $\mathcal{R}_i$ to determine a permutation π that yields a better compression for the partial colors $\mathcal{P}_i$. In fact, while the goal of clustering and partitioning is to factor out repeated sub-patterns within the colors, the goal of the ordering step is to assign nearby identifiers to references that tend to co-occur within the partial colors (as already mentioned in Sect. 3.3).

Specific Framework Instance. In this work, we use the following specific instance of this framework. We build *hyper-log-log* [14] sketches of $W = 2^{10}$ bytes each. As clustering algorithm, we use a *divisive* K-means approach that does not need an a-priori number of clusters to be supplied as input. At the beginning of the algorithm, the whole input forms a single cluster that is recursively split into two clusters until the mean squared error (MSE) between the sketches in the cluster and the cluster's centroid is not below a prescribed threshold (which we fix to 10% of the MSE at the start of the algorithm). Let r be the number of found clusters. The complexity of the algorithm depends on the topology of the binary tree representing the hierarchy of splits performed. In the worst case, the topology is completely unbalanced and the complexity is $O(WNr)$; in the best case, the topology is perfectly balanced instead, for a cost of $O(WN \log r)$. Note that the worst-case bound is very pessimistic because, in practice, the formed clusters tend to be reasonably well-balanced in size.

In the current version of the work, we did not perform any ordering of the references within each cluster. We leave the investigation of this opportunity as future work.

4 Experiments

This section presents the results of experiments conducted to assess the performance of the Mac-dBG. We fixed the k-mer length to $k = 31$. All experiments were run on a machine equipped with Intel Xeon Platinum 8276L CPUs (clocked at 2.20 GHz), 500 GB of RAM, and running Linux 4.15.0.

Datasets. We build Mac-dBGs with the proposed SCPO framework on the following pangenomes: 3,682 *E. Coli* (EC) genomes from NCBI [1]; different collections of *S. Enterica* (SE) genomes (from 5,000 up to 150,000 genomes) from the collection by Blackwell et al. [7]. Additionally, we also include a much more diverse collection of 30,691 genomes assembled from human gut samples (GB), originally published by Hiseni et al. [15].

Other Evaluated Tools. We compare the Mac-dBG against the following indexes: Fulgor [13], Themisto [2], MetaGraph [17–19], and COBS [6]. Links to the corresponding software libraries can be found in the References. We use the C++ implementations from the respective authors. All software was compiled with gcc 11.1.0.

We provide some details on the tested tools. Both Themisto and COBS were built under default parameters as suggested by the authors, that is: option -d 20 for Themisto which enables the sampling of k-mer colors in the SBWT

Table 1. Index space in GB, broken down by space required for indexing the k-mers in the dBG (SSHash for both Fulgor and Mac-dBG, SBWT for Themisto, and BOSS for MetaGraph) and data structures required to encode colors and map k-mers to colors.

	Genomes	Mac-dBG			Fulgor			Themisto			MetaGraph			COBS
		dBG	Colors	Total	dBG	Colors	Total	dBG	Colors	Total	dBG	Colors	Total	Total
EC	3,682	0.29	0.52	0.81	0.29	1.36	1.65	0.22	1.85	2.08	0.10	0.23	0.33	7.53
SE	5,000	0.16	0.16	0.32	0.16	0.59	0.75	0.14	1.29	1.43	0.07	0.19	0.26	9.11
	10,000	0.35	0.33	0.68	0.35	1.66	2.01	0.32	3.50	3.81	0.13	0.38	0.51	18.68
	50,000	1.26	2.14	3.40	1.26	17.03	18.30	1.07	32.42	33.48	0.36	1.95	2.31	88.61
	100,000	1.72	3.83	5.55	1.72	40.70	42.44	1.35	75.94	77.28	0.45	3.50	3.95	173.58
	150,000	2.03	5.37	7.40	2.03	68.60	70.66	1.58	125.16	126.74	—	—	—	265.49
GB	30,691	21.31	7.85	29.16	21.31	15.45	36.85	18.33	30.88	49.21	5.23	4.77	10.00	21.23

for better space effectiveness; in COBS, we have shards of at most 1024 references where each Bloom filter has a false positive rate of 0.3 and one hash function. MetaGraph indexes were built with the *relaxed row-diff* BRWT data structure [18] using a workflow available at https://github.com/theJasonFan/metagraph-workflows that we wrote with the input of the MetaGraph authors.

Index Size. Table 1 reports the total *on disk* index size for all of the methods evaluated. Compared to the most recent indexes, Fulgor and Themisto, that where previously shown to achieve the most desirable space/time trade-offs, Mac-dBG substantially improves on the space (and, as we shall see next, without any negative impact on query time). In fact, the only index smaller on disk than Mac-dBG is MetaGraph in the relaxed row-diff BRWT configuration—at least in the cases where we were able to construct the latter within the construction resource constraints. However, unlike the other indexes evaluated, the *on disk* index size MetaGraph is not representative of the working memory required for query when using the (recommended and default) batch mode query.

The COBS index, despite being approximate, is consistently and considerably larger than all of the other (exact) indexes, except for the Gut bacteria collection (GB). The differing behavior on GB likely derives from the fact that the diversity of that data cause the exact indexes to spend a considerable fraction of their total size on the representation of the k-mer dictionary itself (e.g., 18–21.3 GB). However COBS, by design, eliminates this component of the index entirely.

Finally we observe that, as the number of references grow in the SE datasets, the already-large savings of Mac-dBG become even more prominent. For example Mac-dBG is 43% of the size of Fulgor (2.34× smaller) for SE 5,000, but is only 10% of the size of Fulgor (9.55× smaller) for SE 150,000. As the size of the collection grows, and more repetitive sub-patterns in the collection of colors appears, the Mac-dBG index is able to better capture and eliminate this redundancy.

Table 2. Total query time (elapsed time) and memory used during query (max. RSS) as reported by `/usr/bin/time -v`, using 16 processing threads. The read-mapping output is written to `/dev/null` for this experiment. We also report the mapping rate in percentage (fraction of mapped read over the total number of queried reads). The query algorithm used here is full-intersection. The "B" query mode of MetaGraph corresponds to the batch mode (with default batch size); the "NB" corresponds to the non-batch query mode instead. In red font we highlight the workloads exceeding the available memory (> 500 GB).

	Genomes	Rate	Mac-dBG		Fulgor		Themisto		MetaG.-B		MetaG.-NB		COBS	
			mm:ss	GB	mm:ss	GB	h:mm:ss	GB	mm:ss	GB	h:mm:ss	GB	h:mm:ss	GB
EC	3,682	98.99	2:40	0.85	2:10	1.68	0:03:40	2.46	22:00	30.44	1:05:41	0.40	0:45:11	34.93
SE	5,000	89.49	1:16	0.37	1:16	0.82	0:03:50	1.82	14:14	36.54	0:20:32	0.33	0:38:34	41.93
	10,000	89.71	2:45	0.75	2:26	2.11	0:07:35	4.16	28:15	92.18	0:43:40	0.61	1:01:14	84.20
	50,000	91.25	14:00	3.65	19:15	18.53	0:42:02	33.14	—	—	4:30:03	2.72	3:54:18	408.82
	100,000	91.41	26:48	6.29	27:30	42.78	1:22:00	75.93	—	—	9:40:06	4.82	8:07:29	522.56
	150,000	91.52	41:30	8.51	42:30	70.55	2:00:13	124.27	—	—	—	—	7:47:14	522.63
GB	30,691	92.91	01:03	28.51	01:10	30.02	0:01:20	48.47	28:55	15.86	0:22:05	9.91	0:34:45	225.57

Query Efficiency. Table 2 reports the query times of the indexes, performing full-intersection pseudoalignment (see Alg. 1 from [13]), on a high-hit workload. The queried reads consist of all FASTQ records in the first read file of the following accessions: SRR1928200 for EC, SRR801268 for SE, and ERR321482 for GB. These files contain several million reads each. Timings are relative to a second run of each experiment, where the indexes are loaded from the disk cache (which benefits the larger indexes more than the smaller ones).

Consistent with previously reported results [13], we find that among existing indexes, Fulgor provides the fastest queries. As expected, Mac-dBG does not sacrifice query efficiency compared to Fulgor. After Mac-dBG and Fulgor, we note that Themisto is the next fastest index, followed by MetaGraph in batch query mode. The query speeds of COBS and of MetaGraph when not executed in batch mode are much lower than that of the other indexes, in some cases being (more than) an order of magnitude slower.

Critically, it is not the case with all indexes evaluated here that the size of the index *on disk* is a good proxy for the memory required to actually query the index. Specifically, for MetaGraph, when used in batch query mode ("B"), the required memory can exceed the on-disk index size by up to 2 orders of magnitude, and in several tests this resulted in the exhaustion of available memory and an inability to complete the queries under the tested configuration. On the other hand, Fulgor, Themisto, Mac-dBG and MetaGraph when not executed in batch mode ("NB") require only a small constant amount of working memory beyond the size of the index present on disk.

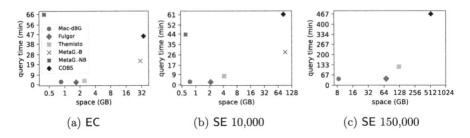

(a) EC   (b) SE 10,000   (c) SE 150,000

Fig. 3. The same data from Table 2 but shown as space vs. time trade-off curves, for some example datasets.

5   Conclusions

We have introduced the Mac-dBG data structure. The Mac-dBG represents a new state-of-the-art representation for answering color queries over large collections of reference sequences, and achieves a considerable improvement over existing work in terms of the space/time trade-off it offers. Specifically, Mac-dBG is almost as small as the smallest variant of MetaGraph—which is the smallest compressed c-dBG representation on disk. Yet, when queried, Mac-dBG requires essentially the same space as is required for the index on disk, while the MetaGraph representation expands manyfold to improve query throughput via batch queries. At the same time, Mac-dBG provides query speed as fast as the fastest existing c-dBG index, Fulgor. This enhanced trade-off can be visualized in Fig. 3. We believe these characteristics make Mac-dBG a very promising data structure for enabling large-scale color queries across a range of applications.

To achieve these substantial improvements over the prior state of the art, the Mac-dBG focuses on providing an improved representation of the color table, the element of the index that tends to grow most quickly as the number of indexed references increases. Specifically, Mac-dBG compresses the colors by factoring out shared sub-patterns that occur across different colors. The color table is represented as a set of *meta* colors and *partial* colors which are combined to recover the original colors exactly. While most interesting formulations of determining the optimal factorization into meta colors and partial colors appear NP-hard, we nonetheless describe a heuristic approach that works well in practice.

Acknowledgement. We are grateful to Laxman Dhulipala for useful comments on an early draft of this paper.

Funding Information. This work is supported by the NIH under grant award numbers R01HG009937 to R.P.; the NSF awards CCF-1750472 and CNS-1763680 to R.P, and DGE-1840340 to J.F. Funding for this research has also been provided by the European Union's Horizon Europe research and innovation programme (EFRA project, Grant Agreement Number 101093026). This work was also partially supported by DAIS – Ca' Foscari University of Venice within the IRIDE program.

Declarations. R.P. is a co-founder of Ocean Genomics inc.

References

1. Alanko, J.N.: 3682 E. Coli assemblies from NCBI (2022). https://zenodo.org/records/6577997
2. Alanko, J.N., Vuohtoniemi, J., Mäklin, T., Puglisi, S.J.: Themisto: a scalable colored K-Mer index for sensitive pseudoalignment against hundreds of thousands of bacterial genomes. Bioinformatics **39**(Supplement_1), i260–i269 (2023). https://github.com/algbio/themisto
3. Almodaresi, F., Sarkar, H., Srivastava, A., Patro, R.: A space and time-efficient index for the compacted colored de Bruijn graph. Bioinformatics **34**(13), i169–i177 (2018)
4. Almodaresi, F., Zakeri, M., Patro, R.: PuffAligner: a fast, efficient and accurate aligner based on the pufferfish index. Bioinformatics **37**(22), 4048–4055 (2021)
5. Baier, U., Beller, T., Ohlebusch, E.: Graphical pan-genome analysis with compressed suffix trees and the burrows-wheeler transform. Bioinformatics **32**(4), 497–504 (2016)
6. Bingmann, T., Bradley, P., Gauger, F., Iqbal, Z.: COBS: a compact bit-sliced signature index. In: Brisaboa, N.R., Puglisi, S.J. (eds.) SPIRE 2019. LNCS, vol. 11811, pp. 285–303. Springer, Cham (2019). https://doi.org/10.1007/978-3-030-32686-9_21
7. Blackwell, G.A., et al.: Exploring bacterial diversity via a curated and searchable snapshot of archived DNA sequences. PLOS Biol. **19**(11), 1–16 (2021). http://ftp.ebi.ac.uk/pub/databases/ENA2018-bacteria-661k
8. Bray, N.L., Pimentel, H., Melsted, P., Pachter, L.: Near-optimal probabilistic RNA-Seq quantification. Nat. Biotechnol. **34**(5), 525–527 (2016)
9. Cleary, A., Ramaraj, T., Kahanda, I., Mudge, J., Mumey, B.: Exploring frequented regions in pan-genomic graphs. IEEE/ACM Trans. Comput. Biol. Bioinf. **16**(5), 1424–1435 (2019)
10. Dede, K., Ohlebusch, E.: Dynamic construction of pan-genome subgraphs. Open Comput. Sci. **10**(1), 82–96 (2020)
11. Dhulipala, L., Kabiljo, I., Karrer, B., Ottaviano, G., Pupyrev, S., Shalita, A.: Compressing graphs and indexes with recursive graph bisection. In: Proceedings of the 22nd ACM SIGKDD International Conference on Knowledge Discovery and Data Mining, pp. 1535–1544 (2016)
12. Fan, J., Khan, J., Pibiri, G.E., Patro, R.: Spectrum preserving tilings enable sparse and modular reference indexing. In: Research in Computational Molecular Biology, pp. 21–40 (2023)
13. Fan, J., Singh, N.P., Khan, J., Pibiri, G.E., Patro, R.: Fulgor: a fast and compact k-mer index for large-scale matching and color queries. In: 23rd International Workshop on Algorithms in Bioinformatics (WABI 2023), pp. 18:1–18:21 (2023). https://github.com/jermp/fulgor
14. Flajolet, P., Fusy, É., Gandouet, O., Meunier, F.: HyperLogLog: the analysis of a near-optimal cardinality estimation algorithm. In: Discrete Mathematics and Theoretical Computer Science, pp. 137–156 (2007)
15. Hiseni, P., Rudi, K., Wilson, R.C., Hegge, F.T., Snipen, L.: HumGut: a comprehensive human gut prokaryotic genomes collection filtered by metagenome data. Microbiome **9**(1), 1–12 (2021). https://arken.nmbu.no/~larssn/humgut/index.htm

16. Holley, G., Melsted, P.: Bifrost: highly parallel construction and indexing of colored and compacted de Bruijn graphs. Genome Biol. **21**(1), 1–20 (2020)
17. Karasikov, M., et al.: MetaGraph: indexing and analysing nucleotide archives at petabase-scale. BioRxiv, pp. 2020–10 (2020)
18. Karasikov, M., Mustafa, H., Joudaki, A., Javadzadeh-no, S., Rätsch, G., Kahles, A.: Sparse binary relation representations for genome graph annotation. J. Comput. Biol. **27**(4), 626–639 (2020). https://github.com/ratschlab/metagraph
19. Karasikov, M., Mustafa, H., Rätsch, G., Kahles, A.: Lossless indexing with counting de Bruijn graphs. Genome Res. **32**(9), 1754–1764 (2022)
20. Lees, J.A., et al.: Improved prediction of bacterial genotype-phenotype associations using interpretable pangenome-spanning regressions. mBio **11**(4), 10–1128 (2020)
21. Liu, B., Guo, H., Brudno, M., Wang, Y.: deBGA: read alignment with de Bruijn graph-based seed and extension. Bioinformatics **32**(21), 3224–3232 (2016)
22. Luhmann, N., Holley, G., Achtman, M.: BlastFrost: fast querying of 100, 000s of bacterial genomes in Bifrost graphs. Genome Biol. **22**(1), 1–15 (2021)
23. Mäklin, T., et al.: High-resolution sweep metagenomics using fast probabilistic inference [version 1; peer review: 1 approved, 1 approved with reservations]. Wellcome Open Res. **5**(14) (2021)
24. Manuweera, B., Mudge, J., Kahanda, I., Mumey, B., Ramaraj, T., Cleary, A.: Pangenome-wide association studies with frequented regions. In: Proceedings of the 10th ACM International Conference on Bioinformatics, Computational Biology and Health Informatics. ACM, September 2019
25. Marcus, S., Lee, H., Schatz, M.C.: SplitMEM: a graphical algorithm for pangenome analysis with suffix skips. Bioinformatics **30**(24), 3476–3483 (2014)
26. Minkin, I., Medvedev, P.: Scalable multiple whole-genome alignment and locally collinear block construction with SibeliaZ. Nat. Commun. **11**(1), 6327 (2020)
27. Minkin, I., Medvedev, P.: Scalable pairwise whole-genome homology mapping of long genomes with BubbZ. iScience **23**(6), 101224 (2020)
28. Pibiri, G.E.: Sparse and skew hashing of k-mers. Bioinformatics **38**(Supplement_1), i185–i194 (2022)
29. Pibiri, G.E.: On weighted k-mer dictionaries. Algorithms Mol. Biol. **18**(3), 3 (2023)
30. Pibiri, G.E., Venturini, R.: Techniques for inverted index compression. ACM Comput. Surv. (CSUR) **53**(6), 125:1–125:36 (2021)
31. Rahman, A., Dufresne, Y., Medvedev, P.: Compression algorithm for colored de Bruijn graphs. In: 23rd International Workshop on Algorithms in Bioinformatics (WABI 2023), pp. 17:1–17:14 (2023)
32. Reppell, M., Novembre, J.: Using pseudoalignment and base quality to accurately quantify microbial community composition. PLoS Comput. Biol. **14**(4), 1–23 (2018)
33. Schaeffer, L., Pimentel, H., Bray, N., Melsted, P., Pachter, L.: Pseudoalignment for metagenomic read assignment. Bioinformatics **33**(14), 2082–2088 (2017)
34. Skoufos, G.: AGAMEMNON: an accurate metaGenomics and MEtatranscriptoMics quaNtificatiON analysis suite. Genome Biol. **23**(1), 39 (2022)

Color Coding for the Fragment-Based Docking, Design and Equilibrium Statistics of Protein-Binding ssRNAs

Taher Yacoub[1,2], Roy González-Alemán[2,3] , Fabrice Leclerc[2] ,
Isaure Chauvot de Beauchêne[4] , and Yann Ponty[1(✉)]

[1] LIX (CNRS UMR 7161), Institut Polytechnique de Paris, Palaiseau, France
`yann.ponty@lix.polytechnique.fr`
[2] Institute for Integrative Biology of the Cell (I2BC – CNRS UMR 9198),
Université Paris Saclay, Gif, France
[3] Laboratorio de Química Computacional y Teórica (LQCT),
Universidad de La Habana, Havana, Cuba
[4] LORIA (CNRS UMR 7503), Université de Lorraine, Nancy, France

Abstract. We revisit the fragment-based docking and design of single-stranded RNA aptamers (ssRNAs), consisting of k nucleotides, onto a rigid protein. Fragments, representing short sequences of (modified) nucleotides, are individually docked as poses onto the protein surface using a force field. Compatible poses are then assembled while optimizing for an additive notion of energy, to obtain stable conformations that can either be constrained to represent an input ssRNA sequence (docking) or left unconstrained (design). However, a brute-force enumeration of clash-free conformations quickly becomes prohibitive due to their super-exponential ($\Theta(n^k)$ worst-case) combinatorial explosion, hindering the potential of fragment-based methods towards docking and design.

In this work, we adapt the color-coding technique, introduced by Alon, Yuster and Zwick, to optimize over self-avoiding fragment assemblies in time/space linear on n the number of poses, and in time only exponential on k the number of fragments. The dynamic programming algorithm at the core of our method is surprisingly simple, and can be extended to produce suboptimal candidates, or modified to perform Boltzmann sampling of candidates assemblies. Using a rejection principle, and further optimized by a clique decomposition of clashing poses, these algorithms can be leveraged into efficient algorithms optimizing over clash-free complexes. The resulting sampling procedure can further be adapted into statistically-consistent estimators for any computable feature of interest.

We showcase some of the capabilities of this new framework by reanalyzing a set of 7 documented ssRNA-protein complexes, demonstrating its practical relevance and versatility.

Keywords: Fragment-based docking · RNA design · RNA-protein interaction · Parameterized complexity algorithms

© The Author(s), under exclusive license to Springer Nature Switzerland AG 2024
J. Ma (Ed.): RECOMB 2024, LNCS 14758, pp. 147–163, 2024.
https://doi.org/10.1007/978-1-0716-3989-4_10

1   Introduction

Fragment-based approach is a powerful strategy, used both in academia and pharmaceutical industry to develop potent compounds from fragments. Five drugs designed with this approach were approved by the FDA (Bollag et al. 2012; Tap et al. 2015; Perera et al. 2017; Schoepfer et al. 2018), one of which as recently as 2021 (Souers et al. 2013). Fragments are usually small compounds with low molecular weight, having about 20 heavy atoms (Kirsch et al. 2019; Schuffenhauer et al. 2005). The principle of this strategy is to dock a library of fragments onto the protein surface, and to select those that specifically bind the target with optimal target affinity. One or several initial poses are then extended to form a complete chemical compound.

While this strategy is generally applied to chemical compounds for the design, fragment-based approach has been utilized to predict complexes formed by ssRNAs of known sequence with RBP (RNA-Binding Protein) (Hall et al. 2015; de Beauchene et al. 2016; Kappel and Das 2019). To predict the interaction of RNA-RBP complexes, fragments libraries must embrace a large diversity of RNA fragments, including for instance chemical modifications for the design. Such a diversity is also crucial towards a fragment-based design of therapeutic molecules, most of which require a good affinity towards the target to achieve the desired activity (e.g. antagonist, agonist).

A recent approach (González-Alemán et al. 2021) initially performs a sampling of mononucleotides with Multiple Copy Simultaneously Search (MCSS). From a library of mononucleotides, the principle of MCSS is to randomly dock copies of each nucleotide to obtain a set of fragment poses docked on the target with known orientation and position. However, the assembly of consecutive nucleotides into an optimal oligonucleotide, either of known (ssRNA docking) or unknown (ssRNA design) sequence, cannot reasonably be performed in a brute-force fashion due to the punishing combinatorial explosion of candidates. The success of fragment-based approaches hinges critically on the density of poses which, in turn, greatly impacts the number of candidate positions/sequences. The issue is even worsened by a consideration of modified nucleotides, increasing the basis of the induced exponential growth.

In this work, we revisit the fragment-based docking and design through the prism of color coding (see Fig. 1), an algorithmic technique introduced by Alon, Yuster and Zwick (Alon et al. 1994) which captures self avoidance, a necessary condition for ssRNA design and docking. This elegant technique initially addressed the problem of finding sparse motifs in graphs, and has been utilized in the context Bioinformatics for searching (Dost et al. 2008; Shlomi et al. 2006) and counting occurrences of motifs in biological networks (Alon et al. 2008). In Sect. 2, we show how to adapt color coding, further optimized by a clique decomposition, to obtain exact and probabilistic algorithms for fragment-based docking through energy minimization. Section 2.3 describes how to perform leverage tour techniques by relaxing the requirement to be compatible with a given nucleotide sequence. The framework is finally further extended to produce equilibrium statistics for virtually any feature of interest. Section 3 illustrates the

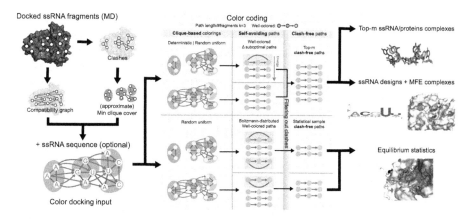

Fig. 1. General workflow: Starting from a graph of docked fragments, for which pairwise connectivity has been assessed by an external tool, our method considers various – random or deterministic – colorings from which solutions to hard computational problems can be obtained.

practicality of proposed algorithms in the context of 7 RNA binding proteins, and Sect. 4 discusses some limitations of the approach, and future extensions.

2 Method and Algorithms

Let us make a few assumptions explicit: Firstly, our docking is assumed to be rigid on the protein level, so that ssRNA fragments (nucleotides or k-mers) can be individually docked onto the protein without overly losing precision; secondly, we assume that the length or nucleotide composition of the input ssRNA forbids the adoption of secondary structure elements; Thirdly, the ssRNA/protein system can be assumed to be at the thermodynamic equilibrium so that minimizing the free-energy coincides with maximizing the probability of the joint configuration. Under these assumptions, the fragment-based docking and design of ssRNAs interacting with a protein can both be reformulated as graph problems.

Definitions and Notations. Namely, we denote as **fragment** f a nucleotide sequence, each associated with a sequence $r(f)$ and a set of relative 3D atomic coordinates. A **fragment pose**, or pose x, represents a fragment docked onto a protein surface, and is defined by the 3D position of its atoms relative to the protein. An ordered pair of poses is said to be **compatible** if their spatial occupancy does not induce unresolvable geometric clashes, and enables the sequential connection of the two fragments into a longer RNA. Compatibility is an oriented relation (associated with the polarity of RNA), whose assessment is a problem in its own right, and the object of specialized tools such as MolPy (Chevrollier 2019) or the upcoming NUCLEAR González-Alemán et al. (2023) in the context of shorter ssRNAs.

Through a systematic docking of fragments, *e.g.* using constrained molecular dynamics, onto the surface of the target protein, followed by an evaluation of the connectivity of resulting fragment poses, one obtains a **poses connectivity graph**. It is defined as a directed graph, *i.e* a pair $G = (V, E)$ where V is a set of fragment poses, and any directed edge $(v, v') \in E$ implies the possibility to connect v and v'. In the following, we denote by $n := |V|$ the number of poses in the graph. Any path of the connectivity graph can be associated with a joint ssRNA/protein conformation, called **complex** in the following.

Next, we associate a notion of **free-energy** $\Delta G(x)$ to any complex $x = (v_1, \ldots, v_k)$, defined as:

$$\Delta G(x) = \sum_{i=1}^{k} \delta(v_i) + \sum_{i=1}^{k-1} \delta'(v_i, v_{i+1})$$

where $\delta : V \to \mathbb{R} \cup \{+\infty\}$ and $\delta' : V \times V \to \mathbb{R} \cup \{+\infty\}$ are terms, specific to a fragment docking procedure, which capture the contributions of individual and pairwise-connected fragments respectively.

However some pairs of fragments may **clash**, occupying overlapping or overly proximal geometric regions in the 3D space, leading some of the paths of the connectivity graph do not always represent promising candidates. Trivial instances of such a clash occur within complexes that reuse the same pose twice. Beyond such a simple cases, pairwise clashes can be modeled using a **clash function** $C : V \times V \to \{\mathsf{True}, \mathsf{False}\}$. A path x of length k is **self-avoiding**, also named a k-**path**, iff it nodes are pairwise distinct. A path is **clash-free** if and only if its nodes are pairwise non-clashing, *i.e.* $\forall 1 \leq i < j \leq k, C(x_i, x_j) = \mathsf{False}$. Note that clash-avoidance induces self-avoidance as long as, for each pose v, one has $C(v, v) = \mathsf{True}$.

Problem Statement and Complexity Aspects. Assuming thermodynamic equilibrium, the most stable/probable complex, for a given nucleotides sequence r of length k, is the one having Minimum Free-Energy. Moreover, fragment assembly should be restricted to complexes compatible with the sequence. The computation of such a complex can be restated as follows:

MFEDOCK **problem**
Input: Pose connectivity graph $G = (V, E)$; Clash function $C : V \times V \to \{\mathsf{True}, \mathsf{False}\}$; Energy function ΔG; Residue sequence $r = r_1, r_2 \ldots r_k$.
Output: Complex $x^* = (v_1^*, v_2^*, \ldots, v_k^*)$ minimizing free-energy

$$x^* = \operatorname*{argmin}_{x=(v_1,\ldots,v_k) \text{ such that}} \Delta G(x)$$

$$\begin{aligned} &v_i \neq v_j \, \forall i \neq j, &&\leftarrow \text{ self avoidance} \\ &C(v_i, v_j) = \mathsf{False}, \forall i \neq j &&\leftarrow \text{ clash-free} \\ &\text{and } r(v_i) = r_i, \forall i &&\leftarrow \text{ nucleotides sequence compatibility} \end{aligned}$$

Computational complexity-wise, for a general input graph, trivial sequence c and unit-valued energy function ($\delta(\cdot) = -1$, $\delta'(\cdot, \cdot) = 0$), MFEDOCK solves the problem of deciding the existence of a HAMILTONIAN PATH in G, implying NP-hardness. The problem remains robustly intractable even when restricted to subclasses of input graphs that can be drawn on a protein surface, such as grid graphs (Itai et al. 1982). Moreover, for the complete compatibility graph and unit-valued energy, solving MFEDOCK answers the existence of a k-set of non-clashing nodes in the graph $(V, \{v, v' \mid C(v, v') = \mathsf{True}\})$, thus solving the MAX INDEPENDENT SET (MIS) problem. However, MIS is not only NP-hard, but also remains intractable (W[1] hard for k) from the perspective of parameterized complexity on geometric instances, *e.g.* graphs stemming from intersections of segments/discs (Marx 2006). Taken together, these results indicate a robust computational hardness of the problem, motivating the exploration of alternatives and heuristics.

2.1   Ensuring Self-avoidance Through Color Coding

Given the dire complexity status of MFEDOCK, we initially address a restricted version of the problem that only considers clashes resulting from the reuse of certain poses. In other words, we optimize the energy optimization over self-avoiding paths, which is equivalent to setting $C(\cdot, \cdot) = \mathsf{False}$. In this setting, the algorithmic problem remains NP-hard but simplifies into a, practically solvable, Fixed-Parameter Tractable (FPT) problem for the path length k, using the color coding technique (Alon et al. 1994).

Classic Color Coding. The key principle of **color coding** is to associate a coloring $\kappa : V \to [1, k]$ to the input graph $G = (V, E)$, and to replace the (hard) search for a path (or motif) of length k (k-path) with the (easier) search of a **colorful path**, using each of the k colors exactly once. Colorful paths can be optimized for, and counted, in time that linear on $n + |E|$, and only exponential on k. For a single coloring, the set of colorful paths is only a subset of k-paths, the optimal k-path may be overlooked. One may then use **derandomization** to turn this approach into an efficient, deterministic and exact algorithm. To that purpose, one needs to construct a family of colorings which, taken as a whole, represents every possible k-path. Naor et al. (1995) propose an explicit construct for such a family, consisting of $e^k k^{\mathcal{O}(\log k)} \log n$ colorings. Iterating the search for optimal colorful paths over the family yields an exact algorithm in overall time $\mathcal{O}((2e)^k k^{\mathcal{O}(\log k)}(n + |E|) \log n)$, critically using $\mathcal{O}(2^k n)$ memory.

Well-Colored Path as a Memory-Frugal Alternative. To work around this substantial memory requirement, we instead consider a variant of color coding based on **well-colored paths**. A well-colored path is a k-path whose colors in κ are not only distinct, but occur in a specific order, assumed to be $1 \to 2 \to \cdots \to k$ without loss of generality. For the sake of simplicity, we say that a coloring κ **hits** (resp. **misses**) a k-path x when x is well-colored (resp. not well-colored) by x. For any given coloring, the optimal/MFE k-path can be obtained in $\mathcal{O}(k.(n + |E|))$ time, *e.g.* using simple dynamic programming. To be well-colored only constrains the colors assigned to the k nodes of x, leaving only one possibility out of the k^k

possible colorings, so the odds of a random uniform coloring hitting x is simply $\mathbb{P}(x \text{ well colored}) = 1/k^k$. Iterating over α independently-draw random colorings $\kappa_1, \ldots, \kappa_\alpha$, the probability of a k-path being missed by all colorings is then

$$\mathbb{P}(x \text{ missed by } \alpha \text{ random colorings}) = \left(1 - \frac{1}{k^k}\right)^\alpha. \tag{1}$$

This property holds for any k-path, including the MFE path $x^\star$. Consequently, for any targeted **tolerance** $\varepsilon \in (0,1)$, it suffices to set

$$\alpha := \left\lceil \frac{\log \varepsilon}{\log\left(1 - \frac{1}{k^k}\right)} \right\rceil \in \Theta(k^k \log 1/\varepsilon)$$

and we obtain a probabilistic algorithm that returns $x^\star$ with probability $1-\varepsilon$, and runs in total time $\mathcal{O}(k^{k+2} \log(1/\varepsilon)(n + |E|))$ and memory linear in both k and n. Derandomization can also be used in the context of well-colored paths. Here, the constructs of Alon et al. (1995), coupled with the earlier results of Schmidt and Siegel (1990), provide a family of $k^{\mathcal{O}(k)} \log n$ colorings that hits every k-path, thus implying an exact deterministic algorithm for MFEDOCK w/o clash constraints. Its complexity is now in $\mathcal{O}(k^{\mathcal{O}(k)} n. \log n)$ for time, marginally higher than for colorful paths, while using a, much reduced, linear memory.

Rejecting from Suboptimals to Produce the Clash-Free MFE Complex. In order to recover the MFE clash-free complex, and thus provide a solution for MFEDOCK, we elicit to extract it from the list of Δ **(self-avoiding) suboptimals**, defined as having energy distance at most Δ from the self-avoiding MFE. The list of Δ-suboptimals can be produced using an adapted version of the Waterman/Byers scheme (Waterman and Byers 1985). It starts by computing the well-colored MFE for a given coloring κ using the following dynamic programming scheme:

$$\text{mfe}_\kappa = \min_{\substack{v \in V \\ \text{such that } r(v)=r_1}} \text{mfe}_\kappa[v, 1] \tag{2}$$

$$\text{mfe}_\kappa[v, m] = \begin{cases} E(v) & [\text{if } m = k] \\ \min_{\substack{(v,v') \in E \text{ s.t.} \\ \kappa(v')=m+1 \\ \text{and } r(v')=r_{m+1}}} \delta(v) + \delta'(v, v') + \text{mfe}_\kappa[v', m+1] & [\text{otherwise}] \end{cases} \tag{3}$$

Once the mfe matrix computed in $\mathcal{O}(k.(n + |E|))$ time, the exhaustive list of Δ-subopts can be obtained using a modified backtrack:

$$\text{subopts}_\kappa(\Delta) \to \bigcup_{\substack{v \in V \text{ s.t} \\ r(v)=r_1}} \text{subopts}_\kappa(v, 1; \Delta') \tag{4}$$

$$[\text{if } \Delta' := \Delta - (\text{mfe}_\kappa[v, 1] - \text{mfe}_\kappa) \geq 0]$$

$$\text{subopts}_\kappa(v, m; \Delta) \to \begin{cases} \{v\} & [\text{if } m = k] \\ \bigcup_{\substack{(v,v') \in E \text{ s.t} \\ \kappa(v')=m+1 \\ \text{and } r(v')=r_{m+1}}} \{v\} \otimes \text{subopts}_\kappa(v', m+1; \Delta') & \\ & [\text{if } m < k \text{ and } \Delta' \geq 0] \end{cases} \tag{5}$$

Such a backtrack essentially runs in time and memory in $\Theta(k\,D)$, where D is the total number of Δ-subopts, and is expected to grow exponentially with Δ.

An exact, exponential-time in the worst-case, algorithm for the clash-free MFE then starts by computing the global self-avoiding MFE $E_{\text{SA}}^\star$, using a derandomizing family $\kappa := (\kappa_i)_i$ of colorings. It then iterates again several times over the whole family using increasing values of Δ until

$$\Delta \geq \Delta_{\max} := E_{\text{clash-free}}^- - E_{\text{SA}}^\star,$$

where $E_{\text{clash-free}}^-$ denotes the clash-free MFE observed for Δ-suboptimals over κ so far. At this point, the algorithm may simply return the clash-free MFE complex within the $\Delta_{\max}$ subopts, $i.e.$ the structure $S^\star$ achieving $E_{\text{clash-free}}^-$, since this structure is then the clash-free MFE, and a valid solution to MFEDOCK.

Indeed, for any clash-free complex $S' \neq S^\star$, if S' is found in the combined list of Δ-suboptimals, then it has higher energy than $E_{\text{clash-free}}^-$ by definition. If S' is not listed as a $\Delta_{\max}$-subopt for κ, then, for any coloring κ that hits S', one has $\text{mfe}_\kappa + \Delta_{\max} \leq \Delta G(S')$. Since $E_{SA}^\star \leq \text{mfe}_\kappa$, one concludes with

$$\Delta G(S^\star) = E_{\text{clash-free}}^- \leq E_{SA}^\star + \Delta_{\max} \leq \text{mfe}_\kappa + \Delta_{\max} \leq \Delta G(S').$$

The energy of any alternative S' is thus higher than that of $S^\star$, from which we conclude that our algorithm is correct.

Of course, the practical performances of the algorithm may critically depend on the $\Delta_{\max}$ value, $i.e.$ the energy difference between the MFE self-avoiding and clash-free complexes. To mitigate the issue, we introduce in the next Sect. 2.2 an optimization based on cliques, which we illustrate in Fig. 2 along with our algorithm.

2.2 Reducing Clashes Through Monochromatic Clique Covers

During the initial docking phase, individual fragments usually cluster around hotspots on the protein surface. On the one hand, such an accumulation is beneficial to the resolution of the selected poses as, to a degree, it enables simulating flexibility. On the other hand, high local densities may result in a combinatorial explosion of clashes, drastically reducing the density of clash-free complexes, all the while hindering the performances of our algorithms. Instead, we would rather focus our effort on a subset of self-avoiding paths featuring a good density of clash-free associated complexes.

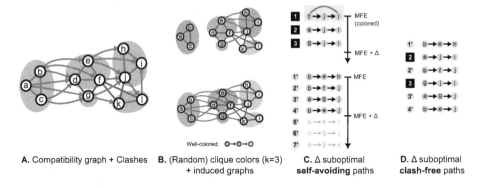

Fig. 2. Example of Δ-**suboptimal color coding based on monochromatic cliques.** From a MFEDOCK instance (A), including compatibility arcs (blue) and clashes edges (red), a clique cover is heuristically computed (gray). A family of coloring is then generated (B; random or deterministic), and a dynamic programming algorithm allows to build a list of (self-avoiding) k-paths (C). Among those, only f → j → l presents a clash (red box) and is filtered out to obtain a merged list of clash-free Δ-suboptimals. Notably, the two colorings above are sufficient to hit all clash-free paths. Moreover, j → l → i, a valid k-path which features two clashing nodes, cannot be well-colored in the current clique cover. (Color figure online)

Cliques of Clashing Nodes Can be Safely Set to a Single Color. To achieve such a goal, we trivially remark that the nodes of a **clashing clique** $\mathcal{C}$, *i.e.* a set of pairwise clashing poses, may not occur more than once within a reasonable candidate complex. Nicely, such clashes can be avoided by enforcing the **monochromaticity** of κ with respect to $\mathcal{C}$, the use of a single color for all $v \in \mathcal{C}$. This restriction is conservative with respect to clash-free complexes, since any clash-free k-path, hit by a coloring κ and featuring a node $v_c \in \mathcal{C}$, is also hit by a monochromatic coloring κ' such that

$$\kappa' : v \to \begin{cases} \kappa(v_c) & \text{if } v \in \mathcal{C} \\ \kappa(v) & \text{otherwise.} \end{cases}$$

Meanwhile, any k-path that borrowed two or more nodes from $\mathcal{C}$ is no longer admissible, thereby increasing the density of clash-free complexes within the search space. Moreover, from the perspective of derandomization, this restriction enables the complete clash-free paths to be hit by a smaller family of colorings, since whole cliques can be treated as a single nodes.

This observation, and overall strategy, provably generalizes to collections of disjoint cliques in the clash graph. Two overlapping cliques $\mathcal{C}$ and $\mathcal{C}'$, however, should not be forced to be simultaneously monochromatic. Indeed the color of $\mathcal{C}$ would, due to its overlap with $\mathcal{C}'$, spread to the latter. This would result in treating $\mathcal{C} \cup \mathcal{C}'$ as a single clique, thereby potentially eliminating some clash-free k-paths from the search space. In order to minimize runtime, and maximize the density of clash-free paths within the runspace, we preprocess clashes by decomposing them as a **clique cover**, a partition of nodes into a set of cliques

$\mathfrak{C} = \{\mathcal{C}_i\}$ while attempting to maximize the number of clashing pairs occurring within a clique $\mathcal{C}_i$. Though not strictly equivalent, this problem is related to MIN CLIQUE COVER and likely hard.

A Pragmatic Solution to Decompose Clashes into Non-overlapping Cliques. To pragmatically solve the problem, we implemented an **greedy heuristic for min clique cover** which initializes the cover $\mathfrak{C} := \varnothing$ and, at each iteration, starts from the node v^+ having max degree node in the remaining graph. It initializes a clique $\mathcal{C} := \{v^+\}$ and a list of common neighbors $\mathcal{N} := \text{neighbors}(v^+)$. Then, until $\mathcal{N} = \varnothing$, it alternates:

1. Choose a node $v \in \mathcal{N}$ having max degree within $\mathcal{N}$, is added to $\mathcal{C}$;
2. Update of list of common neighbors through $\mathcal{N} := \mathcal{N} \cap \text{neighbors}(v)$;

The clique $\mathcal{C}$ is then added to the cover $\mathfrak{C}$, removed from the clique graph for future iterations (choice of v^+, construction of $\mathcal{C}$...) until all nodes have been removed from the clash graph and added as part of a clique to $\mathfrak{C}$. While this heuristic does not provide formal guarantees regarding its result, we found it performs adequately for our typical instances, as shown in Sect. 3.2.

2.3   Rational ssRNA Design as a Relaxation of Docking

Rational design in the context of a fragment-based docking usually requires two properties to be fulfilled by the designed RNA aptamer: **Positive design** requires the ligand to have optimal affinity, or low interaction free-energy, towards the target protein or targeted pocket; **Negative design** constrains the ligand to be specifically binding to a given region of the protein. Interestingly, both criteria are at least partially addressed by a simple relaxation of the MFEDOCK problem.

The required modification simply consists in partially specifying (*e.g.* using IUPAC codes), or even disregarding altogether (*e.g.* poly-N mask), the input ssRNA sequence without added complexity. In this setting, solving the MFE-DOCK problem provides an MFE complex, from which both an ssRNA sequence $r^\star := r(x_1).r(x_2) \cdots r(x_k)$ and its MFE conformation can be derived. More precisely, we can show that: i) No alternative sequence has higher affinity than $r^\star$ towards the protein (positive design); ii) The binding site induced on the protein surface by $x^\star$ is the most likely target for $r^\star$ (negative design). Admittedly, this approach does not enable targeting of a specific site or pocket, since the best complex location of the returned designs is induced by the MFE criterion. Nevertheless, by generating suboptimals and only retaining the first occurrence of each sequence (*i.e* associated with their MFE complex), one can produce a diversity of sequences that are both stable, and specifically target various sites.

2.4   Equilibrium Statistics

While clearly an important – computationally challenging – problem, docking through energy minimization is hindered by its single focus on the MFE conformation. Indeed, at the thermodynamic equilibrium, the probability of a clash-free complex x follows a Boltzmann distribution

$$\mathbb{P}(X = x \mid r) = \frac{e^{-\beta.\Delta G(x)}}{\mathcal{Z}_r} \text{ where } \mathcal{Z}_r = \sum_{\substack{x' \text{ clash-free} \\ \text{and comp. with } r}} e^{-\beta.\Delta G(x')}$$

is the partition function for a nucleotide sequence r, $\mu = RT$ with R the Boltzmann constant and T the absolute temperature. Since the number of valid complexes typically grows (at least) exponentially with k, the probability of the MFE complex becomes abysmally small in larger systems. As an extreme example, for the clique input graph, the number of complexes grows in $\Theta(n^k)$ when $k \ll n$, and even $n! \asymp (n/e)^n$ when $k = n$, thereby completely crushing the probability of any single complex.

Boltzmann Statistics. This motivates a computation of **equilibrium statistics**, *i.e* expected properties of the system under a Boltzmann distribution. Such properties are measured by a set of real-valued **feature functions** $\{f_1, f_2, \ldots\}$, each mapping a valid complex to some numerical value in $\mathbb{R}$. Features can represent any relevant quantity (free-energy, %occupancy of druggable pocket...), provided that they can be effectively computed from a fully-specified complex. The **expectation of a feature** f is defined as:

$$\mathbb{E}(f(X) \mid r) = \sum_{\substack{x \text{ self avoiding} \\ \text{and comp. with } r}} f(x) \times \mathbb{P}(X = x \mid r)$$

and can be interpreted as a collective variables. Probabilities can also be computed as expectations of $(0/1)$-valued features. Indeed, setting $f_c(r) = 1$ or 0 depending on the presence/absence of a contact with a targeted residue A, the expectation simplifies into

$$\mathbb{E}(f_c(X) \mid r) = \sum_x f_c(x) \times \mathbb{P}(x \mid r) = \sum_{x \text{ s.t. } f_c(x)=1} \mathbb{P}(x \mid r) = \mathbb{P}\left(f_c(X) = 1 \mid r\right).$$

Higher moments of the distributions can finally be computed from the expectations of $f, f^2, f^3 \ldots$ enabling access to finer characteristics of the distribution, such as its variance/stddev, skewness, kurtosis... or even correlations between multiple features. Complexity-wise, computing the partition function is provably harder than its, already-hard, optimization version (MFEDOCK). Worse, as defined for optimization, families of coloring used for derandomization would typically introduces a bias in the subsequent estimates, and thus cannot be used.

Statistical Estimators from Colored Statistics. To work around those hurdles, we adopt an approach that estimates the expectation based on a sequence of random colorings $\kappa_1, \kappa_2 \ldots$ Namely, we introduce the **color-restricted expectation** of a feature f given a coloring κ as:

$$\mathbb{E}(f(X) \mid r, \kappa) = \sum_{\substack{x \text{ clash-free,} \\ \text{comp. with } r \\ \text{well col. by } \kappa}} f(x)\, \mathbb{P}(x \mid r, \kappa) = \sum_{\substack{x \text{ clash-free,} \\ \text{comp. with } r \\ \text{well col. by } \kappa}} f(x) \frac{e^{-\beta \Delta G(x)}}{\mathcal{Z}_{r,\kappa}} \text{ where } \mathcal{Z}_{r,\kappa} = \sum_{\substack{x' \text{ clash-free,} \\ \text{comp. with } r \\ \text{well col. by } \kappa}} e^{-\beta \Delta G(x')}.$$

To estimate this quantity, we first introduce a dynamic programming scheme to compute the (coloring-restricted) partition function:

$$\mathcal{Z}_\kappa = \sum_{\substack{v \in V \\ \text{such that } r(v) = r_1}} \mathcal{Z}_{v,1} \quad \text{and} \quad \mathcal{Z}_{v,m} = \begin{cases} e^{-\beta E(v)} & \text{if } m = k \\ \displaystyle\sum_{\substack{(v,v') \in E \text{ s.t.} \\ \kappa(v') = m+1 \\ \text{and } r(v') = r_{m+1}}} e^{-\beta(E(v) + E'(v,v'))} \mathcal{Z}_{v',m+1} & \text{otherwise} \end{cases}$$

(6)

A stochastic backtrack then consists in, starting from $\mathcal{Z}_k$, the repeated choice a node with probability proportional to its contribution to $\mathcal{Z}_\kappa$, recursing until the $m = k$ condition is met. The returned random complex is then Boltzmann distributed within well-colored k-paths. The average value of f on a set of generated complexes, further filtered to retain only clash-free paths, represents an unbiased estimator for $\mathbb{E}(f(X) \mid r, \kappa)$. Our, provably consistent, final estimator takes a collection of random uniformly-distributed colorings, and returns:

$$\widehat{f}(\kappa_1, \kappa_2 \ldots \kappa_M) = \frac{\sum_{i=1}^{M} \mathcal{Z}_{r,\kappa_i} \times \mathbb{E}(f(X) \mid r, \kappa_i)}{\sum_{j=1}^{M} \mathcal{Z}_{r,\kappa_j}}$$

(7)

3   Results

Implementation. We implemented our algorithms for MFEDOCK (optimization; subopts; $\pm$ sequence constraints) and statistical estimators into the ColorDocking software, a collection of Python scripts interfacing C code, freely downloadable with datasets and further information to reproduce experiments at https://gitlab.inria.fr/amibio/colordocking. All experiments were performed on a PBS cluster with a Linux kernel, using 125 GB of memory. Each calculation was done on a single CPU.

Datasets. We selected seven ssRNA/protein complexes to validate our method. Among them, six complexes are RNA-RRM complexes (RRM; 1B7F, 1CVJ, 2MGZ, 2YH1, 3NNH and 4BS2) and the remaining one is a Pumilio domain (PUF; 3BX3). This generally coincides with the benchmark selected by de Beauchene et al. (2016), removing two structures: 4N0T, which natively interacts with a double-stranded RNA; and 5BZV, another PUF which we saw as redundant with 3BX3. To provide a realistic setting for docking, proteins were prepared and minimised using the CHARMM36 force field in the absence of the ssRNA ligand and solvent. As a result, the protein surface at the RNA binding site may have been altered, and in a more specific way at some specific position of the RNA chain.

For each of our targets, we used the MCSS (Miranker and Karplus 1991) method to generate a distribution of 10.000 fragment poses. These fragments are composed of Adenine (A), Cytosine (C), Guanine (G) and Uracil (U). Only the first 4.000 fragments poses (2.000 anti-conformations and 2.000 syn-conformations) were used for this study. From these, the python package NUCLEAR

(González-Alemán et al. 2023) was used to cluster poses within 0.5Å RMSD, and to build matrices (connectivity, clashes, scores) using 4.5Å as a max. value for the $O3'$-$C5'$ distance. The max contact distance between the protein and a fragment was set to 3.5Å. All atoms of amino acids were considered, as well as for nucleotides, except for the terminal patch which was omitted to improve connectivity. All NUCLEAR runs were constrained to only generate the various matrices (run_type = partial option).

A directed graph (+ clash matrix) was then generated and fed as input to our implementation of ColorDocking algorithm, using collections of clique-level random uniform colorings. We uniformly set the tolerance to $\varepsilon = 0.01$, *i.e.* the clash-free MFE complex was predicted with probability of $p = 99\%$. Clash-free MFE candidates were produced, based on a suboptimality cutoff $\Delta = 10$ kcal.mol^{-1}.

3.1   Stability Analysis

Setting the RNA length to $k = 5$ enables the execution of our algorithm in modest time (about a dozen seconds per run). Such a runtime enables a comparison the results obtained over successive executions, in order to assess the impact of the random generation of colorings on the stability of predictions. Namely, for all of the 7 complexes, and setting $k = 5$, we performed 100 independent experiments. In addition, we used a brute-force approach to compute both self-avoiding and clash-free MFE complexes. As expected, we consistently recover the clash-free MFE complex in our experiments, namely between 97/100 and 100/100 of experiments over all targets. Such a behavior is expected from our choice of $\varepsilon = 0.01$, implying a 1% chance of missing the MFE but could, at least

Table 1. Summary of our benchmark and paths cardinality analysis.

Complex	k	#Poses	Target Seq.	α	#Paths	#SA (cliques)	#Clash-Free
1B7F	5	2 171	UUUUU	14 388	$5.22.10^8$	$1.49.10^8$	$6.98.10^6$
1CVJ	5	2 031	AAAAA	14 388	$9.44.10^7$	$2.24.10^7$	$1.46.10^6$
2MGZ	5	4 329	GGUGU	14 388	$1.84.10^7$	$4.89.10^6$	$3.20.10^5$
2YH1	5	2 064	UUUUU	14 388	$1.57.10^8$	$2.97.10^7$	$1.22.10^6$
3BX3	5	7 464	UAUAU	14 388	$1.42.10^8$	$5.39.10^7$	$5.21E.10^6$
3NNH	5	4 606	UUUUG	14 388	$5.58.10^7$	$1.85.10^7$	$3.64.10^6$
4BS2	5	8 150	GAAUG	14 388	$2.37.10^7$	$8.65.10^6$	$1.03.10^6$
1B7F	7	2 171	GUUUUUU	3 792 553	–	–	–
1CVJ	8	2 031	AAAAAAAA	77 261 93	–	–	–
1CVJ	8	5 785	AAAAAAAA	77 261 93	–	–	–
1CVJ	8	26 570	AAAAAAAA	77 261 93	–	–	–
2MGZ	7	4 329	UGGUGUG	3 792 553	–	–	–
3BX3	8	7 464	UGUAUAUA	77 261 93	–	–	–
3NNH	6	4 606	UUUUGU	214 856	–	–	-

in theory, have been affected by setting Δ to a fixed value. Setting $\varepsilon = 0.63$ expectedly reduces the runtime by a factor 10, at the cost of degraded performances, with the MFE clash-free structure being only found between $25/100$ and $47/100$ of experiments.

In a second analysis, we investigated whether the top-100 clash-free complex present a strong overlap across independent executions of the algorithm. We filtered the output of Δ-suboptimal version of the MFEDOCK algorithm ($\Delta = 10$, $\varepsilon = 0.01$) to produce the 100 lowest-energy clash-free complexes. We iterated the experiment 100 times, and found the average pairwise overlap between two runs to be of 98%, with very limited variations.

3.2 Impact of Monochromatic Clique Covers

Next we turn to an investigation of the effect of clique-based coloring on the density of clash-free paths, the runtime and energy distance between the self-avoiding MFE and the clash-free MFE. To investigate those points, in addition to the MFE obtained as above, we used a brute-force approach to compute the numbers of unconstrained, self-avoiding and clash-free paths.

We first report in Table 2 the clique covers returned by our greedy heuristic. While the number of poses is in the order of (dozens of) thousands, the number of clashing cliques scales between 40 and 100, with larger cliques representing a sizeable proportion of the vertex set (10 to 20%). Moreover, a large proportion (50% to 70%) of clashing edges are internal to a clique. Such clashes can no longer occur upon restricting to clique-based coloring, substantially reducing the probability of a k-path featuring a clash.

As can be seen in Table 1, the number of paths is typically reduced by 75% when clique-monochromatic self-avoidance is ensured. This results in a runtime reduction an overall factor 1.5 to 4. Meanwhile, as can be seen in Table 2, the energy distance between the self-avoiding and clash-free MFEs can be greatly reduced (*e.g.* $-10\,\mathrm{kcal.mol}^{-1}$ for 2 MGZ) when cliques are used to reduce the search space. Overall, the consideration of monochromatic cliques represents a very positive addition: it greatly improves the runtime and purifies self-avoiding paths to increase the density of clash-free paths.

3.3 Docking Through Energy-Minimization Under Different Fragment Definitions

We showcased the versatility of our approach by supplementing the MCSS set of poses with the connectivity graphs associated with overlapping trinucleotide fragments, following de Beauchene et al. (2016). For 1CVJ, we used the ATTRACT software (de Vries et al. 2015) to generate 1.000.000 non-redundant (0.2Å RMSD threshold) fragment poses, in coarse-grained representation. We built a connectivity matrix, using as connectivity criteria a 1.8Å RMSD cutoff for overlapping nucleotides between consecutive fragments. We created a directed graph of connected poses, using the ssRNATTRACT package as described in de Beauchene et al. (2016). We used a new fragment library of RNA trinucleotides extracted from

Table 2. Properties and impact of cliques cover on runtime. Values observed for $k = 5$, averaged over 100 iterations (std dev ≈ 1).

Complex	#Poses	#Cliques	Max clique size	% Clique edges	Avg time (sec)		$|MFE_{clash\text{-}free} - MFE_{SA}|$	
					+cliques	−cliques	+cliques	−cliques
1B7F	2 171	49	298	54.56	10.63	16.37	9.15	11.45
1CVJ	2 031	40	344	60.38	6.75	30.00	1.37	1.37
2MGZ	4 329	63	584	57.64	2.40	5.40	8.45	18.74
2YH1	2 064	49	312	66.40	8.60	15.53	5.2	9.6
3BX3	7 464	70	889	49.29	16.71	18.02	5.3	10.97
3NNH	4 606	55	629	57.62	3.61	12.73	2.52	7.25
4BS2	8 150	98	625	53.79	6.19	12.28	2.07	8.68
1CVJ	5 785	44	1 109	71.50	−	−		

the PDB with the `ProtNAff` software (Moniot et al. 2022), using our Radius clustering method.

From the 1.000.000 initial poses, 5327 could be assembled in a 5-fragments chain, and were therefore retained in the final graph of connected poses. We then constructed a clash matrix of those poses, using a 1.5 Å distance criteria between two clashing heavy atoms (excluding overlapping nucleotides of connected poses). In addition, we considered a pair of poses as incompatible if both can be connected only at the same position in a 5-fragments chain, since they can not be together in the same chain. The full matrix of poses incompatibility (either clashing or only at the same position in chains) was used to define cliques of incompatible poses.

The resulting MFEDOCK instance only needs to be executed for $k = 6$, since each fragment represents a trinucleotide, and assembling 6 fragments is sufficient to reach the size of 8 nucleotides. This allows to execute our algorithm in as little as 34 s. Meanwhile, the runtime required by 1CVJ for our MCSS dataset, implying $k = 8$, is of 2.10^3 s, or approximately 33 min. Beyond the demonstrated ability of `ColorDocking` to support multiple fragment definition, we did not analyze further the quality of the produced fragments (*e.g.* RMSD to native complex), since our goal is not to compare different force fields/fragment definitions.

3.4   Design

To illustrate the capacity of MFEDOCK to address design, we considered a design study recently published by Perzanowska et al. (2022), where an oligonucleotide targeting a poly(A)-binding protein (PDBID: 1CVJ) was designed. Since this study included modified nucleotides, we considered an extended list of nucleotides: two without modification (A,G), and 5 with modifications: adenosine and guanosine with a phosphorothioate (A_P, G_P), protonated adenosine (A_ψ), N6-methyladenosine (m^6A), N6-methyladenosine including phosphorothioate (m^6A_P), 2'O-methyladenosine (Am) and 2'O-methyladenosine including phosphorothioate (Am$_P$). All were used in anti- and syn-conformations, for a total of 1 000 poses (500 syn/500 anti) per nucleotide type. They were clustered at 0.5 Å RMSD for a remaining number of 5 785 individual poses.

To generate solutions of length k = 8, we considered a maximum value of $\Delta_{max} := 3$, and gradually increased Δ by unit steps, to reach a maximum of 100 clash-free per coloring. We initially did not consider sequence constraints. The number of unique sequences was 75 out of 562 clash-free solutions. We report below the top 10 of unique sequence, along with their minimum free energy:

A$_\psi$-A-A$_P$-G$_P$-A$_P$-m^{6}A-m^{6}A-A -178.405	m^{6}A$_P$-m^{6}A-A-G$_P$-A$_P$-m^{6}A-m^{6}A-A -178.404
A$_\psi$-A-G$_P$-G$_P$-A$_P$-m^{6}A-m^{6}A-A -178.377	G-m^{6}A$_P$-m^{6}A-A-A$_P$-A$_P$-m^{6}A-m^{6}A -178.055
A$_\psi$-A-A$_P$-G$_P$-A$_P$-A$_m$-A$_m$-m^{6}A -178.052	A$_m$$_P$-A$_m$-A-G$_P$-A$_P$-A$_m$-A$_m$-m^{6}A -178.050
A$_m$$_P$-A$_m$-A-A$_P$-A$_P$-A$_m$-A$_m$-A -178.030	A$_\psi$-A-G$_P$-G$_P$-A$_P$-A$_m$-A$_m$-m^{6}A -178.023
A$_P$-A$_m$$_P$-A$_m$-A-G$_P$-A$_P$-A$_m$-A$_m$ -177.864	A$_\psi$-A-A$_P$-G$_P$-A$_m$$_P$-A$_m$-A$_m$-A -177.812

Interestingly, those differ from the sequences investigated by Perzanowska et al. (2022). In particular, the pair of sequences having highest affinity in the study, was not found in our list. This is not entirely surprising, since the authors limited their investigation to a single modified nucleotide per design. We further analyzed their two best sequences, running a sequence-constrained instance of MFEDOCK

A-A-A-A-A-A-m^{6}A-A -161.252   m^{6}A-A-A-A-A-A-A-A -151.976

and found that their MFE is significantly higher ($+16/+26\,\mathrm{kcal.mol^{-1}}$), suggesting that our ability to tame the combinatorial explosion grants us access to promising alternatives.

4   Conclusions and Perspectives

We have introduced a new algorithmic framework, based on color coding, to solve natural combinatorial problems arising in the context of fragment-based docking and design of ssRNAs interacting with a protein conformation. We have illustrated their utility in the context of seven RNA binding proteins, showing that color coding provides a versatile toolkit for the study and design of ssRNAs. Our method is not restricted to individually docked nucleotides, and could accommodate other fragment libraries, as demonstrated on trinucleotide fragments.

A key strength of our exact algorithm resides in its linear complexity on the number of pairwise connected poses, only being exponential on the length k of the ssRNA to ensure self-avoidance. As such, it can be seen as a parameterized complexity algorithm, showing that the MFEDOCK problem is Fixed Parameter Tractable (FPT) for the ssRNA length k. On a practical level, much larger sets of poses/connections could be supported, allowing to explore the impact of various sampling depth/density of poses on the quality of predictions.

Acknowledgments. This work was supported by a 2020 PhD Grant from the *Fondation Vaincre Alzheimer* (#FR-19059) and by the PaRNAssus project funded by *Agence Nationale de la Recherche* (ANR-19-CE45-0023). The authors are greatly indebted to Laurent Bulteau for suggesting well-colored paths as a memory-efficient alternative to colorful paths, and to Sebastian Will for debunking an earlier, but ultimately erroneous, epiphany.

References

Alon, N., Yuster, R., Zwick, U.: Color-coding. In: Proceedings of the Twenty-Sixth Annual ACM Symposium on Theory of Computing - STOC 1994. ACM Press (1994). https://doi.org/10.1145/195058.195179

Alon, N., Yuster, R., Zwick, U.: Color-coding. J. ACM **42**(4), 844–856 (1995). https://doi.org/10.1145/210332.210337. ISSN 0004-5411

Alon, N., Dao, P., Hajirasouliha, I., et al.: Biomolecular network motif counting and discovery by color coding. Bioinformatics **24**(13):i241–i249 (2008). https://doi.org/10.1093/bioinformatics/btn163

Bollag, G., Tsai, J., Zhang, J., et al.: Vemurafenib: the first drug approved for BRAF-mutant cancer. Nat. Rev. Drug Discov. **11**(11), 873–886 (2012). https://doi.org/10.1038/nrd3847

Chevrollier, N.: Développement et application d'une approche de docking par fragments pour modéliser les interactions entre protéines et ARN simple-brin. Theses, Université Paris-Saclay, May 2019. https://tel.archives-ouvertes.fr/tel-02436914

de Beauchene, I.C., de Vries, S.J., Zacharias, M.: Fragment-based modelling of single stranded RNA bound to RNA recognition motif containing proteins. Nucleic Acids Res. **44**(10), 4565–4580 (2016). https://doi.org/10.1093/nar/gkw328

de Vries, S.J., Schindler, C.E., de Beauchêne, I.C., Zacharias, M.: A web interface for easy flexible protein-protein docking with attract. Biophys. J. **108**(3), 462–465 (2015). https://doi.org/10.1016/j.bpj.2014.12.015. https://www.sciencedirect.com/science/article/pii/S0006349514047602. ISSN 0006-3495

Dost, B., Shlomi, T., Gupta, N., et al.: QNet: a tool for querying protein interaction networks. J. Comput. Biol. **15**(7), 913–925 (2008). https://doi.org/10.1089/cmb.2007.0172

González-Alemán, R., Chevrollier, N., Simoes, M., et al.: MCSS-based predictions of binding mode and selectivity of nucleotide ligands. J. Chem. Theory Comput. **17**(4), 2599–2618 (2021). https://doi.org/10.1021/acs.jctc.0c01339

González-Alemán, R., Montero-Cabrera, L., Leclerc, F.: NUCLEAR: a NUCLeotide AssembleR (2023). https://github.com/rglez/nuclear

Hall, D., Li, S., Yamashita, K., et al.: RNA-LIM: a novel procedure for analyzing protein/single-stranded RNA propensity data with concomitant estimation of interface structure. Anal. Biochem. **472**, 52–61 (2015). https://doi.org/10.1016/j.ab.2014.11.004

Itai, A., Papadimitriou, C.H., Szwarcfiter, J.L.: Hamilton paths in grid graphs. SIAM J. Comput. **11**(4), 676–686 (1982). https://doi.org/10.1137/0211056

Kappel, K., Das, R.: Sampling native-like structures of RNA-protein complexes through Rosetta folding and docking. Structure **27**(1), 140-151.e5 (2019). https://doi.org/10.1016/j.str.2018.10.001

Kirsch, P., Hartman, A.M., Hirsch, A.K.H., Empting, M.: Concepts and core principles of fragment-based drug design. Molecules **24**(23), 4309 (2019). https://doi.org/10.3390/molecules24234309

Marx, D.: Parameterized complexity of independence and domination on geometric graphs. In: Bodlaender, H.L., Langston, M.A. (eds.) Parameterized and Exact Computation, vol. 4169, pp. 154–165. Springer, Heidelberg (2006). https://doi.org/10.1007/11847250_14. ISBN 978-3-540-39101-2

Miranker, A., Karplus, M.: Functionality maps of binding sites: a multiple copy simultaneous search method. In: Proteins: Structure, Function, and Genetics 11(1), 29–34 (1991). https://doi.org/10.1002/prot.340110104

Moniot, A., Guermeur, Y., de Vries, S.J., Chauvot de Beauchene, I.: ProtNAff: protein-bound Nucleic Acid filters and fragment libraries. Bioinformatics 38(16), 3911–3917 (2022). https://doi.org/10.1093/bioinformatics/btac430. ISSN 1367-4803

Naor, M., Schulman, L., Srinivasan, A.: Splitters and near-optimal derandomization. In: Proceedings of IEEE 36th Annual Foundations of Computer Science. IEEE Comput. Soc. Press, October 1995. https://doi.org/10.1109/sfcs.1995.492475

Perera, T.P., Jovcheva, E., Mevellec, L., et al.: Discovery and pharmacological characterization of JNJ-42756493 (erdafitinib), a functionally selective small-molecule FGFR family inhibitor. Mol. Cancer Ther. 16(6), 1010–1020 (2017). https://doi.org/10.1158/1535-7163.mct-16-0589

Perzanowska, O., Smietanski, M., Jemielity, J., Kowalska, J.: Chemically modified poly(A) analogs targeting PABP: structure activity relationship and translation inhibitory properties. Chem. Eur. J. 28(42), e202201115 (2022)

Schmidt, J.P., Siegel, A.: The spatial complexity of oblivious k-probe hash functions. SIAM J. Comput. 19(5), 775–786 (1990)

Schoepfer, J., Jahnke, W., Berellini, G., et al.: Discovery of Asciminib (ABL001), an allosteric inhibitor of the tyrosine kinase activity of BCR-ABL1. J. Med. Chem. 61(18), 8120–8135 (2018). https://doi.org/10.1021/acs.jmedchem.8b01040

Schuffenhauer, A., Ruedisser, S., Marzinzik, A., et al.: Library design for fragment based screening. Curr. Top. Med. Chem. 5(8), 751–762 (2005). https://doi.org/10.2174/1568026054637700

Shlomi, T., Segal, D., Ruppin, E., Sharan, R.: QPath: a method for querying pathways in a protein-protein interaction network. BMC Bioinform. 7(1) (2006). https://doi.org/10.1186/1471-2105-7-199

Souers, A.J., Leverson, J.D., Boghaert, E.R., et al.: ABT-199, a potent and selective BCL-2 inhibitor, achieves antitumor activity while sparing platelets. Nat. Med. 19(2), 202–208 (2013). https://doi.org/10.1038/nm.3048

Tap, W.D., Wainberg, Z.A., Anthony, S.P., et al.: Structure-guided blockade of CSF1r kinase in tenosynovial giant-cell tumor. N. Engl. J. Med. 373(5), 428–437 (2015). https://doi.org/10.1056/nejmoa1411366

Waterman, M.S., Byers, T.H.: A dynamic programming algorithm to find all solutions in a neighborhood of the optimum. Math. Biosci. 77(1–2), 179–188 (1985). https://doi.org/10.1016/0025-5564(85)90096-3

Automated Design of Efficient Search Schemes for Lossless Approximate Pattern Matching

Luca Renders[1]($^{(\boxtimes)}$) (ID), Lore Depuydt[1] (ID), Sven Rahmann[2] (ID), and Jan Fostier[1] (ID)

[1] Ghent University - imec, Technologiepark 126, 9052 Ghent, Belgium
{luca.renders,lore.depuydt,jan.fostier}@ugent.be
[2] Center for Bioinformatics Saar, Saarland University, Saarland Informatics Campus, 66123 Saarbrücken, Germany
sven.rahmann@uni-saarland.de

Abstract. We present a novel method for the automated design of search schemes for lossless approximate pattern matching. Search schemes are combinatorial structures that define a series of searches, each of which specifies lower and upper bounds on the number of errors in each part of a partitioned search pattern, and the processing order of these parts. Collectively, these searches guarantee that all approximate occurrences of a search pattern up to a predefined number of k errors are identified. Because generating efficient search schemes is increasingly computationally expensive for larger k, search schemes have been proposed in literature for only up to $k = 4$ errors.

To design search schemes allowing more errors, we combine a greedy algorithm and a new Integer Linear Programming (ILP) formulation. Efficient, ILP-optimal search schemes for up to $k = 7$ errors are proposed and shown to outperform alternative strategies, both in theory and in practice. Additionally, we propose a technique to dynamically select an appropriate search scheme given a specific search pattern. These combined approaches result in reductions of up to 53% in runtime for higher values of k.

We introduce Hato, an open-source software tool (AGPL-3.0 license) to automatically generate search schemes. It implements the greedy algorithm and solves the ILP formulation using CPLEX. Furthermore, we present Columba 1.2, an open-source lossless read mapper (AGPL-3.0 license) implemented in C++. Columba can identify all approximate occurrences of 100 000 Illumina reads (150 bp) in the human reference genome in 24 s (maximum edit distance of 4) and in 75 s (edit distance of 6) using a single CPU core, thereby outperforming existing state-of-the-art tools for lossless approximate matching by a large margin.

Keywords: search scheme · integer linear program · approximate pattern matching · sequence alignment

© The Author(s), under exclusive license to Springer Nature Switzerland AG 2024
J. Ma (Ed.): RECOMB 2024, LNCS 14758, pp. 164–184, 2024.
https://doi.org/10.1007/978-1-0716-3989-4_11

1   Introduction

We consider the Approximate Pattern Matching (APM) problem: given a search pattern P (e.g., a read) and a text T (e.g., a reference (pan-)genome), find all approximate occurrences of P in T with at most k errors under the Hamming (only substitutions) or edit/Levenshtein distance (substitutions and/or indels).

We focus on *lossless* APM, where *all* such approximate occurrences are guaranteed to be identified. Many bioinformatics tools, such as BLAST [2], Bowtie [10] and BWA [11] are *lossy* in nature: they rely on fast heuristics to quickly detect some, but not necessarily all, approximate matches of P within T. Lossy algorithms are popular because they are fast. Nevertheless, lossless algorithms offer opportunities for applications in bioinformatics that benefit from a comprehensive overview of all candidate alignment positions, such as the Minimum Bait Cover Problem [1], HLA genotyping [3], or alignment to pangenomes [4]. Because different lossless APM algorithms have identical output, the research task at hand is to improve computational performance. This work further closes the performance gap between lossy and lossless approaches.

The simplest approach to lossless APM is naive backtracking: using a full-text index, exhaustively generate, character by character, candidate occurrences of P in T, thus forming a search trie. Its runtime is governed by the size of the search space, i.e., the total number of sequences that are generated during the search process. However, naive backtracking leads to exploring an excessive number of (mostly unsuccessful) branches near the dense root of this trie. This renders backtracking computationally impractical, even for modest values of k [14].

Lam et al. [9] recognized the potential of bidirectional indexes in significantly accelerating lossless APM. This enhancement is rooted in the classical "pigeonhole principle": by dividing pattern P into $k + 1$ non-overlapping parts, with k the maximum number of allowed errors, at least one part must be error-free. By initially performing an *exact* search for each of these $k + 1$ parts and subsequently extending those matches using branching and backtracking, a significant reduction in search space size is achieved.

Kucherov et al. generalized these ideas by introducing the concept of *search schemes* [8]. Search schemes divide the pattern P into a certain number of parts and define how these parts are matched using a bidirectional full-text index, enabling the rapid elimination of unsuccessful branches in the search trie and therefore minimizing runtime. Kucherov et al. presented efficient search schemes for up to $k = 4$ errors. Kianfar et al. [7] proposed a mixed integer linear programming (MILP) formulation to generate search schemes for up to $k = 4$ errors tailored to the Hamming distance metric. The aforementioned APM based on the pigeonhole principle can also be expressed as search schemes [14], and the same is true for the work by Vroland et al. on 01*0 seeds [19]. Even though search schemes based on the pigeonhole principle and the 01*0 seeds can easily be defined for arbitrary k, they are not computationally optimal. Therefore, the design of efficient search schemes for $k > 4$ is still an open research question.

In earlier work, we introduced Columba [15, 16], a lossless read-mapper that supports arbitrary search schemes for both the edit and Hamming distance. In present work, we make following new contributions:

1. We propose a greedy algorithm to improve the computational performance of existing search schemes. Even though this algorithm cannot guarantee optimality, it is able to quickly generate lossless search schemes for up to $k = 13$ errors with good computational performance. We show that for $k = 5, 6$ and 7 errors, the search space (and thus: runtime) is reduced by respectively 55%, 63% and 71%, compared to the best previously known search schemes (i.e., either pigeonhole principle based or 01*0 seed based)

2. We present a novel ILP formulation to generate search schemes. In contrast to the greedy algorithm, these search schemes are guaranteed to be optimal under the set of used constraints. Using the ILP algorithm, we generated for the first time efficient search schemes for $k = 5, 6$ and 7 errors that demonstrate superior performance in a practical scenario. For $k = 7$ errors, the search space is further reduced with up to 16% as compared to the search scheme generated using our greedy algorithm.

3. For a given value of k, multiple, co-optimal ILP solutions can be generated. Even though co-optimal search schemes are equally fast *on average*, their individual performance may vary among different search patterns P. We propose a *dynamic selection* method where, for each pattern P, the expected best performing search scheme is chosen. We show that this heuristic can reduce the search space by up to 11% as compared to the static use of a search scheme.

4. We present Hato (Japanese for "pigeon") and Columba (Latin for "pigeon") 1.2, two open source C++11 tools[1] under AGPL-3.0 license. Hato implements the greedy algorithm and the ILP solver using CPLEX 22.1.1 [6]. Columba 1.2 is a lossless read-mapper that implements dynamic selection, on top of other improvements described in [16] and [15]. We demonstrate that Columba, using dynamic selection and the novel search schemes generated by Hato, significantly outperforms other state-of-the-art lossless alignment implementations, such as GEM [13], Yara [18], BWA aln (in lossless mode) [11] and Bwolo [19], in the task of identifying all occurrences of 150 bp Illumina reads in the human reference genome. Additionally, we demonstrate superior performance to BWA in lossy mem mode for $k \leq 3$ and a similar runtime for $k = 4$.

2   Preliminaries

We assume that up to k errors are allowed over pattern P and that P is divided into a fixed number of parts p. It is useful, but not strictly required, to choose $p \geq k + 1$ to have at least one error-free part. We use square brackets for indexing sequences, and indexing starts at 0, i.e. $s[0]$ is the first character of sequence

---

[1] available at https://github.com/biointec/hato and https://github.com/biointec/columba, respectively.

s. Sequences of single-digit integers are written without interpunctuation, e.g. $s = (0, 0, 1)$ is written as $s = 001$.

Definition 1. *Given parameters p, k, a **search** is a triplet of sequences $S = (\pi, L, U)$. The π-sequence is a permutation of $\{0, \ldots, p-1\}$ and indicates the order in which the parts of the pattern are processed. To ensure that a search can be performed with a bidirectional index, this permutation must satisfy the **connectivity property**: for every $i > 0$, $\pi[i]$ is either $(\min_{j<i} \pi[j] - 1)$ or $(\max_{j<i} \pi[j] + 1)$. The U- and L-sequences are sequences of length p over $\{0, \ldots, k\}$; they respectively provide upper and lower bounds on the cumulative number of errors in the parts in π-order. Because they are cumulative, both L and U must be non-decreasing, and they must satisfy $L[i] \leq U[i]$ for all i.*

Example 1. Consider the search $S = (102, 001, 012)$ defined for $k = 2$ and $p = 3$. The search starts by handling part $\pi[0] = 1$. As $U[0] = 0$, an exact match of this part is searched. If such a match is found, the search continues with part $\pi[1] = 0$, where $U[1] = 1$ errors are allowed. Finally, the search continues with part $\pi[2] = 2$. Here, up to two cumulative errors are allowed ($U[2] = 2$), but at the end at least one error ($L[2] = 1$) should have been encountered.

Definition 2. *An **error distribution** e, defined for at most k errors over p parts, is an integer sequence over $\{0, \ldots, k\}$ of length p, for which $\sum_{i=0}^{p-1} e[i] \leq k$.*

Example 2. Consider error distribution 101 defined for 2 errors and 3 parts. This distribution has one error in the leftmost part and one error in the rightmost part.

Lemma 1. *There are $Q = \binom{p+k}{k}$ distinct error distributions for p parts with at most k errors [5].*

Definition 3. *A search $S = (\pi, L, U)$ **covers** an error distribution if and only if for all $0 \leq i < p$: $L[i] \leq \sum_{j=0}^{i} e[\pi[j]] \leq U[i]$.*

Example 3. The error distribution from Example 2 is covered by the search from Example 1. We have $L[0] \leq e[\pi[0]] \leq U[0]$ (spelling out $0 \leq e[1] = 0 \leq 0$); then $L[1] \leq e[\pi[0]] + e[\pi[1]] \leq U[1]$ (spelling out $0 \leq 1 \leq 1$); and finally $L[2] \leq \sum_j e[j] \leq U[2]$ (spelling out $1 \leq 1 \leq 2$).

Definition 4. *A **search scheme** S is a set of searches defined for fixed k and p. A search scheme is **valid** if each error distribution with p parts and at most k errors is covered by at least one search of S.*

Example 4. The most intuitive search schemes are based on the **pigeonhole principle**. Given k, these schemes consist of $p = k + 1$ parts and $k + 1$ searches. Since there are only k errors to distribute, each possible error distribution must leave at least one of the parts error-free. Hence each search starts by matching a different part exactly. The other parts can then be processed allowing at most k errors. All searches have lower and upper bounds $L = 00 \ldots 0$ and $U = 0k \ldots k$. For $k = 2$, this results in $S = \{S_0, S_1, S_2\}$ with $S_0 = (012, 000, 022)$, $S_1 = (102, 000, 022)$, $S_2 = (210, 000, 022)$.

Example 5. For the same $k = 2$, $p = 3$, Kucherov et al. [8] proposed the following scheme: $\mathcal{S}_0 = (012, 000, 022)$; $\mathcal{S}_1 = (102, 001, 012)$; $\mathcal{S}_2 = (210, 000, 012)$. While $\mathcal{S}_0$ is identical to the previous example, the lower and upper bounds are tighter for the subsequent searches, making them more efficient than the search scheme based on the pigeonhole principle. By checking all error distributions, it is shown that this search scheme is still valid.

These definitions were first formalized by Kucherov et al. [8] Search schemes are designed to systematically manage the number of allowed errors during the search process. The primary idea is to incrementally increase the number of permissible errors, a notion reflected in the U-sequence. By doing so, search schemes enable the efficient elimination of unsuccessful branches within the search trie. Additionally, the L-sequences serve a crucial role in preventing redundant coverage of error distributions. A well-constructed search scheme aims to include just one covering search for each error distribution, ensuring efficiency and effectiveness.

We aim to optimize search schemes for practical scenarios, specifically targeting repetitive and complex genomes like the human genome. In our earlier work [15,16] we found that fast growth rates of the U-sequence lead to larger search spaces, resulting in increased computational requirements. On the other hand, fast-growing L-sequences reduce the search space. Hence, our goal is to minimize the U-sequences and maximize the L-sequences. We call the resulting schemes **minU search schemes**. In Sect. 3, we introduce a greedy heuristic for improving the U and L sequences, given an initial search scheme. In Sect. 4, we present an ILP formulation that incorporates these objectives into the objective function. Section 5 discusses the dynamic selection method, which identifies the expected best performing search scheme for a given pattern P from a set of co-optimal schemes. The practical performance of the newly designed search schemes and the dynamic selection method is evaluated and compared to the current state-of-the-art in Sect. 6. Finally, Sect. 7 provides a summary of the overall findings.

3   A Greedy Heuristic for Improving Search Schemes

We propose a greedy heuristic for designing search schemes. This algorithm takes as input any valid search scheme, whose U- and L-values are then decreased resp. increased by greedy local changes. We may start with the search scheme based on the pigeonhole principle or from the 01*0 seeds strategy [19]. The π-sequences of the searches are not modified by this heuristic.

The algorithm tracks which searches cover which error distributions. If a distribution is covered by only one search, it is labeled as *critical* for that search. First, we aim to minimize the U-sequences by iterating through positions $i = 0, \ldots, p - 1$. Before each iteration, searches are sorted lexicographically by decreasing U-sequences. In case of a tie, they are sorted by increasing L-sequences. For each search $\mathcal{S}_x$ in this list, we assess the possibility of reducing

$U_x[i]$ without violating the monotonicity of the bounds or losing coverage of critical error distributions. If $U_x[i]$ is decreased, we update the list of covering searches for each error distribution previously covered by $\mathcal{S}_x$. In the event that an error distribution e is now exclusively covered by another search $\mathcal{S}_y$, it will be added to $\mathcal{S}_y$'s list of critical error distributions.

Following this, we seek to maximize the L-sequences. This process is analogous but involves iterating over decreasing positions $i = p - 1, \ldots, 1, 0$ (to guarantee maintaining monotonicity of L), and we check by how much we can increase $L_x[i]$ without violating any properties.

We have generated search schemes for up to $k = 13$ using this technique. Pseudo-code for the algorithm as well as the greedily adapted search schemes are available in the appendix. The complexity of this algorithm is dominated by the number of error distributions $\binom{p+k}{k}$.

4   Integer Linear Program Formulation

Kianfar et al. [7] introduced a Mixed Integer Linear Programming (MILP) model to find optimal search schemes in a specific sense: Their model minimized the (recursively defined) expected number of enumerated substrings for a given pattern length. This expected number of explored branches is computed based on the assumption that both T and P are random sequences. However, in the context of sequence alignment, both P and T are not random; and moreover, we expect P to have an approximate occurrence in T, thus the assumption of randomness typically does not hold. As estimating the number of expected branches is computationally very expensive, Kianfar et al. only generated search schemes for up to $k = 4$ and $S = |\mathbb{S}| = 3$. For $k = 3$ and $k = 4$, this resulted in search schemes for which at least one of the searches did not start with an exact match. We proved in earlier work [16] that such search schemes result in non-competitive runtimes on repetitive and complex genomes such as the human genome.

Therefore, we propose a novel Integer Linear Programming (ILP) formulation to design practical and effective search schemes with a different objective. As stated earlier, our goal is to minimize the U-sequences and maximize the L-sequences. As an additional objective, we want to minimize the number of error distributions that are redundantly covered. Our Integer Linear Programming formulation (Table 1) aims to identify a search scheme that efficiently identifies all approximate matches with up to k errors, considering S searches and p parts. The remainder of this section provides a technical explanation of the ILP model. For brevity, we abbreviate the set $\{0, 1, \ldots, n - 1\}$ by $[n]$.

ILP Details. The total number of possible error distributions is denoted as $Q = \binom{p+k}{k}$ (Lemma 1). For $q \in [Q]$, e_q denotes the q-th error distribution (in some fixed enumeration), and $E_{q,j}$ denotes the cumulative number of errors encountered in e_q up to and including index j. These are precomputed constants.

For the *variables*, we partially adopt the modeling by Kianfar et al. for U, L and λ, where $U_{s,i}$ and $L_{s,i}$ respectively denote the upper and lower bound of

Table 1. ILP formulation to design search schemes with minimized U-sequences, maximized L-sequences and a small number of redundantly covered error distributions.

Variables:		
U- and L-sequences	$U_{s,i}, L_{s,i} \in [k+1]$	$s \in [S], i \in [p]$
encoded π-sequences	$y_{s,i} \in \{0,1\}$	$s \in [S], i \in [p-1]$
covering indicators	$\lambda_{q,s} \in \{0,1\}$	$q \in [Q], s \in [S]$
cumulative number of errors in e_q after stage i of $\mathcal{S}_s$	$\epsilon_{q,s,i} \in [k+1]$	$q \in [Q], s \in [S], i \in [p]$
indicators of $L_{s,i} \leq \epsilon_{q,s,i}$ and $\epsilon_{q,s,i} \leq U_{s,i}$	$\mu^L_{q,s,i}, \mu^U_{q,s,i} \in \{0,1\}$	$q \in [Q], s \in [S], i \in [p]$
indicator for $(\max_{i' \leq i} \pi_s[i']) = j$	$r'_{s,i,j} \in \{0,1\}$	$s \in [S], i \in [p], j \in [p]$

Objective:

$$\text{Minimize} \quad \sum_{s=0}^{S-1}\sum_{i=0}^{p-1}(k+1)^{(p-i-1)} \cdot U_{s,i} - \sum_{s=0}^{S-1}\sum_{i=0}^{p-1}(p-i) \cdot L_{s,i} + \sum_{q=0}^{Q-1}\sum_{s=0}^{S-1}\lambda_{q,s},$$

subject to

$$L_{s,i} \leq U_{s,i} \qquad\qquad s \in [S], i \in [p] \qquad (1)$$

$$L_{s,i} \leq L_{s,i+1} \qquad\qquad s \in [S], i \in [p-1] \qquad (2)$$

$$U_{s,i} \leq U_{s,i+1} \qquad\qquad s \in [S], i \in [p-1] \qquad (3)$$

$$\sum_{s=0}^{S-1}\lambda_{q,s} \geq 1 \qquad\qquad q \in [Q] \qquad (4)$$

$$\lambda_{q,s} \leq \mu^L_{q,s,i} \qquad\qquad q \in [Q], s \in [S], i \in [p] \qquad (5)$$

$$\lambda_{q,s} \leq \mu^U_{q,s,i} \qquad\qquad q \in [Q], s \in [S], i \in [p] \qquad (6)$$

$$\lambda_{q,s} \geq \sum_{i=0}^{p-1}(\mu^L_{q,s,i} + \mu^U_{q,s,i}) - 2p + 1 \qquad\qquad q \in [Q], s \in [S] \qquad (7)$$

$$(k+1) \cdot \mu^L_{q,s,i} \geq 1 + \epsilon_{q,s,i} - L_{s,i} \qquad\qquad q \in [Q], s \in [S], i \in [p] \qquad (8)$$

$$k \cdot \mu^L_{q,s,i} \leq k + \epsilon_{q,s,i} - L_{s,i} \qquad\qquad q \in [Q], s \in [S], i \in [p] \qquad (9)$$

$$(k+1) \cdot \mu^U_{q,s,i} \geq 1 - \epsilon_{q,s,i} + U_{s,i} \qquad\qquad q \in [Q], s \in [S], i \in [p] \qquad (10)$$

$$k \cdot \mu^U_{q,s,i} \geq k - \epsilon_{q,s,i} + U_{s,i} \qquad\qquad q \in [Q], s \in [S], i \in [p] \qquad (11)$$

$$(p-1) - \sum_{h=0}^{p-2} y_{s,h} = \sum_{j=0}^{p-1} j \cdot r'_{s,i,j} \qquad\qquad s \in [S], i \in [p] \qquad (12)$$

$$\sum_{j=0}^{p-1} r'_{s,i,j} = 1 \qquad\qquad s \in [S], i \in [p] \qquad (13)$$

$$r'_{s,i,j} = 0 \qquad\qquad s \in [S], i \in [p], j \in [i] \qquad (14)$$

$$\epsilon_{q,s,i} = \sum_{j=i}^{p-1} r'_{s,i,j} \cdot E_{q,j} - \sum_{j=0}^{p-i-2} r'_{s,i,j+i+1} \cdot E_{q,j} \qquad\qquad q \in [Q], s \in [S], i \in [p] \qquad (15)$$

$$\sum_{i=0}^{p-2} y_{s+1,i} \cdot 2^i \geq 1 + \sum_{i=0}^{p-2} y_{s,i} \cdot 2^i \qquad\qquad s \in [S-1] \qquad (16)$$

$\mathcal{S}_s$ for the i-th part (in π_s-order), and $\lambda_{q,s}$ is a boolean variable that indicates whether e_q is covered by $\mathcal{S}_s$.

To model the permutations π_s with the additional connectivity restriction, we use a novel direct encoding and introduce $p-1$ binary variables $y_{s,i}$ per search $\mathcal{S}_s$. The total number of zeros in the sequence y_s corresponds to $\pi_s[0]$.

A 1-bit in the sequence corresponds to an extension to the right, whereas a 0-bit in the sequence is an extension to the left. For example, for $p = 5$, the sequence $y = 0110$ corresponds to $\pi = 21340$: We have $\pi[0] = 2$, as there are two zeros in y; then the interval $[2, 2]$ is extended to the left, right, right, and left, which gives $1, 3, 4, 0$. In this way, connected permutations on $[p]$ are in a 1-to-1 correspondence with bit-vectors of length $p - 1$.

Our new *objective function* consists of three components. The first component aims to minimize the upper bounds across all searches, with higher importance given to earlier upper bounds within a search. The weighting factor $(k+1)^{(p-i-1)}$ ensures that lexicographically smaller U-sequences are preferred over lexicographically larger ones, and give a high overall weight to the U-sequences. The second component maximizes the lower bounds. Here, a weighting factor of $(p-i)$ is used to give (slightly) higher importance to bounds earlier in the search. The third component aims to minimize the coverage of error distributions by multiple searches. By minimizing the coverage, the objective function encourages the utilization of fewer searches to handle each error distribution, thereby enhancing efficiency and reducing redundancy.

The *constraints* (and auxiliary variables to express the constraints) together ensure that the search scheme is valid. Constraints (1), (2) and (3) state the obvious properties of the L- and U-sequences.

The next Constraints (4)–(7) ensure that the search scheme is valid, i.e., that each error distribution is covered by at least one search. Here, (4) directly models this coverage constraint using the λ-variables, and the other constraints express that $\lambda_{q,s} = 1$ if and only if $\mu_{q,s,i}^{L} = \mu_{q,s,i}^{U} = 1$ for all $i \in [p]$, which we then constrain to be indicators of $L_{s,i} \leq \sum_{j \leq i} e_q[\pi_s[j]]$ and $\sum_{j \leq i} e_q[\pi_s[j]] \leq U_{s,i}$, respectively.

Indeed, Constraints (8)–(11) do exactly this using auxiliary variables $\epsilon_{q,s,i} := \sum_{j \leq i} e_q[\pi_s[j]]$ (which remain to be constrained to satisfy this definition). In particular, Constraints (8) and (9) ensure $\mu_{q,s,i}^{L} = 1$ if and only if $L_{s,i} \leq \epsilon_{q,s,i}$, whereas Constraints (10) and (11) ensure $\mu_{q,s,i}^{U} = 1$ if and only if $\epsilon_{q,s,i} \leq U_{s,i}$.

Now, for the hardest part Constraints (12)–(15): As mentioned above, we need variables $\epsilon_{q,s,i} := \sum_{j \leq i} e_q[\pi_s[j]]$ that contain the cumulative number of errors of the q-th error distribution in the i-th part of search s in π_s-order, but π_s is encoded in the y_s-variables. Fortunately, we can express the right border (call it $r_{s,i}$) of the interval $\pi_s[0, \ldots, i]$ using the y-variables. As $\pi_s[0]$ corresponds to the number of zeros in y_s, and each 1-bit extends the interval to the right, we have $r_{s,0} = (p-1) - \sum_{h=0}^{p-2} y_{s,h}$ and $r_{s,i+1} = r_{s,i} + y_{s,i}$ for $i \in [p-1]$. Combining these two gives $r_{s,i} = (p-1) - \sum_{h=i}^{p-2} y_{s,h}$ for $i \in [p]$ (with the empty sum taking a value of 0 as usual). For the left interval borders we have $\ell_{s,i} = r_{s,i} - i$. We can now write $\epsilon_{q,s,i}$ as the difference between the number of errors encountered up until the right border minus the number of errors encountered before the left border: $\epsilon_{q,s,i} = E_{q,r_{s,i}} - E_{q,(\ell_{s,i}-1)}$, using the precomputed constants $E_{q,j}$. To select the correct $E_{q,j}$ values to subtract from each other using linear relations, we convert the interval endpoint $r_{s,i}$ into a sequence of binary indicator variables $r'_{s,i,j}$ with $r'_{s,i,j} = 1$ if and only if $r_{s,i} = j$. This relation is modeled by (12) and (13). As we must have $r_{s,i} \geq i$, we have $r'_{s,i,j} = 0$ for $j < i$, which is (14). Similarly, the left boundary $\ell_{s,i}$ can be converted into a binary sequence $\ell'_{s,i,j}$. However, it is not necessary to do this explicitly because $\ell_{s,i} = r_{s,i} - i$ and hence $\ell'_{s,i,j} = r'_{s,i,j+i}$ for $j \in [p-i]$. Together, we obtain Constraint (15): $\epsilon_{q,s,i} = E_{q,r_{s,i}} - E_{q,\ell_{s,i}-1} = \sum_{j=0}^{p-1} (r'_{s,i,j} - \ell'_{s,i-1,j}) E_{q,j} = \sum_{j=i}^{p-1} r'_{s,i,j} E_{q,j} - \sum_{j=0}^{p-i-2} r'_{s,i,j+i+1} E_{q,j}$.

Finally, Constraint (16) is a symmetry-breaking constraint enforcing a monotone order of the permutations π_s across the S searches by enforcing that the y_s-sequences (interpreted as binary numbers) are strictly increasing. (Recall that a search scheme is a set of searches in which the order of searches is unimportant; so we prescribe a canonical ordering to avoid symmetric solutions.)

Limiting the Scope of the ILP-Model. The ILP in Table 1 is general and works in principle for any parameter combination of k, p and S. In practice, we are mostly interested in the special case with $p = k + 1$ parts (one guaranteed error-free part) and $S = p$ searches, each of which starts with a distinct error-free part. Under these assumptions, we can introduce extra constraints that reduce the time needed to solve the ILP to optimality. We remove the symmetry-breaking Constraints (16) and add the following explicit ones:

$$U_{s,0} = 0, \quad s \in [S], \tag{17}$$

$$U_{s,k} = k, \quad s \in [S], \tag{18}$$

$$(p - 1) - \sum_{i=0}^{p-2} y_{s,i} = s, \quad s \in [S], \tag{19}$$

$$y_{0,i} = 1, \quad i \in [p-1], \tag{20}$$

$$y_{S-1,i} = 0, \quad i \in [p-1]. \tag{21}$$

Constraint (17) ensures that each search starts with an exact match. Constraint (18) ensures that each search allows up to k errors in the last part; this is necessary for $S = p = k + 1$ to cover all error distributions with k 1s and a single 0. Constraint (19) enforces that each search starts with a different part by setting $\pi_s[0] = s$. Constraints (20) and (21) then respectively model the explicit π-sequence of the first search (all extensions to the right) and of the last search (all extensions to the left), as these are the only possibilities when we start on the left resp. right end.

Kucherov et al. defined the *critical sequence* of a search scheme $\mathbb{S}$ as its lexicographically maximal U-sequence. They showed that the minimal critical sequence in a valid search scheme for $p = k + 1$ is $013355\ldots kk$ for odd k and $02244\ldots kk$ for even k [8], and in an optimal search scheme, some search, called the *critical search*, has this U-sequence. Thus, we add the following constraints if k is odd, as the critical sequence starts with $01\ldots$:

$$U_{s,1} \leq 1, \quad s \in [S]; \tag{22}$$

If k is even, we distinguish between the critical search s' with U-sequence $U_{s'} = 02\ldots$ and the other (non-critical) searches s, starting with $U_s = 01\ldots$. By looping over the different non-redundant possibilities for s' (see below), we define a sequence of ILPs (one for each s') with constraints

$$U_{s,1} \leq 1, \qquad s \in [S], \, s \neq s', \tag{23}$$

$$U_{s',1} = 2. \tag{24}$$

It is sufficient to find those schemes where the critical search $\mathcal{S}_{s'}$ starts with a part in the first half (including part $k/2$) of the pattern, as the other schemes can be constructed by mirroring the permutations, i.e., using $\bar{\pi}[i] := (p-1) - \pi[i]$, but keeping the same U- and L-sequences.

Implementation. We use the CPLEX 22.1.1 solver, implementing the ILP model in C++ with the Concert Technology API [6]. The solver uses up to 32 threads (the maximum for CPLEX) on a 64-core Intel® Xeon® E5-2698 v3 CPU, running at a base clock frequency of 2.30 GHz CPU.

To speed up solving the model to optimality, we provide a warm start. This start can be any valid search scheme. The given scheme is then first greedily improved (using only the upper bounds loop) before starting the ILP. As a first step, the ILP is solved with all lower bounds fixed to zero. Afterwards, the found search scheme is again greedily adapted. This solution with improved lower bounds is then given as initial solution (warm start) to the main ILP, which then computes the overall optimum. This last step, solving the full ILP, may be omitted for large values of k to get good (but sub-optimal) solutions fast, as solving the full ILP takes the majority of the running time. Resulting search schemes are presented in Sect. 6.2. For $k = 6$, the program finished within 1 h, for $k = 7$ the optimal solution was found within 1.5 h.

5 Dynamic Selection

In scenarios where there are multiple co-optimal search schemes that each have a notable load imbalance among their searches, dynamic selection of search schemes proves to be a valuable strategy. These co-optimal solutions are equivalent (from the ILP's point of view), but differ in which search is critical, which may lead to different performance on specific patterns and texts. This variability arises from the fact that (for practically usable search schemes) each search starts with an exact search of one of the parts (each U_s starts with 0), and the number of exact matches for each part can be very different depending on the contents of P and T, while the ILP does not consider these contents. Hence, the size of the search space for the corresponding search also fluctuates.

The crucial insight here is that when the critical search, determined by the lexicographically highest U-sequence, notably differs from the other searches, it typically dominates the overall search time, as it results in an expected broader search trie structure and consequently a larger search space (i.e. more nodes visited). By preemptively identifying the part of P with the fewest exact matches, we can select the co-optimal search scheme for which the critical search starts with this part, to reduce the expected search space size, as only very few exact matches have to be extended by a large number of errors in the next part.

One notable instance is when k is even and $k + 1 = p = S$. In this specific scenario, co-optimal solutions arise, for which the critical search's U-string starts with 02, while all other U-strings start with 01.

Example 6. Consider a DNA read that starts with a low-complexity part (say, a repeat of CA) with *many* exact matches in the reference genome, but all other parts are highly specific and contain differences with respect to the reference genome, so there are *no* exact matches. Assume that we want to find all occurrences of the read within edit distance 4, using 5 parts and 5 searches, where each search starts with a different part. Consider the following two minU search schemes (co-optimal with equal ILP objective value), in which the critical search is marked with an asterisk:

s	Scheme A			Scheme B		
	π_s	L_s	U_s	π_s	L_s	U_s
0	01234	01114	01444	01234	00222	02244*
1	10234	00003	01444	12034	00000	01244
2	23410	01111	02244*	21034	01111	01244
3	32410	00000	01244	34210	00003	01444
4	43210	00222	01244	43210	01114	01444

In Scheme A, the critical search (which covers error distribution 02020) has index $s = 2$. It first searches part 2 exactly and finds zero exact matches (according to our scenario) and immediately stops. Search $s = 0$ that first searches part 0 exactly and finds many exact matches, extends all of these to part 1, allowing only 1 error, which creates much less work than extending them allowing 2 errors. In contrast, in Scheme B, the critical search has index $s = 0$. It first searches part 0 exactly and finds many exact matches, all of which have to be extended allowing up to 2 errors in part 1. With dynamic selection scheme A will be chosen. We observed search space reductions of up to 88% in practice in such scenarios using dynamic selection.

6   Experiments and Results

6.1   Dataset and Computational Environment

All benchmarks were done using a dataset of 100 000 Illumina NovaSeq 6000 reads (151 bp) randomly sampled from a larger whole genome sequencing dataset (SRR9091899). We exhaustively identified approximate read occurrences up to an edit distance of $k = 2, 3, \ldots, 7$ on both strands of the human reference genome (GRCh38) [17] where non-ACGT characters (e.g., Ns) were replaced with a

Table 2. Average number of visited nodes (proportional to search time) for different search schemes. Search schemes above the middle line have been proposed in the literature (-: results not available), while those below the line are proposed in this work. Approximately co-optimal values are highlighted in boldface; values improved from standard minU by dynamic selection (only for even k) are highlighted in bold italics (N/A: not applicable for odd k).

Search scheme	Source	$k = 2$	$k = 3$	$k = 4$	$k = 5$	$k = 6$	$k = 7$
Kucherov $k + 1$	[8]	689	1472	4500	-	-	-
Kucherov $k + 2$	[8]	858	1627	5020	-	-	-
Pigeonhole principle	[9]	847	3073	10467	31200	81908	191668
01*0	[19]	808	2183	5729	13861	31104	67347
Man$_{Best}$	[14]	-	-	5030	-	-	-
Kianfar	[7]	**637**	9359	36967	-	-	-
Greedy Kucherov $k + 1$	here	**640**	**1287**	3643	-	-	-
Greedy Pigeonhole	here	**640**	1433	3493	6572	13592	21723
Greedy 01*0	here	711	1528	3246	6281	11426	19622
minU (ILP)	here	**638**	**1287**	**2943**	**6041**	**9978**	**16542**
minU + dynamic	here	*567*	N/A	*2859*	N/A	*9618*	N/A

randomly selected nucleotide. The chromosomes were concatenated into a single sequence. Spurious occurrences that span the borders of adjacent chromosomes can be easily filtered during post-processing.

Performance benchmarks were obtained using a single core of a 64-core Intel® Xeon® E5-2698 v3 CPU, operating at a base clock frequency of 2.30 GHz. Each benchmark run was repeated 20 times. We report the average wall clock time and the standard deviation.

6.2   Better Search Schemes

In our comparative analysis of search schemes we explore an array of approaches. From literature, we included Kucherov et al.'s schemes with $k + 1$ and $k + 2$ parts [8], the pigeonhole principle-based schemes [9], the 01*0-seeds-based schemes [19], Kianfar et al.'s scheme for $k + 1$ parts, and Man$_{Best}$, a manual adaptation of the scheme by Kianfar et al. for $k = 4$ [14]. Additionally, we include the search schemes created by our greedy algorithm, namely the greedy adaptions of the search schemes by Kucherov et al. with $k + 1$ parts, the search schemes based on the pigeonhole principle ($p = k + 1$) and the search schemes based on 01*0-seeds ($p = k + 2$). Finally, we include the minU scheme created by the ILP (only one of the co-optimal solutions is shown). All search schemes, including the co-optimal minU schemes, are listed in the appendix in Tables 4, 5, 6, 7, 8, 9, 10 and 11.

To assess the different search schemes, Table 2 lists, for different values of k, the average number of nodes visited in the search trie across the approximate matching procedure of all sequences and their reverse complements. This metric directly reflects the size of the search space and serves as an objective measure of efficiency, regardless of implementation quality. Smaller search spaces indicate more efficient search schemes. Each visited node represents a single character extension, which, using a bidirectional FM-index, is executed in constant time. Consequently, reducing the search space results in shorter runtimes. Note that for even values of k, the number of nodes are averaged out over the globally co-optimal minU schemes.

Overall, the minU schemes consistently yield the smallest search space across all values of k, confirming that minimizing the U-sequence leads to better performing search schemes in practice. Notably, for $k > 2$, the simple greedy adaptations of the pigeonhole principle and the 01*0 seeds already outperform all other search schemes previously proposed in literature, demonstrating the power of this fast algorithm.

For $k = 2$, the scheme by Kianfar et al., the greedy adaptations with $k + 1$ parts, and the minU schemes are equivalent. Small performance differences that can be observed are due to minor differences (e.g. mirroring) and the specific dataset that was used. For $k = 3$ and $k = 4$, the schemes by Kucherov et al. were, prior to this work, the fastest search schemes available. Our ILP-optimal minU schemes reduce the search space by respectively 12.6% and 34.6%. For $k = 3$, the greedy adaptation of Kucherov et al.'s search scheme leads to the same search scheme as the one discovered by the ILP, and hence to the same search space size. For $k \geq 5$, no prior efficient search schemes had been proposed in the literature. As a baseline, we make use of the pigeonhole principle and the 01*0-strategy, where the 01*0-strategy can be considered the prior state-of-the-art. The greedy adaptations of the 01*0 schemes reduce the search space by 54.7%, 63.3% and 70.9% for $k = 5$, 6 and 7, respectively. The minU schemes reduce the search space by 56.4%, 67.9% and 75.4% for $k = 5$, 6 and 7, respectively.

Dynamic selection of minU schemes for even k reduces the search space even more (Table 2, last row), by an additional 11.1%, 2.9% and 3.6% for $k = 2$, 4 and 6, respectively.

In conclusion, our results demonstrate that the minU schemes, along with the greedy adaptations, outperform prior state-of-the-art approaches in terms of reducing the search space. This reduction in the number of visited nodes within the search trie translates to significantly improved runtimes.

6.3   Application to Lossless Read Mapping

We benchmark the runtime of these search schemes using our read aligner Columba 1.2. The previous version Columba 1.1 [15] implements a cache-friendly BWT representation and a dynamic partitioning strategy [16], and it relies on bit-parallel edit distance computations and in-text verification. Columba 1.2 can handle arbitrary (valid) search schemes, including the minU schemes with

Table 3. Runtime comparison of state-of-the-art lossless alignment tools, with the exception of BWA in 'mem' mode, which is a lossy alignment algorithm. For the lossless alignment tools, the footnotes mention with which parameters the tools were ran. The Mem. column indicates the peak-RAM usage. The smaller value between brackets indicates the percentage of mapped reads with the lossless aligners.

Tool	Lang.	Mem.	$k = 2$ (90.5%)	$k = 3$ (93.1%)	$k = 4$ (94.8%)	$k = 5$ (95.9%)	$k = 6$ (96.7%)
Columba 1.2[a]	C++	22.9 GB	6.5 ± 0.1 s	12.6 ± 0.1 s	24.0 ± 0.2 s	46.4 ± 4.2 s	74.6 ± 3.7 s
Columba 1.1[b]	C++	21.5 GB	7.5 ± 1.2 s	12.9 ± 0.1 s	27.9 ± 0.2 s	72.9 ± 0.7 s	160.1 ± 6.1 s
BWA[c]	C	3.0 GB	135.9 ± 3.0 s	1473.1 ± 29.5 s	DNC (>3 h)	DNC (>3 h)	DNC (>3 h)
Bwolo	C++	6.7 GB	25.0 ± 1.0 s	63.9 ± 2.0 s	189.2 ± 4.9 s	631.2 ± 14.2 s	3336.2 ± 85.1 s
GEMv3[d]	C	13.3 GB	19.8 ± 2.2 s	37.0 ± 2.7 s	83.4 ± 5.1 s	crash	crash
Yara v0.9.11[e]	C++	4.8 GB	21.6 ± 1.6 s	84.2 ± 5.0 s	542.3 ± 22.6 s	774.8 ± 34.5 s	4666.4 ± 181.0 s
BWA mem (lossy)	C	5.1 GB	31.4 ± 0.5 s (independent of k)				

[a] `-e` $[k]$ `-i 5 -ss multiple /path/to/minU/schemes` for even k
`-e` $[k]$ `-i 5 -ss custom /path/to/minU/scheme` for odd k
[b] `-e` $[k]$ `-i 5 -ss custom /path/to/kuch_k+1_adapted/` for $k \le 4$
`-e` k `-i 5 -ss custom /path/to/01star0/` for $k \ge 5$
[c] `aln -N -n` $[k]$ `-i 0 -l 150 -k` $[k]$
[d] `-t 1 -e` $[k]$ `-s` $[k]$ `--alignment-model edit --mapping-mode complete -M 1000`
[e] `-e` $[k]$ `-s` $[k]$ `-y full -t 1`

dynamic selection. It features a 64-bit mode to handle larger (pan-)genomes and supports outputs in SAM format [12].

We compare Columba to Bwolo [19], GEM [13], Yara [18] and BWA [11] in all-mapping mode. Note that Bwolo does not report the CIGAR string of the alignments whereas all other tools do. For the GEM aligner, not all occurrences could be reported as the tool failed when using the **all** parameter. Therefore, GEM was configured to report at most 1000 occurrences per read. For $k \ge 5$, GEM failed even with this restriction. The results for Columba 1.1 use the best known search schemes prior to this work. These are manual adaptations based on the schemes by Kucherov et al. for $k \le 4$ and the 01*0 seeds for $k \ge 5$.

Table 3 shows the runtimes and peak RAM-usage for different tools and different values of k. Note that Columba is currently not optimized for memory. Both versions of Columba show superior performance in terms of runtime over other lossless aligners. Columba 1.2 outperforms its predecessor for $k = 2, 4, 5$ and 6 and matches it for $k = 3$. For $k = 2$, the reduced runtime can be mainly attributed to the dynamic selection technique as the used search schemes are highly similar. For $k = 3$ the search schemes used by Columba 1.1 and 1.2 are similar, resulting in comparable runtimes. Starting from $k = 4$, we start to see the effects of the newly designed search schemes. Columba 1.2 is 14.0% faster than its predecessor for $k = 4$. For $k = 5$ and $k = 6$ the improvements are even higher, respectively 36.4% and 53.4%, as previously no optimized search schemes were available for these values.

Columba outperforms existing lossless aligners for all values of $k \ge 2$. Among the competing tools, GEM is the fastest, but it cannot handle the large number of occurrences for some reads. Bwolo and Yara require respectively 55 and 78 min to align reads with up to $k = 6$ errors; Columba 1.2 performs this task in only 75 s and is hence approximately $45\times$ faster. BWA in all-mapping mode is outperformed by the tools specifically designed for lossless APM, and it does not finish the alignment of the 100 000 reads for $k \geq 4$ errors in 3 h. The analysis for $k = 1$ is not included as its optimal search scheme is trivial. In earlier work, we found that Yara outperformed Columba for this case, likely due to the overhead of a bidirectional index used in Columba [15].

BWA-mem (which is lossy) does not require specifying a maximum error threshold k and typically reports only a single candidate alignment position per read. The runtime reported for BWA-mem includes the time it takes to read the index structure from disk, which is not the case for Columba 1.2. BWA-mem can handle paired-end reads, a feature not yet present in Columba 1.2. Columba 1.1 outperforms BWA-mem in terms of speed for $k = 2$ and $k = 3$. Moreover, When k is set to 4, Columba 1.2 is over 20% faster than BWA-mem, while the runtime for Columba 1.1 is similar to that of BWA-mem. Even for higher values of k, the runtime of Columba 1.2 is less than three times the runtime of BWA mem. Strikingly, BWA-mem, as a lossy tool, outputs only 100 086 alignment positions, whereas Columba 1.2 outputs respectively 6 to 60 times as many alignment positions, depending on the specific choice of k.

7   Conclusion

We have introduced novel methods for designing efficient search schemes for lossless approximate pattern matching, allowing a larger number of errors than previously possible, up to $k = 13$, filling a critical gap in this field. We presented two novel approaches: a greedy algorithm and an ILP formulation, implemented in Hato, a versatile open source tool capable of crafting search schemes using a combination of these approaches.

Furthermore, we introduced the concept of dynamic selection, tailoring the choice of search scheme to the characteristics of each input read. The reduction in search space achieved through our newly designed search schemes and dynamic selection collectively amounts to 69% for $k = 6$ errors. These ideas are implemented in Columba 1.2, which significantly outperforms existing lossless read aligners.

Our results suggest a narrowing performance gap between lossless and lossy alignment tools. The inclusion of a strata-based search strategy, where k is dynamically selected per read, could result in a read alignment tool with stronger guarantees for optimality. Given the performance advances in lossless approximate pattern matching, and given the fact that most Illumina reads can be aligned with few errors, next-generation lossless mappers need not be slower than state-of-the-art lossy mappers such as Bowtie or BWA.

Acknowledgments. Luca Renders and Lore Depuydt are funded by the Research Foundation - Flanders (FWO), through a PhD Fellowship SB (1SE7822N) and a PhD Fellowship FR (1117322N), respectively.

Appendix

Algorithm 1 Algorithm to greedily adapt a search scheme.

Input: A valid search scheme S for p parts and upto k errors. This scheme is updated during the procedure.
Input: The adapted search scheme.
Generate all error distributions E.
for each error distribution e in E **do**
   Create an empty list e.covering
for each search $\mathcal{S}_x$ in S **do**
   Create empty lists x.covering and x.critical
for each error distribution e in E **do**
   for each search $\mathcal{S}_x$ in S **do**
     if $\mathcal{S}_x$ covers e **then**
       add x to e.covering.
       add e to x.covering.
   if $|e$.covering$| = 1$ **then**
     add e to $e[0]$.critical.
for $i \leftarrow 0$ to $p - 1$ **do**
   Sort the searches in S on decreasing U-string and increasing L-string.
   for each search $\mathcal{S}_x$ in S **do**
     while true **do**
       Decrease the value at $U_x[i]$ by 1.
       if $U_x[i] < 0$ or invalid bounds or not (all e in x.critical are covered by $\mathcal{S}_x$) **then**
         Increase $U_x[i]$ by 1
         Break the while loop
     for all error distributions e in x.covering **do**
       if $\mathcal{S}_x$ does not cover e **then**
         Remove x from e.covering.
         Remove e from x.covering
         if $|e$.covering$| = 1$ **then**
           add e to $e[0]$.critical.
for $i \leftarrow p - 1$ to 0 **do**
   Sort the searches in S on decreasing U-string and increasing L-string.
   for each search $\mathcal{S}_x$ in S **do**
     while true **do**
       Increase the value at $L_x[i]$ by 1.
       if $L_x[i] > k$ or invalid bounds or not (all e in x.critical are covered by $\mathcal{S}_x$) **then**
         Decrease $L_x[i]$ by 1
         Break the while loop
     for all error distributions e in x.covering **do**
       if $\mathcal{S}_x$ does not cover e **then**
         Remove x from e.covering.
         Remove e from x.covering
       if $|e$.covering$| = 1$ **then**
         add e to $e[0]$.critical.

Table 4. The search schemes by Kucherov et al. [8]

	$k = 2$	$k = 3$	$k = 4$
$p = k + 1$	(012, 000, 022) (210, 000, 012) (102, 001, 012)	(0123, 0000, 0133) (1023, 0011, 0133) (2310, 0000, 0133) (3210, 0011, 0133)	(01234, 00000, 02244) (43210, 00000, 01344) (10234, 00133, 01334) (01234, 00133, 01334) (32410, 00011, 01244) (21034, 00013, 01244) (10234, 00124, 01244) (01234, 00034, 00444)
$p = k + 2$	(0123, 0000, 0112) (3210, 0000, 0122) (1230, 0001, 0012) (0123, 0002, 0022)	(01234, 00000, 01233) (12340, 00000, 01223) (23410, 00001, 01133) (34210, 00012, 00333)	(012345, 000000, 012344) (123450, 000000, 012344) (543210, 000001, 012244) (345210, 000012, 011344) (234510, 000023, 011244) (453210, 000133, 003344) (012345, 000333, 003344) (012345, 000044, 002444) (231045, 000124, 002244) (453210, 000044, 001444)

Table 5. The used search schemes by Kianfar et al. [7] and the manual adaptation ("Man$_{Best}$") of the search scheme for $k = 4$ [14].

$k = 2$	$k = 3$	$k = 4$	Man$_{Best}$ $k = 4$
			(012345, 000004, 033344)
(012, 002, 012)	(0123, 0003, 0233)	(01234, 00004, 03344)	(123450, 000000, 022334)
(210, 000, 022)	(1230, 0000, 1233)	(12340, 00000, 22334)	(213450, 011111, 022334)
(120, 011, 012)	(2310, 0022, 0033)	(43210, 00033, 00444)	(321450, 012222, 012334)
			(543210, 000033, 004444)

Table 6. The search schemes based on the pigeonhole principle and the greedy adaptions of these schemes found by using Hato for up to $k = 7$. The left column is the original scheme and the right column is the greedily adpated search scheme.

	Original	Greedily adapted
$k = 2$	(012, 000, 022)	(012, 012, 022)
	(120, 000, 022)	(102, 000, 012)
	(210, 000, 022)	(210, 001, 012)
$k = 3$	(0123, 0000, 0333)	(0123, 0000, 0133)
	(1023, 0000, 0333)	(1230, 0023, 0223)
	(2310, 0000, 0333)	(2310, 0001, 0133)
	(3210, 0000, 0333)	(3210, 0112, 0133)
$k = 4$	(01234, 00000, 04444)	(01234, 01234, 02344)
	(12340, 00000, 04444)	(10234, 00123, 01444)
	(23410, 00000, 04444)	(21034, 00000, 01244)
	(34210, 00000, 04444)	(32104, 00011, 01334)
	(43210, 00000, 04444)	(43210, 00002, 01344)
$k = 5$	(012345, 000000, 055555)	(012345, 000000, 012555)
	(234510, 000000, 055555)	(123450, 000034, 014445)
	(123450, 000000, 055555)	(234510, 000001, 013355)
	(453210, 000000, 055555)	(345210, 002345, 022555)
	(345210, 000000, 055555)	(453210, 000112, 013555)
	(543210, 000000, 055555)	(543210, 011223, 013555)
$k = 6$	(0123456, 0000000, 0666666)	(0123456, 0123456, 0235666)
	(1234560, 0000000, 0666666)	(1023456, 0012345, 0145666)
	(2345610, 0000000, 0666666)	(2103456, 0000012, 0126666)
	(3456210, 0000000, 0666666)	(3210456, 0001123, 0133666)
	(4563210, 0000000, 0666666)	(4321056, 0000234, 0134466)
	(5643210, 0000000, 0666666)	(5432106, 0000000, 0125556)
	(6543210, 0000000, 0666666)	(6543210, 0000001, 0125666)
$k = 7$	(01234567, 00000000, 07777777)	(01234567, 00000000, 01237777)
	(12345670, 00000000, 07777777)	(12345670, 00000012, 01266667)
	(23456710, 00000000, 07777777)	(23456710, 00000001, 01255577)
	(34567210, 00000000, 07777777)	(34567210, 00003456, 01444777)
	(45673210, 00000000, 07777777)	(45673210, 00000123, 01337777)
	(56743210, 00000000, 07777777)	(56743210, 00234567, 02257777)
	(67543210, 00000000, 07777777)	(67543210, 00011234, 01357777)
	(76543210, 00000000, 07777777)	(76543210, 01122345, 01357777)

Table 7. The search schemes based on 01*0 seeds [14,19] and the greedy adaptions of these schemes found by using Hato for up to $k = 7$. The left column is the original scheme and the right column is the greedily adapted search scheme.

	Original	Greedily adapted
$k = 2$	(0123, 0000, 0122) (1230, 0000, 0122) (2310, 0000, 0022)	(0123, 0002, 0122) (1230, 0011, 0112) (2310, 0000, 0022)
$k = 3$	(01234, 00000, 01333) (12340, 00000, 01333) (23410, 00000, 01333) (34210, 00000, 00333)	(01234, 00003, 01233) (12340, 00022, 01223) (23410, 00111, 01133) (34210, 00000, 00333)
$k = 4$	(012345, 000000, 014444) (123450, 000000, 014444) (234510, 000000, 014444) (345210, 000000, 014444) (453210, 000000, 004444)	(012345, 000004, 012444) (123450, 000033, 012334) (234510, 000222, 012244) (345210, 001111, 011444) (453210, 000000, 003444)
$k = 5$	(0123456, 0000000, 0155555) (1234560, 0000000, 0155555) (2345610, 0000000, 0155555) (3456210, 0000000, 0155555) (4563210, 0000000, 0155555) (5643210, 0000000, 0055555)	(0123456, 0000004, 0123555) (1234560, 0000045, 0124445) (2345610, 0000333, 0123355) (3456210, 0002222, 0122555) (4563210, 0011111, 0115555) (5643210, 0000000, 0035555)
$k = 6$	(01234567, 00000000, 01666666) (12345670, 00000000, 01666666) (23456710, 00000000, 01666666) (34567210, 00000000, 01666666) (45673210, 00000000, 01666666) (56743210, 00000000, 01666666) (67543210, 00000000, 00666666)	(01234567, 00000005, 01236666) (12345670, 00000044, 01235556) (23456710, 00000456, 01244666) (34567210, 00003333, 01233666) (45673210, 00022222, 01226666) (56743210, 00111111, 01156666) (67543210, 00000000, 00356666)
$k = 7$	(012345678, 000000000, 017777777) (123456780, 000000000, 017777777) (234567810, 000000000, 017777777) (345678210, 000000000, 017777777) (456783210, 000000000, 017777777) (567843210, 000000000, 017777777) (678543210, 000000000, 017777777) (786543210, 000000000, 007777777)	(012345678, 000000004, 012347777) (123456780, 000000056, 012366667) (234567810, 000000445, 012355577) (345678210, 000004567, 012444777) (456783210, 000033333, 012337777) (567843210, 000222222, 012277777) (678543210, 001111111, 011577777) (786543210, 000000000, 003577777)

Table 8. The greedy adaptations of the search schemes by Kucherov et al. with $p = k + 1$.

$k = 2$	$k = 3$	$k = 4$
(012, 012, 022) (102, 001, 012) (210, 000, 012)	(0123, 0000, 0133) (1023, 0111, 0133) (2310, 0002, 0133) (3210, 0113, 0133)	(01234, 00002, 02244) (01234, 00334, 01334) (01234, 00344, 00444) (10234, 01334, 01334) (10234, 01224, 01244) (21034, 00113, 01244) (32410, 00111, 01244) (43210, 00000, 01344)

Table 9. The minU schemes for $k + 1$ parts found by Hato. For $k = 4$ and $k = 6$, two co-optimal variants are given. For all k, symmetric variants can be created by reverse-mapping the π-strings.

$k = 2$	(012, 011, 022) (102, 000, 012) (210, 002, 012)	
$k = 3$	(0123, 0000, 0133) (1023, 0111, 0133) (2310, 0002, 0133) (3210, 0113, 0133)	
$k = 4$	(01234, 00222, 02244) (12034, 00000, 01244) (21034, 01111, 01244) (34210, 00003, 01444) (43210, 01114, 01444)	(01234, 01114, 01444) (10234, 00003, 01444) (23410, 01111, 02244) (32410, 00000, 01244) (43210, 00222, 01244)
$k = 5$	(012345, 000222, 013555) (102345, 011333, 013555) (231045, 000000, 013355) (321045, 011111, 013355) (453210, 000004, 013555) (543210, 011115, 013555)	
$k = 6$	(0123456, 0022226, 0226666) (1203456, 0111115, 0126666) (2103456, 0000004, 0126666) (3456210, 0000000, 0133666) (4356210, 0111111, 0133666) (5643210, 0002222, 0133666) (6543210, 0113333, 0133666)	(0123456, 0111115, 0126666) (1023456, 0000004, 0126666) (2103456, 0022226, 0226666) (3456210, 0002222, 0133666) (4356210, 0113333, 0133666) (5643210, 0000000, 0133666) (6543210, 0111111, 0133666)
$k = 7$	(01234567, 00000000, 01337777) (10234567, 01111111, 01337777) (23104567, 00022222, 01337777) (32104567, 01133333, 01337777) (45673210, 00000004, 01337777) (54673210, 01111115, 01337777) (67543210, 00022226, 01337777) (76543210, 01133337, 01337777)	

Table 10. The greedy adaptations of the search schemes based on the pigeonhole principle, for $8 \le k \le 9$, found by using Hato.

$k = 8$	$k = 9$
(012345678, 012345678, 023578888) (102345678, 001234567, 014578888) (210345678, 000001234, 012678888) (321045678, 000112345, 013378888) (432105678, 000023456, 013448888) (543210678, 000000012, 012555888) (654321078, 000000123, 012566688) (765432108, 000000000, 012377778) (876543210, 000000001, 012388888)	(0123456789, 0000000000, 0123499999) (1234567890, 0000000012, 0123888889) (2345678910, 0000000001, 0123777799) (3456789210, 0000001234, 0126666999) (4567893210, 0000000123, 0125559999) (5678943210, 0000345678, 0144499999) (6789543210, 0000012345, 0133799999) (7896543210, 0023456789, 0225799999) (8976543210, 0001123456, 0135799999) (9876543210, 0112234567, 0135799999)

Table 11. The greedy adaptations of the search schemes based on the pigeonhole principle, for $10 \leq k \leq 13$, found by using Hato.

	Greedily adapted

```
                  Greedily adapted

        ( 0 1 2 3 4 5 6 7 8 9 10 , 0 1 2 3 4 5 6 7 8 9 10 , 0 2 3 5 7  9 10 10 10 10 10)
        ( 1 0 2 3 4 5 6 7 8 9 10 , 0 0 1 2 3 4 5 6 7 8  9 , 0 1 4 5 7  9 10 10 10 10 10)
        ( 2 1 0 3 4 5 6 7 8 9 10 , 0 0 0 0 0 1 2 3 4 5  6 , 0 1 2 6 7  9 10 10 10 10 10)
        ( 3 2 1 0 4 5 6 7 8 9 10 , 0 0 0 1 1 2 3 4 5 6  7 , 0 1 3 3 7  9 10 10 10 10 10)
k = 10  ( 4 3 2 1 0 5 6 7 8 9 10 , 0 0 0 0 2 3 4 5 6 7  8 , 0 1 3 4 4  9 10 10 10 10 10)
        ( 5 4 3 2 1 0 6 7 8 9 10 , 0 0 0 0 0 0 0 1 2 3  4 , 0 1 2 5 5  5 10 10 10 10 10)
        ( 6 5 4 3 2 1 0 7 8 9 10 , 0 0 0 0 0 0 1 2 3 4  5 , 0 1 2 5 6  6 6 10 10 10 10)
        ( 7 6 5 4 3 2 1 0 8 9 10 , 0 0 0 0 0 0 0 0 1  2 , 0 1 2 3 7  7 7 7 10 10 10)
        ( 8 7 6 5 4 3 2 1 0 9 10 , 0 0 0 0 0 0 0 1 2  3 , 0 1 2 3 8  8 8 8 8 10 10)
        ( 9 8 7 6 5 4 3 2 1 0 10 , 0 0 0 0 0 0 0 0 0  0 , 0 1 2 3 4  9 9 9 9 9 10)
        (10 9 8 7 6 5 4 3 2 1 0  , 0 0 0 0 0 0 0 0 0 0  1 , 0 1 2 3 4 10 10 10 10 10 10)

        ( 0  1  2  3  4  5  6  7  8  9 10 11 , 0 0 0 0 0 0 0 0 0 0  0  0 , 0 1 2 3 4  5 11 11 11 11 11 11)
        ( 1  2  3  4  5  6  7  8  9 10 11  0 , 0 0 0 0 0 0 0 0 0 0  1  2 , 0 1 2 3 4 10 10 10 10 10 10 11)
        ( 2  3  4  5  6  7  8  9 10 11  1  0 , 0 0 0 0 0 0 0 0 0 0  0  1 , 0 1 2 3 4  9 9 9 9 9 9 11)
        ( 3  4  5  6  7  8  9 10 11  2  1  0 , 0 0 0 0 0 0 0 0 1 2  3  4 , 0 1 2 3 8  8 8 8 8 11 11 11)
        ( 4  5  6  7  8  9 10 11  3  2  1  0 , 0 0 0 0 0 0 0 0 0 1  2  3 , 0 1 2 3 7  7 7 11 11 11 11 11)
k = 11  ( 5  6  7  8  9 10 11  4  3  2  1  0 , 0 0 0 0 0 0 1 2 3 4  5  6 , 0 1 2 6 6  6 6 11 11 11 11 11)
        ( 6  7  8  9 10 11  5  4  3  2  1  0 , 0 0 0 0 0 0 0 1 2 3  4  5 , 0 1 2 5 5  5 11 11 11 11 11 11)
        ( 7  8  9 10 11  6  5  4  3  2  1  0 , 0 0 0 0 3 4 5 6 7 8  9 10 , 0 1 4 4 4  9 11 11 11 11 11 11)
        ( 8  9 10 11  7  6  5  4  3  2  1  0 , 0 0 0 0 0 1 2 3 4 5  6  7 , 0 1 3 3 7  9 11 11 11 11 11 11)
        ( 9 10 11  8  7  6  5  4  3  2  1  0 , 0 0 2 3 4 5 6 7 8 9 10 11 , 0 2 2 5 7  9 11 11 11 11 11 11)
        (10 11  9  8  7  6  5  4  3  2  1  0 , 0 0 0 1 1 2 3 4 5 6  7  8 , 0 1 3 5 7  9 11 11 11 11 11 11)
        (11 10  9  8  7  6  5  4  3  2  1  0 , 0 1 1 2 2 3 4 5 6 7  8  9 , 0 1 3 5 7  9 11 11 11 11 11 11)

        ( 0  1  2  3  4  5  6  7  8  9 10 11 12 , 0 1 2 3 4 5 6 7 8 9 10 11 12 , 0 2 3 5 7  9 11 12 12 12 12 12 12)
        ( 1  0  2  3  4  5  6  7  8  9 10 11 12 , 0 0 1 2 3 4 5 6 7 8  9 10 11 , 0 1 4 5 7  9 11 12 12 12 12 12 12)
        ( 2  1  0  3  4  5  6  7  8  9 10 11 12 , 0 0 0 0 0 1 2 3 4 5  6  7  8 , 0 1 2 6 7  9 11 12 12 12 12 12 12)
        ( 3  2  1  0  4  5  6  7  8  9 10 11 12 , 0 0 0 1 1 2 3 4 5 6  7  8  9 , 0 1 3 3 7  9 11 12 12 12 12 12 12)
        ( 4  3  2  1  0  5  6  7  8  9 10 11 12 , 0 0 0 0 2 3 4 5 6 7  8  9 10 , 0 1 3 4 4  9 11 12 12 12 12 12 12)
        ( 5  4  3  2  1  0  6  7  8  9 10 11 12 , 0 0 0 0 0 0 0 1 2 3  4  5  6 , 0 1 2 5 5  5 11 12 12 12 12 12 12)
k = 12  ( 6  5  4  3  2  1  0  7  8  9 10 11 12 , 0 0 0 0 0 0 1 2 3 4  5  6  7 , 0 1 2 5 6  6 6 12 12 12 12 12 12)
        ( 7  6  5  4  3  2  1  0  8  9 10 11 12 , 0 0 0 0 0 0 0 0 1  2  3  4 , 0 1 2 3 7  7 7 7 12 12 12 12 12)
        ( 8  7  6  5  4  3  2  1  0  9 10 11 12 , 0 0 0 0 0 0 0 1 2  3  4  5 , 0 1 2 3 8  8 8 8 8 12 12 12 12)
        ( 9  8  7  6  5  4  3  2  1  0 10 11 12 , 0 0 0 0 0 0 0 0 0  1  2  3 , 0 1 2 3 4  9 9 9 9 9 12 12 12)
        (10  9  8  7  6  5  4  3  2  1  0 11 12 , 0 0 0 0 0 0 0 0 0 0  1  2  3 , 0 1 2 3 4 10 10 10 10 10 10 12 12)
        (11 10  9  8  7  6  5  4  3  2  1  0 12 , 0 0 0 0 0 0 0 0 0 0  0  0  1 , 0 1 2 3 4  5 11 11 11 11 11 11 12)
        (12 11 10  9  8  7  6  5  4  3  2  1  0 , 0 0 0 0 0 0 0 0 0 0  0  0  1 , 0 1 2 3 4  5 12 12 12 12 12 12 12)

        ( 0  1  2  3  4  5  6  7  8  9 10 11 12 13 , 0 0 0 0 0 0 0 0 0 0  0  0  0 , 0 1 2 3 4  5  6 13 13 13 13 13 13 13)
        ( 1  2  3  4  5  6  7  8  9 10 11 12 13  0 , 0 0 0 0 0 0 0 0 0 0  0  1  2 , 0 1 2 3 4  5 12 12 12 12 12 12 12 13)
        ( 2  3  4  5  6  7  8  9 10 11 12 13  1  0 , 0 0 0 0 0 0 0 0 0 0  0  0  1 , 0 1 2 3 4  5 11 11 11 11 11 11 13)
        ( 3  4  5  6  7  8  9 10 11 12 13  2  1  0 , 0 0 0 0 0 0 0 0 0 1  2  3  4 , 0 1 2 3 4 10 10 10 10 10 10 13 13)
        ( 4  5  6  7  8  9 10 11 12 13  3  2  1  0 , 0 0 0 0 0 0 0 0 0 1  2  3 , 0 1 2 3 4  9 9 9 9 9 13 13 13)
        ( 5  6  7  8  9 10 11 12 13  4  3  2  1  0 , 0 0 0 0 0 0 0 1 2 3  4  5  6 , 0 1 2 3 8  8 8 8 8 13 13 13 13)
        ( 6  7  8  9 10 11 12 13  5  4  3  2  1  0 , 0 0 0 0 0 0 0 1 2 3  4  5 , 0 1 2 3 7  7 7 7 13 13 13 13 13)
k = 13  ( 7  8  9 10 11 12 13  6  5  4  3  2  1  0 , 0 0 0 0 0 0 1 2 3 4  5  6  7 , 0 1 2 6 6  6 6 13 13 13 13 13 13)
        ( 8  9 10 11 12 13  7  6  5  4  3  2  1  0 , 0 0 0 0 0 0 0 1 2 3  4  5  6  7 , 0 1 2 5 5  5 11 13 13 13 13 13 13)
        ( 9 10 11 12 13  8  7  6  5  4  3  2  1  0 , 0 0 0 3 4 5 6 7 8 9 10 11 12 , 0 1 4 4 4  9 11 13 13 13 13 13 13)
        (10 11 12 13  9  8  7  6  5  4  3  2  1  0 , 0 0 0 0 1 2 3 4 5 6  7  8  9 , 0 1 3 3 7  9 11 13 13 13 13 13 13)
        (11 12 13 10  9  8  7  6  5  4  3  2  1  0 , 0 0 2 3 4 5 6 7 8 9 10 11 12 13 , 0 2 2 5 7  9 11 13 13 13 13 13 13)
        (12 13 11 10  9  8  7  6  5  4  3  2  1  0 , 0 0 0 1 1 2 3 4 5 6  7  8  9 10 , 0 1 3 5 7  9 11 13 13 13 13 13 13)
        (13 12 11 10  9  8  7  6  5  4  3  2  1  0 , 0 1 1 2 2 3 4 5 6 7  8  9 10 11 , 0 1 3 5 7  9 11 13 13 13 13 13 13)
```

References

1. Alanko, J.N., Slizovskiy, I.B., Lokshtanov, D., Gagie, T., Noyes, N.R., Boucher, C.: Syotti: scalable bait design for DNA enrichment. Bioinformatics **38**(Suppl. 1), i177–i184 (2022). https://doi.org/10.1093/bioinformatics/btac226
2. Altschul, S.F., Gish, W., Miller, W., Myers, E.W., Lipman, D.J.: Basic local alignment search tool. J. Mol. Biol. **215**(3), 403–10 (1990)
3. Claeys, A., Merseburger, P., Staut, J., Marchal, K., den Eynden, J.V.: Benchmark of tools for *in silico* prediction of MHC class I and class II genotypes from NGS data. BMC Genomics **24**, 247 (2023). https://doi.org/10.1186/s12864-023-09351-z
4. Depuydt, L., Renders, L., Abeel, T., Fostier, J.: Pan-genome de Bruijn graph using the bidirectional FM-index. BMC Bioinform. **24**(1), 400 (2023). https://doi.org/10.1186/s12859-023-05531-6
5. Feller, W.: An Introduction to Probability Theory and Its Applications, 3rd edn., vol. 1. Wiley, New York (1968)

6. IBM-ILOG: CPLEX (2022). https://www.ibm.com/docs/en/icos/22.1.1?topic=documentation-introducing-ilog-cplex-optimization-studio-2211. Accessed 2 Jul 2023

7. Kianfar, K., Pockrandt, C., Torkamandi, B., Luo, H., Reinert, K.: FAMOUS: fast approximate string matching using optimum search schemes. CoRR (2017). http://arxiv.org/abs/1711.02035

8. Kucherov, G., Salikhov, K., Tsur, D.: Approximate string matching using a bidirectional index. In: Kulikov, A.S., Kuznetsov, S.O., Pevzner, P. (eds.) CPM 2014. LNCS, vol. 8486, pp. 222–231. Springer, Cham (2014). https://doi.org/10.1007/978-3-319-07566-2_23

9. Lam, T., Li, R., Tam, A., Wong, S., Wu, E., Yiu, S.: High throughput short read alignment via bi-directional BWT. In: IEEE International Conference on Bioinformatics and Biomedicine, December 2009, pp. 31–36 (2009). https://doi.org/10.1109/BIBM.2009.42

10. Langmead, B.: Aligning short sequencing reads with Bowtie. Curr. Protoc. Bioinform. **32**(1), 11–7 (2010)

11. Li, H., Durbin, R.: Fast and accurate short read alignment with Burrows-Wheeler transform. Bioinformatics **25**(14), 1754–1760 (2009). https://doi.org/10.1093/bioinformatics/btp324

12. Li, H., et al.: 1000 genome project data processing subgroup: the sequence alignment/map format and SAMtools. Bioinformatics **25**(16), 2078–2079 (2009)

13. Marco-Sola, S., Sammeth, M., Guigó, R., Ribeca, P.: The GEM mapper: fast, accurate and versatile alignment by filtration. Nat. Meth. **9**(12), 1185–1188 (2012). https://doi.org/10.1028/nmeth.2221

14. Pockrandt, C.M.: Approximate string matching: improving data structures and algorithms. Ph.D. thesis, Freien Universität Berlin (2019). http://dx.doi.org/10.17169/refubium-2185

15. Renders, L., Depuydt, L., Fostier, J.: Approximate pattern matching using search schemes and in-text verification. In: Rojas, I., Valenzuela, O., Rojas, F., Herrera, L.J., Ortuño, F. (eds.) Bioinformatics and Biomedical Engineering, IWBBIO 2022. LNCS, pp. 419–435. Springer, Cham (2022). https://doi.org/10.1007/978-3-031-07802-6_36

16. Renders, L., Marchal, K., Fostier, J.: Dynamic partitioning of search patterns for approximate pattern matching using search schemes. iScience **24**(7), 102687 (2021). https://doi.org/10.1016/j.isci.2021.102687

17. Schneider, V., et al.: Evaluation of GRCh38 and de novo haploid genome assemblies demonstrates the enduring quality of the reference assembly. Genome Res. **27** (2017). https://doi.org/10.1101/gr.213611.116

18. Siragusa, E.: Approximate string matching for high-throughput sequencing. Ph.D. thesis (2015)

19. Vroland, C., Salson, M., Bini, S., Touzet, H.: Approximate search of short patterns with high error rates using the 01*0 lossless seeds. J. Discrete Algorithms **37**, 3–16 (2016). https://doi.org/10.1016/j.jda.2016.03.002

CELL-E: A Text-to-Image Transformer for Protein Image Prediction

Emaad Khwaja[1,2(✉)], Yun S. Song[2,3,4], and Bo Huang[4,5,6(✉)] (iD)

[1] UC Berkeley - UCSF Joint Graduate Program in Bioengineering,
San Francisco, CA 94143, USA
emaad@berkeley.edu

[2] Computer Science Division, UC Berkeley, Berkeley, CA 94720, USA

[3] Department of Statistics, UC Berkeley, Berkeley, CA 94720, USA

[4] Chan Zuckerberg Biohub - San Francisco, San Francisco, CA 94158, USA

[5] Department of Pharmaceutical Chemistry, UCSF, San Francisco,
CA 94143, USA
bo.huang@ucsf.edu

[6] Department of Biochemistry and Biophysics, UCSF, San Francisco, CA 94143, USA

Abstract. Accurately predicting cellular activities of proteins based on their primary amino acid sequences would greatly improve our understanding of the proteome. In this paper, we present CELL-E, a text-to-image transformer model that generates 2D probability density images describing the spatial distribution of proteins within cells. Given an amino acid sequence and a reference image for cell or nucleus morphology, CELL-E predicts a more refined representation of protein localization, as opposed to previous *in silico* methods that rely on pre-defined, discrete class annotations of protein localization to subcellular compartments.

Keywords: text-to-image synthesis · transformers · single-cell imaging · generative models

1 Introduction

In recent years, advancements in sequencing technologies have allowed for the comprehensive cataloging of proteins and their amino acid sequences across a wide range of organisms [10]. Despite this progress, the exact functions and cellular dynamics of many proteins remain unclear. In order to gain a deeper understanding of these proteins, researchers have sought ways to predict their properties, including structure, interactions, subcellular localization, and trafficking patterns, from their amino acid sequences. This type of computational analysis has the potential to shed light on the "dark matters" of the proteome and enable large-scale screening before expensive experimental validation. These tools have numerous applications in biomedical research, such as drug design and therapeutic target discovery [18].

In this study, our focus is on predicting subcellular localization of proteins from their amino acid sequences, which serves as the spatial context for their

© The Author(s), under exclusive license to Springer Nature Switzerland AG 2024
J. Ma (Ed.): RECOMB 2024, LNCS 14758, pp. 185–200, 2024.
https://doi.org/10.1007/978-1-0716-3989-4_12

cellular functions. The localization of a protein to a specific subcellular compartment can be driven by either active transport or passive diffusion in conjunction with specific protein-protein interactions, often involving localization "signals" in the amino acid sequence [4]. In many cases, however, the exact mechanisms for sequence recognition and trafficking are not yet fully understood [9]. For example, there is ongoing debate about the mechanism behind the import of proteins via the nuclear localization sequence (NLS) [16]. Given these challenges, machine learning utilizing existing knowledge of protein localization has become a particularly useful tool.

Although computational prediction of protein subcellular localization from primary amino acid sequences is an active area of research, most works train the model with class annotation of subcellular compartments (e.g., nucleus, plasma membrane, endoplasmic reticulum, etc.) [1] which are available from databases such as UniProt [27]. This approach has two major limitations. First, many proteins are present in different and variable amounts across multiple subcellular compartments. Second, protein localization could be highly heterogeneous and dynamic depending on the cell type and cell state (including cell cycle state). Neither of these two aspects have been captured by existing discrete class annotations. Consequently, machine-learning-based protein localization prediction still has limited applications. Furthermore, to assist mechanistic discoveries, it is highly desirable for the machine learning models to be explainable.

To investigate the relationship between sequence and subcellular localization, we present CELL-E, a text-to-image transformer model which predicts the probability of protein localization on a per-pixel level from a given amino acid sequence and a conditional reference image for the cell or nucleus morphology and location (Fig. 1). It relies on transfer learning via amino acid embeddings from a pre-trained protein language model and two quantized image encoders trained from a live-cell imaging dataset. By generating a two-dimensional probability density function (2D PDF) atop the reference image, CELL-E naturally accounts for multi-compartment localization and the cell type/state information implicitly encoded by the cell morphology. We demonstrate the capability of CELL-E to predict localization of proteins, identify changes in localization due to mutations, and uncover sequence features correlated with the specification of subcellular protein localization.

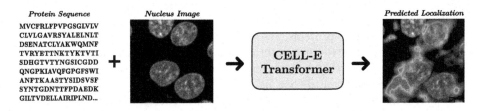

Fig. 1. Given an amino acid sequence and a reference nucleus image, CELL-E makes a prediction of protein localization with respect to the nucleus as a 2D probability density function, shown as heatmap, with color indicating relative confidence for each pixel.

2   Results

2.1   The CELL-E Model

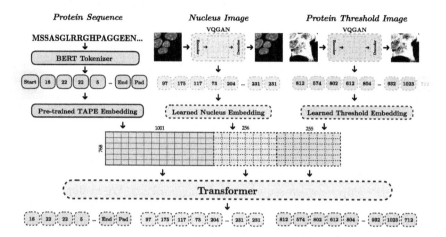

Fig. 2. Graphical depiction of CELL-E. Solid lines correspond to pre-trained components. Gray dashed lines are learned in Phase 1 and 2 (Reference Image and Protein Threshold VQGANs). Black dashed lines correspond to components learned in Phase 3. A start token is prepended to the sequence and the final protein image token is removed. The amino acid sequence embedding from the model is preserved, and embedding spaces for the image tokens are cast in the same depth and concatenated with the amino acid sequence embedding. The transformer is tasked with reproducing the original sequence of tokens (e.g., the input sequence with start token shifted to the right one position). (Color figure online)

CELL-E (Fig. 2) is inspired by the text-to-natural-image generation model of DALL-E [21]. Similar to DALL-E, our model autoregressively learns text and image tokens as a single stream of data. On the other hand, While the goal of general text-to-image models is to produce images with high perceptual strength, they do not necessarily aim for quantitative accuracy [6,20,21]. Therefore, CELL-E was designed with the following considerations:

1. **Transfer learning.** Training CELL-E requires a library of cellular images and corresponding morphological reference images for a large number of proteins. For this purpose, we utilized the recently established OpenCell library [5], which contains a library of 1,311 CRISPR-edited HEK293T human cell lines, each having one target protein fluorescently tagged and imaged by confocal microscopy with accompanying DNA staining as the reference for nuclei morphology. The high image quality and consistency makes OpenCell a good choice as the training and validation dataset. Still, data availability in this domain remains a large obstacle. For example, DALL-E was trained

on 250 million text-images pairs [21], orders of magnitude larger than the OpenCell dataset. Even the largest publicly available dataset with annotated protein images in human cells, Human Protein Atlas (HPA), contains 12,003 unique proteins with just 82,000 immunofluorescence staining and confocal microscopy (ICC-IF) images [28]. Additionally, image captions are often much shorter than full amino acid sequences sequences. CogView and DALL-E relied on text encoding which were only 256 word tokens in length. amino acid sequences can contain upwards of 600 amino acid residues, where any portion could have functional and localization-critical domains [29]. Another difference is NLP utilize dictionaries which contain thousands of possible words, whereas a protein language model only needs to encode at least 20 entries for the canonical amino acids. We utilize transfer learning by incorporating frozen embeddings from a pre-trained protein language model as the input representation of the amino acid text sequence. This approach reduces the number of learned parameters, thereby alleviating the burden for CELL-E to also learn the amino acid sequence space. This allows training to be concentrated on the relationship between sequence and image tokens. We evaluated multiple protein language models and eventually chose the BERT-based model from Rao et. al. [22], which we refer to as the TAPE model, for subsequent work.

2. **Morphological reference.** In our initial efforts, we found that a transformer using just the amino acid tokens and protein image tokens is capable of generating cell-like images from the amino acid sequence alone (Fig. ??). However, quantifying protein localization information in the generated images is challenging. Furthermore, an estimation of a single snapshot of protein localization is not necessarily a quantifiable indication of global behavior. Therefore, in addition to amino acid tokens and protein image tokens, we add a 3rd embedding space to include tokens representing the overall cell morphology from a reference image. The reference image provides the model with information regarding the localization of subcellular structures and compartments. Moreover, cell morphology implicitly provides the cell type and cell state context for CELL-E predictions.

3. **Image model.** Instead of the Vector Quantized Variational Autoencoder (VQVAE) previously used to analyze OpenCell imaging data [14], we chose to use Vector Quantized Generative Adversarial Network (VQGAN) [8] which produces images with comparatively higher spatial frequency. To simplify the task of the protein image VQGAN, we let it predict per-pixel binary representations of protein localization (i.e., a thresholded image). This allows us to use the marginal probabilities predicted for each image token from CELL-E to create a weighted sum on the image tokens. This latent space linear combination is then used to generate a continuous 2D probability density function of protein localization, which resembles a gray-scale image (Fig. 8).

2.2   Performance Evaluation

Figure 3 and Fig. 4 show the CELL-E predictions for several proteins in the validation dataset. High similarities can be seen between the predictions and the ground truth. Even though the reference images only depict the nuclei, which is a limitation of the OpenCell training data, CELL-E can reasonably paint the shape of the cell for cytoplasmic proteins. Interestingly, the case of Mitogen-Activated Protein Kinase 9 (MAPK9) contains a cell in metaphase (top row of Fig. 3). CELL-E correctly predicts the round shape of its distribution around the mitotic chromosomes instead of the more expanded distribution for the adjacent interphase cell. This result suggests that CELL-E can indeed capture cell state information from the morphological reference images.

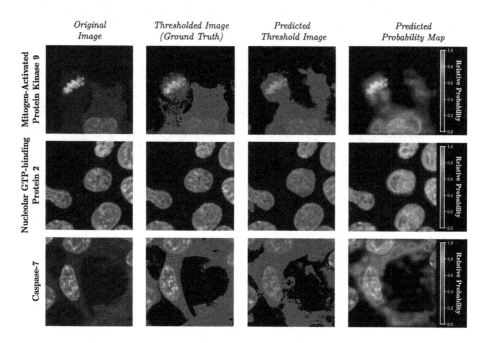

Fig. 3. Prediction results of several types of proteins from the validation set, unseen to the model during training. The nucleus channel is depicted in grayscale, and the protein channel is shown as an overlay in red (Fig. ?? for clarification). The thresholded image (Column 2) is designated "Ground Truth" because those are the types of images exposed to the model during training. The predicted probability map is obtained from a weighted sum of potential image patches and normalized to 1. (Color figure online)

We used several metrics to evaluate the reconstruction performance of CELL-E, summarized in Table 1. Among the metrics, nucleus proportion accuracy measures how close the estimated proportion of pixel intensity within the nucleus is to the ground truth thresholded image. We believe this is the most relevant metric as it is not obscured by small spatial variations and nucleus boundaries can

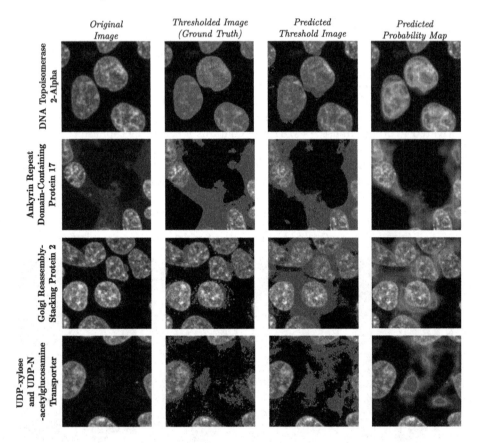

Fig. 4. More prediction results from the validation set. We observe a high degree of spatial awareness from the model, notably in UDP-xylose-acetylglucosamine Transporter, which accurately predicts signal between cell nuclei with high confidence.

be obtained from the reference images. Using these metrics, we performed ablations studies to optimize our model architecture and choice of protein language embedding (not shown because of the page limit).

While CELL-E is not specifically trained as a discrete localization classifier, we also performed naive comparison between CELL-E model and 1D protein localization classifiers MuLoc [12] and Subcons [26] specifically trained with annotated protein localizations. We focused on nuclear classification using a simple classification criteria on CELL-E output, and the results are summarized in Table 2. We observed a relatively high degree of accuracy from this method compared to the task-specific models. CELL-E was a close second for validation set proteins despite not seeing localization annotations during training.

Table 1. Image Accuracy

	Train		Validation	
	CELL-E	VQGAN	CELL-E	VQGAN
Nucleus Proportion Accuracy	0.94 ± 0.05	0.99 ± 0.01	0.81 ± 0.18	0.99 ± 0.01
Predicted Threshold Pixel Accuracy	0.77 ± 0.06	0.87 ± 0.08	0.77 ± 0.05	0.88 ± 0.08
Predicted 2D PDF Pixel Accuracy	0.68 ± 0.10		0.63 ± 0.10	
Structual Similarity Index Measure	0.32 ± 0.21	0.55 ± 0.25	0.25 ± 0.16	0.56 ± 0.25
Inception Score	2.77 ± 0.07	4.17 ± 0.17	2.13 ± 0.07	3.87 ± 0.17
Fréchet Inception Distance	107	15	156	23

Performance is reported as mean ± standard deviation where applicable. The VQGAN columns indicate the value of these metrics evaluated on the ground truth threshold image passed through the protein threshold VQGAN. As CELL-E selects tokens from this VQGAN to produce its outputs, these values represent the best possible performance for our model.

Table 2. Nuclear Localization Prediction Accuracy

VQGAN	Train	Validation
	0.99 ± 0.08	0.99 ± 0.09
CELL-E	$\mathbf{0.89 \pm 0.31}$	0.72 ± 0.45
MuLoc	0.71 ± 0.45	$\mathbf{0.79 \pm 0.41}$
Subcons	0.43 ± 0.49	0.69 ± 0.46

VQGAN indicates the accuracy evaluated on the ground truth threshold image passed through the VQGAN image encoder. As CELL-E selects tokens from this VQGAN to produce its outputs, these values represent the best possible performance for our model.

2.3 Analysis of NLS Using CELL-E

As a first test to show that CELL-E can recognize specific, functional sequence features, we let it predict the images for Green Fluorescent Protein (GFP), which is non-native to human and does not contain known localization signals, as well as GFP appended with two commonly used NLS's KRPAATKKAGQAKKKK from nucleoplasmin [7] and PAAKRVKLD from N-Myc [23]) that drive nuclear localization of a protein. We also appended a randomly generated sequence as a control. A randomly chosen nuclear image from the OpenCell dataset was used as the morphological reference. CELL-E does not localization of GFP (or random sequence + GFP) to a specific subcellular compartment with high confidence, whereas the two NLS-GFP fusions are clearly predicted to be localized within the nucleus (Fig. 5). Therefore, CELL-E has the potential to perform computational insertion screenings for the functional sufficiency of putative localization sequence features.

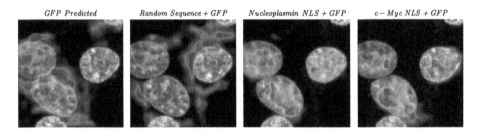

Fig. 5. Predicted localization of GFP and modified-GFP sequences.

Next, we examined whether CELL-E can identify NLS in a protein by computationally performing truncation/deletion studies. For this purpose, we chose DNA Topoisomerase I (TOP1), whose N-terminal intrinsically disordered region (amino acid (aa) 1–199) is essential for its nuclear localization [2]. An experimental study generated a series of deletion mutants for this region and imaged the subcellular localization in HeLa cells when fused to eGFP [17]. To computationally reproduce this study, we fed the exact sequences of the deletion mutants to CELL-E. As shown in Fig. 6, the predictions were largely consistent with the experimental data, recapturing the inability for *aa 1–67* to drive nuclear localization despite containing a putative NLS, as well as the sufficiency of *aa 148–199* as an NLS.

Lastly, we demonstrate a more direct approach than computational insertion or deletion studies to identify putative sequence features responsible for protein localization. Specifically, we split the generated image patches into two groups, one with the target protein being present and the other being absent based on the average pixel intensity within the 16 × 16 image patch. Then, we calculated the difference of attention weights for each amino acid token to contribute to the two groups. Figure 7 highlights the amino acids with higher weights for the "present" group. The highlighted amino acids include the three putative NLSs (Motifs II, III, and IV) in the experimentally verified *aa 148–199* range, as well as part of the new *aa 117–146* NLS identified in [17]. On the other hand, the putative NLS (Motif I) in the experimentally invalidated *aa 1–69* range are not activated. The attention map also suggest that *aa 89–107* (KIKKE) could be another NLS in this protein. We must point out that the calculation of attention map was simply based on a protein being "present" or "not present" in image patches and did not specify "nuclear localization" at all. Therefore, it should be capable of serving as a general approach to discover putative sequence features driving protein localization to a variety of subcellular compartments.

3   Discussion

CELL-E's performance seems to be currently limited by the scope of the Open-Cell dataset, which only accounts for a handful of proteins within a single cell type and imaging modality. As the OpenCell project is an active development,

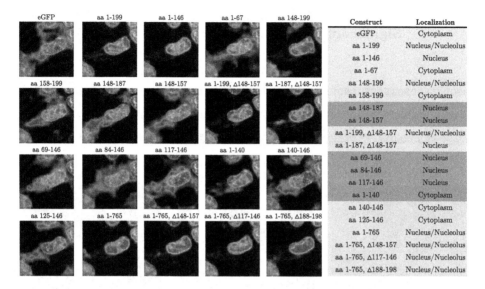

Construct	Localization
eGFP	Cytoplasm
aa 1-199	Nucleus/Nucleolus
aa 1-146	Nucleus
aa 1-67	Cytoplasm
aa 148-199	Nucleus/Nucleolus
aa 158-199	Cytoplasm
aa 148-187	Nucleus
aa 148-157	Nucleus
aa 1-199, Δ148-157	Nucleus/Nucleolus
aa 1-187, Δ148-157	Nucleus
aa 69-146	Nucleus
aa 84-146	Nucleus
aa 117-146	Nucleus
aa 1-140	Cytoplasm
aa 140-146	Cytoplasm
aa 125-146	Cytoplasm
aa 1-765	Nucleus/Nucleolus
aa 1-765, Δ148-157	Nucleus/Nucleolus
aa 1-765, Δ117-146	Nucleus/Nucleolus
aa 1-765, Δ188-198	Nucleus/Nucleolus

Fig. 6. CELL-E's predicted localization (images) of eGFP fusions from [17] and corresponding localization annotations (table) from the original paper. In the table on the right hand side, green indicates agreement between CELL-E and experimental results, while red indicates disagreement. *aa 1-199* contains the entire N-terminus region. *aa 1-146* only contains Motifs I and V. *aa 1-67* only contains Motif-I. *aa 148-199* contains Motif II, III, IV and V.

we expect stronger performance as more data become available. The availability of brightfield (e.g., phase-contrast) images as the morphological reference will also likely improve the prediction of cytoplasmic protein localization compared to using nuclei images. Furthermore, the utility of the model comes in terms of linking embedding spaces of dependent data. One could imagine follow up experiments where rather than images being the prediction, other signatures such as protein mass spec could be predicted. Additionally, other sources of information, such as structural embeddings could be incorporated to bolster CELL-E's capabilities.

4   Methods

We utilized 4×NVIDIA RTX 3090 TURBO 24G GPUs for this study. 2 GPUs were utilized for training VQGANS via distributed training. Only a single GPU is ever used to train CELL-E models. Our computer also contained 2×Intel Xeon Silver and 8×32768 mb 2933 MHz DR×4 Registered ECC DDR4 RAM. We use a multi-phase training approach similar to DALL-E, but our model also uses pre-trained language-model input embeddings for the amino acid text sequences via TAPE:

DNA Topoisomerase I
Significant Tokens for Nuclear Localization

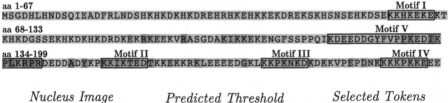

Sequence
N-Terminus

aa 1-67   Motif I
MSGDHLHNDSQIEADFRLNDSHKHKDKHKDREHRHKEHKKEKDREKSKHSNSEHKDSE[KKHKEKE]KT

aa 68-133   Motif V
KHKDGSSEKHKDKHKDRDKEK[R]KEEKV[R]ASGDAKIKKEKENGFSSPPQI[KDEEDDGYFVPPKEDIK]

aa 134-199   Motif II   Motif III   Motif IV
[PLKRPR]DEDDADYKP[KKIKTEDT]KKEKKRKLEEEEDGKL[KKPKNKD]KDKKVPEPDNK[KKKPKKE]EE

Nucleus Image   *Predicted Threshold*   *Selected Tokens*

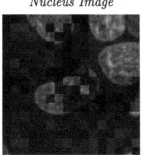      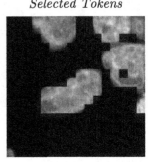

Fig. 7. Attention weights for significant tokens when patches containing a large percentage of protein are selected (bottom-right figure). Previous computationally identified putative NLSs are boxed in black (top figure). These are *aa 59–65* (Motif I, KKHKEKE), *aa 150–156* (Motif II, KKIKTED), *aa 174–180* (Motif III, KKPKNKD), and *aa 192–198* (Motif IV, KKKPKKE). Additionally, the new NLS identified in Mo et al. [17], Motif V (*aa 117–146*), is highlighted.

– **Phase 1** A Vector Quantized-Generative Adversarial Network (VQGAN) [8] is trained to represent a single channel 256×256 nucleus image as a grid comprised of 16 × 16 image tokens, each of which could be one of 512 tokens.
– **Phase 2** A similar VQGAN is trained on images corresponding to binarized versions of protein images. These tokens represent the spatial distribution of the protein.
– **Phase 3** The VQGAN image tokens are concatenated to 1000 amino acid tokens for the autoregressive transformer which models a joint distribution over the amino acids, nucleus image, and protein threshold image tokens.

4.1 Model Specifics

The optimization problem is modelled as maximizing the evidence lower bound (ELBO) [13,24] on a joint likelihood distribution over protein threshold images u, nucleus images x, amino acids y, and tokens z for the protein threshold image:

Theorem 1.

$$p_{\theta,\psi}(u, x, y, z) = p_{\theta}(u \mid x, y, z)p_{\psi}(x, y, z)$$

This is bounded by:

Theorem 2.

$$\ln \, p_{\theta,\psi}(u, x, y) \geq \underset{z \sim q_{\phi}(z|u)}{\mathbb{E}}[\ln \, p_{\theta}(u \mid x, y, z)] - KL(q_{\phi}(x, y, z \mid u), \, p_{\psi}(x, y, z))$$

where q_{ϕ} is the distribution 16×16 image tokens from the VQGAN corresponding to the threshold protein image u, p_{θ} is the distribution over protein threshold generated by the VQGAN given the image tokens, and p_{ψ} indicates the joint distribution over the amino acid, nucleus, and protein threshold tokens within the transformer.

4.2   Nucleus Image Encoder

Training both image VQGANs maximizes ELBO with respect to ϕ and θ. The VQGAN improves upon existing quantized autoencoders by introducing a learned discriminator borrowed from GAN architectures [8]. The Nucleus Image Encoder is a VQGAN which represents 256×256 nucleus reference images as 256 16×16 image patches. The VQGAN codebook size was set to $n = 512$ image patches. The model was trained on random 256×256 crops of 512×512 nuclei images.

4.3   Protein Threshold Image Encoder

The protein threshold image encoder learns a dimension reduced representation of a discrete binary PDF of per-pixel protein location, represented as an image image. We adopt a VQGAN architecture identical to the Nucleus VQGAN. The VQGAN serves to approximate the total set of binarized image patches. While in theory a discrete lookup of each pixel arrangement is possible, this would require $\sim 1.16 \times 10^{77}$ entries, which is computationally infeasible. Furthermore, some distributions of pixels might be so improbable that having a discrete entry would be a waste of space.

Protein images are binarized with respect to a mean-threshold, via:

$$\bar{u}_{i,j} = \begin{cases} 1, & u_{i,j} \geq \mu, \\ 0, & u_{i,j} < \mu, \end{cases}$$

$\forall$ pixels $u \in$ image U of size $i \times j$, where μ is the mean pixel intensity in the image.

The 16×16 image patches learned within the VQGAN codebook therefore correspond to local protein distributions. In Sect. 4.6, we detail how a weighted sum over these binarized image patches is used to determine a final probability density map. The model was trained on random 256×256 crops of 512×512 nuclei images.

4.4   Amino Acid Embedding

For language transformers, it is necessary to learn both input embedding representations of a text vector as well as attention weights between embeddings [30]. In practice, this creates a need for very large datasets [19]. The OpenCell dataset contains 1,311 proteins, while the human body is estimated to contain upwards of 80,000 unique proteins. It is unlikely that such a small slice could account for the large degrees of variability found in nature.

In order to overcome this obstacle, we opted for a transfer learning strategy, where fixed amino acid embeddings from a pre-trained language model exposed to a much larger dataset were utilized. We found the strongest performance came from TAPE embeddings [22]. Utilizing pre-trained embeddings had the two-fold benefit of giving our model a larger degree of protein sequence context, as well as reducing the number of trained model parameters, which allowed us to scale the depth of our network.

We tried training using random initialization for amino acid embeddings, however, we noted overfitting on the validation set image reconstruction and high loss on validation sequences. We also experimented with other types of protein embeddings, including UniRep [3] and ESM1-b [25].

In TAPE embeddings, there are 30 possible codebook values for amino acids within this model, with 25 corresponding to amino acids and 5 corresponding to special tokens (i.e. padding). amino acid sequence length was limited to 1000 amino acids, which is longer than 96% of sequences within the dataset. For amino acid sequences shorter than 1000 amino acids, an end token (if utilized by the language model) was appended, followed by padding tokens. For amino acid sequences longer than 1000 amino acids, we randomly cropped a 1000 length subsection. If the right end of the crop ended before the true end of the amino acid sequence, no end token was applied. A start token is then prepended to all 1000 length sequence. The TAPE model used represents input embeddings as vectors with dimension $n \times 768$, where n is the number of amino acids. The sequence embedding for the TAPE based models therefore had embedding vector sizes of 1001×768. Input amino acids were tokenized and their embeddings were retrieved from the language models. This input embedding is fixed.

4.5   CELL-E Transformer

The transformer (p_ϕ) utilizes an input comprised of amino acid tokens, a 256×256 nucleus image crop, and the 256×256 corresponding protein image threshold crop. In this phase, ϕ and θ are fixed, and a prior over all tokens is learned by maximizing ELBO with respect to ϕ. It is a decoder-only model [15].

The model is trained on a concatenated sequence of text tokens, nucleus image tokens, and protein threshold image tokens, in order. Within the CELL-E transformer, image token embeddings were cast into the same dimensionality as the language model embedding to in order to maintain the larger protein context information, however the embeddings corresponding to the image tokens within this dimension are learned (See Fig. 2).

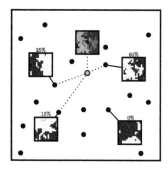

Fig. 8. Simplified example of probability map calculation. Each circle corresponds to an image token within the quantized VQGAN embedding space. Each PDF patch (yellow) is obtained as a weighted sum over all protein threshold image VQGAN codebook vectors. (Color figure online)

4.6   Probability Density Maps

When generating images, the model is provided with the amino acid sequence and nucleus image. The transformer autoregressively predicts the protein-threshold image. In order to select a token, the model outputs logits which contain probability values corresponding to the codebook identity of the next token. The image patch v_i is selected by filtering for the top 25% of tokens and applying top-k sampling with gumbel noise [11].

Ordinarily, the final image is generated by converting the predicted codebook indices of the protein threshold image to the VQGANs decoder. However, to generate the probability density map $\bar{v}$, we include the full range of probability values corresponding to image patches, $p(v_i)$, obtained from the output logits. The values are clipped between 0 and 1 and multiplied by the embedding weights within the VQGAN's decoder, w_i:

Theorem 3.

$$\bar{v} = w \cdot p(v) = \sum_{i=1}^{n} w_i \, p(v_i)$$

This output is normalized and displayed as a heatmap (Fig. 8).

Acknowledgements. B.H. is supported by the National Institutes of Health (R01GM131641). Y.S.S. and B.H. are Chan Zuckerberg Biohub - San Francisco Investigators. Y.S.S. is supported by NIH grant R35-GM134922.

Code availability. Our model is a heavily modified version of an open source text-to-image transformer [31], available via the MIT license (Copyright (c) 2021 Phil Wang). Our code and more detailed descriptions of the training process are available at https://github.com/BoHuangLab/Protein-Localization-Transformer via the MIT license (Copyright (c) 2022 Emaad Khwaja, Yun Song, & Bo Huang).

Author information. E.K. played a key role in the advancement of the approach, carrying out the majority of the coding, designing and conducting a significant number of the experiments, and producing an initial version of the manuscript. The remaining authors also offered consistent input on all aspects of the project, assessed the code, and helped with the final draft of the manuscript.

References

1. Almagro Armenteros, J.J., Sønderby, C.K., Sønderby, S.K., Nielsen, H., Winther, O.: DeepLoc: prediction of protein subcellular localization using deep learning. Bioinformatics **33**(21), 3387–3395 (2017). https://doi.org/10.1093/bioinformatics/btx431, https://doi.org/10.1093/bioinformatics/btx431

2. Alsner, J., Svejstrup, J.Q., Kjeldsen, E., Sørensen, B.S., Westergaard, O.: Identification of an N-terminal domain of eukaryotic DNA topoisomerase I dispensable for catalytic activity but essential for in vivo function. J. Biol. Chem. **267**(18), 12408–12411 (1992)

3. Bepler, T., Berger, B.: Learning the protein language: Evolution, structure, and function. Cell Syst. **12**(6), 654–669.e3 (2021). https://doi.org/10.1016/j.cels.2021.05.017, https://linkinghub.elsevier.com/retrieve/pii/S2405471221002039

4. Chacinska, A., Koehler, C.M., Milenkovic, D., Lithgow, T., Pfanner, N.: Importing mitochondrial proteins: machineries and mechanisms. Cell **138**(4), 628–644 (2009). https://doi.org/10.1016/j.cell.2009.08.005, https://www.sciencedirect.com/science/article/pii/S0092867409009672

5. Cho, N.H., et al.: OpenCell: endogenous tagging for the cartography of human cellular organization. Science (New York, N.Y.) **375**(6585), eabi6983 (2022). https://doi.org/10.1126/science.abi6983

6. Ding, M., et al.: CogView: mastering Text-to-Image Generation via Transformers (Nov 2021). arXiv:2105.13290, http://arxiv.org/abs/2105.13290

7. Dingwall, C., Robbins, J., Dilworth, S.M., Roberts, B., Richardson, W.D.: The Nucleoplasmin nuclear location sequence is larger and MoreComplex than that of SV-40 large T antigen. J. Cell Biol. **107**, 9 (1988)

8. Esser, P., Rombach, R., Ommer, B.: Taming transformers for high-resolution image synthesis (Jun 2021). arXiv:2012.09841, http://arxiv.org/abs/2012.09841

9. Gardy, J.L., Brinkman, F.S.L.: Methods for predicting bacterial protein subcellular localization. Nat. Rev. Microbiol. **4**(10), 741–751 (Oct 2006). https://doi.org/10.1038/nrmicro1494, https://www.nature.com/articles/nrmicro1494, bandiera_abtest: a Cg_type: Nature Research Journals Number: 10 Primary_atype: Reviews Publisher: Nature Publishing Group

10. Hu, T., Chitnis, N., Monos, D., Dinh, A.: Next-generation sequencing technologies: an overview. Hum. Immunol. **82**(11), 801–811 (Nov 2021). https://doi.org/10.1016/j.humimm.2021.02.012, https://www.sciencedirect.com/science/article/pii/S0198885921000628

11. Jang, E., Gu, S., Poole, B.: Categorical reparameterization with gumbel-softmax (Aug 2017). arXiv:1611.01144, http://arxiv.org/abs/1611.01144

12. Jiang, Y., Wang, D., Wang, W., Xu, D.: Computational methods for protein localization prediction. Comput. Struct. Biotechnol. J. **19**, 5834–5844 (Jan 2021). https://doi.org/10.1016/j.csbj.2021.10.023, https://www.sciencedirect.com/science/article/pii/S2001037021004451

13. Kingma, D.P., Welling, M.: Auto-encoding variational Bayes (May 2014). arXiv:1312.6114, http://arxiv.org/abs/1312.6114

14. Kobayashi, H., Cheveralls, K.C., Leonetti, M.D., Royer, L.A.: Self-supervised deep learning encodes high-resolution features of protein subcellular localization. preprint, Cell Biol. (Mar 2021). https://doi.org/10.1101/2021.03.29.437595, http://biorxiv.org/lookup/doi/10.1101/2021.03.29.437595

15. Liu, P.J., et al.: Generating Wikipedia by summarizing long sequences (Apr 2023). https://openreview.net/forum?id=Hyg0vbWC-

16. Lu, J., et al.: Types of nuclear localization signals and mechanisms of protein import into the nucleus. Cell Commun. Signal. **19**(1), 60 (May 2021). https://doi.org/10.1186/s12964-021-00741-y, https://doi.org/10.1186/s12964-021-00741-y

17. Mo, Y.Y., Wang, C., Beck, W.T.: A novel nuclear localization signal in human DNA Topoisomerase I*. J. Biol. Chem. **275**(52), 41107–41113 (Dec 2000). https://doi.org/10.1074/jbc.M003135200, https://www.sciencedirect.com/science/article/pii/S0021925819556435

18. Palma, C.A., Cecchini, M., Samorì, P.: Predicting self-assembly: from empirism to determinism. Chemical Society Reviews **41**(10), 3713–3730 (Apr 2012). https://doi.org/10.1039/C2CS15302E, https://pubs.rsc.org/en/content/articlelanding/2012/cs/c2cs15302e, publisher: The Royal Society of Chemistry

19. Popel, M., Bojar, O.: Training tips for the transformer model. Prague Bull. Math. Linguist. **110**(1), 43–70 (Apr 2018). https://doi.org/10.2478/pralin-2018-0002, http://content.sciendo.com/view/journals/pralin/110/1/article-p43.xml

20. Ramesh, A., Dhariwal, P., Nichol, A., Chu, C., Chen, M.: Hierarchical text-conditional image generation with CLIP Latents (Apr 2022). https://doi.org/10.48550/arXiv.2204.06125, http://arxiv.org/abs/2204.06125, arXiv:2204.06125

21. Ramesh, A., et al.: Zero-shot text-to-image generation (Feb 2021). arXiv:2102.12092, http://arxiv.org/abs/2102.12092

22. Rao, R., et al.: evaluating protein transfer learning with TAPE (Jun 2019). arXiv:1906.08230, http://arxiv.org/abs/1906.08230

23. Ray, M., Tang, R., Jiang, Z., Rotello, V.M.: Quantitative tracking of protein trafficking to the nucleus using cytosolic protein delivery by nanoparticle-stabilized nanocapsules. Bioconjug. Chem. **26**(6), 1004–1007 (2015). https://doi.org/10.1021/acs.bioconjchem.5b00141

24. Rezende, D.J., Mohamed, S., Wierstra, D.: Stochastic backpropagation and approximate inference in deep generative models. In: Proceedings of the 31st International Conference on Machine Learning, pp. 1278–1286. PMLR (Jun 2014). https://proceedings.mlr.press/v32/rezende14.html, iSSN: 1938-7228

25. Rives, A., et al.: Biological structure and function emerge from scaling unsupervised learning to 250 million protein sequences. Proc. Nat. Acad. Sci. **118**(15), e2016239118 (2021). https://doi.org/10.1073/pnas.2016239118, https://www.pnas.org/doi/abs/10.1073/pnas.2016239118, _eprint: https://www.pnas.org/doi/pdf/10.1073/pnas.2016239118

26. Salvatore, M., Warholm, P., Shu, N., Basile, W., Elofsson, A.: SubCons: a new ensemble method for improved human subcellular localization predictions. Bioinformatics **33**(16), 2464–2470 (2017). https://doi.org/10.1093/bioinformatics/btx219

27. The UniProt Consortium: UniProt: the universal protein knowledgebase. Nucleic Acids Res. **45**(D1), D158–D169 (2017). https://doi.org/10.1093/nar/gkw1099

28. Thul, P.J., Lindskog, C.: The human protein atlas: a spatial map of the human proteome. Protein Sci.: Publ. Protein Soc. **27**(1), 233–244 (2018). https://doi.org/10.1002/pro.3307

29. Tiessen, A., Pérez-Rodríguez, P., Delaye-Arredondo, L.J.: Mathematical modeling and comparison of protein size distribution in different plant, animal, fungal and microbial species reveals a negative correlation between protein size and protein number, thus providing insight into the evolution of proteomes. BMC Res. Notes 5(1), 1–23 (Dec 2012). https://doi.org/10.1186/1756-0500-5-85, https://bmcresnotes.biomedcentral.com/articles/10.1186/1756-0500-5-85

30. Vaswani, A., et al.: Attention is all you need. In: Guyon, I., Luxburg, U.V., Bengio, S., Wallach, H., Fergus, R., Vishwanathan, S., Garnett, R. (eds.) Advances in Neural Information Processing Systems, vol. 30. Curran Associates, Inc. (2017). https://proceedings.neurips.cc/paper/2017/file/3f5ee243547dee91fbd053c1c4a845aa-Paper.pdf

31. Wang, P.: DALL-E in Pytorch (Apr 2022). https://github.com/lucidrains/DALLE-pytorch, original-date: 2021-01-05T20:35:16Z

A Scalable Optimization Algorithm for Solving the Beltway and Turnpike Problems with Uncertain Measurements

C. S. Elder[1], Minh Hoang[2], Mohsen Ferdosi[1], and Carl Kingsford[1]

[1] Ray and Stephanie Lane Computational Biology Department,
Carnegie Mellon University, Pittsburgh, PA 15213, USA
{celder,mferdosi,carlk}@cs.cmu.edu
[2] Computer Science Department, Carnegie Mellon University,
Pittsburgh, PA 15213, USA
qhoang@andrew.cmu.edu

Abstract. The BELTWAY and TURNPIKE problems entail the reconstruction of circular and linear one-dimensional point sets from unordered pairwise distances. These problems arise in computational biology when the measurements provide distances but do not associate those distances with the entities that gave rise to them. Such applications include molecular structure determination, genomic sequencing, tandem mass spectrometry, and molecular error-correcting codes (since sequencing and mass spec technologies can give lengths or weights, usually without connecting them to endpoints). Practical algorithms for TURNPIKE are known when the distance measurements are accurate, but both problems become strongly NP-hard under any level of measurement uncertainty. This is problematic since all known applications experience some degree of uncertainty from uncontrollable factors. Traditional algorithms cope with this complexity by exploring a much larger solution space, leading to exponential blowup in terms of both time and space. To alleviate both issues, we propose a novel alternating optimization algorithm that can scale to large, uncertain distance sets with as many as 100,000 points. This algorithm is space and time-efficient, with each step running in $\mathcal{O}(m \log(m))$ time and requiring only $\mathcal{O}(\sqrt{m})$ working space for a distance set of size m. Evaluations of this approach on synthetic and partial digest data showcase improved accuracy and scalability in the presence of uncertain, duplicated, and missing distances. Our implementation of the algorithm is available at https://github.com/Kingsford-Group/turnpikesolvermm.

Keywords: Inverse Problem · Optimization · Beltway · Turnpike

1 Introduction

The TURNPIKE problem is to reconstruct n unknown points on a line from all $\binom{n}{2}$ pairwise distances between them provided without labels. The BELTWAY problem is a variant where the points lie on a circle instead of a line. These problems

© The Author(s), under exclusive license to Springer Nature Switzerland AG 2024
J. Ma (Ed.): RECOMB 2024, LNCS 14758, pp. 201–216, 2024.
https://doi.org/10.1007/978-1-0716-3989-4_13

arise frequently in computational biology applications when the measurement (e.g. mass spectrometry or sequencing) provides distances but does not associate those distances with the entities that gave rise to them. In the tandem mass spec application, for example, when sequencing an unknown peptide $a_1 a_2 \ldots a_n$, the "points" are the weights of the fragments $a_i, a_i a_{i+1}, a_i a_{i+1} a_{i+2}, \ldots$ — reconstructing those points would suggest the identity of each amino acid a_i via its weight. However, the MS/MS measurement provides the weights of every fragment $a_i \ldots a_j$ (which can be treated as "distances" between points i and j) without associating that measurement with i or j. Various heuristics for this problem are applied to structure estimation of biomolecules [13], *de novo* sequencing of linear and cyclic peptides [9,17], and reconstructing DNA sequences from their partially digested fragments [20,22]. Some versions of the problem provide additional labeling information and reduced distance subsets, such as the labeled partial digest problem that separates the endpoint distances from the all-pairs distance set and the simplified partial digest problem [4] that returns only a subset of the distances. Other variants of the TURNPIKE problem are applied to quantum phase estimation [26] and molecular error-correcting codes used for databases [11].

The EXACT TURNPIKE variant of the problem, where all distances are observed without error, can be solved exactly via a backtracking algorithm that alternates between placing the largest remaining distance and matching derived and ground truth distances [21]. While there exist pathological cases for which it incurs exponential runtimes [25], this algorithm is generally efficient in practice with an expected run time of $\mathcal{O}(n^2 \log n)$ for random instances [20]. Various extensions to the backtracking algorithm have been proposed to improve both expected and worst case runtimes, including a variant based on breadth-first search [1], that are empirically faster. One extension efficiently solves known pathological instances [18]. In contrast, algorithms for BELTWAY are not efficient, with a worst case runtime of $\mathcal{O}(n^n \log n)$ that is often realized in practice [9]. Other approaches to TURNPIKE include a fixed-parameter tractable algorithm that works by factoring a polynomial and scales with the largest distance in the set [14]. Regrettably, this approach is highly susceptible to numerical precision errors [15]. This restricts its practical applicability whenever floating point arithmetic is used. A semidefinite relaxation also exists that is able to solve some instances but is known to be numerically unstable and suffer from runtimes far exceeding the backtracking algorithm in practice [13].

When the distance measurements are uncertain, we have the NOISY TURNPIKE and NOISY BELTWAY problems, which are both strongly NP-complete as demonstrated by a reduction from the three-partition problem [6]. Skiena et al. modified the backtracking approach to use intervals instead of points to accommodate measurement uncertainty [20], but these modifications lead to the consideration of exponentially many paths, limiting the algorithm's efficiency and practical applicability [13]. Pandurangan et al. assumed that the partial digestion results from both ends of the double stranded DNA sample are observed [19]. Fomin et al. performed the equivalent modifications for NOISY BELTWAY and reduce the running time by removing redundant measurements, but as with the exact case, only very small NOISY BELTWAY instances can be solved with this algorithm [10]. More recently, Huang et al. model both the NOISY TURNPIKE and NOISY BELTWAY problems as probabilistic inference of the point assignments using discrete bins that quantize the input domain [13]. In this approach, the bin size is set to be smaller than the smallest distance, and hence it was assumed that no bin can contain more than one point. However, this only holds true when the observation error is sufficiently small in magnitude relative to the smallest distances. As such, the accuracy of this algorithm deteriorates in noisier instances. In addition, it also struggles to efficiently solve larger problem instances, with $n > 500$ out of reach at present.

In Sect. 2, we propose a novel approach to solving the NOISY TURNPIKE and NOISY BELTWAY problems using a bilevel optimization scheme that alternates between estimating the point-distance correspondence and recovering the original point set given this assignment. Our formulation's non-convex optimization landscape contains many saddle points and local optima. We accommodate for this by introducing a divide-and-conquer step to recursively correct small-scale mistakes that lead to low-quality solutions. Our algorithm runs in time $\mathcal{O}(n^2 \log n)$ for each step, with time dominated by a low-cost sorting step.

In Sect. 3, we empirically demonstrate the performance of our Minorization-Maximization algorithm (MM) in various synthetic and realistic biological settings, such as the partial digestion task [13]. Our algorithm arrives at highly accurate solutions even in extremely noisy observation conditions. We also demonstrate that the proposed algorithm runs more efficiently than previous approaches and empirically matches our theoretical runtime expectation. Most notably, the proposed algorithm can efficiently process partial digestion instances with up to a hundred thousand digested fragments, which is realistically on the scale of a whole genome and has never been achieved by previous methods. Moreover, we provide an extension of the method in Appendix C [8] to problem variants that provide additional labeling information and reduced distance sets. In summary, this algorithm advances the capacity to address both the NOISY TURNPIKE and NOISY BELTWAY problems, and thereby improves the accuracy and scalability of various biological tasks that make use of these formulations.

2 Method

2.1 Problem Setting

Let $m = n(n-1)/2$ and $D \in \mathbb{R}^m$ be a vector of pairwise distances between n points. We denote the ground truth vector containing the points to be recovered as $z \in \mathbb{R}^n$. Without loss of generality, we assume that $z_1 \leq \cdots \leq z_n$, $\sum_{k=1}^{n} z_k = 0$, and $\|z\|_2 = 1$; that is, the unknown points are named in sorted order, centered around zero, and have unit norm. These assumptions do not fundamentally change the problem, but are nonetheless important as they prevent trivial non-uniqueness. The first and second assumptions hold because the distance set is invariant to translation and permutation of the points, allowing us to look for a centered, sorted solution vector z. The third assumption follows because we can construct a scaled distance set $\bar{D} = \sqrt{n}\,\|D\|_2^{-1} D$ from the original distances that generates $\bar{z} = z/\|z\|_2$, using the fact that z is centered:

$$\|D\|_2^2 = \sum_{i \leq j}^n (z_j - z_i)^2 = n\|z\|_2^2 + \sum_{i,j}^n z_i z_j = n\|z\|_2^2 + \left(\sum_{k=0}^n z_k\right)^2 = n\|z\|_2^2 \,.$$

Let $\mathcal{Z}$ be the set of vectors in $\mathbb{R}^n$ that satisfy all three assumptions above (treating dimensions of vectors in $\mathcal{Z}$ as the point locations), and let $\mathcal{S}_m$ denote the set of all permutation matrices of m items. We use TURNPIKE to refer to both the EXACT TURNPIKE and NOISY TURNPIKE variants, when statements apply to both. The EXACT TURNPIKE problem is formalized as finding a vector $\hat{z} \in \mathcal{Z}$ such that $Q\hat{z} = PD$ for some $P \in \mathcal{S}_m$, and where $Q \in \mathbb{R}^{m \times n}$ is a fixed incidence matrix defined as follows. Each row in Q corresponds to a pair of indices $j > i$. For convenience, we let the function $\alpha(i,j)$ map the index pair (i,j) to its (arbitrary) row index in Q. The incidence matrix Q is constructed such that $Q_{\alpha(i,j),j} = 1$ and $Q_{\alpha(i,j),i} = -1$ are the only non-zero entries in $Q_{\alpha(i,j)}$. It follows that $Q_{\alpha(i,j)}\hat{z} = \hat{z}_j - \hat{z}_i$, and $Q\hat{z}$ contains all the pairwise distances generated by $\hat{z}$. Furthermore, if $\hat{z}$ recovers the ground truth z, then $Q\hat{z}$ must also be a permutation of D, which explains the role of P in the objective above. In the NOISY TURNPIKE case, which is the focus of this paper, exact recovery is not possible in general due to the corrupted observations. Therefore, the objective can be written in the form of an optimization task:

$$\hat{z} = \underset{z' \in \mathcal{Z}}{\operatorname{argmax}} \ \max_{P \in \mathcal{S}_m} \ \langle Qz', PD \rangle, \tag{1}$$

where $\langle \cdot, \cdot \rangle$ denotes the inner product of two vectors. This is equivalent to minimizing the ℓ_2 distance between Qz' and PD because the norm of P, Q and D are constant, z' is normalized based on our previous assumptions, and optimality in the exact case will take place when $Qz' = PD$.

2.2   Minorization-Maximization Scheme for Solving Turnpike

We first observe that Eq. (1) is bilinear because fixing either P or z reduces the problem to a linear function. This motivates a bilevel minorization-maximization (MM) scheme [23] to optimize this objective. In particular, we relax our objective into two alternating subproblems. At iteration $t + 1$, for $t > 0$, the first subproblem fixes an estimation z^t and solves for

$$P_t = \underset{P \in S_m}{\operatorname{argmax}} \ \langle Qz^t, PD \rangle, \tag{2}$$

which has a closed-form solution, as shown in Proposition 1 below. This closed form is a variant of the rearrangement inequality [12] used in Lemma 1.

Lemma 1. *Let* $y = \langle y_1, y_2, \dots, y_n \rangle \in \mathbb{R}^n$ *such that* $y_1 \leq y_2 \leq \dots \leq y_n$. *The objective* $\underset{P \in \mathcal{S}_m}{\operatorname{argmax}} \ \langle Px, y \rangle$ *is solved by* P_x *such that* $P_x x$ *is in sorted order.*

Algorithm 1. Minorization-Maximization (MM)

Input: Distance vector D, initial estimate z^0, tolerance $\epsilon > 0$
1: $t \leftarrow 0$
2: $D \leftarrow D^\uparrow$ $\triangleright$ Replace D with its sorted equivalent $D^\uparrow$
3: **while not** converged **do**
4:      $P_t \leftarrow \Pi_{Qz^t}^\top$ $\triangleright$ Calculate and sort Qz^t using Alg. 2
5:      $z^{t+1} \leftarrow Q^\top P_t D$ $\triangleright$ Estimate the next point vector
6:      $t \leftarrow t+1$
7:      converged $\leftarrow \|z^{t+1} - z^t\|_2 < \epsilon$
8: **end while**
9: **return** unit(z^t)

Proof. Let $P \in \mathcal{S}_m$ be a non-sorting permutation, meaning there exist indices $i < j$ where $(Px)_i > (Px)_j$. Notice that transposing elements i and j increases the objective because

$$((Px)_j - (Px)_i)(y_j - y_i) \leq 0 \implies (Px)_j y_j + (Px)_i y_i \leq (Px)_i y_j + (Px)_j y_i.$$

Thus the permutation that first applies P then transposes elements i and j is no worse than P. Iterating this argument leads to a sorting permutation that is also no worse than P. As the initial permutation was arbitrary, this shows that there exists a globally maximizing permutation that sorts x. To finish the proof, notice that any two sorting permutations P_1 and P_2 must have the same objective value since sortedness implies $P_1 x = P_2 x$.   □

Proposition 1. *Let $\Pi^\top$ be a permutation that puts Qz into sorted order. The permutation Π is a globally maximizing solution to Eq. (2).*

Proof. Without loss of generality, we assume that D is sorted as a preprocessing step to the NOISY TURNPIKE problem. We can rewrite the expression in Eq. (2) as $\langle Qz^t, PD \rangle = \langle P^\top(Qz^t), D \rangle$. By Lemma 1, any permutation $\Pi^\top$ that sorts Qz must be a global maximizer of the right-hand side. Notice the transpose Π is the equivalent solution on the left-hand side, proving the claim.   □

On the other hand, the second subproblem fixes an estimation for P_t, which is the closed-form solution derived above, and solves for:

$$z^{t+1} = \operatorname*{argmax}_{\hat{z} \in \mathcal{Z}} \langle Q\hat{z}, P_t D \rangle \equiv \operatorname*{argmax}_{\hat{z} \in \mathcal{Z}} \langle \hat{z}, Q^\top P_t D \rangle . \tag{3}$$

Since the inner product of two vectors is maximized when they are parallel and $\|\hat{z}\|_2 = 1$ by assumption, the maximum objective value is obtained when $\hat{z} = \mathrm{unit}(Q^\top P_t D)$, where unit$(\cdot)$ scales a vector to unit norm.

As objectives (2) and (3) have closed-form solutions, they motivate a practical bilevel optimization routine described in Algorithm 1. Note that the unit projection does not affect the permutation in the next iteration, so we omit it until the vector is returned. We avoid storing both the incidence matrix and intermediate distance vector by using implicit matrix multiplication and a problem-specific matching algorithm, Algorithm 2. The runtime of the optimization inner loop is derived in Proposition 2. In the same proposition, we also derive a memory efficient implementation that avoids storing intermediate values during optimization.

Lemma 2. *The priority queue in Algorithm 2 uses z^t interval order, i.e., $(i,j) \leq (i',j') \iff (z^t[j] - z^t[i]) \leq (z^t[j'] - z^t[i'])$. This ordering satisfies $i \leq i'$, $j' \leq j$ and implies $(i,j) \leq (i',j')$ when z^t is sorted.*

Proof. For $i \leq i'$ and $j' \leq j$, we have $z^t[i] \leq z^t[i']$ and $z^t[j'] \leq z^t[j]$, which implies that $z^t[j'] - z^t[i'] \leq z^t[j] - z^t[i]$. This is the definition of $(i',j') \leq (i,j)$. $\square$

Proposition 2. *Upon termination of Algorithm 2, the vector z^{t+1} contains $Q^\top \Pi_{Qz^t}^\top D$. Moreover, the algorithm runs in $O(n^2 \log n)$ time and uses only $\mathcal{O}(n)$ nonnegative integers for non-constant storage, where n is the number of points.*

Proof. We first prove that the priority queue pops the tth smallest distance during iteration t. To that end, we define the sequences $I^k = (k, k+t)_{t=1}^{n-1}$. We note that the sequences $I^1, \ldots, I^{n-1}$ partition the $\binom{n}{2}$ possible intervals. Lemma 2 establishes that these chains are in interval sorted order, and thus implies Algorithm 2 produces the smallest unseen interval at each iteration. This holds because the queue holds the smallest element from each sequence, and we add the next one until each sequence has been exhausted.

By the discussion above, during iteration t, (i,j) is the (potentially non-unique) t^{th} smallest interval. Thus the sorting permutation will send interval (i,j) to index t, and its transpose (i.e., inverse) will send index t to interval (i,j), implying $D[t]$ will be used as the (i,j) distance. When multiplying by $Q^\top$, the (i,j) distance entry contributes only to the ith and j^{th} points. Specifically, the (i,j) entry is subtracted from $z^{t+1}[i]$ and added to $z^{t+1}[j]$, which is immediately performed in Algorithm 2's loop. Thus the algorithm terminates with $z^{t+1} = Q^\top P_t D$ since we initially zero it out and accumulate all the entries that contribute to it.

The algorithm performs $\mathcal{O}(n \log n)$ work before the main loop, which takes $\mathcal{O}(n^2 \log n)$ time because the priority queue takes $\mathcal{O}(\log n)$ time per iteration using standard implementations. This is unaffected by the constant-time interval comparison function. The priority queue uses the only non-constant memory, as it needs to store $\mathcal{O}(n)$ non-negative integers for the intervals. $\square$

Proposition 3. *The outer loop of Algorithm 1 terminates within a finite number of steps. The inner-loop takes $\mathcal{O}(n^2 \log n)$ time and $\mathcal{O}(n)$ non-constant storage.*

Proof. For the first claim, notice that the sorting permutation in each iteration fully decides the point vector that is produced in the next step, meaning the set of possible output vectors is finite. We also know that the permutation and point vector must improve the objective at each step. This means the algorithm cannot continue to make progress indefinitely and will terminate when $z^t = z^{t+1}$.

For the second claim, notice that steps 4 and 5 take $O(n^2 \log n)$ time and need only $\mathcal{O}(n)$ non-negative integers of non-constant storage by the result of Proposition 2. We only need to keep two n-dimensional floating point vectors to calculate step 7. □

In practice, we observed that Algorithm 1 converges quickly but is prone to becoming trapped in local maxima. To prevent this, we further propose a divide-and-conquer heuristic formally described in Algorithm 3. In particular, after each pass of Algorithm 1, we partition the estimation $\hat{z}$ into non-overlapping subsets $\hat{z}_l$ and $\hat{z}_r$. In our implementation, the median is used to form the partitions, but any rule works with this framework. No matter the choice, this segments the distance set D into three portions: (a) D_{ll} contains the distances among points in $\hat{z}_l$; (b) D_{rr} contains the distances among points in $\hat{z}_r$; and (c) D_{lr} contains the distances between pairs of points respectively in $\hat{z}_l$ and $\hat{z}_r$. Even though we do not have the ground truth assignment of the point-distance correspondence, we can use the estimated permutation matrix P to perform this segmentation.

Intuitively, if $\hat{z}$ and P are the optimal TURNPIKE solution, then subsequent applications of Algorithm 1 on (z_l, D_{ll}) and (z_r, D_{rr}) will not alter this solution. Otherwise, the recursive sub-routines will likely not get trapped in the same local maxima as the parent routine and will serve as a self-correcting mechanism for Algorithm 1 by returning the adjusted permutations P_l and P_r. At this point, we can adjust $\hat{z}_l$ and $\hat{z}_r$ by solving the following regression tasks:

$$\hat{z}_l^+ = \underset{z_l'}{\operatorname{argmin}} \; \|Q_l z_l' - P_l D_{ll}\| \quad \text{and} \quad \hat{z}_r^+ = \underset{z_r'}{\operatorname{argmin}} \; \|Q_r z_r' - P_r D_{rr}\|,$$

where Q_l and Q_r are the respective incidence submatrices corresponding to $\hat{z}_l$ and $\hat{z}_r$. To avoid storing the incidence matrices, we can use any matrix-free solver such as the conjugate gradient method [24] (see Alg. 4 in Appendix A [8] for the matrix-free oracles). As the adjusted estimation $\hat{z}^+ = (\hat{z}_l^+, \hat{z}_r^+)$ breaks away from potential local maxima, this routine is repeated until convergence, as described in Algorithm 3 below. We provide a visualization of how this improves solutions in Appendix B [8].

Remark. An alternative approach (which will be compared against our method in Sect. 3) to solving Eq. (1) applies Birkhoff's theorem [3], which states that the polytope $\mathcal{B}_m$ of $m \times m$ doubly stochastic matrices is the convex hull of $\mathcal{S}_m$. This motivates a relaxation of Eq. (1) to optimize for P on $\mathcal{B}_m$:

$$\hat{z} = \underset{z' \in \mathcal{Z}}{\operatorname{argmin}} \; \underset{P \in \mathcal{B}_m}{\max} \; \langle Qz', PD \rangle, \tag{4}$$

which allows for a differentiable permutation learning framework that combines (a) stochastic gradient descent over the space of square matrices; and (b) projection onto $\mathcal{B}_m$ with the Sinkhorn operator [16]. In the case of the TURNPIKE and NOISY TURNPIKE problems, this approach requires the algorithm to optimize an $m \times m$ matrix, which holds an infeasibly large $\Theta(n^4)$ entries. We refer to this alternative as the "gradient descent" method in the results below.

Algorithm 2. $Q^\top$ applied to matched D

Input: m-Distance vector D; n-Point vectors z^t, z^{t+1}

1: $z^{t+1}[:] \leftarrow 0$ ▷ Zero out the vector
2: $z^t \leftarrow \text{sort}(z^t)$ ▷ Sort the incoming point vector
3: frontier ← Min-Interval-Priority-Queue(n, z^t) ▷ z^t interval order, n interval
    allocation
4: **for** $i \in [1, \ldots, n-1]$ **do**
5:     enqueue(frontier, $(i, i+1)$)
6: **end for**
7: **for** $t \in [1, \ldots, m]$ **do**
8:     $(i, j) \leftarrow$ Min-Pop(frontier)
9:     $z^{t+1}[i] \leftarrow z^{t+1}[i] - D[t]$
10:    $z^{t+1}[j] \leftarrow z^{t+1}[j] + D[t]$
11:    **if** $j < n$ **then**
12:        enqueue(frontier, $(i, j+1)$)
13:    **end if**
14: **end for**

1: **procedure** INTERVAL-COMPARE$(z, (i_1, j_1), (i_2, j_2))$
2:     ▷ Interval comparison function based on z
3:     **return** $(z[j_1] - z[i_1]) \leq (z[j_2] - z[i_2])$
4: **end procedure**

2.3   Extension to Other Variants

In the BELTWAY problem, we are given $n(n-1)$ unlabeled arc lengths (distances) between n points $p_1, \ldots, p_n$ on a circle. Note that we receive double the number of distances as in the Turnpike case because there are two different arcs between any two points (i.e., clockwise and counter-clockwise). The BELTWAY problem can be solved within our framework (Sect. 2.2) with minor modifications. We also extend our method to a general variant of the TURNPIKE problem that handles both labeled and missing distances. This extension captures the labeled partial digest problem [19] and simplified partial digest problem [4]. We refer to Appendix C [8] for the details of these extensions.

2.4   Initializer Sampling

The choice of an initializer for Algorithm 3 plays a critical role in achieving good convergence and overall performance. A well-chosen initializer can lead to faster convergence, improved stability, and a more accurate solution. Here, we consider three practical initializing schemes. The first scheme samples a random Gaussian vector and sorts it. Though efficient to implement, this scheme is unlikely to produce a good initializer if the ground set exhibits pathological features such as having spread-out point clusters. On the other hand, if the points are well-spread, this scheme often finds a close starting point. The second scheme provides a random permutation P_0 to the sub-problem in Eq. (2) and sets z^0 as its closed-form solution. This incorporates the combinatorial nature of TURN-PIKE and potentially encourages more diverse exploration of the solution space.

Algorithm 3. Minorization-Maximization Divide-and-Conquer (MMDQ)

Input: Distance vector D, initial estimate z^0, tolerance ϵ
1: $D \leftarrow D^\uparrow$ ▷ Replace D with its sorted equivalent $D^\uparrow$
2: $t \leftarrow 0$
3: **while not** converged **do**
4:       $z^{t+1}, P_{t+1} \leftarrow \text{MM}(D, z^t, \epsilon)$ ▷ Alg. 1
5:       $z_l, z_r \leftarrow \text{PARTITION}(z^{t+1})$ ▷ as described above
6:       $D_{ll}, D_{rr}, D_{lr} \leftarrow \text{SEGMENT}(z_l, z_r, D, P_{t+1})$ ▷ as above
7:       $P_l, \_ \leftarrow \text{MMDQ}(D_{ll}, z_l, \epsilon)$ ▷ recursive call on left set
8:       $P_r, \_ \leftarrow \text{MMDQ}(D_{rr}, z_r, \epsilon)$ ▷ recursive call on right set
9:       $z^{t+1} \leftarrow$ solve Eq. (4)   ▷ "consensus" point set
10:      $t \leftarrow t + 1$
11:      converged $\leftarrow \|z^{t+1} - z^t\| < \epsilon$
12: **end while**
13: **return** P_t, z^t

Nevertheless, selecting random permutations does not guarantee proximity to the optimal solution or even proximity to a valid distance permutation. The final scheme is a greedy-search method inspired by the classical backtracking approach [20]. That is, we sequentially fit the largest distance in D onto a line segment configuration (i.e., placing a new point to the left or to the right end of the segment based on this distance). However, unlike the original formulation—which uses backtracking to find the optimal placement—we make greedy choices to generate an initializer that will be polished with our algorithm afterwards, thus avoiding potentially exponential runtime.

3   Empirical Results

Experimental Design. We assessed the performance of our proposed algorithm on the Turnpike, Beltway, and Labeled Partial Digest problems. As a baseline, we used synthetic data to validate our proposed algorithm's performance on uncertain measurements and compared it to the backtracking method [20], the distribution matching method [13], and our projected gradient descent baseline using the Gumbel-Sinkhorn relaxation [16]. To evaluate the performance of our method in genome reconstruction, we conducted a series of experiments that simulated the reconstruction of a DNA sequence from fragments generated by enzymes. All experiments were implemented in Python 3.10 using a C++20 library implementing the algorithm integrated with Python using PyBind11 and conducted on a computer equipped with 1.0 TB of RAM, two Intel Xeon E5-2699A v4 CPUs, and a GTX 3080 GPU.

Synthetic Data. Synthetic datasets were generated by sampling n points on the real line from three distributions: the Cauchy distribution, the standard normal distribution, and the uniform distribution on $[0, 1]$. The uniform distribution was chosen to align with the setting explored by Huang et al. [13]. The normal distribution was chosen to generate point sets with tightly-clustered points. The Cauchy distribution was selected to generate point sets with varying scales, i.e., sets where some points are much larger than others. This is important to test since outlying values often pose a challenge for ℓ_2 optimization methods [5].

We examined sample sizes ranging from 50 to 2,000 points (in increments of 50) and three additional large sample sizes of 5,000, 10,000, and 100,000 to demonstrate the method's scalability. To simulate measurement uncertainty of magnitude $\epsilon = 10^{-k}$ for integer $k \in [1, 12]$, we added a Gaussian noise vector $g \sim \mathcal{N}(0, \epsilon \mathbf{I})$ to the given vector of pairwise distances [7]. We rounded the distance to zero when the amount of uncertainty exceeded the magnitude of the distance, which simulates missing distances. We predicted the points for each set of distribution, size, and uncertainty for 10 independent test cases. We run each algorithm 10 times and output the best estimate, which we quantified with the ℓ_2 distance between the estimated and uncertain distance sets (the algorithms are deterministic, but the choice of initializer is random as described above). We recorded the mean absolute error (MAE) and mean squared error (MSE) between the estimated and ground point sets. The MAE is a continuous alternative to the binning distance [13] and is more suitable for our method since we do not explicitly assign points to bins. Since the distribution matching method produces bins as its output, we use the midpoint of each bin as the predicted point.

Study of Different Initialization Schemes. We investigated the three initialization strategies (Sect. 2.4) to select one for subsequent experiments. We boosted the Gaussian point vector and permutation point vector initializer by drawing n distinct samples that were scored by solving Problem 2 for each and taking the maximum value. The sample with the maximum score from each strategy was used as the initializer. We used the Gaussian initializer as the starting point for the greedy-search initializer. We tested the strategies across all settings described previously. Figure 1 shows the cosine distances between the estimated and uncertain distance vectors. Among the three approaches, the permutation strategy exhibited the worst similarity scores, with an average magnitude 13 times larger than that of the greedy-search strategy. The Gaussian strategy demonstrated an average error magnitude that was 8 times larger than the greedy-search initialization.

A better initial score does not necessarily guarantee a better reconstruction after optimization. To assess the efficacy of each initializer, we analyzed whether lower pre-optimization errors translated to reduced post-optimization errors. The cosine distance after optimization is also shown in Fig. 1. The permutation initialization had the highest errors and the greedy-search approach had the lowest errors, which is consistent with the pre-optimization cosine distance. We used the greedy-search initializer for our experiments since it exhibited the lowest post-optimization distance. The greedy-search strategy's lower error comes at a computational cost. Table 1 shows the median runtime for the greedy-search initializer, Gaussian initializer, and optimization loop across a representative set of problem sizes. For all sizes, the greedy-search initialization takes more time than running the optimization, whereas the Gaussian initialization strategy runs in

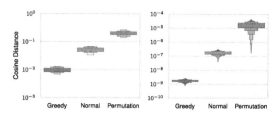

Fig. 1. Cosine distances between estimated distance vectors ($\hat{D}$) and ground distance vectors (D), before (left) and after (right) MM optimization under three different initialization schemes.

Table 1. Median runtimes (in seconds) for the MM optimizer (Opt.), Gaussian and Greedy initializations over different sample sizes.

Points	Opt.	Gauss.	Greedy
100	0.40	0.54	0.23
500	8.40	2.54	17.56
1000	16.49	4.63	36.49
1500	25.39	7.53	55.72
2000	42.38	18.53	84.06

an order of magnitude less time than the optimization. This is due to the inherently serial nature of the greedy-search initializer, which requires all previous steps to be considered first. This is in contrast to the optimization loop, which has a runtime dominated by sorting, which is parallelized.

Evaluating Noisy Turnpike Solutions on Synthetic Instances. We tested how accurately the MM (Sect. 2.2), backtracking, distribution matching [13], and gradient descent methods were able to reconstruct point sets. Table 2 shows the median MAE normalized by the uncertainty for a representative set of problem sizes and uncertainties. Each method had 1 h to solve each instance, with the exception of 10,000 and 100,000 point instances, which were given 90 and 6,000 min respectively. The backtracking method was able to solve instances with 1,000 or fewer points, but exhibited larger errors than our method. The gradient descent method solved all instances with 500 or fewer points with residual error that ranged between 10 and 1,000 times higher than the MM approach. The distribution matching method performed similarly to our method but could not

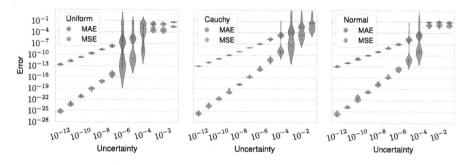

Fig. 2. Mean absolute error (blue) and mean squared error (orange) between the estimated and ground vectors across all levels of measurement uncertainty for Uniform, Cauchy and Normal data distributions. (Color figure online)

scale past 100 points. Our method was able to solve instances with 2,000 points with a median MAE that is 10 times lower than the uncertainty level up to a magnitude of 10^{-4}, after which the scaling becomes distribution dependent.

Table 2. Median MAE normalized by the magnitude of measurement uncertainty ϵ across different point set sizes and uncertainties. We compare our method (MM), distribution matching (DM), backtracking (BT), and gradient descent (GD) approaches. A dash indicates that a method did not finish solving any instances of this size due to either memory or runtime constraints.

$n/100$	10^{-6}				10^{-5}				10^{-4}			
	MM	DM	BT	GD	MM	DM	BT	GD	MM	DM	BT	GD
1	0.2	0.49	26.4	1270	0.19	0.51	26.6	186	2.09	0.68	56.7	1.54
2	0.1	—	26.4	462	0.14	—	26.5	39	1.54	—	55.7	5.72
5	0.11	—	36.4	312	0.09	—	31.5	40	0.94	—	34.7	3.08
10	0.06	—	36.4	—	0.04	—	36.5	—	0.08	—	36.7	—
50	0.08	—	—	—	0.08	—	—	—	0.86	—	—	—
100	0.08	—	—	—	0.11	—	—	—	0.82	—	—	—
1000	0.12	—	—	—	0.08	—	—	—	0.11	—	—	—

Table 3. Normalized MAE for 5 sizes and 4 uncertainty levels using the MM and gradient descent (GD) algorithms on simulated partial digestions of a cDNA.

n	MM (10^{-7})	GD (10^{-7})	MM (10^{-6})	GD (10^{-6})	MM (10^{-5})	GD (10^{-5})	MM (10^{-4})	GD (10^{-4})
10	0.148	0.087	0.159	0.096	0.168	0.145	0.232	0.284
15	0.157	0.072	0.150	0.078	0.140	0.160	0.202	0.274
20	0.214	0.031	0.186	0.032	0.123	0.068	0.224	0.231
38	0.113	0.043	0.128	0.094	0.135	0.112	0.178	0.243
54	0.101	0.053	0.102	0.078	0.186	0.203	0.146	0.581

Figure 2 shows our method's MAE and MSE over all settings plotted with respect to the magnitude of uncertainty. We observed that uncertainty in the distances correlated with reconstruction error, but the MAE is an order of magnitude lower than the uncertainty on average when the uncertainty is 10^{-4} or less. Instance size also affects the method's error scaling. As the sample size varied between 50 and 100,000 points, the median MAE shown in Table 2 demonstrates a downward trend for fixed error rates. This suggests the method scales at least as well as it does on small point sets as the number of points grows. This is because the distance measurement linear system is highly overdetermined, which makes it resilient to uncertainty [24]. Last, we report the mean and standard deviation of the runtimes of different solvers in Table 5. The MM mean runtime was lowest across all point sizes and MM is the only method that successfully solved the 5,000, 10,000, and 100,000 point instances.

Table 4. Normalized MAE for 10 sizes and 4 uncertainty magnitudes using the MM and gradient descent (GD) algorithms on simulated partial digestions of a linear genome. A dash indicates that the algorithm did not finish due to memory constraints or runtime constraints.

n	MM (10^{-7})	GD (10^{-7})	MM (10^{-6})	GD (10^{-6})	MM (10^{-5})	GD (10^{-5})	MM (10^{-4})	GD (10^{-4})
10	0.152	2.31×10^6	0.148	1.54×10^5	0.163	1.70×10^4	0.142	1.34×10^3
64	0.213	1.89×10^5	0.219	6.42×10^4	0.220	1.87×10^3	0.232	4.20×10^2
142	0.358	8.22×10^5	0.359	3.44×10^4	0.357	9.28×10^3	0.365	6.12×10^2
183	0.282	1.28×10^6	0.268	1.75×10^5	0.288	9.37×10^3	0.290	1.34×10^3
530	0.071	—	0.070	—	0.080	—	0.066	—
959	0.119	—	0.121	—	0.125	—	0.139	—
1209	0.119	—	0.132	—	0.127	—	0.115	—
1451	0.059	—	0.061	—	0.043	—	0.072	—
2669	0.048	—	0.039	—	0.050	—	0.048	—

Table 5. Runtime (in seconds) across point sizes for various Turnpike solvers.

$n/100$	MM	DM	BT	GD
1	0.8 ± 3.9	1680.3 ± 32.1	2.8 ± 10.2	16.3 ± 0.4
2	21.2 ± 13.0	—	$53. \pm 32.3$	114.9 ± 0.5
5	204.3 ± 74.4	—	304.9 ± 20.3	4366.6 ± 8.6
10	552.3 ± 112.4	—	1052.5 ± 50.9	—
50	1992.1 ± 51.2	—	—	—
100	3543.8 ± 712.3	—	—	—
1000	5912.3 ± 52.4	—	—	—

Partial Digestion Experiments. We tested the effectiveness of our algorithms for reconstructing genomes via data generated by an enzyme that digests DNA into fragments at restriction sites [2]. The fragment lengths give the distances between all restriction sites, which are at unknown positions. The genome is assembled from the fragments after inferring the restriction site locations from the distances, a process equivalent to solving the TURNPIKE problem for linear genomes and the BELTWAY problem for circular genomes [13]. We simulated partial digestion instances to test our algorithms. For TURNPIKE instances, we used the human X chromosome's centromere, and for BELTWAY instances, we used the full genome of the bacteria *Carsonella ruddii*. In both cases, we used 15-base-long enzymes and simulated the digestion process by sampling the DNA sequence such that each restriction site occurred between 10 and 500 times. We obtained digested DNA fragments by splitting the sequence at all of its occurrences. We added a signed Poisson random vector to simulate when enzymes cut too many or too few bases, both frequent occurrences in practice [6].

The TURNPIKE experiments were performed with our method and the gradient descent baseline due to runtime constraints. The BELTWAY experiments were performed with our algorithm and the distribution matching algorithm, as they are the only ones designed for uncertain BELTWAY instances. Table 4 shows normalized MAE for the TURNPIKE experiments on instances with 10–2,669 fragments. Our method recovered fragment locations with an MAE that scaled linearly to the uncertainty present in the measurements, performing orders of magnitude better than the gradient descent baseline. Table 3 shows normalized MAE for the BELTWAY experiments, which were performed on instances with 10–54 fragments. Our method performed competitively with the gradient descent approach.

Labeled Partial Digestion Experiment. Pandurangan et al. [19] performed a labeled partial digestion problem (LPDP) recovery experiment using the restriction sites of the enzyme HindIII on the bacteriophage λ. For each distance d, they simulated relative uncertainty of order $r \in [0, 1]$ by replacing d with a uniformly sampled integer in $[(1 - r)\,d, (1 + r)\,d]$. They varied r between 0% and 5% to mimic experimental settings, where 2% to 5% is expected.

Each experiment was repeated 100 times. A success is reported when the recovered distances were within the relative uncertainty of the ground truth set. We repeated this experiment using our base algorithm (MM) and our partition-update formulation (PMM) given in Appendix C [8]. Our base algorithm does not use additional labeling information. The results are shown in Table 6. We observe that our method performs competitively without additional labels and further improves when it is provided with the labels. All instances ran in less than 1 s across all uncertainty levels and across all solvers.

Table 6. Recovery success rate of our base solver (MM), our partition solver (PMM), and Pandurangan et al.'s solver [19] at various relative error levels.

r	MM	PMM	LPDP
0%	100%	100%	100%
1%	99%	99%	98%
2%	96%	97%	96%
3%	95%	96%	94%
4%	92%	94%	91%
5%	89%	92%	87%

4   Conclusion

NOISY BELTWAY and NOISY TURNPIKE are NP-hard problems that aim to recover a set of one-dimensional points based on a corrupted pairwise distances. These problems find application in widespread biological contexts. We introduced a novel optimization formulation and an alternating algorithm built from sorting and implicit matrix multiplication. This leads to an asymptotic runtime of $\mathcal{O}(n^2 \log n)$ time per iteration with $\mathcal{O}(n)$ auxiliary memory. To escape low-quality local optima, we introduced a divide-and-conquer step to fix common errors. We performed large-scale experiments with approximately 25 billion distances (equivalent to 100,000 points) to showcase the efficiency of our method. In contrast, previous methods are infeasible with as few as 125,000 distances (equivalent to 500 points). We also demonstrated the method's robustness and scalability in a variety of challenging situations, including large-scale uncertainty and distance duplication. Our algorithm efficiently solves large distance sets with realistic levels of uncertainty, opening up new avenues of research into biological applications of TURNPIKE and computational geometry problems.

Acknowledgements. This work was supported in part by the US National Science Foundation [DBI-1937540, III-2232121], the US National Institutes of Health [R01HG012470] and by the generosity of Eric and Wendy Schmidt by recommendation of the Schmidt Futures program. Disclosure of interests: C.K. is a co-founder of Ocean Genomics, Inc.

References

1. Abbas, M.M., Bahig, H.M.: A fast exact sequential algorithm for the partial digest problem. BMC Bioinform. **17**(19), 510 (2016)
2. Alizadeh, F., Karp, R.M., Weisser, D.K., Zweig, G.: Physical mapping of chromosomes using unique probes. J. Comput. Biol. **2**(2), 159–184 (1995)
3. Birkhoff, G.: Three observations on linear algebra. Univ. Nac. Tacuman, Rev. Ser. A **5**, 147–151 (1946)
4. Blazewicz, J., Burke, E., Kasprzak, M., Kovalev, A., Kovalyov, M.: Simplified partial digest problem: enumerative and dynamic programming algorithms. IEEE/ACM Trans. Comput. Biol. Bioinf. **4**, 668–680 (2007)
5. Boyd, S., Boyd, S.P., Vandenberghe, L.: Convex Optimization. Cambridge University Press, Cambridge (2004)
6. Cieliebak, M., Eidenbenz, S.: Measurement errors make the partial digest problem NP-hard. In: Farach-Colton, M. (ed.) LATIN 2004. LNCS, vol. 2976, pp. 379–390. Springer, Heidelberg (2004). https://doi.org/10.1007/978-3-540-24698-5_42
7. Dokmanic, I., Parhizkar, R., Ranieri, J., Vetterli, M.: Euclidean Distance Matrices: essential theory, algorithms, and applications. IEEE Signal Process. Mag. **32**(6), 12–30 (2015)
8. Elder, C.S., Hoang, M., Ferdosi, M., Kingsford, C.: A scalable optimization algorithm for solving the beltway and turnpike problems with uncertain measurements. bioRxiv (2024)
9. Fomin, E.: Reconstruction of sequence from its circular partial sums for cyclopeptide sequencing problem. J. Bioinform. Comput. Biol. **13**(1), 1540008 (2015)
10. Fomin, E.: A simple approach to the reconstruction of a set of points from the multiset of pairwise distances in n^2 steps for the sequencing problem: III. Noise inputs for the beltway case. J. Comput. Biol. **26**(1), 68–75 (2019)
11. Gabrys, R., Pattabiraman, S., Milenkovic, O.: Mass error-correction codes for polymer-based data storage. In: 2020 IEEE International Symposium on Information Theory (ISIT), pp. 25–30, June 2020. ISSN 2157-8117
12. Hardy, G.H., Littlewood, J.E., Pólya, G.: Inequalities. Cambridge University Press, Cambridge (1952)
13. Huang, S., Dokmanić, I.: Reconstructing point sets from distance distributions. IEEE Trans. Signal Process. **69**, 1811–1827 (2021)
14. Lemke, P., Skiena, S.S., Smith, W.D.: Reconstructing sets from interpoint distances. In: Aronov, B., Basu, S., Pach, J., Sharir, M. (eds.) Discrete and Computational Geometry: The Goodman-Pollack Festschrift. Algorithms and Combinatorics, pp. 597–631. Springer, Heidelberg (2003). https://doi.org/10.1007/978-3-642-55566-4_27

15. Lenstra, A.K., Lenstra, H.W., Lovász, L.: Factoring polynomials with rational coefficients. Math. Ann. **261**(4), 515–534 (1982)
16. Mena, G., Snoek, J., Linderman, S., Belanger, D.: Learning latent permutations with Gumbel-Sinkhorn networks. In: International Conference on Learning Representation, vol. 2018 (2018)
17. Mohimani, H., et al.: Multiplex de novo sequencing of peptide antibiotics. J. Comput. Biol. **18**(11), 1371–1381 (2011)
18. Nadimi, R., Fathabadi, H.S., Ganjtabesh, M.: A fast algorithm for the partial digest problem. Jpn. J. Ind. Appl. Math. **28**, 315–325 (2011)
19. Pandurangan, G., Ramesh, H.: The restriction mapping problem revisited. J. Comput. Syst. Sci. **65**(3), 526–544 (2002)
20. Skiena, S.S., Sundaram, G.: A partial digest approach to restriction site mapping. In: Proceedings. International Conference on Intelligent Systems for Molecular Biology, vol. 1, pp. 362–370 (1993)
21. Skiena, S.S., Smith, W.D., Lemke, P.: Reconstructing sets from interpoint distances (extended abstract). In: Proceedings of the Sixth Annual Symposium on Computational Geometry, SCG 1990, pp. 332–339, New York, NY, USA, May 1990. Association for Computing Machinery (1990)
22. Smith, H.O., Birnstiel, M.L.: A simple method for DNA restriction site mapping. Nucleic Acids Res. **3**(9), 2387–2398 (1976)
23. Sun, Y., Babu, P., Palomar, D.P.: Majorization-minimization algorithms in signal processing, communications, and machine learning. IEEE Trans. Signal Process. **65**(3), 794–816 (2017)
24. Wendland, H.: Numerical Linear Algebra: An Introduction. Cambridge University Press, Cambridge (2017)
25. Zhang, Z.: An exponential example for a partial digest mapping algorithm. J. Comput. Biol. **1**(3), 235–239 (1994)
26. Zintchenko, I., Wiebe, N.: Randomized gap and amplitude estimation. Phys. Rev. A **93**(6), 62306 (2016)

Overcoming Observation Bias for Cancer Progression Modeling

Rudolf Schill[1]([✉]), Maren Klever[3], Andreas Lösch[2], Y. Linda Hu[2],
Stefan Vocht[2], Kevin Rupp[1], Lars Grasedyck[3], Rainer Spang[2],
and Niko Beerenwinkel[1]

[1] Department of Biosystems Science and Engineering, ETH Zürich, Basel,
Switzerland
{Rudolf.Schill,Niko.Beerenwinkel}@bsse.ethz.ch
[2] Department of Statistical Bioinformatics, University of Regensburg, Regensburg,
Germany
[3] Institute for Geometry and Applied Mathematics, RWTH Aachen, Aachen,
Germany

Abstract. Cancers evolve by accumulating genetic alterations, such as mutations and copy number changes. The chronological order of these events is important for understanding the disease, but not directly observable from cross-sectional genomic data. Cancer progression models (CPMs), such as Mutual Hazard Networks (MHNs), reconstruct the progression dynamics of tumors by learning a network of causal interactions between genetic events from their co-occurrence patterns. However, current CPMs fail to include effects of genetic events on the observation of the tumor itself and assume that observation occurs independently of all genetic events. Since a dataset contains by definition only tumors at their moment of observation, neglecting any causal effects on this event leads to the "conditioning on a collider" bias: Events that make the tumor more likely to be observed appear anti-correlated, which results in spurious suppressive effects or masks promoting effects among genetic events. Here, we extend MHNs by modeling effects from genetic progression events on the observation event, thereby correcting for the collider bias. We derive an efficient tensor formula for the likelihood function and learn two models on somatic mutation datasets from the MSK-IMPACT study. In colon adenocarcinoma, we find a strong effect on observation by mutations in TP53, and in lung adenocarcinoma by mutations in EGFR. Compared to classical MHNs, this explains away many spurious suppressive interactions and uncovers several promoting effects.

The data, code, and results are available at https://github.com/cbg-ethz/ObservationMHN.

Keywords: Cancer progression model · Selection bias · Collider bias

---

Supplementary Information The online version contains supplementary material available at https://doi.org/10.1007/978-1-0716-3989-4_14.

1   Introduction

Cancer progression models (CPMs) aim to describe and reproduce the evolutionary development of a healthy tissue into a malignant tumor, driven by a series of genetic (or epigenetic) events such as mutations or copy number alterations [4]. While these events occur randomly due to cellular replication errors, their establishment in the tumor cell population is not entirely random. It depends on the selective advantage they confer in the given environment and the genetic background [37]. Fixation of a genetic alteration in the tumor is often enabled or suppressed by previous events, making some chronological sequences and patterns of events more likely than others [43].

For instance, an initial mutation might promote tumor growth until it is starved for oxygen, whereupon subsequent mutations become beneficial that facilitate blood vessel formation. Access to blood vessels in turn sets the stage for further events culminating in metastasis. Conversely, some events can also suppress one another. This can result, e.g., from synthetic lethality, where some events aid the tumor cell individually but become fatal when they occur together. Or, events may target genes in the same regulatory pathway; whichever event occurs first disrupts the whole pathway, reducing selective pressure on the other event.

Such interactions between events are still poorly characterized, and learning them from data is the goal of CPMs. The challenge lies in the inherent limitations of available data. Datasets with many patients typically provide only bulk genotypes and do not resolve clonal structures. Most datasets are also cross-sectional: They provide a snapshot of many different tumors at a single time point each, but do not track tumors over multiple stages of their evolution.

While we do not know the time at which a tumor was observed relative to the start of its progression, it is also not entirely random: Tumors are usually detected rather late in this process, such that most data comes from later stages of the progression. Up to this point, the tumor has already grown, undergone changes and accumulated events. Some of these events have actually caused the tumor to grow. Thus, our ability to observe and study tumors depends on the events that occurred before we could detect the tumor. This dependence introduces a systematic bias to cancer progression models, which we resolve in this paper.

So far, CPMs have been developed that can be learned from bulk genotypes [16] but assume that tumors were observed at a random time independent of their progression events. They are trained on the co-occurrence patterns of events and model the probabilities of future events as functions of events already present. These functions define a causal network. CPMs build on the seminal work of Fearon and Vogelstein [18] who manually inferred from genetic and clinical data that colorectal cancer tends to progress along a chain of mutations in the genes APC $\rightarrow$ KRAS $\rightarrow$ TP53.

Oncogenetic Trees [3,15] extend such chains and allow each event to be a necessary precursor to more than one successor event. In Conjunctive Bayesian Networks (CBNs) [2,20,40] events may also require multiple precursors, thus extending trees to directed acyclic graphs (DAGs). CAPRESE [35] and CAPRI

[46] are similar tree and DAG models where precursor events are not strictly necessary for successor events but raise their probabilities. Other DAG models with different functional forms are Disjunctive Bayesian Networks [42], Monotone Bayesian Networks [17] and Bayesian Mutation Landscapes [38]. Pathway Linear Progression Models [47] infer groups of mutually exclusive events and arrange them in a chain. PathTiMEx [14] generalizes this to CBNs of groups of mutually exclusive events. Network Aberration Models (NAMs) [28] are cyclic causal networks with promoting effects. HyperTraPS [24,31] and Mutual Hazard Networks (MHNs) [50] generalize this to cyclic networks with promoting and suppressive effects. Similar approaches [1,39] allow higher-order rather than pairwise interactions between events. TreeMHN [36] infers MHNs from intra-tumor phylogenetic trees derived from single-cell, multi-region or bulk sequencing data.

Here we address a fundamental oversight in all these CPMs: They do not include the observation of the tumor itself into their causal networks. Instead, we regard observation of the tumor as an event indicating that the tumor was biopsied, sequenced, and eventually included into the dataset. It implies that the tumor has become conspicuous due to its size, morphology, or symptoms such as weight loss, fatigue or pain. Since a dataset contains by definition only tumors at their moment of observation, neglecting any causal effects on this event makes CPMs prone to the notorious "conditioning on a collider" bias [27]. This bias is also known as Berkson's paradox and refers to spurious associations between any variables that affect another conditioned variable. Joseph Berkson originally described it for a hospital in-patient population which showed a negative association between diabetes and cholecystitis [5], see Fig. 1. However, since diabetes is known to increase the risk for cholecystitis [12], one would naturally expect a positive association. The explanation for the spurious negative association is that diabetes and cholecystitis are both separate causes to be in the hospital and therefore to be observed in this study. Learning of one cause explains away the need for the other cause.

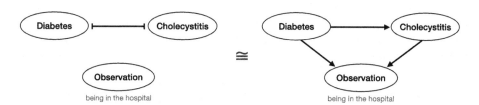

Fig. 1. Berkson's original example of a collider bias [5]: The negative association between diabetes and cholecystitis observed in hospital patients could be spuriously explained (left) by suppressive effects between the diseases, if the inclusion of a patient in the dataset were independent of both diseases. Alternatively, the same negative association can be correctly explained (right) by taking into account that both diseases have a promoting effect on being in the hospital, and thus observed in the dataset. The spurious association masks the actual promoting effect of diabetes on cholecystitis.

Similarly, the inference of CPMs from statistical associations can be grossly distorted when the observation should be a part of the causal network but is not properly accounted for. CBNs and MHNs are models in continuous time which do have a random observation event, but its rate is fixed at 1 and cannot be affected by other events. Timed Hazard Networks [11] extend MHNs by hidden variables for the observation times of all tumors, but these are also not affected by other events. NAMs [28] have an observation event whose rate depends on the total number of events that have occurred, but not on which particular events have occurred.

In this paper, we extend Mutual Hazard Networks by causal effects between its progression events and its observation event. Each event occurs at its base rate and has multiplicative effects on the rate of every other event. These effects can be greater than 1 (promoting), less than 1 (suppressive), or equal to 1 (neutral) and define a causal network with cycles. An MHN is a generative model of cancer progression in the form of a continuous-time Markov chain. We provide an analytical formula for its probability distribution over tumor states, explicitly conditioned on their times of observation. This formula uses tensor expressions which allows us to efficiently infer base rates and multiplicative effects between events via maximum likelihood estimation.

We demonstrate our approach on two datasets of colon adenocarcinoma (COAD) and lung adenocarcinoma (LUAD) from the MSK-IMPACT study [41,51]. Compared to classical MHNs, we find results that offer drastically different interpretations. In COAD, we find that TP53 strongly promotes observation, which explains away suppressive interactions and uncovers promoting effects between APC and TP53. For LUAD, the new model identifies EGFR mutations as principal observation drivers, which explains away its suppressive interactions with most other events but retains suppressive effects with KRAS.

2   Methods

We first summarize the definition of classical Mutual Hazard Networks from [50]. Then we extend MHNs by effects on the observation and derive a formula for their likelihood function. Finally, we show that such models are not uniquely identifiable from cross-sectional data and resolve this by a regularization that favors parsimony.

2.1   Classical MHNs with Unaffected Observation

Mutual Hazard Networks (MHN) [50] model cancer progression as a continuous-time Markov chain that describes how a tumor accumulates n possible progression events. Over the course of its progression, a tumor can be in any of 2^n states $\mathbf{x} \in \{0,1\}^n$ where $\mathbf{x}_i = 0$ encodes that event $i \in \{1, \ldots, n\}$ has not yet occurred and $\mathbf{x}_i = 1$ that it has. We assume that every tumor starts at time $t = 0$ in the healthy state $(0, \ldots, 0)^\top \in \{0,1\}^n$, accumulates events irreversibly one after another, and is finally observed at a random time t which is unknown.

Let $\mathbf{p}(t)$ be a vector of size 2^n that denotes the transient probability distribution over states at time $t \geq 0$. Here we use a lexicographic order on $\{0,1\}^n$ with the leftmost bit cycling fastest, see Fig. 2 (bottom left). An entry $\mathbf{p}(t)_\mathbf{x}$ denotes the probability that a tumor is in state $\mathbf{x}$ at time $t \geq 0$. The initial distribution

$$\mathbf{p}(0) := (1, 0, \ldots, 0)^\top \in [0, 1]^{2^n} \tag{1}$$

is concentrated on the healthy state. Its change over time is governed by the Kolmogorov forward equation:

$$\frac{d\mathbf{p}(t)}{dt} = Q\mathbf{p}(t) \quad \text{with solution} \quad \mathbf{p}(t) = \exp(tQ)\mathbf{p}(0). \tag{2}$$

Here, $Q \in \mathbb{R}^{2^n \times 2^n}$ is the transition rate matrix, where an off-diagonal entry $Q_{\mathbf{x}_{+i}, \mathbf{x}}$ is the transition rate from a state $\mathbf{x} = (\ldots, \mathbf{x}_{i-1}, 0, \mathbf{x}_{i+1}, \ldots)^\top$, which lacks event i, to the state $\mathbf{x}_{+i} := (\ldots, \mathbf{x}_{i-1}, 1, \mathbf{x}_{i+1}, \ldots)^\top$, which differs from $\mathbf{x}$ only in the additional event i. By assumption, events accumulate irreversibly one at a time, and thus all other off-diagonal entries are 0 and Q is lower-triangular. Its diagonal entries are defined such that each column sums to 0.

Our aim is to learn for each event i how its rate depends on already present events in $\mathbf{x}$. To this end, an MHN with parameters $\Theta \in \mathbb{R}^{n \times n}$ defines the functional form

$$Q_{\mathbf{x}_{+i}, \mathbf{x}} = \Theta_{ii} \prod_{\mathbf{x}_j = 1} \Theta_{ij}, \tag{3}$$

where $\Theta_{ii} > 0$ is the base rate of event i and $\Theta_{ij} > 0$ is the multiplicative effect of event j on the rate of event i.

In order to learn Θ from data via maximum likelihood estimation, we have to compute the probability distribution over all possible tumor states at the time of their observation. The observation in a classical MHN occurs randomly at a time which is exponentially distributed with a fixed rate of 1. Marginalizing over the unknown observation time $t \sim \text{Exp}(1)$ yields the time-marginal distribution

$$\mathbf{p} := \int_0^\infty e^{-t} \mathbf{p}(t) \, dt \tag{4}$$

$$= \int_0^\infty \exp(-tI) \exp(tQ) \, dt = \int_0^\infty \exp(-t[I - Q]) \, dt \tag{5}$$

$$= [I - Q]^{-1} \mathbf{p}(0). \tag{6}$$

Note that Eq. (5) is only valid for a fixed observation rate, since it relies on the fact that Q commutes with the identity matrix I. The log-likelihood of Θ for a dataset $\mathcal{D}$ of observed tumor states is then

$$\ell_\mathcal{D}(\Theta) = \frac{1}{|\mathcal{D}|} \sum_{\mathbf{x} \in \mathcal{D}} \log \mathbf{p}_\mathbf{x}. \tag{7}$$

Maximizing the log-likelihood of Θ, e.g. via gradient ascent or quasi-Newton methods, requires operations that involve the huge matrix Q. To this end, we make use of the following representation of Q as a sum of tensor products:

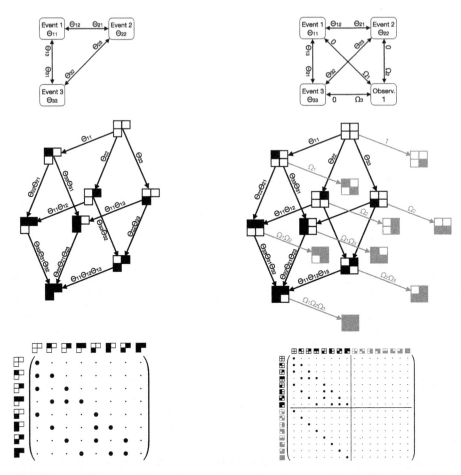

Fig. 2. Comparative illustration for $n = 3$ progression events. Left: A cMHN with parameters Θ and implicit observation event whose rate is fixed at 1. Right: An oMHN with the observation as an explicit fourth event and parameters (Θ, Ω). For the cMHN and oMHN each; top: the corresponding causal interaction networks between events; middle: the transition rates of the corresponding Markov chains; bottom: the structure of the corresponding transition rate matrices for a lexicographic order of the state space.

$$Q = \sum_{i=1}^{n} \bigotimes_{j=1}^{i-1} \begin{pmatrix} 1 & 0 \\ 0 & \Theta_{ij} \end{pmatrix} \otimes \begin{pmatrix} -\Theta_{ii} & 0 \\ \Theta_{ii} & 0 \end{pmatrix} \otimes \bigotimes_{j=i+1}^{n} \begin{pmatrix} 1 & 0 \\ 0 & \Theta_{ij} \end{pmatrix}. \tag{8}$$

Using efficient tensor operations [9], Θ can be learned with a time and storage complexity only exponential in the number of events that have occurred for each tumor, rather than exponential in $2n$ [49].

2.2 MHNs with Effects on Observation

Here, we extend the classical MHN (cMHN) introduced in the previous section to an observation MHN (oMHN). We include the observation event into its causal network as an explicit $(n+1)^{\text{th}}$ event. Its base rate is defined as 1 in order to standardize the time scale. We introduce additional parameters $\Omega \in \mathbb{R}^n$, where $\Omega_j > 0$ is the multiplicative effect of the progression event $j \in \{1, \ldots, n\}$ on the rate of observation.

Because now the observation rate depends on the state, we can no longer use Eq. (6) to compute the probabilities of tumor states at their time of observation. Instead we use the following construction: We set the outgoing effects of the observation on all genetic progression events to 0. Once the observation occurs, it prevents all other events from ever occurring by multiplying their rates with 0, which freezes the data generating process at the time of observation[1]. The probability distribution at observation now equals the stationary distribution at infinity, which can be computed as follows.

Formally, we define the extended Markov chain on the state space

$$\{0,1\}^{n+1} = \underbrace{(\{0,1\}^n \times \{0\})}_{=:A} \cup \underbrace{(\{0,1\}^n \times \{1\})}_{=:B}, \qquad (9)$$

where A includes all states before observation and B all states after observation. The extended transition rate matrix $\bar{Q}$ is of size $2^{n+1} \times 2^{n+1}$ and has the following block structure:

$$\bar{Q} = \begin{array}{c} \\ \left(\begin{array}{cc} \overbrace{T}^{A} & \overbrace{0}^{B} \\ U & 0 \end{array} \right) \begin{array}{l} \} A \\ \} B \end{array} \end{array} \quad \text{with} \quad U := \bigotimes_{j=1}^{n} \begin{pmatrix} 1 & 0 \\ 0 & \Omega_j \end{pmatrix} \text{ and } T := Q - U, \qquad (10)$$

where each block is of size $2^n \times 2^n$, see Fig. 2 (bottom right). The block U contains all transitions that introduce the observation event. It is diagonal with strictly positive eigenvalues and hence invertible. The block T contains all transitions that introduce a progression event, given by Q in Eq. (8), and U is subtracted from its diagonal so that each column of $\bar{Q}$ sums to 0. T is lower-triangular with strictly negative eigenvalues and hence also invertible.

The transient distribution $\bar{\mathbf{p}}(t)$ of the extended Markov chain can also be organized by blocks and is governed by the Kolmogorov forward equation:

$$\frac{d\bar{\mathbf{p}}(t)}{dt} = \bar{Q}\bar{\mathbf{p}}(t) = \begin{pmatrix} T & 0 \\ U & 0 \end{pmatrix} \begin{pmatrix} \bar{\mathbf{p}}_A(t) \\ \bar{\mathbf{p}}_B(t) \end{pmatrix} = \begin{pmatrix} T\bar{\mathbf{p}}_A(t) \\ U\bar{\mathbf{p}}_A(t) \end{pmatrix}, \qquad (11)$$

---

[1] This construction is only needed for learning the model. In order to extrapolate the progression of a tumor into the future beyond its observation, one would "unfreeze" the process again by setting the outgoing effects of the observation to 1. Ideally one would include effects from the treatment of the patient instead.

where $\bar{\mathbf{p}}_A(t)$ and $\bar{\mathbf{p}}_B(t)$ are each of size 2^n and denote the transient distribution restricted to A and B respectively. Given the initial distribution $\bar{\mathbf{p}}(0) = (1, 0, \ldots, 0)^\top$, i.e.,

$$\bar{\mathbf{p}}_A(0) = \mathbf{p}(0) \quad \text{and} \quad \bar{\mathbf{p}}_B(0) = (0, \ldots, 0)^\top,$$

the solution to the Kolmogorov equation reads

$$\bar{\mathbf{p}}_A(t) = \exp(tT)\bar{\mathbf{p}}_A(0) = \exp(tT)\mathbf{p}(0), \tag{12}$$

$$\bar{\mathbf{p}}_B(t) = \bar{\mathbf{p}}_B(0) + \int_0^t U\bar{\mathbf{p}}_A(s)\,\mathrm{d}s = \int_0^t U\exp(sT)\bar{\mathbf{p}}_A(0)\,\mathrm{d}s \tag{13}$$

$$= U\left(\int_0^t \exp(sT)\,\mathrm{d}s\right)\mathbf{p}(0) = -U\big(I - \exp(tT)\big)T^{-1}\mathbf{p}(0). \tag{14}$$

Because all eigenvalues of T are strictly negative, we can calculate the stationary distribution by

$$\bar{\mathbf{p}}_A(\infty) := \lim_{t\to\infty} \bar{\mathbf{p}}_A(t) = \lim_{t\to\infty} \underbrace{\exp(tT)}_{\to 0}\mathbf{p}(0) = (0, \ldots, 0)^\top,$$

$$\bar{\mathbf{p}}_B(\infty) := \lim_{t\to\infty} \bar{\mathbf{p}}_B(t) = \lim_{t\to\infty} -U\big(I - \underbrace{\exp(tT)}_{\to 0}\big)T^{-1}\mathbf{p}(0)$$

$$= -UT^{-1}\mathbf{p}(0) = U[U - Q]^{-1}\mathbf{p}(0) = [I - QU^{-1}]^{-1}\mathbf{p}(0)$$

$$= \left[I - \sum_{i=1}^n \bigotimes_{j=1}^{i-1} \begin{pmatrix} 1 & 0 \\ 0 & \Theta_{ij}/\Omega_j \end{pmatrix} \otimes \begin{pmatrix} -\Theta_{ii} & 0 \\ \Theta_{ii} & 0 \end{pmatrix} \otimes \bigotimes_{j=i+1}^n \begin{pmatrix} 1 & 0 \\ 0 & \Theta_{ij}/\Omega_j \end{pmatrix}\right]^{-1}\mathbf{p}(0). \tag{15}$$

The log-likelihood of a dataset $\mathcal{D}$ of observed tumor states is then

$$\ell_\mathcal{D}(\Theta, \Omega) = \frac{1}{|\mathcal{D}|} \sum_{\mathbf{x}\in\mathcal{D}} \log \bar{\mathbf{p}}_B(\infty)_\mathbf{x}. \tag{16}$$

Computing and maximizing the log-likelihood to learn Θ and Ω has the same complexity as for a cMHN, i.e., it is exponential in the number of events that have occurred for each tumor.

2.3 Non-identifiability and Regularization

Note that the formula for the stationary distribution of an oMHN (15) is the same as the formula for the time-marginal distribution of a cMHN (6) where the parameters Θ_{ij} are replaced by the fractions Θ_{ij}/Ω_j. It follows that an oMHN is not uniquely identifiable from cross-sectional data alone. For any oMHN with parameters Θ and Ω, we can construct a likelihood-equivalent cMHN with $\Theta_{ij}^* = \Theta_{ij}/\Omega_j$ for $i \neq j$ and $\Theta_{ii}^* = \Theta_{ii}$, see Fig. 3. Although both models generate exactly the same observational data, they have very different causal interpretations. That is, if we intervened experimentally on the system, the two models would then differ in their future dynamics.

Fig. 3. Example of a cMHN (left) and an oMHN (right) which generate the same observational data but differ in their causal interpretation. They imply different experimental predictions: A drug treatment which suppresses event 2 would increase the probabilities of events 1 and 3 according to the left model, but not according to the right model. (Both networks are fully connected, but neutral effects of multiplicative strength 1 are not drawn.)

In order to decide on a particular causal model, we cannot rely on data alone but have to incorporate background knowledge or preferences in the form of a Bayesian prior or a penalty on the likelihood. Following the principle of parsimony (Occam's razor), we prefer simple models that postulate the least number of causal mechanisms for explaining the data. This means that MHNs should be sparse, in the sense that many effects $\Theta_{ij} = 1$ and $\Omega_j = 1$ for $i \neq j$. In the example of Fig. 3, we would hence prefer the model on the right.

Moreover, we prefer symmetric models where many effects $\Theta_{ij} = \Theta_{ji}$ since these are likely due to a single causal mechanism that is inherently symmetric, such as synthetic lethality or functional equivalence among mutations. While such effects presumably do not vary in strength whether event i or j occurs first, there may be important exceptions [29,45]. Hence, we do not want to impose strict symmetry on Θ.

To this end, we propose maximizing the log-likelihood regularized by the following penalty which induces sparsity and soft symmetry:

$$\ell_{\mathcal{D}}(\Theta, \Omega) - \lambda \left(\sum_{i \neq j} \sqrt{\theta_{ij}^2 + \theta_{ji}^2 - \theta_{ij}\theta_{ji}} + \sum_{j=1}^{n} \sqrt{\omega_j^2} \right), \qquad (17)$$

where $\theta_{ij} := \log(\Theta_{ij})$, $\omega_j := \log(\Omega_j)$ and $\lambda > 0$ is a hyperparameter. Similar to the Group Lasso [56], this penalty promotes sparsity such that many logarithmic effects are 0 (hence multiplicative effects are 1) but pairs of effects θ_{ij} and θ_{ji} are selected together. The additional term $-\theta_{ij}\theta_{ji}$ ensures that symmetric effects of equal strength and sign are penalized only as strongly as a single effect θ_{ij} with $\theta_{ji} = 0$.

In this paper, we choose λ in 5-fold cross-validation according to the One Standard Error Rule [26], which selects the largest value for λ such that its average log-likelihood is within one standard error of the optimum. We use this rule because the optimal λ tends to 0 for larger datasets as it becomes less necessary to prevent overfitting, but we still want to favor simple models to mitigate non-identifiability.

3   Results

We provide a new version of Mutual Hazard Networks with a corresponding efficient learning algorithm. These models shed new light on cancer progression by telling us which genetic events are most responsible for the clinical observation of a tumor. The models are thereby corrected for a collider bias and offer more realistic interpretations of cancer progression, showing fewer spurious interactions and more genuine interactions that had been previously overlooked.

Specifically, we applied our method and learned two models from somatic mutation data of colon adenocarcinoma (COAD) and lung adenocarcinoma (LUAD), which were originally collected by the Memorial Sloan Kettering Cancer Center [41] and retrieved through AACR GENIE [51]. We selected one primary tumor sample for each of the 2269 COAD patients and 3662 LUAD patients. As mutational events, we considered only likely pathogenic variants and selected the 12 most commonly affected genes in each of COAD and LUAD, as described in Supplementary S1.

Although oMHN models are more realistic than cMHNs, they are in principle equally powerful for explaining the data, so we did not necessarily expect results with higher likelihood. Nevertheless, we validated their model fit by splitting each dataset in half into a training and test set. We trained a cMHN and an oMHN on the training set and evaluated their log-likelihoods on the test set. For COAD, the cMHN achieved a log-likelihood of -5.14 while the oMHN achieved a slightly better -5.10. For reference, the independence model[2] achieved -6.02 and the best possible performance was the entropy -4.48 of the test set. For LUAD, the cMHN achieved a log-likelihood of -3.96 and the oMHN achieved a slightly better -3.94. The independence model achieved -4.50 and the entropy of the test set was -3.74.

In the following, we report the models trained on the full datasets.

3.1   Colon Adenocarcinoma

Mutations in APC, KRAS and TP53 are long thought to be the cornerstones of conventional COAD progression [18]. The three events are abundant in the dataset (42%–72%) but enriched in samples with few events overall, see Supplementary S2. TP53 in particular is anti-correlated with most other events.

Although cMHN and oMHN both fit the data similarly well, they offer drastically different causal interpretations (Fig. 4): cMHN suggests that APC, KRAS and TP53 strongly antagonize each other as well as other events. oMHN instead proposes that APC, KRAS and especially TP53 lead to observation. This explains away many of their suppressive interactions and even uncovers a synergy between APC und TP53.

The different causal models also imply different chronological orders of events. For a given tumor genotype, we consider the probability of every possible chronological order according to each model, see Table 1. The most probable orders for

---

[2] In the independence model, events occur independently of each other with rates equal to their odds in the dataset.

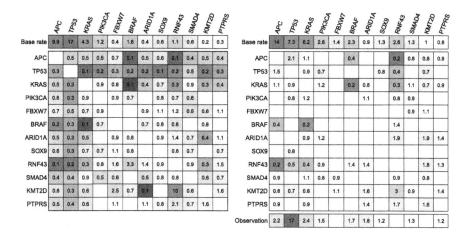

Fig. 4. Heatmap visualization of the cMHN (left) and the oMHN (right) for the COAD dataset. In the main heatmap bodies, each cell shows the multiplicative effect Θ_{ij} from the column event j on the row event i. Promoting effects > 1 are coded in red, suppressive effects < 1 in blue and neutral effects $= 1$ are blank. The additional top row indicates base rates Θ_{ii} and the bottom row indicates effects Ω_j from each column event j on the observation event. Values are rounded to the first decimal. (Color figure online)

common genotypes in the dataset are shown in Fig. 5. Contrary to cMHN, the oMHN suggests that APC tends to occur early in the progression and that TP53 tends to occur late, despite its prevalence. This is because TP53 triggers and therefore immediately precedes the observation.

Unlike for cMHN, the interpretations drawn from oMHN are in line with common conceptions about COAD genetic progression. It has been repeatedly suggested that APC inactivation is a gatekeeper which starts the transformation in healthy tissues and is a prerequisite for subsequent alterations, like TP53, which then elicit aggressive growth and invasion [10,53,55]. The synergy between APC and TP53 is further supported by a systematic study of conditional selection effects in cancer genomes [29] which found that TP53 mutations are under particularly strong positive selection in APC-mutated colorectal cancers, and vice versa. However, oMHN also suggests that TP53 alterations are able to generate clinically conspicuous tumors on their own.

Table 1. All possible chronological orders to reach the genotype that contains exactly the events APC, KRAS, TP53 and was observed. The probabilities of these orders according to cMHN and oMHN are computed as in Supplementary S3 and rounded to the 3rd decimal.

Chronological order			cMHN	oMHN
APC	→ KRAS	→ TP53	0.068	0.312
KRAS	→ APC	→ TP53	0.064	0.262
APC	→ TP53	→ KRAS	0.198	0.149
KRAS	→ TP53	→ APC	0.075	0.113
TP53	→ APC	→ KRAS	0.383	0.101
TP53	→ KRAS	→ APC	0.212	0.064

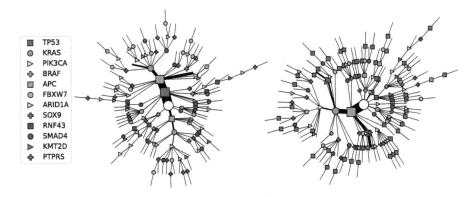

Fig. 5. Most probable chronological order of events for the COAD dataset according to the cMHN (left) and oMHN (right). Each path from the root of the tree (white circle) to a leaf represents the progression of a tumor in the dataset. The symbols along the path indicate events whose most probable chronological order was computed from the trained models. To avoid clutter, the observation event at every leaf is implied without drawing a symbol and only tumors whose state is shared by at least 3 patients are drawn. The size of the edges and symbols along a path scale in the total number of patients with that tumor state.

Despite these differences, some interactions remain consistent between cMHN and oMHN. Most notably, both models suggest a "double antagonism" between the KRAS-APC and BRAF-RNF43 pairs: each event in one pair suppresses both members of the other pair. In fact, the two event pairs likely produce similar consequences through alternative means: both event pairs deregulate the RAS and Wnt pathways. These are synergistic milestones in COAD progression [30,33]. Specifically, KRAS and BRAF mutations are alternative ways of RAS pathway deregulation [13,44] and APC and RNF43 are alternative ways of Wnt signalling deregulation [21,23]. Additionally, the synergy within the pairs as well as the antagonism between them are clearly reflected in the conditional selection analysis of [29]. Both points, functional similarity and conditional selection effects, support genuine antagonism between these pairs.

Interestingly, the BRAF-RNF43 pair is associated with a distinct mode of COAD progression, the Serrated Neoplasia Pathway. These cancers develop from serrated sessile lesions, with different histopathological and prognostic properties [34]. Unlike in conventional COADs, APC mutations are rare here while BRAF mutations are thought to be initial [6,8]. Experimental evidence suggests that specifically MLH1-deficient, microsatellite-instable serrated COADs rely on BRAF and RNF43 mutations in their progression [7,54].

Taken together, these findings suggest that there are two prototypical ways of genetic progression in COAD. On the one hand, any combination of the synergistic triplet APC-KRAS-TP53 can be sufficient to elicit observation, although APC tends to be the initiating factor and TP53 the observation driver. On the other hand, crucial pathway deregulation can also be achieved by alternatives like BRAF and RNF43. In these cases, there is no main observation driver and typically more alterations are accumulated before observation.

3.2 Lung Adenocarcinoma

In the models on lung adenocarcinoma (LUAD), Fig. 6, we also observed a shift from widespread suppressive interactions in cMHN to observation rate increases in oMHN, most notably for EGFR mutations. EGFR mutations appear mutually exclusive with many other events in the input data. cMHN models this with widespread suppressive interactions while oMHN explains these away by an observation rate increase. For EGFR and TP53, oMHN even suggests synergy instead of the antagonism proposed by cMHN.

The chronological orders differ between cMHN and oMHN mainly for EGFR and KRAS. These events tend to occur later according to oMHN because they trigger observation, see Fig. 7. According to oMHN, EGFR has a strong effect on observation on its own. Conversely, KRAS-positive LUADs elicit observation in a more concerted manner supported by e.g., ATM, STK11 and KEAP1. Moreover, there are also interactions that remain consistent between cMHN and oMHN, most prominently the suppressive relationship between EGFR and KRAS. In fact, experimental demonstration of synthetic lethality [52] and conditional selection analysis [29] both support a genuine antagonism.

Heatmap cMHN (left):

	TP53	KRAS	EGFR	STK11	RBM10	KEAP1	ATM	SMARCA4	PTPRD	NF1	PIK3CA	BRAF
Base rate	1.3	1.5	1.2	0.3	0.2	0.2	0.1	0.1	0.1	0.1	0.1	0.1
TP53		0.3	0.6	0.3	0.3	0.6	0.4	0.9			0.8	0.6
KRAS	0.2		0	0.8	0.8	0.5		0.8	0.8	0.3	0.8	0.2
EGFR	0.5	0		0.1	0.7	0.1	0.4	0.5	0.4	0.1		0.1
STK11	0.4	0.8	0.1		0.7	3.2	0.9	1.1		0.7	0.7	0.9
RBM10	0.3	0.8	0.8	0.7		0.8						0.9
KEAP1	0.6	0.5	0.1	3.7	0.6		0.8	1.7			0.9	0.8
ATM	0.4		0.3	0.9		0.7						
SMARCA4	0.9	0.8	0.4	1.2		2.2						
PTPRD		0.8	0.3							1.1		
NF1		0.3	0.1	0.7					1.1			
PIK3CA	0.8	0.8		0.6		0.9						
BRAF	0.6	0.2	0.1	0.9	0.9	0.8						

Heatmap oMHN (right):

	TP53	KRAS	EGFR	STK11	RBM10	KEAP1	ATM	SMARCA4	PTPRD	NF1	PIK3CA	BRAF
Base rate	2	1.6	1.1	0.5	0.5	0.2	0.2	0.2	0.2	0.2	0.2	0.2
TP53		0.6	1.7	0.4	0.4		0.7	1.1				
KRAS	0.5		0.1	1.1			1.8			0.4		0.6
EGFR	1.6	0.1		0.1	1.2	0.3		0.9	0.6	0.2	1.6	0.6
STK11	0.5	1.1	0.2		0.7	3.8		1.3		0.8	0.7	
RBM10	0.5		1.2	0.7		0.8						
KEAP1		0.4	6	0.8				2.3				
ATM	0.7	2										
SMARCA4			0.9	1.4		2.4						
PTPRD	1.1		0.7								1.2	
NF1	0.5	0.3	0.8						1.2			
PIK3CA			1.6	0.7								
BRAF	0.6	0.7										
Observation	1.9	3.4	11	1.2	1.1	2.2	1.6			1.2	1.1	4.1

Fig. 6. Heatmap visualization of the cMHN (left) and the oMHN (right) for the LUAD dataset. In the main heatmap bodies, each cell shows the multiplicative effect Θ_{ij} from the column event j on the row event i. Promoting effects > 1 are coded in red, suppressive effects < 1 in blue and neutral effects $= 1$ are blank. The additional top row indicates base rates Θ_{ii} and the bottom row indicates effects Ω_j from each column event j on the observation event. Values are rounded to the first decimal. (Color figure online)

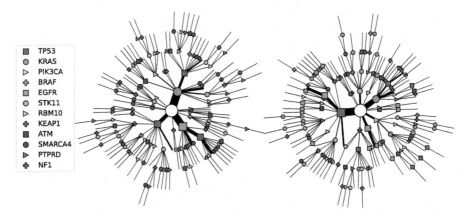

- ◼ TP53
- ◯ KRAS
- ▷ PIK3CA
- ✛ BRAF
- ◻ EGFR
- ◎ STK11
- ▷ RBM10
- ✛ KEAP1
- ◼ ATM
- ● SMARCA4
- ▷ PTPRD
- ✛ NF1

Fig. 7. Most probable chronological orders of events for the LUAD dataset according to the cMHN (left) and oMHN (right). Each path from the root of the tree (white circle) to a leaf represents the progression of a tumor in the dataset. The symbols along the path indicate events whose most probable chronological order was computed from the trained models. To avoid clutter, the observation event at every leaf is implied without drawing a symbol and only tumors whose state is shared by at least 3 patients are drawn. The size of the edges and symbols along a path scale in the total number of patients with that tumor state.

4   Discussion

Large cancer genomics datasets offer a valuable opportunity for modeling cancer progression, but many of them are observational, drawn from routine clinical practice rather than controlled trials [51]. This makes them prone to pervasive biases [25], such as the notorious confounder bias, which is due to unaccounted effects from latent variables, and the collider bias, which is due to unaccounted effects on a conditioned outcome. In this paper, we have resolved an important instance of the collider bias by learning which genetic events cause the clinical observation of a tumor. This is an important biological insight on its own, since the observation of a tumor is often tied to its size and aggressiveness. In addition, and perhaps more consequentially, learning their effects explains away spurious interactions between many other events and uncovers interactions that were previously hidden.

While resolving the collider bias is a crucial step towards more reliable cancer progression models, other sources of confounding may still remain. Future work should combine our approach with the modeling of latent variables such as environmental factors, mutational processes, or the tumor's cell type of origin. Further non-identifiability could be mitigated by exploiting known time intervals between consecutive observations [48], such as biopsies of primary tumors and metastases. Surprisingly, [22] have shown that the identifiability of classical MHNs can also be improved simply by including more events, which becomes possible through efficient learning algorithms [19,22,32]. Moreover, our approach could also be applied to models of subclonal tumor compositions [36].

More realistic models will ultimately allow us to not only understand and predict the course of cancer progression, but also to steer it towards favorable outcomes through treatment.

Acknowledgements. This work was supported by the Swiss National Science Foundation grant 179518, the Swiss Cancer League grant KFS-2977-08-2012 and the German Research Foundation grants TRR-305 and GR-3179/6-1.

References

1. Alfaro-Murillo, J.A., Townsend, J.P.: Pairwise and higher-order epistatic effects among somatic cancer mutations across oncogenesis, January 2022. https://doi.org/10.1101/2022.01.20.477132
2. Beerenwinkel, N., Eriksson, N., Sturmfels, B.: Conjunctive Bayesian networks. Bernoulli **13**(4), 893–909 (2007). https://doi.org/10.3150/07-BEJ6133
3. Beerenwinkel, N., et al.: Learning multiple evolutionary pathways from cross-sectional data. J. Comput. Biol. **12**(6), 584–598 (2005). https://doi.org/10.1089/cmb.2005.12.584
4. Beerenwinkel, N., Schwarz, R.F., Gerstung, M., Markowetz, F.: Cancer evolution: mathematical models and computational inference. Syst. Biol. **64**(1), e1–e25 (2014). https://doi.org/10.1093/sysbio/syu081
5. Berkson, J.: Limitations of the application of fourfold table analysis to hospital data. Biometrics Bull. **2**(3), 47 (1946). https://doi.org/10.2307/3002000

6. Bettington, M., et al.: Clinicopathological and molecular features of sessile serrated adenomas with dysplasia or carcinoma. Gut **66**(1), 97–106 (2015). https://doi.org/10.1136/gutjnl-2015-310456

7. Bleijenberg, A.G., et al.: The earliest events in BRAF-mutant colorectal cancer: exome sequencing of sessile serrated lesions with a tiny focus dysplasia or cancer reveals recurring mutations in two distinct progression pathways. J. Pathol. **257**(2), 239–249 (2022). https://doi.org/10.1002/path.5881

8. Bond, C.E., et al.: RNF43 and ZNRF3 are commonly altered in serrated pathway colorectal tumorigenesis. Oncotarget **7**(43), 70589–70600 (2016). https://doi.org/10.18632/oncotarget.12130

9. Buis, P.E., Dyksen, W.R.: Efficient vector and parallel manipulation of tensor products. ACM Trans. Math. Softw. **22**(1), 18–23 (1996). https://doi.org/10.1145/225545.225548

10. Bürtin, F., Mullins, C.S., Linnebacher, M.: Mouse models of colorectal cancer: Past, present and future perspectives. World J. Gastroenterol. **26**(13), 1394–1426 (2020). https://doi.org/10.3748/wjg.v26.i13.1394

11. Chen, J.: Timed hazard networks: incorporating temporal difference for oncogenetic analysis. PLoS ONE **18**(3), e0283004 (2023). https://doi.org/10.1371/journal.pone.0283004

12. Cho, J.Y.: Risk factors for acute cholecystitis and a complicated clinical course in patients with symptomatic cholelithiasis. Arch. Surg. **145**(4), 329 (2010). https://doi.org/10.1001/archsurg.2010.35

13. Cicenas, J., et al.: KRAS, NRAS and BRAF mutations in colorectal cancer and melanoma. Med. Oncol. **34**(2) (2017). https://doi.org/10.1007/s12032-016-0879-9

14. Cristea, S., Kuipers, J., Beerenwinkel, N.: pathTiMEx: joint inference of mutually exclusive cancer pathways and their progression dynamics. J. Comput. Biol. **24**(6), 603–615 (2017). https://doi.org/10.1089/cmb.2016.0171

15. Desper, R., Jiang, F., Kallioniemi, O.P., Moch, H., Papadimitriou, C.H., Schäffer, A.A.: Inferring tree models for oncogenesis from comparative genome hybridization data. J. Comput. Biol. **6**(1), 37–51 (1999). https://doi.org/10.1089/cmb.1999.6.37

16. Diaz-Colunga, J., Diaz-Uriarte, R.: Conditional prediction of consecutive tumor evolution using cancer progression models: what genotype comes next? PLoS Comput. Biol. **17**(12), e1009055 (2021). https://doi.org/10.1371/journal.pcbi.1009055

17. Farahani, H.S., Lagergren, J.: Learning oncogenetic networks by reducing to mixed integer linear programming. PLoS ONE **8**(6), e65773 (2013). https://doi.org/10.1371/journal.pone.0065773

18. Fearon, E.R., Vogelstein, B.: A genetic model for colorectal tumorigenesis. Cell **61**(5), 759–767 (1990). https://doi.org/10.1016/0092-8674(90)90186-i

19. Georg, P.: Tensor train decomposition for solving high-dimensional mutual hazard networks (2022). https://doi.org/10.5283/EPUB.53004. https://epub.uni-regensburg.de/id/eprint/53004

20. Gerstung, M., Baudis, M., Moch, H., Beerenwinkel, N.: Quantifying cancer progression with conjunctive Bayesian networks. Bioinformatics **25**(21), 2809–2815 (2009). https://doi.org/10.1093/bioinformatics/btp505

21. Giannakis, M., et al.: RNF43 is frequently mutated in colorectal and endometrial cancers. Nat. Genet. **46**(12), 1264–1266 (2014). https://doi.org/10.1038/ng.3127

22. Gotovos, A., Burkholz, R., Quackenbush, J., Jegelka, S.: Scaling up continuous-time Markov chains helps resolve underspecification, July 2021. https://doi.org/10.48550/arXiv.2107.02911

23. Grant, A., et al.: Molecular drivers of tumor progression in microsatellite stable APC mutation-negative colorectal cancers. Sci. Rep. **11**(1) (2021). https://doi.org/10.1038/s41598-021-02806-x

24. Greenbury, S.F., Barahona, M., Johnston, I.G.: HyperTraPS: inferring probabilistic patterns of trait acquisition in evolutionary and disease progression pathways. Cell Syst. **10**(1), 39–51.e10 (2020). https://doi.org/10.1016/j.cels.2019.10.009

25. van de Haar, J., Canisius, S., Yu, M.K., Voest, E.E., Wessels, L.F., Ideker, T.: Identifying epistasis in cancer genomes: a delicate affair. Cell **177**(6), 1375–1383 (2019). https://doi.org/10.1016/j.cell.2019.05.005

26. Hastie, T., Tibshirani, R., Friedman, J.: The Elements of Statistical Learning. Springer Series in Statistics. Springer, New York (2009). https://doi.org/10.1007/978-0-387-84858-7

27. Hernán MA, R.J.: Causal Inference: What If. Chapman & Hall/CRC, Boca Raton (2020)

28. Hjelm, M., Höglund, M., Lagergren, J.: New probabilistic network models and algorithms for oncogenesis. J. Comput. Biol. **13**(4), 853–865 (2006). https://doi.org/10.1089/cmb.2006.13.853

29. Iranzo, J., Gruenhagen, G., Calle-Espinosa, J., Koonin, E.V.: Pervasive conditional selection of driver mutations and modular epistasis networks in cancer. Cell Rep. **40**(8), 111272 (2022). https://doi.org/10.1016/j.celrep.2022.111272

30. Jeong, W.J., Ro, E.J., Choi, K.Y.: Interaction between wnt/β-catenin and RAS-ERK pathways and an anti-cancer strategy via degradations of β-catenin and RAS by targeting the wnt/β-catenin pathway. npj Precis. Oncol. **2**(1) (2018). https://doi.org/10.1038/s41698-018-0049-y

31. Johnston, I.G., Williams, B.P.: Evolutionary inference across eukaryotes identifies specific pressures favoring mitochondrial gene retention. Cell Syst. **2**(2), 101–111 (2016). https://doi.org/10.1016/j.cels.2016.01.013

32. Klever, M., Georg, P., Grasedyck, L., Schill, R., Spang, R., Wettig, T.: Low-rank tensor methods for Markov chains with applications to tumor progression models. J. Math. Biol. **86**(1) (2022). https://doi.org/10.1007/s00285-022-01846-9

33. Lee, S.K., Hwang, J.H., Choi, K.Y.: Interaction of the wnt/β-catenin and RAS-ERK pathways involving co-stabilization of both β-catenin and RAS plays important roles in the colorectal tumorigenesis. Adv. Biol. Regul. **68**, 46–54 (2018). https://doi.org/10.1016/j.jbior.2018.01.001

34. Leggett, B., Whitehall, V.: Role of the serrated pathway in colorectal cancer pathogenesis. Gastroenterology **138**(6), 2088–2100 (2010). https://doi.org/10.1053/j.gastro.2009.12.066

35. Loohuis, L.O., et al.: Inferring tree causal models of cancer progression with probability raising. PLoS ONE **9**(10), e108358 (2014). https://doi.org/10.1371/journal.pone.0108358

36. Luo, X.G., Kuipers, J., Beerenwinkel, N.: Joint inference of exclusivity patterns and recurrent trajectories from tumor mutation trees. Nat. Commun. **14**(1) (2023). https://doi.org/10.1038/s41467-023-39400-w

37. Mina, M., Iyer, A., Ciriello, G.: Epistasis and evolutionary dependencies in human cancers. Curr. Opin. Genet. Dev. **77**, 101989 (2022). https://doi.org/10.1016/j.gde.2022.101989

38. Misra, N., Szczurek, E., Vingron, M.: Inferring the paths of somatic evolution in cancer. Bioinformatics **30**(17), 2456–2463 (2014). https://doi.org/10.1093/bioinformatics/btu319

39. Moen, M.T., Johnston, I.G.: HyperHMM: efficient inference of evolutionary and progressive dynamics on hypercubic transition graphs. Bioinformatics **39**(1) (2022). https://doi.org/10.1093/bioinformatics/btac803
40. Montazeri, H., et al.: Large-scale inference of conjunctive Bayesian networks. Bioinformatics **32**(17), i727–i735 (2016). https://doi.org/10.1093/bioinformatics/btw459
41. Nguyen, B., Sanchez-Vega, C.F.F., Schultz, N., et al.: Genomic characterization of metastatic patterns from prospective clinical sequencing of 25,000 patients. Cell **185**(3), 563–575.e11 (2022). https://doi.org/10.1016/j.cell.2022.01.003
42. Nicol, P.B., et al.: Oncogenetic network estimation with disjunctive Bayesian networks. Comput. Syst. Oncol. **1**(2) (2021). https://doi.org/10.1002/cso2.1027
43. Nowell, P.C.: The clonal evolution of tumor cell populations. Science **194**(4260), 23–28 (1976). https://doi.org/10.1126/science.959840
44. Oliveira, C., et al.: KRAS and BRAF oncogenic mutations in MSS colorectal carcinoma progression. Oncogene **26**(1), 158–163 (2006). https://doi.org/10.1038/sj.onc.1209758
45. Ortmann, C.A., et al.: Effect of mutation order on myeloproliferative neoplasms. N. Engl. J. Med. **372**(7), 601–612 (2015). https://doi.org/10.1056/nejmoa1412098
46. Ramazzotti, D., et al.: CAPRI: efficient inference of cancer progression models from cross-sectional data. Bioinformatics **31**(18), 3016–3026 (2015). https://doi.org/10.1093/bioinformatics/btv296
47. Raphael, B.J., Vandin, F.: Simultaneous inference of cancer pathways and tumor progression from cross-sectional mutation data. J. Comput. Biol. **22**(6), 510–527 (2015). https://doi.org/10.1089/cmb.2014.0161
48. Rupp, K., et al.: Differentiated uniformization: a new method for inferring Markov chains on combinatorial state spaces including stochastic epidemic models (2021). https://doi.org/10.48550/ARXIV.2112.10971. https://arxiv.org/abs/2112.10971
49. Schill, R.: Mutual hazard networks: Markov chain models of cancer progression (2022). https://doi.org/10.5283/EPUB.53417. https://epub.uni-regensburg.de/id/eprint/53417
50. Schill, R., Solbrig, S., Wettig, T., Spang, R.: Modelling cancer progression using mutual hazard networks. Bioinformatics **36**(1), 241–249 (2019). https://doi.org/10.1093/bioinformatics/btz513
51. The AACR Project GENIE Consortium, et al.: AACR project genie: powering precision medicine through an international consortium. Cancer Discov. **7**(8), 818–831 (2017). https://doi.org/10.1158/2159-8290.CD-17-0151
52. Unni, A.M., Lockwood, W.W., Zejnullahu, K., Lee-Lin, S.Q., Varmus, H.: Evidence that synthetic lethality underlies the mutual exclusivity of oncogenic KRAS and EGFR mutations in lung adenocarcinoma. eLife **4** (2015). https://doi.org/10.7554/elife.06907
53. Vogelstein, B., Papadopoulos, N., Velculescu, V.E., Zhou, S., Diaz, L.A., Kinzler, K.W.: Cancer genome landscapes. Science **339**(6127), 1546–1558 (2013). https://doi.org/10.1126/science.1235122
54. Yamamoto, D., et al.: Characterization of RNF43 frameshift mutations that drive Wnt ligand- and RS-spondin-dependent colon cancer. J. Pathol. **257**(1), 39–52 (2022). https://doi.org/10.1002/path.5868
55. Yang, L., et al.: An enhanced genetic model of colorectal cancer progression history. Genome Biol. **20**(1) (2019). https://doi.org/10.1186/s13059-019-1782-4
56. Yuan, M., Lin, Y.: Model selection and estimation in regression with grouped variables. J. R. Stat. Soc. Ser. B Stat Methodol. **68**(1), 49–67 (2005). https://doi.org/10.1111/j.1467-9868.2005.00532.x

Inferring Metabolic States from Single Cell Transcriptomic Data via Geometric Deep Learning

Holly R. Steach[1], Siddharth Viswanath[2], Yixuan He[3], Xitong Zhang[4],
Natalia Ivanova[5], Matthew Hirn[1,2,3,4,5,6,7,8,9], Michael Perlmutter[6,7],
and Smita Krishnaswamy[1,2,8,9(✉)]

[1] Department of Genetics, Yale University, New Haven, USA
smita.krishnaswamy@yale.edu
[2] Department of Computer Science, Yale University, New Haven, USA
[3] Department of Statistics, University of Oxford, Oxford, UK
[4] Department of Computational Mathematics, Science, and Engineering,
Michigan State University, East Lansing, USA
[5] Department of Biochemistry and Molecular Biology, University of Georgia,
Athens, USA
[6] Department of Mathematics, Boise State University, Boise, USA
[7] Program in Computing, Boise State University, Boise, USA
[8] Wu Tsai Institute, Yale University, New Haven, USA
[9] Program for Computational Biology and Bioinformatics, Yale University,
New Haven, USA

Abstract. The ability to measure gene expression at single-cell resolution has elevated our understanding of how biological features emerge from complex and interdependent networks at molecular, cellular, and tissue scales. As technologies have evolved that complement scRNAseq measurements with things like single-cell proteomic, epigenomic, and genomic information, it becomes increasingly apparent how much biology exists as a product of multimodal regulation. Biological processes such as transcription, translation, and post-translational or epigenetic modification impose both energetic and specific molecular demands on a cell and are therefore implicitly constrained by the metabolic state of the cell. While metabolomics is crucial for defining a holistic model of any biological process, the chemical heterogeneity of the metabolome makes it particularly difficult to measure, and technologies capable of doing this at single-cell resolution are far behind other multiomics modalities. To address these challenges, we present GEFMAP (Gene Expression-based Flux Mapping and Metabolic Pathway Prediction), a method based on geometric deep learning for predicting flux through reactions in a global metabolic network using transcriptomics data, which we ultimately apply to scRNAseq. GEFMAP leverages the natural graph structure of metabolic networks to learn both a biological objective for each cell and estimate a mass-balanced relative flux rate for each reaction in each cell using novel deep learning models.

H. R. Steach and S. Viswanath—Co-lead author.
M. Perlmutter and S. Krishnaswamy—Co-senior author.

Keywords: metabolomics · single-cell omics · transcriptomics

1   Introduction

Technologies that measure gene expression at single-cell resolution have massively expanded over the last decade and are now broadly available to researchers. However, at this time, no method exists that accurately measures the entire metabolome at single-cell resolution. One possible remedy is to utilize the wide availability of single-cell RNA sequencing data (scRNAseq) to develop computational tools for predicting and modeling the metabolic states of individual cells via the transcriptome. Indeed, metabolic reactions are catalyzed by enzymes whose expression is available in the scRNA-seq measurements. Here, we use this idea to understand not only what gene pathways are being upregulated by the cell but also gain specific insights on the metabolic pathways being engaged as a result of the gene expression. Additionally, after formulating a metabolic objective, we can estimate flux through the entire network and assess the effects of transcription network-wide.

Learning about the metabolome is particularly challenging for multicellular organisms in part because we do not know a priori what objective each cell is trying to optimize. This is in contrast to the setting of single-cell organisms where researchers have effectively used cell growth (biomass accumulation) as an objective [6,24,28]. This motivates us to introduce GEFMAP - Gene Expression-based Flux Mapping and Metabolic Pathway Prediction. GEFMAP consists of two sub-networks, the first of which infers a plausible metabolic objective from the dynamically regulated portions of the transcriptomic profile, and the second of which solves this objective in order to infer network-wide metabolic flux rates.

The first subnetwork *infers the cellular metabolic objective* based on the intuition that the cell upregulates expression of catalytic enzymes (genes) for producing its desired metabolic state. Here, we formulate this as the problem of finding a highly-weighted, highly-connected subgraph in the metabolic network graph where the nodes representing individual reactions are given weights according to the expression levels of associated genes. This allows us to essentially infer the cellular objective from its transcriptomic profile. To do this, we utilize a deep neural network based on the geometric scattering transform [7,8,34] to estimate a large highly-connected subnetwork by solving a maximum weighted subgraph, a relaxed version of the maximum weighted clique problem. We then formulate a cellular objective function corresponding to maximizing the reactivity in this subgraph.

Our second subnetwork *solves the cellular objective* by identifying a set of reaction rates $\mathbf{v}$ that maximizes the objective, given the constraint that our solution $\mathbf{v}$ must satisfy mass balance within the system. We impose this using a matrix of reaction stoichiometries S, where a solution $\mathbf{v}$ satisfies the mass balance constraint if $S\mathbf{v} = 0$, inspired by flux balance analysis (FBA). We therefore consider a basis for the null space, $S\mathbf{v} = 0$, and design a novel network that operates in this null space to find the coefficients of the solution with respect to this basis. Thus, GEFMAP is able to utilize both the structure of the network and the geometric constraint that $\mathbf{v}$ lies within the null space of S to predict the metabolic fluxes. In essence this allows us to predict the entire metabolic state based on the inferred objective, which will include maximizing reactions of a subnetwork and may have pervasive effects on system-wide flux.

Main Contributions. The main contributions in this paper are summarized as follows:

1. We create a dual system of complementary neural networks to both infer a cellular metabolic objective as well as predict steady-state flux rates that result from the metabolic objective using deep neural network models.
2. For infering a transcriptionally regulated cellular objective, we model gene expression values as features on a node-weighted graph and estimate a relaxed maximum weighted clique by modifying a graph neural network designed to compute a maximum clique.
3. For solving the objective, we use a neural network that operates within the null space of the stoichiometry matrix S in order to predict mass-balanced reaction rates that maximize flux through reactions corresponding to the objective.
4. We apply these networks to synthetic data, bulk RNA sequencing of E. coli, and single cell RNA sequencing of human cells to both identify known biology and generate novel hypotheses.

2   Problem Setup

The difficulty of direct metabolomics measurements, particularly at single-cell resolution, motivates the development of computational methods that leverage gene expression data to estimate metabolic network states. A large portion of metabolic reactions are catalyzed by enzymes, where expression of reaction-associated genes is a rate-limiting factor. A given cell will therefore transcriptionally upregulate metabolic genes in order to increase activity of a particular set of reactions in response to some stimulus. However, the relationship between transcript levels and reaction rates is influenced by several other features and is not a sufficient predictor of flux. Therefore, in order to model cellular metabolic activity from transcriptional data we define two major challenges. The first is to identify a set of reactions that a cell is actively engaging, which we refer to as the **cellular metabolic objective**. Once known, the second challenge is to determine how the cell is accomplishing this objective, which we do by predicting flux rates for all reactions in the metabolic network. By subjecting these predictions to a set of constraints that include expression of reaction-associated genes and mass conservation within the system, we identify which reactions support the cellular objective and are likely to have high activity and which reactions are counter to the objective and are likely to be competitively downregulated.

Since metabolites and their fluxes form a network, all components of this problem can be modeled using graph representations. Here, we leverage previously curated genome-scale metabolic models (GEM) that represent the global set of reactions, the substrate/product stoichiometries, and the associated genes involved. Tools such as constraint-based reconstruction and analysis (COBRA) [10] include methods to parse GEM, however, we require a non-standard method of mapping gene expression to reactions. A single reaction may be catalyzed by a single gene; however, many reactions involve multiple enzymes. In the latter setting, it is sometimes the case that all of the enzymes are necessary, such as in the case of an enzyme complex, and other times it is the case that the enzymes act redundantly. Therefore, the models must be parsed in a way that we can use to map gene expression values onto reactions in a manner that reflects their biological relationships. To do this, we build a method that extracts rules from a given GEM and applies them to expression value assignments as part of GEFMAP.

A common method for predicting metabolic network activity is flux balance analysis (FBA) [24], in which flux through a metabolic network is formulated as a linear optimization problem. In this framework, we consider a system of m metabolites $\{\mu_i\}_{i=1}^m$ and n reactions $\{R_j\}_{j=1}^n$, and we let S denote and $m \times n$ stoichiometry matrix so that $S_{i,j}$ is the activity level of the metabolite μ_i in the reaction R_j. Generally S is provided as part of a curated genome-scale metabolic model (GEM). We let $\mathbf{v}$ denote an $n \times 1$ flux vector where v_j denotes the rate of the reaction R_j (metabolite concentration per unit of time). Our goal is to estimate $\mathbf{v}$ based on S and other available information. In FBA, we assume that $\mathbf{v}$ is the solution to an optimization problem of the form, $\max_{\mathbf{v}} Z(\mathbf{v}) = \sum_{j=1}^n c_j |v_j|$, subject to certain constraints.

By construction,

$$(S\mathbf{v})_i = \sum_j S_{i,j} v_j = \sum_j \text{change of } \mu_i \text{ in reaction } j \times \text{rate of reaction } j$$

is the overall net rate change of μ_i in the system. In our analysis, we will assume that the system is at steady state, i.e., the mass entering the system (cellular import) is equal to the mass accumulating in or leaving the system (growth, storage, cellular export). Thus, $\mathbf{v}$ must satisfy the constraint

$$S\mathbf{v} = 0,$$

i.e., $\mathbf{v}$ must lie in the the null space of S. Additionally, we often have upper and lower constraints for each of the rates v_j based on known biological features such as environmental nutrient availability or gene expression, i.e.,

$$v_j^{(\text{lb})} \leq v_j \leq v_j^{(\text{ub})}.$$

Notably, in the case where R_j is reversible, we will take $v_j^{(\text{lb})} = -v_j^{(\text{ub})}$ and otherwise we will have $v_j^{(\text{lb})} \geq 0$.

Various cell types in different states such as quiescence, activation, and differentiation engage different metabolic pathways to support their respective energetic and biomolecular needs. These metabolic programs comprise subsets of the global metabolic network and can be modeled as an objective function that the cell is optimizing under constraints parameterized by the external environment and bioenergetic features such as reaction kinetics. This leads to a cellular objective function

$$Z(\mathbf{v}) = \sum_{j=1}^{n} c_j |v_j|. \tag{1}$$

In the idealized case, $\mathbf{c}$ would be an indicator vector whose j-th entry is 1 if the cell is trying to maximize the reaction R_j and is zero otherwise. In practice, since the true cellular objective function is unknown, we will interpret $c_j \in [0,1]$ as the probability that the cell is trying to maximize reaction j. FBA thus identifies the vector $\mathbf{v}$ within the solution space that describes the mass balanced metabolic network state most capable of engaging the objective biological processes under the given conditions by optimizing

$$\max Z(\mathbf{v}) = \sum_{j=1}^{n} c_j |v_j|, \quad \text{Subject to:} \quad S\mathbf{v} = 0, \ \mathbf{v}^{(\text{lb})} \leq \mathbf{v} \leq \mathbf{v}^{(\text{ub})}, \tag{2}$$

$\mathbf{v}^{(\text{lb})}$ and $\mathbf{v}^{(\text{ub})}$ are vectors with entries $v_j^{(\text{lb})}$ and $v_j^{(\text{ub})}$ and the inequalities are defined componentwise.

Most FBA applications take a single network, where $\mathbf{c}$ and other parameters are known, and model phenotypic effects of modulating those parameters such as simulating a genetic/pharmacological perturbation or identifying optimal conditions to maximize some process (e.g., production of a specific molecule). FBA is most effective when reaction rates are predicted using a known objective function and constraints. Under well-studied conditions, we may safely assume certain biological objectives, such as a bacterium in nutrient-rich growth media optimizing growth and biomass accumulation [6]. However, when environmental variables change or cells are acting cooperatively in a multicellular system, these objectives change and become difficult to determine a priori.

One possible approach might be to try to estimate $\mathbf{c}$ and the corresponding reaction flux rates $\mathbf{v}$ based on gene product levels. The relationship between gene product levels and reaction flux in a reaction R_j is described by the Michaelis-Menten equation,

$$v_j = \frac{d[\text{substrate}]}{dt} = \frac{K_{\text{cat}}[\text{enzyme}][\text{substrate}]}{K_M + [\text{substrate}]} = \frac{V_{\text{max}}[\text{substrate}]}{K_M + [\text{substrate}]},$$

where the reaction rate v_j is a non-linear function of the substrate concentration [substrate], the concentration [enzyme] and experimentally-defined kinetic rate constant K_{cat} for the catalyzing enzyme, and the Michaelis constant K_M, the later two being commonly expressed using the product term V_{max}. Enzyme concentration is subject to regulatory processes beyond transcription that include post-transcriptional/translational modification, stability, and turnover. Additionally, K_{cat} can only be derived experimentally and is not available for many enzymes, making it difficult to implement in large genome-scale metabolic network models. For these reasons, gene expression values are typically an unreliable predictor of reaction rates.

We therefore consider dynamic gene expression changes between a given cell and a specified reference state, using relative expression values as a metric of active regulation, in order to learn a cellular objective function and concordant network state (i.e., first learn $\mathbf{c}$ and then learn $\mathbf{v}$). We note that the objective function itself is informative of metabolic regulation, and the utility of predicting precise flux rates will vary based on the data and experimental system. Therefore, we approach the separate problems with independent methods that can be combined or used independently for different applications. In summary, our goals are two-fold:

1. First, we aim to learn a vector $\mathbf{c}$ that describes which reactions the cell is trying to maximize.
2. Then, given $\mathbf{c}$, we aim to find $\mathbf{v}$ by solving the constrained optimization problem (2).

3   Related Work

Historically, metabolic phenotypes in transcriptional data have been identified using differential gene expression with pathway enrichment methods such as GSEA [29]. Some methods are specifically designed to focus on metabolic pathways such as KEGG [13], MetaboAnalyst [19], or Reactome [5]. More recently, various methods have been developed to integrate transcriptomic data and constraint-based modeling. For bulk population analysis, variations on FBA such as parsimonious FBA (pFBA), dynamic FBA (dFBA), or flux variability analysis (FVA) are able to incorporate gene expression information, as reviewed in [26].

Compass [30], a recently developed method, provides an extension of gene expression-constrained FBA to single-cell transcriptomics. In order to circumvent the previously discussed caveats with defining cellular objective functions in mammalian cells, i.e., that $\mathbf{c}$ is unknown, Compass instead estimates a score for each reaction in each cell representing the propensity of a cell to engage that reaction using serial rounds of linear optimization. First, an initial set of transcription-agnostic 'maximal fluxes' $\{v_j^{\mathrm{opt}}\}_{j=1}^{n}$ is calculated using network stoichiometries and user-defined parameters such as nutrient uptake limits. Gene expression values are then mapped to reactions and converted into penalty scores, where low expression of genes involved in a reaction incurs a high penalty, and, for every reaction R_j in every cell i, Compass solves a linear optimization problem that minimizes reaction penalties (i.e., minimizes use of lowly expressed genes) while preserving a specified proportion ω of the maximum flux, such that $v_j \geq v_j^{\mathrm{opt}} \cdot \omega$. The magnitude of v_j represents the maximal flux that reaction R_j may carry with minimal resistance from the cell, where $\{v_j\}_{j=1}^{n}$ can be inverted and scaled within each cell to produce a set of scores signifying the relative capacity of a given cell to carry flux through each reaction.

While Compass does avoid the pitfalls of estimating metabolic state using a blanket objective function such as biomass accumulation and does notably capture both known and novel biochemical phenotypes, iteration through each reaction in each cell generates a substantial computational cost and renders scalability difficult. Additionally, the capacity of a cell to engage a metabolic reaction transcriptionally does not necessarily imply a biological imperative to do so. For this reason, we hypothesize that identifying a cellular objective function based on dynamic gene expression will provide useful information about metabolic programs that mechanistically drive processes such as cellular differentiation and effector functionality, while simultaneously mitigating the computational burden of serial linear optimization.

To address these challenges, we propose a deep learning method for high-throughput prediction of metabolic network activity from scRNAseq data. We first build an (undirected) graph $G = (V, E)$ of a given metabolic network where the nodes V represent reactions and edges E represent the production/consumption of a metabolite. Here, we define edges $\{v_i, v_j\} \in E$ if either reaction generates a product that the other consumes as a substrate, and edge weights represent metabolite flux, or the amount of metabolite moving between nodes v_i and v_j per arbitrary unit of time. We define node features as the relative gene expression between a given cell and a specified reference cell, which we map to the reactions catalyzed by each gene product to obtain a vertex-weighted graph that can be used to learn cellular objective functions and subsequent flux-balanced network state solutions.

4 GEFMAP: Gene Expression-Based Flux Mapping and Metabolic Pathway Prediction

In this section, we outline our method, which is illustrated in Fig. 1. Our approach is based on using a GNN to find a large, highly connected subgraph in a graph derived from the metabolic network, using the output of this GNN to derive a cellular objective function, and then solving this objective function via neural network which is geometrically constrained in order to preserve mass balance in the system.

4.1 Metabolic Network Graph Generation

Given a network with m metabolites and n reactions, we treat the nodes of the graph as the reactions and the edges of the graph as the amount of metabolites flowing through them. We let $\hat{S}$ denote a Boolean stoichiometry matrix defined by

$$\hat{S}_{j,k} = \begin{cases} 1 & \text{if } |S_{j,k}| > 0 \\ 0 & \text{otherwise} \end{cases},$$

and we calculate an $n \times n$ reaction adjacency matrix, A defined as in [25] by

$$A = \hat{S}^T \hat{S}.$$

We note that $A_{j,k}$ is nonzero if and only if reactions R_j and R_k utilize a common metabolite in a producer/consumer relationship. The resulting graph represents the connectivity of the metabolic network.

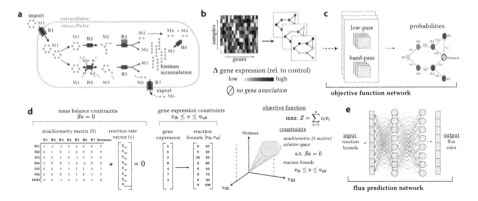

Fig. 1. Illustration of methods starting with (a.) a set of enzyme-catalyzed reactions and their associated substrate/product metabolites and constructing a node-weighted graph (b.) where node weights represent gene expression values, (c.) determining which reactions a cell is trying to maximize (a cellular metabolic objective) via a graph neural network (d.) using stoichiometric constraints to formulate an objective function and (4) using a neural network to find flux rates which optimize this objective.

Nodes corresponding to reactions that are catalyzed by a gene-encoded enzyme have gene expression features, and we assign values w_j to each node using the reaction gene associations provided in the genome-scale models (GEM). If a reaction can be catalyzed by multiple enzymes separately (A or B), we use the maximum expression value for the set of genes, and if the enzymes form a complex (A and B), we take the minimum expression value. We apply ℓ^1-normalization and min-max scaling to expression values across reactions; reactions without gene associations are assigned a value of 0 for estimating the objective function and 1 for predicting the flux rates.

4.2 Inferring the Objective Function

The first key component of GEFMAP is a graph neural network which uses the geometry of the metabolic network to infer cellular metabolic objective $\mathbf{c}$ in (2). We formulate an approach based on [20], which uses a GNN to find the maximum clique (largest fully connected subgraph) in a given graph. In the metabolic context this would identify a set of interconnected reactions that are upregulated, i.e., an upregulated metabolic pathway for example, rather than an isolated set of reactions. Note that cliques may not be possible in metabolic graphs due to chemical and enzymatic constraints, since not every substrate leads to every product. For this, we relax the problem to we consider the maximum weighted subgraph, which is defined as

$$C^* = \arg\max_C \sum_{j \in C} w_j \tag{3}$$

where the max is taken over all cliques, i.e., sets $C \subseteq V$ such that $A_{j,k} > 0$ for all $j, k \in C$, and the node weights w_j are the normalized reaction expression features described in the previous subsection.

The input to our GNN is an $n \times 4$ feature matrix X where the columns of X represent the eccentricity, clustering coefficient, node weight, and weighted degree of the nodes (defined as the sum of weights across neighboring nodes $\sum_j A_{i,j}$). This differs from [20] which used an $n \times 3$ matrix with unweighted node degree and omitted the node weight column. The output is vector $\mathbf{p}$ where p_j is to be thought of as the *probability* that the j-th node is a member of C^*.

The GNN used to compute $\mathbf{p}$, i.e. probability of subgraph membership of a node. In each layer, the network uses two types of filters: (i) low-pass filters inspired by Kipf and Welling's Graph Convolutional Network (GCN) [11] and (ii) band-pass wavelet filters inspired by the geometric scattering transform [8] (see also [7,34]). The low-pass filters, which are similar to those used in standard message-passing neural networks (see, e.g., [31]) are constructed by applying powers of the normalized adjacency matrix and aim to smooth the node features, i.e., to ensure that the GNN's representation of node j is similar to node k if there is an edge between j and k. The band-pass filters, which are constructed using diffusion wavelets [2], i.e. differences between different scales of random walks. To understand the importance of these band-pass filters and their capacity to capture different information than the GCN filters, consider the case where C^* consists of 30 nodes and some node j is a neighbor of 29 of them. A network which is solely based on low-pass smoothing operations will produce a hidden representation of node j which is similar to its neighbors. Therefore, it is highly likely to mistakenly think that j is a member of the clique. By contrast, the band-pass filters do not smooth the node features and allow the network to detect some manner in which x_j is different than the values of $\mathbf{x}$ at the neighbors of j.

Since the low-pass and band-pass filters can be seen as serving competing goals, promoting smoothness in features versus preserving informative oscillations, we use a localized attention mechanism to balance the importance of the various filters in the network. For each filter f, the attention mechanism computes a score vector $\boldsymbol{\alpha}_f$ (where $(\boldsymbol{\alpha}_f)_j$ is the importance of filter f and node j) and uses these scores to reweight the hidden representation of each vertex. The network then passes this hidden representation through a multi-layer perceptron (MLP) before applying another GNN layer. For further details on the layers utilized in this GNN (which also includes readout layers and an initial transformation of the node features parameterized by an MLP), we refer the readers to Section 3 of [20].

Unlike more common GNN tasks such as node-classification, there is no obvious loss function to use while training the GNN to solve (3). Similar to [20] we use a mass concentration loss function, that ensures that the cellular objective is a coherent set of reactions that are not too dispersed. In particular, the objective contains two parts, one part maximizes connections within likely clique members, and the second part minimizes the probabilities outside of a clique. Given the membership probability vector p and graph adjacency A the loss function is given by, with hyperparameters β choosing the importance of each term.

$$L(p) := L_1(p) + \beta L_2(p) = -p^T W p + \beta p^T \overline{W} p \qquad (4)$$

Notably, our network relaxes many of the constraints of the max-weighted clique network of [20]. First, we do not require a single maximum weighted clique, indeed a cell can upregulate many metabolic pathways, second we do not need these reactions to form a "true clique," this is in fact not possible due to the structure of metabolic reactions, instead we simply want a highly interconnected weighted subgraph. Thus, in particular we do not need parts of the network that process p into a combinatorially accurate maximum clique as is done in [20].

4.3   Null Space Network for Solving the Objective Function

Having found the objective $\mathbf{c}$ by the method from the previous subsection, here, we will now use deep learning to solve the optimization problem (2). Note that given a metabolic objective, solving for flux is a constrained optimization problem. In specific cases of solving FBA, one can use a linear program. However, solving a linear program for each cell becomes computationally infeasible. This motivates the use of a neural network that efficiently mimics a linear program. Additionally, with a neural network more flexibility is available. For instance, we can bias the system towards a sparse solution such that the number of reactions taken to achieve the metabolic objective is energy efficient. Thus, here we formulate a null space network for this goal. Note that rather than using penalties to respect stoichiometric constraints, this network operates in the null space of the stoichiometric matrix, i.e., an alternate coordinate system where all points respect metabolic constraints. We note that such spaces could be further constrained by, e.g., thermodynamic constraints in the future.

Thus second component of GEFMAP is a neural network which maximizes $\sum_i c_i |v_i|$ over $\mathbf{v}$ lying in the null space of S. In order to account for the geometric mass-balance constraint, $S\mathbf{v} = 0$, we first compute an orthonormal basis for $\text{Null}(S)$, $\mathbf{b_1}, \dots, \mathbf{b_K}$, and note that any $\mathbf{v} \in \text{Null}(S)$ may be written as

$$\mathbf{v} = \sum_{k=1}^{K} \theta_k \mathbf{b_k}$$

for some $\theta_1, \dots, \theta_k \in \mathbb{R}$. We calculate the flux vector $\mathbf{v}$ for a small subset of the data using a linear program similar to FBA, which is then used to train a multi-layer perceptron (MLP). The MLP consists of 3 fully connected hidden layers and ReLU activations and the outputs of this network are the flux vectors v which are the estimated flux values based on the pre-computed null space vectors of the stoichiometric matrix.

5   Experiments

5.1   Experimental Setup

Extensive experiments on GEFMAP are performed on a synthetic toy data set, an augmented E. coli data set, and a human embryoid body data set to validate the model's efficacy in modeling complex metabolic networks. For code needed to reproduce our experiments, please see https://github.com/KrishnaswamyLab/ metabolic_GNN; for further detail we refer the reader to the supplemental methods in Sect. A.1. The first subnetwork of GEFMAP computes the cell's metabolic objective that can be solved using the second subnetwork. All of the graphs generated from these data sets are treated as undirected by all the networks except in the case of one of the baselines MagNet [33], which is a directed graph neural network that is capable of dealing with directed edges (where the direction of the edge corresponds to the direction of the reaction). For all of the solver methods, we use the upper and lower bounds $\mathbf{v}^{ub}$ and $\mathbf{v}^{lb}$ as input features. As a loss function, we use the mean squared error between $\mathbf{v}$ and the optimal ground truth solution $\mathbf{v}^*$ (where the ground truth vectors for training are generated via a direct linear solver).

Baselines. To evaluate the physiological relevance of our objective function, we compare flux distributions calculated to maximize our MWS objective to the established biomass objective [6]. We use a dataset containing bulk RNA sequencing from E. coli where experimental parameters and measurements are available in order to determine how well these objectives recapitulate the biology.

For the objective function solver null space network, we compare to both an off-the-shelf linear solver as well as several other deep-learning architectures. We first compare to a simple multilayer perceptron (MLP) that does not use the geometry of the metabolic network. We next compare to a graph convolutional network (GCN) [11], a widely used message-passing network for node-level tasks on undirected graphs. We also consider MagNet [33], which aims to incorporate directional information into the geometric deep learning framework. To apply MagNet, we view the metabolic network as a directed graph, where edge direction corresponds to the direction of the flow, i.e., there is a directed edge from R_i to R_j if R_i produces a metabolite which is then utilized by R_j. Given the directed graph, MagNet then uses a complex Hermitian matrix known as the magnetic Laplacian [3,16,21] to define a notion of convolution on a directed graph (building off of several previous works, such as [4,14], which uses the standard graph Laplacian on an undirected graph).

5.2 Validating Our Objective Function on Core E. Coli Network

Here, we evaluate the biological relevance of the objective function introduced in Sect. 4.2, which is based on maximum weighted subgraph (MWS). We compare this to the biomass objective, which takes as an assumption that cells aim to maximize growth [6]. We first test our methods using gene expression from the PRECISE compendium of E. coli cultured under various conditions [27]. For these experiments, we use absolute rather than relative expression values due to the experimental absence of a reference transcriptome. Using the E. coli core metabolic model [23], we construct a $m \times n$ reaction adjacency matrix A representative of $m = 72$ metabolites and $n = 95$ reactions. Expression of 137

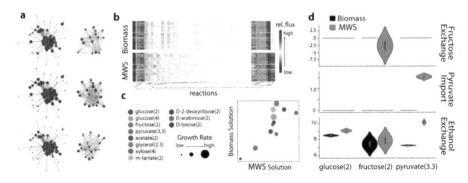

Fig. 2. Maximum Weighted Subgraph (MWS) Objective in E. Coli. (a) Illustration of vertex-weighted metabolic network graphs (left) constructed from the core E. coli metabolic network and associated max-weighted cliques (right) Node colors denote MWS probabilities, node sizes denote reaction-associated gene expression; (left) red node borders denote inclusion in an approximated ground truth max-weighted clique. (b.) Predicted reaction flux rates from E. coli RNA sequencing samples to maximize the flux through highly-connected subnetworks (top) or biomass/growth objectives (bottom). (c.) Correlation between maximal objective solutions for different objectives. Datapoints are colored by experimental growth condition and datapoint size represents experimentally-measured relative growth rates. (d.) Predicted flux rates for reactions involved in central carbon metabolism for bacteria grown in the presence of either glucose, fructose, or pyruvate. (Color figure online)

genes was mapped onto the 95 reactions, examples illustrated in (Fig. 2a), and reaction expression values were used to compute **c**.

To test the result of the MWS (in isolation of the null space network), we next use FBA with an off-the-shelf linear solver to estimate reaction flux rates across the network that maximized either flux through the relaxed max clique or, as a comparison, maximized biomass accumulation (growth). When maximizing with respect to our MWS objective, we observe a general concordance between the predicted flux distributions and those determined using the biomass objective (Fig. 2b). This trend was expected, as bacteria grown in nutrient-replete cell culture are expected to be in a growth state [6], although we note distinct differences in certain samples. Indeed, using both objective functions we observed a general correlation between experimentally measured growth rates and flux rates (Fig. 2c). However, when optimizing for biomass, there are a number of samples for which we are able to find transcriptionally-constrained flux solutions that predict high levels of biomass increase despite the fact that the measured growth rates are low, reinforcing the utility of considering alternative metabolic objectives. To further explore this, we look specifically at bacteria cultured with either 2 g/L glucose, fructose, or pyruvate and compare differences in the predicted rate of reactions involved in these different components of central carbon metabolism (Fig. 2d). For both fructose and pyruvate, the only conditions in which we observe predicted activity in the reactions that mediate cellular import are in the presence of the nutrient and with solutions that maximize flux through the maximum weighted subgraph, suggesting that this method is able to capture the cellular metabolic response to environmental nutrient availability.

5.3 Learning FBA Solution Flux Estimations

For the purposes of validating our null space network, we generated a synthetic data set comprised of 892 graphs with each graph having $n = 8$ reactions and $m = 12$ metabolites. Gene expression values were chosen by random sampling of a normal distribution, and ground truth reaction flux rates were determined by flux balance analysis (FBA) using an arbitrary objective function. We additionally test the augmented E. coli data that consists of over 3000 graphs with 95 reactions, 72 metabolites, and 2204 edges where the ground truth reaction flux rates were computed using the geometric scattering GNN. We evaluate accuracy via the metric used to compare the Pearson Correlation Coefficient (PCC) between predicted flux values and the ground truth for both the null space network and the baseline models.

Table 1. Results of flux predictions (PCC with ground truth) over five runs (mean ± standard deviation). The best-performing method is highlighted in bold.

Data Model name	Synthetic	E. coli
Null Space	**0.928 ± 0.016**	**0.939 ± 0.001**
MagNet	0.841 ± 0.014	0.920 ± 0.005
GCN	0.643 ± 0.021	0.741 ± 0.019
MLP	0.308 ± 0.011	0.409 ± 0.004

The results in Table 1 show the mean ± standard deviation PCC of the models, run five times on each data set, employing different random states each time during the train-test split process. GCN performs considerably better than the simple MLP, due to its ability to incorporate the network structure of the data, and MagNet performs better than GCN likely due to its ability to incorporate the direction of the reactions. The null space network, which also incorporates the structure of the network via the constraint $S\mathbf{v} = 0$, is the top performing model on both data sets.

5.4 Human Embryoid Networks

To test the strength of GEFMAP on real-world data, we use a previously published scRNAseq data set of human embryonic stem cells (hESCs) gathered at 5 timepoints over 27 days [22]. We generate a human metabolic network graph using Recon3 [1] that consists of 5835 metabolites and 10600 reactions. We consider dynamic gene expression between a given timepoint and precursor embryonic stem (ES) cells sequenced at the initial timepoint ($t = 0$), which are

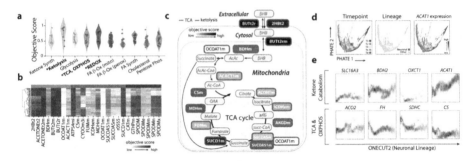

Fig. 3. Human embryoid body data implicates ketone metabolism in regulation of neuronal lineage differentiation. (a.) Objective score (MWS prediction) values for different metabolic pathways. Individual data points represent reactions, and objective score values represent median score across all cells. (b.) Heatmap showing objective scores for individual reactions. Left side bar denotes pathway association (blue = ketone catabolism, red = TCA, green = REDOX). (c.) Illustration showing catabolism of the ketone β-hydroxybutrate (BHB) for utilization as a carbon substrate for the TCA. Reaction border color denotes pathway associate (blue = ketone catabolism, red = TCA) (d.) PHATE embeddings [22] colored by experimental timepoint (left), neuronal lineage identity (center), and expression of ketone metabolic gene *ACAT1* (right). (e.) DREVI [12] visualization of the relationship between expression of neuronal lineage marker *ONECUT2* and expression of genes catalyzing reactions involved in ketolytis (left column) or the TCA (right column). (Color figure online)

used as the input for GEFMAP. We define an objective score as the likelihood values that each reaction is included in the max weighted clique, representing the relative likelihood a cell is actively engaging a given reaction.

We first aggregate reaction scores across all neuronal lineage (NL) cells and group reactions by pathways that were manually curated using Metabolic Atlas [15] (Fig. 3a). Of the pathways analyzed, we observe the highest objective scores in reactions involved in ketolysis (ketone consumption), as well as notable trends towards higher scores in TCA/OXPHOS (tricarboxylic acid cycle and oxidative phosphorylation) and REDOX (oxidation-reduction) regulation (Fig. 3a,b).

Ketone bodies (ketones), Beta-hydroxybutyrate (βHB) and acetoacetate (AcAc), are short-chain fatty acids that are synthesized mainly in the liver and provide an alternative fuel source to glucose [9]. Ketones are actively imported into the cell via MCT transporters and transported into the mitochondria, where they are converted to acetyl-CoA and enter the TCA for production of energy via ATP (Fig. 3c). Human patients fed a ketogenic diet show improvement in cognitive function as well as reduced pathology resulting from neuronal damage or neurodegenerative disease [18], mechanistically attributed to neuronal preference for βHB as a carbon source for mitochondrial metabolism. Additional roles have been described that include regulation of neuronal excitability [32] and response to oxidative stress. In accordance with literature [17], we observed lower objective scores for glycolysis and fatty acid oxidation modules (Fig. 3A). Within the ketolytic pathway, objective scores vary between individual reactions with the highest scores observed in reactions that move βHB between cellular compartments (Fig. 3b,c).

To explore the specificity of this pathway in the neuronal lineage, we embed cells based on transcriptional similarity using PHATE [22] and identify NL cells using the lineage marker *ONECUT2* (Fig. 3d). Visualizing expression of the enzyme *ACAT1*, which reversibly converts acetoacetyl-Coa into 2 acetyl-CoA (reaction ACACT1m), shows high expression in the NL as opposed to other populations at late experimental timepoints. We further visualize the relationship between expression of *ONECUT2* and metabolic genes using conditional-Density Resampled Visualization of Mutual Information (DREVI) [12]. Although co-expression patterns are variable, we observe trends towards an increase in ketolytic genes and decrease in TCA/OXPHOS genes as NL cells differentiate and begin expressing *ONECUT2*. Results suggest that neuronal cells switch their TCA cycle from pyruvate to βHB, and we hypothesize that this may regulate differentiation programs.

6   Conclusions and Future Work

In this paper we introduce GEFMAP (Gene Expression-based Flux Mapping and Metabolic Pathway Prediction), a novel geometric deep learning method to estimate cellular metabolic states from single cell gene expression data. GEFMAP is a two-part neural network; the first component is a geometric scattering-based GNN that finds a large highly connected subnetwork with high levels of gene expression in order to determine the cell's metabolic objective from dynamic gene expression values, and the second component is a fully connected MLP that operates in the null space of the metabolic stoichiometric matrix to solve the objective to estimate the resultant flux rate. Experiments using on synthetic and complex real-world data sets show the ability of GEFMAP to determine the metabolic objective and estimate the flux rate with high accuracy.

Acknowledgements. Yixuan He is supported by a Clarendon scholarship from the University of Oxford. Michael Perlmutter and Smita Krishnaswamy were partially funded by NSF DMS 2327211. Additionally, Smita Krishnaswamy was partially supported by NSF Career Grant 2047856, by NIH 1R01GM130847-01A1, and by NIH 1R01GM135929-01.

A   Supplemental Information

A.1   Supplemental Methods

Source code, GEM files, datasets, and other resources are openly available at our Github repository (https://github.com/KrishnaswamyLab/metabolic_GNN).

Transcriptomic Data. Bulk RNA sequencing data was obtained from the Precision RNA-seq Expression Compendium for Independent Signal Exploration (PRECISE) [27] that was collected from 15 studies conducted in the same laboratory using a standardized protocol and includes information on experimental conditions and measured growth rates. The original data contains over 250 samples and approximately 150 experimental conditions, which we augmented to over 3000 samples by adding Gaussian noise to gene expression values.

Single cell RNA sequencing data from human embryoid body cells was obtained from [22]; filtering and normalization was done identically to the original publication.

Objective Function Prediction Network. The graph neural network used to infer the objective c takes in torch geometric graph objects as input and utilizes the RMSProp optimizer. For all experiments, a learning rate $lr = 0.0001$ trained on 3 epochs with a batch size of 80 as training parameters with a (60-20-20) train-test-validation split. For E. coli data the parameter β in the loss function was set to 0.1, and for human EB data was set to 0.25.

Objective Function Solver Networks. All four flux prediction/estimation models utilize the Adam optimizer with a learning rate $lr = 0.01$ trained on 100 epochs. A train/test split of 80-20 is applied to the dataset. In order to compute the training losses, we use the mean squared error between the predicted and ground truth values. The performance metrics are computed by taking the mean and standard deviation of the Pearson Correlation Coefficient (PCC) between the predicted and ground truth values over 5 runs of each model.

References

1. Brunk, E., et al.: Recon3D enables a three-dimensional view of gene variation in human metabolism. Nat. Biotechnol. **36**(3), 272–281 (2018)
2. Coifman, R.R., Maggioni, M.: Diffusion wavelets. Appl. Comput. Harmon. Anal. **21**(1), 53–94 (2006)
3. Cucuringu, M., Li, H., Sun, H., Zanetti, L.: Hermitian matrices for clustering directed graphs: insights and applications. In: International Conference on Artificial Intelligence and Statistics, pp. 983–992. PMLR (2020)
4. Defferrard, M., Bresson, X., Vandergheynst, P.: Convolutional neural networks on graphs with fast localized spectral filtering. In: Advances in Neural Information Processing Systems, vol. 29, pp. 3844–3852 (2016)
5. Fabregat, A., et al.: The reactome pathway knowledgebase. Nucleic Acids Res. **46**(D1), D649–D655 (2017). https://doi.org/10.1093/nar/gkx1132
6. Feist, A.M., Palsson, B.O.: The biomass objective function. Curr. Opin. Microbiol. **13**(3), 344–349 (2010). https://doi.org/10.1016/j.mib.2010.03.003
7. Gama, F., Ribeiro, A., Bruna, J.: Diffusion scattering transforms on graphs. In: 7th International Conference on Learning Representations, ICLR 2019 (2019)
8. Gao, F., Wolf, G., Hirn, M.: Geometric scattering for graph data analysis. In: International Conference on Machine Learning, pp. 2122–2131. PMLR (2019)

9. García-Rodríguez, D., Giménez-Cassina, A.: Ketone bodies in the brain beyond fuel metabolism: from excitability to gene expression and cell signaling. Front. Mol. Neurosci. **14**, 732120 (2021)

10. Heirendt, L., et al.: Creation and analysis of biochemical constraint-based models using the COBRA toolbox v.3.0. Nat. Protoc. **14**(3), 639–702 (2019). https://doi.org/10.1038/s41596-018-0098-2

11. Kipf, T.N., Welling, M.: Semi-supervised classification with graph convolutional networks. In: 5th International Conference on Learning Representations, ICLR 2017, Toulon, France, 24–26 April 2017, Conference Track Proceedings (2017)

12. Krishnaswamy, S., et al.: Conditional density-based analysis of t cell signaling in single-cell data. Science **346**(6213) (2014). https://doi.org/10.1126/science.1250689

13. Kyoto Encyclopedia of Genes and Genomes (KEGG): Kyoto encyclopedia of genes and genomes. https://www.genome.jp/kegg/

14. Levie, R., Monti, F., Bresson, X., Bronstein, M.M.: Cayleynets: graph convolutional neural networks with complex rational spectral filters. IEEE Trans. Signal Process. **67**(1), 97–109 (2019). https://doi.org/10.1109/TSP.2018.2879624

15. Li, F., Chen, Y., Anton, M., Nielsen, J.: Gotenzymes: an extensive database of enzyme parameter predictions. Nucleic Acids Res. **51**(D1), D583–D586 (2022). https://doi.org/10.1093/nar/gkac831

16. Lieb, E.H., Loss, M.: Fluxes, Laplacians, and Kasteleyn's theorem. In: Nachtergaele, B., Solovej, J.P., Yngvason, J. (eds.) Statistical Mechanics, pp. 457–483. Springer, Heidelberg (1993). https://doi.org/10.1007/978-3-662-10018-9_28

17. Maffezzini, C., Calvo-Garrido, J., Wredenberg, A., Freyer, C.: Metabolic regulation of neurodifferentiation in the adult brain. Cell. Mol. Life Sci. **77**, 2483–2496 (2020)

18. Mattson, M.P., Moehl, K., Ghena, N., Schmaedick, M., Cheng, A.: Intermittent metabolic switching, neuroplasticity and brain health. Nat. Rev. Neurosci. **19**(2), 81–94 (2018). https://doi.org/10.1038/nrn.2017.156

19. MetaboAnalyst: Metaboanalyst: A comprehensive tool suite for metabolomic data analysis. https://www.metaboanalyst.ca/

20. Min, Y., Wenkel, F., Perlmutter, M., Wolf, G.: Can hybrid geometric scattering networks help solve the maximum clique problem? In: NeurIPS (2022). http://papers.nips.cc/paper_files/paper/2022/hash/8ec88961d36d9a87ac24baf45402744f-Abstract-Conference.html

21. Mohar, B.: A new kind of Hermitian matrices for digraphs. Linear Algebra Appl. **584**, 343–352 (2020)

22. Moon, K.R., et al.: Visualizing structure and transitions in high-dimensional biological data. Nat. Biotechnol. **37**(12), 1482–1492 (2019). https://doi.org/10.1038/s41587-019-0336-3

23. Orth, J.D., Fleming, R.M.T., Palsson, B.Ø.: Reconstruction and use of microbial metabolic networks: the core Escherichia coli metabolic model as an educational guide. EcoSal Plus **4**(1) (2010). https://doi.org/10.1128/ecosalplus.10.2.1

24. Orth, J.D., Thiele, I., Palsson, B.Ø.: What is flux balance analysis? Nat. Biotechnol. **28**(3), 245–248 (2010). https://doi.org/10.1038/nbt.1614

25. Palsson, B.O.: Systems Biology: Properties of Reconstructed Networks. Cambridge University Press, New York (2006)

26. Sahu, A., Blätke, M.A., Szymański, J.J., Töpfer, N.: Advances in flux balance analysis by integrating machine learning and mechanism-based models. Comput. Struct. Biotechnol. J. **19**, 4626–4640 (2021). https://doi.org/10.1016/j.csbj.2021.08.004

27. Sastry, A.V., et al.: The Escherichia coli transcriptome mostly consists of independently regulated modules. Nat. Commun. **10**(1) (2019). https://doi.org/10.1038/s41467-019-13483-w

28. Schuetz, R., Zamboni, N., Zampieri, M., Heinemann, M., Sauer, U.: Multidimensional optimality of microbial metabolism. Science **336**(6081), 601–604 (2012). https://doi.org/10.1126/science.1216882

29. Subramanian, A., et al.: Gene set enrichment analysis: a knowledge-based approach for interpreting genome-wide expression profiles. Proc. Natl. Acad. Sci. **102**(43), 15545–15550 (2005). https://doi.org/10.1073/pnas.0506580102

30. Wagner, A., et al.: Metabolic modeling of single TH17 cells reveals regulators of autoimmunity. Cell **184**(16), 4168–4185.e21 (2021). https://doi.org/10.1016/j.cell.2021.05.045

31. Xu, K., Hu, W., Leskovec, J., Jegelka, S.: How powerful are graph neural networks? In: 7th International Conference on Learning Representations, ICLR 2019, New Orleans, LA, USA, 6–9 May 2019 (2019)

32. Yudkoff, M., et al.: Response of brain amino acid metabolism to ketosis. Neurochem. Int. **47**(1–2), 119–128 (2005)

33. Zhang, X., He, Y., Brugnone, N., Perlmutter, M., Hirn, M.: Magnet: a neural network for directed graphs. Adv. Neural. Inf. Process. Syst. **34**, 27003–27015 (2021)

34. Zou, D., Lerman, G.: Graph convolutional neural networks via scattering. Appl. Comput. Harmon. Anal. **49**(3), 1046–1074 (2020). https://doi.org/10.1016/j.acha.2019.06.003

Computing Robust Optimal Factories in Metabolic Reaction Networks

Spencer Krieger[1](✉) and John Kececioglu[2]

[1] Ray and Stephanie Lane Computational Biology Department,
Carnegie Mellon University, Pittsburgh, PA 15213, USA
`skrieger@andrew.cmu.edu`
[2] Department of Computer Science, The University of Arizona,
Tucson, AZ 85721, USA
`kece@cs.arizona.edu`

Abstract. Perhaps the most fundamental model in synthetic and systems biology for inferring pathways in metabolic reaction networks is a metabolic *factory*: a system of reactions that starts from a set of source compounds and produces a set of target molecules, while conserving or not depleting intermediate metabolites. Finding a shortest factory—that minimizes a sum of real-valued weights on its reactions to infer the most likely pathway—is NP-complete. The current state-of-the-art for shortest factories solves a mixed-integer linear program with a major drawback: it requires the user to set a critical parameter, where too large a value can make optimal solutions infeasible, while too small a value can yield degenerate solutions due to numerical error.

We present the first *robust algorithm* for optimal factories that is both *parameter-free* (relieving the user from determining a parameter setting) and *degeneracy-free* (guaranteeing it finds an optimal nondegenerate solution). We also give for the first time a *complete characterization* of the graph-theoretic structure of shortest factories via cuts of *hypergraphs* that reveals two important classes of degenerate solutions which were overlooked and potentially output by the prior state-of-the-art. In addition we settle the relationship between the two established pathway models of *hyperpaths* and factories by proving that hyperpaths are actually a subclass of factories. Comprehensive experiments over all instances from the standard metabolic reaction databases in the literature demonstrate our algorithm is *fast in practice*, quickly finding optimal factories in large real-world networks containing thousands of reactions.

A preliminary implementation of our algorithm for robust optimal factories in a new tool called `Freeia` is available free for research use at http://freeia.cs.arizona.edu.

1 Introduction

Metabolic pathways are cornerstones of synthetic and systems biology. They inform metabolic engineering, govern cellular environmental response, and their perturbation has been implicated in the cause of disease [19]. Reactions in such

J. Ma (Ed.): RECOMB 2024, LNCS 14758, pp. 253–269, 2024.
https://doi.org/10.1007/978-1-0716-3989-4_16

pathways are typically annotated with stoichiometry ratios for their participating molecules, that specify the relative number of copies that are consumed and produced. Networks of metabolic pathways are traditionally represented using conventional graphs [23,24], though such graphs do not accurately model multiway reactions that have multiple reactants and multiple products [8,22]. Directed *hypergraphs* (a generalization of directed graphs) in contrast fully capture multiway reactions [8], and represent such a reaction by a single hyperedge, directed from its set of input reactants to its set of output products.

A fundamental task on metabolic networks is to infer the most likely pathway that produces specific target molecules from the source compounds available to the cell, while not exhausting intermediate metabolites. Computationally this corresponds to the *shortest factory* problem we consider here: Given a metabolic network represented by a directed hypergraph with annotated stoichiometries, and a set of sources and targets, find a metabolic factory (a collection of reactions that conserve or do not deplete intermediate metabolites) that produces all the targets from the sources, while minimizing a weighted sum over its reactions.

Next we briefly summarize related work, and then state our contributions.

Related Work. The two main hypergraph models for pathway inference in metabolic networks are hyperpaths and factories. (For a further review, see [9].)

Hyperpaths informally are a set of reactions that produces all targets from the sources, where the reactions can be ordered so that the inputs to each reaction are produced as outputs of preceding reactions. Italiano and Nanni [6] proved that finding shortest hyperpaths is NP-complete. Ritz et al. [20,21] gave the first practical exact algorithm for *acyclic* shortest hyperpaths. Krieger and Kececioglu developed the first methods for *general* shortest hyperpaths that allow cycles: both an efficient heuristic that is close to optimal in practice [10,13,14], and a practical exact algorithm that uses a cutting-plane approach [15–17].

Factories informally are a set of reactions that produces all targets from the sources, while conserving or not depleting intermediate metabolites. Factories have been studied in the context of *min-source* factories (which use the fewest possible source compounds), and *min-edge* factories (which use the fewest possible reactions). Cottret et al. [4] proved that finding a min-source factory is NP-complete, while Acuña et al. [1] and Andrade et al. [2] developed methods to enumerate all min-source factories. Krieger and Kececioglu [12] proved that finding a min-edge factory is NP-complete, and developed a practical exact algorithm that finds optimal factories while also incorporating negative regulation. All these methods (whether explicitly or implicitly) rely on specifying the value of a critical *parameter*, whose default value can exclude valid factories. Furthermore these methods may return *degenerate* solutions that are either non-physical, or correspond to an equilibrium state where targets do not actually accrue.

We will unify these two pathway models—hyperpaths and factories—by later proving that hyperpaths are in fact a *subclass* of factories.

Our Contributions. In contrast to prior work, we give the first robust method for optimal factories that never fails due to poor parameter choices, and always delivers nondegenerate solutions. We also resolve the relationship between hyperpaths and factories via a new structural characterization of shortest factories. More specifically, we make the following contributions.

- We develop the first *robust algorithm* for shortest factories with no user-specified parameters, whose solution is guaranteed to be nondegenerate.

- We derive the first *complete characterization* of the graph-theoretic structure of reactions in shortest factories in terms of crossing hypergraph cuts.

- We leverage this characterization to unify the main hypergraph models for pathway inference, showing hyperpaths are actually a *subclass* of factories.

- Our computational results reveal the current *state-of-the-art fails* to find factories when they exist, due to brittleness in default parameter settings.

- Our new algorithm is *fast in practice*, as comprehensively demonstrated on the standard pathway databases, with a median runtime under 5 seconds.

A preliminary implementation of our robust algorithm for optimal factories in a new tool called `Freeia` (short for "robust optimal factories in metabolic reaction networks") is freely available at http://freeia.cs.arizona.edu.

Plan of the Paper. The next section presents our new *parameter-free* algorithm for optimal factories. Section 3 gives a complete *characterization* of the structure of shortest factories, proves hyperpaths comprise a subclass of factories, and develops an algorithm for optimal *nondegenerate* factories. Section 4 evaluates our algorithm on real biological benchmarks, highlighting instances where factories were missed by the prior state-of-the-art. Finally Sect. 5 concludes.

2   Computing Optimal Parameter-Free Factories

We next provide the necessary background on factories and hypergraphs, and then present our parameter-free algorithm for shortest factories.

2.1   Factories and Hypergraphs

Informally, a *factory* in a metabolic network is a collection of reactions that produces a set of target molecules starting from a set of source compounds, properly taking into account the stoichiometries of intermediate metabolites in reactions. The reactions in the factory may form cycles, and effectively can proceed simultaneously. This is in contrast to the notion of a *hyperpath*, which is also a collection of reactions that produces the targets from the sources, but without taking into account stoichiometry, and whose reactions must have an ordering in which for each successive reaction all its input reactants are formed as output products of prior reactions in the ordering.

For the intermediate metabolites involved in a factory (the substances other than sources and targets), the stoichiometry ratios for the input reactants and output products of the factory's reactions must be such that one of two conditions are met: either intermediate metabolites neither build up nor get depleted as the factory continues to produce the targets, known as *conservation*; or intermediate metabolites are allowed to build up, but not be depleted, known as *accumulation*. Under conservation or accumulation, by continuously supplying just the source compounds to the factory, all targets will be produced indefinitely.

To properly represent the reactions in a metabolic network, where a given reaction can have multiple input reactants and multiple output products, requires a generalization of ordinary directed graphs known as a directed *hypergraph* $G = (V, E)$, consisting of a set of directed *hyperedges* E, corresponding to the reactions of the network, and a set of vertices V, corresponding to the substances participating in the reactions. Each hyperedge $e \in E$ is an ordered pair (X, Y) where both $X, Y \subseteq V$ are nonempty sets of vertices, and e is directed from set X to set Y. Here X is called the *tail* of e, and Y is called its *head*, given by functions $\text{tail}(e) = X$ and $\text{head}(e) = Y$. We refer to the in-edges of a vertex $v \in V$ by $\text{in}(v) = \{e \in E : v \in \text{head}(e)\}$, and its out-edges by $\text{out}(v) = \{e \in E : v \in \text{tail}(e)\}$.

For a reaction represented in hypergraph G by hyperedge e, the set $\text{tail}(e)$ is all its input reactants, while $\text{head}(e)$ is all its output products. For a reversible reaction, we represent it in G by a pair of hyperedges $e = (X, Y)$ and its reverse hyperedge $\text{rev}(e) = (Y, X)$. Typically for a metabolic network represented by hypergraph G, the *sources* $S \subseteq V$ of the network are vertices with no in-edges, while *targets* $T \subseteq V$ are often (but not always) vertices with no out-edges.

Figure 2 in Sect. 4.2 shows a directed hypergraph.

Key to metabolic factories is the notion of *flux*: the relative rate at which each reaction is used in its forward direction by the factory. In a hypergraph, we represent the flux for a factory by a nonnegative real-valued vector $f = (f_e)_{e \in E}$ with all $f_e \geq 0$. For a metabolic network represented by a hypergraph, the stoichiometry ratios of the substances in the reactions of the network can be summarized by *stoichiometry matrix* $M = (r_{ve})_{v \in V, e \in E}$ where r_{ve} is the stoichiometry ratio for substance v in reaction e. We express this quantity as $r_{ve} := r_{ve}^+ - r_{ve}^-$, with r_{ve}^+ being the nonnegative stoichiometry ratio for $v \in \text{head}(e)$, where v is produced as an output product of reaction e; and r_{ve}^- being the nonnegative ratio for $v \in \text{tail}(e)$, where v is consumed as an input reactant of e. In all other cases, r_{ve}^+ and r_{ve}^- are zero. Their net difference in r_{ve} is positive when e produces more v than it consumes, and negative in the opposite situation.

Using stoichiometry matrix M, we can express whether flux f for a factory satisfies conservation or accumulation. For a set $I \subseteq V$ of intermediate metabolites, denote by $M|_I$ matrix M restricted to rows in I. Then matrix-vector product $M|_I f$ is a vector giving for each intermediate metabolite $v \in I$ the relative excess of v produced by reactions in the factory under flux f. Condition $M|_I f = 0$ captures *conservation*, while $M|_I f \geq 0$ captures *accumulation*.

A hyperedge e with nonzero flux $f_e > 0$ is called an *active edge*, meaning its corresponding reaction is used by the factory.

We now formally define the problem of finding an optimal factory in a metabolic network. This problem has two versions, according to whether we require conservation or accumulation of intermediate metabolites.

Definition 1 (Shortest Factory). *The* Shortest Factory *problem is as follows.*

The input is a metabolic network represented by hypergraph $G = (V, E)$ *with stoichiometries* M, *sources* $S \subseteq V$, *targets* $T \subseteq V - S$, *and edge weight function* ω.

The output is nonnegative flux f *such that: for all intermediate metabolites* $I = V - (S \cup T)$, *either accumulation* $M|_I f \geq 0$, *or conservation* $M|_I f = 0$ *holds; for each target* $t \in T$, *the production requirement* $\sum_{e \in \text{in}(t)} r_{te} f_e > 0$ *is met; and the total weight of active hyperedges* $\sum_{e \in E \,:\, f_e > 0} \omega(e)$ *is minimum.* □

This finds a metabolic factory, given by flux f, that produces all targets T from the sources S, while minimizing the total weight of its active edges. We call this total active edge weight the *length* of the factory.

Figure 2 in Sect. 4.2 illustrates an optimal factory as well.

For *nonuniform* edge weights, under a simple likelihood model where $P(e)$ is the probability that reaction e occurs given its input reactants, and assuming independence of reactions, a shortest factory for weights $\omega(e) = -\log P(e)$ corresponds to a metabolic factory of *maximum likelihood*.

For *uniform* edge weights, the *Minimum-Hyperedge Factory* problem is Shortest Factory with unit weights $\omega(e) = 1$ for all $e \in E$. This finds a factory that uses the least number of reactions, corresponding to a factory of *maximum parsimony*. We call an optimal solution to this problem a *min-edge factory*.

Shortest Factory—even for unit edge weights—is NP-complete [12], so there is likely no algorithm that finds optimal factories and is worst-case efficient.

We note that factories satisfying conservation tend to exist far less frequently than factories satisfying accumulation, as shown in Sect. 4.1 through Table 2.

2.2 Parameter-Free Shortest Factories

We now give the first parameter-free algorithm for Shortest Factory, which solves mixed-integer linear programs (MILPs). We first review the MILP for the state-of-the-art *parameter-based* algorithm, then present the MILPs for our *parameter-free* algorithm for min-edge factories, and finally extend it to *weighted* factories.

Parameter-Based Algorithm. Given an instance of Shortest Factory, the current state-of-the-art parameter-based algorithm [12] constructs an MILP consisting of variables, constraints, and an objective function, as we review below.

The *variables* are grouped into flux vector $f = (f_e)_{e \in E}$ with real-valued variables f_e, and active-edge vector $x = (x_e)_{e \in E}$ with integer-valued variables x_e.

The basic *constraints* are in the following classes. The domain constraints are $0 \leq f_e \leq 1$ and $0 \leq x_e \leq 1$ for all hyperedges $e \in E$ (which ensures $x_e \in \{0, 1\}$). For the intermediate metabolites $I = V - (S \cup T)$, we have either the conservation constraints $M|_I f = 0$, or the accumulation constraints $M|_I f \geq 0$. For hyperedges $e \in E$, the active edge constraints $x_e \geq f_e$ ensure $x_e = 1$ for an active edge e with $f_e > 0$. Lastly for pairs of reverse hyperedges e and $\text{rev}(e)$ that model a single reversible reaction, the reversible-reaction constraints $x_e + x_{\text{rev}(e)} \leq 1$ prevent trivial cycles that send flux through both e and its reverse.

The *objective function* minimizes $\sum_{e \in E} \omega(e) x_e$, the total active edge weight.

All prior methods for optimal factories [2,4,12,25] are *parameter-based*—which explicitly or implicitly depend on a parameter that either must be set by the user or is hard-coded into their implementation—and effectively use a target production constraint for each target $t \in T$ of the form $\sum_{e \in \text{in}(t)} r_{te} f_e \geq \epsilon$, for a small target production constant $\epsilon > 0$, to ensure their solution produces all targets. (This nonzero ϵ is necessary because MILPs cannot accurately represent strict inequalities of the form $\sum_e r_{te} f_e > 0$.) Such a dependence on *parameter* ϵ is a serious shortcoming, as an ill-suited value for ϵ that is too large can prevent the MILP solver from finding an optimal factory (when no optimal factory produces that much of its targets with bounded fluxes), while a value too small can cause the MILP solver to return an invalid factory (due to numerical rounding error).

Parameter-Free Algorithm. Instead our parameter-free algorithm overcomes this through the following approach, using one additional variable, two additional types of constraints, and now solving a small *series* of MILPs. We add a real-valued variable δ, and for each target $t \in T$ we replace the target production constraint by $\sum_{e \in \text{in}(t)} r_{te} f_e \geq \delta$. Then for Minimum-Hyperedge Factory, we add a length constraint $\sum_{e \in E} x_e \leq \ell$, for an integer ℓ that is determined below.

The new objective function now maximizes the value of variable δ.

Notice the objective function value δ^* of an optimal solution to this new MILP gives the maximum possible flux that can be sent to all the targets by a factory with at most ℓ active hyperedges. If δ^* is zero, we know there is no factory of length at most ℓ that produces all the targets. Once we find the smallest ℓ for which δ^* exceeds zero, we know we have found an optimal min-edge factory.

We can find the unknown length ℓ^* of a min-edge factory in two phases, as follows. The first phase uses doubling, starting from $\ell = 1$, multiplying ℓ by a factor of 2 in the next iteration, where each iteration solves an MILP instance of the above form, until δ^* for the current limit ℓ is greater than zero. This yields an upper bound u on ℓ^*, satisfying $u < 2\ell^*$. The second phase then performs binary search on interval $[0, u]$, again solving MILP instances as above, to find ℓ^*.

To find a min-edge factory, whose optimal number of reactions is k, this solves just $\Theta(\log k)$ instances of the above MILP. For a hypergraph of n vertices and m hyperedges, each MILP instance has $\Theta(m)$ variables and $\Theta(m+n)$ constraints.

Extending to Weighted Factories. We can extend this further to factories with positively *weighted* reactions. We use length constraint $\sum_e \omega(e) x_e \leq \ell$, for real ℓ. Then given upper bound u on the shortest factory length, such as $\sum_e \omega(e)$, we perform bisection on $[0, u]$ to find optimal length ℓ^*. This yields a shortest factory, for machine precision ϵ, after solving $O(\log(u/\epsilon))$ instances of MILPs.

3   Characterizing Optimal Factories

We next give a complete *characterization* of the structure of shortest factories, that captures for the first time exactly which sets of reactions correspond to optimal factories. We then relate *hyperpaths* to factories, showing they actually comprise a subclass of metabolic factories. Finally we build on this characterization to develop the first practical algorithm for optimal *nondegenerate* factories.

3.1   The Structure of Shortest Factories

To simplify our structural characterization, we first note that the multiple-source and multiple-target factory problem can be reduced to a simpler *single-source* and *single-sink* version, where both problems are under accumulation. (We omit the reduction due to page limits.) Consequently, the s, t-factory problem with a single source s and a single sink t that we work with below is fully general—and leads to a cleaner characterization.

We next define the notions of cuts, crossing a cut, reachability, cycles, and intact sets that are essential to the characterization of factories. (The following terminology is in distinction to the notions of strongly-crossing a cut and strong-reachability that are defined for hyperpaths in Sect. 3.2.)

An s, t-*cut* of hypergraph $G = (V, E)$ with source $s \in V$ and sink $t \in V - \{s\}$ is a bipartition $(C, \overline{C})$ of its vertices V, where $C \subseteq V$ and $\overline{C} := V - C$, with $s \in C$ and $t \in \overline{C}$. We often refer to such a cut by just specifying its source-side C.

Hyperedge e *weakly-crosses* s, t-cut C if tail$(e) \not\subseteq \overline{C}$ and head$(e) \not\subseteq C$. In other words, hyperedge e weakly-crosses source-sink cut C if some vertex in tail(e) is on the source-side C, while some vertex in head(e) is on the sink-side $\overline{C}$. A set of hyperedges F *weakly-crosses* C if some $e \in F$ weakly-crosses C.

Vertex w is *weakly-reachable* from vertex v by hyperedges $F \subseteq E$ if $v = w$, or recursively, if $w \in$ head(e) for a hyperedge $e \in F$ with a vertex in tail(e) that is weakly-reachable from v by F. We also say F *weakly-reaches* w from v. Similarly v is *weakly-backward-reachable* from w if F weakly-reaches w from v.

A *cycle* is a minimal set of hyperedges $F \subseteq E$ where for all distinct $e, f \in F$ both of the following hold: F weakly-reaches some vertex in tail(f) from some vertex in head(e), and vice versa F weakly-reaches some vertex in tail(e) from some vertex in head(f). In other words, in a cycle, for every pair of hyperedges, both are weakly-reachable from the other within the cycle (while this does not hold for any proper subset of the cycle).

A set $F \subseteq E$ is s, t-*intact* with respect to source s and sink t if F has an in-edge to t, and an in-edge to every vertex other than s that is touched by F. In other words, an intact set is closed with respect to in-edges, as the sink and every vertex it touches other than the source has an in-edge within the set.

We now define the three solution classes that can arise as shortest factories.

Definition 2 (Trails, Whirls, and Eddies). *Consider a directed hypergraph $G = (V, E)$ with source $s \in V$, sink $t \in V - \{s\}$, and hyperedge subset $F \subseteq E$.*

An s, t-trail is an s, t-intact set F that weakly-crosses every s, t-cut.

An s, t-whirl is an s, t-intact set F that does not *weakly-cross every s, t-cut, but contains a cycle $C \subseteq F$ that touches sink t and does not touch source s.*

An s, t-eddy is an s, t-intact set F that does not *weakly-cross every s, t-cut, does* not *contain a cycle touching t and not s, but contains a cycle $C \subseteq F$ that touches neither s nor t yet touches a vertex from which F weakly-reaches t.* □

Fig. 1. The three classes of factories. Every shortest factory is either a *trail* (shown in red), *whirl* (in blue), or *eddy* (in black). Conversely, every trail, whirl, or eddy is a shortest factory for some edge weights and stoichiometries. A general factory instance can always be reduced to an equivalent one with a single source s and a single target t. (Color figure online)

Figure 1 illustrates these three classes. (Hyperedges are drawn to indicate multiple head- and tail-vertices.) These classes are distinct, and together they capture all s, t-intact sets (as the proof below shows).

We can now state our main theorem, which completely characterizes the structure of the active hyperedges of shortest factories for *general* edge weights and stoichiometries, where edge weights are arbitrary reals that can be negative.

(Due to page limits, we only give sketches of the proofs for the theorems in this proceedings paper. Full proofs will appear in the journal paper.)

Theorem 1 (Characterization of Shortest Factories). *Let* $G = (V, E)$ *be a hypergraph with source* $s \in V$ *and sink* $t \in V - \{s\}$. *Then* $F \subseteq E$ *is the set of active hyperedges of a shortest* s, t-*factory in* G *under accumulation for some edge weights and stoichiometries if and only if* F *is an* s, t-*trail, -whirl, or -eddy.*

Proof. (Sketch) For the *forward* implication, accumulation forces the the active hyperedges F of an s, t-factory to be s, t-intact. Start at sink t and collect the set $R \subseteq V$ of vertices weakly-backward-reachable from t by F. If $s \in R$, we can show F weakly-crosses every s, t-cut, so F is an s, t-trail. Otherwise when $s \notin R$, set F does not weakly-cross all s, t-cuts, and on collecting R depth-first backward from t, the backward search must encounter a cycle $C \subseteq F$; this implies F is an s, t-whirl or -eddy, which proves the forward implication.

For the *reverse* implication, given any s, t-intact set F, we construct flux f, edge weights ω, and stoichiometries M, as follows. For the flux, $f_e = 1$ if $e \in F$; otherwise $f_e = 0$. For the weights, $\omega(e) = -1$ if $e \in F$; otherwise $\omega(e) = 1$. For the stoichiometries, $M = (r_{ve})$ for all $v \in V$ and $e \in E$, with $r_{ve} := r_{ve}^+ - r_{ve}^-$, where: $r_{ve}^+ = 1/|\text{in}(v) \cap F|$ if $e \in \text{in}(v) \cap F$, otherwise $r_{ve}^+ = 0$; and $r_{ve}^- = 1/|\text{out}(v) \cap F|$ if $e \in \text{out}(v) \cap F$, otherwise $r_{ve}^- = 0$. For this flux f, its active hyperedges are exactly set F, and the flux into sink t is nonzero (as F is s, t-intact). One can show that this flux f satisfies accumulation for these stoichiometries M, and that for these edge weights ω, its active hyperedges F are a minimum-weight s, t-factory. Thus F is the active hyperedge set of a shortest s, t-factory f under accumulation for edge weights ω and stoichiometries M. Finally any s, t-trail, -whirl, or -eddy is an s, t-intact set, which proves the reverse implication.   □

Among the three classes of solutions in Theorem 1, only a *trail* corresponds to a legitimate factory that produces the targets by supplying the sources.

A *whirl*, for physically-valid stoichiometries that conserve mass, corresponds to an equilibrium solution that just maintains the existing amount of targets without increasing their production on supplying sources.

An *eddy*, whose active edges produce a nonzero amount of the targets without consuming sources, is impossible under accumulation unless its reactions fail to conserve mass, which can only arise when the network has been misannotated with erroneous physically-invalid stoichiometries.

In brief, Theorem 1 reveals that a shortest factory solver may return a legitimate solution in the form of a trail—or a *degenerate solution* in the form of a whirl or eddy, both of which have been overlooked by all prior approaches to shortest factories, and potentially output as purported solutions. Later Sect. 3.3 presents the first algorithm that finds an *optimal trail*—guaranteeing it delivers an optimal nondegenerate factory.

3.2   Hyperpaths Are Factories

An unexpected consequence of the characterization in Theorem 1 is that every *hyperpath* is a factory—for *some* choice of stoichiometries. Here we show below in Theorem 2 a much stronger result: that given a metabolic network G with stoichiometries M, every s,t-hyperpath is an s,t-factory under accumulation—for the *fixed* stoichiometries M of G. In other words, surprisingly, hyperpaths are actually a *subclass* of factories.

Formally, an s,t-*hyperpath* is a minimal set $P = \{e_1, \ldots, e_k\}$ of hyperedges that can be ordered so that $\mathrm{tail}(e_1) = \{s\}$, $\mathrm{head}(e_k) \supseteq \{t\}$, and for all $1 < i \leq k$, hyperedge e_i satisfies $\mathrm{tail}(e_i) \subseteq \{s\} \cup \bigcup_{1 \leq j < i} \mathrm{head}(e_j)$. We say P *strongly-reaches* t from s. Hyperedge e *strongly-crosses* cut C if $\mathrm{tail}(e) \subseteq C$ and $\mathrm{head}(e) \not\subseteq C$. Set $S \subseteq E$ strongly-crosses cut C if some hyperedge $e \in S$ does. Equivalently, s,t-hyperpaths are exactly minimal sets that strongly-cross all s,t-cuts [16,17].

Theorem 2 (Hyperpaths Are Factories). *Consider a directed hypergraph $G = (V, E)$ with source $s \in V$, sink $t \in V - \{s\}$, stoichiometries M, and any s,t-hyperpath $P \subseteq E$. Then P is the set of active hyperedges of an s,t-factory in G for M under accumulation.*

Proof. (Sketch) Given s,t-hyperpath P, we construct a flux f whose active hyperedges are exactly P with nonzero flux into t that satisfies accumulation under $M = (r_{ve})$. The construction of f processes the edges of $P = \{p_1, \ldots, p_k\}$, making use of their ordering $p_1 \prec p_2 \prec \ldots \prec p_k$ given by the definition of a hyperpath, where it processes them in *reverse order* as successively $p_k, \ldots, p_2, p_1$. For each hyperedge $e \in E$, define the following (possibly empty) subset of its head by $H(e) := \{v \in \mathrm{head}(e) : r_{ve} > 0\} - \{s, t\}$. Let ϵ be any real value with $\epsilon > 0$.

Before processing the hyperedges of P, initialize the flux to $f_e = 0$ for all $e \in E$. Then when processing the next hyperedge $e \in P$ in reverse order, set its flux by,

$$f_e := \max \left\{ \epsilon, \; \max_{v \in H(e)} \left\{ -\sum_{h \in P \,:\, h \succ e} r_{vh} f_h \Big/ r_{ve} \right\} \right\}. \tag{1}$$

On setting f_e by the above rule, we can show accumulation holds for all $v \in H(e)$.

With each hyperedge $e = p_i \in P$, associate the following set $W_i \subseteq V$, consisting of all vertices that are only in H-sets of the hyperedges $p_i, p_{i+1}, \ldots, p_k$ processed up through e: namely, $W_i := \bigcup_{h \in P : h \succeq e} H(h) - \bigcup_{g \in P : g \prec e} H(g)$.

We can then prove by induction for decreasing $i \in \{k, \ldots, 2, 1\}$ that after processing $e = p_i \in P$ by setting f_e using (1), accumulation is satisfied for all $v \in W_i$.

Consequently after processing all $e \in P$, accumulation is satisfied for every vertex in W_1, which is all vertices touched by P except s and t. Any vertex not touched by P trivially satisfies accumulation, as it has zero flux on all incident hyperedges. When processing is finished, $f_e \geq \epsilon > 0$ for $e \in P$, so there is nonzero flux into t; also $f_e = 0$ for $e \notin P$. Thus f is an s,t-factory under accumulation for G whose active hyperedges are exactly hyperpath P. $\qquad\square$

An immediate consequence of Theorem 2 is that for any edge weights ω, the length of a shortest s,t-factory is always at most the length of a shortest s,t-hyperpath. So a min-edge factory can potentially use *fewer reactions* than a hyperpath (but never more). Furthermore factories can potentially exist for *more sets* of sources and targets than hyperpaths (but never fewer). The latter is demonstrated empirically in Sect. 4.1 through Table 2.

3.3   Guaranteeing Nondegeneracy

We now give the first algorithm that is guaranteed to find an optimal *nondegenerate* factory under accumulation, which by our characterization theorem is an optimal *trail*. This relies on a parameter-free algorithm for correctly finding a shortest factory such as from Sect. 2.2 (that may return a degenerate solution), which the nondegenerate algorithm calls as a subroutine.

Our approach to finding a shortest s,t-trail in essence generates *next-best* s,t-factories $f^{(1)}, f^{(2)}, \ldots$ in order of increasing length $\omega(f^{(1)}) \leq \omega(f^{(2)}) \leq \cdots$, stopping at the first $f^{(i)}$ whose active hyperedges form an s,t-trail. This $f^* = f^{(i)}$ is a *shortest* s,t-trail, hence f^* is output as an optimal nondegenerate s,t-factory.

Testing whether the active hyperedges F of a factory under accumulation form an s,t-trail is equivalent to checking whether F weakly-reaches t from s. (Under accumulation, the active hyperedges F of an s,t-factory are s,t-intact. So it suffices to check whether F weakly-crosses all s,t-cuts, which is equivalent to weak-reachability.) Determining whether t is weakly-reachable from s by F can be done in time linear in the total size of hyperedge set F (see [10,13]). So the key is how to generate factories by increasing length to find a shortest trail.

Given a shortest factory for a problem-instance $\mathcal{P}$ whose active hyperedges F are a degenerate *whirl* or *eddy*, the next-best factory for $\mathcal{P}$ whose active hyperedges $F' \neq F$ are a *trail* must either: (1) use a proper *subset* of F, and other hyperedges outside F to weakly-reach t from s; or (2) use a proper *superset* of F. Hence we can find the best trail for $\mathcal{P}$ by solving these two subproblems (1) and (2), which we call respectively $\mathcal{P}_F^{\subset}$ and $\mathcal{P}_F^{\supset}$, finding a shortest trail for both of $\mathcal{P}_F^{\subset}$ and $\mathcal{P}_F^{\supset}$, and returning the better of these two trails.

Table 1. Dataset Summaries

	C_Rud	S_Mue	B_Aph	B_Cic	S_Cer	H_Sap	E_Col	Reactome
Vertices	263	314	460	700	936	1,618	1,877	20,458
Hyperedges	229	273	447	755	1,250	2,132	2,999	11,802
Sources	40	45	45	58	128	171	65	8,296
Targets	44	48	51	67	227	344	73	5,066

	med	max	med	max	med	max	med	max	med	max	med	max	med	max	med	max
Tail size	2	4	2	4	2	6	2	6	1	2	1	2	2	7	2	26
Head size	2	5	2	5	2	6	2	6	1	3	1	3	2	95	1	28
In-degree	1	41	1	49	1	67	1	156	1	15	1	13	1	806	1	1,056
Out-degree	1	64	1	72	1	104	1	142	1	8	1	18	1	511	1	1,167

We can solve subset subproblem $\mathcal{P}' := \mathcal{P}_F^{\subseteq}$, and superset subproblem $\mathcal{P}' := \mathcal{P}_F^{\supseteq}$, by constructing a modified MILP for the parameter-free algorithm, and examining its solution F'. (We omit details of the modified MILP due to page limits.) If F' is a trail, we can show it is an optimal solution to subproblem $\mathcal{P}'$. Otherwise, we recursively solve the two further subproblems $(\mathcal{P}')_{F'}^{\subseteq}$ and $(\mathcal{P}')_{F'}^{\supseteq}$.

We implement this whole process using a heap H of such subproblems, where the priority of subproblem $\mathcal{P}$ on H is the *length* (or total weight) of the best (possibly degenerate) factory for $\mathcal{P}$ found by the parameter-free algorithm. The nondegenerate algorithm repeatedly extracts from H the subproblem $\mathcal{P}$ of minimum priority, and fetches the corresponding optimal factory f^* for $\mathcal{P}$. If f^* is a trail, the nondegenerate algorithm halts and outputs f^*. Otherwise, subproblems $\mathcal{P}_F^{\subseteq}$ and $\mathcal{P}_F^{\supseteq}$ are inserted into H, and the algorithm continues.

This heap-based approach can find an optimal nondegenerate factory quickly, when shortest factories have few hyperedges, and there are few near-optimal factories—both of which are typically the case.

4   Experimental Results

We now present results from computational experiments on biological benchmark datasets. We highlight an example of a shortest factory instance where the prior state-of-the-art fails, and evaluate the speed of our parameter-free algorithm. (In addition, we also performed experiments that investigated imputing unit stoichiometry ratios, and further differences between the parameter-based and parameter-free approaches, which will appear in the full journal paper.)

4.1   Experimental Setup

Datasets.   We evaluate our parameter-free algorithm for shortest factories on eight standard datasets, which we now briefly describe. (For a full description of these datasets, and their transformation into hypergraphs, see [12].) Seven of the datasets are metabolic networks for model organisms from MetExplore [3]. We use an abbreviation of the organism name to identify these datasets (namely, first letter of genus, underscore, followed by first three letters of species). The final dataset contains curated human signaling pathways from Reactome [7].

Table 2. Target Instance Feasibility

	C_Rud	S_Mue	B_Aph	B_Cic	vS_Cer	H_Sap	E_Col	Reactome
Target instances	40	48	51	67	142	344	73	5,066
Factory, accumulation	6	17	25	40	131	273	48	3,955
Factory, conservation	0	0	0	13	127	235	1	1,632
Hyperpath	0	0	2	1	129	267	1	2,432

We consider any vertex with no in-edges a *source*, and any vertex with no out-edges a *target*. A problem *instance* then involves finding a factory (or hyperpath) from all of the sources to a given target. (When computing hyperpaths, we created a supersource, and a zero-weight hyperedge with the supersource as its tail, and all source vertices in its head.)

Table 1 gives statistics on the hypergraphs constructed for each dataset, listed in order of increasing size. Overall, the hypergraphs tend to have fewer hyperedges than vertices, suggesting potentially low connectivity between nodes.

Table 2 reports for each dataset the number of instances having a factory (either under accumulation or conservation), or a hyperpath. As expected, there are more instances with factories under accumulation than under conservation, and more instances with factories under accumulation than hyperpaths.

Implementation. Our new tool `Freeia` [18] implements the parameter-free algorithm for min-edge factories from Sect. 2.2, though it first runs two heuristics described below to quickly: (1) check feasibility, or the existence of any factory; and (2) bound the minimum number of active hyperedges, potentially tightly.

The first heuristic tests feasibility by solving the parameter-free MILP from Sect. 2.2, but without a length constraint on the number of active hyperedges. If the objective function value of an optimal solution with no length constraint is zero, `Freeia` reports no factory exists that produces the targets.

The second heuristic has two steps. It first runs `Odinn` [11] (the current state-of-the-art for optimal factories, which may exclude valid factories due to its parameter choice), to get an upper bound $\tilde{k}$ on the number of active hyperedges in a min-edge factory. Then it solves the parameter-free MILP from Sect. 2.2 where its length constraint has $\ell := \tilde{k} - 1$. If the objective function under this constraint is zero, we know `Odinn`'s solution is optimal, and is output by `Freeia`. Otherwise, `Freeia` runs the full parameter-free algorithm with binary search.

`Freeia` comprises around 300 lines of Python code. For the experiments, we used `Mmunin` [16] to compute shortest hyperpaths. For directed hypergraph representations, we used Halp (https://github.com/Murali-group/halp). MILPs were solved using `CPLEX` 12.6, run on an M1 processor with 8 GB of memory.

4.2   `Freeia` Finds Factories Missed by the Prior State-of-the-Art

The current state-of-the-art for min-edge factories (that produce the targets using the fewest reactions) is `Odinn` [11,12], which has a target production

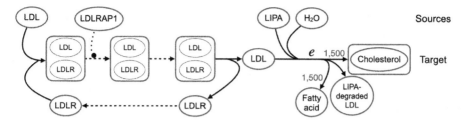

Fig. 2. Shortest factory to the target "Cholesterol" in `Reactome`. Sources are shown along the top of the figure; the target is at the far right. Dashed hyperedges represent transport between cellular compartments. The dotted curve from LDLRAP1 ending in a disc indicates it is a positive regulator. All stoichiometry ratios are unit, except for hyperedge e where "Fatty acid" and "Cholesterol" both have stoichiometry ratio 1,500.

parameter ϵ (settable by the user) that specifies the minimum amount of all targets that must be produced by a legitimate factory. Assigning parameter ϵ can be difficult, since setting it too high excludes factories that produce the target in a nonzero amount less than ϵ, while setting it too low allows for numerical tolerances within `CPLEX` to exclude valid factories. Other methods for finding optimal factories also have an equivalent parameter that instead upper bounds the maximum allowable flux on any hyperedge. `Freeia` avoids these issues, and includes all valid factories in its space of feasible solutions.

Figure 2 highlights an instance where `Freeia` finds an optimal factory, yet `Odinn` (being parameter-based) reports no valid factory exists. The figure shows a shortest factory to "Cholesterol" in the pathway "Transport of small molecules" from `Reactome`. Sources are along the top of the figure, and the target is at the far right. Dashed hyperedges represent transport from one cellular compartment to another. The dotted portion of the hyperedge involving LDLRAP1 indicates it acts as a positive regulator of this reaction. All stoichiometries are unit, except on the final hyperedge to the target, where "Fatty acid" and "Cholesterol" each have stoichiometry 1,500. Note that this factory is not a hyperpath, due to the cycle involving LDLR (and no hyperpath for this target exists).

Biologically, the reactions in this pathway lead to the accumulation of excess cholesterol in atherosclerosis [5]. The process begins with the migration of low density lipoproteins (LDLs) across an injured artery endothelium, after binding to the LDL receptor (LDLR). Once transported into the subendothelial space, these LDLs undergo hydrolysis by lysosomal acid lipase (LIPA), causing a massive release of cholesterol and fatty acids.

`Odinn` fails to return a valid factory for this instance due to numerical issues in `CPLEX` caused by the high stoichiometry ratio for Cholesterol on its in-edge e. (We note that this stoichiometry ratio may be an incorrect annotation.) The default value for the target production parameter in `Odinn` is $\epsilon := 5 \times 10^{-4}$, meaning a factory is feasible only if it produces target t in quantity at least ϵ. This high stoichiometry ratio allows sufficient target production with a very small amount of flux on final hyperedge e, namely $f_e = \epsilon / r_{te} = 3 \times 10^{-7}$. In `Odinn`,

Table 3. Running Time

	C_Rud		S_Mue		B_Aph		B_Cic		S_Cer		H_Sap		E_Col		Reactome	
	med	max	med	max	med	max	med	max	med	max	med	max	med	vmax	med	max
Freeia, accum.	0.1	0.1	0.1	0.2	0.1	0.5	0.2	28	0.1	0.4	0.3	2.3	37	3,168	4.4	4,141
Odinn, accum.	0.1	0.1	0.1	0.1	0.1	0.2	0.1	2.3	0.1	0.1	0.1	0.2	3.1	2,943	3.1	6.6
Freeia, conserv.	†	†	†	†	†	†	0.2	0.5	0.2	47	0.4	75	0.7	0.7	4.3	97
Odinn, conserv.	†	†	†	†	†	†	0.1	0.1	0.1	0.3	0.1	0.5	0.2	0.2	2.9	4.1
Mmunin	†	†	†	†	0.1	0.1	0.1	0.1	0.1	525	0.1	314	0.1	0.1	9	776

† Either no factory under conservation, or no hyperpath, exists for any target in this dataset.
Time is in seconds.

each hyperedge e in the hypergraph has both a real-valued variable f_e, giving the flux on e, and an integer-valued variable x_e, indicating whether e is active. (Odinn minimizes its number of active hyperedges.) These variables are related by constraint $x_e \geq f_e$, which should force $x_e = 1$ when $f_e > 0$. Unfortunately due to numerical tolerances in CPLEX, small values for f_e do not force $x_e = 1$, so hyperedge e is not considered active, and Odinn fails to output a valid factory.

Strikingly, we experimentally confirmed that there is *no default value* for the target production parameter ϵ at which Odinn returns an optimal factory for all instances in Reactome. The largest possible value for ϵ was calculated using Freeia, where the objective function value of our parameter-free MILP gives an upper bound on target production for any factory with an optimal number of reactions. (For any higher ϵ-value, Odinn either returns a suboptimal factory that creates the target in a larger quantity, or reports no factory exists.) The smallest value for ϵ was found by running Odinn and observing when CPLEX returned an invalid factory due to numerical errors. The following table lists, for various ϵ-values, the number of Reactome instances on which Odinn experiences the following *failure* modes: finding an invalid factory, when ϵ is too low; or a suboptimal factory, or no factory, when ϵ is too high.

Target production parameter ϵ	$\leq 10^{-5}$	5×10^{-4}	0.0125	0.025	0.05	0.1	0.2	0.4	0.8
Odinn failures (out of 5,066 instances)	all	1	2	15	35	143	378	714	1,040

More precisely, Odinn fails on at least one Reactome instance for *every possible ϵ-value*: it fails on the instance from Fig. 2 for $\epsilon \leq 0.03$, and fails on a separate instance for $\epsilon \geq 0.0125$. In distinction, Freeia never returns invalid or suboptimal solutions, or reports no solution exists on an instance with a valid factory.

4.3   Speed of Computing Parameter-Free Factories

Computing robust optimal factories with Freeia is fast in practice, with a median running time across all instances of under five seconds. Table 3 compares running times on datasets for: Freeia, our new parameter-free tool; Odinn, the prior state-of-the-art for optimal factories; and Mmunin, the current state-of-the-art for shortest hyperpaths. (Running times are reported in seconds.) For all datasets except E_Col and Reactome, the Freeia tool has median running time under a second, with its maximum time just over a minute. For the more challenging datasets, Freeia maintains a fast median time, but its maximum time rises to just over an hour for an isolated instance in Reactome. The time for these longer-running instances is typically dominated by solving the MILP from the second heuristic implemented in Freeia, which checks if a valid factory exists with one-fewer active hyperedge than Odinn's factory. We noticed that the computational cost of this MILP typically scales with the number of active hyperedges in an optimal factory, and that the shortest factory for any instance taking more than 1,000 seconds contains at least 20 hyperedges.

Surprisingly, Freeia tends to be faster than finding shortest hyperpaths with Mmunin. This is interesting, since by Theorem 2 every hyperpath is a factory, which implies that for any instance its space of feasible factories is larger than of feasible hyperpaths. This difference in running time appears due to algorithmic differences in Mmunin and Freeia, as Mmunin typically solves more MILPs per instance than Freeia (though Freeia's MILPs occasionally take longer to solve).

5   Conclusion

We have presented the first *robust algorithm* for optimal factories, that is free of parameter settings and guarantees nondegeneracy. We also for the first time characterized the graph-theoretic structure of shortest factories, establishing hyperpaths are a subclass of factories. Comprehensive experiments demonstrate our algorithm is fast in practice, and finds solutions missed by the prior state-of-the-art.

Further Research. A major open problem is the characterization of shortest factories for the case of *positive edge weights* (which arise under both parsimony and maximum likelihood). While there is likely no constant-factor approximation algorithm for Shortest Factory (since its NP-completeness proof [12] shows it is as hard to approximate as Set Cover), a *fast heuristic* for shortest factories (like for shortest hyperpaths [13]) would be useful, since all current approaches solve mixed-integer linear programs, whose time could potentially explode in practice.

Acknowledgments. We thank Anna Ritz for sharing the BioPax parser, and the anonymous referees for their useful comments. Research supported by the National Science Foundation through grants CCF-1617192 and IIS-2041613 to JK.

References

1. Acuña, V., Milreu, P.V., Cottret, L., et al.: Algorithms and complexity of enumerating minimal precursor sets in genome-wide metabolic networks. Bioinformatics **28**(19), 2474–2483 (2012)
2. Andrade, R., Wannagat, M., Klein, C.C., et al.: Enumeration of minimal stoichiometric precursor sets in metabolic networks. Alg. for Mol. Bio. **11**(1), 25 (2016). https://doi.org/10.1186/s13015-016-0087-3

3. Cottret, L., Frainay, C., Chazalviel, M., et al.: MetExplore: collaborative edition and exploration of metabolic networks. Nucleic Acids Res. **46**(W1), W495–W502 (2018)

4. Cottret, L., Vieira Milreu, P., Acuña, V., et al.: Enumerating precursor sets of target metabolites in a metabolic network. In: Proceedings of the 8th Workshop on Algorithms in Bioinformatics (WABI), pp. 233–244 (2008)

5. Dubland, J.A., Francis, G.A.: Lysosomal acid lipase: at the crossroads of normal and atherogenic cholesterol metabolism. Front. Cell Dev. Bio. **3**, 3 (2015)

6. Italiano, G.F., Nanni, U.: Online maintenance of minimal directed hypergraphs. Department of Computer Science, Columbia University, Tech. rep. (1989)

7. Joshi-Tope, G., Gillespie, M., Vastrik, I., et al.: Reactome: a knowledgebase of biological pathways. Nucleic Acids Res. **33**, D428-432 (2005)

8. Klamt, S., Haus, U.U., Theis, F.: Hypergraphs and cellular networks. PLoS Comput. Biol. **5**(5), e1000385 (2009)

9. Krieger, S.: Algorithmic Inference of Cellular Reaction Pathways and Protein Secondary Structure. PhD dissertation, Department of Computer Science, The University of Arizona (July 2022)

10. Krieger, S., Kececioglu, J.: Fast approximate shortest hyperpaths for inferring pathways in cell signaling hypergraphs. In: Proceedings of the 21st ISCB Workshop on Algorithms in Bioinformatics (WABI). Leibniz International Proceedings in Informatics, vol. 201, pp. 1–20 (2021)

11. Krieger, S., Kececioglu, J.: **Odinn**: optimal minimum-hyperedge factories in metabolic networks with negative regulation, version 1.0 (2021). http://odinn.cs.arizona.edu

12. Krieger, S., Kececioglu, J.: Computing optimal factories in metabolic networks with negative regulation. Bioinformatics **38**(Suppl. 1), i369–i377 (2022). Proceedings of the 30th ISCB Conference on Intelligent Systems for Molecular Biology (ISMB)

13. Krieger, S., Kececioglu, J.: Heuristic shortest hyperpaths in cell signaling hypergraphs. Algorithms Mol. Biol. **17**(1), 12 (2022). https://doi.org/10.1186/s13015-022-00217-9

14. Krieger, S., Kececioglu, J.: **Hhugin**: hypergraph heuristic for general shortest source-sink hyperpaths, version 1.0 (2022). http://hhugin.cs.arizona.edu

15. Krieger, S., Kececioglu, J.: **Mmunin**: integer-linear-programming-based cutting-plane algorithm for shortest source-sink hyperpaths, version 1.0 (2022). http://mmunin.cs.arizona.edu

16. Krieger, S., Kececioglu, J.: Computing shortest hyperpaths for pathway inference in cellular reaction networks. In: Proceedings of the 27th Conference on Research in Computational Molecular Biology (RECOMB), LNBI 13976, pp. 155–173. Springer, Cham (2023). https://doi.org/10.1007/978-3-031-29119-7_10

17. Krieger, S., Kececioglu, J.: Shortest hyperpaths in directed hypergraphs for reaction pathway inference. J. Comput. Biol. **30**(11), 1–28 (2023)

18. Krieger, S., Kececioglu, J.: **Freeia**: robust optimal factories in metabolic reaction networks, version 1.0 (2023). http://freeia.cs.arizona.edu

19. Li, Y., McGrail, D.J., Latysheva, N., et al.: Pathway perturbations in signaling networks: linking genotype to phenotype. Sem. in Cell Dev. Bio. **99**, 3–11 (2020)

20. Ritz, A., Avent, B., Murali, T.: Pathway analysis with signaling hypergraphs. IEEE/ACM Trans. Comp. Bio. Bioinf. **14**(5), 1042–1055 (2017)

21. Ritz, A., Murali, T.: Pathway analysis with signaling hypergraphs. In: Proceedings of the 5th ACM Conference on Bioinformatics, Computational Biology, and Health Informatics (ACM-BCB), pp. 249–258 (2014)

22. Ritz, A., Tegge, A.N., Kim, H., et al.: Signaling hypergraphs. Trends Biotechnol. **32**(7), 356–362 (2014)
23. Sharan, R., Ideker, T.: Modeling cellular machinery through biological network comparison. Nat. Biotechnol. **24**(4), 427–433 (2006)
24. Vidal, M., Cusick, M.E., Barabási, A.L.: Interactome networks and human disease. Cell **144**(6), 986–998 (2011)
25. Zarecki, R., Oberhardt, M.A., Reshef, L., et al.: A novel nutritional predictor links microbial fastidiousness with lowered ubiquity, growth rate, and cooperativeness. PLoS Comput. Biol. **10**(7), 1–12 (2014)

Undesignable RNA Structure Identification via Rival Structure Generation and Structure Decomposition

Tianshuo Zhou[1] , Wei Yu Tang[1] , David H. Mathews[3,4,5] ,
and Liang Huang[1,2(✉)]

[1] School of EECS, Oregon State University, Corvallis, OR 97330, USA
liang.huang.sh@gmail.com
[2] Department of Biochemistry and Biophysics, Oregon State University,
Corvallis, OR 97330, USA
[3] Department of Biochemistry and Biophysics,
University of Rochester Medical Center, Rochester, NY 14642, USA
[4] Center for RNA Biology, University of Rochester Medical Center,
Rochester, NY 14642, USA
[5] Department of Biostatistics and Computational Biology,
University of Rochester Medical Center, Rochester, NY 14642, USA

Abstract. RNA design is the search for a sequence or set of sequences that will fold into predefined structures, also known as the inverse problem of RNA folding. While numerous RNA design methods have been invented to find sequences capable of folding into a target structure, little attention has been given to the identification of undesignable structures according to the minimum free energy (MFE) criterion under the Turner model. In this paper, we address this gap by first introducing mathematical theorems outlining sufficient conditions for recognizing undesignable structures, then proposing efficient algorithms, guided by these theorems, to verify the undesignability of RNA structures. Through the application of these theorems and algorithms to the Eterna100 puzzles, we demonstrate the ability to efficiently establish that 15 of the puzzles indeed fall within the category of undesignable structures. In addition, we provide specific insights from the study of undesignability, in the hope that it will enable more understanding of RNA folding and RNA design.

Availability: Our source code is available at https://github.com/shanry/RNA-Undesign.

Keywords: RNA Design · Inverse Folding · Undesignability · Designability

Supplementary Information The online version contains supplementary material available at https://doi.org/10.1007/978-1-0716-3989-4_17.

J. Ma (Ed.): RECOMB 2024, LNCS 14758, pp. 270–287, 2024.
https://doi.org/10.1007/978-1-0716-3989-4_17

1   Introduction

Ribonucleic Acid (RNA) plays essential roles in the core activities within living cells such as transcription and translation [6], catalyzing reactions [7], and controlling gene expression [18]. Given a target structure, RNA design aims to find sequences that can fold into that structure. This problem, however, has been proved NP-hard [5] when the simplest model of energy is adopted. The importance of RNA structure and the hardness of RNA design problem have motivated various RNA design methods [3,4,8,10,13,16,17,19,24,25].

While extensive research has been dedicated to designing RNA based on a target structure, there is a notable scarcity of literature investigating the undesignability of RNA design using realistic energy models. Undesignability refers to the inability to find an RNA sequence that can fold into a desired structure using a realistic energy model. Initially, specific cases of undesignability were discovered by the work [1] attempting to extend RNA-SSD [3], which identified two undesignable motifs and proposed alternative motifs that would consistently be favored by the conventional Turner energy models [20]. Later work [9] has presented additional motifs that prevent designability, as observed using the maximum base pair model, which is not necessarily realistic. Recent works [22,23] outlined a method to verify undesignability for short motifs through exhaustive enumeration and folding. To the best of our knowledge, the examination of undesignable structures or motifs based on the nearest neighbor model [14,15,20] has not been thoroughly explored thus far.

To bridge the gap between RNA design and undesignability, we propose a systematic and scientifically grounded approach known as "Rival Structure Generation and Structure Decomposition" (RIGENDE). Our methodology operates on the principle of "proof by construction," whereby undesignability is confirmed by the identification of rival structures that consistently outperform the target structure for any possible RNA sequence. RIGENDE can not only serve as a sanity check for empirical RNA design methods, allowing for the avoidance of executing heuristic-based algorithms in situations where no feasible solution exists, but also provide deeper insights into the energy models themselves. This, in turn, contributes to a more profound understanding of thermodynamic models used for the prediction of RNA secondary structures. The main contributions of this paper are:

1. Theorems. We establish the theoretical grounds for Undesignable RNA Structure Identification, characterizing the importance of rival structure(s) and structure decomposition.
2. Algorithms. Driven by the proposed theorems, we designed and implemented highly efficient algorithms to verify undesignability automatically.
3. Application. When applying to the puzzles from Eterna100 [2] benchmark, RIGENDE is able to prove 15 of them are undesignable. Remarkably, the verification process for each puzzle was completed within a matter of seconds or minutes.

2   RNA Design

2.1   Secondary Structure, Loop and Free Energy

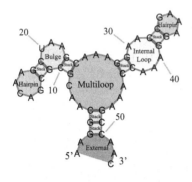

Fig. 1. An example of secondary structure and loops.

Table 1. Critical positions of loops in Fig. 1

Loop Type	Critical Positions	
	Closing Pairs	Mismatches (Unpaired)
External	(3, 50)	2, 51
Stack	(3, 50), (4, 49)	
Stack	(4, 49), (5, 48)	
Multi	(5, 48), (9, 24), (28, 44)	4, 49, 8, 25, 27, 45
Stack	(9, 24), (10, 23)	
Bulge	(10, 23), (11, 19)	
Stack	(11, 19), (12, 18)	
Hairpin	(12, 18)	13, 17
Stack	(28, 44), (29, 43)	
Internal	(29, 43), (32, 39)	30, 42, 31, 40
Stack	(32, 39), (33, 38)	
Hairpin	(33, 38)	34, 37

Table 2. Critical positions for each type of loops under Turner model implemented in ViennaRNA Special hairpins [15] of triloops, tetraloops and hexaloops are not considered here

Loop Type	Critical Positions	
	Closing Pairs	Mismatches
External	$(i_1, j_1), (i_2, j_2), \ldots, (i_k, j_k)$	$i_1 - 1, j_1 + 1, i_2 - 1, j_2 + 1, \ldots, i_k - 1, j_k + 1$
Hairpin	(i, j)	$i + 1, j - 1$
Stack	$(i, j), (k, l)$	
Bulge	$(i, j), (k, l)$	
Internal	$(i, j), (k, l)$	$i + 1, j - 1, k - 1, l + 1$
Multi	$(i, j), (i_1, j_1), (i_2, j_2), \ldots, (i_k, j_k)$	$i + 1, j - 1, i_1 - 1, j_1 + 1, i_2 - 1, j_2 + 1, \ldots, i_k - 1, j_k + 1$

An RNA sequence $\boldsymbol{x}$ of length n is specified as a string of base nucleotides $x_1 x_2 \ldots x_n$, where $x_i \in \{A, C, G, U\}$ for $i = 1, 2, \ldots, n$. A secondary structure $\mathcal{P}$ for $\boldsymbol{x}$ is a set of paired indices where each pair $(i, j) \in \mathcal{P}$ indicates two distinct bases $x_i x_j \in \{CG, GC, AU, UA, GU, UG\}$ and each index from 1 to n can only be paired once. A secondary structure is pseudoknot-free if there are no two pairs $(i, j) \in \mathcal{P}$ and $(k, l) \in \mathcal{P}$ such that $i < k < j < l$. In short, a pseudoknot-free secondary structure is a properly nested set of pairings in an RNA sequence. Alternatively, $\mathcal{P}$ can be represented as a string $\boldsymbol{y} = y_1 y_2 \ldots y_n$, where a pair of indices $(i, j) \in \mathcal{P}$ corresponds to $y_i = $ "(", $y_j = $ ")" and any unpaired index k corresponds to $y_k = $ ".". The unpaired indices in $\boldsymbol{y}$ are denoted as *unpaired*$(\boldsymbol{y})$

and the set of paired indices in y is denoted as $pairs(y)$, which is equal to $\mathcal{P}$. In nature, some RNA structures contain crossing pairings called pseudoknots. Since the computational model we use does not allow these, we do not consider them. Henceforth we elide pseudoknot-free secondary structure to just secondary structure or structure for brevity.

The *ensemble* of an RNA sequence x is the set of all secondary structures that x can possibly fold into, denoted as $\mathcal{Y}(x)$. The *free energy* $\Delta G(x, y)$ is used to characterize the stability of $y \in \mathcal{Y}(x)$. The lower the free energy $\Delta G(x, y)$, the more stable the secondary structure y for x. In the nearest neighbor energy model [20], a secondary structure is decomposed into a collection of loops, where each loop is usually a region enclosed by some base pair(s). Depending on the number of pairs on the boundary, main types of loops include hairpin loop, internal loop and multiloop, which are bounded by 1, 2 and 3 or more base pairs, respectively. In particular, the external loop is the most outside loop and is bounded by two ends (5' and 3') and other base pair(s). Thus each loop can be identified by a set of pairs. Figure 1 showcases an example of secondary structure with various types of loops, where the some of the loops are notated as

1. Hairpin: $H\langle(12, 18)\rangle$.
2. Bulge: $B\langle(10, 23), (11, 19)\rangle$.
3. Stack: $S\langle(3, 50), (4, 49)\rangle$.
4. Internal Loop: $I\langle(29, 43), (32, 39)\rangle$.
5. Multiloop: $M\langle(5, 48), (9, 24), (28, 44)\rangle$.
6. External Loop: $E\langle(3, 50)\rangle$.

The function $loops(y)$ is used to denote the set of loops in a structure y. The free energy of a secondary structure y is the sum of the free energy of each loop,

$$\Delta G(x, y) = \sum_{z \in loops(y)} \Delta G(x, z), \qquad (1)$$

where each term $\Delta G(x, z)$ is the energy for one specific loop in $loops(y)$. See Supplementary Section B for detailed energy functions for different types of loops in the Turner model implemented in ViennaRNA [13]. The energy of each loop is typically determined by nucleotides on the positions of enclosing pairs and their adjacent mismatch positions, which are named as *critical positions* in this article. Table 1 lists the critical positions for all the loops in Fig. 1 and Table 2 shows the indices of critical positions for each type of loops. Additionally, some special hairpins [15] of unstable triloops and stable tetraloops and hexaloops in Turner model have a separate energy lookup table (See Supplementary Section B.2). When evaluating the energy of a loop, it suffices to input only the nucleotides on its critical positions, i.e.,

$$\Delta G(x, y) = \sum_{z \in loops(y)} \Delta G(x \vdash critical(z), z), \qquad (2)$$

where $critical(z)$ denotes the critical positions of loop z and $x \vdash critical(z)$ denotes the nucleotides from x that are "projected" onto $critical(z)$. See Supplementary Section A for the detailed functionality of projection operator. The projection (⊢) allows us to focus on the relevant nucleotides for energy evaluation. For instance,

$$critical(H\langle(12,18)\rangle) = \{12,13,17,18\}, \tag{3}$$

$$critical(I\langle(29,43),(32,39)\rangle) = \{29,30,31,32,39,40,42,43\}. \tag{4}$$

For convenience of later discussion, we also interchangeably put paired positions in brackets, i.e.,

$$critical(H\langle(12,18)\rangle) = \{(12,18),13,17\}, \tag{5}$$

$$critical(I\langle(29,43),(32,39)\rangle) = \{(29,43),(32,39),30,31,40,42\}. \tag{6}$$

2.2   MFE and Structure Distance

The structure with the *minimum free energy* is the most stable structure in the ensemble. A structure $y^\star$ is an MFE structure of x, i.e. $\mathrm{MFE}(x)$, if and only if

$$\forall y \in \mathcal{Y}(x) \text{ and } y \neq y^\star, \Delta G(x,y^\star) \leq \Delta G(x,y). \tag{7}$$

RNA design is the inverse problem of RNA folding. Given a target structure $y^\star$, RNA design aims to find suitable RNA sequence x such that $y^\star$ is an MFE structure of x. For convenience, we define $\mathcal{X}(y)$ as the set of all RNA sequences whose ensemble contains y, i.e., $\mathcal{X}(y) = x \mid y \in \mathcal{Y}(x)$. Here we follow a more strict definition of MFE criterion adopted in some previous studies [5,9,21,23,25] on the designability of RNA, i.e., x is a correct design if and only if y is the only MFE structure of x, which we call unique MFE (uMFE) criterion to differentiate it from the traditional MFE criterion. Formally, $\mathrm{uMFE}(x) = y^\star$ if and only if

$$\forall y \in \mathcal{Y}(x) \text{ and } y \neq y^\star, \Delta G(x,y^\star) < \Delta G(x,y). \tag{8}$$

From the perspective of optimization, the satisfaction of MFE criterion requires that the structure distance between target structure $y^\star$ and MFE structure of x is minimized to 0. Therefore, many methods focus on optimizing $d(y^\star, \mathrm{MFE}(x))$. The function $d(y', y'')$ represents the distance between two secondary structures y' and y'', which is defined as

$$d(y',y'') = n - 2 \cdot |pairs(y') \cap pairs(y'')| - |unpaired(y') \cap unpaired(y'')|, \tag{9}$$

where y' and y'' have the same length $|y'| = |y''| = n$.

3   Undesignability

Based the uMFE criterion in Eq. 8, the straightforward meaning of undesignability is that such a condition can not be satisfied for any RNA sequence x given a target structure $y^\star$. Alternatively, we give the formal definition of undesignability as follows.

Definition 1. *An RNA secondary structure $\boldsymbol{y}^\star$ is undesignable by* uMFE *criterion if and only if*

$$\forall \boldsymbol{x} \in \mathcal{X}(\boldsymbol{y}^\star), \exists \boldsymbol{y}' \neq \boldsymbol{y}^\star, \Delta G(\boldsymbol{x}, \boldsymbol{y}') \leq \Delta G(\boldsymbol{x}, \boldsymbol{y}^\star). \tag{10}$$

Similarly, we have the definition of undesignability under MFE criterion.

Definition 2. *An RNA secondary structure $\boldsymbol{y}^\star$ is undesignable by* MFE *criterion if and only if*

$$\forall \boldsymbol{x} \in \mathcal{X}(\boldsymbol{y}^\star), \exists \boldsymbol{y}' \neq \boldsymbol{y}^\star, \Delta G(\boldsymbol{x}, \boldsymbol{y}') < \Delta G(\boldsymbol{x}, \boldsymbol{y}^\star). \tag{11}$$

Following previous work [9] on undesignability, the discussions in this paper are under the setting of the uMFE criterion and Definition 1. However, all discussions can be straightforwardly adapted to Definition 2.

4   Theorems and Algorithms for Undesignability

4.1   Algorithm 0: Exhaustive Search

Given a target structure $\boldsymbol{y}^\star$ of length n, the designed sequence $\boldsymbol{x}$ should have the same length. Therefore, the most straightforward method is to enumerate all RNA sequences of length n, and check whether there exist at least one RNA sequence that can fold into $\boldsymbol{y}^\star$. Considering the designed sequence should at least satisfy that nucleotides at the paired position of the target structure should be matchable, the number of brute-force enumeration is $6^{|pairs(\boldsymbol{y}^\star)|} \times 4^{|unpaired(\boldsymbol{y}^\star)|}$, as there are 6 choices for a pair and 4 types of nucleotides. Notice that $2 \cdot |pairs(\boldsymbol{y}^\star)| + |unpaired(\boldsymbol{y}^\star)| = n$ and the RNA folding algorithms typically have a cubic time complexity with respect to sequence length n, the overall complexity $\mathcal{O}(6^{|pairs(\boldsymbol{y}^\star)|} \times 4^{|unpaired(\boldsymbol{y}^\star)|} \cdot n^3)$ makes brute-force search impractical even for very short structures.

4.2   Theorem 1 and Algorithm 1: Identify One Rival Structure

One observation from RNA design is that when the designed RNA sequence $\boldsymbol{x}$ can not fold into the target structure $\boldsymbol{y}^\star$, sometimes $\boldsymbol{x}$ tends to fold into another structure $\boldsymbol{y}'$. Another observation is that $\boldsymbol{y}'$ can be very close to $\boldsymbol{y}^\star$, i.e., their structure distance $d(\boldsymbol{y}^\star, \boldsymbol{y}')$, can be very small. For example, when designing the puzzle "Simple Single Bond" (shown as $\boldsymbol{y}^\star$ in Fig. 2) from the benchmark Eterna100, the designed sequence (shown as $\boldsymbol{x}$ in Fig. 2) tends to fold into another similar structure (shown as $\boldsymbol{y}'$ in Fig. 2).

In this instance, we know that at least for $\boldsymbol{x}$, $\boldsymbol{y}'$ is a more advantageous choice than $\boldsymbol{y}^\star$. We further hypothesize that $\boldsymbol{y}'$ is superior to $\boldsymbol{y}^\star$ for any RNA sequence that can possibly fold into $\boldsymbol{y}^\star$. If the hypothesis holds, then we can assert that $\boldsymbol{y}^\star$ is undesignable under uMFE criterion. This leads to the first theorem we proposed.

```
y* : ...... (......... (((( ..... )))) ......... ) ....................
y' : ................ (((( ..... )))) ....................
x : AUAAGCGGUAAAAAAAGUGCGAAAAGCAUGAAAAAAAACAGAAAAAAAAAAAAAAAAAAAA
```

Fig. 2. Example for Theorem 1 and Algorithm 1

Theorem 1. *A structure* $y^\star$ *is undesignable, if*

$$\exists y' \neq y^\star, \forall x \in \mathcal{X}(y^\star), \Delta G(x, y') \leq \Delta G(x, y^\star). \tag{12}$$

It is worth noting that the condition in Theorem 1 is a special case of the condition in Definition 1, despite both employing the same notations but in different order. The correctness of Theorem 1 can be proven by the Definition 1. Whether the undesignability can be approached by Theorem 1 can be formulated as an optimization or feasibility problem.

$$\begin{aligned} \text{find} \quad & y' \\ \text{subject to} \quad & \Delta G(x, y') \leq \Delta G(x, y^\star), \forall x \in \mathcal{X}(y^\star) \end{aligned} \tag{13}$$

If Theorem 1 can be applied, the problem of undesignability boils down to showing that y' is superior to $y^\star$ for any RNA sequence, we can rewrite the inequality in Eq. 12 as

$$\Delta\Delta G(y', y^\star) \overset{\Delta}{=} \Delta G(x, y') - \Delta G(x, y^\star) \leq 0. \tag{14}$$

Combining Eq. 2, Eq. 14 can be written as the difference of two sets of energy units,

$$\sum_{z' \in loops(y')} \Delta G(x \vdash critical(z'), z') - \sum_{z^\star \in loops(y^\star)} \Delta G(x \vdash critical(z^\star), z^\star) \leq 0. \tag{15}$$

Fig. 3. Venn diagram of loops in y' and $y^\star$.

Table 3. Example of design constraint

I	11	12	13	14	19	20	21	22
$\hat{x}^1$	G	G	C	G	C	C	A	U
$\hat{x}^2$	G	C	C	C	G	G	A	U
$\hat{x}^3$	G	C	U	C	G	G	A	U
$\hat{x}^4$	G	C	C	A	U	G	A	U
$\hat{x}^5$	G	C	U	A	U	G	A	U

The loops in $loops(y')$ and $loops(y^\star)$ are compared via the Venn diagram in Fig. 3. As we can see, the loops in y' and $y^\star$ overlap a lot. As a result, we can simplify Eq. 15 by canceling those intersected loops,

$$\sum_{z' \in loops(y') \setminus loops(y^\star)} \Delta G(x \vdash critical(z'), z') - \sum_{z^\star \in loops(y^\star) \setminus loops(y')} \Delta G(x \vdash critical(z^\star), z^\star) \leq 0. \tag{16}$$

By Eq. 16, the energy difference does not necessarily involve each nucleotide of $\boldsymbol{x}$. It is equivalent to consider only the nucleotides participating the calculation of energy difference in Eq. 16, which can be written as

$$\hat{\boldsymbol{x}} = \boldsymbol{x} \vdash \Delta(\boldsymbol{y}', \boldsymbol{y}^\star), \Delta\Delta G(\hat{\boldsymbol{x}}, \boldsymbol{y}', \boldsymbol{y}^\star) \leq 0, \tag{17}$$

where

$$\Delta(\boldsymbol{y}', \boldsymbol{y}^\star) \triangleq \bigcup_{\boldsymbol{z} \in loops(\boldsymbol{y}^\star) \ominus loops(\boldsymbol{y}')} critical(\boldsymbol{z}), \tag{18}$$

and

$$\Delta\Delta G(\hat{\boldsymbol{x}}, \boldsymbol{y}', \boldsymbol{y}^\star) \triangleq \sum_{\boldsymbol{z}' \in loops(\boldsymbol{y}') \setminus loops(\boldsymbol{y}^\star)} \Delta G(\hat{\boldsymbol{x}} \vdash critical(\boldsymbol{z}'), \boldsymbol{z}') - \sum_{\boldsymbol{z}^\star \in loops(\boldsymbol{y}^\star) \setminus loops(\boldsymbol{y}')} \Delta G(\hat{\boldsymbol{x}} \vdash critical(\boldsymbol{z}^\star), \boldsymbol{z}^\star). \tag{19}$$

We name $\Delta(\boldsymbol{y}', \boldsymbol{y}^\star)$ as *differential positions* as it is a set of all the positions whose nucleotides are involved in calculating the free energy difference between $\boldsymbol{y}'$ and $\boldsymbol{y}^\star$. Accordingly, each nucleotide of $\hat{\boldsymbol{x}}$ corresponds to one position in $\Delta(\boldsymbol{y}', \boldsymbol{y}^\star)$, and the number of nucleotides in $\hat{\boldsymbol{x}}$ is the same as the size of $\Delta(\boldsymbol{y}', \boldsymbol{y}^\star)$. Equation 17 implies that enumerating all possible ($\hat{\boldsymbol{x}}$ is equivalent to enumerating all possible $\boldsymbol{x}$. Suppose the number of paired positions and unpaired positions in $\Delta(\boldsymbol{y}', \boldsymbol{y}^\star)$ are p and q, the total number of enumeration would be $p^6 \times q^4$. Moreover, the time cost of evaluating Eq. 19 is almost $\mathcal{O}(1)$ as $loops(\boldsymbol{y}')$ and $loops(\boldsymbol{y}^\star)$ only need to be computed once. As a result, it would be not hard to determine whether $\boldsymbol{y}'$ satisfies Theorem 1 when $|\Delta(\boldsymbol{y}', \boldsymbol{y}^\star)|$ is small, which motivates our first algorithm to efficiently verify undesignability, as described in Algorithm 1. In the case of example in Fig. 2, $\Delta(\boldsymbol{y}', \boldsymbol{y}^\star) = \{(7, 39), (17, 29), 6, 8, 16, 30, 38, 40\}$, total number of enumerations of $\hat{\boldsymbol{x}}$ in Eq. 17 is 147456 which can be finished within 1 second on a single computer in our experiments. To give a specific complexity, $\hat{\mathcal{X}}^{\Delta(\boldsymbol{y}', \boldsymbol{y}^\star)}$ is used to denote the all possible nucleotide compositions at the positions in $D(\boldsymbol{y}', \boldsymbol{y}^\star)$, we have

$$|\hat{\mathcal{X}}^{\Delta(\boldsymbol{y}', \boldsymbol{y}^\star)}| = 6^{|pairs(\Delta(\boldsymbol{y}', \boldsymbol{y}^\star))|} \times 4^{|unpaired(\Delta(\boldsymbol{y}', \boldsymbol{y}^\star))|}. \tag{20}$$

To prevent excessive runtime, our implementation selects only $\boldsymbol{y}'$ that is sufficiently close to $\boldsymbol{y}^\star$ as input to Algorithm 1, specifically when $\hat{\mathcal{X}}^{\Delta(\boldsymbol{y}', \boldsymbol{y}^\star)} > M$, where M is a large integer.

Algorithm 1: Identify One Rival Structure

Input	: $\boldsymbol{y}^\star, \boldsymbol{y}'$; // $\boldsymbol{y}' = \text{MFE}(\boldsymbol{x})$, $\boldsymbol{x}$ comes from RNA Design
Output	: $(I, \hat{X})$; // $\hat{X}$ will store all the $\hat{\boldsymbol{x}}$ that violates Theorem 1

1 $\hat{X} \leftarrow \varnothing$;
2 $I \leftarrow \Delta(\boldsymbol{y}', \boldsymbol{y}^\star)$;
3 **foreach** $\hat{\boldsymbol{x}} \in \{\boldsymbol{x} \vdash I \mid \boldsymbol{x} \in \mathcal{X}(\boldsymbol{y}^\star)\}$ **do**
4   **if** $\Delta\Delta G(\hat{\boldsymbol{x}}, \boldsymbol{y}', \boldsymbol{y}^\star) > 0$ **then**   // If Eq. 17 violated, insert $\hat{\boldsymbol{x}}$ into $\hat{X}$
5       $\hat{X} \leftarrow \hat{X} \cup \{\hat{\boldsymbol{x}}\}$
6 **return** $(I, \hat{X})$;   // If $\hat{X}$ is empty then $\boldsymbol{y}^\star$ is undesignable

In fact, if y' is always superior to $y^\star$, any sequence $x \in \mathcal{X}(y^\star)$ must be able to fold into y', which leads to the following corollary.

Corollary 1. *If y' satisfies the condition in Theorem 1, then we have $pairs(y') \subset pairs(y^\star)$.*

Proof. Suppose there exists a pair (i, j) such that $(i, j) \in pairs(y')$ but $(i, j) \notin pairs(y^\star)$. For any sequence x where $x_i x_j$ is not among the allowed base pairs, i.e. $x_i x_j \notin \{CG, GC, AU, UA, GU, UG\}$, x cannot fold into y' because $\Delta G(x, y') = \infty$. Therefore, if x prefers y' to $y^\star$, then y' cannot have any pair (i, j) not in $pairs(y^\star)$. Since $y' \neq y^\star$, it follows that $pairs(y') \subset pairs(y^\star)$.   □

4.3   Theorem 2 and Algorithm 2: Identify Multiple Rival Structures

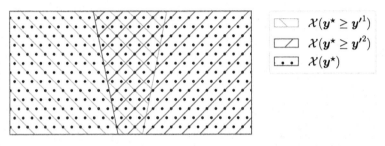

Fig. 4. Undesignability proven by 2 rival structures, $\mathcal{X}(y^\star \geq y'^1) \bigcup \mathcal{X}(y^\star \geq y'^2) = \mathcal{X}(y^\star)$

While Algorithm 1 is effective in verifying the potential rival structure y', it is important to acknowledge that an arbitrary structure y' does not necessarily always have a lower free energy than the target structure $y^\star$. Generally, the entire search space consisting of all possible RNA sequences can be divided into two subsets depending on whether each sequence x prefers $y^\star$ to y'.

Proposition 1. *Given a target structure $y^\star$ and another structure $y' \neq y^\star$, the RNA design space $\mathcal{X}(y^\star)$ can be divided into the two sets below.*

1. $\mathcal{X}(y^\star < y') = \{x \mid \Delta G(x, y^\star) < \Delta G(x, y'), x \in \mathcal{X}(y^\star)\}$;
2. $\mathcal{X}(y^\star \geq y') = \{x \mid \Delta G(x, y') \leq \Delta G(x, y^\star), x \in \mathcal{X}(y^\star)\}$.

Following Proposition 1, the feasibility problem in Eq. 13 is equivalent to

$$\begin{aligned} &\text{find} \quad y' \\ &\text{subject to} \quad \mathcal{X}(y^\star \geq y') = \mathcal{X}(y^\star) \text{ or } \mathcal{X}(y^\star < y') = \emptyset \end{aligned} \tag{21}$$

In cases when no feasible y' satisfying Eq. 21 can be found, we consider extending Theorem 1 and feasibility problem 21 to multiple rival structures identification.

Theorem 2. *A structure $\boldsymbol{y}^\star$ is undesignable, if*

$$\exists Y = \{\boldsymbol{y}'^1, \boldsymbol{y}'^2, .., \boldsymbol{y}'^k\} \text{ and } \boldsymbol{y}^\star \notin Y, \text{ such that } \forall \boldsymbol{x} \in \mathcal{X}(\boldsymbol{y}^\star), \Delta G(\boldsymbol{x}, \boldsymbol{y}') \leq \Delta G(\boldsymbol{x}, \boldsymbol{y}^\star) \text{ for some } \boldsymbol{y}' \in Y.$$

Theorem 2 can also be proven by the Definition 1. The corresponding optimization formulation is

$$\text{find} \quad Y = \{\boldsymbol{y}'^1, \boldsymbol{y}'^2, .., \boldsymbol{y}'^k\}$$
$$\text{subject to} \quad \bigcup_{\boldsymbol{y}' \in Y} \mathcal{X}(\boldsymbol{y}^\star \geq \boldsymbol{y}') = \mathcal{X}(\boldsymbol{y}^\star) \text{ or } \bigcap_{\boldsymbol{y}' \in Y} \mathcal{X}(\boldsymbol{y}^\star < \boldsymbol{y}') = \emptyset. \quad (22)$$

Figure 4 shows a venn diagram when we can prove undesignability by finding a set of 2 rival structures $Y = \{\boldsymbol{y}'^1, \boldsymbol{y}'^2\}$. When $\mathcal{X}(\boldsymbol{y}^\star \geq \boldsymbol{y}'^1) \bigcup \mathcal{X}(\boldsymbol{y}^\star \geq \boldsymbol{y}'^2) = \mathcal{X}(\boldsymbol{y}^\star)$ or $\mathcal{X}(\boldsymbol{y}^\star < \boldsymbol{y}'^1) \bigcap \mathcal{X}(\boldsymbol{y}^\star < \boldsymbol{y}'^2) = \emptyset$, for any sequence $\boldsymbol{x} \in \mathcal{X}(\boldsymbol{y}^\star)$, either $\boldsymbol{y}'^1$ or $\boldsymbol{y}'^2$ would have lower free energy than $\boldsymbol{y}^\star$.

Given input $\boldsymbol{y}^\star$ and $\boldsymbol{y}'$, we call the output of Algorithm 1 a *design constraint*, which characterizes the set $\mathcal{X}(\boldsymbol{y}^\star < \boldsymbol{y}')$. For example, Fig. 5 contains a target structure $\boldsymbol{y}^\star$ from Eterna puzzle "Zigzag Semicircle", along with a designed sequence $\boldsymbol{x}$ and $\boldsymbol{y}' = \text{MFE}(\boldsymbol{x})$. Upon applying Algorithm 1, the output is a tuple consisting of $I = \Delta(\boldsymbol{y}', \boldsymbol{y}^\star) = \{(11, 22), (12, 20), 13, (14, 19), 21\}$ and a set $\hat{X} = \{\hat{\boldsymbol{x}}^1, \hat{\boldsymbol{x}}^2, .., \hat{\boldsymbol{x}}^{90}\}$. Table 3 displays 5 nucleotides compositions in $\hat{X}$. The functionality of Algorithm 1 ensures that any sequence $\boldsymbol{x} \in \mathcal{X}(\boldsymbol{y}^\star < \boldsymbol{y}')$ must satisfy the design constraint $(I, \hat{X})$ and any sequence satisfying the design constraint $(I, \hat{X})$ is in $\mathcal{X}(\boldsymbol{y}^\star < \boldsymbol{y}')$. As a result, we can use $(I, \hat{X})$ to represent the set $\mathcal{X}(\boldsymbol{y}^\star < \boldsymbol{y}')$ and conduct set operations such as intersection and union.

```
y* : .... ( ( ( ( ( ( ( ( ( . ( .... ) ) . ) . ) . ) ) ) ) ) ....
y' : .... ( ( ( ( ( ( ( ( .. ( .... ) .. ) . ) . ) ) ) ) ) ....
 x : AAAAUGAGCCCCACGAAAGGAGAGUGCUCACAAA
```

Fig. 5. Example for Theorem 2 and Algorithm 2

A high level algorithm for solving Eq. 22 is shown in Algorithm 2. Starting from a seed $\boldsymbol{x}$ and $\boldsymbol{y}' = \text{MFE}(\boldsymbol{x})$, Algorithm 2 repeatedly calls Algorithm 1 to get new potential $\boldsymbol{y}'$ and corresponding design constraint $\mathcal{X}(\boldsymbol{y}^\star < \boldsymbol{y}')$. Each new design constraint is intersected (line 13) with all the other design constraints previously found. An example of design constraint intersection is show in Table 4. Refer to Supplementary Section A for specific steps of constraint intersection. The algorithm stops if no new rival structure candidate can be found or there are too many rival structures in Y. Algorithm 2 has 3 parameters: (1) M is the maximum enumeration allowed for Algorithm 1; (2) N is maximum number of rival structures allowed in Y; (3) K is the number of sampled sequences from design space $\mathcal{X}$. At most N set intersections are executed, and at most NK sequences are sampled and folded. Assuming hash sets are used, the time complexity of set intersection is $\mathcal{O}(M)$. Therefore, the overall complexity of Algorithm 2 is $\mathcal{O}(NM + NKn^3)$, where n is the length of the input target structure.

Table 4. Example of design constraint intersection: $C_1', C_2' = \text{Intersection}(C_1, C_2)$ The composition for positions $28, 29$ can only be GC or GU

Constraint C_1					Constraint C_2					Constraint C_1'					Constraint C_2'				
I	28	29	30	31	I	28	29	32	51	I	28	29	30	31	I	28	29	32	51
$\hat{x}^1$	G	C	C	C	$\hat{x}^1$	G	C	A	G	$\hat{x}^1$	G	C	C	C	$\hat{x}^1$	G	C	A	G
$\hat{x}^2$	G	U	C	U	$\hat{x}^2$	G	C	A	U	$\hat{x}^2$	G	U	C	U	$\hat{x}^2$	G	C	A	U
$\hat{x}^3$	G	G	U	U	$\hat{x}^3$	G	U	U	C						$\hat{x}^3$	G	U	U	C
$\hat{x}^4$	G	G	U	C	$\hat{x}^4$	A	G	U	U										

Algorithm 2: Identify Multiple Rival Structures

    Input   : $y^\star, x$;   // x come from (unsuccessful) RNA design
    Output   : undesignable/designable/unknown
1 $\mathcal{X} \leftarrow \mathcal{X}(y^\star)$;   // Design (search) space for $y^\star$
2 $Y \leftarrow \varnothing$;   // Contains all potential rival structures y'
3 $Q \leftarrow \{x\}$;   // A queue contains RNA sequences for folding
4 **while** Q *is not empty* **do**
5 | $x \leftarrow \text{pop}(Q)$;
6 | **if** $\text{uMFE}(x) = y^\star$ **then**
7 | | **return** designable;   // Identify designable case
8 | $y' = \text{MFE}(x)$;
9 | **if** $y' \in Y$ **then break**;   // Stop if no new y'
10 | **if** $|\hat{\mathcal{X}}^{\Delta(y', y^\star)}| > M$ **then** // Continue if too many enumeration in
               Algorithm 1
11 | | **continue**
12 | $\mathcal{X}(y^\star < y') \leftarrow$ **Algorithm 1**$(y^\star, y')$;
13 | $\mathcal{X} \leftarrow \mathcal{X} \cap \mathcal{X}(y^\star < y')$;   // Set intersection
14 | $Y \leftarrow Y \cup \{y'\}$;
15 | **if** $\mathcal{X} = \varnothing$ **then return** undesignable;
16 | **if** $|Y| > N$ **then break**;   // Stop if Y is too large
17 | **if** Q *is empty* **then**
18 | | **for** $i = 1$ **to** K **do**   // Sample at most K sequences
19 | | | Sample $x_{new} \in \mathcal{X}$;
20 | | | $Q \leftarrow \text{push}(Q, x_{new})$;
21 **return** unknown

4.4   Theorem 3 and Algorithm 3: Structure Decomposition

While Algorithm 1 and 2 are efficient when the input $\Delta(y^\star, \text{MFE}(x))$ is small, it is not practical otherwise. For instance, Fig. 6 showcases the puzzle "multilooping fun" from Eterna100 benchmark. The difference between $y^\star$ and y' is so huge that is not suitable as input for Algorithm 1 and 2. It is worth noting that a base pair $(i, j) \in y^\star$ divides the free energy $\Delta G(x, y^\star)$ into two uncoupled parts: one within and one outside $\boldsymbol{y^\star}_{i \to j} = \boldsymbol{y^\star}_i \boldsymbol{y^\star}_{i+1} \cdots \boldsymbol{y^\star}_j$, respectively,

$$\Delta G(\boldsymbol{x}, \boldsymbol{y^\star}) = \sum_{z \in loops(\boldsymbol{y^\star}), z \in loops(\boldsymbol{y^\star}_{i \to j})} \Delta G(\boldsymbol{x}, z) + \sum_{z \in loops(\boldsymbol{y^\star}), z \notin loops(\boldsymbol{y^\star}_{i \to j})} \Delta G(\boldsymbol{x}, z).$$
(23)

When it is impractical to apply Algorithm 1 and 2 to the entire structure $\boldsymbol{y^\star}$, it might be beneficial to search for rival structures for a pair-bounded *substructure* $\boldsymbol{y^\star}_{i \to j}$. For example, if another pair-bounded $\boldsymbol{y''}_{i \to j}$ is always more advantageous, then replacing $\boldsymbol{y^\star}_{i \to j}$ with $\boldsymbol{y''}_{i \to j}$ in $\boldsymbol{y^\star}$ will yield another structure $\boldsymbol{y''}$ that qualifies as a rival structure for $\boldsymbol{y^\star}$. However, the crucial point for such a decomposition and combination is that both $\boldsymbol{y^\star}_{i \to j}$ and $\boldsymbol{y''}_{i \to j}$ must be enclosed by a pair, ensuring that the free energy is the sum of the energy of loops within the pair and outside the pair (i, j). Therefore, we propose to decompose a target structure by base pairs such that the undesignability of a pair-bounded substructure can assure the undesignability of the original target structure.

$$
\begin{aligned}
\boldsymbol{y^\star}: &\quad \texttt{((.(..\underline{(.(....).(....).)}..).(....).))} \\
\boldsymbol{y'}: &\quad \texttt{((............((....))............))} \\
\boldsymbol{y^\star}_{i \to j}: &\quad \texttt{(.(....).(....).)} \\
\boldsymbol{y''}_{i \to j}: &\quad \texttt{(...............)} \\
\boldsymbol{y''}: &\quad \texttt{((.(..\underline{(...............)}..).(....).))}
\end{aligned}
$$

Fig. 6. Example for Theorem 3 and Algorithm 3

Definition 3. *A structure* $\boldsymbol{y} = \boldsymbol{y}_1 \boldsymbol{y}_2 \cdots \boldsymbol{y}_n$ *is context-constrained if* $(1, n) \in pairs(\boldsymbol{y})$, *i.e., its first and last positions are paired.*

For a sequence $\boldsymbol{x} = \boldsymbol{x}_1 \boldsymbol{x}_2 \ldots \boldsymbol{x}_n$ satisfying $\boldsymbol{x}_1 \boldsymbol{x}_n \in \{CG, GC, AU, UA, GU, UG\}$, its *context-constrained ensemble* is defined as $\mathcal{Y}_{CC}(\boldsymbol{x}) = \{\boldsymbol{y} \mid (1, n) \in pairs(\boldsymbol{y}), \boldsymbol{y} \in \mathcal{Y}(\boldsymbol{x})\}$. A context-constrained structure $\boldsymbol{y^\star}$ is a context-constrained MFE structure of $\boldsymbol{x}$, i.e., $\text{MFE}_{CC}(\boldsymbol{x})$, if and only if

$$\forall \boldsymbol{y} \in \mathcal{Y}_{CC}(\boldsymbol{x}) \text{ and } \boldsymbol{y} \neq \boldsymbol{y^\star}, \text{ then } \Delta G(\boldsymbol{x}, \boldsymbol{y^\star}) \leq \Delta G(\boldsymbol{x}, \boldsymbol{y}).$$
(24)

A context-constrained structure $\boldsymbol{y^\star}$ is the context-constrained uMFE structure of $\boldsymbol{x}$, i.e., $\text{uMFE}_{CC}(\boldsymbol{x})$, if and only if

$$\forall \boldsymbol{y} \in \mathcal{Y}_{CC}(\boldsymbol{x}) \text{ and } \boldsymbol{y} \neq \boldsymbol{y^\star}, \text{ then } \Delta G(\boldsymbol{x}, \boldsymbol{y^\star}) < \Delta G(\boldsymbol{x}, \boldsymbol{y}).$$
(25)

Accordingly, we can define context-constrained undesignability by uMFE criterion.

Definition 4. *A context-constrained structure* $\boldsymbol{y^\star}$ *is context-constrained-undesignable if and only if*

$$\forall \boldsymbol{x} \in \mathcal{X}(\boldsymbol{y^\star}), \exists \boldsymbol{y'} \neq \boldsymbol{y^\star} \text{ and } \boldsymbol{y'} \text{ is context-constrained}, \Delta G(\boldsymbol{x}, \boldsymbol{y'}) \leq \Delta G(\boldsymbol{x}, \boldsymbol{y^\star}).$$

Algorithm 3: Identify Rival Structures with Structure Decomposition

---

    Input   : $y^\star, x$;   // x comes from RNA Design
    Output   : undesignable/unknown

1 **foreach** $(i,j) \in pairs(y^\star)$ **do**
2 | **if** $H\langle(i,j)\rangle \notin loops(y^\star)$ **and** $S\langle(i,j),(i+1,j-1)\rangle \notin loops(y^\star)$ **then**
    | // Hairpin&stack excluded
3 | | **if** $y^\star_{i \to j} \neq \text{uMFE}_{\text{CC}}(x_{i \to j})$ **then**   // Constrained folding
4 | | **if Algorithm2**$(y^\star_{i \to j}, x_{i \to j}) = $ undesignable **then**   // Use
    | | MFE_{CC}&uMFE_{CC} in Alg.2
5 | | | **return** undesignable
6 **return** unknown;

The above definitions allow us to succinctly express the idea of proving undesignability via structure decomposition in Theorem 3.

Theorem 3. *A structure $y^\star$ is undesignable if there exists a pair $(i,j) \in pairs(y^\star)$ such that the structure $y^\star_{i \to j}$ is context-constrained undesignable, where $y^\star_{i \to j} = y^\star_i y^\star_{i+1} \cdots y^\star_j$.*

Proof. By Definition 4, $\forall x_{i \to j} \in \mathcal{X}(y^\star_{i \to j}), \exists y'_{i \to j} \neq y^\star_{i \to j}$ and $y'_{i \to j}$ is context-constrained, $\Delta G(x_{i \to j}, y'_{i \to j}) \leq \Delta G(x_{i \to j}, y^\star_{i \to j})$. We can construct a structure $y'' \neq y^\star$ by substituting $y^\star_{i \to j}$ within $y^\star$ with $y'_{i \to j}$ such that $loops(y'') = loops(y^\star) \setminus loops(y^\star_{i \to j}) \cup loops(y'_{i \to j})$. As a result, $\forall x \in \mathcal{X}(y^\star), \exists y'' \neq y, \Delta G(x, y'') - \Delta G(x, y^\star) = \Delta G(x_{i \to j}, y'_{i \to j}) - \Delta G(x_{i \to j}, y^\star_{i \to j})) \leq 0$. □

The algorithm for Theorem 3 is presented in Algorithm 3. Each substructure of the target structure bounded by a pair (i,j) can be regarded as a context-constrained structure, which is input to Algorithm 2. For efficiency we excluded those pairs enclosing a hairpin loop or a stack loop. The target structure is then proven undesignable if one decomposed substructure is verified to be context-constrained undesignable. Since Algorithm 2 is called at most $n/2$ times, the overall complexity of Algorithm 3 is $\mathcal{O}(NMn + NKn^4)$.

5 Experiments on Eterna100 Dataset

5.1 Setting

We applied the three algorithms described in Sect. 4 to structures from the Eterna100 dataset [2], a well-known benchmark for RNA inverse folding. Eterna100 contains a list of 100 secondary structure design challenges (also called puzzles) with a wide range of difficulties.

A previous study [12] identified 19 puzzles were never successfully designed with the folding parameters of ViennaRNA 2.5.1. We took a step further and tried to prove that it is impossible to solve some of Eterna100 puzzles under the uMFE criterion.

For each target structure $y^\star$ in Eterna100, we first attempted RNA design using two state-of-the-art methods NEMO [16] and SAMFEO [25]. We chose the two because our previous studies show that they were able to solve the most puzzles [25]. We adopted the same setting as the RNA design experiments in SAMFEO [25]. Eventually, we obtained 22 structures that neither of the two programs designed successfully under the uMFE criterion with ViennaRNA 2.5.1 parameters. For each unsolved puzzle $y^\star$, we selected the output x such that its MFE structure y' has the minimal structure distance $d(y^\star, y')$, then we used $y^\star$, y', and x as the input to our algorithms.

The three algorithms are implemented in C++ and running on Linux, with 3.40 GHz Intel Xeon E3-1231 CPU and 32G memory. Our implementation also utilized OpenMP to achieve parallelization and the program was ran with 8 CPUs. In Algorithm 2, we used LinearFold [11] (beam size set as 0, which means exact search without beam pruning) with the energy parameter from ViennaRNA 2.5.1 to find MFE(x) and uMFE(x). LinearFold also provides the functionality for constraint folding, which is used in Algorithm 3 to obtain $\text{MFE}_{CC}(x_{i \to j})$ and $\text{uMFE}_{CC}(x_{i \to j})$. Notice our algorithms do not rely on any specific folding package, our released implementation also support using ViennaRAN package for folding and constrained folding which will yield the same output. To prevent the algorithms from running indefinitely, we set the parameters in Algorithm 2 as follows: $M = 10^{10}$, $N = 10^5$, $K = 500$.

5.2   Results

The results of applying our algorithms are presented in Table 5. In total, we identified that 15 out of those the 22 puzzles are undesignable using ViennaRNA 2.5.1 parameters. The algorithms identified the rival structure(s) for 14 out of those 15 undesignable puzzles automatically. For the Puzzle 87, the algorithms took the puzzle and a candidate rival (sub)structure we manually selected then proved the puzzle is undesignable according to Theorem 3.

The implementation of our algorithm also enable turning off special hairpins in energy model. As a result, in addition to the aforementioned 15 undesignable puzzles, our algorithms can automatically prove the Puzzle 50 is undesignable when special hairpins are not considered.

An additional noteworthy finding is that Algorithm 2 can also identify a uMFE (or MFE) solution (line 7) in the process of searching rival structure candidates by folding new sequences. Remarkably, the puzzle "Short String 4" (in the 22 unsolved puzzles) turned out to be designable, i.e., Algorithm 2 successfully generated an RNA sequence that adopts the target structure as the unique MFE structure. See Supplementary Section C for the structure of "Short String 4" along with the designed sequence. Finally, the designability of remaining 5 puzzles remains uncertain, whose puzzles names are Taraxacum officinale, Mat-Lot2-2B, Gladius, Hoglafractal, and Teslagon.

Table 5. List of Eterna100 puzzles that we prove to be undesignable, with context-constrained-undesignable substructures highlighted. If #Rivals is 1, the rival structure can be obtained by removing the red-colored pair(s) from the target structure.

Id	Puzzle	Length	#Rivals	Algorithm	Time (sec.)	Structure
50	1, 2, 3 and 4 bulges[a]	105	1	alg 1	0.08	
52	[RNA] Repetitious Seqs. 8/10	80	1	alg 1	0.03	
57	multilooping fun	36	1	alg 3	22.74	
60	Mat - Elements & Sections	105	8	alg 2	1.82	
61	Chicken feet	67	1	alg 3	231.61	
67	Simple Single Bond	61	1	alg 1	0.10	
72	Loop next to a Multiloop[b]	73	1	alg 1	0.19	
80	Spiral of 5's	397	1	alg 1	0.17	
81	Campfire	212	9	alg 3	0.25	
86	Methaqualone $C_{16}H_{14}N_2O$	355	1	alg 3	17.66	
87	Cat's Toy 2	97	1	alg 3	9.68	
88	Zigzag Semicircle	34	9	alg 2	1.51	
91	Thunderbolt	392	1	alg 3	1.04	
92	Mutated chicken feet	100	1	alg 3	223.57	
96	Cesspool	358	1	alg 3	14.27	
99	Shooting Star	364	2	alg 3	7.77	

[a] This puzzle is proven undesignable if we ignore energies of special hairpins.
[b] Though this puzzle is proven undesignable by the uMFE criterion, it is designable by the MFE criterion.

5.3   Insights

For those puzzles proven undesignable by our three algorithms, we further compared the identified rival structures[1] with original target structures. Main insights are summarized as follows.

1. The undesignability identified by Algorithm 1 is usually caused by some lonely pair or double pairs in the target structure, which is consistent to the observation of previous study [2] on the difficulty of puzzles. For example, the y' in Fig. 2 has one less pair compared to $y^\star$. However, our approach can provide loop-level reasoning and quantitative explanation, which goes beyond heuristics.
2. However, contrary to the principle [2] that symmetry is a feature of difficulty for RNA design, we found that the undesignability is usually caused by some independent local region in a target structures, as is highlighted in the structures plot in Table 5.
3. If an undesignable structure can be proven by identifying multiple rival structures, the number of the rivals tends to be small and those rival structures can be very similar to each other. There are 4 cases with multiple rival structures in Table 5, and their number of rivial structures are $8, 9, 9, 2$ respectively.
4. The constrained-context undesignable structures identified by Algorithm 3 often contains some hairpin enclosed by a single pair or double pairs as the cases highlighted in Table 5. However, it is hard to locate those regions by attempting RNA design and find a y' similar to target structure $y^\star$, which demonstrates the cruciality of structure decomposition.

6   Conclusions and Future Work

Following the core idea of proof by construction, we propose three efficient and explainable algorithms (RIGENDE) for **proving undesignability** in the context of RNA design with the nearest neighbor model. Theoretically, the theorems we introduced can shed some light on why and how some structures are not designable. The establishment of those concepts such as **rival structure, designability constraint, and context-constrained undesignability** can be regarded as a milestone for automatically verifying undesignability. Applied to Eterna100 benchmark, RIGENDE can prove 15 of them are actually undesignable using popular Turner model implemented in ViennaRNA 2.5.1 and LinearFold. Without doubt, the found rival structures can help humans understand more about RNA folding and RNA design. The main drawbacks of RIGENDE include:

1. The rival structure candidates are crucial for the algorithms to work, and the selection of candidates is dependent on the results of RNA design.

---

[1] We released those rival structures at https://github.com/shanry/RNA-Undesign/tree/main/data/results/rigend.

2. The structure decomposition in Algorithm 3 only considers a pair-bounded substructure, which may not be able to cover other sophisticated cases.

In the future, we would address those drawbacks. We will not only prove more cases of undesignability on structure level but also examine the undesignability on the level of structure motifs.

1. Design better ways to find rival structure candidates, such as devising approaches that eliminate the necessity of relying on external RNA design methods.
2. Decompose structures according to the topology of loops instead of splitting the entire structure into two via a base pair.
3. Experiment with more puzzles and RNA design settings to search for more general regularities of designability and undesignability.

References

1. Aguirre-Hernández, R., Hoos, H.H., Condon, A.: Computational RNA secondary structure design: empirical complexity and improved methods. BMC Bioinform. **8**(1), 1–16 (2007)
2. Anderson-Lee, J., et al.: Principles for predicting RNA secondary structure design difficulty. J. Mol. Biol. **428**(5), 748–757 (2016)
3. Andronescu, M., Fejes, A.P., Hutter, F., Hoos, H.H., Condon, A.: A new algorithm for RNA secondary structure design. J. Mol. Biol. **336**(3), 607–624 (2004)
4. Bellaousov, S., Kayedkhordeh, M., Peterson, R.J., Mathews, D.H.: Accelerated RNA secondary structure design using preselected sequences for helices and loops. RNA **24**(11), 1555–1567 (2018)
5. Bonnet, É., Rzazewski, P., Sikora, F.: Designing RNA secondary structures is hard. J. Comput. Biol. **27**(3), 302–316 (2020)
6. Crick, F.: Central dogma of molecular biology. Nature **227**(5258), 561–563 (1970)
7. Doudna, J.A., Cech, T.R.: The chemical repertoire of natural ribozymes. Nature **418**(6894), 222–228 (2002)
8. Garcia-Martin, J.A., Clote, P., Dotu, I.: RNAiFOLD: a constraint programming algorithm for RNA inverse folding and molecular design. J. Bioinform. Comput. Biol. **11**(02), 1350001 (2013)
9. Haleš, J., Maňuch, J., Ponty, Y., Stacho, L.: Combinatorial RNA design: designability and structure-approximating algorithm. In: Cicalese, F., Porat, E., Vaccaro, U. (eds.) CPM 2015. LNCS, vol. 9133, pp. 231–246. Springer, Cham (2015). https://doi.org/10.1007/978-3-319-19929-0_20
10. Hofacker, I.L., Fontana, W., Stadler, P.F., Bonhoeffer, L.S., Tacker, M., Schuster, P.: Fast folding and comparison of RNA secondary structures. Monatshefte für Chemie/Chemical Monthly **125**(2), 167–188 (1994)
11. Huang, L., et al.: LinearFold: linear-time approximate RNA folding by 5'-to-3' dynamic programming and beam search. Bioinformatics **35**(14), i295–i304 (2019). https://doi.org/10.1093/bioinformatics/btz375
12. Koodli, R.V., Rudolfs, B., Wayment-Steele, H.K., Designers, E.S., Das, R.: Redesigning the EteRNA100 for the Vienna 2 folding engine. BioRxiv, pp. 2021–08 (2021)

13. Lorenz, R., et al.: ViennaRNA Package 2.0. Algorithms for Molecular Biology **6**(1), 1 (2011)

14. Mathews, D., Sabina, J., Zuker, M., Turner., D.: Expanded sequence dependence of thermodynamic parameters improves prediction of RNA secondary structure. J. Mol. Biol. **288**(5), 911–940 (1999)

15. Mathews, D.H., Disney, M.D., Childs, J.L., Schroeder, S.J., Zuker, M., Turner, D.H.: Incorporating chemical modification constraints into a dynamic programming algorithm for prediction of RNA secondary structure. Proc. Nat. Acad. Sci. USA **101**(19), 7287–7292 (2004)

16. Portela, F.: An unexpectedly effective Monte Carlo technique for the RNA inverse folding problem. BioRxiv, p. 345587 (2018)

17. Rubio-Largo, Á., Vanneschi, L., Castelli, M., Vega-Rodríguez, M.A.: Multiobjective metaheuristic to design RNA sequences. IEEE Trans. Evol. Comput. **23**(1), 156–169 (2018)

18. Serganov, A., Patel, D.J.: Ribozymes, riboswitches and beyond: regulation of gene expression without proteins. Nat. Rev. Genet. **8**(10), 776–790 (2007)

19. Taneda, A.: MODENA: a multi-objective RNA inverse folding. In: Advances and Applications in Bioinformatics and Chemistry: AABC, vol. 4, p. 1 (2011)

20. Turner, D.H., Mathews, D.H.: NNDB: the nearest neighbor parameter database for predicting stability of nucleic acid secondary structure. Nucleic Acids Res. **38**(suppl_1), D280–D282 (2010)

21. Ward, M., Courtney, E., Rivas, E.: Fitness Functions for RNA Structure Design. bioRxiv (2022)

22. Yao, H.T.: Local decomposition in RNA structural design. Ph.D. thesis, McGill University (Canada) (2021)

23. Yao, H.T., Chauve, C., Regnier, M., Ponty, Y.: Exponentially few RNA structures are designable. In: Proceedings of the 10th ACM International Conference on Bioinformatics, Computational Biology and Health Informatics. pp. 289–298 (2019)

24. Zadeh, J.N., Wolfe, B.R., Pierce, N.A.: Nucleic Acid Sequence Design via Efficient Ensemble Defect Optimization. J. Comput. Chem. **32**(3), 439–452 (2010)

25. Zhou, T., Dai, N., Li, S., Ward, M., Mathews, D.H., Huang, L.: RNA design via structure-aware multifrontier ensemble optimization. Bioinformatics **39**(Supplement_1), i563–i571 (2023)

Structure- and Function-Aware Substitution Matrices via Learnable Graph Matching

Paolo Pellizzoni[✉], Carlos Oliver, and Karsten Borgwardt

Department of Machine Learning and Systems Biology,
Max Planck Institute of Biochemistry, Martinsried, Germany
{pellizzoni,oliver,borgwardt}@biochem.mpg.de

Abstract. Substitution matrices, which are crafted to quantify the functional impact of substitutions or deletions in biomolecules, are central component of remote homology detection, functional element discovery, and structure prediction algorithms. In this work we explore the use of biological structures and prior knowledge about molecular function (e.g. experimental data or functional annotations) as additional information for building more expressive substitution matrices compared to the traditional frequency-based methods. External prior knowledge in the form of family annotations have been exploited for specialized sequence alignment methods, and substitution matrices on structural alphabets have led to advances in remote homology detection. However, no method has integrated both structural information as well as external priors without the need of pre-curated alignments.

Here we propose a general algorithmic framework for learning structure-based substitution matrices automatically conditioned on any prior knowledge. In particular, we represent the structures of interest as graphs and we learn, using graph neural networks, suitable substitution cost matrices such that the resulting graph matching metric correlates with the prior at hand. Our method shows promising performance in functional similarity classification tasks and molecular database searching and shows potential for interpreting the functional importance of substructures.
Code and data are available at:
https://github.com/BorgwardtLab/GraphMatchingSubstitutionMatrices.

Keywords: Substitution matrices · Graph matching · Graph neural networks

1 Introduction

Understanding the functional roles of biomolecules and their substructures is a core challenge in bioinformatics. To this end, alignment algorithms seek to

---

P. Pellizzoni and C. Oliver—Equal contribution.

J. Ma (Ed.): RECOMB 2024, LNCS 14758, pp. 288–307, 2024.
https://doi.org/10.1007/978-1-0716-3989-4_18

identify conservation at the primary, secondary, and tertiary structure level by leveraging substitution matrices which quantify the biological impact of changes in sequence and structure alphabets. The quality of alignments therefore depends the degree to which underlying substitution matrices accurately capture the functional impact of changes within their respective alphabets [17].

Widely used substitution matrices are built with the intuition that the frequency of a modification within a *pre-aligned* set of molecules deemed homologous is an indicator of their functional impact [19]. Looking for low frequency changes in a given set of alignments, is then a hint for selective pressure and thus an indication that such changes are likely to impact the function of the molecule. Conversely, substitutions that occur at frequencies close to those expected by chance do not show signs of selection, allowing alignment algorithms to match such entities without incurring a strong penalty.

From this intuition came many proposals for substitution matrices in several domains. For amino acid sequences, BLOSUM62 and PAM [42,47], for DNA the BLASTN matrix [14], for base pair substitution matrices for RNA [21] and for chemical group substitution matrices [40]. Most alignment tools and hence substitution matrices have been applied on sequence data, but with the growing availability of structural data in RCSB [37] came the motivation for modeling the impact of modifications on *structural* alphabets. These efforts are motivated by the fact that structure is more tightly conserved than sequence [22] and hence lies closer to the function of a molecule than sequence alone. Methods such as Blast3D, SSLALN [34,44], and the custom 3Di structural alphabet in Foldseek [45] have been successful at detecting remote homologs (i.e. proteins with low sequence identity but with a common structure). These substitution matrices are built from manually curated sets of aligned homologous proteins and then the process of substitution frequency calculation is repeated, but this time on an alphabet of structural fragments rather than residues. Further substitution matrix conditioning settings have been explored for specific protein families [23], organisms [43] and phylogenetic knowledge [24].

Another powerful family of methods for understanding the impact of substructures on function comes from adopting an alignment-free methodology. Given prior knowledge about some set of molecules (e.g. enzyme classifications, pathway information, experimental assays, etc.), alignment-free models automatically learn the associations between a given structure and the functional outcome in a classification setting. Methods such as DeepFRI [16], DeepGO [26] for proteins, RNAmigos [32] for RNA binding sites, ChemBERT for chemicals [12] are trained to predict the function of a given biomolecule using neural networks and prior functional knowledge as labels. The advantage of these large parametric models is that they are very sensitive to subtle and possibly complex structure-function associations that are hard to model explicitly *a priori*. Furthermore, they allow one to model structure-function relationships conditioned on a user-defined task without the need of alignments, which could allow one to pick up on patterns that a generalist approach such as BLOSUM may not. With these benefits of course comes the cost of model interpretability which limits their use in the construction of expressive substitution matrices.

Ideally one would like the best of both worlds: *a substitution matrix algorithm on structural alphabets that can use prior knowledge to circumvent the need of pre-curated alignments*. The first efforts to this end were made with DEDAL [28] which fine-tunes substitution costs using Pfam [2] annotations. However, the method works only on sequence data and still requires pre-fabricated alignments for training. To take such efforts further, in this work we explore the potential of metric learning algorithms on graphs as substitution matrix generators. We make a connection with the graph edit distance literature [9,31], where efforts have been made at automatically learning optimal edit costs conditioned on prior knowledge. In particular, we are interested in graph learning frameworks which are well-suited for incorporating domain knowledge in the form of classification labels.

Several works have explored the approximation of the graph edit distance in a learning-based setting. Some methods, such as SimGNN [1] and GREED [35], focus on estimating directly the edit distance, without actually providing an alignment between graphs. Other methods, such as GOT-Sim [13] are based on graph matching methods and can provide alignments. All of these methods though require the ground truth graph edit distances, which is often unrealistic.

Graph Matching Networks [27] propose a method to learn graph matchings based on graph labels alone, but provides no edit cost matrix. In [36], the authors propose a model, based on a soft-assignment heuristic, to approximate graph edit distances according to graph labels. Finally, a recent preprint proposed EPIC [20], a model that learns edit costs based on graph labels, which are then used in the context of dataset augmentation.

Until now, no differentiable graph matching framework has been proposed for the purpose of generating alignment-free and interpretable substitution matrix on biomolecules.

1.1   Contributions

In this work, we tackle the problem of automatically obtaining task-specific substitution matrices for biological structures, bridging the gap between learning-based algorithms for graph matching and structural bioinformatics. In particular we:

1. design a model, GMSM (Graph Matching Substitution Matrices), that provides an interpretable substitution matrix and alignment between the pairs of structures it receives as input. Moreover, we provide a theoretical analysis of the expressiveness of the model and of its suitability to a learning objective.
2. provide experimental validation to the soundness of the graph metric induced by the learned substitution matrices in proteins, RNA structure, and chemical compounds datasets.
3. give a first analysis of the learned substitution matrices.

2 Preliminaries

In this section, we define some preliminaries on graph theory and on machine learning on graphs. In what follows, we denote as a graph a tuple $G = (V, E)$, with V the set of nodes and E the set of undirected edges, meaning unordered pairs from V representing some form of relation between the nodes. Both node and edges can have discrete labels. We define $\mathcal{V}$ as the set of such labelled nodes and $\mathcal{G}$ as the set of graphs.

2.1 Graph Neural Networks

Graph neural networks (GNNs) are a generalization of neural networks designed to work on graphs [15,46,49]. Most common GNN architectures can be described using the message passing framework, where the model iteratively produces for each node v, at each level $\ell = 1, \ldots, L$, the embeddings $h_v^\ell \in \mathbb{R}^{d_\ell}$ by taking into account *messages* coming from its neighbors $\mathcal{N}(v)$. More formally, the message at iteration t received by node v is

$$m_v^t = f_{\text{agg}}\left(h_v^{t-1}, \{(h_u^{t-1}, e_{uv}) : u \in \mathcal{N}(v)\}\right),$$

with e_{uv} the attribute of the edge between u and v. Then, the embedding of node v is updated as

$$h_v^t = f_{\text{update}}\left(h_v^{t-1}, m_v^t\right),$$

where f_{agg} and f_{update} are the aggregate and the update operations, respectively. The first layer of the GNN is fed with the initial node embeddings h_v^0, e.g. one-hot encodings of the node labels. Finally, one can get a graph-level readout by aggregating the output node embeddings, e.g. using their mean or their sum.

We denote $\psi_\theta(v, G)$ as the output embedding for node v for a GNN with parameters θ. Note that the map $G = (V, E) \to \{\{\psi(v, G) : v \in V\}\}$ is not injective on isomorphism classes of graphs, i.e. there can be two non-isomorphic graphs that are mapped to the same set of node embeddings. In particular, message passing neural networks are known to be at most as expressive as the Weisfeiler-Lehman (WL) isomorphism test [49]. We will denote $(v, G_1) =_\psi (u, G_2)$ if $\psi(v, G_1) = \psi(u, G_2)$, and denote by $\mathcal{V}_{\psi_\theta}$ the set of equivalence classes induced by $=_\psi$. Moreover, we will denote, with abuse of notation, $G_1 =_\psi G_2$ if $\{\{\psi(v, G_1 = (V_1, E_1)) : v \in V_1\}\} = \{\{\psi(v, G_2 = (V_2, E_2)) : v \in V_2\}\}$, and denote for brevity with $\mathcal{G}_\psi$ the set $\mathcal{G}/=_\psi$ of equivalence classes induced by $=_\psi$ on graphs.

2.2 Graph Edit Distance

The *graph edit distance* [9,31] is a distance that assesses the similarity between two graphs. In particular, it is computed as the minimum cumulative cost of the edit operations required to transform one graph into another, with legal edit operations being node and edge insertion, deletion, and substitution, each with an associated cost.

When the edit costs form a metric [6], the graph edit distance can be equivalently defined as a bipartite graph matching problem:

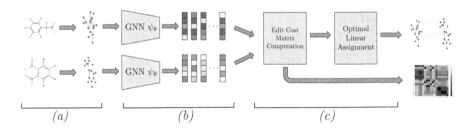

(a)   (b)   (c)

Fig. 1. Architecture of GMSM. *(a)* Biochemical structures are transformed into graphs. *(b)* For each graph, its nodes are represented as a structure-aware embeddings using the same GNN. *(c)* The model computes the substitution matrix from node embeddings and obtains the graph alignment with respect to the learned substitution matrix.

Definition 1 (Graph Edit Distance [8]). *Let $G_1 = (V_1, E_1)$ and $G_2 = (V_2, E_2)$ be the source and the target graphs respectively. Let $|V_1| = n_1$ and $|V_2| = n_2$. Let $V_1^+ = V_1 \cup \{\varepsilon_1, \ldots, \varepsilon_{n_2}\}$ be the vertex set of G_1 enriched with n_2 dummy nodes ε to allow for insertion and deletions. Let the same hold for V_2^+, with n_1 dummy nodes. The graph edit distance (GED) between G_1 and G_2 is defined by*

$$GED(G_1, G_2) = \min_{\pi \in \Pi} \sum_{v_i \in V_1^+} c_v(v_i, \pi(v_i)) + \sum_{v_i, v_j \in V_1} c_e(v_i, v_j, \pi(v_i), \pi(v_j)),$$

where Π denotes the set of bijections from V_1^+ to V_2^+, and c_v denotes the cost function for node edit operations and c_e for edge edit operations.

The graph edit distance is a quadratic assignment problem, and therefore is known to be NP-hard [9]. The *bipartite graph matching* heuristic [6] to the graph edit distance is an heuristic technique to get approximate GEDs in polynomial time. The main idea is to transform the problem into a linear assignment problem, which is well-known to be polynomial-time solvable (e.g. with the Hungarian algorithm), by disregarding edge edit operations and only considering node edit ones.

Then, the linear assignment problem to be solved is

$$d_C(G_1, G_2) := \min_{\pi \in \Pi} \langle C, \pi \rangle = \min_{\pi \in \Pi} \sum_{v_i \in V_1^+} c_{v_i, \pi(v_i)},$$

with $\langle \cdot, \cdot \rangle$ being the Frobenius inner product, and with cost matrix C defined as

$$C = \left[\begin{array}{ccc|ccc} c_{1,1} & \cdots & c_{1,n_2} & c_{1,\varepsilon} & \cdots & \infty \\ \vdots & \ddots & \vdots & \vdots & \ddots & \vdots \\ c_{n_1,1} & \cdots & c_{n_1,n_2} & \infty & \cdots & c_{n_1,\varepsilon} \\ \hline c_{\varepsilon,1} & \cdots & \infty & 0 & \cdots & 0 \\ \vdots & \ddots & \vdots & \vdots & \ddots & \vdots \\ \infty & \cdots & c_{\varepsilon,n_2} & 0 & \cdots & 0 \end{array} \right]$$

where $c_{i,j}$ denotes the cost of a node substitution $v_i \rightarrow v_j$, $c_{i,\varepsilon}$ denotes the cost of a node deletion $u_i \rightarrow \varepsilon$, and $c_{\varepsilon,j}$ denotes the costs of a node insertion $\varepsilon \rightarrow v_j$ with $v_i \in V_1$ and $v_j \in V_2$; and where Π is the set of permutation matrices of size $|V_1| + |V_2|$, representing bijections from V_1^+ to V_2^+.

If one chooses $c_{i,j} = c_v(v_i, v_j)$, i.e. setting the cost of assigning node v_i to node v_j as the node edit cost in the original problem, then $d_C(G_1, G_2)$ lower bounds $GED(G_1, G_2)$.

Many approximation algorithms to the GED modify the node assignment costs in order to account for edge edit operations [4]. The common technique is to represent the nodes as some local substructure around them, such as neighborhoods [5] or subgraphs [10], and to compute the assignment costs accordingly. In many practical applications, representing the graph as such a bag of local structures is enough to compute a good approximation to the true edit distance [4].

3   Methods

In this section, we describe our methodological contributions towards obtaining task-specific substitution matrices for biochemical structures.

3.1   GMSM Architecture

In this section, we describe the architecture of our method GMSM, which is designed to learn expressive substitution matrices for biological structures and, at the same time, when given two such graph-represented structures, to output an interpretable alignment of the two graphs based on such substitution matrices.

Taking inspiration from the bipartite graph matching heuristic for graph edit distance, we represent our graphs as bag of *learnable* node features, and compute the edit distance between graphs by computing the optimal assignment between such features.

More formally, given a graph G we represent each node $v \in V$ as a parametric function $\psi_\theta(v, G)$, which is implemented by a graph neural network (GNN) parametrized by θ. For a pair of graphs G_1, G_2, the set of node features is computed using the same parametric function, which is usually called a *siamese network* [11], as shown in Fig. 1.

Then, the cost of substituting v with u is given by $c_{u,v} = \|\psi_\theta(v, G_1) - \psi_\theta(u, G_2)\|_2$. Node insertion and deletion costs are obtained by computing the distance to a learnable embedding for a dummy isolated node ε, that is $c_{v,\varepsilon} = c_{\varepsilon,v} = \|\psi_\theta(v, G_1) - \psi_\theta(\varepsilon)\|_2$. This yields a global learnable substitution matrix $C(\psi_\theta) = (c_{u,v})_{u,v \in \mathcal{V}_{\psi_\theta}}$ of costs between elements of $\mathcal{V}_{\psi_\theta} \cup \{\varepsilon\}$, which correspond to nodes and their rooted subgraph explored by the GNN. In particular, given two graphs G_1, G_2, the model computes the corresponding edit cost matrix $C_{G_1,G_2}(\psi_\theta) = (c_{u,v})_{u \in V_1^+, v \in V_2^+}$, which is a submatrix of $C(\psi_\theta)$.

Finally, the optimal matching between the node features is computed using the Hungarian algorithm, as described in Sect. 2.2, as

$$d_{\psi_\theta}(G_1, G_2) := d_{C_{G_1,G_2}(\psi_\theta)}(G_1, G_2) = \min_{\pi \in \Pi} \langle C_{G_1,G_2}(\psi_\theta), \pi \rangle.$$

Note that if ψ is a 0-layer GNN, i.e. the output node embedding is a function only of the original node label, then the model implements a node-level substitution matrix and the optimal assignments computes a similarity between sets of nodes.

The time complexity of extracting the node embeddings for a graph depends on the choice of the graph neural network, and for the most common architectures is linear in the number of edges of graph. Computing the cost substitution matrix takes time $O(n_1 n_2 \ell)$, where ℓ is the dimensionality of the node embeddings. Finally, if one computes the optimal assignment between the nodes using the Hungarian algorithm, the time complexity of the distance calculation is $O((n_1 + n_2)^3)$, which usually dominates the other two phases. In fact, since the $c_{u,v}$ costs satisfy the triangle inequality, one can notice that it suffices to add dummy nodes to the graph with less nodes, which reduces the complexity to $O(\max(n_1, n_2)^3)$.

The following theorem shows that the function $d_{\psi_\theta}(\cdot, \cdot)$ is indeed well-behaved.

Theorem 1. *Let $\mathcal{G}$ be the set of graphs. Then, $(\mathcal{G}, d_{\psi_\theta})$ is a pseudometric space.*

Proof. We drop the subscript d_{ψ_θ} where clear from the context. We show that if $G_1 = G_2$ then $d(G_1, G_2) = 0$. By permutation equivariance of message-passing GNNs, if $G_1 = G_2$, then $G_1 =_{\psi_\theta} G_2$ and their set of node embeddings will be the same. The optimal linear assignment cost is then 0. Note that $d(G_1, G_2) = 0$ does not imply $G_1 = G_2$. Moreover, since C_{G_1,G_2} is symmetric, $d(G_1, G_2) = d(G_2, G_1)$.

We now show that triangle inequality holds, namely that $d(G_1, G_3) \leq d(G_1, G_2) + d(G_2, G_3)$, for any $G_1, G_2, G_3 \in \mathcal{G}$. Let π_{12}^*, π_{13}^* and π_{23}^* the maps that realize the optimal assignments between the graphs. We show a map $\pi : V_1^+ \to V_3^+$ with associated cost less or equal to $d(G_1, G_2) + d(G_2, G_3)$.

Let $V_1^{++} = V_1 \cup \{\varepsilon_1^2, \ldots, \varepsilon_{|V_2|}^2, \varepsilon_1^3, \ldots, \varepsilon_{|V_3|}^3\}$, $V_2^{++} = V_2 \cup \{\varepsilon_1^1, \ldots, \varepsilon_{|V_1|}^1, \varepsilon_1^3, \ldots, \varepsilon_{|V_3|}^3\}$ and $V_3^{++} = V_3 \cup \{\varepsilon_1^1, \ldots, \varepsilon_{|V_1|}^1, \varepsilon_1^2, \ldots, \varepsilon_{|V_2|}^2\}$. Let $\pi_{12}^+ : V_1^{++} \to V_2^{++}$ be defined as $\pi_{12}^+(u) = \pi_{12}^*$ if $u \in V_1 \cup \{\varepsilon_1^2, \ldots, \varepsilon_{|V_2|}^2\}$ and $\pi_{12}^+(u) = u$ otherwise. Let π_{23}^+ be defined as $\pi_{23}^+(u) = \pi_{23}^*$ if $u \in V_2 \cup \{\varepsilon_1^3, \ldots, \varepsilon_{|V_3|}^3\}$ and $\pi_{23}^+(u) = u$ otherwise.

Then we construct a bijective map $\pi_{13}^+ : V_1^{++} \to V_3^{++}$ as $\pi_{13}^+ = \pi_{12}^+ \circ \pi_{23}^+$. Note that $\sum_{u \in V_1^{++}} c_{u, \pi_{13}^+(u)} \leq \sum_{u \in V_1^{++}} c_{u, \pi_{12}^+(u)} + c_{\pi_{12}^+(u), \pi_{23}^+(\pi_{12}^+(u))} = d(G_1, G_2) + d(G_2, G_3)$, since the costs satisfy the triangle inequality.

Finally, we note that there are at least V_2 dummy nodes in V_1^{++} whose image of π_{13}^+ is also a dummy node. If we discard such V_2 dummy nodes from the domain and codomain, and relabel the remaining dummy nodes, we obtain the desired map $\pi : V_1^+ \to V_3^+$, which has the same cost as π_{13}^+.

Moreover, one can obtain a metric space on $\mathcal{G}_{\psi_\theta}$ as follows. Let ψ_θ be such that $\psi_\theta(\varepsilon) \neq \psi_\theta(v, G)$, $\forall v \in V, \forall G = (V, E) \in \mathcal{G}$, i.e. insertion and deletion costs are positive.

Then $G_1 =_{\psi_\theta} G_2$ if and only if $d_{\psi_\theta}(G_1, G_2) = 0$. If $G_1 =_{\psi_\theta} G_2$ their set of node embeddings will be the same and the optimal linear assignment cost is 0. Conversely, if $G_1 \neq_{\psi_\theta} G_2$, then their node embeddings sets will be different. Let without loss of generality $|V_1| \geq |V_2|$, then $\exists v \in V_1$ such that $\psi_\theta(v, G_1) \neq \psi_\theta(w, G_2)$, $\forall w \in V_2$. Then, $\min_{w \in V_2} c_{v,w} > 0$. Since insertions and deletion costs are non-zero, $\min_{w \in V_2^+} c_{v,w} > 0$ and the optimal assignment cost must be positive.

Therefore, the equivalence relation $=_{\psi_\theta}$ is the metric identification of the pseudometric, and $\mathcal{G}_{\psi_\theta}$ is the quotient space of $\mathcal{G}$ with respect to such equivalence relation. Then, if we let $d^*([G_1], [G_2]) = d(G_1, G_2)$, the space $(\mathcal{G}_{\psi_\theta}, d^*)$ is a metric space.

Note that the distance d depends on the size of the graphs that are being compared. In practice, it is useful [13] to normalize the distance by the sum of the number of nodes of the two graphs and to use the *graph dissimilarity*

$$\hat{d}(G_1, G_2) = \frac{1}{|V_1| + |V_2|} d(G_1, G_2)$$

as the output of the GMSM model rather than the unnormalized distance.

3.2 Training GMSM

Informally, we want that the graph dissimilarity induced by the learned substitution matrix $C(\psi_\theta)$ correlates with the conditioning information at hand. In this work, we restrict the conditioning information to be discrete class labels, such as Pfam families or EC numbers for proteins.

In particular, we would like for graphs belonging to the same class to have low distance, and for graphs belonging to different classes to have higher distance, as common in the *metric learning* setting [18].

Common losses for metric learning are the contrastive loss [18] and the triplet loss [39], which act on pairs and triplets of graphs, respectively. We use the *margin loss* proposed in [48], which reportedly yields better results than the contrastive one. Moreover, it can work with randomly sampled pairs, while the triplet loss usually requires hard or semi-hard sample mining to work properly [48].

In particular, for a pair of graphs G_1, G_2, the loss is defined as

$$\ell_{margin}(G_1, G_2) = \max\left(0, \alpha + y(\hat{d}_C(G_1, G_2) - \beta)\right),$$

with $y = 1$ for positive pairs, i.e. both graphs belonging to the same class, and $y = -1$ for negative pairs. This loss strives to push the graph dissimilarities of graphs belonging to the same class to be less than $\beta - \alpha$ and the dissimilarities of graphs belonging to different classes to be more than $\beta + \alpha$.

Crucially, since one wants the cost matrix C to be *learnt* based on the data at hand, the function $\hat{d}_C(G_1, G_2)$ should allow the existence of the gradient with respect to C to allow for its optimization. Clearly, solving the optimal assignment involves non-differentiable operations. Nonetheless, we propose a well-defined proxy for the gradient that allows us to optimize the model parameters.

Proposition 1. *Let* $d_C(G_1, G_2) = \min_{\pi \in \Pi} \langle C, \pi \rangle$ *and let* C *such that* $\operatorname{argmin}_{\pi \in \Pi} \langle C, \pi \rangle$ *is unique. Then the function* $d_C(G_1, G_2)$ *is differentiable with gradient*

$$\nabla_C d_C(G_1, G_2) = \operatorname{argmin}_{\pi \in \Pi} \langle C, \pi \rangle.$$

We define $\pi_A^*(C)$ the solution returned by an assignment algorithm A (e.g. Hungarian algorithm) when applied to the problem $\min_{\pi \in \Pi} \langle C, \pi \rangle$. Clearly, $\pi_A^*(C)$ is unique, and $\pi_A^*(C) = \operatorname{argmin}_{\pi \in \Pi} \langle C, \pi \rangle$ for all C such that argmin is unique. We define $\tilde{\nabla}_C d_C(G_1, G_2) = \pi_A^*(C)$ and apply gradient descent to GMSM with this re-defined gradient.

4   Experimental Evaluation

In this section, we provide some experimental evidence that the substitution matrices learned by our method indeed distill useful information about the conditioning priors on which the model was trained. To do so, we show results on distance-based classification and retrieval tasks for both macromolecules and small molecules.

4.1   Datasets

In our experimental evaluation, we use three protein datasets, one RNA dataset and three small molecule datasets. All datasets are split into training, validation and test sets at random and with ratios $\{0.8, 0.1, 0.1\}$.

The protein structure datasets are taken from the ProteinShake library [25]. Pfam is a dataset of proteins from The Protein Data Bank [37] annotated with Pfam families. EC is a dataset of proteins annotated with Enzyme Commission numbers; we take the top level of the EC hierarchy as the label. SCOP is a dataset of protein domains annotated according to evolutionary and structural criteria. We use the SF (superfamily) classifications level as label. The RNA dataset is built using rnaglib [29] and contains small molecule binding sites classified according to the chemical family of the bound small molecule. The small molecules datasets are obtained from the TUDataset [30] and contain molecules annotated with a label on mutagen activity (Mutagenicity), on activity against non-small cell lung cancer (NCI1) and on evidence of anti-HIV activity (AIDS).

All structures are represented as graphs using domain-specific choices described as follows.

Proteins: Proteins can be represented as labeled undirected graphs. In this representation, the nodes represent the residues of the protein, with node labels encoding the amino acid types. An edge is drawn between two nodes when the Euclidean distance between the corresponding residues remains within a specified threshold. In what follows, this threshold is set at 8.0 Angstroms, primarily because a majority of local intermolecular interactions manifest within this range [3].

RNA: to encode an RNA molecule's atomic structure as a graph we use the Leontis-Westhof base pair nomenclature which is thought to capture the essential features of an RNA's 3D geometry [38]. Under this scheme, each node in the graph corresponds to a nucleotide (residue) and an edge is formed between pairs of consecutive residues along the covalent backbone, as well as base pairs undergoing hydrogen bonding. The relative orientation of the bases along the hydrogen bond defines the edge attributes and falls in one of 18 possible discrete categories according to [38]. Each node is also annotated with its nucleotide type {A, C, G, U}. Datasets of RNA graphs are managed by rnaglib [29].

Molecules: we represent molecules as undirected graphs simply by considering atoms as nodes and the bonds between them as edges. Nodes and edges are labeled according to the element number and the bond type for nodes and edges, respectively.

4.2   Experimental Setup

Tasks. The first task we tackle is the similarity-based classification task. Given two graphs, the task is to predict whether or not they belong to the same class, solely as a function of their learned distance. In particular, we evaluate two metrics. The first one is the triplet accuracy. Namely, given an anchor graph, one graph from the same class of the anchor (positive pair) and one graph from another class (negative pair), the triplet of graphs is considered a successful prediction if the distance of the positive pair is lower than the one of the negative pair. The second is pair AUROC, the area under the ROC curve for classifying pairs of graphs as similar or not based on a distance threshold. The goal of this task is to evaluate whether the learned dissimilarity between graphs correlates, at both the short-range and long range scale, with the conditioning priors on which it was trained on.

The second task we evaluate is the retrieval task. In particular, given a query graph, the task is to return a set of graphs that are the most similar to the query one. The goal of this task is to evaluate the quality of the learned graph dissimilarity at very short scales.

Implementation Details. Our model, GMSM, is implemented as follows. The GNN is implemented by a GAT model [46] with k layers, where k is a hyperparameter, followed by a concatenation of the embeddings to the one-hot

Table 1. Similarity-based classification on macromolecules

Method	EC		Pfam		SCOP		RNA	
	Trip. acc.	AUROC	Trip. acc.	AUROC	Trip. acc.	AUROC	Trip. acc.	AUROC
WL kernel	0.503	0.505	0.771	0.708	0.652	0.604	0.579	0.575
Seq. alignment (BLOSUM64)	0.470	0.478	0.587	0.541	0.470	0.478	–	–
Siamese-GNN	0.643	0.622	0.869	0.855	0.800	0.794	0.672	0.663
GMSM (uniform costs)	0.520	0.518	0.868	0.857	0.804	0.790	0.609	0.606
GMSM (node level)	0.520	0.518	0.864	0.855	0.799	0.789	0.606	0.603
GMSM (GNN)	0.584	0.570	0.904	0.904	0.846	0.851	0.669	0.642

Table 2. Similarity-based classification on small molecules

Method	Mutagenicity		NCI1		AIDS	
	Trip. acc.	AUROC	Trip. acc.	AUROC	Trip. acc.	AUROC
WL kernel	0.532	0.532	0.591	0.581	0.827	0.820
Molecular fingerprint	0.559	0.558	0.623	0.609	0.993	0.992
Siamese-GNN	0.698	0.677	0.652	0.632	0.431	0.450
GMSM (uniform costs)	0.572	0.562	0.528	0.517	0.775	0.741
GMSM (node level)	0.568	0.558	0.540	0.534	0.833	0.815
GMSM (GNN)	0.668	0.653	0.604	0.592	0.848	0.838

encodings of the labels and by a linear layer to obtain the final embeddings $\psi(v, G)$. The embeddings are then normalized to have norm 1. The cost matrix C is computed by taking the Euclidean distance between embeddings and the optimal assignment is obtained using the Hungarian algorithm.

The model is trained taking the same number of random positive and negative pairs from the training set, and optimized with respect to the margin loss, using $\beta = 0.5$ and $\alpha = 0.1$. The best model is selected using the validation set pair AUROC metric using early stopping.

The models are evaluated and tested using the same sampling strategy for random positive and negative pairs from the validation and test set, respectively.

Baselines. We now describe the baselines we compare GMSM to. We used a combination of established graph-based methods and domain-specific ones.

WL Kernel: The WL kernel [41] is a simple nonparametric graph kernel that is based on the WL refinement procedure. It serves as a simple baseline to assess the hardness of a task. It is used as a task-independent baseline across datasets.

Sequence Alignment: We perform sequence alignment using the Smith-Waterman algorithm with the BLOSUM64 matrix [42]. We use this as a protein-specific baseline.

Molecular Fingerprint: We compute molecular fingerprints using RDKit (www. rdkit.org) and compare them using the Tanimoto similarity. We use this as a small-molecule-specific baseline.

Siamese-GNN: This model uses the same GNN architecture as GMSM, but instead of computing the distance using linear assignment, it simply uses a graph mean-pooling operator to encode graphs as a single embedding. Distances are then computed as the euclidean distance between embeddings. The model is trained using the same hyperparameters and loss as GMSM, for a fair comparison, in an end-to-end fashion. This model is more expressive than GMSM, as it is not constrained by the linear assignment step, but it does not provide cost matrices nor graph matchings.

Moreover, we test two simple versions of GMSM as additional baselines. The first one uses uniform costs at the node level, meaning that the cost of matching two nodes is 0 if they have the same label and 1 otherwise. This method computes a dissimilarity that is related to the Jaccard similarity of the sets of nodes of the two graphs. The second one allows for learnable node-level substitution costs, which allows to account for e.g. similarities between residue types. Since these two methods work at the node level, they cannot take into account the graph structure, as opposed to the full version of the model, which we denote with GMSM (GNN).

4.3   Similarity-Based Classification

Table 1 reports the results of our models and of the baselines on the macromolecular datasets, while Table 2 reports the results of our models and of the baselines on the small molecule datasets.

Firstly, one can see that GMSM, when run with a GNN to extract node features, consistently outperforms the versions of GMSM with uniform costs and with residue-level substitution matrices. This means that representing the graph as a bag of subgraphs rather than just as the set of its nodes improves significantly performance, suggesting that taking structure into account is indeed crucial to understanding function. Secondly, on the structure-based Pfam and SCOP datasets GMSM outperforms the Siamese-GNN, which shares the same architecture except for the graph dissimilarity computation. This suggests that the additional inductive bias given by the fact that the graph dissimilarity is being calculated as a linear assignment problem might be beneficial on some tasks. On the other hand, on some more complex tasks this might hinder the expressiveness of the model. Indeed, on EC, RNA and on two small molecule datasets, GMSM fails to reach its accuracy. Moreover, on the AIDS dataset the Siamese-GNN heavily overfits on the training set, while the stronger inductive bias of GMSM allows it to avoid overfitting.

Finally, we note that the performance of our model is in general better than the simple baselines given by the WL kernel and the task-specific baselines, namely BLOSUM64-based sequence alignment and molecular fingerprints.

Moreover, we analyze the performance of GMSM in a transfer learning setting, where it is trained on one dataset and tested on another. In particular, we use the three protein datasets EC, Pfam and SCOP. Figure 2 reports the relative performance, in terms of triplet accuracy and pair AUROC, with respect to the performance of the model when trained and tested on the same dataset. As expected, testing the model on a dataset different from the one on which it was

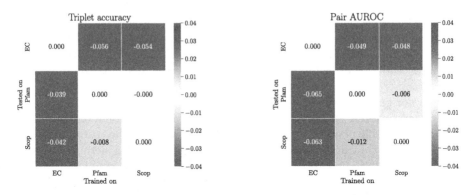

Fig. 2. Transfer learning performance on similarity-based classification on protein datasets. Relative performance with respect to training and testing on the same dataset.

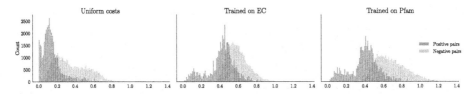

Fig. 3. Distribution of graph dissimilarities for positive and negative pairs on the Pfam test dataset. We report, from left to right, the results for GMSM with uniform costs, trained on EC and trained on Pfam.

trained on yields sub-par performance. This further reinforcing the claim that the costs that GMSM learns are indeed task-specific.

Interestingly, the model trained on Pfam seems to perform in a satisfactory way on SCOP, and vice-versa, while the gap with EC is wider. This indeed makes sense as Pfam families and SCOP annotations are quite strongly correlated.

Finally, Fig. 3 reports the distributions of the graph dissimilarities for positive and negative pairs on the test Pfam dataset. We report the distribution yielded by the model with uniform costs, by GMSM when trained on EC (and tested on Pfam) and by GMSM when trained on the dataset on which is tested, Pfam. As expected from the results of Table 1, trained models show a better separation between distributions compared to the uniform cost model, and the model trained on the correct dataset shows a better separation than the model trained on a different dataset.

Table 3. Retrieval

Method	EC		Pfam		SCOP		RNA	
	APR@10	APR@50	APR@10	APR@50	APR@10	APR@50	APR@10	APR@50
WL kernel	0.530	0.406	0.629	0.484	0.119	0.08	0.550	0.279
Siamese-GNN	0.586	0.473	0.762	0.631	0.254	0.162	0.380	0.195
GMSM (uniform costs)	0.580	0.451	0.799	0.650	0.309	0.179	0.317	0.192
GMSM (residue level)	0.578	0.449	0.775	0.620	0.297	0.169	0.330	0.191
GMSM (GNN)	0.606	0.475	0.887	0.776	0.387	0.221	0.481	0.258

Table 4. Retrieval on small molecules

Method	Mutagenicity		NCI1		AIDS	
	APR@10	APR@50	APR@10	APR@50	APR@10	APR@50
WL kernel	0.699	0.642	0.682	0.614	0.909	0.802
Molecular fingerprint	0.711	0.630	0.682	0.614	0.916	0.841
Siamese-GNN	0.677	0.649	0.616	0.588	0.875	0.805
GMSM (uniform costs)	0.644	0.613	0.598	0.575	0.997	0.991
GMSM (residue level)	0.644	0.611	0.602	0.571	0.999	0.992
GMSM (GNN)	0.714	0.649	0.680	0.626	0.994	0.991

4.4 Retrieval

We evaluate the retrieval task. In particular, given a query graph, the task is to return a set of graphs that are the most similar to the query. The goal of this task is to evaluate the quality of the learned graph similarity at very short scales. Indeed, for the retrieval task it does not matter if some positive pairs are at a high distance as long as there are enough positive pairs at a very short distance, which will be returned as hits by the retrieval procedure.

Table 3 and Table 4 report the results on the retrieval tasks on the macro-molecular datasets and on the small molecule datasets, respectively. To evaluate the quality of the returned set, we use the precision@k metric, that is the pro-portion of the top-k returned hits belonging to the same class as the query graph.

In particular, we take as queries the graphs of the test set, and search for the hits in the training set, which serves then as the searchable database. In the tables we report the average precision@k (APR@k) over all the queries, for $k \in \{10, 50\}$.

As observed in the classification task, GMSM consistently outperforms its node-level variants. Moreover, for the retrieval task, it outperforms also the Siamese-GNN model, which is based on the same GNN architecture, suggesting that the learned substitution matrices are indeed meaningful.

We note that the performance figures falls short of the state-of-the-art. For example, Foldseek [45], an efficient protein alignment method based on linearized 3D structures and a structure-based substitution matrix, achieves significantly higher precision values. Indeed, it achieves an APR@10 of 0.839, 0.976 and 0.913 on EC, Pfam and SCOP, respectively.

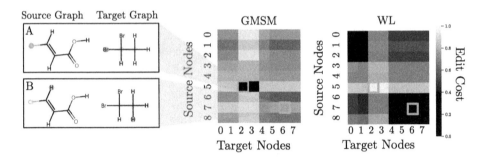

Fig. 4. Two sample chemical graphs from the Mutagenicity dataset, shown on the left, and the cost matrices between them, shown on the right calculated by GMSM and by the WL kernel. Center nodes are marked in red and their neighbourhoods in yellow. We highlight two learned pairwise costs and the subgraphs involved in the computation. (Color figure online)

An interesting research avenue is to combine the powerful structure extractors of purpose-engineered state-of-the-art methods with the graph matching stage of GMSM, as it should allow to get more meaningful local substructure representations compared to the simple GNN model we use, potentially achieving better performance.

5   Analysis of the Edit Cost Matrices

In this section, we first provide an intuition for interpreting the learned costs, then a preliminary analysis of the substitution matrices and of the graph alignments obtained with GMSM.

GMSM is trained to output small dissimilarities for graphs belonging to the same class and large ones for graphs belonging to different classes. These graph dissimilarities are a function of pairwise substructure assignment costs which are in turn a function of a GNN with *shared* parameters. The key observation here is that the shared nature of the GNN parameters means that the edit costs of a particular pair of substructures (more formally, elements of $\mathcal{V}_{\psi_\theta}$) are *global*, i.e. will be the same for all pairs of graphs across the dataset, allowing us to identify dataset-level patterns. Moreover, because the model is conditioned on a specific task, as shown in Sect. 4.3 such costs can tell us about the relationship between substructures and the task labels (function).

We show an example in Fig. 4 to illustrate that our cost matrices result in structurally sound alignments while also showing potential for capturing task-specific substructures. Using the Mutagenicity dataset of small molecules for ease of visualization, and using solely the test set to avoid overfitting artifacts, we inspect the substitution costs proposed by GMSM and the WL kernel for two pairs of substructures on the same source and target graphs. In Fig. 4 we highlight examples of substructures where WL (fully structure-driven) diverges from the structure and function-based edit costs of GMSM. In particular we note

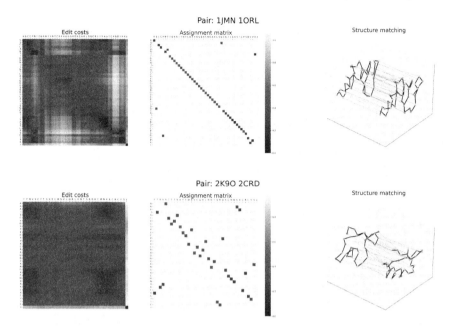

Fig. 5. Edit cost matrices and graph alignments returned by GMSM on two pairs of proteins belonging to the same Pfam family. On the right, we plot the pairwise matching between the 3D structures obtained from the graph alignments.

in Fig. 4A that GMSM assigns a low edit cost to substructures centered around halogens (Br and Cl) which we hypothesize is due to the known mutagenic effect of halogens [7] and thus substituting halogen for halogen would not be likely to affect the class label. On the other hand in Fig. 4B we show examples where WL assigns low edit costs, likely due to the fact that the subgraphs are both rooted around H atoms with two C atoms as neighbors, yet GMSM introduces a large cost, again presumably due to the presence of the Cl atom in the source graph. This is meant as an illustration of the hypothesis generation potential of GMSM and a rigorous analysis remains for future work.

We find similar behaviour when plotting protein alignments from the Pfam test set. Indeed, pairs of proteins belonging to the same class, two of which we plot in Fig. 5 as an example, can show meaningful graph alignments, with low edit costs corresponding to conserved structures and high edit costs corresponding to differing substructures. In particular, the first two plotted proteins, 1JMN and 1ORL, two variants of Viscotoxin, have high sequence identity, and GMSM recovers most of the sequence alignment, with some misaligned amino acids likely due to small differences in the structures. The second pair of proteins, 2K9O and 2CRD, two proteins belonging to the scorpion short toxin protein family, present very low sequence similarity. Nonetheless, GMSM assigns low costs between the amino acids, leading to a low predicted distance. Most notably, the lower

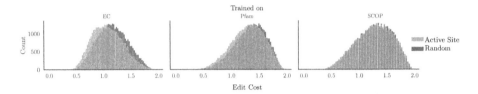

Fig. 6. Distribution of residue substitution costs of residue pairs sampled from inside active sites (Catalytic Site Atlas [33]) vs random sites on the protein. Each plot shows the same distribution when conditioned on models trained with the EC, Pfam and SCOP datasets respectively (left to right).

substitution costs concentrate in C-terminal region of the two proteins, where indeed the two sequences are more similar.

Finally for a more quantitative perspective, we use the Catalytic Site Atlas [33] on the EC test dataset to test whether our learned costs generally correlate with known catalytic sites. We show in Fig. 6 (left panel) that there is indeed a significant difference between the costs the model assigns to pairs of residues belonging to catalytic sites versus other sites in the same proteins despite this information being absent during training. Furthermore, this effect is lost when the model used to generate the costs was conditioned on non-specific datasets (namely Pfam or SCOP). This analysis serves as preliminary evidence that task-specific learned costs could point automatically towards functional substructures and serve to improve the quality of downstream alignments and interpretability of learned models.

6   Discussion and Conclusions

In this paper, we have presented the first algorithmic framework for automatically (i.e. without pre-curated alignments) obtaining substitution matrices for biochemical structures that are conditioned to functional information of interest.

Our model GMSM shows promising performance in classification and retrieval tasks across domains, and most importantly yields substitution matrices and structure alignments that are interpretable, and show, in preliminary analysis, correspondence with known functional sites.

Nonetheless, our method has limitations that should be addressed in future work. First, although classification and retrieval performance are better than simple baselines, GMSM struggles to reach metrics that match those of purpose-built state-of-the-art methods. This shortcoming should be addressed by specializing our general framework to data-specific models such as Foldseek [45] that leverage specialized alignment algorithms and domain-specific design.

Secondly, the time complexity of GMSM is cubic in the number of nodes of the graphs to be matched, which makes it impractical to train and to run for large graphs. Although we managed to work on proteins with up to a thousand residues, this could be addressed by adapting the matching with domain-specific speedups.

While the focus of this work was on high-level evaluation of the learned substitution matrices, we envision that future work closely analysing the resulting costs along with more functional readouts (e.g. binding sites, reactive groups, chemical modifications) could reveal new functional mechanisms and inform downstream alignment algorithms.

References

1. Bai, Y., Ding, H., Bian, S., Chen, T., Sun, Y., Wang, W.: SimGNN: a neural network approach to fast graph similarity computation. In: Proceedings of the Twelfth ACM International Conference on Web Search and Data Mining, pp. 384–392 (2019)
2. Bateman, A., et al.: The PFAM protein families database. Nucleic Acids Res. **32**(suppl_1), D138–D141 (2004)
3. Bissantz, C., Kuhn, B., Stahl, M.: A medicinal chemist's guide to molecular interactions. J. Med. Chem. **53**(14), 5061–5084 (2010)
4. Blumenthal, D.B., Boria, N., Gamper, J., Bougleux, S., Brun, L.: Comparing heuristics for graph edit distance computation. VLDB J. **29**(1), 419–458 (2020)
5. , D.B., Gamper, J.: Improved lower bounds for graph edit distance. IEEE Trans. Knowl. Data Eng. **30**(3), 503–516 (2017)
6. Bougleux, S., Brun, L., Carletti, V., Foggia, P., Gaüzère, B., Vento, M.: Graph edit distance as a quadratic assignment problem. Pattern Recogn. Lett. **87**, 38–46 (2017). Advances in Graph-Based Pattern Recognition
7. Brem, H., Stein, A.B., Rosenkranz, H.S.: The mutagenicity and DNA-modifying effect of haloalkanes. Cancer Res. **34**(10), 2576–2579 (1974)
8. Bunke, H., Riesen, K.: Graph classification based on dissimilarity space embedding. In: da Vitoria Lobo, N., et al. (eds.) SSPR /SPR 2008. LNCS, vol. 5342, pp. 996–1007. Springer, Heidelberg (2008). https://doi.org/10.1007/978-3-540-89689-0_103
9. Bunke, H., Riesen, K.: Graph edit distance–optimal and suboptimal algorithms with applications. In: Analysis of Complex Networks: From Biology to Linguistics, pp. 113–143 (2009)
10. Carletti, V., Gaüzère, B., Brun, L., Vento, M.: Approximate graph edit distance computation combining bipartite matching and exact neighborhood substructure distance. In: Liu, C.-L., Luo, B., Kropatsch, W.G., Cheng, J. (eds.) GbRPR 2015. LNCS, vol. 9069, pp. 188–197. Springer, Cham (2015). https://doi.org/10.1007/978-3-319-18224-7_19
11. Chicco, D.: Siamese neural networks: an overview. In: Cartwright, H. (ed.) Artificial Neural Networks. MMB, vol. 2190, pp. 73–94. Springer, New York (2021). https://doi.org/10.1007/978-1-0716-0826-5_3
12. Chithrananda, S., Grand, G., Ramsundar, B.: ChemBERTa: large-scale self-supervised pretraining for molecular property prediction. arXiv preprint arXiv:2010.09885 (2020)
13. Doan, K.D., Manchanda, S., Mahapatra, S., Reddy, C.K.: Interpretable graph similarity computation via differentiable optimal alignment of node embeddings. In: Proceedings of the 44th International ACM SIGIR Conference on Research and Development in Information Retrieval, pp. 665–674 (2021)
14. Eklund, A.C., Friis, P., Wernersson, R., Szallasi, Z.: Optimization of the BLASTN substitution matrix for prediction of non-specific DNA microarray hybridization. Nucleic Acids Res. **38**(4), e27–e27 (2010)

15. Gilmer, J., Schoenholz, S.S., Riley, P.F., Vinyals, O., Dahl, G.E.: Neural message passing for quantum chemistry. In: International Conference on Machine Learning, pp. 1263–1272. PMLR (2017)
16. Gligorijević, V., et al.: Structure-based protein function prediction using graph convolutional networks. Nat. Commun. **12**(1), 3168 (2021)
17. Gotoh, O.: Multiple sequence alignment: algorithms and applications. Adv. Biophys. **36**, 159–206 (1999)
18. Hadsell, R., Chopra, S., LeCun, Y.: Dimensionality reduction by learning an invariant mapping. In: 2006 IEEE Computer Society Conference on Computer Vision and Pattern Recognition (CVPR'06), vol. 2, pp. 1735–1742. IEEE (2006)
19. Henikoff, S., Henikoff, J.G.: Amino acid substitution matrices. Adv. Protein Chem. **54**, 73–98 (2000)
20. Heo, J., Lee, S., Ahn, S., Kim, D.: EPIC: graph augmentation with edit path interpolation via learnable cost. arXiv preprint arXiv:2306.01310 (2023)
21. Hofacker, I.L., Bernhart, S.H.F., Stadler, P.F.: Alignment of RNA base pairing probability matrices. Bioinformatics **20**(14), 2222–2227 (2004)
22. Illergård, K., Ardell, D.H., Elofsson, A.: Structure is three to ten times more conserved than sequence-a study of structural response in protein cores. Proteins Struct. Function Bioinform. **77**(3), 499–508 (2009)
23. Keul, F., Hess, M., Goesele, M., Hamacher, K.: PFASUM: a substitution matrix from PFAM structural alignments. BMC Bioinform. **18**, 1–14 (2017)
24. Koshi, J.M., Goldstein, R.A.: Context-dependent optimal substitution matrices. Protein Eng. Des. Sel. **8**(7), 641–645 (1995)
25. Kucera, T., Oliver, C., Chen, D., Borgwardt, K.: ProteinShake: building datasets and benchmarks for deep learning on protein structures. In: Thirty-Seventh Conference on Neural Information Processing Systems Datasets and Benchmarks Track (2023)
26. Kulmanov, M., Hoehndorf, R.: DeepGOPlus: improved protein function prediction from sequence. Bioinformatics **36**(2), 422–429 (2020)
27. Li, Y., Gu, C., Dullien, T., Vinyals, O., Kohli, P.: Graph matching networks for learning the similarity of graph structured objects. In: International Conference on Machine Learning, pp. 3835–3845. PMLR (2019)
28. Llinares-López, F., Berthet, Q., Blondel, M., Teboul, O., Vert, J.-P.: Deep embedding and alignment of protein sequences. Nat. Methods **20**(1), 104–111 (2023)
29. Mallet, V., Oliver, C., Broadbent, J., Hamilton, W.L., Waldispühl, J.: RNAglib: a Python package for RNA 2.5 D graphs. Bioinformatics **38**(5), 1458–1459 (2022)
30. Morris, C., Kriege, N.M., Bause, F., Kersting, K., Mutzel, P., Neumann, M.: Tudataset: a collection of benchmark datasets for learning with graphs. arXiv preprint arXiv:2007.08663 (2020)
31. Neuhaus, M., Bunke, H.: A probabilistic approach to learning costs for graph edit distance. In: Proceedings of the 17th International Conference on Pattern Recognition. ICPR 2004, vol. 3, pp. 389–393. IEEE (2004)
32. Oliver, C., et al.: Augmented base pairing networks encode RNA-small molecule binding preferences. Nucleic Acids Res. **48**(14), 7690–7699 (2020)
33. Porter, C.T., Bartlett, G.J., Thornton, J.M.: The catalytic site atlas: a resource of catalytic sites and residues identified in enzymes using structural data. Nucleic Acids Res. **32**(suppl_1), D129–D133 (2004)
34. Qiu, J., Elber, R.: SSALN: an alignment algorithm using structure-dependent substitution matrices and gap penalties learned from structurally aligned protein pairs. Proteins Struct Function Bioinform. **62**(4), 881–891 (2006)

35. Ranjan, R., Grover, S., Medya, S., Chakaravarthy, V., Sabharwal, Y., Ranu, S.: Greed: a neural framework for learning graph distance functions. In: Advances in Neural Information Processing Systems, vol. 35, pp. 22518–22530 (2022)

36. Riba, P., Fischer, A., Lladós, J., Fornés, A.: Learning graph edit distance by graph neural networks. Pattern Recogn. **120**, 108132 (2021)

37. Rose, P.W., et al.: The RCSB protein data bank: new resources for research and education. Nucleic Acids Res. **41**(D1), D475–D482 (2012)

38. Sarver, M., Zirbel, C.L., Stombaugh, J., Mokdad, A., Leontis, N.B.: FR3D: finding local and composite recurrent structural motifs in RNA 3D structures. J. Math. Biol. **56**, 215–252 (2008)

39. Schroff, F., Kalenichenko, D., Philbin, J.: Facenet: a unified embedding for face recognition and clustering. In: Proceedings of the IEEE Conference on Computer Vision and Pattern Recognition, pp. 815–823 (2015)

40. Sheridan, R.P.: The most common chemical replacements in drug-like compounds. J. Chem. Inf. Comput. Sci. **42**(1), 103–108 (2002)

41. Shervashidze, N., Schweitzer, P., Van Leeuwen, E.J., Mehlhorn, K., Borgwardt, K.M.: Weisfeiler-Lehman graph kernels. J. Mach. Learn. Res. **12**(9) (2011)

42. Song, D., et al.: Parameterized blosum matrices for protein alignment. IEEE/ACM Trans. Comput. Biol. Bioinform. **12**(3), 686–694 (2014)

43. Sutormin, R.A., Rakhmaninova, A.B., Gelfand, M.S.: Batmas30: amino acid substitution matrix for alignment of bacterial transporters. Proteins Struct Function Bioinform. **51**(1), 85–95 (2003)

44. Tung, C.-H., Huang, J.-W., Yang, J.-M.: Kappa-alpha plot derived structural alphabet and blosum-like substitution matrix for rapid search of protein structure database. Genome Biol. **8**(3), 1–16 (2007)

45. van Kempen, M., et al.: Fast and accurate protein structure search with Foldseek. Nat. Biotechnol. pp. 1–4 (2023)

46. Veličković, P., Cucurull, G., Casanova, A., Romero, A., Lio, P., Bengio, Y.: Graph attention networks. arXiv preprint arXiv:1710.10903 (2017)

47. Wilbur, W.J.: On the PAM matrix model of protein evolution. Mol. Biol. Evol. **2**(5), 434–447 (1985)

48. Wu, C.-Y., Manmatha, R., Smola, A.J., Krahenbuhl, P.: Sampling matters in deep embedding learning. In: Proceedings of the IEEE International Conference on Computer Vision, pp. 2840–2848 (2017)

49. Xu, K., Hu, W., Leskovec, J., Jegelka, S.: How powerful are graph neural networks? In: International Conference on Learning Representations (2018)

Secure Discovery of Genetic Relatives Across Large-Scale and Distributed Genomic Datasets

Matthew M. Hong[1], David Froelicher[1,2], Ricky Magner[2], Victoria Popic[2(✉)], Bonnie Berger[1,2(✉)], and Hyunghoon Cho[3(✉)]

[1] MIT, Cambridge 02139, USA
bab@mit.edu
[2] Broad Institute of MIT and Harvard, Cambridge 02142, USA
vpopic@broadinstitute.org
[3] Yale University, New Haven 06510, USA
hoon.cho@yale.edu

Abstract. Finding related individuals in genomic datasets is a necessary step in many genetic analysis workflows and has broader societal value as a tool for retrieving lost relatives. However, detecting such relationships is often infeasible when the dataset is distributed across multiple entities due to privacy concerns. Although cryptographic techniques for secure computation offer ways to jointly analyze distributed datasets with privacy guarantees, the sheer computational burden of operations required for identifying kinship, such as pairwise sequence comparison of all individuals across large datasets, presents key challenges to developing a practical privacy-preserving solution. We introduce SF-Relate, a secure federated algorithm for identifying genetic relatives across data silos (Fig. 1) that scales efficiently to large datasets that include hundreds of thousands of individuals. We leverage the key insight that the number of individual pairs to compare can be vastly reduced, while maintaining accurate detection, through innovative locality-sensitive hashing of individuals who are likely to be related together into buckets and then testing relationships only between individuals in corresponding buckets across parties. To this end, we construct an effective hash function that captures identity-by-descent (IBD) segments in genetic sequences, which, along with our novel *micro-bucketing* strategy is key to achieving accurate and practical private relative detection. To guarantee privacy, we devise an efficient algorithm based on multiparty homomorphic encryption (MHE) to allow the parties to cooperatively compute the relatedness coefficients between pairs of individuals, and to further classify their degrees of relatedness, all without sharing any private data. We demonstrate the accuracy and practical runtimes of SF-Relate on real genomic datasets of varying sizes, from the UK Biobank and All of Us datasets. On the largest dataset of 200K individuals split between two parties, SF-Relate securely detects 94.9% of third degree relatives, and 99.9% of relatives second-degree or closer within 15 h of runtime. Our work enables secure identification of relatives across large-scale genomic

M. M. Hong and D. Froelicher—Equal contribution.

datasets. Our code is available at https://github.com/froelich/sf-relate, and the full manuscript preprint is available at https://doi.org/10.1101/2024.02.16.580613.

1 Methods

SF-Relate efficiently scales to large datasets by drastically reducing the number of kinship computations between pairs of individuals, from quadratic to linear, while preserving accuracy. Each party locally assigns their samples to buckets such that related samples are more likely to be assigned to the same bucket, via *locality sensitive hashing* (LSH) [4], and then securely estimates kinship only between samples that end up in the corresponding buckets across parties. We devised a data encoding scheme for LSH aimed at capturing identity-by-descent (IBD) segments in genetic sequences, thus effectively grouping together samples that are likely to be related.

Furthermore, we introduce a new strategy for bucket assignment, in which local buckets obtained through multiple LSH trials are merged and filtered to obtain a set of size-one buckets (referred to as *micro-buckets*). Since related samples typically share several unique IBD segments, they are typically assigned to matching small-size buckets multiple times, which helps to ensure that they remain together in at least one of those buckets even after filtering. This technique guarantees a high probability of detecting related samples, minimizes computational overhead, and ensures that no private information is revealed between the parties.

Finally, to estimate kinship coefficients between pairs of samples in the corresponding buckets across parties without sharing data, we introduce a provably secure approach that leverages homomorphic encryption based on the CKKS scheme [2], implemented in the Lattigo library [5]. With this approach, SF-Relate keeps each party's data confidential throughout the kinship computation, revealing only the final output to each party, which includes only the list of their own samples that have at least one relative in another dataset.

Next, we provide further details of our algorithm, as illustrated in Fig. 2:

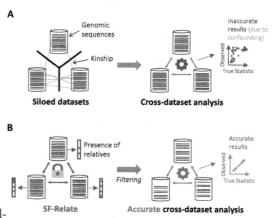

Fig. 1. SF-Relate overview. When genetic relatives across datasets cannot be identified due to data sharing restrictions, joint studies can suffer from bias and confounding (**A**). SF-Relate enables secure identification of cross-dataset relatives to enhance downstream analysis (**B**).

Step 1: Hashing and bucketing. In this step, each party locally evaluates a series of hash functions on each individual's haplotype sequences to assign the individual to buckets across a collection of hash tables, such that related individuals are more likely to be assigned to the same bucket index. Only individuals in the same bucket across parties are compared in a later step. This step consists of two parts. In **Step 1a**, SF-Relate assigns individuals to buckets using a locality sensitivity hash (LSH). LSH functions map similar items to the same value more frequently based on a similarity notion. Specifically, the Hamming LSH, which relies on the Hamming similarity (defined as the number of equal coordinates between vectors), projects a vector onto one random coordinate and uses its value as the output. SF-Relate applies an encoding scheme that results in highly similar Hamming vectors for related samples. This encoding captures the biological signal of IBD distributions, and can be seen as a variant of the encoding in [8]. We describe the details of this encoding in the full manuscript. The output of this hashing procedure is a list of hash tables, each consisting of buckets storing sample IDs. In **Step 1b**, to prevent leakage of private information, the parties need to compare the samples in corresponding buckets without exposing any additional information about their datasets, such as the distribution of non-empty buckets and their sizes. This requires that the buckets created in the previous step be padded to a fixed size by adding dummy samples. However, to keep the sample identities hidden, all pairs of samples in a bucket between the parties need to be compared, which leads to both quadratic scaling of comparisons with the bucket size and a large amount of wasted computation involving dummy samples. To address this issue, SF-Relate merges buckets with the same index across multiple hash tables and then filters every bucket down to a *single* element. Dummy samples are added only at the end to pad empty bucket to size one. This effectively transforms the parties' local bucket assignments into an ordered list of samples to be securely compared against the corresponding list obtained by the other party in an element-wise fashion. The approach avoids the quadratic scaling while minimizing the addition of dummy samples due to the merging of buckets (i.e., a bucket is filled if at least one sample is assigned to it in one of the hash tables). Despite the extreme level of filtering applied to each bucket during this process, our strategy enables accurate detection of relatives with remarkable efficiency. At the end of this process, each party in SF-Relate obtains a single hash table with a linear number of size-one buckets.

Step 2: Secure kinship evaluation. In this step, the parties perform element-wise comparisons between their ordered list of samples from Step 1. They first randomly project the SNP panel down into a sketched version, on which they jointly evaluate kinship coefficients for each pair (**MHE-Phase 1**, in Fig. 2 and Results). Then, they aggregate the results to obtain an indicator for each individual reflecting the presence of a close relative in the other dataset (**MHE-Phase 2**). To compute on encrypted data in a secure manner, SF-Relate builds upon multiparty homomorphic encryption (MHE) [3,7], extending the CKKS scheme [2]. In SF-Relate, all exchanged data are encrypted under the collective encryption key and only the final result can be decrypted with the cooperation

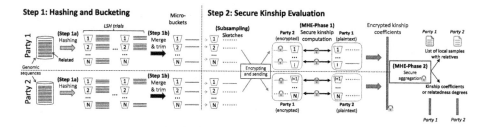

Fig. 2. SF-Relate's workflow. In Step 1, the parties perform multiple trials of LSH to bucket samples (Step 1a) before merging and trimming to obtain buckets of size 1 (Step 1b; micro-buckets). In Step 2, each sample is sketched (subsampled) and securely compared against the other party's sample in the same bucket to evaluate kinship (MHE-Phase 1). Finally, parties securely aggregate the results to obtain per-individual output (MHE-Phase 2).

of all parties. We describe our protocols in detail in the full manuscript. The key to our protocols' efficiency is that we minimize the cryptographic overhead by maximizing the use of locally available plaintext data and balancing the workload between the parties. Although we focus on the two-party setting, our protocols naturally extend to settings with more than two parties.

2   Results

To evaluate SF-Relate, we obtained three genomic datasets of varying sizes, including a dataset of 20K samples (individuals) with 1M SNPs from the All of Us Research Program (AoU) and two datasets from the UK Biobank (UKB) [1] including 100K and 200K samples, respectively, both with 650K SNPs. The two UKB datasets were uniformly sampled from the full UK Biobank release v3 ($n = 488,377$), and the AoU dataset comprises the first 20K individuals in the All of Us release v5 ($n = 98,590$). We then evenly split each dataset into two parts to emulate a cross-dataset analysis involving two parties. We compute the ground-truth kinship and degree of relatedness by evaluating all pairwise KING kinship estimation [6] in plaintexts on a set of ancestry agnostic SNPs, as in UK Biobank's pipeline [1]. All experiments were performed using virtual machines (VMs) on the Google Cloud Platform (GCP). For UKB, we used two VMs (one for each party) with 128 virtual CPUs (vCPUs) and 856 GB of memory (n2-highmem-128) co-located in the same zone in GCP. For AoU, we emulated the two parties in a single VM with 96 vCPUs and 624GB memory due to the constraints of the provided data analysis platform.

Across all three datasets, SF-Relate obtains near-perfect recall and precision (both exceeding 97% in all cases) for detecting the presence of 3rd-degree or closer relationships between two parties (Table 1). Calculating the recall separately for each relatedness degree from 0th (monozygotic twins) to 3rd, we observe that most missing relationships are for the 3rd degree. The recall metric for third-degree relationships remains high—above 94% for all three datasets.

Despite the overhead of cryptographic protocols for secure computation, the runtime of SF-Relate remains practical for all three datasets, resulting in 5.8, 7.3, and 14.5 h of runtime for AoU-20K, UKB-100K, and UKB-200K, respectively (Table 2). Although the observed communication costs are not negligible, they are primarily attributed (over 99%) to the exchange of encrypted hash tables, a process achievable within a single round of communication. We therefore expect the impact of high communication on runtime to be minimal even in a wide-area network (WAN). Furthermore, we highlight that without the hashing and bucketing strategy we introduced in SF-Relate, it would not be feasible to securely detect relatives between datasets by all-pairwise computation of the kinship coefficient (**All-pairwise** in Table 2). Even with our efficient MHE implementation of the kinship calculation over the sketched haplotypes, performing all-pairwise comparisons for the UKB-200K dataset is estimated to cost 1.3 years (and 65 PB of communication) on the same computational setting. Taken together, these results demonstrate SF-Relate's accurate and efficient relative detection performance across a range of datasets, which is achieved without revealing any private information between the two parties due to SF-Relate's use of secure computation techniques when jointly analyzing the two datasets.

Table 1. SF-Relate achieves near-perfect accuracy for identifying close relatives in UK Biobank and All of Us datasets. Ground-truth relatedness degrees for recall and precision metrics are obtained using the KING method [6] and assigning each sample to the lowest degree of relatedness observed. Recall represents the fraction of samples with a close relative in the other dataset (as determined by the baseline KING-robust method given a threshold) that SF-Relate successfully identifies. Precision represents the fraction of samples identified by SF-Relate as having a close relative in the other dataset that actually have such a relationship according to the baseline method. SF-Relate obtains accurate results while performing only a small fraction of comparisons compared to **all-pairwise** comparison between datasets.

Dataset	Recall (%, counts)					Precision	% of comparisons
	Relatedness degree				Overall		w.r.t.
	0th	1st	2nd	3rd		(%, counts)	all-pairwise
UKB-200K	100.0%	100.0%	99.8%	94.9%	97.0%	98.5%	0.13%
	16/16	4702/4702	1709/1711	8475/8925	14902/15354	14902/15129	
UKB-100K	100.0%	100.0%	100.0%	95.1%	97.2%	98.7%	0.26%
	6/6	1243/1243	404/404	2169/2279	3822/3932	3822/3872	
AoU-20K	100.0%	100.0%	100.0%	94.1%	98.0%	100.0%	1.28%
	14/14	209/209	93/93	145/154	461/470	461/461	

Table 2. SF-Relate scales efficiently to large datasets. We measured the elapsed wall-clock time and the total number of bytes sent from one party to another (given the symmetry of SF-Relate's computation) for runtime and communication costs, respectively. The runtime and communication costs for setting up the cryptographic keys are 40.4 s and 1.7 GB, respectively, constant across all experiments. We also show the estimated total costs of running **all-pairwise** comparisons and determining the closest relationship for each individual both using MHE.

Dataset	SF-Relate								All-pairwise	
	Runtime				Communication				Runtime (est. total)	Comm. (est. total)
	Step 1	Step 2 (MHE)		Total	Step 1	Step 2 (MHE)		Total		
		Phase 1	Phase 2			Phase 1	Phase 2			
UKB-200K	1.8 m	14.0 h	0.5 h	14.5 h	—	46.6 TB	0.5 GB	46.6 TB	1.3 y	32.5 PB
UKB-100K	49.5 s	7.05 h	0.23 h	7.29 h	—	23.85 TB	241.7 MB	23.85 TB	112 d	9.8 PB
AoU-20K	18.6 s	5.65 h	0.11 h	5.79 h	—	6.2 TB	77.6 MB	6.2 TB	18.8 d	2.31 PB

Acknowledgements. This work is supported by NIH R01 HG010959 (to B.B.) and NIH DP5 OD029574 and RM1 HG011558 (to H.C.) and the Broad Institute Schmidt Fellowship (to V.P.).

References

1. Bycroft, C., et al.: The UK Biobank resource with deep phenotyping and genomic data. Nature **562**(7726), 203–209 (2018)
2. Cheon, J.H., Kim, A., Kim, M., Song, Y.: Homomorphic encryption for arithmetic of approximate numbers. In: Takagi, T., Peyrin, T. (eds.) Advances in Cryptology – ASIACRYPT 2017, pp. 409–437 (2017)
3. Froelicher, D., et al.: Scalable privacy-preserving distributed learning. In: Proceedings on Privacy Enhancing Technologies Symposium (PET 2021), vol. 2, pp. 323–347 (2021)
4. Indyk, P., Motwani, R.: Approximate nearest neighbors: towards removing the curse of dimensionality. In: Proceedings of the Thirtieth Annual ACM Symposium on Theory of Computing. STOC 1998 (1998)
5. Lattigo v4. EPFL-LDS, Tune Insight SA (Aug 2022). https://github.com/tuneinsight/lattigo
6. Manichaikul, A., Mychaleckyj, J.C., Rich, S.S., Daly, K., Sale, M., Chen, W.M.: Robust relationship inference in genome-wide association studies. Bioinformatics **26**(22), 2867–2873 (2010)
7. Mouchet, C., Troncoso-pastoriza, J.R., Bossuat, J.P., Hubaux, J.P.: Multiparty homomorphic encryption from ring-learning-with-errors. In: Proceedings on Privacy Enhancing Technologies Symposium (PET 2021) (2021)
8. Shemirani, R., Belbin, G.M., Avery, C.L., Kenny, E.E., Gignoux, C.R., Ambite, J.L.: Rapid detection of identity-by-descent tracts for mega-scale datasets. Nat. Commun. **12**(1), 1–13 (2021)

GFETM: Genome Foundation-Based Embedded Topic Model for scATAC-seq Modeling

Yimin Fan[1,4], Yu Li[4], Jun Ding[2(✉)], and Yue Li[1,3(✉)]

[1] School of Computer Science, McGill University, Montreal, Canada
yueli@cs.mcgill.ca
[2] Department of Medicine, McGill University, Montreal, Canada
jun.ding@mcgill.ca
[3] Mila - Quebec AI Institute, Montreal, Canada
[4] Department of Computer Science and Engineering,
The Chinese University of Hong Kong, Hong Kong, China

1 Introduction

Single-cell Assay for Transposase-Accessible Chromatin with sequencing (scATAC-seq) has emerged as a powerful technique for investigating open chromatin landscapes at the single-cell level. Yet, scATAC-seq cell representation learning and its downstream tasks remain challenging due to the inherent high dimensional, sparse, and noisy properties of the data. The scarcity of available datasets compared to scRNA-seq further underscores the importance of applying transfer learning from abundant reference data to enhance scATAC-seq analyses across diverse biological scenarios. However, variations in computational methods and inherent biological differences between scATAC-seq samples intensify the difficulty in effectively implementing transfer learning strategies. Genome Foundation Models (GFMs), which are pre-trained on millions of DNA sequences in a self-supervised manner, have proven effective in applications involving genomic sequences, yet their application in single-cell biology remains underexplored. Given that highly accessible chromatin regions often harbour salient sequence features, we hypothesize that leveraging GFMs' nucleotide sequence embeddings may improve scATAC-seq data modeling and its transferability. In this study, we introduce the Genome Foundation Embedded Topic Model (GFETM), an interpretable and transferable deep neural network framework that combines GFMs with the Embedded Topic Model (ETM) for scATAC-seq data analysis. We show that by probing and integrating the DNA sequence embedding extracted by GFMs from open chromatin regions, GFETM not only achieves state-of-the-art performance of scATAC-seq cell representation learning on benchmarking datasets of various scales but also demonstrates generalizability and transferability to single-cell transcriptomes and across different subjects, tissues, and species. Code is available at https://github.com/fym0503/GFETM. The full paper is online at https://www.biorxiv.org/content/10.1101/2023.11.09.566403v1.

© The Author(s), under exclusive license to Springer Nature Switzerland AG 2024
J. Ma (Ed.): RECOMB 2024, LNCS 14758, pp. 314–319, 2024.
https://doi.org/10.1007/978-1-0716-3989-4_20

2   Methods

GFETM is an interpretable and transferrable deep neural network framework for single-cell ATAC-seq modeling. The overall architecture of GFETM is shown in Fig. 1a. GFETM is composed of two main components, the ETM component [6] and the GFM component, which take the cell-by-peak matrix and the peak sequences as input, respectively. The ETM encoder projects the peak vector of each cell onto the latent cell topic mixture. The cell topic mixture is then passed to the ETM decoder and then combined with the sequence embeddings from the pre-trained GFM component to compute expected rate of the peaks in the cell. The training objective is to maximize the evidence lower bound (ELBO) of the log marginal likelihood of the input cell-by-peak data.

2.1   The ETM Component

We model the scATAC-seqs data as a cells-by-peaks matrix $\mathbf{X} \in \{0,1\}^{N \times M}$ with N cells and M peaks. We model the peak data using multinomial distribution with the expected peak rate parameterized as $\mathbf{R} \in [0,1]^{N \times M}$. We decompose $\mathbf{R}$ into cells-by-topics $\theta \in [0,1]^{N \times K}$ and topics-by-peaks $\boldsymbol{\beta} \in [0,1]^{K \times M}$ (i.e., $\mathbf{R} = \theta\boldsymbol{\beta}$). The two matrices are softmax-normalized over K topics (i.e., columns) and M peaks (i.e., rows), respectively. Specifically, for each cell $c \in \{1,\ldots,N\}$, the cell topic mixture is $\boldsymbol{\theta}_{c,.}$ such that $\sum_{k=1}^{K} \theta_{c,k} = 1$; for each topic $\boldsymbol{\beta}_{k,.}$, where $k \in \{1,\ldots,K\}$, $\sum_{p=1}^{M} \beta_{k,p} = 1$. We further decompose the topic distribution into the topic embedding $\boldsymbol{\alpha} \in \mathbb{R}^{K \times L}$ and peak embedding $\boldsymbol{\rho} \in \mathbb{R}^{L \times M}$, where L denotes the size of the embedding space. Thus, the probability of a peak belonging to a topic is proportional to the dot product between the topic embedding and the peak embedding ($\boldsymbol{\beta}_{k,.} \propto \boldsymbol{\alpha}_{k,.}\boldsymbol{\rho}$). Formally, the data generative process of each scATAC-seq profile of cell $c \in \{1,\ldots,N\}$ can be described as follows:

1. Draw a latent cell type mixture $\boldsymbol{\theta}_c$ for a cell c from logistic normal $\boldsymbol{\theta}_c \sim \mathcal{LN}(0,\mathbf{I})$: $\boldsymbol{\delta}_c \sim \mathcal{N}(0,\mathbf{I})$, $\boldsymbol{\theta}_c = \text{softmax}(\boldsymbol{\delta}_c)$, where $\theta_{c,k} = \frac{\exp(\delta_{c,k})}{\sum_{k=1}^{K} \exp(\delta_{c,k})}$

2. For each peak token $w_{c,i}$, where $i \in \{1,\ldots,N_c\}$ among the N_c peaks observed in cell c, draw peak index $p \in \{1,\ldots,M\}$ from a categorical distribution $\text{Cat}(\mathbf{r}_c)$. $w_{c,i} \sim \prod_{p=1}^{M} r_{c,p}^{[w_{c,i}=p]}$, where $r_{c,p} = \boldsymbol{\theta}_{c,.}\boldsymbol{\beta}_{.,p} = \sum_k \theta_{c,k}\beta_{k,p}$ denotes the categorical rate for cell c and peak p and $\beta_{k,p} = \frac{\exp(\boldsymbol{\alpha}_{k,.}\boldsymbol{\rho}_{.,p})}{\sum_p \exp(\boldsymbol{\alpha}_{k,.}\boldsymbol{\rho}_{.,p})}$.

Given $\mathbf{x}_c \in [0,N_c]^{1 \times M}$, as the vector of the peak count over all M peaks for cell c, the likelihood over the N_c peak tokens $w_{c,i}$'s follows a multinomial likelihood: $p(\mathbf{x}_c|\mathbf{r}_c) = \prod_{i=1}^{N_c} \prod_{p=1}^{M} r_{c,p}^{[w_{c,i}=p]} = \prod_{p=1}^{M} r_{c,p}^{\sum_{p=1}^{N_c}[w_{c,i}=p]} = \prod_{p=1}^{M} r_{c,p}^{x_{c,p}}$ When integrating multiple scATAC-seq datasets, in order to account for batch effect, the chromatin accessibility $r_{c,p}$ is further parameterized as $\hat{r}_{c,p} = \boldsymbol{\theta}_c\boldsymbol{\alpha}\boldsymbol{\rho}_p + \lambda_{b_c,p}$ and $r_{c,p} = \frac{\exp(\hat{r}_{c,p})}{\sum_{p'} \exp(\hat{r}_{c,p'})}$ where $\boldsymbol{\lambda}_{b_c,.} \in \mathbb{R}^{1 \times M}$ is an optional parameter which depends on the batch index $b_c \in \{1,\ldots,B\}$ of cell c. The log marginal

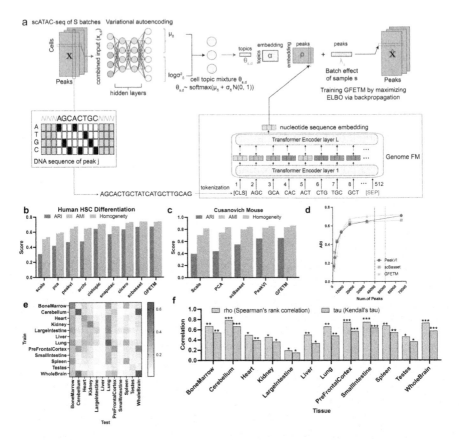

Fig. 1. Study overview. a. Overview of GFETM: GFETM models the scATAC-seq data matrices using an ETM approach. Each scATAC-seq profile serves as an input to a variational autoencoder (VAE) as the normalized peak count. The encoder network produces the latent topic mixture for clustering cells. The GFM takes the peak sequence as input and output peak embeddings ρ. Given the cell topic mixture $\theta_{s,d}$ of cell d from batch s and the peak sequence embedding ρ, the linear decoder learns topic embedding α as its weights to reconstruct the input. The encoder, decoder and GFM are jointly optimized by maximizing the ELBO of the scATAC data log marginal likelihood. **b.** GFETM performance on Human HSC Differentiation dataset. **c.** GFETM performance on Cusanovich-Mouse dataset. **d.** Scalability of GFETM on peaks using 60K cells from the Cusanovich-Mouse dataset. **e.** Cross-tissue zero-shot transfer learning in mice. **f.** Correlation between cell type similarity and zero-shot transfer learning performance on mouse adult tissues. The number of asterisks indicate significance of the p-value based on chi-squared test at the order of 10 (i.e., *, **, *** indicate p-value $= 0.1, 0.001, 0.0001$, respectively).

likelihood is approximated by ELBO: $\log p(\mathbf{x}_c) \geq \mathbb{E}_{q(\theta_c|\mathbf{x}_c)}[\log p(\mathbf{x}_c, \theta_c)] - \mathbb{E}_{q(\theta_c|\mathbf{x}_c)}[\log q(\theta_c|\mathbf{x}_c)]$, where $q(\theta_c|\mathbf{x}_c)$ is a proposed distribution to approximate the true posterior distribution $p(\theta_c|\mathbf{x}_c)$. Using the VAE framework [4], the variational distribution is defined as $q(\boldsymbol{\delta}_c|\mathbf{x}_c) = \mathcal{N}(\boldsymbol{\delta}_c; \boldsymbol{\mu}_c, \mathrm{diag}(\boldsymbol{\sigma}_c))$, where $\boldsymbol{\mu}_c$ and $\boldsymbol{\sigma}_c$ are the outputs of a neural network function (i.e., the encoder): $[\boldsymbol{\mu}_c, \log \boldsymbol{\sigma}_c] = f(\hat{\mathbf{x}}_c|\mathbf{W})$. Here $\hat{\mathbf{x}}_c$ is the normalized Term Frequency - Inverse Document Frequency (TF-IDF) count. The variational likelihood is approximated by Monte Carlo, where we use sampled $\tilde{\boldsymbol{\delta}}_c \sim \boldsymbol{\mu}_c + \boldsymbol{\sigma}_c^2 \mathcal{N}(0, \mathbf{I})$ from the proposed distribution to evaluate the likelihood: $\mathbb{E}_{q(\boldsymbol{\theta}_c|\mathbf{x}_c)}[\log p(\mathbf{x}_c|\boldsymbol{\theta}_c)] \approx \log p(\mathbf{x}_c|\tilde{\boldsymbol{\theta}}_c)$. Note that $\tilde{\boldsymbol{\theta}}_c$ is deterministic given $\tilde{\boldsymbol{\delta}}_c$. Training of the encoder network is done by stochastic gradient descent.

2.2   The GFM Component

We use a pre-trained GFM to extract peak nucleotide sequence embeddings. Specifically, given input peak p containing the chromosome index and start/end position information, we extract the corresponding DNA sequence from the reference genome. The sequence is then tokenized into input tokens by specific tokenization algorithms in specific GFM. The input tokens are then fed into the pre-trained GFM to obtain the token embedding. The sequence embedding $\boldsymbol{\rho}_p$ for each peak is computed by average pooling the token embeddings. In this study, we have experimented many GFMs and chose DNABERT [3] as the GFM component in GFETM for downstream experiments because it is fairly light weighted and based on the standard transformers architecture.

2.3   Leveraging the Peak Embedding from GFM in ETM

To further integrate the ETM component and GFM component and improve the model performance, we developed a joint-training and fine-tuning strategy for the ETM and GFM components, respectively. Specifically, we fine-tuned the last two transformer layers from GFM together with the ETM component. This allows the GFM and ETM to jointly optimize the ELBO objective function. Specifically, we use the following method to amortize the peak embedding learning on the GFM: $\hat{r}_{c,p} = \boldsymbol{\theta}_c \boldsymbol{\alpha} \mathrm{GFM}(\mathbf{s}_\mathrm{p}) + \lambda_{\mathrm{bc,p}}$ and $r_{c,p} = \frac{\exp(\hat{r}_{c,p})}{\sum_{p'} \exp(\hat{r}_{c,p'})}$ where $\mathrm{GFM}(\mathbf{s}_\mathrm{p})$ is the output of the last layer of the GFM for the peak embedding $\boldsymbol{\rho}_p$ based on the one-hot sequence matrix $\mathbf{s}_p$. We adopted a minibatch peak sampling strategy for scalable training. Given a minibatch of cells, we first randomly sample $M' \leq M$ peaks among these cells and obtain the nucleotide sequence embedding $\boldsymbol{\rho}'_i$ of those M' peaks through forward pass of the GFM. The sequence embedding $\boldsymbol{\rho}'_i$ from the GFM are then multiplied with the latent topic mixture $\boldsymbol{\theta}$ and topic embedding $\boldsymbol{\alpha}$ from the ETM to obtain the expected transcription rate. In practice, to reduce the computational costs of joint-training, we sample 384 peaks in each iteration (M'=384). We use pre-trained DNABERT as GFM because it is fairly light weighted and the model architecture is more general (vanilla transformers).

2.4   Transfer Learning of GFETM

We performed transfer learning of GFETM in zero-shot and transfer-train settings. In the zero-shot transfer setting, the GFETM model was first trained on a source scATAC-seq dataset. The model parameters were then frozen and the model was tested on the target scATAC-seq dataset from different species or tissues. In the transfer-train setting, the GFETM model was first trained on the source scATAC-seq dataset and then trained on the target scATAC-seq dataset from different species or tissues. The model was evaluated on the target scATAC-seq dataset. Note that ATAC-seq peaks in different species or experiments are different. Therefore, we aligned different peaks from different datasets to enable the transfer learning. We also aligned scRNA-seq and scATAC-seq datasets for the same study to perform cross-omic transfer learning. Details are described in the online full version.

3   Results

GFETM Improves Cell Representational Learning. We conducted experiments on several scATAC-seq datasets in the full study. In this abstract, we showcased the performance on the Human HSC Differentiation dataset [1] and Cusanovich Mouse dataset [2]. We evaluated the quality of the inferred cell embeddings by comparing Louvain clustering results with ground-truth cell-type labels using the Adjusted Rand Index (ARI), Adjusted Mutual Information (AMI) and cell type Average Silhouette Width (ASW) (Fig. 1b,c). The sequence-informed deep learning methods, including our GFETM and an existing state-of-the-art (SOTA) scBasset [5] outperform all other baseline methods by a large margin, which demonstrates the advantage of integrating peak DNA sequence information in scATAC-seq modeling.

Scalability on Large Scale Datasets. Early scATAC-seq studies have limited yield in terms of cell numbers (less than 10k) and sequencing depth. The recent advancements in sequencing technologies generated several large atlas-level scATAC-seq datasets [2], encompassing up to millions of cells, along with millions of peaks. To evaluate the scalability of GFETM on large-scale datasets, we utilized the Cusanovich-Mouse dataset. As shown in Fig. 1d, on a subset of 60000 cells, we compared the performance of GFETM with the SOTA methods scBasset and PeakVI. As the number of selected highly variable peaks increases from 1k to 70k, GFTM consistently outperforms scBasset and PeakVI with increasing number of peaks, especially when the peak number is larger than 30k.

Cross-Tissue Transfer Learning. We performed zero-shot transfer learning across mouse tissues (Fig. 1e). As expected, transfer learning on the target tissues, which has similar functions as the source tissues, led to better results compared to distinct tissues. For example, PreFrontalCortex, Cerebellum and WholeBrain all contain cells in the nervous system, while BoneMarrow, Spleen and Lung are all closely related to immune system and hematopoietic system. Therefore, the tissues with more similar cell types are more readily transferable between each other. Indeed, we observed statistically significant positive correlation between cell-type similarity and zero-shot transfer learning performance in terms of ARI for most tissues (Fig. 1f).

References

1. Buenrostro, J.D., et al.: Integrated single-cell analysis maps the continuous regulatory landscape of human hematopoietic differentiation. Cell **173**(6), 1535-1548.e16 (2018). https://doi.org/10.1016/j.cell.2018.03.074
2. Cusanovich, D.A., et al.: A Single-cell atlas of in vivo mammalian chromatin accessibility. Cell **174**(5), 1309-1324.e18 (2018). https://doi.org/10.1016/j.cell.2018.06.052
3. Ji, Y., Zhou, Z., Liu, H., Davuluri, R.V.: DNABERT: pre-trained bidirectional encoder representations from transformers model for DNA-language in genome. Bioinformatics **37**(15), 2112–2120 (2021)
4. Kingma, D.P., Welling, M.: Auto-encoding variational Bayes. arXiv preprint arXiv:1312.6114 (2013)
5. Yuan, H., Kelley, D.R.: scBasset: sequence-based modeling of single-cell ATAC-seq using convolutional neural networks. Nat. Methods **19**(9), 1088–1096 (2022). https://doi.org/10.1038/s41592-022-01562-8
6. Zhao, Y., Cai, H., Zhang, Z., Tang, J., Li, Y.: Learning interpretable cellular and gene signature embeddings from single-cell transcriptomic data. Nat. Commun. **12**(1), 5261 (2021). https://doi.org/10.1038/s41467-021-25534-2

SEM: Size-Based Expectation Maximization for Characterizing Nucleosome Positions and Subtypes

Jianyu Yang[1], Kuangyu Yen[2(✉)], and Shaun Mahony[1(✉)]

[1] Center for Eukaryotic Gene Regulation, Department of Biochemistry and Molecular Biology, Pennsylvania State University, University Park, PA, USA
mahony@psu.edu

[2] State Key Laboratory of Experimental Hematology, National Clinical Research Center for Blood Diseases, Haihe Laboratory of Cell Ecosystem, Institute of Hematology & Blood Diseases Hospital, Chinese Academy of Medical Sciences & Peking Union Medical College, Tianjin 300020, China
kuangyuyen@ihcams.ac.cn

1 Introduction

Nucleosome landscapes across the genome are typically characterized using micrococcal nuclease sequencing (MNase-seq). MNase is an endo-exonuclease that preferentially digests accessible DNA between nucleosomes. After size selection, mononucleosome-sized DNA fragments are retained for high-throughput sequencing [1, 2]. However, depending on the composition of the nucleosome and the factors engaging the nucleosome, not all nucleosomes protect the canonical 147 bp of DNA. Most current nucleosome-calling software packages still assume that nucleosomes uniformly protect ~147 bp of DNA [3–5]. Current approaches use this rigid assumption when estimating the locations and occupancy properties of nucleosomes, making their performance sub-optimal when characterizing nucleosomes of non-canonical DNA length.

2 Methods

To resolve the lack of an effective method for characterizing nucleosome subtypes, we introduce a new nucleosome-calling package called Size-based Expectation Maximization (SEM). SEM is a hierarchical Gaussian Mixture Model, which probabilistically models the positions, occupancy, fuzziness, and subtype identities of nucleosomes from MNase-seq data (Fig. 1A). The components of the mixture model represent individual nucleosomes; the properties of each nucleosome are modeled based on the mapped locations and lengths of MNase-seq fragments. Specifically, each nucleosome component is defined by its dyad location, occupancy, fuzziness, and the probability of belonging to each nucleosome subtype. Nucleosome subtypes are represented by normal distributions of nucleosome-protected DNA fragment lengths.

The distributions of nucleosome subtypes can be inferred from the overall fragment size distribution of the MNase-seq experiment through a Gaussian Mixture Model with

J. Ma (Ed.): RECOMB 2024, LNCS 14758, pp. 320–323, 2024.
https://doi.org/10.1007/978-1-0716-3989-4_21

a user pre-defined number of components or via a Dirichlet Process Mixture Model. A Generalized Expectation Maximization algorithm is used to calculate the latent assignment of MNase-seq fragments to nucleosomes and to estimate the various properties associated with each nucleosome (Fig. 1A). Additionally, several priors are integrated into the model to better reflect the biological properties of nucleosomes, including a sparse prior on nucleosome occupancy to eliminate nucleosomes with weak occupancy and another sparse prior on subtype probability to encourage each nucleosome to be a member of an individual subtype. An exclusion zone is also taken into consideration to ensure neighboring nucleosomes do not overlap in the model.

3 Results

The performance of SEM was evaluated against other existing nucleosome calling packages on both simulated and real MNase-seq data. In simulated datasets, SEM accurately predicted nucleosome dyad location, occupancy, and fuzziness, with performance comparable to two other nucleosome-calling packages, DANPOS [4] and PuFFIN [6]. When evaluated on real MNase-seq data, all tested nucleosome calling packages exhibited comparable performance on predicting nucleosome dyad locations. Furthermore, SEM demonstrated high accuracy in distinguishing nucleosome subtypes in simulated MNase-seq datasets. Overall, these results suggest that SEM performs comparably with existing nucleosome-calling packages in terms of conventional nucleosome metrics while additionally having the ability to characterize nucleosome subtypes.

We further applied SEM to a low-dose MNase-H2B-ChIP-seq dataset obtained from mouse embryonic stem cells (mESCs) [7], detecting three nucleosome subtypes: short fragment nucleosomes (~115 bp mean size); canonical nucleosomes (~185 bp mean size); and di-nucleosomes (~295 bp mean size). In comparison with hard fragment size cut-offs, SEM's detection of nucleosome subtypes more clearly separates nucleosomes belonging to each subtype at TSSs and CTCF sites (Fig. 1B).

We continued subcategorizing SEM's nucleosome subtypes according to their association with potential regulatory regions by overlapping with mESC ATAC-seq peaks [8]. Short fragment nucleosomes that overlap accessible regions display high MNase sensitivity, similar to the so-called "fragile nucleosomes" that were defined in the original study. Approximately 33% of SEM-defined accessible short fragment nucleosomes occupy non-TSS/CTCF sites, including sites displaying proximal and distal enhancer-like signatures. Accessible short fragment nucleosomes are also associated with active histone modifications. Additionally, chromatin remodelers such as Ep400 are enriched at these nucleosome dyad locations, indicating a mechanism for their destabilization (Fig. 1C). Moreover, several mESC-specific transcription factors are highly enriched at accessible short fragment nucleosome sites, which suggests accessible short fragment nucleosome sites are hotspots for transcription regulation.

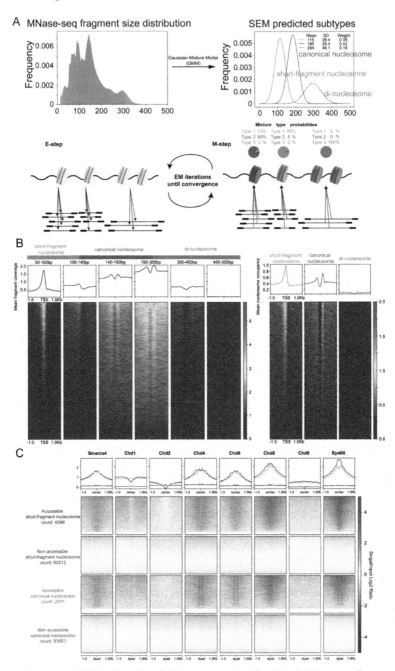

Fig. 1. A) Overview of SEM algorithm. **B)** Heatmap and profile plot of MNase-seq fragments split by fragment size (left panel) and each nucleosome subtype as determined by SEM (right panel). **C)** Heatmap and profile plots of chromatin remodeler ChIP-seq enrichment around nucleosome dyads.

4 Conclusion

When compared with other nucleosome-calling packages, SEM exhibits comparable performance on conventional nucleosome-calling metrics while uniquely providing an automatic annotation of nucleosome subtype identity. Our results on mESC MNase-ChIP-seq data demonstrate that SEM's genome-wide probabilistic approach to nucleosome subtype calling provides clear advantages over the typically employed fragment length threshold approaches. In summary, SEM provides an effective platform for exploration of non-standard nucleosome subtypes.

SEM is publicly available from https://github.com/YenLab/SEM and a preprint version of the full manuscript is available at https://doi.org/10.1101/2023.10.17.562727.

Acknowledgments. This work was supported by NIH R35-GM144135 and National Science Foundation DBI CAREER 2045500 (to S.M.). Any opinions, findings and conclusions or recommendations expressed in this material are those of the authors and do not necessarily reflect the views of the funders. This work was initiated by J.Y. as a Master's student in K.Y.'s lab at the Department of Developmental Biology, School of Basic Medical Sciences, Southern Medical University, Guangzhou, China. Work by the Yen lab is supported by the National Natural Science Foundation of China (grants 31522031 & 31571526). The authors thank the members of the Center for Eukaryotic Gene Regulation at Penn State for helpful feedback and discussions.

References

1. Jiang, C., Pugh, B.F.: A compiled and systematic reference map of nucleosome positions across the Saccharomyces cerevisiae genome. Genome Biol. **10**, 1–11 (2009)
2. Mavrich, T.N., et al.: Nucleosome organization in the Drosophila genome. Nature **453**, 358–362 (2008)
3. Becker, J., Yau, C., Hancock, J.M., Holmes, C.C.: NucleoFinder: a statistical approach for the detection of nucleosome positions. Bioinformatics **29**, 711–716 (2013)
4. Chen, K., et al.: DANPOS: dynamic analysis of nucleosome position and occupancy by sequencing. Genome Res. **23**, 341–351 (2013)
5. Zhou, X., Blocker, A.W., Airoldi, E.M., O'Shea, E.K.: A computational approach to map nucleosome positions and alternative chromatin states with base pair resolution. Elife **5**, 1–28 (2016)
6. Polishko, A., Bunnik, E.M., Le Roch, K.G., Lonardi, S.: PuFFIN - a parameter-free method to build nucleosome maps from paired-end reads. BMC Bioinform. **15**, 1–10 (2014)
7. Ishii, H., Kadonaga, J.T., Ren, B.: MPE-seq, a new method for the genome-wide analysis of chromatin structure. Proc. Natl. Acad. Sci. U.S.A. **112**, E3457–E3465 (2015)
8. Ostapcuk, V., et al.: Activity-dependent neuroprotective protein recruits HP1 and CHD4 to control lineage-specifying genes. Nature **557**, 739–743 (2018)

Centrifuger: Lossless Compression of Microbial Genomes for Efficient and Accurate Metagenomic Sequence Classification

Li Song[1,2,3]($\boxtimes$) (iD) and Ben Langmead[4] (iD)

[1] Department of Biomedical Data Science, Dartmouth College, Hanover, NH 03755, USA
Li.Song@dartmouth.edu
[2] Department of Computer Science, Dartmouth College, Hanover, NH 03755, USA
[3] Department of Microbiology and Immunology, Dartmouth College, Hanover, NH 03755, USA
[4] Department of Computer Science, Johns Hopkins University, Baltimore, MD 21218, USA
langmea@cs.jhu.edu

Abstract. Centrifuger is an efficient taxonomic classification method that compares sequencing reads against a microbial genome database. Due to the increasing availability of microbial genomes, classification methods tend to store the genome database in an approximate way, keeping the memory footprint within a practical range. In contrast, Centrifuger losslessly compresses the Burrows-Wheeler transformed (BWT) sequence from microbial genomes using a novel compression algorithm called run-block compression. We prove that the run-block compression achieves sublinear space complexity, $O(\frac{n}{\sqrt{l}})$ words, where n is the sequence length and l is the average run length. This space complexity falls between the no-compression wavelet tree representation using $O(n)$ words and the run-length compression representation using $O(\frac{n}{l})$ words. Run-block compression is effective at compressing microbial databases like RefSeq, where the average run length of the BWT sequence is low, e.g., about 6.8. Combining this compression method with other strategies for compacting the Ferragina-Manzini (FM) index, Centrifuger reduces the index size by half compared to its predecessor, Centrifuge. Lossless compression helps Centrifuger achieve greater accuracy than competing methods at lower taxonomic levels such as species and genus. Additionally, run-block compression supports rapid rank queries in $O(log\sigma)$time, the same order as the wavelet-tree rank query. Despite its use of a compressed data structure, Centrifuger is as fast as Centrifuge in terms of processing speed.

Keywords: FM-index · r-index · metagenomic · compact data structure

Taxonomic classification labels each sequencing read with taxonomy IDs representing its most likely taxon of origin. This has become an important step in translating raw sequencing data, like metagenomic sequencing data, into meaningful microbiome profiles [1]. Classification is usually conducted by comparing the read sequence to all the sequences in a database of microbial reference genomes, such as RefSeq [2]. The growth of available microbial reference genomes creates a strong need for memory-efficient structures. Many methods turn to lossy representations of the database. For

© The Author(s), under exclusive license to Springer Nature Switzerland AG 2024
J. Ma (Ed.): RECOMB 2024, LNCS 14758, pp. 324–327, 2024.
https://doi.org/10.1007/978-1-0716-3989-4_22

example, Kraken2 [3] reduces the space by storing minimizers [4] instead of all the k-mers. We previously co-developed the taxonomic classification method Centrifuge [5] that used the memory-efficient Burrows-Wheeler transformed (BWT) sequence [6] and the Ferragina-Manzini (FM) index [7]. However, the FM-index grows linearly with the database size and the lossy compression strategy proposed in Centrifuge is not scalable, making Centrifuge less usable in the context of large and growing genome databases.

Related genomes share similar sequences, giving genome databases a degree of repetitiveness and compressibility. R-index [8] exploits this feature, builds upon the run-length compressed BWT (RLBWT), and fits in O(r) words, where r is the number of runs in the BWT sequence. However, microbial genomes are diverse, so applying RLBWT may take more space than the uncompressed wavelet tree [9]. Therefore, we designed the compact data structure, called run-block compressed BWT (RBBWT), to effectively compress the BWT sequence for the intermediate level of repetitiveness characteristic of microbial genome databases.

In run-block compression, the input sequence T, of length n and alphabet set Σ of size σ, , is firstly partitioned into equal-size substrings (blocks), $T_1, T_2, \ldots, T_m$, where $m = \lceil \frac{n}{b} \rceil$ and b is the block size. We use a bit vector B_R of size m to indicate whether the corresponding block is a run block, i.e. a block consisting of one alphabet character repeated b times. We will then split T into two substrings, by concatenating run blocks and non-run blocks, i.e., $T_{R\prime} = T_{i_1} T_{i_2} \ldots T_{i_l}$, $T_P = T_{j_1} T_{j_2} \ldots T_{j_{m-l}}$, and T_{i_k} is the k-th run blocks in T with the alphabet σ_{i_k}. $T_{R\prime}$ can be lossless represented as $T_R = \sigma_{i_1} \sigma_{i_2} \ldots \sigma_{i_l}$, where $|T_R| = \frac{|T_{R\prime}|}{b}$. The space saving comes from using one character to represent a run block of size b, a strategy we call run-block compression. We apply this run-block compression scheme to the BWT sequence and produce its representation RBBWT. RBBWT supports rank query in $O(log\sigma)$ time by combining the corresponding ranks on T_R and T_P guided by B_R. Furthermore, RBBWT reduces the size of the raw BWT to $O(\frac{n}{\sqrt{l}})$ words, where l is the average run length, i.e. $l = \frac{n}{r}$. The block size yielding this sublinear-space representation can also be efficiently determined.

We compared the computational efficiency of RBBWT against the uncompressed wavelet tree, RLBWT, and the hybrid RLBWT. When varying the average run length of the BWT sequence, RBBWT was the most memory-efficient representation when l was less than or around 10 (Fig. 1A,B). In line with the theoretical analysis, the rank query on RBBWT was three times slower than on the uncompressed representation but about five times faster than on RLBWT (Fig. 1C).

Inspired by this observation, we developed the software tool Centrifuger (Centrifuge with RBBWT), which rapidly assigned the taxonomy IDs for a sequencing read while consuming half the memory of a conventional FM-index. We applied RBBWT to reduce the size needed to store the BWT sequence. For the sampled suffix array in the FM-index, we save space by storing only the sequence ID for each sampled position on the BWT sequence (Fig. 2 right). The classification algorithm scans the read twice, once for the original sequence and once for the reverse-complement sequence. Each scan looks for semi-maximal matches, by repeatedly extending the match with the backward search until reaching a mismatch, then skipping the base immediately after the point where the backward search terminates (Fig. 2 left). For each match, Centrifuger retrieves the sequence IDs associated with entries in the matching BWT interval. Centrifuger adds

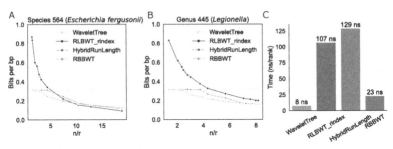

Fig. 1. Computational efficiency of the wavelet tree, RLBWT, hybrid RLBWT, and RBBWT (A) Bits used to represent one base pair (bp) when representing increasingly more genomes with species ID 564 (*Escherichia fergusonii*). (B) Bits used to represent one bp when representing genomes with genus ID 445 (*Legionella*). (C) Rank query time

a score, which is a quadratic function of the match length, for each retrieved sequence ID. The highest-scoring taxonomy IDs translated from the sequence IDs are reported as the classification result. Compared with other taxonomic classification methods like Kraken2, Centrifuger achieved higher accuracy and significantly better results at the species level and the genus level. Centrifuger was memory efficient, reducing the memory footprint of classifying reads against the 140 Gbp RefSeq prokaryotic genome database from Centrifuge's 83 GB to 43 GB. While being much more memory-efficient and using a losslessly compressed data structure, Centrifuger was only about two times slower than Centrifuge when using 8 threads.

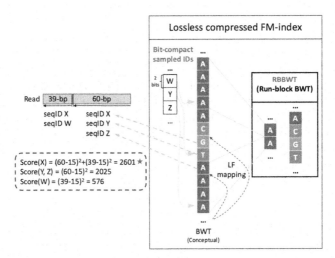

Fig. 2. Overview of Centrifuger. Left: Classification procedure. Right: FM-index with RBBWT.

Centrifuger is free and open-source software released under the MIT license and is available at https://github.com/mourisl/centrifuger. The link to the full manuscript on Biorxiv is https://www.biorxiv.org/content/https://doi.org/10.1101/2023.11.15.567129 [10].

Acknowledgments. This work is supported by the NIH grants P20GM130454 (Dartmouth), 3P20GM130454-05WS (Dartmouth), R01HG011392 (B.L.), and R35GM139602 (B.L.).

Disclosure of Interests. The authors have no competing interests to declare that are relevant to the content of this article.

References

1. Knight, R., et al.: Best practices for analysing microbiomes. Nat. Rev. Microbiol. **16**, 410–422 (2018). https://doi.org/10.1038/s41579-018-0029-9
2. Pruitt, K.D., Tatusova, T., Maglott, D.R.: NCBI reference sequences (RefSeq): a curated non-redundant sequence database of genomes, transcripts and proteins. Nucleic Acids Res. **35**, D61–D65 (2007). https://doi.org/10.1093/nar/gkl842
3. Wood, D.E., Lu, J., Langmead, B.: Improved metagenomic analysis with Kraken 2. Genome Biol. **20**, 257 (2019). https://doi.org/10.1186/s13059-019-1891-0
4. Roberts, M., Hayes, W., Hunt, B.R., Mount, S.M., Yorke, J.A.: Reducing storage requirements for biological sequence comparison. Bioinformatics **20**, 3363–3369 (2004). https://doi.org/10.1093/bioinformatics/bth408
5. Kim, D., Song, L., Breitwieser, F.P., Salzberg, S.L.: Centrifuge: rapid and sensitive classification of metagenomic sequences. Genome Res. **26**, 1721–1729 (2016). https://doi.org/10.1101/gr.210641.116
6. Burrows, M., Wheeler, D.J.: A block-sorting lossless data compression algorithm. SRS Research Report. 124 (1994)
7. Ferragina, P., Manzini, G.: Opportunistic data structures with applications. In: Proceedings 41st Annual Symposium on Foundations of Computer Science, pp. 390–398 (2000). https://doi.org/10.1109/SFCS.2000.892127
8. Gagie, T., Navarro, G., Prezza, N.: Optimal-Time Text Indexing in BWT-runs Bounded Space (2017). http://arxiv.org/abs/1705.10382
9. Grossi, R., Gupta, A., Vitter, J.S.: High-order entropy-compressed text indexes. In: Proceedings of the Fourteenth Annual ACM-SIAM Symposium on Discrete Algorithms, pp. 841–850. Society for Industrial and Applied Mathematics, USA (2003)
10. Song, L., Langmead, B.: Centrifuger: lossless compression of microbial genomes for efficient and accurate metagenomic sequence classification (2023). https://www.biorxiv.org/content/10.1101/2023.11.15.567129v1, https://doi.org/10.1101/2023.11.15.567129

BONOBO: Bayesian Optimized Sample-Specific Networks Obtained by Omics Data

Enakshi Saha[1], Viola Fanfani[1], Panagiotis Mandros[1], Marouen Ben-Guebila[1], Jonas Fischer[1], Katherine H. Shutta[1,2], Kimberly Glass[1,2,3], Dawn L. DeMeo[2,3], Camila M. Lopes-Ramos[1,2,3], and John Quackenbush[1,2,4(✉)]

[1] Department of Biostatistics, Harvard T.H. Chan School of Public Health, Boston, MA, USA
johnq@hsph.harvard.edu
[2] Channing Division of Network Medicine, Brigham and Women's Hospital, Boston, MA, USA
[3] Department of Medicine, Harvard Medical School, Boston, MA, USA
[4] Department of Data Science, Dana-Farber Cancer Institute, Boston, MA, USA

Abstract. Correlation networks can provide important insights into biological systems by uncovering intricate interactions between genes and their molecular regulators. However, methods for estimating co-expression networks generally derive an aggregate population-specific network that represents the mean regulatory properties of the entire population and hence falls short in capturing heterogeneity across individuals. While numerous methods have been proposed to estimate sample-specific co-expression networks, they fail to estimate positive semidefinite correlation networks and, hence, are subject to misinterpretation. To fill this gap in co-expression network inference, we introduce BONOBO (Bayesian Optimized Networks Obtained By assimilating Omics data), a scalable Bayesian model for deriving individual sample-specific co-expression networks by acknowledging heterogeneity in molecular interactions across individuals. For each sample, BONOBO imposes a Gaussian distribution on the log-transformed, centered gene expression and a conjugate Inverse Wishart prior distribution on the sample-specific co-expression matrix constructed from assimilating all other samples in the data. BONOBO yields a closed-form solution for the posterior distribution of the sample-specific co-expression matrices by combining the sample-specific gene expression with the prior distribution. We demonstrate the advantages of BONOBO using several simulated and real datasets. BONOBO is computationally scalable and available as open-source software through the Network Zoo package (from netZooPy v0.10.0; netzoo.github.io). A preprint associated with this abstract can be found on bioRxiv (doi: 10.1101/2023.11.16.567119v1).

Keywords: Gene regulatory network · Co-expression · individual-specific network · Bayesian inference · posterior distribution

---

E. Saha and V. Fanfani—These authors contributed equally.

J. Ma (Ed.): RECOMB 2024, LNCS 14758, pp. 328–331, 2024.
https://doi.org/10.1007/978-1-0716-3989-4_23

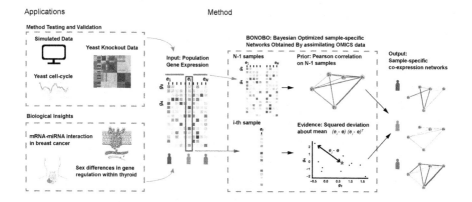

1 Introduction

Co-expression networks are effective tools for uncovering interactions between genes and molecular regulators and thus can provide important insights into the mechanisms of complex traits and diseases. Methods for estimating co-expression networks typically derive an aggregate network representing the mean regulatory properties of the population and hence fail to capture the individual-specific heterogeneity in regulatory patterns. Further, methods to infer individual sample-specific co-expression networks [1–3] suffer from limitations such as non-positive definite estimates of co-expression and/or correlation values that fall beyond $(-1, 1)$, thus posing significant challenges in downstream analyses and interpretation. Other methods for deriving sample-specific networks [4,5] require an external reference population and hence are susceptible to varying inference depending on the reference used. BONOBO (Bayesian Optimized Networks Obtained By assimilating Omics data) is an empirical Bayesian model that derives individual sample-specific co-expression networks. BONOBO derives positive definite co-expression networks without using any external reference datasets.

2 BONOBO

Let $x_1, x_2, \ldots, x_N \sim \mathbb{R}^g$ represent the log-transformed bulk gene expression values of g genes for N samples. For every sample $i \in \{1, 2, \ldots, N\}$, we assume the centered expression vector $x_i - \bar{x}$ to follow a multivariate normal distribution with mean zero and a sample-specific covariance matrix V_i, which is unknown:

$$x_i - \bar{x} \sim N_g\left(\mathbf{0}_g, V_i\right), \qquad (1)$$

where $\mathbf{0}_g \in \mathbb{R}^g$ represents a vector of all zeros and $\bar{x} = \frac{1}{n}\sum_{i=1}^{n} x_i$ denotes the mean expression computed across all samples. The primary goal is to estimate V_i, the sample-specific covariance matrix of gene expression for the i-th sample.

For every sample $i \in \{1, 2, \ldots, N\}$, we impose an inverse Wishart prior distribution on the sample-specific covariance matrix V_i, given all other samples

$j \in \{1, 2, \ldots, N\} \setminus \{i\},$

$$V_i \sim InvWishart\left((\nu_i - g - 1)S_i, \nu_i\right), \tag{2}$$

where $\nu_i \geq g+1$ represents the degrees of freedom and S_i represents the sample covariance matrix computed from the remaining $N - 1$ samples after excluding the i-th sample from the data. With this assumption, the prior mean of the covariance matrix for the i-th sample is given by $\mathbb{E}[V_i] = S_i$, meaning that for each individual, the correlation between any pair of genes is centered around the correlation between these same pair of genes across the entire population.

Under assumptions (1) and (2), the posterior distribution of the sample-specific covariance matrix V_i turns out to be

$$V_i | \{x_1, \ldots, x_N\} \sim InvWishart\left((\nu_i - g)\Sigma_i, \nu_i + 1\right), \tag{3}$$

where $\Sigma_i = \frac{(x_i - \bar{x})(x_i - \bar{x})^T + (\nu_i - g - 1)S_i}{\nu_i - g}$ is the posterior mean of V_i.

From (3) we note that the posterior mean of V_i is a linear combination of the prior mean S_i, which consolidates information from all other samples except the i-th sample and a sample-specific component $(x_i - \bar{x})(x_i - \bar{x})^T$, which encapsulates the association between pairwise genes within the i-th sample alone:

$$\Sigma_i = \delta_i (x_i - \bar{x})(x_i - \bar{x})^T + (1 - \delta_i)S_i, \tag{4}$$

where $\delta_i = \frac{1}{\nu_i - g}$. As $\nu_i - g \geq 1$, we have $0 \leq \delta_i \leq 1$, which represents the relative contributions of the sample-specific information and the prior information in estimating the posterior mean of V_i. We introduce an empirical Bayes approach for tuning the hyperparameters δ_i for every sample i.

BONOBO constructs a complete network with edges between every pair of genes, where edge weights correspond to σ_{jk}, the posterior mean of the covariance between genes j and k. We can generate a sparse covariance network by pruning out edges for which the correlation values are zero with high posterior probability.

BONOBO is implemented in Python and it is available as open-source software through the Network Zoo package [6] (from netZooPy v0.10.0; net-zoo.github.io).

3   Results and Discussion

BONOBO is a Bayesian parametric model designed to construct personalized sample-specific gene co-expression networks for single samples, which not only enables us to capture individual-specific variations in gene co-expression but also serves as a key step for the estimation of personalized gene regulatory networks. Unlike other methods, BONOBO yields positive semidefinite correlation networks along with posterior credible intervals for the individual-specific correlation estimates. First, we benchmark BONOBO's performance on simulated and experimental data [7], and show that it is a scalable algorithm that outperforms competing methods. Then, we showcase the ability of our method to generate sample-specific co-expression networks from human datasets, that not only yield correlation values between all gene pairs but can also be used to provide valuable insights into disease mechanisms. Using paired miRNA-mRNA expression data [8] from breast cancer we demonstrate that BONOBO can uncover individual-specific differences in multiomic interactions with prognostic significance. Furthermore, we show that our sample-specific correlation networks can be readily used in combination with GRN estimation methods, such as PANDA to derive individual-specific gene regulatory networks. Using RNA-seq data from thyroid tissue samples from GTEx, we show that the estimated gene regulatory networks reveal regulatory differences between males and females which help explain the clinically observed sex disparity in the risk of thyroid diseases [9].

Acknowledgments. This work was supported by grants from the National Institutes of Health (R35CA220523, U24CA231846, P50CA127003, R01HG011393, R01HG 125975, P01HL114501, T32HL007427, K01HL166376, K24HL171900, R01HL155749) and the American Lung Association grant (LCD-821824).

References

1. Kuijjer, M.L., Tung, M.G., Yuan, G.C., Quackenbush, J., Glass, K.: Estimating sample-specific regulatory networks. Iscience **14**, 226–240 (2019). https://doi.org/10.1016/j.isci.2019.03.021
2. Yu, X., Zeng, T., Wang, X., Li, G., Chen, L.: Unravelling personalized dysfunctional gene network of complex diseases based on differential network model. J. Transl. Med. **13**, 1–13 (2015). https://doi.org/10.1186/s12967-015-0546-5
3. Chen, H., et al.: SWEET: a single-sample network inference method for deciphering individual features in disease. Briefings Bioinform. **24**(2) (2023). https://doi.org/10.1093/bib/bbad032
4. Liu, X., Wang, Y., Ji, H., Aihara, K., Chen, L.: Personalized characterization of diseases using sample-specific networks. Nucleic Acids Res. **4422**, e164–e164 (2016). https://doi.org/10.1093/nar/gkw772
5. Lee, W., Huang, D., Han, K.: Constructing cancer patient-specific and group-specific gene networks with multi-omics data. BMC Med. Genomics **13**, 1–12 (2020). https://doi.org/10.1186/s12920-020-00736-7
6. Guebila, M.B., et al.: The Network Zoo: a multilingual package for the inference and analysis of gene regulatory networks. Genome Biol. **231**, 45 (2023). https://doi.org/10.1186/s13059-023-02877-1
7. Jackson, C.A., Castro, D.M., Saldi, G., Bonneau, R., Gresham, D.: Gene regulatory network reconstruction using single-cell RNA sequencing of barcoded genotypes in diverse environments. eLife **9**(2020). https://doi.org/10.7554/eLife.51254
8. Enerly, E., et al.: miRNA-mRNA integrated analysis reveals roles for miRNAs in primary breast tumors. PLoS ONE **6**(2) (2011). https://doi.org/10.1371/journal.pone.0016915
9. Shobab, L., Burman, D.K., Wartofsky, L.: Sex differences in differentiated thyroid cancer. Thyroid **323**, 224–235 (2022). https://doi.org/10.1089/thy.2021.0361

regLM: Designing Realistic Regulatory DNA with Autoregressive Language Models

Avantika Lal[1]([⊠])[iD], David Garfield[2], Tommaso Biancalani[1], and Gokcen Eraslan[1]([⊠])

[1] Biology Research, AI Development, gRED Computational Sciences, Genentech, South San Francisco, CA 94080, USA
{lal.avantika,eraslan.gokcen}@gene.com
[2] OMNI Bioinformatics and Department of Regenerative Medicine, Genentech, South San Francisco, CA 94080, USA

Abstract. We present regLM, a framework to design synthetic CREs with desired properties, such as high, low or cell type-specific activity, using autoregressive language models in conjunction with supervised sequence-to-function models. Using regLM, we designed synthetic yeast promoters of defined strength, as well as cell type-specific human enhancers. We show that the synthetic CREs generated by regLM contain biological features similar to experimentally validated CREs.

1 Introduction

Cis-regulatory elements (CREs), such as promoters and enhancers, are DNA sequences that regulate gene expression. Their activity is influenced by the presence, order, and spacing of sequence motifs [10] that bind to proteins called transcription factors (TFs). Synthetic CREs with defined properties are needed for biomanufacturing as well as numerous therapeutic applications including cell and gene therapy; for example, to maximize activity of a therapeutic gene in the target cell type.

Such CREs are often designed manually based on prior knowledge [3]. Recent studies have used directed evolution [8,9] and gradient-based approaches [4,5,7] for CRE design, in which supervised models are trained to predict the activity of a CRE from its sequence, and are then used to edit sequences iteratively to achieve the desired prediction. However, such approaches are not truly generative and do not necessarily learn the overall sequence distribution of the desired CREs. Instead they may only optimize specific features that have high predictive value. Consequently, the resulting CREs may be out-of-distribution and unrealistic, leading to unpredictable behavior when they are experimentally tested in a cell.

Autoregressive language models, such as Generative Pre-trained Transformer (GPT) can produce realistic content in natural languages [2]. Here, we present regLM, a framework to design synthetic CREs with desired properties, such as high, low or cell type-specific activity, using autoregressive language models in

J. Ma (Ed.): RECOMB 2024, LNCS 14758, pp. 332–335, 2024.
https://doi.org/10.1007/978-1-0716-3989-4_24

conjunction with supervised models. To our knowledge, this is the first time language modeling has been used for DNA in a generative setting.

2   Methods

Figure 1 illustrates the regLM framework. Given a dataset of DNA sequences labeled with their measured activity, we encode the label in a sequence of categorical 'prompt tokens', which is prefixed to the DNA sequence. We then train or fine-tune a HyenaDNA model [6] to perform next token prediction beginning with the prompt tokens. This formulation allows us to use any prior knowledge on sequences in the model explicitly. Once trained, the language model can be prompted with the sequence of tokens representing any desired function. The model, now conditioned on the prompt tokens, generates a DNA sequence one nucleotide at a time. In parallel, we train a supervised sequence-to-activity regression model on the same dataset, and apply it to the generated sequences to select those that best match the desired activity. Finally, we provide several approaches to evaluate the generated sequences as well as the model itself.

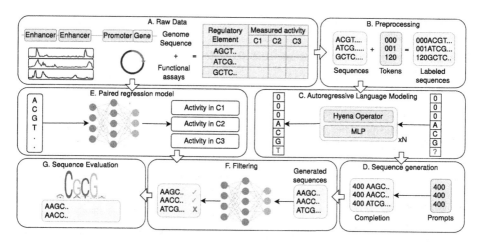

Fig. 1. Schematic of regLM. A, B) DNA sequences are prefixed with a sequence of prompt tokens representing functional labels. C) A HyenaDNA model is trained or fine-tuned to perform next token prediction on the labeled sequences. D) The trained model is prompted with a sequence of prompt tokens to generate sequences with desired properties. E, F) A sequence-to-function regression model trained on the same dataset is used to check and filter the generated sequences. G) The regulatory content of generated sequences is evaluated.

3   Results

We applied the regLM framework to two datasets: first, a dataset of DNA sequences and their measured promoter activities in yeast cells [1,9], and second, a dataset of human enhancers and their measured activity in three cell lines

(K562, HepG2 and SK-N-SH) [4]. By training regLM models on these datasets and prompting them with specific tokens, we generated synthetic yeast promoters with precisely defined levels of activity, as well as synthetic human enhancers specific to each of the three cell types.

Using independent regression models trained on fully separate data, as well as classification models trained on related genomic modalities such as chromatin accessibility, we predicted that the synthetic CREs generated by regLM are likely to have the desired level of activity. In addition, we examined the generated CREs and identified known binding motifs for species- and cell type- specific transcription factors consistent with the desired activity.

Finally, we compared the putative CREs generated by regLM to CREs with similar activity generated using five state-of-the-art approaches (Directed evolution, Ledidi [7], AdaLead, FastSeqProp, and Simulated Annealing) as well as to synthetic CREs generated in previous studies [4,9]. Based on numerous measures of similarity, such as GC content, k-mer content and TF-binding motif content, we found regLM generated CREs to be the most functionally similar to experimentally validated CREs with the same function.

4   Preprint

https://www.biorxiv.org/content/10.1101/2024.02.14.580373.

5   Code Availability

regLM is available at https://github.com/Genentech/regLM. Model weights and code to perform the experiments in this paper are available at https://zenodo.org/records/10669334.

References

1. de Boer, C.G., Vaishnav, E.D., Sadeh, R., Abeyta, E.L., Friedman, N., Regev, A.: Deciphering eukaryotic gene-regulatory logic with 100 million random promoters. Nat. Biotechnol. **38**(1), 56–65 (2020)
2. Brown, T., et al.: Language models are few-shot learners. Adv. Neural. Inf. Process. Syst. **33**, 1877–1901 (2020)
3. Fornes, O., et al.: Ontarget: in silico design of minipromoters for targeted delivery of expression. Nucleic Acids Res. gkad375 (2023)
4. Gosai, S.J., et al.: Machine-guided design of synthetic cell type-specific cis - regulatory elements. bioRxiv (2023)
5. Linder, J., Seelig, G.: Fast activation maximization for molecular sequence design. BMC Bioinform. **22**(1), 510 (2021)
6. Nguyen, E., et al.: HyenaDNA: long-range genomic sequence modeling at single nucleotide resolution. arXiv (2023)
7. Schreiber, J., Lu, Y.Y.: Ledidi: designing genomic edits that induce functional activity (2020)

8. Taskiran, I.I., Spanier, K.I., Christiaens, V., Mauduit, D., Aerts, S.: Cell type directed design of synthetic enhancers (2022)
9. Vaishnav, E.D., et al.: The evolution, evolvability and engineering of gene regulatory DNA. Nature **603**(7901), 455–463 (2022)
10. Wittkopp, P.J., Kalay, G.: Cis-regulatory elements: molecular mechanisms and evolutionary processes underlying divergence. Nat. Rev. Genet. **13**(1), 59–69 (2012)

DexDesign: A New OSPREY-Based Algorithm for Designing *de novo* D-peptide Inhibitors

Nathan Guerin[1], Henry Childs[3], Pei Zhou[4], and Bruce R. Donald[1,2,3,4]($\boxtimes$)

[1] Department of Computer Science, Duke University, Durham, NC 27708, USA
brd+recomb24@cs.duke.edu
[2] Department of Mathematics, Duke University, Durham, NC 27708, USA
[3] Department of Chemistry, Duke University, Durham, NC 27708, USA
[4] Department of Biochemistry, Duke University School of Medicine, Durham, NC 22710, USA

Abstract. D-peptide inhibitors offer unique advantages as therapeutics, including increased metabolic stability and low immunogenicity. We introduce DexDesign, an OSPREY-based algorithm for computationally designing *de novo* D-peptide inhibitors, and use it to design inhibitors of two biomedically important PDZ domains. Novel techniques enabling exponential reductions in peptide search space are presented: Minimum Flexible Set, Inverse Alanine Scans, and K*-based Mutational Scans. Designed D-peptide inhibitors are predicted to significantly improve binding affinity (K_D) over the endogenous ligand.

Keywords: protein:ligand binding · *de novo* peptide design · OSPREY

1 Introduction

1.1 Benefits of Including D-amino Acids in Peptides

Despite many advantages [1], peptide therapeutics have poor stability, oral bioavailability, membrane permeability, and retention [2]. The inclusion of D-amino acids can increase peptide stability by decreasing substrate recognition by proteolytic enzymes [3]. Therefore, changing the chirality of L-amino acids to their D counterparts is a strategy used to improve stability and binding affinity of inhibitory peptides [4]. The ubiquitous peptide-recognition PDZ domains [5] are excellent targets for D-peptides.

1.2 OSPREY (Open-Source Protein REdesign for You)

OSPREY is a widely-used, open-source software program containing a suite of computational protein design algorithms developed in our lab [6]. Until now, it has not had the capability to design D-peptides. In this paper we present an algorithm, DexDesign (see Fig. 1), for designing *de novo* D-peptides in OSPREY. We designed 30 D-peptide inhibitors for CALP [7] and MAST2 [8] PDZ domains.

Full Text. The Full Article is Available in BioRxiv: https://doi.org/10.1101/2024.02.12.579944.

© The Author(s), under exclusive license to Springer Nature Switzerland AG 2024
J. Ma (Ed.): RECOMB 2024, LNCS 14758, pp. 336–339, 2024.
https://doi.org/10.1007/978-1-0716-3989-4_25

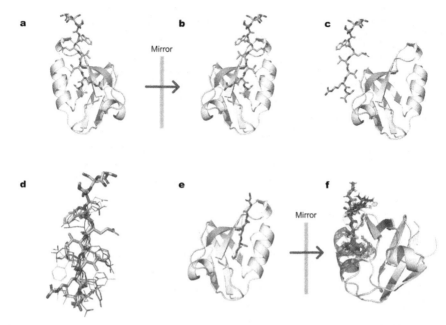

Fig. 1. DexDesign on CALP. **a)** The inhibitor L-kCAL01 (pink) bound to L-CALP (cyan). **b)** The complex is reflected to D-space. **c)** The peptide and protein components are split. **d)** MASTER [9] uses D-kCAL01 to query an L-protein database, returning substructure that are similar to D-kCAL01 (pink sticks). Ten L-segments matches (multicolored wires) are overlaid. **e)** L-matches are aligned to D-kCAL01, which is then removed. An L-peptide (purple) is selected for redesign. **f)** The L-peptide:D-CALP complex is reflected to form a D-peptide:L-CALP complex. The K* provable binding affinity algorithm [10], alongside novel techniques (see Sect. 2.2), is invoked to optimize D-peptide binding. Two mutations, with interactions visualized with Molprobity dots [11], improved predicted binding affinity (K_D) 9-fold. (Color figure online)

2 Methods

2.1 Energy-Equivariant Geometric Transformations, MASTER, and K*

Energy-equivariant geometric transformations, such as reflection, are isometries that do not change structural energy due to symmetry in the energy field [12]. For example, an energy function will compute the same energy of protein structure s and s reflected over the Cartesian x-y plane. OSPREY algorithms mimic this physics precisely, allowing us to add the ability to design on mixed-chirality systems.

The MASTER algorithm [9] searches a database of protein structures using a user-specified query structure and is guaranteed to find all protein substructures in the database with a backbone RMSD below a cutoff threshold. DexDesign invokes MASTER to generate D-peptide scaffolds with backbone conformations similar to their L-peptide counterpart, and then invokes K* to optimize amino acid sequences and side chain conformations on these scaffolds. The DexDesign algorithm is specified as:

1. Let s_n be a protein structure with n residues. We define substructure $s_{i,j}$ of s, where $1 \leq i < j \leq n$, to be a structure of residues i through j of s.

2. Let $r(s, a)$ be a function that reflects all atoms in protein structure s across a plane a. Without loss of generality, we let a be the x-y plane and define $r(s) = r(s, a)$ henceforth. Then, $r(s)$ reflects all L-amino acids, including those with multiple stereocenters (*viz.*, threonine and isoleucine), into their corresponding D-versions, and vice-versa.

3. Let $M(DB, s, c)$ be the MASTER subroutine. M returns a set of substructures from the database (DB) with backbone RMSD, when optimally aligned with protein substructure s, less than c Å.

4. Let $\mathcal{O}(p,t)$ be the OSPREY K* subroutine. $\mathcal{O}$ redesigns peptide p towards increased binding affinity with protein target t by searching over mutated and continuously minimized amino acid sidechains, and returns a set of mutant sequences (and structural molecular ensembles) derived from p that have improved binding with t.

2.2 Novel Features and Design Techniques in OSPREY

In the process of developing DexDesign, we have added the capability of OSPREY to use customizable conformation libraries. Design parameters (i.e., mutable residues, flexible residues, etc.) are now a user-modifiable input to the algorithm, unlocking new design capabilities. Further, we have formulated three new techniques that allow for rapid *de novo* design of scaffolds.

Minimum Flexible Set: The unique set of residues that must be modeled as continuously flexible to resolve clashes from MASTER-returned scaffolds. This enables selection of scaffolds amenable to low-cost design, saving compute resources for location of mutations that increase binding affinity.

Inverse Alanine Scanning: Inspired by experimental alanine scans, this technique determines point mutations on the peptide that increase predicted binding given high flexibility. This is deemed *Inverse* because all of the peptide's residues, except the residue of interest, are mutated to alanine. The target residue is evaluated at all 20 D-amino acid identities. This provides data on effective mutations and protein flexibility, implementing combinatorial reductions in the conformational search space.

K-based Mutational Scanning*: This technique systematically mutates each residue in the scaffold to all 19 other D-amino acids. Positive mutations are used in subsequent K* designs with simultaneous peptide mutations, optimizing binding. This resulted in significant improvements to predicted binding.

3   Results

The D-peptide inhibitors produced by DexDesign are predicted to outcompete endogenous ligands and establish desirable hydrogen bonds while exploiting the unique geometry of D-amino acids to form novel, favorable contacts. The best designs for MAST2 and CALP are predicted to improved K_D 5- and 46-fold, respectively, over the endogenous ligand.

Acknowledgments. We thank all members of the Donald lab for helpful discussions and the NIH (grants R35-GM144042 to BRD and AI139216 to PZ) for funding.

Software Availability. OSPREY can be found at github.com/donaldlab/OSPREY3.

Disclosure of Interests. BRD is a founder of Ten63 therapeutics, Inc. NSG was employed by Ten63 therapeutics, Inc. In 2024.

References

1. Fosgerau, K., Hoffmann, T.: Peptide therapeutics: current status and future directions. Drug Discov. Today **20**, 122–128 (2015). https://doi.org/10.1016/j.drudis.2014.10.003
2. Craik, D.J., Fairlie, D.P., Liras, S., Price, D.: The future of peptide-based drugs. Chem. Biol. Drug Des. **81**, 136–147 (2013). https://doi.org/10.1111/cbdd.12055
3. Di, L.: Strategic approaches to optimizing peptide ADME properties. AAPS J. **17**, 134–143 (2014). https://doi.org/10.1208/s12248-014-9687-3
4. Liu, M., et al.: D-peptide inhibitors of the p53-MDM2 interaction for targeted molecular therapy of malignant neoplasms. Proc. Natl. Acad. Sci. U.S.A. **107**, 14321–14326 (2010). https://doi.org/10.1073/pnas.1008930107
5. Amacher, J.F., Brooks, L., Hampton, T.H., Madden, D.R.: Specificity in PDZ-peptide interaction networks: computational analysis and review. J. Struct. Biol. X **4**, 100022 (2020). https://doi.org/10.1016/j.yjsbx.2020.100022
6. Hallen, M.A., et al.: OSPREY 3.0: open-source protein redesign for you, with powerful new features. J. Comput. Chem. **39**, 2494–2507 (2018). https://doi.org/10.1002/jcc.25522
7. Holt, G.T., et al.: Computational analysis of energy landscapes reveals dynamic features that contribute to binding of inhibitors to CFTR-associated ligand. J. Phys. Chem. B **123**, 10441–10455 (2019). https://doi.org/10.1021/acs.jpcb.9b07278
8. Valiente, M., et al.: Binding of PTEN to specific PDZ domains contributes to PTEN protein stability and phosphorylation by microtubule-associated Serine/Threonine Kinases. J. Biol. Chem. **280**, 28936–28943 (2005). https://doi.org/10.1074/jbc.M504761200
9. Zhou, J., Grigoryan, G.: Rapid search for tertiary fragments reveals protein sequence–structure relationships. Protein Sci. Publ. Protein Soc. **24**, 508–524 (2015). https://doi.org/10.1002/pro.2610
10. Gainza, P., Roberts, K.E., Donald, B.R.: Protein design using continuous rotamers. PLoS Comput. Biol. **8**, e1002335 (2012). https://doi.org/10.1371/journal.pcbi.1002335
11. Jou, J.D., Guerin, N., Roberts, K.E.: Protein Design Plugin (2023)
12. Noether, E.: Gesammelte Abhandlungen - Collected Papers, 1st edn. Springer, Berlin, Heidelberg (1983)

Memory-Bound and Taxonomy-Aware K-Mer Selection for Ultra-Large Reference Libraries

Ali Osman Berk Şapcı[2] and Siavash Mirarab[1,2(✉)]

[1] Bioinformatics and Systems Biology Graduate Program, UC San Diego, San Diego, CA 92093, USA
[2] Department of Electrical and Computer Engineering, UC San Diego, San Diego, CA 92093, USA
{asapci,smirarab}@ucsd.edu

Abstract. Classifying sequencing reads based on k-mer matches to a reference library is widely used in applications such as taxonomic profiling. Given the ever-increasing number of genomes publicly available, it is increasingly impossible to keep all or a majority of their k-mers in memory. Thus, there is a growing need for methods for selecting a subset of k-mers while accounting for taxonomic relationships. We propose k-mer RANKer (KRANK), a method that uses a set of heuristics to efficiently and effectively select a size-constrained subset of k-mers from a diverse and imbalanced taxonomy that suffers biased sampling. Empirical evaluations demonstrate that a fraction of all k-mers in large reference libraries can achieve comparable accuracy to the full set.

Keywords: k-mer selection · k-mer minimization · Reference library construction · Taxonomic classification · Abundance profiling · Metagenomics

Motivation and Background. Matching sequencing reads to reference libraries of genomes is used in many applications, including metagenomic taxonomic profiling and contamination detection. The number of available genomes has been growing dramatically in recent years, providing an opportunity to better identify *query* sequences. It has been long appreciated that the accuracy of many applications heavily depends on having access to dense reference sets and utilizing those reference sets effectively [3]. This opportunity, however, faces a practical obstacle as computational resources, especially the memory, needed to build ultra-large reference libraries can grow beyond what is available.

Several leading methods for taxonomic read classification rely on matching k-mers from query sequences to k-mers extracted from reference genomes using easily searchable data structures such as hash tables [2,5,6]. Many of these methods use various strategies to select a subset of all k-mers to be saved in the reference library, which ultimately needs to be kept in the memory. Kraken-II [6], for

© The Author(s), under exclusive license to Springer Nature Switzerland AG 2024
J. Ma (Ed.): RECOMB 2024, LNCS 14758, pp. 340–343, 2024.
https://doi.org/10.1007/978-1-0716-3989-4_26

Algorithm 1. KRANK algorithm. Functions are described in the text.
1: **procedure** BUILDLIBRARY(t)
2:    **if** $t \in S$ **then**   ▷ Checks if t is a member of the bottom rank: species.
3:       $\mathcal{K}_t \leftarrow$ EXTRACTKMERS(t)   ▷ Extract k-mers from genomes for species t.
4:       **return** ($\mathbf{H}_t \leftarrow$ CONSTRUCTTABLE($\mathcal{K}_t$))   ▷ Computes encodings and LSHs.
5:    **for all** $t' \in$ child(t) **do**
6:       $\mathbf{H}_{t'} \leftarrow$ BUILDLIBRARY(t')   ▷ Recursively calls BUILDLIBRARY for each child.
7:    $\mathbf{H}_t \leftarrow$ an empty table with 2^{2h} rows
8:    **for all** $t' \in$ child(t) **do**
9:       $\mathbf{H}_t \leftarrow$ UNIONTABLES($\mathbf{H}_{t'}, \mathbf{H}_t$) ▷ Takes the union of parent and children tables.
10:   $M(t) \leftarrow$ ADAPTIVESIZECONSTRAINT(t) ▷ Computes the maximum allowed size.
11:   $n \leftarrow |\mathbf{H}_t| - M(t)$ ▷ Computes number of extra k-mers currently in the table
12:   **if** $n > 0$ **then**   ▷ Checks if there are more k-mers than if the allowed size.
13:      FILTERBYRANK($\mathbf{H}_t, n$) ▷ Ranks and removes k-mers to satisfy the constraint.
14:   **return** $\mathbf{H}_t$

instance, uses the widely-adopted minimizers [4,7]. We argue that beyond minimization, which focuses on reducing overlap between selected k-mers, we need to consider the evolutionary dimension as well. Such a goal is most relevant when a library consists of taxonomically diverse sets of species. A notable attempt in selecting k-mers in a taxonomy-aware fashion is seeking discriminative k-mers [2] specific to a taxonomic group but not found in other groups.

Building representative libraries needs to contend with peculiarities of available taxonomies (e.g., the vast diversity of genomes within some groups), and the heavily biased and imbalanced sampling of species in reference sets (e.g., 35947 *Escherichia* genomes in RefSeq) [1]. Our goal is to find k-mer subsets that do not leave out poorly sampled groups, work across taxonomic ranks, and keep the required information to enable classifying relatively novel reads. To this end, we developed k-mer RANKer (KRANK), which takes a taxonomy and a set of genomes labeled with the taxonomy as input. KRANK selects a size-constrained subset of k-mers from these genomes based on its ranking strategy. The tool is implemented as a highly optimized C++ software.

KRANK Algorithm. We are given a taxonomic tree and a set of genomes $\mathcal{G}$ labeled by the taxonomy. Let $\mathcal{T}$ denote the set of all nodes of the taxonomy. Let $\mathcal{S} \subseteq \mathcal{T}$ be the set of species, and for $t \in \mathcal{T}$, let $\mathcal{S}_t \subset \mathcal{S}$ be the subset of species under node t. We define $\mathcal{K}$ as the set all of distinct k-mers across all genomes $g \in \mathcal{G}$. $\mathcal{K}_t$ denotes the set of k-mers of all genomes labeled by a taxon $t \in \mathcal{T}$. Algorithm 1 shows the overall KRANK strategy. We next discuss three main aspects of the algorithm.

Hierarchical k-mer Selection. The backbone of KRANK's algorithm is a postorder traversal of a given taxonomic tree. During the traversal, KRANK recursively combines selected k-mer sets of sibling taxa to construct parent's k-mer set, and finally, at the root, it returns the selected subset of reference k-mers with the desired size. At leaves of the tree, defined to be $\mathcal{S}$, KRANK simply extracts the k-mer set from all genomes belonging to the corresponding species ($t \in \mathcal{S}$), and builds a hash table $\mathbf{H}_t$, using locality-sensitive hashing (LSH) as implemented through the bit-sampling approach. In order to keep the size of the final table within the memory-bound, KRANK removes *some* k-mers at each internal node. The number of k-mers kept for each internal node, denoted by $M(t)$, is defined by a heuristic, discussed next. When the size of the table at t, $|\mathbf{H}_t|$, exceeds its size constraint $M(t)$, KRANK ranks k-mers based on criteria discussed below and removes enough low-ranked k-mers to satisfy size constraints.

Adaptive Size Constraint. We need to decide how many k-mers should be kept at taxon t. Clearly, the upper bound is the total budget, $M(t) \leq M$, and we wish to use the entire budget for the final table: $M(\text{root}) = M$. We define $r : \mathcal{T} \rightarrow (0, 1]$ to assign a portion of the entire budget M to each node t; any function r is valid as long as it takes the value 1 at the root (i.e., $r(\text{root}) = 1$) and increases as we move up the tree. Furthermore, if the budget assigned to the parent is bounded by the sum of its children, k-mers will be gradually removed moving up. We set

$$M(t) = \begin{cases} |\mathcal{K}_t| & t \in \mathcal{S}, \\ \sqrt{r(t)}M & \text{otherwise,} \end{cases} \tag{1}$$

noting that $\sum_{t' \in \text{child}(t)} M(t') \geq M(t)$ due to the concavity of the square root, making the size constraint more restrictive as we move up. For $r(t)$, KRANK chooses the following quantity among alternatives based on empirical evaluation:

$$r(t) = \frac{\sum_{s \in \mathcal{S}_t} |\mathcal{K}_s|}{\sum_{s \in \mathcal{S}} |\mathcal{K}_s|}.$$

Which k-mers to filter? Three options immediately present themselves — removing randomly, keeping *discriminative* k-mers unique to some taxa, or conversely, keeping *shared* k-mers present in many taxa. To assess how discriminative or shared a k-mer x is, we simply use the number of species that have x in at least one genome. For a k-mer $x \in \mathcal{K}$ and a set of taxa $\mathcal{T}' \subset \mathcal{T}$, we define $\mathrm{R}(x, t) = |\{y : x \in \mathcal{K}_y, y \in \mathcal{S}_t\}|$, denoting the cardinality of the subset of species under t which have x. Ranking k-mers by this value at an internal node, and removing k-mers with low or high $\mathrm{R}(x, t)$ corresponds to filtering discriminative k-mers or shared k-mers, respectively. Our extensive empirical investigation reveals that neither option is better than random filtering, and filtering shared k-mers significantly degrades the taxonomic identification performance. Thus, we need a better approach. In addition to maximizing total species coverage, we also wish to ensure that no species is left uncovered. While this can be imposed as a complex set covering problem, in the interest of running time, we opt for a simple approach using weighted sums. We rank k-mers based on the following quantity

$$R^* (x, t) = \sum_{t' \in \text{child}(t)} w_{t'}(x) \cdot R(x, t')$$

where $w_{t'}$ down-weights groups that are highly sampled among surviving k-mers. We define the weight of a k-mer x locally for its row by setting it to be inversely proportional to the *coverage* of each child taxon among k-mers of that row:

$$w_{t'}(x) = 1/|\{x' \ : \ x' \in \mathbf{H}_{t'}, \text{LSH}(x) = \text{LSH}(x')\}|$$

These weights favor children with fewer surviving k-mers by making them more likely to get covered by the parent.

Empirical Results. Using a moderately large dataset [8], we demonstrated the ability of KRANK to reduce the size without sacrificing accuracy. In particular, we showed that KRANK, when paired with CONSULT-II's algorithm, can reduce memory use from 140.7 Gb to 51.2 Gb without sacrificing the accuracy in both read classification and taxonomic profiling. Further reducing the memory down to 12 Gb reduces the F1 classification accuracy by only 2.5%.

Availability. The tool is available under https://github.com/bo1929/KRANK and data are available under https://github.com/bo1929/shared.KRANK. The full paper is available at http://doi.org/10.1101/2024.02.12.580015.

References

1. Nasko, D.J., Koren, S., Phillippy, A.M., Treangen, T.J.: RefSeq database growth influences the accuracy of k-mer-based lowest common ancestor species identification. Genome Biol. **19**(1), 165 (2018). https://doi.org/10.1186/s13059-018-1554-6
2. Ounit, R., Lonardi, S.: Higher classification sensitivity of short metagenomic reads with CLARK-S. Bioinformatics (Oxford, England) **32**(24), 3823–3825 (2016). https://doi.org/10.1093/bioinformatics/btw542
3. Pachiadaki, M.G., et al.: Charting the complexity of the marine microbiome through single-cell genomics. Cell **179**(7), 1623-1635.e11 (2019). https://doi.org/10.1016/j.cell.2019.11.017
4. Roberts, M., Hayes, W., Hunt, B.R., Mount, S.M., Yorke, J.A.: Reducing storage requirements for biological sequence comparison. Bioinformatics (Oxford, England) **20**(18), 3363–3369 (2004). https://doi.org/10.1093/bioinformatics/bth408
5. Şapcı, A.O.B., Rachtman, E., Mirarab, S.: CONSULT-II: accurate taxonomic identification and profiling using locality-sensitive hashing. bioRxiv (2024). https://doi.org/10.1101/2023.11.07.566115
6. Wood, D.E., Lu, J., Langmead, B.: Improved metagenomic analysis with Kraken 2. Genome Biol. **20**(1), 257 (2019). https://doi.org/10.1186/s13059-019-1891-0
7. Zheng, H., Marçais, G., Kingsford, C.: Creating and using minimizer sketches in computational genomics. J. Comput. Biol., cmb.2023.0094 (2023). https://doi.org/10.1089/cmb.2023.0094
8. Zhu, Q., et al.: Reference phylogeny for microbes (data pre-release) (2019)

SpaCeNet: Spatial Cellular Networks from Omics Data

Stefan Schrod[1]⬤, Niklas Lück[1], Robert Lohmayer[2]⬤, Stefan Solbrig[3],
Tina Wipfler[3], Katherine H. Shutta[4,5], Marouen Ben Guebila[4]⬤,
Andreas Schäfer[3]⬤, Tim Beißbarth[1,6]⬤, Helena U. Zacharias[7]⬤,
Peter J. Oefner[8]⬤, John Quackenbush[4]⬤, and Michael Altenbuchinger[1(✉)]⬤

[1] Department of Medical Bioinformatics, University Medical Center Göttingen,
Göttingen, Germany
michael.altenbuchinger@bioinf.med.uni-goettingen.de
[2] Leibniz Institute for Immunotherapy, 93053 Regensburg, Germany
[3] Institute of Theoretical Physics, University of Regensburg, Regensburg, Germany
[4] Department of Biostatistics, Harvard T.H. Chan School of Public Health,
Boston, MA, USA
[5] Channing Division of Network Medicine, Department of Medicine,
Brigham and Women's Hospital, Boston, MA, USA
[6] Campus Institute Data Science (CIDAS), University of Göttingen,
Göttingen, Germany
[7] Peter L. Reichertz Institute for Medical Informatics of TU Braunschweig
and Hannover Medical School, Hannover Medical School, Hannover, Germany
[8] Institute of Functional Genomics, University of Regensburg, Regensburg, Germany

Abstract. We propose SpaCeNet as a method for analyzing patterns of correlation in spatial transcriptomics data. SpaCeNet extends the concept of conditional independence to spatially distributed information, and disentangles conditional independence relations between inter- and intra-cellular variables. Moreover, SpaCeNet addresses the various length scales over which intercellular communication occurs via flexible interaction potentials in combination with appropriate regularization strategies.

Keywords: Spatial Transcriptomics · Intercellular Interactions

1 Introduction

Recent advances in spatial transcriptomics (ST) have enabled the molecular profiling of single cells in their spatial context. Cells exchange signals, which induce downstream effects and thereby determine their molecular phenotypes. Thus, ST data opens a window into the effects of interactions between cells in shaping the transcriptional landscape. We introduce the theoretical foundations needed to resolve cell-cell interactions from ST data and propose SpaCeNet as an efficient algorithmic solution [4]. The full manuscript is available at https://doi.org/10.1101/2022.09.01.506219, and our implementation at https://github.com/sschrod/SpaCeNet.

S. Schrod and N. Lück—These authors contributed equally to this work and share first authorship.

© The Author(s), under exclusive license to Springer Nature Switzerland AG 2024
J. Ma (Ed.): RECOMB 2024, LNCS 14758, pp. 344–347, 2024.
https://doi.org/10.1007/978-1-0716-3989-4_27

2   Methods

We assume potentially high-dimensional single-cell resolved molecular data annotated with spatial information (e.g., transcriptomic profiles of single cells together with their positions in space). We denote the molecular variables as X_i with $i = 1, \ldots, p$. Further, let $\mathbf{X} = [\mathbf{x}^1, \ldots, \mathbf{x}^n]^\top \in \mathbb{R}^{n \times p}$ be a data matrix with n profiles $\mathbf{x}^a$ in its rows, each annotated with the position r_a of cell a.

Spatial Conditional Independence: Conditional independence (CI) is key to the inference of molecular networks, as it allows the disentanglement of direct and indirect statistical relationships [1]. CI between variables X_i and X_j given all remaining variables can be expressed as $X_i \perp X_j|\{\text{rest}\}$, where "rest" refers to the set of all variables in X except X_i and X_j. We extend this language to intra- and intercellular spatial conditional independence (SCI):

Intracellular SCI relations between variables X_i^a and X_j^a measured within one cell a are expressed as $X_i^a \perp X_j^a|\{\text{rest}\}$ with the term "rest" referring to all other variables of cell a and to all variables of all other cells.

Intercellular SCI relations between variables X_i^a and X_j^b measured in different cells a and b, conditioned on all remaining variables, are denoted as $X_i^a \perp X_j^b|\{\text{rest}\}$ with $a \neq b$ and "rest" referring to all variables of cell a except X_i^a, all variables of cell b except X_j^b, and all variables of all remaining cells.

Joint Probability Distribution: Gaussian graphical models (GGMs) assume data to follow a multivariate normal distribution. SpaCeNet is an np-dimensional GGM that encodes SCI relationships in the joint probability density

$$f_{\text{full}}(\mathbf{X}|\mathbf{R}) = \sqrt{\frac{\det \boldsymbol{\Lambda}}{(2\pi)^{np}}} \exp\left\{ -\frac{1}{2}(\boldsymbol{\xi} - \mathbf{m})^\top \boldsymbol{\Lambda}(\boldsymbol{\xi} - \mathbf{m}) \right\}. \tag{1}$$

The precision matrix $\boldsymbol{\Lambda}$, which is required to be symmetric and positive definite, captures both intra- and intercellular SCI relations. In f_{full}, the individual cells' profiles $\mathbf{x}^a \in \mathbb{R}^p, a = 1, \ldots, n$, are stacked vertically in $\boldsymbol{\xi} = \text{vec}(\mathbf{X}^\top) \in \mathbb{R}^{np}$, and we use a global, location-agnostic mean vector $\boldsymbol{\mu}$ for all $\mathbf{x}^a$ such that $\mathbf{m} = \mathbf{1}_n \otimes \boldsymbol{\mu} = (\mu_1, \ldots, \mu_p, \mu_1, \ldots, \mu_p, \ldots)^\top$. All pairwise cell-cell distances are collected in a matrix $\mathbf{R} = (r_{ab}) \in \mathbb{R}^{n \times n}$, where r_{ab} is the Euclidean distance between cells a and b. We decompose the precision matrix $\boldsymbol{\Lambda} \in \mathbb{R}^{np \times np}$ into $\boldsymbol{\Lambda} = \boldsymbol{\Lambda}_{\text{within}} + \boldsymbol{\Lambda}_{\text{between}}$, where $\boldsymbol{\Lambda}_{\text{within}} = \mathbb{I}_n \otimes \boldsymbol{\Omega}$ represents intracellular (within-cell) associations and

$$\boldsymbol{\Lambda}_{\text{between}} = \begin{pmatrix} \mathbf{0}_{p \times p} & \boldsymbol{\Lambda}_{\text{between}}^{12} & \cdots & \boldsymbol{\Lambda}_{\text{between}}^{1n} \\ \boldsymbol{\Lambda}_{\text{between}}^{21} & \mathbf{0}_{p \times p} & & \vdots \\ \vdots & & \ddots & \boldsymbol{\Lambda}_{\text{between}}^{(n-1)n} \\ \boldsymbol{\Lambda}_{\text{between}}^{n1} & \cdots & \boldsymbol{\Lambda}_{\text{between}}^{n(n-1)} & \mathbf{0}_{p \times p} \end{pmatrix} \tag{2}$$

contains the intercellular (between-cell) associations. The parametrization of Λ_{within} implies that the same matrix $\boldsymbol{\Omega} = (\omega_{ij}) \in \mathbb{R}^{p \times p}$ encodes the intracellular associations for all cells (i.e., $\omega_{ij} = 0 \Leftrightarrow X_i^a \perp X_j^a | \{\text{rest}\} \; \forall a$).

Key to SpaCeNet is a meaningful parametrization of Λ_{between}. We assume that the intercellular association of gene i in any cell a with gene j in any other cell b can be described by a function of the cells' Euclidean distance r_{ab}. With a set of radial cell-cell interaction potentials $\rho_{ij}(r)$, we parametrize $\Lambda_{\text{between}}^{ab} = (\rho_{ij}(r_{ab})) \in \mathbb{R}^{p \times p}$. From Eq. (1), we see that

$$X_i^a \perp X_j^b | \{\text{rest}\} \quad \text{with} \quad a \neq b \quad \Leftrightarrow \quad \rho_{ij}(r_{ab}) = 0 \,,$$

where the term "rest" refers to all variables of cell a except X_i^a, all variables of cell b except X_j^b, and all variables of all other cells. Thus, all intercellular SCI relations are encoded in the set of $p(p+1)/2$ independent functions $\rho_{ij}(r) = \rho_{ji}(r)$. Since cells that are infinitely separated do not interact, we require $\rho_{ij}(r) = 0$ for $r \to \infty$. To approximate $\rho_{ij}(r)$, we use a power-series in $(1 - e^{-r/r_0}) \frac{r_0}{r}$, given by $\rho_{ij}^*(r) = \sum_{l=1}^{L} \Delta\rho_{ij}^{(l)} \left(1 - e^{-r/r_0}\right)^l \left(\frac{r_0}{r}\right)^l$, where l is the order in the series expansion and $\boldsymbol{\Delta\rho}^{(l)} = (\Delta\rho_{ij}^{(l)}) \in \mathbb{R}^{p \times p}$ the corresponding coefficient matrix (required to be symmetric). This leads to an approximation for the intercellular precision matrix Λ_{between} given by

$$\Lambda_{\text{between}}^* = \sum_{l=1}^{L} \boldsymbol{\Theta}^{(l)} \otimes \boldsymbol{\Delta\rho}^{(l)} \tag{3}$$

with $\Theta_{aa}^{(l)} = 0$ for all a and $\Theta_{ab}^{(l)} = (1 - e^{-r_{ab}/r_0})^l \left(\frac{r_0}{r_{ab}}\right)^l$ for $a \neq b$. This expansion naturally fulfills $\lim_{r \to \infty} \rho_{ij}^*(r) = 0$ and $\lim_{r \to 0} \rho_{ij}^*(r) = c_{ij}$ with constants $c_{ij} = \sum_{l=1}^{L} \Delta\rho_{ij}^{(l)}$. Note, an expansion in $(1 - e^{-r/r_0}) \frac{r_0}{r}$ has the advantage that terms do not diverge for $r \to 0$, which is in contrast to an expansion in $1/r$. Thus, the factor $(1 - e^{-r/r_0})$ smoothes the divergence and the amount of smoothing is determined by the length-scale parameter r_0.

The precision matrix Λ is of size $np \times np$, which makes a naive maximum-likelihood-based estimate intractable for reasonably large p and n. We address this issue via pseudo-log-likelihood (PLL), which is a computationally efficient and consistent estimator formed by products of all conditional distributions [2, 3]. Let $\mathbf{X}^{\backslash a}$ denote all gene expression levels in all cells except cell a, and $\mathbf{x}_{\backslash j}^a$ denote all gene expression levels in cell a except gene j. Then, the densities

$$f_c(x_j^a | \mathbf{R}, \mathbf{X}^{\backslash a}, \mathbf{x}_{\backslash j}^a) = \sqrt{\frac{\omega_{jj}}{2\pi}} \exp\left\{ -\frac{1}{2}\omega_{jj}\left(x_j^a - \mu_j \right.\right.$$

$$\left.\left. + \frac{1}{\omega_{jj}}\left[\sum_{k \neq j}^{p} \omega_{jk}(x_k^a - \mu_k) + \sum_{b=1}^{n}\sum_{l=1}^{L}\sum_{k=1}^{p}(\Theta_{ab}^{(l)}\Delta\rho_{jk}^{(l)})(x_k^b - \mu_k)\right]\right)^2\right\} \tag{4}$$

yield the PLL $\ell(\boldsymbol{\Omega}, \boldsymbol{\Delta\rho}^{(\cdot)}, \boldsymbol{\mu}) = \sum_{a=1}^{n} \sum_{j=1}^{p} \log\left(f_{c}(x_{j}^{a}|\mathbf{R}, \mathbf{X}^{\backslash a}, \mathbf{x}_{\backslash j}^{a})\right)$. For S independent ST slides, the full optimization goal of SpaCeNet becomes

$$\underset{\boldsymbol{\Omega}, \boldsymbol{\Delta\rho}^{(\cdot)}, \boldsymbol{\mu}}{\text{minimize}} \left\{ -\sum_{s=1}^{S} \ell_{s}(\boldsymbol{\Omega}, \boldsymbol{\Delta\rho}^{(\cdot)}, \boldsymbol{\mu}) + nS \left(\alpha \sum_{i<j} |\omega_{ij}| + \beta \sum_{i\leq j} \sqrt{\sum_{l=1}^{L} \left(\Delta\rho_{ij}^{(l)}\right)^{2}} \right) \right\},$$

which penalizes the off-diagonal elements of the intracellular precision matrix $\boldsymbol{\Omega}$ via L_1 regularization [5] and the intercellular interactions via group-lasso terms [6], where the groups contain the interaction coefficients at different orders $l = 1, \ldots, L$. This induces sparseness in the potentials ρ_{ij} and not just in the different orders of its expansion, where α and β calibrate the regularization.

3   Summary

We developed SpaCeNet – a statistical framework to model cell-cell interactions in a spatial context. With approaches such as SpaCeNet, new upcoming ST data can be analyzed to improve our understanding of cellular functioning, growth, development, and disease processes.

Acknowledgments. HUZ, MA, and PJO were supported by the German Federal Ministry of Education and Research (BMBF) (01ZX1912A, 01ZX1912C, and 01EJ2202B). SS, NL, and MA were funded by the Deutsche Forschungsgemeinschaft (DFG) [AL 2355/1-1]. JQ, MBG, and KHS were supported by the NCI under awards U24CA231846 (JQ, MBG) and R35CA220523 (JQ, MBG, KHS). JQ was supported by the NHGRI (R01HG011393) of the US NIH. KHS was supported by the US NHLBI (P01HL114501 and T32HL007427).

The authors declare no competing interests.

References

1. Altenbuchinger, M., Weihs, A., Quackenbush, J., Grabe, H.J., Zacharias, H.U.: Gaussian and mixed graphical models as (multi-) omics data analysis tools. Biochimica et Biophysica Acta (BBA)-Gene Regulatory Mechanisms **1863**(6), 194418 (2020)
2. Besag, J.: Statistical analysis of non-lattice data. J. Roy. Stat. Soc. Ser. D (Stat.) **24**(3), 179–195 (1975)
3. Lee, J.D., Hastie, T.J.: Learning the structure of mixed graphical models. J. Comput. Graph. Stat. **24**(1), 230–253 (2015)
4. Schrod, S., et al.: Spacenet: spatial cellular networks from omics data. bioRxiv (2024). https://doi.org/10.1101/2022.09.01.506219
5. Tibshirani, R.: Regression shrinkage and selection via the lasso. J. Roy. Stat. Soc. Ser. B (Methodol.) **58**(1), 267–288 (1996)
6. Yuan, M., Lin, Y.: Model selection and estimation in regression with grouped variables. J. Roy. Stat. Soc. Ser. B (Stat. Methodol.) **68**(1), 49–67 (2006)

Discovering and Overcoming the Bias in Neoantigen Identification by Unified Machine Learning Models

Ziting Zhang, Wenxu Wu, Lei Wei, and Xiaowo Wang$^{(\boxtimes)}$

Ministry of Education Key Laboratory of Bioinformatics; Center for Synthetic and Systems Biology; Bioinformatics Division, Beijing National Research Center for Information Science and Technology; Department of Automation, Tsinghua University, Beijing, China
xwwang@tsinghua.edu.cn

Abstract. Neoantigens, formed by genetic mutations in tumor cells, are abnormal peptides that can trigger immune responses. Precisely identifying neoantigens from vast mutations is the key to tumor immunotherapy design. There are three main steps in the neoantigen immune process, i.e., binding with MHCs, extracellular presentation, and induction of immunogenicity. Various machine learning methods have been developed to predict the probability of one of the three events, but the overall accuracy of neoantigen identification remains far from satisfactory. To gain a systematic understanding of the key factors of neoantigen identification, we developed a unified transformer-based machine learning framework ImmuBPI that comprised three tasks and achieved state-of-the-art performance. Through cross-task model interpretation, we have discovered an underestimation of data bias for immunogenicity prediction, which has led to skewed discriminatory boundaries of current machine learning models. We designed a mutual information-based debiasing strategy that performed well on mutation variants immunogenicity prediction, a task where current methods fell short. Clustering immunogenic peptides with debiased representations uncovers unique preferences for biophysical properties, such as hydrophobicity and polarity. These observations serve as an important complement to the past understanding that accurately predicting neoantigen is constrained by limited data, highlighting the necessity of bias control. We expect this study will provide novel and insightful perspectives for neoantigen prediction methods and benefit future neoantigen-mediated immunotherapy designs.

Keywords: neoantigen identification · data bias · machine learning · attention mechanism

1 Introduction

Tumor immunotherapy is a promising, rapidly growing generation of cancer treatment that aims to kill cancer cells by leveraging one's own immune system [6]. To achieve precise killing effects, the immune system relies on specific

© The Author(s), under exclusive license to Springer Nature Switzerland AG 2024
J. Ma (Ed.): RECOMB 2024, LNCS 14758, pp. 348–351, 2024.
https://doi.org/10.1007/978-1-0716-3989-4_28

markers called neoantigens. They are a subset of abnormal peptides originating from genetic mutations within tumor cells. Accurately identifying neoantigens from vast tumor mutations can significantly contribute to immunotherapy development [5].

There are three main steps in the neoantigen immune process, i.e., binding with Major Histocompatibility Complexes (MHCs), which is also called Human Leukocyte Antigen (HLA) in humans, extracellular presentation, and induction of immunogenicity by forming interactions with the T cell receptor (TCR). In recent years, a plethora of machine learning methods have been developed to predict each of the above three processes related to neoantigens [1–4,8], each of which contributes to neoantigen identification from different perspectives. However, the overall accuracy of neoantigen identification remains far from satisfactory [9].

One limitation in this field is the lack of a systematic view and understanding of the complicated, multi-step processes involved in neoantigen identification. Contrary to the intensive focus on improving model performance for individual tasks, few studies have explored relationships among models trained for diverse immunological tasks (Fig. 1A). Another challenge arises from substantial data bias, caused by inevitable batch effect and high experimental cost with immunological assays [5] (Fig. 1B). To address these challenges, we established a unified machine learning framework, named ImmuBPI (**Immu**ne predictors for **B**inding, **P**resentation, and **I**mmunogenicity), to model three key steps of the neoantigen immune response process.

2   Methods

We designed a transformer encoder-based model backbone with an attention-pooling mechanism to build the ImmuBPI framework (Fig. 1C). To achieve a high classification performance, we chose an interaction-based model rather than a representation-based model [7]. The primary motivation for building a unified framework was to make our analysis as universal as possible with popular and standard model architecture and to leverage the attention mechanism for interpretability.

We measured the unbalancedness and detected the bias candidate by mutual information (MI) between the label y and some parts of the features $\mathbf{x}$ (denoting as x'). We can consider the marginal-conditional formulation of MI:

$$I(x'; y) = H(y) - H(y|x') = -H(y|x') - (-H(y)) \qquad (1)$$

The entropy of a distribution measures its uniformity. Therefore, the MI between feature x' and label y quantifies the increase in imbalance of y when transitioning from an unknown x' to a given x'. High MI suggests that feature x' is a potential candidate for either being a biased feature or a pivotal feature influencing the label y. In this work, we showed that both the HLA allele and peptide anchor positions exhibited a high MI score but weak causal relationships with the label. These features were masked before input as a debiasing strategy.

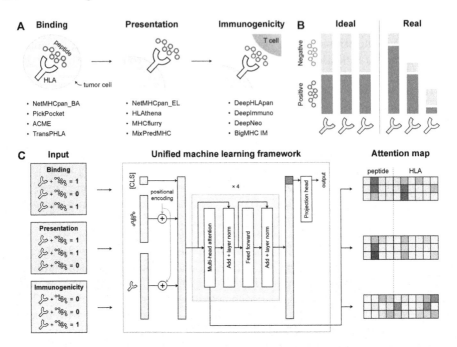

Fig. 1. (A) Various models have been applied to model three immunological tasks involved in neoantigen predictions. (B) An ideal distribution (left) should achieve a balance in both the number of peptides related to different HLA alleles and the ratio of positive peptides to negative peptides given a specific HLA allele. Dataset distributions in real-world scenarios (right). (C) The overview of ImmuBPI framework.

3   Results

ImmuBPI demonstrated superior predictive power with attention mechanisms as a powerful model indicator. Through interpretability analysis across different tasks, we have identified a significant bias in the immunogenicity dataset that could lead data-driven models to learn skewed discriminatory boundaries (Fig. 2). As the ratio between the number of positive and negative peptides given a specific HLA allele constitutes a highly variable feature for different HLA alleles, we demonstrated that the model may learn shortcuts to make decisions using this feature. To address the challenge, we developed a mutual information-based debiasing strategy that enabled the model to perform sensitive immunogenicity predictions on mutation variants, a task where current state-of-the-art methods fell short. After debiasing, clustering immunogenic peptides with immunogenicity-encoded representations uncovers unique preferences for biophysical properties, such as hydrophobicity and polarity. The code of our work is available at https://github.com/WangLabTHU/ImmuBPI. The full preprint is available at https://www.biorxiv.org/content/10.1101/2024.02.07.579420v1.

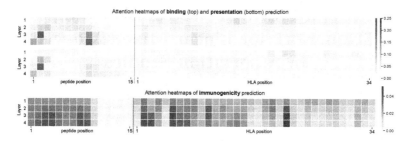

Fig. 2. Visualization of attention weights in heatmaps for binding, presentation, and immunogenicity prediction. The heatmap showed the contribution of each position on the peptide and HLA sequence to the [CLS] token. In immunogenicity prediction, HLA demonstrated abnormally high attention weights compared with binding and presentation results.

References

1. Albert, B.A., et al.: Deep neural networks predict class I major histocompatibility complex epitope presentation and transfer learn neoepitope immunogenicity. Nat. Mach. Intell. **5**, 861–872 (2023)
2. Chu, Y., et al.: A transformer-based model to predict peptide-HLA class i binding and optimize mutated peptides for vaccine design. Nat. Mach. Intell. **4**(3), 300–311 (2022)
3. Gfeller, D., et al.: Improved predictions of antigen presentation and TCR recognition with MixMHCpred2. 2 and PRIME2. 0 reveal potent SARS-CoV-2 CD8+ t-cell epitopes. Cell Syst. **14**(1), 72–83 (2023)
4. Kim, J.Y., et al.: MHC II immunogenicity shapes the neoepitope landscape in human tumors. Nat. Genet. **55**(2), 221–231 (2023)
5. Lang, F., Schrörs, B., Löwer, M., Türeci, Ö., Sahin, U.: Identification of neoantigens for individualized therapeutic cancer vaccines. Nat. Rev. Drug Discov. **21**(4), 261–282 (2022)
6. Mellman, I., Coukos, G., Dranoff, G.: Cancer immunotherapy comes of age. Nature **480**(7378), 480–489 (2011)
7. Qiao, Y., Xiong, C., Liu, Z., Liu, Z.: Understanding the behaviors of BERT in ranking. arXiv preprint arXiv:1904.07531 (2019)
8. Reynisson, B., Alvarez, B., Paul, S., Peters, B., Nielsen, M.: NetMHCpan-4.1 and NetMHCIIpan-4.0: improved predictions of MHC antigen presentation by concurrent motif deconvolution and integration of MS MHC eluted ligand data. Nucleic Acids Res. **48**(W1), W449–W454 (2020)
9. Wells, D.K., et al.: Key parameters of tumor epitope immunogenicity revealed through a consortium approach improve neoantigen prediction. Cell **183**(3), 818–834 (2020)

MaSk-LMM: A Matrix Sketching Framework for Linear Mixed Models in Association Studies

Myson Burch[1], Aritra Bose[1], Gregory Dexter[2], Laxmi Parida[1],
and Petros Drineas[2(✉)]

[1] IBM T.J. Watson Research Center, Yorktown Heights, NY, USA
{myson.burch,a.bose}@ibm.com, parida@us.ibm.com
[2] Department of Computer Science, Purdue University, West Lafayette, IN, USA
{gdexter,pdrineas}@purdue.edu

Abstract. Linear mixed models have been widely used in genome-wide association studies to control for population stratification and cryptic relatedness. Unfortunately, estimating LMM parameters is computationally expensive, necessitating large-scale matrix operations to build the genetic relatedness matrix. Randomized Linear Algebra has provided alternative approaches to such matrix operations by leveraging *matrix sketching*, which often results in provably accurate fast and efficient approximations. We leverage *matrix sketching* to develop a fast and efficient LMM method called **Matrix-Sketching LMM (MaSk-LMM)** by sketching the genotype matrix to reduce its dimensions and speed up computations. Our framework provides theoretical guarantees and a strong empirical performance compared to current methods.

Keywords: Linear Mixed Models · Matrix Sketching · GWAS

1 Introduction

Linear Mixed Models (LMMs) are widely used when conducting genome-wide association studies (GWAS) for quantitative traits in the presence of population structure. Population structure plays an important role in confounding results and generating false positive associations [10]. LMMs are able to capture and correct such confounders in the data, while decomposing phenotypic correlations into genetic and non-genetic components. These desirable properties have resulted in wide use of LMMs in human and plant genetics, as well as in other biological applications [4–6,8,9].

Although they are a popular tool for GWAS, LMMs have well-known limitations that we attempt to address in our work. Most prominent among those limitations are the increased computational requirements in terms of computational time and memory space that these models necessitate. LMMs require multiple $\mathcal{O}(n^3)$ or $\mathcal{O}(mn^2)$ matrix operations such as large matrix inversions, multiplications, etc. (here m is the number of Single Nucleotide Polymorphisms or genetic markers and n is the number of individual samples in the study).

© The Author(s), under exclusive license to Springer Nature Switzerland AG 2024
J. Ma (Ed.): RECOMB 2024, LNCS 14758, pp. 352–355, 2024.
https://doi.org/10.1007/978-1-0716-3989-4_29

We propose a method based on *Matrix-Sketching LMM (MaSk-LMM)*, to approximately solve LMMs by applying sketching to the genotype matrix to reduce both its dimensions, while preserving the relevant properties of the original matrix. We provide theoretical support to our sketching approach by proving that sketching the genetic markers (columns) of the genotype matrix results in bounded accuracy loss for the underlying LMM. To the best of our knowledge, this is the first theoretical result of its type, arguing that dimensionality reduction on the genetic marker space (which is typically massive in modern genetic datasets) is feasible without a significant loss in accuracy.

Beyond our theoretical guarantees, we demonstrate, through the use of simulated data, that solving the LMM using the sketched matrix results in a similar number of causal and spurious genetic associations compared to solving it using the original matrix. When applied to data for complex diseases, we recover previously known associations which are possibly linked with coronary artery disease and hypertension. In both synthetic and real data, we observe speed-ups using our approach compared to Regenie, BOLT-LMM and FaST-LMM.

2 Methods

2.1 Mixed-Model Association

Linear mixed models (LMMs) are formed using the following simple linear model:

$$\mathbf{y} = \mathbf{X}\boldsymbol{\beta} + \mathbf{Z}\mathbf{u} + \mathbf{e}, \tag{1}$$

where[1] $\mathbf{y} \in \mathbb{R}^n$ is the measured phenotype (response); $\mathbf{X} \in \mathbb{R}^{n \times k}$ is the matrix of the k covariates (*e.g.* principal components, age, sex, etc.) with the corresponding vector of fixed effects $\boldsymbol{\beta} \in \mathbb{R}^k$; $\mathbf{Z} \in \mathbb{R}^{n \times m}$ is the genotype matrix of n individuals genotyped on m genetic markers with $\mathbf{u} \in \mathbb{R}^m$ being the corresponding genetic effects vector; and $\mathbf{e} \in \mathbb{R}^n$ is the error vector or the component of $\mathbf{y}$ which cannot be explained by the model. We assume $\mathbf{u}$ and $\mathbf{e}$ are independent vectors and moreover that[2] $\mathbf{u} \sim \mathcal{N}\left(\mathbf{0}, \sigma_g^2 \mathbf{I}_m\right)$ and $\mathbf{e} \sim \mathcal{N}\left(\mathbf{0}, \sigma_e^2 \mathbf{I}_n\right)$ with scalars σ_g^2 and σ_e^2 being the heritable and non-heritable components of $\mathbf{u}$ and $\mathbf{e}$ respectively. In the LMM setting, some form of maximum likelihood estimation is used to estimate the random and fixed effects of the model to identify genetic associations while correcting for confounding effects.

2.2 MaSk-LMM

Our approach, MaSk-LMM, mitigates the computational complexity of LMMs by using sample and marker sketching on the input genotype matrix $\mathbf{Z}$, as well

---

[1] We use bold letters for vectors and matrices; a vector $\mathbf{x} \in \mathbb{R}^n$ is an n-dimensional real vector, while a matrix $\mathbf{X} \in \mathbb{R}^{n \times m}$ is an $n \times m$ real matrix.

[2] We use the notation $\mathcal{N}(\mu, \boldsymbol{\Sigma})$ to denote a multivariate normal distribution with mean vector μ and covariance matrix $\boldsymbol{\Sigma}$. $\mathbf{I}_n$ denotes the $n \times n$ identity matrix.

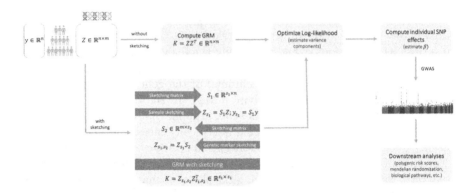

Fig. 1. MaSk-LMM Framework. We use sketching to speed up the standard pipeline of LMM computations (peach). Our alternative pipeline uses sketching on both the sample and marker space of the genotype matrix $\mathbf{Z}$ to speed-up computations (green). (Color figure online)

as on the response vector $\mathbf{y}$. This allows us to significantly reduce the dimensions of the genotype matrix, as well as of the relatedness or kinship matrix (GRM). As discussed in the introduction, sketching reduces the dimensions of the input while maintaining sufficient information to approximate functions of the original input accurately. Let $\mathbf{S}_1 \in \mathbb{R}^{s_1 \times n}$ and $\mathbf{S}_2 \in \mathbb{R}^{m \times s_2}$ be two sketching matrices, with $s_1 \ll n$ and $s_2 \ll m$. Here s_1 and s_2 are the sketching dimensions and are user-controlled parameters. Simple constructions for $\mathbf{S}_1$ and $\mathbf{S}_2$ are to have their entries drawn in independent identical trials from a Gaussian distribution of zero mean and variance $1/s_1$ and $1/s_2$, respectively. We can then use $\mathbf{S}_1$ and $\mathbf{S}_2$ to sketch the input genotype matrix as follows:

$$\mathbf{Z}_{s_1,s_2} = \mathbf{S}_1 \mathbf{Z} \mathbf{S}_2 \in \mathbb{R}^{s_1 \times s_2}. \tag{2}$$

$\mathbf{Z}_{s_1,s_2}$ is computed in blocks so the entire original input does not need to be loaded into memory alleviating a portion of the computational burden of this approach. Notice that $\mathbf{Z}_{s_1,s_2}$ is now a much smaller $s_1 \times s_2$ matrix which can be used in downstream computations instead of $\mathbf{Z}$. For example, we can approximate the GRM as follows:

$$\mathbf{K} = \mathbf{Z}_{s_1,s_2} \mathbf{Z}_{s_1,s_2}^{\mathsf{T}} = \mathbf{S}_1 \mathbf{Z} \mathbf{S}_2 \mathbf{S}_2^{\mathsf{T}} \mathbf{Z}^{\mathsf{T}} \mathbf{S}_1^{\mathsf{T}} \in \mathbb{R}^{s_1 \times s_1}. \tag{3}$$

We also sketch the n-dimensional response vector $\mathbf{y}$ to construct the s_1-dimensional response vector $\mathbf{y}_{s_1} = \mathbf{S}_1 \mathbf{y}$ to be used in downstream computations instead of $\mathbf{y}$. It is worth noting that there is a long line of research on matrix sketching methods, including gaussian sketching, the use of the subsampled randomized hadamard transforms, the count-min sketch, etc. and its application in human genetics [1–3]. In our work, we evaluated both the count-min sketch and the gaussian sketch. Both methods performed similarly and we chose to report results on gaussian sketching only, because it is conceptually simpler as well as easier to implement and theoretically analyze. See [7] for a discussion of other sketching methods. Figure 1 summarizes our framework.

3   Discussion

We have developed a framework for linear mixed-model associations using matrix sketching. MaSk-LMM applies both sample and marker sketching to reduce the dimensions of the genotype matrix prior to performing LMM analysis. Such sketching speeds up the GRM computation and the estimation of the LMM parameters without a significant loss in accuracy. MaSk-LMM is an important advance and contribution to the space of genomics, specifically when conducting genome-wide association studies. MaSk-LMM source code is available at https://github.com/IBM/mask-lmm and full-version available at https://www.medrxiv.org/content/10.1101/2023.11.13.23298469v1.

Funding. PD and MB were partially supported by NSF 10001674, NSF 10001225, an IBM Faculty Award to PD, and an NSF GRFP to MB. AB and LP were supported by IBM Research.

Disclosure of Interests. The authors have no competing interests to declare that are relevant to the content of this article.

References

1. Bose, A., Burch, M., Chowdhury, A., Paschou, P., Drineas, P.: Structure-informed clustering for population stratification in association studies. BMC Bioinform. **24**, 1–13 (2023)
2. Bose, A., Kalantzis, V., Kontopoulou, E.M., Elkady, M., Paschou, P., Drineas, P.: TeraPCA: a fast and scalable software package to study genetic variation in tera-scale genotypes. Bioinformatics **35**(19), 3679–3683 (2019)
3. Bose, A., Platt, D.E., Parida, L., Drineas, P., Paschou, P.: Integrating linguistics, social structure, and geography to model genetic diversity within India. Mol. Biol. Evol. **38**(5), 1809–1819 (2021)
4. Lipper, C.: Fast linear mixed models for genome-wide association studies. Nat. Methods **8**, 833 (2011). https://doi.org/10.1038/nmeth.1681
5. Runcie, D.E.: MegaLMM: mega-scale linear mixed models for genomic predictions with thousands of traits. Genome Biol. **22**(1), 1–25 (2021)
6. Runcie, D.E., Crawford, L.: Fast and flexible linear mixed models for genome-wide genetics. PLoS Genet. **15**(2), e1007978 (2019)
7. Woodruff, D.P., et al.: Sketching as a tool for numerical linear algebra. Found. Trends® Theor. Comput. Sci. **10**(1–2), 1–157 (2014)
8. Yamamoto, E., Matsunaga, H.: Exploring efficient linear mixed models to detect quantitative trait locus-by-environment interactions. G3 **11**(8), jkab119 (2021)
9. Yang, J.: GCTA: a tool for genome-wide complex trait analysis. Am. J Hum. Genet. **88**, 76–82 (2011)
10. Yang, J.: Advantages and pitfalls in the application of mixed-model association methods. Nat. Genet. **46**(2), 100–106 (2014). https://doi.org/10.1038/ng.2876

Community Structure and Temporal Dynamics of Viral Epistatic Networks Allow for Early Detection of Emerging Variants with Altered Phenotypes

Fatemeh Mohebbi[1,2], Alexander Zelikovsky[1], Serghei Mangul[2],
Gerardo Chowell[3], and Pavel Skums[1,4(✉)]

[1] Department of Computer Science, Georgia State University, Atlanta, GA, USA
[2] Titus Family Department of Clinical Pharmacy, USC Alfred E. Mann School
of Pharmacy and Pharmaceutical Sciences, University of Southern California,
Los Angeles, CA, USA
[3] School of Public Health, Georgia State University, Atlanta, GA, USA
[4] School of Computing, University of Connecticut, Storrs, CT, USA
pavel.skums@uconn.edu

Abstract. In this study, we demonstrated that SARS-CoV-2 emerging variants can be detected or predicted by examining the community structure of viral coordinated substitution networks. These variants can be linked to dense network communities, which become discernible earlier than their associated viral variants reach noticeable prevalence levels. From these insights, we developed HELEN (Heralding Emerging Lineages in Epistatic Networks), a computational framework that identifies densely connected communities of SAV alleles and merges them into haplotypes using a combination of statistical inference, population genetics, and discrete optimization techniques. Our methodology can be employed to detect emerging and circulating strains of any highly mutable pathogen with adequate genomic surveillance data, while offering greater scalability than phylogenetic lineage tracing methods.

Keywords: SARS-CoV-2 · Genomic surveillance · Haplotype forecasting · Epistasis · Network community

1 Introduction

Development of models to predict directions of viral evolution is an immensely important challenge directly associated with our ability to forecast and control the spread of infectious diseases [7,14]. The case of severe acute respiratory syndrome coronavirus 2 (SARS-CoV-2) provides a telling example. The successive waves of COVID-19 have been driven by the emerging variants of interest (VOIs) or variants of concern (VOCs) that have been associated with altered phenotypic features, including transmissibility [4,5], antibody resistance and immune

---

Partially supported by NSF grants NSF 2047828 and 2212508.

J. Ma (Ed.): RECOMB 2024, LNCS 14758, pp. 356–359, 2024.
https://doi.org/10.1007/978-1-0716-3989-4_30

escape [11]. Genomic epidemiology has been crucial for monitoring the emergence and spread of SARS-CoV-2 variants. Viral genomes sampled around the globe have been analyzed by a plethora of phylogenetic, phylodynamic, and epidemiological models [6] to detect spreading lineages and measure their reproductive numbers and other characteristics. However, these methods, powerful and valuable as they are, usually allow to *detect* growing lineages only when they are already sufficiently prevalent. In contrast, the task of *early detection* or *forecasting* involves the proactive identification of SARS-CoV-2 genomic variants that have the potential to become prevalent in the future. Several studies dedicated to SARS-CoV-2 evolutionary forecasting problem have been published [1,2,7,10,14,16]; however, most of them have focused on *individual mutations* under the assumption that mutations accumulate independently or that the effects of their interactions can be averaged out over their genomic backgrounds.

Meanwhile, a number of studies have highlighted the significance of *epistasis*, i.e., the non-additive phenotypic effects of combinations of mutations, for SARS-CoV-2 by suggesting the existence of an epistatic network that includes many genomic sites in the receptor-binding domain of the spike protein that is associated with increased binding affinity to angiotensin-converting enzyme 2 (ACE2) receptor [8,9,12–14]. Given the role of epistasis, it can be argued that selection often acts on combinations of mutations, or *haplotypes*, rather than on individual mutations. Therefore, effective evolutionary forecasting requires focusing on viral haplotypes instead of solely on SAVs.

2   Methods

Our study focuses on predicting emerging viral haplotypes using a novel approach based on analyzing structures of *coordinated substitution networks* of viral genomes [3,9,12]. We found that it is possible to accurately predict haplotypes that exhibit new phenotypes by identifying these haplotypes as dense communities of coordinated substitution networks. To achieve this, we introduce HELEN (Heralding Emerging Lineages in Epistatic Networks), a computational framework designed to infer viral haplotypes as these dense communities using techniques from graph theory, statistical inference, and population genetics.

The computational pipeline of HELEN consists of several distinct phases. Initially, we construct a coordinated substitution network (CSN) from aligned sequences. This is achieved through a statistical test designed to ascertain if non-reference alleles co-occur more frequently than would be expected by random chance. This step produces networks with rich community structures, providing a foundation for the next stages.

Following this, we generate a collection of candidate dense CSN subgraphs of varying sizes. This task is accomplished by producing multiple solutions a specially formulated Integer Linear Programming problem. The subsequent phase involves refining these subgraphs. Our goal here is twofold: to amalgamate subgraphs that pertain to the same haplotype and to split those that represent different haplotypes. This goal is achieved by constructing and processing a "graph of subgraphs", where edges denote pairs of subgraphs with significant overlap. This graph is decomposed into clusters using a series of graph clustering techniques, with each cluster reflecting a unique haplotype. The final stage is the reconstruction of that haplotype for each cluster by finding the densest core community in the union of subgraphs forming that cluster. Beyond the development of HELEN, we also introduce a method to statistically validate the significance of the inferred associations between haplotypes and their respective network communities.

Importantly, the computational complexity of most intensive stages of our method depends on genome length rather than the number of sequences, making it significantly faster than traditional phylogenetic methods for variant detection and enabling it to handle millions of currently available SARS-CoV-2 genomes.

3   Results and Discussion

HELEN was validated by accurately identifying known SARS-CoV-2 Variants of Concern and Vaiants of Interest up to months before they reached high prevalences and were designated by the WHO. These results demonstrate that network density is a more precise, sensitive, and scalable measure than lineage frequency, allowing for reliable early detection or prediction of potential variants of concern before they become prevalent.

We believe that the methodology proposed in this study is not limited to SARS-CoV-2 and can be extended to other pathogens. The high sensitivity of HELEN should make it particularly suitable for detecting emerging and circulating strains of pandemic viruses, including HIV, Hepatitis C, and Influenza. This capability is particularly valuable in the context of seasonal vaccine development, where accurate and timely forecasts can play a crucial role in the selection of strains for vaccine formulation.

Acknowledgments. We gratefully acknowledge all data contributors, i.e., the authors and their originating laboratories responsible for obtaining the specimens, and their submitting laboratories for generating the genetic sequence and metadata and sharing via the GISAID Initiative [15], on which this research is based.

Data Availability Statement. The developed tool is freely available at https://github.com/compbel/HELEN. Full preprint can be found at https://doi.org/10.1101/2023.04.02.535277.

References

1. Ahmed, S.F., Quadeer, A.A., McKay, M.R.: Covidep: a web-based platform for real-time reporting of vaccine target recommendations for sars-cov-2. Nat. Protoc. **15**(7), 2141–2142 (2020)
2. Bai, C., et al.: Predicting mutational effects on receptor binding of the spike protein of sars-cov-2 variants. J. Am. Chem. Soc. **143**(42), 17646–17654 (2021)

3. Campo, D., Dimitrova, Z., Mitchell, R.J., Lara, J., Khudyakov, Y.: Coordinated evolution of the hepatitis c virus. Proc. Natl. Acad. Sci. **105**(28), 9685–9690 (2008)

4. Davies, N.G., et al.: Estimated transmissibility and impact of sars-cov-2 lineage b. 1.1. 7 in england. Science **372**(6538), eabg3055 (2021)

5. Hoffmann, M., Kleine-Weber, H., Pöhlmann, S.: A multibasic cleavage site in the spike protein of sars-cov-2 is essential for infection of human lung cells. Molecular Cell (2020)

6. Knyazev, S., et al.: Unlocking capacities of genomics for the Covid-19 response and future pandemics. Nat. Methods **19**(4), 374–380 (2022)

7. Maher, M.C.,et al.: Predicting the mutational drivers of future sars-cov-2 variants of concern. Science Trans. Med. **14**(633), eabk3445 (2022)

8. Moulana, A., et al.: Compensatory epistasis maintains ace2 affinity in sars-cov-2 omicron ba. 1. Nature Commun. **13**(1), 7011 (2022)

9. Neverov, A.D., Fedonin, G., Popova, A., Bykova, D., Bazykin, G.: Coordinated evolution at amino acid sites of sars-cov-2 spike. Elife **12**, e82516 (2023)

10. Obermeyer, F., et al.: Analysis of 6.4 million sars-cov-2 genomes identifies mutations associated with fitness. Science **376**(6599), 1327–1332 (2022)

11. Planas, D., et al.: Reduced sensitivity of sars-cov-2 variant delta to antibody neutralization. Nature **596**(7871), 276–280 (2021)

12. Rochman, N.D., Faure, G., Wolf, Y.I., Freddolino, P.L., Zhang, F., Koonin, E.V.: Epistasis at the sars-cov-2 receptor-binding domain interface and the propitiously boring implications for vaccine escape. MBio **13**(2), e00122–e00135 (2022)

13. Rochman, N.D., Wolf, Y.I., Faure, G., Mutz, P., Zhang, F., Koonin, E.V.: Ongoing global and regional adaptive evolution of sars-cov-2. Proc. National Acad. Sci. **118**(29) (2021)

14. Rodriguez-Rivas, J., Croce, G., Muscat, M., Weigt, M.: Epistatic models predict mutable sites in sars-cov-2 proteins and epitopes. Proc. Natl. Acad. Sci. **119**(4), e2113118119 (2022)

15. Shu, Y., McCauley, J.: Gisaid: global initiative on sharing all influenza data–from vision to reality. Eurosurveillance **22**(13) (2017)

16. Yarmarkovich, M., Warrington, J.M., Farrel, A., Maris, J.M.: Identification of sars-cov-2 vaccine epitopes predicted to induce long-term population-scale immunity. Cell Reports Med. **1**(3), 100036 (2020)

Maximum Likelihood Inference
of Time-Scaled Cell Lineage Trees
with Mixed-Type Missing Data

Uyen Mai, Gillian Chu, and Benjamin J. Raphael[✉]

Princeton University, Princeton, NJ 08544, USA
braphael@princeton.edu

Abstract. Recent dynamic lineage tracing technologies combine CRISPR-based genome editing with single-cell sequencing to track cell divisions during development. A key problem in lineage tracing is to infer a cell lineage tree from the measured CRISPR-induced mutations. Several features of lineage tracing data distinguish this problem from standard phylogenetic tree inference: CRISPR-induced mutations are *non-modifiable* and can result in distinct sets of possible mutations at each target site; the number of mutations decreases over time due to non-modifiability; and CRISPR-based genome-editing and single-cell sequencing results in high rates of both heritable and non-heritable (dropout) missing data. To model these features, we introduce the Probabilistic Mixed-type Missing (PMM) model. We describe an algorithm, LAML (Lineage Analysis via Maximum Likelihood), to compute a maximum likelihood tree under the PMM model. LAML combines an Expectation Maximization (EM) algorithm with a heuristic tree search to jointly estimate tree topology, branch lengths and missing data parameters.

Keywords: cell phylogeny inference · evolutionary model · maximum likelihood

Lineage tracing, or the problem of tracing the history of cell divisions resulting in a multicellular organism, is a key problem in developmental biology, and has proven to be challenging both experimentally [1–5,8,10,11,14,16] and computationally [6,7,9,12,13,15,17]. Currently, there is no method for lineage tracing data can overcome the following three challenges: (i) a distinct set of *non-modifiable* mutations at each target site, (ii) the existence of two distinct sources of missing data, and (iii) the decay in the number of editable target sites. We propose the first probabilistic method that accounts for these key features of recent developments in lineage tracing data.

U. Mai and G. Chu—These authors contributed equally to this work.

J. Ma (Ed.): RECOMB 2024, LNCS 14758, pp. 360–363, 2024.
https://doi.org/10.1007/978-1-0716-3989-4_31

1   Problem Formulation

Cell lineage tree inference is the computational problem of constructing the rooted cell lineage tree topology T and estimating its branch lengths from the given $N \times K$ *character matrix* $\mathbf{D}$, where N is the number of sequenced cells and K is the number of target sites. We solve this problem using a probabilistic approach: first, we introduce a generative model that generates $\mathbf{D}$ from topology T and other parameters $\boldsymbol{\Theta}$ of the model, and second, we develop a maximum likelihood algorithm to infer T and $\boldsymbol{\Theta}$ from $\mathbf{D}$ under this model.

2   The PMM Model

Our Probabilistic Mixed-type Missing (PMM) model generates $\mathbf{D}$ from T and $\boldsymbol{\Theta}$ in two layers: layer 1 models the CRISPR/Cas9 editing process and layer 2 models the single-cell sequencing process. In addition to the tree topology T, the other parameters of PMM model, $\boldsymbol{\Theta}$, comprises the followings: the branch length δ_e of every branch e, the mutation rate λ, the silencing rate ν, and the dropout rate ϕ. As such, $\boldsymbol{\Theta} = (\{\delta_e\}, \lambda, \nu, \phi)$.

2.1   Layer 1: The CRISPR/Cas9 Editing Process

Layer 1 describes the CRISPR/Cas9 editing process. Let λ be the editing rate and t_e be the length of a branch e in time units. We assume λ is shared across all sites and branches, t_e for each branch e is shared across all sites, and each site k mutates following a CTMC with the following transition rate matrix $\mathbf{Q}^{(k)}$:

$$
\mathbf{Q}^{(k)} =
\begin{array}{c}
\\
0 \\
1 \\
\vdots \\
M^{(k)} \\
-1
\end{array}
\begin{array}{c}
\begin{array}{ccccc}
0 & 1 & \dots & M^{(k)} & -1
\end{array} \\
\left[
\begin{array}{ccccc}
-(1+\nu)\, q_1^{(k)} & \dots & q_{M^{(k)}}^{(k)} & \nu \\
0 & -\nu & \dots & 0 & \nu \\
\vdots & \vdots & \ddots & \vdots & \vdots \\
0 & 0 & \dots & -\nu & \nu \\
0 & 0 & \dots & 0 & 0
\end{array}
\right]
\end{array},
\tag{1}
$$

where $q_1^{(k)}, q_2^{(k)}, ..., q_{M^{(k)}}^{(k)}$ are the rates of transitioning from 0 to each of the mutated states for site k (i.e. $\sum_{m=1}^{M^{(k)}} q_m^{(k)} = 1$) and ν is the rate of transitioning to the heritable silenced state -1, which is shared across all sites. On edge e of T at target site k, the transition probabilities of every pair of states are determined by the *transition probability matrix*, $\boldsymbol{\Psi}_e^{(k)}$, computed from $\mathbf{Q}^{(k)}$ as $\boldsymbol{\Psi}_e^{(k)} = e^{\mathbf{Q}^{(k)} \lambda t_e}$.

2.2   Layer 2: The Single-Cell Sequencing Process

The second layer describes the stochastic generation of dropout during sc-Seq. After sc-Seq, characters in the silent state (i.e. -1) will be observed in the missing state with probability 1, while all other states have some probability of being observed in the missing state depending on the dropout rate of sc-Seq. We use ϕ to represent the *dropout rate* and represent the transition probabilities during sc-Seq by the following matrix:

$$
\boldsymbol{\Phi} = \begin{array}{c} \\ 0 \\ 1 \\ \vdots \\ M^{(k)} \\ -1 \end{array} \begin{array}{ccccc} 0 & 1 & \dots & M^{(k)} & ? \\ \left[\begin{array}{ccccc} 1-\phi & 0 & \dots & 0 & \phi \\ 0 & 1-\phi & 0 & \dots & \phi \\ \vdots & \vdots & \vdots & \vdots & \vdots \\ 0 & 0 & \dots 1-\phi & \phi \\ 0 & 0 & \dots & 0 & 1 \end{array}\right] \end{array} \tag{2}
$$

3   Maximum Likelihood Inference

LAML is a maximum likelihood algorithm to infer T and $\boldsymbol{\Theta}$ from an observed character matrix $\boldsymbol{D}$ under the PMM model. LAML iterates over the following steps: (i) propose a new tree topology T' using nearest neighbor interchanges (NNI); (ii) optimize $\hat{\boldsymbol{\Theta}}$ on T' using an EM algorithm and compute the log-likelihood of the observed data; (iii) accept/reject the new topology according to simulated annealing. Importantly, our newly derived EM algorithm for branch length estimation is efficient. Specifically, at each iteration of the E-step, we compute the expected value for transitions on every edge. Since Ψ_e and Φ are both sparse, we group the transition types in order to compute each transition's posterior probability independently from alphabet size, reducing the E-step complexity to linear time. For the M-step, in the case of no heritable missing data we derive a closed-form solution which can be computed in linear time. In the general case, we show that the optimization problem in the M-step is convex with respect to ϕ, all δ_e, and ν separately and use block coordinate ascent to solve it.

Acknowledgements. This research was supported by NIH/NCI grant U24CA248453 to B.J.R. U.M. was funded by the Presidential Postdoctoral Fellowship at Princeton University. G.C. was funded by the NSF GRFP DGE grant 2039656. We thank Palash Sashittal and Henri Schmidt for help with running the Startle code; Sophie Seidel for help with running the TiDeTree code; and Michelle Chan for helpful discussion.

Preprint, Software, and Data Availability. The full paper is available on bioRxiv at https://www.biorxiv.org/content/10.1101/2024.03.05.583638v1. The software is available on Github at https://github.com/raphael-group/LAML. All data used in this research is available at https://github.com/raphael-group/laml-experiments.

References

1. Alemany, A., Florescu, M., Baron, C.S., Peterson-Maduro, J., Van Oudenaarden, A.: Whole-organism clone tracing using single-cell sequencing. Nature **556**(7699), 108–112 (2018)

2. Bowling, S., et al.: An engineered crispr-cas9 mouse line for simultaneous readout of lineage histories and gene expression profiles in single cells. Cell **181**(6), 1410–1422 (2020)
3. Chan, M.M., et al.: Molecular recording of mammalian embryogenesis. Nature **570**(7759), 77–82 (2019)
4. Choi, J., et al.: A time-resolved, multi-symbol molecular recorder via sequential genome editing. Nature **608**(7921), 98–107 (2022)
5. Ke-Huan, K C., et al. Imaging cell lineage with a synthetic digital recording system. Science **372**(6538), eabb3099 (2021)
6. Feng, J., DeWitt, W.S., III., McKenna, A., Simon, N., Willis, A.D., Matsen, F.A., IV.: Estimation of cell lineage trees by maximum-likelihood phylogenetics. Annals Appli Stat. **15**(1), 343–362 (2021)
7. Gong, W., Kim, H.J., Garry, D.J., Kwak, I.-Y.: Single cell lineage reconstruction using distance-based algorithms and the r package, dclear. BMC Bioinform. **23**(1), 103 (2022)
8. He, Z., et al.: Lineage recording in human cerebral organoids. Nat. Methods **19**(1), 90–99 (2022)
9. Jones, M.G., et al.: Inference of single-cell phylogenies from lineage tracing data using cassiopeia. Genome Biol. **21**(1), 1–27 (2020)
10. McKenna, A., Findlay, G.M., Gagnon, J.A., Horwitz, M.S., Schier, A.F., Shendure, J.: Whole-organism lineage tracing by combinatorial and cumulative genome editing. Science **353**(6298), aaf7907 (2016)
11. Raj, B., et al.: Simultaneous single-cell profiling of lineages and cell types in the vertebrate brain. Nat. Biotechnol. **36**(5), 442–450 (2018)
12. Sashittal, P., Schmidt, H., Chan, M., Raphael, B.J.: Startle: a star homoplasy approach for crispr-cas9 lineage tracing. Cell Syst. **14**(12), 1113–1121 (2023)
13. Seidel, S., Stadler, T.: TiDeTree: a bayesian phylogenetic framework to estimate single-cell trees and population dynamic parameters from genetic lineage tracing data. Proc. R. Soc. B **289**(1986), 20221844 (2022)
14. Spanjaard, B., et al.: Simultaneous lineage tracing and cell-type identification using crispr-cas9-induced genetic scars. Nat. Biotechnol. **36**(5), 469–473 (2018)
15. Wang, R., Zhang, R.Y., Khodaverdian, A., Yosef, N.: Theoretical guarantees for phylogeny inference from single-cell lineage tracing. bioRxiv (2021)
16. Yang, D., et al.: Lineage tracing reveals the phylodynamics, plasticity, and paths of tumor evolution. Cell **185**(11), 1905–1923 (2022)
17. Zafar, H., Lin, C., Bar-Joseph, Z.: Single-cell lineage tracing by integrating crispr-cas9 mutations with transcriptomic data. Nat. Commun. **11**(1), 1–14 (2020)

TRIBAL: Tree Inference of B Cell Clonal Lineages

Leah L. Weber[1] , Derek Reiman[2] , Mrinmoy S. Roddur[1] ,
Yuanyuan Qi[1] , Mohammed El-Kebir[1](✉) , and Aly A. Khan[2,3](✉)

[1] University of Illinois at Urbana-Champaign, Champaign, IL 61801, USA
melkebir@illinois.edu
[2] Toyota Technological Institute at Chicago, Chicago, IL 60637, USA
[3] University of Chicago, Chicago, IL 60637, USA
aakhan@uchicago.edu

Abstract. B cells are a critical component of the adaptive immune system. Single cell RNA-sequencing (scRNA-seq) has allowed for both profiling of B cell receptor (BCR) sequences and gene expression. However, understanding the adaptive and evolutionary mechanisms of B cells in response to specific stimuli remains a significant challenge in the field of immunology. We introduce a new method, TRIBAL, which aims to infer the evolutionary history of clonally related B cells from scRNA-seq data. The key insight of TRIBAL is that inclusion of isotype data into the B cell lineage inference problem is valuable for reducing phylogenetic uncertainty that arises when only considering the receptor sequences. Consequently, the TRIBAL inferred B cell lineage trees jointly capture the somatic mutations introduced to the B cell receptor during affinity maturation and isotype transitions during class switch recombination. In addition, TRIBAL infers isotype transition probabilities that are valuable for gaining insight into the dynamics of class switching. Via *in silico* experiments, we demonstrate that TRIBAL infers isotype transition probabilities with the ability to distinguish between direct versus sequential switching in a B cell population. This results in more accurate B cell lineage trees and corresponding ancestral sequence and class switch reconstruction compared to competing methods. Using real-world scRNA-seq datasets, we show that TRIBAL recapitulates expected biological trends in a model affinity maturation system. Furthermore, the B cell lineage trees inferred by TRIBAL were equally plausible for the BCR sequences as those inferred by competing methods but yielded lower entropic partitions for the isotypes of the sequenced B cell. Thus, our method holds the potential to further advance our understanding of vaccine responses, disease progression, and the identification of therapeutic antibodies.

This work was partially supported by NIH grant DP2AI177884 (A.A.K.) and by the National Science Foundation grant CCF-2046488 (M.E-K.). This work used resources, services, and support provided via the Greg Gulick Honorary Research Award Opportunity supported by a gift from Amazon Web Services.
M. El-Kebir and A. A. Khan—Joint senior authorship.

J. Ma (Ed.): RECOMB 2024, LNCS 14758, pp. 364–367, 2024.
https://doi.org/10.1007/978-1-0716-3989-4_32

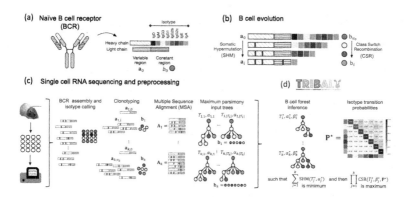

Fig. 1. TRIBAL infers B cell lineage trees and isotype transition probabilities for scRNA-seq data. (a) A Naive BCR consists of paired heavy and light immunoglobulin chains, each chain comprised of a variable and constant region. (b) BCRs undergo somatic hypermutation/affinity maturation and class switch recombination. (c) Following scRNA-seq, BCRs are assembled, clustered into k clonotypes and aligned. Alignments are used to generate a maximum parsimony forest for each clonotype j. Also, the isotype of each B cell is identified. (d) TRIBAL jointly infers a B cell lineage tree T_j^* for each clonotype j and population-specific isotype transition probabilities $\mathbf{P}^*$ with maximum parsimony for MSA $\mathbf{A}_j$ and maximum likelihood for isotypes $\mathbf{b}_j$.

Backgound. A B cell receptor (BCR) is comprised of two paired heavy and light immunoglobulin chains, each consisting of a variable and constant region (Fig. 1a). To enhance their effectiveness, B cells undergo affinity maturation (Fig. 1a,b) [6], an evolutionary process involving repeated cycles of *somatic hypermutation* (SHM) and cellular divisions. SHM introduces mutations in the variable region BCR genes, selecting for B cells expressing high-affinity BCRs, while eliminating those with low affinity. Concurrently, B cells have the ability for *class switch recombination* (CSR) (Fig. 1b) [5], which diversifies their response by altering the antibody's functional class or *isotype*. CSR is an irreversible processes whereby any heavy chain constant region locus between the current isotype and the new isotype in the genome is removed via a recombination process (Fig. 1b) and offers a distinct milestone in its evolutionary history.

Method. To comprehensively model the evolutionary history of a collection of n B cells clustered into k clonotypes, TRIBAL aims to solve the following problem.

*Problem 1 (*B CELL LINEAGE FOREST INFERENCE *(BLFI)).* Given multiple sequence alignments $\mathbf{A}_1, \ldots, \mathbf{A}_k$ and isotypes $\mathbf{b}_1, \ldots, \mathbf{b}_k$ for k clonotypes, find isotype transition probabilities $\mathbf{P}^*$ for r isotypes and lineage trees $T_1^*, \ldots, T_k^*$ for $(\mathbf{A}_1, \mathbf{b}_1), \ldots, (\mathbf{A}_k, \mathbf{b}_k)$ whose nodes are labeled by sequences $\alpha_1^*, \ldots, \alpha_k^*$ and isotypes $\beta_1^*, \ldots, \beta_k^*$, respectively, such that $\sum_{j=1}^{k} \text{SHM}(T_j^*, \alpha_j^*)$ is minimum and then $\prod_{j=1}^{k} \text{CSR}(T_j^*, \beta_j^*, \mathbf{P}^*)$ is maximum.

TRIBAL has two inputs (Fig. 1c). First, an MSA $\mathbf{A}_j$ is generated by concatenating the DNA sequences of the variable regions of the heavy and light chain of the B cell receptor (BCR) of the n_j B cells comprising clonotype j that descend from the same naive B cell post V(D)J recombination with sequence $\mathbf{a}_{j,0}$. Second, isotypes $b_{j,i} \in [r] = \{1, \ldots, r\}$ are called from existing tools. For humans, there are $r = 8$ isotypes linearly encoded from 1 to 8 as IgM/D, IgG3, IgG1, IgA1, IgG2, IgG4, IgE and IgA2.

TRIBAL infers a *lineage tree* T_j for the n_j B cells of each clonotype j, describing the joint evolution of the given DNA sequences $\mathbf{A}_j = [\mathbf{a}_{j,0}, \mathbf{a}_{j,1}, \ldots, \mathbf{a}_{j,n_j}]^\top$ and isotypes $\mathbf{b}_j = [b_{j,0}, b_{j,1}, \ldots, b_{j,n_j}]^\top$. Specifically, T_j is a rooted tree whose nodes v are labeled by a DNA sequence $\alpha(v)$ and isotype $\beta(v)$ such that the root v_0 is labeled by $\alpha(v_0) = \mathbf{a}_0$ and $\beta(v_0) = b_0 = 1$. The n_j leaves $L(T_j) = \{v_1, \ldots, v_{n_j}\}$ are labeled by DNA sequence $\alpha(v_i) = \mathbf{a}_{j,i}$ and isotype $\beta(v_i) = b_{j,i}$ for each B cell $i \in [n_j]$. In addition, due to irreversibilty of class switch recombination (CSR), the isotype $\beta(u)$ of an ancestral cell u must be less than or equal to the isotype $\beta(v)$ of its descendants v, i.e., $\beta(u) \leq \beta(v)$ for all edges $(u, v) \in E(T_j)$.

Lineage trees typically have shallow depth due to the limited number of mutations introduced during somatic hypermutation (SHM) [1,2,4], making unweighted parsimony a reasonable evolutionary model for SHM. Thus, $\mathrm{SHM}(T, \alpha)$ counts the total number of nucleotide substitutions in the lineage tree T labeled by sequences α. To model CSR, we use isotype transition probabilities $\mathbf{P} = [p_{s,t}]$ that capture the conditional probability of a descendant isotype t given the isotype of its parent s subject to irreversible isotype evolution. Using independence along the edges $E(T)$ of a lineage tree T allows us to define the joint likelihood $\mathrm{CSR}(T, \beta, \mathbf{P})$ of the observed isotypes $\mathbf{b}$ for isotype transition probabilities $\mathbf{P}$ and any lineage tree T whose leaves have isotypes $\mathbf{b}$ as $\prod_{(u,v) \in E(T)} p_{\beta(u), \beta(v)}$.

TRIBAL is based on two key ideas that allow us to effectively solve the BLFI problem. First, the lexicographical ordering of our two objectives—optimizing for SHM followed by CSR—enables one to use the following two-stage approach (Fig. 1c). In the first stage, we use existing maximum parsimony methods to generate a set $\mathcal{T}$ of input trees—also called a *maximum parsimony forest*—for each clonotype such that each tree $T \in \mathcal{T}$ minimizes the objective $\mathrm{SHM}(T, \alpha)$. To do so, we provide these methods only the sequence information $\mathbf{A}$ to enumerate a solution space $\mathcal{T}$ of trees whose nodes are labeled by sequences $\alpha_1, \ldots, \alpha_{|\mathcal{T}|}$ (Fig. 1c). In the second stage, we incorporate isotype information $\mathbf{b}$ to further operate on the set $\mathcal{T}$ and additionally optimize $\mathrm{CSR}(T, \beta, \mathbf{P})$ in such a manner that maintains optimality of the SHM objective.

We note that a lexicographically optimal lineage tree T^* does not necessarily need to be an element of $\mathcal{T}$, but instead it suffices that the evolutionary relationships in tree T^* are a refinement of the evolutionary relationships described by some tree T among the set $\mathcal{T}$ of input trees. More specifically, a *refinement* T' of tree T is obtained by zero or more EXPAND operations such that EXPAND(v) results in splitting node v into v and v', joining them with an edge (v, v') and then reassigning a (potentially empty) subset of the children of v to be children of v'. Importantly, one can obtain a refinement T' of T maintaining the SHM objective, i.e., $\mathrm{SHM}(T, \alpha) = \mathrm{SHM}(T', \alpha')$ by setting $\alpha(v') = \alpha(v)$ for each node v' of T' obtained via the EXPAND operation applied to node v of T. Therefore, our sought lineage tree T^* that first optimizes SHM and then CSR must be a refinement of some tree T in the set $\mathcal{T}$ of unrefined trees with optimal SHM scores.

The second key idea is that the inference of optimal lineage trees $T_1^*, \ldots, T_k^*$ is conditionally independent when given isotype transition probabilities $\mathbf{P}$. This motivates the use of a coordinate ascent algorithm where we randomly initialize isotype transition probabilities $\mathbf{P}^{(1)}$. Then, at each iteration ℓ, we use isotype transition probabilities $\mathbf{P}^{(\ell)}$ and the input set $\mathcal{T}_j$ of trees to independently infer an optimal lineage tree $T_j^{(\ell)}$ for each clonotype j. Briefly, this is achieved by solving the intermediate NP-hard problem of finding the most parsimonious refinement of a each tree T in the maximum parsimony forest $\mathcal{T}$ utilizing a graph-based approach. This is then followed by estimating updated isotype transition probabilities $\mathbf{P}^{(\ell+1)}$ given trees $T_1^{(\ell)}, \ldots, T_k^{(\ell)}$ via maximum likelihood estimation. We terminate upon convergence of our CSR objective or when exceeding a specified number of maximum iterations.

Results. In this work, we introduced TRIBAL, a method to infer B cell lineage trees and isotype transition probabilities from scRNA-seq data. We formulated and proved that the problem of finding a refinement maximizing the CSR likelihood is NP-hard. Via *in silico* experiments, we showed the importance of tree refinement for both accurately estimating isotype transition probabilities and outperforming existing methods on lineage tree inference. Furthermore, we demonstrated on experimental data that TRIBAL returns lineage trees with similar HLP19 [3] likelihoods, despite utilizing a less complex model for sequence evolution but yield a reduction in the entropy of the isotype leaf labelings.

Data Availibility Statement. https://github.com/elkebir-group/TRIBAL.
Paper: https://doi.org/10.1101/2023.11.27.568874.

References

1. Davidsen, K., Matsen, F.A., IV.: Benchmarking tree and ancestral sequence inference for B cell receptor sequences. Front. Immunol. **9**, 2451 (2018)
2. DeWitt, W.S., III., et al.: Using genotype abundance to improve phylogenetic inference. Mol. Biol. Evol. **35**(5), 1253–1265 (2018)
3. Hoehn, K.B., et al.: Repertoire-wide phylogenetic models of B cell molecular evolution reveal evolutionary signatures of aging and vaccination. Proc. Natl. Acad. Sci. **116**(45), 22664–22672 (2019)
4. Hoehn, K.B., et al.: Phylogenetic analysis of migration, differentiation, and class switching in B cells. PLoS Comput. Biol. **18**(4), e1009885 (2022)
5. Stavnezer, J., Guikema, J.E., Schrader, C.E.: Mechanism and regulation of class switch recombination. Annu. Rev. Immunol. **26**, 261 (2008)
6. Victora, G.D., Nussenzweig, M.C.: Germinal centers. Annu. Rev. Immunol. **30**(1), 429–457 (2012)

Mapping the Topography of Spatial Gene Expression with Interpretable Deep Learning

Uthsav Chitra[1], Brian J. Arnold[1,2], Hirak Sarkar[1,3], Cong Ma[1],
Sereno Lopez-Darwin[4], Kohei Sanno[1], and Benjamin J. Raphael[1(✉)]

[1] Department of Computer Science, Princeton University, Princeton, NJ, USA
braphael@cs.princeton.edu
[2] Center for Statistics and Machine Learning, Princeton University,
Princeton, NJ, USA
[3] Ludwig Cancer Institute, Princeton Branch, Princeton University,
Princeton, NJ, USA
[4] Lewis-Sigler Institute, Princeton University, Princeton, NJ, USA

Abstract. Spatially resolved transcriptomics technologies provide high-throughput measurements of gene expression in a tissue slice, but the sparsity of this data complicates the analysis of spatial gene expression patterns. We address this issue by deriving a *topographic map* of a tissue slice—analogous to a map of elevation in a landscape—using a novel quantity called the *isodepth*. Contours of constant isodepth enclose spatial domains with distinct cell type composition, while gradients of the isodepth indicate spatial directions of maximum change in gene expression. We develop GASTON, an unsupervised and interpretable deep learning algorithm that simultaneously learns the isodepth, spatial gene expression gradients, and piecewise linear functions of the isodepth. GASTON models both continuous gradients and discontinuous spatial variation in the expression of individual genes. We show that GASTON accurately identifies spatial domains and marker genes in multiple SRT datasets.

Keywords: Spatial transcriptomics · gene expression topography · expression gradients · deep learning

1 Introduction

Gene expression varies spatially across a tissue due to both the discrete spatial organization of cell types into *spatial domains* and continuous variation in cell state through processes such as differentiation and cell-cell communication [16]. Spatially resolved transcriptomics (SRT) technologies measure the number of RNA transcripts at thousands of locations in a 2-D tissue slice, enabling the inference of spatial domains and continuous variation in gene expression within and across spatial domains [6–9,13,15]. In this work, we introduce *"gene*

© The Author(s), under exclusive license to Springer Nature Switzerland AG 2024
J. Ma (Ed.): RECOMB 2024, LNCS 14758, pp. 368–371, 2024.
https://doi.org/10.1007/978-1-0716-3989-4_33

expression topography", a novel approach for modeling spatial variation in gene expression. We derive GASTON, an unsupervised and interpretable deep learning algorithm that learns a *topographic map* of a tissue slice and simultaneously learns continuous gradients and discontinuous variation in gene expression.

2   Methods

We briefly describe our model of gene expression topography and the GASTON algorithm. We model spatial gene expression with a *gene expression function* $\mathbf{f} : \mathbb{R}^2 \to \mathbb{R}^G$, where $\mathbf{f}(x, y) = (f_1(x, y), \ldots, f_G(x, y)) \in \mathbb{R}^G$ is the gene expression vector of G genes at location (x, y) in tissue $T \subseteq \mathbb{R}^2$. We assume the gene expression function $\mathbf{f}$ may be factored as

$$\mathbf{f}(x, y) = \mathbf{h}(d(x, y)), \tag{1}$$

where $d : \mathbb{R}^2 \to \mathbb{R}$ is a *scalar* function and $\mathbf{h} : \mathbb{R} \to \mathbb{R}^G$ is a univariate function. We call the scalar function d *isodepth*, which describes the *topography* of gene expression. We call the function $\mathbf{h} : \mathbb{R} \to \mathbb{R}^G$ a *1-D gene expression function*, since $\mathbf{h}(w) = (h_1(w), \ldots, h_G(w))$ is a function of a single spatial variable, i.e. the isodepth, in contrast to the gene expression function $\mathbf{f}(x, y)$ which is a function of two spatial variables x and y. We further assume the 1-D gene expression function $\mathbf{h}$ is a *piecewise linear* function with P pieces, where each piece corresponds to a spatial domain of the tissue. See [5] for a rigorous derivation of our model and for further details.

Given a gene expression matrix $\mathbf{A} = [a_{ig}] \in \mathbb{R}^{N \times G}$ and spatial locations $\mathbf{s}_1 = (x_1, y_1), \ldots, \mathbf{s}_N = (x_N, y_N) \in \mathbb{R}^2$ for N spots and G genes, and a number P of pieces, GASTON computes maximum likelihood estimators (MLEs) for an isodepth function d and piecewise linear 1-D gene expression function $\mathbf{h}$:

$$\underset{\substack{d \in C^1(\mathbb{R}^2, \mathbb{R}) \\ b_1 < b_2 < \cdots < b_{P-1} \\ \mathbf{h} = (h_1, \ldots, h_G) \in \mathcal{L}(b_1, \ldots, b_{P-1})}}{\arg \max} \sum_{g=1}^{G} \left(\sum_{i=1}^{N} \log \mathbb{P}\Big(a_{i,g} \mid h_g\big(d(x_i, y_i)\big)\Big) \right), \tag{2}$$

where $C^1(\mathbb{R}^2, \mathbb{R})$ is the space of continuously differentiable functions from $\mathbb{R}^2$ to $\mathbb{R}$, and $\mathcal{L}(b_1, \ldots, b_{P-1})$ is the space of piecewise linear functions with breakpoints $b_1, \ldots, b_{P-1}$, i.e. a piecewise linear function with P pieces.

For computational efficiency, we solve (2) using the following two-step procedure. First, we estimate the isodepth d and breakpoints $b_1, \ldots, b_{P-1}$ using the top generalized linear model principal components (GLM-PCs) [14], which also yields a piecewise linear 1-D GLM-PC function $\mathbf{h}'$, and then we estimate the 1-D gene expression function $\mathbf{h}$. Specifically, in the first step, we run GLM-PCA and obtain the top-$2P$ GLM-PCs $\mathbf{u}_j = [u_{i,j}] \in \mathbb{R}^N$ for $j = 1, \ldots, 2P$, and we compute a maximum likelihood estimator (MLE) for the isodepth d and 1-D expression function $\mathbf{h}'$ using the GLM-PCs under a Gaussian error model

$u_{i,j} \sim N(h'_j(d(x_i, y_i)), \sigma^2)$ with shared variance parameter σ^2. That is, we solve the following problem:

$$\underset{\substack{d \in C^1(\mathbb{R}^2, \mathbb{R}) \\ b_1 < b_2 < \cdots < b_{P-1} \\ \mathbf{h}' = (h'_1, \ldots, h'_{2P}) \in \mathcal{L}(b_1, \ldots, b_{P-1})}}{\arg\max} \sum_{j=1}^{2P} \left(\sum_{i=1}^{N} \log \mathbb{P}\left(u_{i,j} \mid h'_j\left(d(x_i, y_i)\right)\right) \right), \quad (3)$$

Note that the value of the variance σ^2 is not needed to solve (3). We solve (3) using deep learning, as described in [5], which yields an estimated isodepth $\hat{d}$ and breakpoints $\hat{b}_1, \ldots, \hat{b}_{P-1}$.

In the second step, we use the estimated isodepth and breakpoints to compute the 1-D expression function $\mathbf{h}$:

$$\underset{\mathbf{h} = (h_1, \ldots, h_G) \in \mathcal{L}(\hat{b}_1, \ldots, \hat{b}_{P-1})}{\arg\max} \sum_{g=1}^{G} \left(\sum_{i=1}^{N} \log \mathbb{P}\left(a_{i,g} \mid h_g\left(\hat{d}(x_i, y_i)\right)\right) \right). \quad (4)$$

where we assume the UMI counts $a_{i,g}$ follow the Poisson expression model $a_{i,g} \sim$ Pois$(N_i e^{h_g(d(x_i, y_i))})$ where N_i is the total UMI count at spot i [11]. Solving (4) is equivalent to solving $G \cdot P$ Poisson regression problems, one problem for each combination of the G genes and P domains. See [5] for further details.

3   Results

We demonstrate that the topographic map of gene expression learned by GAS-TON reveals the geometry and continuous gene expression gradients of multiple tissues across multiple SRT technologies including 10x Visium [1], Slide-SeqV2 [10,12], and Stereo-Seq [4]. Using SRT data from the mouse cerebellum [2,3] and olfactory bulb [4], we show that GASTON more accurately identifies spatial domains (larger spatial coherency) and marker genes (larger AUPRC) compared to existing methods. Moreover, GASTON derives a map of spatial cell type organization and reveals novel spatial gradients of neuronal differentiation. See [5] for details.

4   Code and Preprint

GASTON is available at https://github.com/raphael-group/GASTON and a preprint [5] is available at https://doi.org/10.1101/2023.10.10.561757.

References

1. 10x Visium Genomics Visium Spatial Gene Expression. https://www.10xgenomics.com/products/spatial-gene-expression

2. Cable, D.M., et al.: Cell type-specific inference of differential expression in spatial transcriptomics. Nat. Methods **19**(9), 1076–1087 (2022)
3. Cable, D.M., et al.: Robust decomposition of cell type mixtures in spatial transcriptomics. Nat. Biotechnol. **40**(4), 517–526 (2022)
4. Chen, A., et al.: Spatiotemporal transcriptomic atlas of mouse organogenesis using DNA nanoball-patterned arrays. Cell **185**(10), 1777–1792 (2022)
5. Chitra, U., et al.: Mapping the topography of spatial gene expression with interpretable deep learning. bioRxiv (2023)
6. Marx, V.: Method of the year: spatially resolved transcriptomics. Nat. Methods **18**(1), 9–14 (2021)
7. Moses, L., Pachter, L.: Museum of spatial transcriptomics. Nat. Methods **19**(5), 534–546 (2022)
8. Palla, G., Fischer, D.S., Regev, A., Theis, F.J.: Spatial components of molecular tissue biology. Nat. Biotechnol. **40**(3), 308–318 (2022)
9. Rao, A., Barkley, D., França, G.S., Yanai, I.: Exploring tissue architecture using spatial transcriptomics. Nature **596**(7871), 211–220 (2021)
10. Rodriques, S.G., et al.: Slide-Seq: a scalable technology for measuring genome-wide expression at high spatial resolution. Science **363**(6434), 1463–1467 (2019)
11. Sarkar, A., Stephens, M.: Separating measurement and expression models clarifies confusion in single-cell RNA sequencing analysis. Nat. Genet. **53**(6), 770–777 (2021)
12. Stickels, R.R., et al.: Highly sensitive spatial transcriptomics at near-cellular resolution with slide-seqv2. Nat. Biotechnol. **39**(3), 313–319 (2021)
13. Tian, L., Chen, F., Macosko, E.Z.: The expanding vistas of spatial transcriptomics. Nat. Biotechnol. **41**(6), 773–782 (2023)
14. Townes, F.W., Hicks, S.C., Aryee, M.J., Irizarry, R.A.: Feature selection and dimension reduction for single-cell RNA-SEq based on a multinomial model. Genome Biol. **20**, 1–16 (2019)
15. Velten, B., Stegle, O.: Principles and challenges of modeling temporal and spatial omics data. Nat. Methods, 1–13 (2023)
16. Zeng, H.: What is a cell type and how to define it? Cell **185**(15), 2739–2755 (2022)

GraSSRep: Graph-Based Self-supervised Learning for Repeat Detection in Metagenomic Assembly

Ali Azizpour[1]([✉]), Advait Balaji[2], Todd J. Treangen[2], and Santiago Segarra[1]

[1] Department of Electrical and Computer Engineering, Rice University, Houston, TX, USA
{aa210,segarra}@rice.edu
[2] Department of Computer Science, Rice University, Houston, TX, USA
{advait,treangen}@rice.edu

Abstract. Repetitive DNA (repeats) poses significant challenges for accurate and efficient genome assembly and sequence alignment. This is particularly true for metagenomic data, where genome dynamics such as horizontal gene transfer, gene duplication, and gene loss/gain complicate accurate genome assembly from metagenomic communities. Detecting repeats is a crucial first step in overcoming these challenges. To address this issue, we propose GraSSRep, a novel approach that leverages the assembly graph's structure through graph neural networks (GNNs) within a self-supervised learning framework to classify DNA sequences into repetitive and non-repetitive categories. Specifically, we frame this problem as a node classification task within a metagenomic assembly graph. In a self-supervised fashion, we rely on a high-precision (but low-recall) heuristic to generate pseudo-labels for a small proportion of the nodes. We then use those pseudo-labels to train a GNN embedding and a random forest classifier to propagate the labels to the remaining nodes. In this way, GraSSRep combines sequencing features with pre-defined and learned graph features to achieve state-of-the-art performance in repeat detection. We evaluate our method using simulated and synthetic metagenomic datasets. The results on the simulated data highlight our GraSSRep's robustness to repeat attributes, demonstrating its effectiveness in handling the complexity of repeated sequences. Additionally, our experiments with synthetic metagenomic datasets reveal that incorporating the graph structure and the GNN enhances our detection performance. Finally, in comparative analyses, GraSSRep outperforms existing repeat detection tools with respect to precision and recall.

Keywords: Metagenomics · Repeat detection · Graph neural network · Self-supervised learning

This work was supported by the NSF under award EF-2126387.

J. Ma (Ed.): RECOMB 2024, LNCS 14758, pp. 372–376, 2024.
https://doi.org/10.1007/978-1-0716-3989-4_34

Motivation

One of the major challenges in the metagenomic assembly is the presence of repeats [3,5], which are sequences of DNA that are similar or identical to sequences elsewhere in the genome [7]. These repetitive elements, while natural and abundant in genomes, complicate the process of genome assembly and comparison [6]. They intricately tangle the assembly graph, making it difficult to distinguish the order, orientation, and copy number variation of genomes comprising the microbiome under study, resulting in fragmented assemblies. Moreover, repeats introduce ambiguities for comparative genomics, hindering differentiation between identical or similar regions and complicating the understanding of gene functions, regulatory elements, and their role in genetic disorders [7]. To overcome these obstacles, precise identification and annotation of repeated sequences is necessary. Previous studies have employed pre-specified graph features in combination with machine learning techniques to address the challenge of detecting repeats, treating it as a node classification problem [1,2]. In this context, the nodes of the graph represent DNA sequences, and the objective is to classify them into repeats and non-repeats. However, given the vast amount of genomic data, there remains ample opportunity for enhancement through learning discriminative graph features. One of the promising ways to achieve this is by employing graph neural networks (GNNs) [8]. GNNs have the unique ability to learn distinctive and valuable features for the nodes within the graphs. Unlike predefined features, GNNs generate these characteristics through trainable iterative computations, making them adaptive to the specific data. However, one of the primary challenges in genomic data analysis is the fact that most of the data is unlabeled, particularly in distinguishing between repeat and non-repeat sequences. In the absence of labeled data points offering insights into each class, these conventional methods become ineffective. To overcome this issue, self-supervised learning emerges as a natural and powerful alternative to leverage the vast unsupervised data [4]. In self-supervised learning, specific data points (nodes) are initially given (potentially noisy) labels. Subsequently, machine learning algorithms are employed, coupled with fine-tuning steps, to refine the model's performance. This approach ensures the ability to classify data points without requiring access to their true labels. In this work, we propose GraSSRep, a novel graph-based algorithm to identify and detect the repeated sequences in the metagenomic assembly in a self-supervised manner by leveraging GNNs, to learn (rather than pre-specify) graph features for repeat detection. An implementation of GraSSRep can be found at https://github.com/aliaaz99/GraSSRep. A preprint of the full paper is available at https://arxiv.org/abs/2402.09381.

Methods

Given paired-end reads, our goal is to identify repeated DNA sequences in the metagenome. An overview of our method specifically designed for this task is illustrated in Fig. 1.

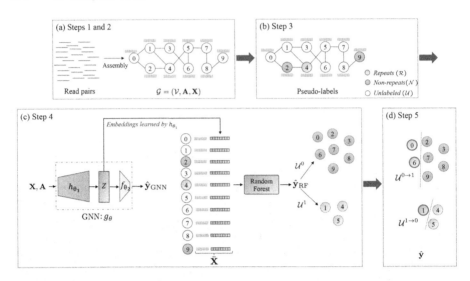

Fig. 1. Overview of GraSSRep. (a) Reads are assembled into unitigs forming the nodes of the unitig graph. Edges are constructed based on the read mapping information. Also, feature vectors are computed for each unitig. (b) Unitigs with distinctive sequencing features are selected as training nodes and labeled. (c) The unitig graph is input into a GNN. Embeddings are generated for each unitig and combined with the initial features. A random forest classifier predicts labels for all unitigs based on the augmented feature vectors. (d) Sequencing features are employed to identify outliers within each predicted class, leading to the reassignment of their class labels.

In the initial step, we construct a unitig graph in order to leverage graph features for repeat detection. First, all reads are assembled into unitigs by using the de Bruijn graph structure, and then we consider these unitigs as the nodes $\mathcal{V}$ of our unitig graph. To form the edges, we map the reads back to the unitigs and define two types of edges between the unitigs. The first set, referred to as adjacency edges, captures potentially neighboring unitigs in the genome. The second set, which we call repeat edges, provides additional relational information for repeat detection.

In the second step, we compute features of the unitigs that are informative in determining which unitigs are repetitive. We consider two types of features: sequencing (unitig length and mean coverage) that are obtained during the sequencing process before constructing the unitig graph, and graph-based, where we incorporate five widely used features in the literature: betweenness centrality, k-core value, degree, weighted degree, and clustering coefficient.

Since we do not have any prior information (labels) on whether any unitig is a repeat or not, in the third step, we generate a set of pseudo-labels using the sequencing features. In defining our pseudo-labels, we rely on the fact that shorter unitigs with higher coverage are highly likely to be repetitive, while very long unitigs with lower coverage are more likely to be non-repeat unitigs [1]. Based on this fact, we divide the unitigs into three sets: the repeats $\mathcal{R}$, the non-repeats $\mathcal{N}$, and the unlabeled $\mathcal{U}$, where we are confident about the labels of the nodes in sets of $\mathcal{R}$ and $\mathcal{N}$, utilizing them as a training set for a machine learning model. The objective is to classify the remaining unitigs in the set $\mathcal{U}$.

To do so, we employ self-supervised learning to classify the unlabeled unitigs. We train a graph-based model on labeled sets $\mathcal{R}$ (repeats) and $\mathcal{N}$ (non-repeats), using a graph neural network (GNN) denoted as g_θ. The GNN takes the graph structure $\mathbf{A}$ and the node features $\mathbf{X}$ as input, producing labels $\hat{\mathbf{y}}_{\text{GNN}}$. The model's parameters θ are learned through end-to-end training based on pseudo-labels. The GNN generates intermediate embeddings $\mathbf{Z}$ representing learned features for each unitig. The parameters θ are optimized to minimize a classification loss, aligning predicted labels with pseudo-labels for $\mathcal{R}$ and $\mathcal{N}$. The optimized parameters $\theta^\star$ yield embeddings that capture relevant features for unitig classification. Then, the augmented feature matrix $\bar{\mathbf{X}}$ is created by concatenating the initial graph-based features $\mathbf{X}$ with the GNN-generated features $\mathbf{Z}$. A random forest (RF) classifier is trained on pseudo-labeled sets $\mathcal{R} \cup \mathcal{N}$ using $\bar{\mathbf{X}}$ as input. The RF combines the explanatory power of the original graph-based features with the learned features from the GNN, producing predicted labels $\hat{\mathbf{y}}_{\text{RF}}$. Sequencing features are excluded from the RF input to prevent the classifier from relying solely on them, ensuring effective generalization of knowledge about graph-based attributes associated with repeats and non-repeats.

In the final step of our method, we enhance the performance of our predictions through a fine-tuning process. We first assign the pseudo-labels of the training nodes in $\mathcal{R}$ and $\mathcal{N}$ as their final predicted labels. Our primary focus is then directed toward the non-training unitigs in $\mathcal{U}$. To do so, sequencing features are reconsidered for $\mathcal{U}$, crucial for accurate labeling. We split $\mathcal{U}$ into sets $\mathcal{U}^1$ (predicted repeats) and $\mathcal{U}^0$ (predicted non-repeats) based on the RF predictions. Consequently, we change the label from repeat to non-repeat ($\mathcal{U}^{1 \to 0}$) for those unitigs that are longer than a threshold and have low coverage within the set of $\mathcal{U}^1$. Similarly, we change the label from non-repeat to repeat ($\mathcal{U}^{0 \to 1}$) for short unitigs with high coverage in $\mathcal{U}^0$.

Summarizing, the final labels $\hat{\mathbf{y}}$ predicted by our model are given by

$$[\hat{\mathbf{y}}]_i = \begin{cases} 1 & \text{for all } i \in \mathcal{R} \cup (\mathcal{U}^1 \setminus \mathcal{U}^{1 \to 0}) \cup \mathcal{U}^{0 \to 1}, \\ 0 & \text{for all } i \in \mathcal{N} \cup (\mathcal{U}^0 \setminus \mathcal{U}^{0 \to 1}) \cup \mathcal{U}^{1 \to 0}. \end{cases} \tag{1}$$

In (1), we see that the unitigs deemed as repeats ($[\hat{\mathbf{y}}]_i = 1$) by our method are those i) assigned a repeat pseudo-label ($\mathcal{R}$), ii) classified as repeats by our RF and not deemed as outliers ($\mathcal{U}^1 \setminus \mathcal{U}^{1 \to 0}$), or iii) classified as non-repeats by RF but later deemed as outliers ($\mathcal{U}^{0 \to 1}$). Conversely, unitigs classified as non-repeats are those i) assigned a non-repeat pseudo-label ($\mathcal{N}$), ii) classified as non-repeats by our RF and not deemed as outliers ($\mathcal{U}^0 \setminus \mathcal{U}^{0 \to 1}$), or iii) classified as repeats by RF but later deemed as outliers ($\mathcal{U}^{1 \to 0}$).

Results

We conduct a comprehensive analysis of our algorithm's performance across various settings. Initially, we utilize a simulated dataset to explore the impact of three critical characteristics beyond our control in real datasets: length of repeats, the copy number of the repeats, and depth of coverage. Our approach exhibits resilience to variations in repeat length and copy number, maintaining stability in all metrics as these parameters vary. Furthermore, the model consistently enhances its performance with increased coverage. Additionally, through an ablation study of the algorithm steps using synthetic metagenomic data, we observe a consistent improvement in algorithm performance throughout the pipeline. This underscores the significance of each step in achieving optimal results. Finally, using real datasets, we compare our method with various existing repeat detection methods. GraSSRep outperforms all other methods, particularly demonstrating superior capability in detecting repeats with a higher recall rate (55% versus the next best alternative [2] at 29.8%). This superiority comes from the combined value of incorporating learnable graph features (through the GNN) and considering a self-supervised framework.

References

1. Ghurye, J., Pop, M.: Better identification of repeats in metagenomic scaffolding. In: Frith, M., Storm Pedersen, C.N. (eds.) WABI 2016. LNCS, vol. 9838, pp. 174–184. Springer, Cham (2016). https://doi.org/10.1007/978-3-319-43681-4_14
2. Ghurye, J., Treangen, T., Fedarko, M., Hervey, W.J., Pop, M.: MetaCarvel: linking assembly graph motifs to biological variants. Genome Biol. **20**(1), 1–14 (2019)
3. Ghurye, J.S., Cepeda-Espinoza, V., Pop, M.: Metagenomic assembly: overview, challenges and applications. Yale J. Biol. Med. **89**(3), 353 (2016)
4. Jaiswal, A., Babu, A.R., Zadeh, M.Z., Banerjee, D., Makedon, F.: A survey on contrastive self-supervised learning. Technologies **9**(1), 2 (2020)
5. Lapidus, A.L., Korobeynikov, A.I.: Metagenomic data assembly-the way of decoding unknown microorganisms. Front. Microbiol. **12**, 613791 (2021)
6. Treangen, T.J., Abraham, A.L., Touchon, M., Rocha, E.P.: Genesis, effects and fates of repeats in prokaryotic genomes. FEMS Microbiol. Rev. **33**(3), 539–571 (2009)
7. Treangen, T.J., Salzberg, S.L.: Repetitive DNA and next-generation sequencing: computational challenges and solutions. Nat. Rev. Genet. **13**(1), 36–46 (2012). https://doi.org/10.1038/nrg3117
8. Wu, Z., Pan, S., Chen, F., Long, G., Zhang, C., Philip, S.Y.: A comprehensive survey on graph neural networks. IEEE Trans. Neural Netw. Learn. Syst. **32**(1), 4–24 (2020)

PRS-Net: Interpretable Polygenic Risk Scores via Geometric Learning

Han Li[1] , Jianyang Zeng[2(✉)], Michael P. Snyder[3(✉)], and Sai Zhang[4,5,6(✉)]

[1] Institute for Interdisciplinary Information Sciences, Tsinghua University, Beijing, China

[2] School of Engineering, Westlake University, Hangzhou, Zhejiang, China
zengjy@westlake.edu.cn

[3] Department of Genetics, Stanford University School of Medicine, Stanford, CA, USA
mpsnyder@stanford.edu

[4] Department of Epidemiology, University of Florida, Gainesville, FL, USA
sai.zhang@ufl.edu

[5] J. Crayton Pruitt Family Department of Biomedical Engineering, University of Florida, Gainesville, FL, USA

[6] The Genetics Institute, University of Florida, Gainesville, FL, USA

Abstract. Polygenic risk score (PRS) serves as a valuable tool for predicting the genetic risk of complex human diseases for individuals, playing a pivotal role in advancing precision medicine. Traditional PRS methods, predominantly following a linear structure, often fall short in capturing the intricate relationships between genotype and phenotype. We present PRS-Net, an interpretable deep learning-based framework designed to effectively model the nonlinearity of biological systems for enhanced disease prediction and biological discovery. PRS-Net begins by deconvoluting the genome-wide PRS at the single-gene resolution, and then it encapsulates gene-gene interactions for genetic risk prediction leveraging a graph neural network, thereby enabling the characterization of biological nonlinearity underlying complex diseases. An attentive readout module is specifically introduced into the framework to facilitate model interpretation and biological discovery. Through extensive tests across multiple complex diseases, PRS-Net consistently outperforms baseline PRS methods, showcasing its superior performance on disease prediction. Moreover, the interpretability of PRS-Net has been demonstrated by the identification of genes and gene-gene interactions that significantly influence the risk of Alzheimer's disease and multiple sclerosis. In summary, PRS-Net provides a potent tool for parallel genetic risk prediction and biological discovery for complex diseases.

Keywords: Polygenic risk score · Complex disease · Graph neural network · Protein-protein interactions

1 Introduction

Complex human diseases display polygenicity in their genetic architectures, characterized by a multitude of common genetic variants with minor individual effects

© The Author(s), under exclusive license to Springer Nature Switzerland AG 2024
J. Ma (Ed.): RECOMB 2024, LNCS 14758, pp. 377–380, 2024.
https://doi.org/10.1007/978-1-0716-3989-4_35

accumulatively influencing the disease risk [1]. Polygenic risk scores (PRSs) are developed to quantitatively characterize the genetic susceptibility of individuals to specific traits or complex diseases based on common genetic variants [2]. This methodology empowers targeted preventive and therapeutic interventions, paving the way towards personalized medicine [3].

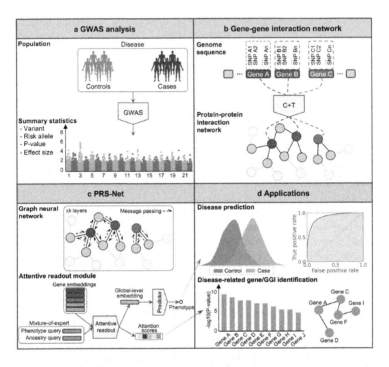

Fig. 1. An illustrative diagram of PRS-Net. **(a)** The proposed framework is based on GWAS summary statistics, including P-values, effect sizes, and standard errors. **(b)** A gene-gene or protein-protein interaction network is constructed based on the public database. Gene-level PRSs are calculated using the clumping and thresholding (C+T) method with different parameters, serving as node features of the network. **(c)** A graph neural network is employed to update node features via message passing and subsequently an attentive readout module is applied to enhance model interpretation. **(d)** The PRS-Net can be applied for disease prediction and disease-relevant gene and gene-gene interaction identification.

PRS is typically calculated based on the summary statistics derived from the genome-wide association study (GWAS) [4], a widely-used statistical method to study genotype-phenotype associations. While GWAS identifies trait- and disease-associated genetic variants, such as single nucleotide polymorphisms (SNPs), that exhibit significant differences in frequencies between cases and controls, these GWAS hits tend to have modest-to-mild effect sizes, resulting in limited prediction power. In an effort to boost predictive modeling, various statistical methods have been proposed to aggregate the effects of individual SNPs. Nonetheless, these techniques primarily rely on univariate effect sizes derived from linear GWAS models, thus overlook potential nonlinear associations between genetic factors and phenotypes, undermining their predictive performance. Additional endeavors have been made to build models capturing nonlinear interactions in PRS calculation. However, these methods only take a limited number of variants as their input, and lack the integration of versatile prior biological knowledge. Indeed, these approaches have demonstrated either comparable or, in many cases, inferior performance in predicting phenotypes compared to linear models [5].

2   Overview of PRS-Net

In this study, we propose PRS-Net (Fig. 1), a geometric deep learning-based framework designed to inherently incorporate nonlinear interactions among genes in predicting disease genetic risk, aiming to deliver a more accurate and interpretable PRS. PRS-Net comprises the two main components:

(i) **Gene-gene interaction network construction.** Based on the GWAS summary statistics, PRS-Net first maps gene-level PRSs, computed by the standard clumping and thresholding (C+T) method, onto a gene-gene interaction (GGI) network. We construct our GGI network based on the protein-protein interactions (PPIs) derived from the STRING database [6], where network nodes stand for protein-coding genes and edges represent protein interactions. To compute gene-level PRSs, we perform linkage disequilibrium (LD) clumping and subsequent thresholding using 11 distinct P-values for variants within the extended region of each gene. This process results in 11 PRSs for each gene within the PPI network, subsequently serving as the input node features for PRS-Net.

(ii) **PRS-Net.** After constructing the GGI network along with node features, a graph isomorphism network (GIN) [7] is employed to iteratively update gene embeddings via message passing, enabling the propagation of genetic information over the GGI network. Next, an attentive readout module is introduced to facilitate the model interpretation. Moreover, we propose a multiple-ancestry variation of PRS-Net named PRS-Net$_{MA}$, which incorporates a mixture-of-expert module [8] to enhance PRS prediction across different ancestries.

3   Experimental Results

We downloaded genotype and phenotype data from the UK Biobank (UKBB) database [9] for six complex diseases, encompassing Alzheimer's disease, atrial fibrillation, rheumatoid arthritis, multiple sclerosis, ulcerative colitis, and asthma. Diseases were defined based on the ICD-10 codes. In our primary experiments, we focused on individuals of Western European ancestry due to the insufficient sample size of non-European ancestry populations. The results revealed that PRS-Net consistently outperformed baseline methods, including PLINK, PRSice-2, LDpred-2, and lassosum, on all disease datasets, resulting in relative improvements ranging from 0.5% to 3.7%. We also curated a mixed-ancestry dataset encompassing Western European, South Asian, and African for asthma to assess the performance of our multiple-ancestry model, PRS-Net$_{MA}$. In these tests, PRS-Net$_{MA}$ exhibited superior performance compared to baseline methods. In summary, our experiments demonstrate the improved prediction power of PRS-Net by incorporating nonlinear gene interactions into the genotype-phenotype modeling.

Next, we sought to evaluate the application of PRS-Net in identifying risk genes and GGIs underlying Alzheimer's disease and multiple sclerosis. Our results unveiled a substantial alignment between disease risk genes and GGIs pinpointed by PRS-Net and the prior research, highlighting the promising capacity of PRS-Net to discover disease genes and offer biological insights into disease mechanisms.

Code: https://github.com/lihan97/PRS-Net.
Preprint: https://www.biorxiv.org/content/10.1101/2024.02.13.580211v1.

References

1. Clarke, R., et al.: Genetic variants associated with lp (a) lipoprotein level and coronary disease. New Engl. J. Med. **361**(26), 2518–2528 (2009)
2. Torkamani, A., Wineinger, N.E., Topol, E.J.: The personal and clinical utility of polygenic risk scores. Nat. Rev. Genet. **19**(9), 581–590 (2018)
3. Gibson, G.: On the utilization of polygenic risk scores for therapeutic targeting. PLoS Genet. **15**(4), e1008060 (2019)
4. Vilhjálmsson, B.J., et al.: Modeling linkage disequilibrium increases accuracy of polygenic risk scores. Am. J. Human Genet. **97**(4), 576–592 (2015)
5. Bellot, P., de Los Campos, G., Pérez-Enciso, M.: Can deep learning improve genomic prediction of complex human traits? Genetics **210**(3), 809–819 (2018)
6. Szklarczyk, D., et al.: The string database in 2023: protein-protein association networks and functional enrichment analyses for any sequenced genome of interest. Nucleic Acids Res. **51**(D1), D638–D646 (2023)
7. Xu, K., Hu, W., Leskovec, J., Jegelka, S.: How powerful are graph neural networks? In: International Conference on Learning Representations (2018)
8. Masoudnia, S., Ebrahimpour, R.: Mixture of experts: a literature survey. Artif. Intell. Rev. **42**, 275–293 (2014)
9. Sudlow, C., et al.: UK biobank: an open access resource for identifying the causes of a wide range of complex diseases of middle and old age. PLoS Med. **12**(3), e1001779 (2015)

Haplotype-Aware Sequence Alignment
to Pangenome Graphs

Ghanshyam Chandra[1], Daniel Gibney[2], and Chirag Jain[1(✉)]

[1] Department of Computational and Data Sciences, Indian Institute of Science,
Bangalore 560012, KA, India
{ghanshyamc,chirag}@iisc.ac.in
[2] Department of Computer Science, The University of Texas at Dallas,
Richardson, TX 75080, USA
daniel.gibney@utdallas.edu

Abstract. Modern pangenome graphs are built using haplotype-resolved genome assemblies. While mapping reads to a pangenome graph, prioritizing alignments that are consistent with the known haplotypes has been shown to improve genotyping accuracy. However, the existing rigorous formulations for sequence-to-graph co-linear chaining and alignment problems do not consider the haplotype paths in a pangenome graph. This often leads to spurious read alignments to those paths that are unlikely recombinations of the known haplotypes.

We present novel formulations and algorithms for haplotype-aware sequence alignment to directed acyclic graphs (DAGs). We consider both sequence-to-DAG chaining and sequence-to-DAG alignment problems. Drawing inspiration from the commonly used models for genotype imputation, we assume that a query sequence is an imperfect mosaic of the reference haplotypes. Accordingly, we extend previous chaining and alignment formulations by introducing a recombination penalty for a haplotype switch. First, we solve haplotype-aware sequence-to-DAG alignment in $O(|Q||E||\mathcal{H}|)$ time where Q is the query sequence, E is the set of edges, and $\mathcal{H}$ is the set of haplotypes represented in the graph. To complement our solution, we prove that an algorithm significantly faster than $O(|Q||E||\mathcal{H}|)$ is impossible under the Strong Exponential Time Hypothesis (SETH). Second, we propose a haplotype-aware chaining algorithm that runs in $O(|\mathcal{H}|N \log |\mathcal{H}|N)$ time after graph preprocessing, where N is the count of input anchors. We then establish that a chaining algorithm significantly faster than $O(|\mathcal{H}|N)$ is impossible under SETH. As a proof-of-concept of our algorithmic solutions, we implemented the chaining algorithm in the Minichain aligner (https://github.com/at-cg/minichain). We demonstrate the advantage of the algorithm by aligning sequences sampled from human major histocompatibility complex (MHC) to a pangenome graph of 60 MHC haplotypes. The proposed algorithm offers better consistency with ground-truth recombinations when compared to a haplotype-agnostic algorithm.

Keywords: Pangenome · Pattern matching · Genome sequencing

A longer version of this paper is available on bioRxiv [3].

J. Ma (Ed.): RECOMB 2024, LNCS 14758, pp. 381–384, 2024.
https://doi.org/10.1007/978-1-0716-3989-4_36

1   Introduction

A pangenome graph is commonly represented either as a directed cyclic graph or a directed acyclic graph (DAG), where each vertex is labeled by a sequence. Recent methods for pangenome graph construction use phased genome assemblies to construct a graph [7]. The corresponding haplotype sequences are stored as paths in the graph. An arbitrary path in a pangenome graph corresponds to either the reference haplotypes or their recombinations. As such, the number of sequences spelled by a graph increases combinatorially with the number of variants, which often results in ambiguity during read mapping [11]. To circumvent this issue, it is important to consider correlations between two or more genetic variants, i.e. where individuals tend to have same genotype. For example, PanGenie is an alignment-free genotyping algorithm that leverages long-range haplotype information inherent in the phased genomes [4].

The primary problem formulation for sequence-to-graph alignment seeks a path in the graph which spells a sequence with minimum edit distance from the query sequence [10]. $O(|V| + |Q||E|)$-time algorithms exist for both exact and approximate pattern matching problems for graphs, where Q denotes the query sequence, E denotes the set of edges, and V denotes the set of vertices [10]. These formulations do not consider the associations between genetic variants and may lead to alignments with spurious recombinations in variant-dense regions. Co-linear chaining is another common technique used in modern aligners [1]. It is used to identify a coherent subset of anchors (exact matches) that can be joined together to produce an alignment. The existing formulations for chaining on graphs share the same limitation of not considering the associations between genetic variants [9]. Some of these known chaining algorithms run in $O(KN \log KN)$ time after graph preprocessing, where K denotes the minimum number of paths required to cover all the vertices and N denotes the count of input anchors [2,8].

2   Contributions

1. To address the above, we develop 'haplotype-aware' formulations for (i) sequence-to-DAG alignment and (ii) sequence-to-DAG chaining problems. Our formulations use the haplotype path information available in modern pangenome graphs. The formulations are inspired from the classic Li-Stephens haplotype copying model [6]. The Li-Stephens model is a probabilistic generative model which assumes that a sampled haplotype is an imperfect mosaic of known haplotypes.

2. Our problem formulation for the haplotype-aware sequence-to-DAG alignment optimizes the number of edits and haplotype switches simultaneously (Fig. 1). We give $O(|Q||E||\mathcal{H}|)$ time dynamic programming algorithm for solving the problem, where $\mathcal{H}$ denotes the set of haplotypes represented in the pangenome DAG. We further prove that the existence of a significantly faster algorithm than $O(|Q||E||\mathcal{H}|)$ is not possible under the strong exponential time

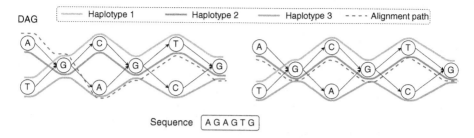

Fig. 1. The left figure shows the optimal alignment of the sequence to the DAG with minimum edit distance. Accordingly, the edit distance is zero and the count of recombinations is two. Next, suppose we use recombination penalty -5 (formally defined in [3]). The right figure shows the new optimal alignment, where there is no recombination because the alignment is consistent with Haplotype 2.

hypothesis (SETH) [12]. The proof involves a reduction from the Orthogonal Vectors problem.

3. We also formulate the haplotype-aware co-linear chaining problem. We solve it in $O(|\mathcal{H}|N \log |\mathcal{H}|N)$ time, assuming that a one-time preprocessing of the DAG is done in $O(|E||\mathcal{H}|)$ time. Our chaining algorithm builds on the sparse dynamic programming framework in [9]. To provide evidence of the near optimality of the proposed algorithm, we prove that it is impossible to solve this problem significantly faster than $O(|\mathcal{H}|N)$ under SETH.

4. We implemented the proposed chaining algorithm in Minichain and evaluated it using simulated and real sequences. We built a pangenome DAG using 60 publicly-available complete major histocompatibility complex (MHC) sequences [5]. We simulated query MHC haplotypes as mosaics of the 60 haplotypes. We demonstrate that introducing recombination penalty in the formulation leads to a much better consistency between the observed recombination events and the ground truth. We achieved Pearson correlation up to 0.94 between the observed recombination count and the ground-truth recombination count, whereas the correlation remained below 0.32 if recombinations are not penalized.

5. We also tested our algorithm using real publicly-available PacBio (SRX5633451, SRR1129212) and Oxford Nanopore (SRR2336508) long reads from CHM13 human genome. Here we demonstrate a better consistency between the ground-truth haplotype (CHM13) and the selected haplotype in the computed chains on the DAG. Our results suggest that haplotype-aware pattern matching to pangenome graphs can be useful to improve read mapping and variant calling accuracy.

Acknowledgements. This work is supported by funding from the National Supercomputing Mission, India under DST/NSM/ R&D_HPC_Applications, the Science and Engineering Research Board (SERB) under SRG/2021/000044, and the Intel India Research Fellowship.

References

1. Abouelhoda, M., Ohlebusch, E.: Chaining algorithms for multiple genome comparison. J. Disc. Algor. **3**(2–4), 321–341 (2005)
2. Chandra, G., Jain, C.: Gap-sensitive colinear chaining algorithms for acyclic pangenome graphs. J. Comput. Biol. **30**(11), 1182–1197 (2023)
3. Chandra, G., Jain, C.: Haplotype-aware sequence-to-graph alignment. In: bioRxiv, pp. 2023-11 (2023). https://doi.org/10.1101/2023.11.15.566493
4. Ebler, J., et al.: Pangenome-based genome inference allows efficient and accurate genotyping across a wide spectrum of variant classes. Nat. Genet. **54**(4), 518–525 (2022)
5. Li, H.: Sample graphs and sequences for testing sequence-to-graph alignment (2022). https://doi.org/10.5281/zenodo.6617246
6. Li, N., Stephens, M.: Modeling linkage disequilibrium and identifying recombination hotspots using single-nucleotide polymorphism data. Genetics **165**(4), 2213–2233 (2003)
7. Liao, W.W., et al.: A draft human pangenome reference. Nature **617**(7960), 312–324 (2023)
8. Ma, J., Cáceres, M., Salmela, L., Mäkinen, V., Tomescu, A.I.: Chaining for accurate alignment of erroneous long reads to acyclic variation graphs. Bioinformatics **39**(8), btad460 (2023)
9. Mäkinen, V., Tomescu, A.I., Kuosmanen, A., Paavilainen, T., Gagie, T., Chikhi, R.: Sparse dynamic programming on DAGs with small width. ACM Trans. Algor. **15**(2), 1–21 (2019)
10. Navarro, G.: Improved approximate pattern matching on hypertext. Theoret. Comput. Sci. **237**(1–2), 455–463 (2000)
11. Pritt, J., Chen, N.C., Langmead, B.: Forge: prioritizing variants for graph genomes. Genome Biol. **19**(1), 1–16 (2018)
12. Williams, V.V.: Hardness of easy problems: basing hardness on popular conjectures such as the strong exponential time hypothesis (invited talk). In: 10th International Symposium on Parameterized and Exact Computation (IPEC 2015). Schloss Dagstuhl-Leibniz-Zentrum fuer Informatik (2015)

Disease Risk Predictions with Differentiable Mendelian Randomization

Ludwig Gräf[1,2], Daniel Sens[1], Liubov Shilova[1,3],
and Francesco Paolo Casale[1,2(✉)]

[1] Helmholtz Munich, Neuherberg, Germany
`francescopaolo.casale@helmholtz-munich.de`
[2] Technical University of Munich, Munich, Germany
[3] Friedrich-Alexander-Universität Erlangen-Nürnberg, Erlangen, Germany

Abstract. Predicting future disease onset is crucial in preventive healthcare, yet longitudinal datasets linking early risk factors to subsequent health outcomes are scarce. To address this challenge, we introduce Differentiable Mendelian Randomization (DMR), an extension of the classical Mendelian Randomization framework for disease risk predictions without longitudinal data. To do so, DMR leverages risk factors and genetic profiles from a healthy cohort, along with results from genome-wide association studies (GWAS) of diseases of interest. In this work, we describe the DMR framework and confirm its reliability and effectiveness in simulations and an application to a type 2 diabetes (T2D) cohort.

1 Introduction

The advent of large biobanks, like UK Biobank [5], has revolutionized access to health metrics and genetic data, enabling advanced studies in healthy populations. Yet, the utility of these biobanks for longitudinal disease risk prediction is constrained by challenges like incomplete follow-ups, missing data, and low disease incidence rates.

Mendelian Randomization (MR) is a powerful tool for discerning causal relationships between risk factors (e.g., LDL cholesterol) and health outcomes (e.g., cardiovascular disease), even when such risk factors and health outcomes are measured in different cohorts. Leveraging this capability, we explore its application for cross-cohort risk prediction as an alternative to longitudinal analysis. We introduce Differentiable Mendelian Randomization (DMR), a new approach for end-to-end learning of disease predictors from multiple risk factors within the MR framework. We here describe the DMR framework and validate it in simulations and real data applications.

L. Gräf, D. Sens, L. Shilova—These authors contributed equally to this work.
Full paper—https://doi.org/10.1101/2024.03.06.583727

J. Ma (Ed.): RECOMB 2024, LNCS 14758, pp. 385–389, 2024.
https://doi.org/10.1007/978-0-7166-3989-4_37

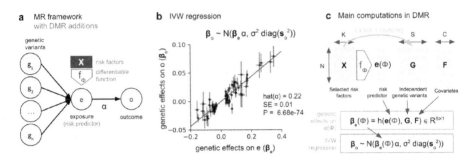

Fig. 1. (a) Schematic illustration of the MR framework with DMR additions highlighted in purple. (b) Visualisation of the IVW regression model used in two-sample MR. (c) Breakdown of the computations involved in DMR, emphasising the main steps for computing the loss function.

2   Methods

Two-Sample MR. Two-sample MR leverages summary statistics of GWAS of a risk factor (exposure) and a health outcome from different cohorts to infer the causal effect of the exposure on the outcome (Fig. 1a). Briefly, assuming S independent genetic variants associated with the exposure, let $\boldsymbol{\beta}_e \in \mathbb{R}^S$ denote the estimated effects of these variants on the exposure, $\boldsymbol{\beta}_o \in \mathbb{R}^S$ the estimated effects on the outcome, and $\boldsymbol{s}_o \in \mathbb{R}^S$ the standard errors of $\boldsymbol{\beta}_o$[1]. The causal effect of the exposure on the outcome can be estimated via the maximum likelihood estimator (MLE) of the slope α in Inverse Variance Weighting (IVW) regression, where $\boldsymbol{\beta}_o$ is regressed on $\boldsymbol{\beta}_e$ accounting for $\boldsymbol{s}_o$ (Fig. 1b). A statistical test for $\alpha \neq 0$ can be used to asses causality of the exposure on the outcome. We refer to [4] for a comprehensive description of the MR framework.

Two-Sample MR for Risk Predictions. We note that two-sample Mendelian Randomization (MR) can be used to build risk predictors without longitudinal data. For example, for L causal risk factors with estimated causal effects $\hat{\alpha}_1, \ldots, \hat{\alpha}_L$, we can build the following linear predictor:

$$f(\mathbf{x}) = \sum_{k=1}^{K_S} \hat{\alpha}_k x_k, \tag{1}$$

which can be utilized to assess risk in new patients.

Differentiable Mendelian Randomization. DMR leverages individual-level data from a genetic cohort of healthy individuals and GWAS summary statistics of a health outcome to learn risk predictors without longitudinal data. To do so, it employs a differentiable function f_ϕ parametrized by ϕ within the MR framework

---

[1] Exposure and outcome statistics should be estimated in different cohorts with no sample overlap from the same underlying population.

to synthesize multiple risk factors into an aggregate risk predictor (Fig. 1a). Briefly, for N individuals, K risk factors $\boldsymbol{E} \in \mathbb{R}^{N \times K}$, C GWAS covariates $\boldsymbol{F} \in \mathbb{R}^{N \times C}$ and S independent genetic variants associated with at least one risk factor $\boldsymbol{G} \in \mathbb{R}^{N \times S}$, the main computations in DMR are (Fig. 1c):

- Compute aggregate risk predictor $\boldsymbol{e}_\phi \in \mathbb{R}^{N \times 1}$ from $\boldsymbol{E}$ using f_ϕ, i.e. $\boldsymbol{e}_{\phi,i} = f_\phi(\boldsymbol{E}_{i:})$;
- Compute genetic effects on the aggregate risk predictor as the MLE of the weights of each variant $\boldsymbol{G}_{:s}$ on $\boldsymbol{e}_\phi$ accounting for covariates $\boldsymbol{F}$ through S marginal linear regressions,[2] which we indicate as $h(\boldsymbol{e}_\phi, \boldsymbol{G}, \boldsymbol{F})$;
- Compute IVW regression loss using the genetic effects on the aggregate predictor and the genetic effects on the outcome:

$$\text{loss}(\phi, \alpha, \sigma^2) = -\log \mathcal{N}\left(\boldsymbol{\beta}_o \mid h(\boldsymbol{e}_\phi, \boldsymbol{G}, \boldsymbol{F})\alpha, \sigma^2 \text{diag}(\boldsymbol{s}_o^2)\right). \tag{2}$$

As the loss is differentiable in the parameters ϕ, α, and σ^2, we can learn f_ϕ through gradient descent. To select independent genetic variants for our analyses, we performed univariate GWAS for each risk factor followed by a multivariate clumping procedure[3]. Prioritizing simplicity and clinical plausibility, we considered the following function for f:

$$f_\phi(\boldsymbol{x}) = \sum_{k=1}^{K} a_k \times \text{elu}(b_k x_k + c_k), \tag{3}$$

with parameters $\phi = \{\boldsymbol{a}, \boldsymbol{b}, \boldsymbol{c}\}$. The elu function can describe scenarios where contributions from single factors remains minimal until a critical threshold and then escalate. Notably, DMR reduces to multivariable Mendelian Randomization (MVMR) [3] when choosing linear function f. For optimization, we trained for 1,000 epochs using the Adam optimizer with learning rate of 0.01 and gradient clipping. All exposures were rank-inverse transformed to a Gaussian distribution prior to model training.

3   Results

Simulations. We evaluated the risk prediction accuracy of DMR and baseline methods through a series of simulations derived from the UK Biobank ($n = 309,865$ unrelated European individuals). We selected 26 blood biomarkers as risk factors, and simulated health outcomes as a linear combination of a subset of these traits, transformed by a J-shaped function to reflect contributions activating beyond specific thresholds. Our evaluation maintained a strict two-sample framework to prevent overlap between cohorts used for determining genetic effects on risk factors and outcomes. Across various simulation conditions, DMR consistently outperformed baseline MR models and showed competitive accuracy compared to a gold standard directly trained on individual-level data (Fig. 2).

---

[2] This mirrors the exposure GWAS step in standard MR. We account for sex, age and the leading 20 genetic PCs as covariates.

[3] To identify independent variants associated with at least one trait, we clumped the minimum P-value across traits using PLINK [2] (clump-p1 $= 5 \times 10^{-8}$, clump-r2 $= 0.05$ and clump-kb $= 5000$).

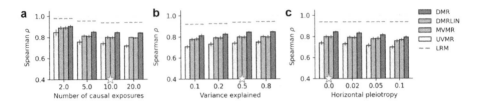

Fig. 2. (a–c) Model accuracy comparison across DMR, its linear variant DMR-LIN, Multivariable MR (MVMR), Univariate MR (UVMR), and a longitudinal reference model (LRM) trained on individual-level data. We varied the number of causal exposures (**a**), outcome variance fraction from risk factors (**b**), and horizontal pleiotropy influence (**c**), measuring Spearman correlation between simulated and estimated risk in a held-out validation set. Stars indicate fixed standard values; error bars show standard deviations from 10 repeat experiments.

T2D Risk Predictions. Next, we evaluated the prediction accuracy of DMR considering a type 2 diabetes (T2D) cohort derived from the UK Biobank dataset. We considered unrelated Europeans with no diabetes diagnosis ($n = 218,665$), and 37 traits including metabolic, anthropometric, and cardiovascular metrics. As external T2D GWAS, we utilized the summary statistics from [1]. Notably, DMR demonstrated superior accuracy of predicting T2D in 5 years over baseline MR methods (AUC of 0.847 ± 0.002 for DMR vs 0.836 ± 0.002 vs MVMR, $P < 10^{-4}$), and showed competitive results against a supervised model trained on individual-level outcome data in scenarios with low numbers of followup labels.

4   Discussion

Our study highlights that it is possible to learn disease risk predictors leveraging genetics rather than relying on longitudinal data. Future directions include leveraging the causal inference capabilities of DMR to address confounding in longitudinal datasets to enable robust and fair risk predictors, setting the stage for significant advancements as richer datasets emerge.

Acknowledgements. This research has been conducted using the UK Biobank Resource (Application Number 87065). F.P.C. and D.S. were funded by the Free State of Bavaria's Hightech Agenda through the Institute of AI for Health (AIH). L.S. acknowledges the support of the Friedrich-Alexander-Universität Erlangen-Nürnberg.

Author contributions. F.P.C. conceived the study and supervised the work. L.G., D.S., F.P.C. implemented the methods. L.G., D.S., L.S. analysed the data. L.G., D.S., L.S., F.P.C. interpreted the results. L.G., D.S., L.S., F.P.C. wrote the paper.

References

1. Mahajan, A., et al.: Fine-mapping type 2 diabetes loci to single-variant resolution using high-density imputation and islet-specific epigenome maps. Nat. Genet. **50**(11), 1505–1513 (2018)
2. Purcell, S.: Plink. http://pngu.mgh.harvard.edu/purcell/plink/
3. Sanderson, E.: Multivariable mendelian randomization and mediation. In: Cold Spring Harbor Perspectives in Medicine, p. a038984 (2020)
4. Sanderson, E., et al.: Mendelian randomization. Nat. Rev. Methods Primers **2**(1), 6 (2022)
5. Sudlow, C., et al.: UK biobank: an open access resource for identifying the causes of a wide range of complex diseases of middle and old age. PLoS Med. **12**(3), e1001779 (2015)

DIISCO: A Bayesian Framework for Inferring Dynamic Intercellular Interactions from Time-Series Single-Cell Data

Cameron Park[1(✉)], Shouvik Mani[2], Nicolas Beltran-Velez[2], Katie Maurer[3], Satyen Gohil[3], Shuqiang Li[3], Teddy Huang[3], David A. Knowles[2,4,5], Catherine J. Wu[3,6], and Elham Azizi[1,2(✉)]

[1] Department of Biomedical Engineering and Irving Institute for Cancer Dynamics, Columbia University, New York, NY, USA
{cyp2111,ea2690}@columbia.edu
[2] Department of Computer Science, Columbia University, New York, NY, USA
[3] Dana-Farber Cancer Institute and Harvard Medical School, Boston, MA, USA
[4] New York Genome Center, New York, NY, USA
[5] Department of Systems Biology, Columbia University, New York, NY, USA
[6] Broad Institute of MIT and Harvard, Cambridge, MA, USA

Abstract. Characterizing cell-cell communication and tracking its variability over time is essential for understanding the coordination of biological processes mediating normal development, progression of disease, or responses to perturbations such as therapies. Existing tools lack the ability to capture time-dependent intercellular interactions, such as those influenced by therapy, and primarily rely on existing databases compiled from limited contexts. We present DIISCO, a Bayesian framework for characterizing the temporal dynamics of cellular interactions using single-cell RNA-sequencing data from multiple time points. Our method uses structured Gaussian process regression to unveil time-resolved interactions among diverse cell types according to their co-evolution and incorporates prior knowledge of receptor-ligand complexes. We show the interpretability of DIISCO in new data collected from CAR-T cells co-cultured with lymphoma cells, demonstrating its potential to uncover dynamic cell-cell crosstalk.
Availability: DIISCO is publicly accessible at https://github.com/azizilab/DIISCO_public. All data will be deposited to GEO upon publication.

Keywords: Cell-cell communication · Single-cell omics · Time-series data · Probabilistic modeling · Variational inference

---

C. Park and S. Mani—These authors contributed equally.

© The Author(s), under exclusive license to Springer Nature Switzerland AG 2024
J. Ma (Ed.): RECOMB 2024, LNCS 14758, pp. 390–395, 2024.
https://doi.org/10.1007/978-1-0716-3989-4_38

1   Introduction

Single-cell RNA sequencing (scRNA-seq) which captures gene expression at the individual cell level, is crucial for delineating heterogeneous cell types and states [1,10]. The expanding landscape of single-cell datasets provides an exciting opportunity to understand temporal dynamics in cell types and cell-cell crosstalk. However, existing computational frameworks lack the ability to effectively integrate single-cell data across varying time points, for example in longitudinal clinical studies [2]. In dynamic systems like the tumor microenvironment, unraveling crosstalk between tumor and immune cells [7] is key to understanding immune dysfunction mechanisms and developing more effective treatment strategies [9,13]. Current methods for predicting cell-cell interactions using scRNA-seq data rely on databases of known interacting protein complexes, predicting based on expression levels of receptor-ligand (R-L) pairs [3,5]. However, these methods have limitations, including overlooking context-dependent nuances in different cell types and the inability to predict dynamic, time-varying interactions.

We introduce DIISCO (Dynamic Intercellular Interactions in Single Cell transcriptOmics), an open-source tool available at https://github.com/azizilab/DIISCO_public. DIISCO jointly infers cell type dynamics and communication patterns, defining cell types as clusters with similar gene expression profiles in scRNA-seq data. To model temporal dynamics, Gaussian Process (GP) regression models are deployed which have proven successful in integrating time-series single-cell datasets [8]. DIISCO further draws inspiration from Gaussian Process Regression Networks (GPRNs) for encoding cell type interactions, allowing for complex, time-dependent correlations between celltypes [12]. Our Bayesian framework infers dynamic interactions in scRNA-seq data from non-uniformly sampled time points. It incorporates prior knowledge on receptor-ligand complexes and quantifies uncertainty in predictions and interpretations (**Fig. 1a**). Performance is demonstrated on a dataset of Chimeric Antigen Receptor (CAR) T cells interacting with lymphoma cells.

2   Materials and Methods

Notations. We assume that we have N measurements of cell type frequencies at time points $t_1, \ldots, t_N$. We define $y(t_i)$ as a K-dimensional vector of observations at time t_i where the k-th dimension corresponds to the frequency of the k-th cell type. Additionally, we assume we have a set of M unobserved time points $t_{N+1}, \ldots, t_{N+M}$, placed anywhere on the time axis, for which we would like to infer the cell type values $y(t_{N+1}), \ldots, y(t_{N+M})$. We denote the set of all time points as $\mathcal{T} = \{t_1, \ldots, t_{N+M}\}$ and call $\mathcal{T}_u$ the set of unobserved time points $\mathcal{T}_u = \{t_{N+1}, \ldots, t_{N+M}\}$ and $\mathcal{T}_o$ the set of observed time points $\mathcal{T}_o = \{t_1, \ldots, t_N\}$. We will use the convention of $\cdot_u$ and $\cdot_o$ to denote unobserved and observed variables respectively.

Additionally, we have a binary matrix Λ of size $K \times K$ where $\Lambda_{k,k'} = 1$ indicates that the k-th cell type might interact with the k'-th cell type and $\Lambda_{k,k'} = 0$ otherwise.

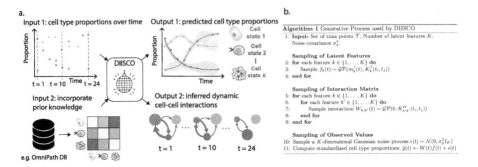

Fig. 1. Overview of DIISCO framework. a General workflow of DIISCO algorithm including inputs and outputs. Cell type proportions are computed from scRNA-seq data in each timepoint. Expression of RL complexes is incorporated to obtain time-resolved interactions between cell types. **b** Algorithm describing the generative process used by DIISCO

Model Specification. DIISCO is a generative model that assumes cell type frequencies, $\hat{y}(t_i)$, are derived from the following process (**Fig.** 1b): For every time point, we sample latent features, $f(t_i) \in \mathbb{R}^K$ where every feature $f(t_i)$, is a Gaussian process. We call this set $\mathcal{F} = \{f(t_i) \mid t_i \in \mathcal{T}\}$. Similarly, we sample at each time point an interaction matrix $W(t_i) \in \mathbb{R}^{K \times K}$ where we also assume that each $W(t_i)$ is a Gaussian process across time. We call this set $\mathcal{W} = \{W(t_i) \mid t_i \in \mathcal{T}\}$. Finally, we sample the standardized cell type proportions $\hat{y}(t_i) \in \mathbb{R}^K$ from a multivariate Gaussian. In other words:

$$\hat{y}(t_i) = W(t_i)f(t_i) + \epsilon(t_i) \tag{1}$$

where $\epsilon(t_i) \sim \mathcal{N}(0, \sigma_y^2 I)$ represents a zero-centered Gaussian noise process. We use $\mathcal{Y} = \{\hat{y}(t_i) \mid t_i \in \mathcal{T}\}$ to denote the set of all standardized cell type proportions across all time points.

Model Interpretation. The latent variable $W(t)_{i,j}$ represents the direction and effect of intercellular interaction (signaling communication) from cell type j to cell type i at time t. In particular, $W(t)_{i,j} > 0$ represents an activating effect, $W(t)_{i,j} < 0$ denotes inhibitory impact, and $|W(t)_{i,j}|$ reflects the strength of the interaction. $f(t)_i$ is a latent variable that represents the normalized proportion of cell type i at time. In constructing the prior for W, we penalize self-interactions $W_{i,i}$, such that $W_{i,j}$ can be interpreted as the impact of other cell types $j \neq i$ on the dynamics of cell type i.

Prior Distribution Over $\mathcal{W}$. To further limit the solution space, and improve model robustness and interpretability, we set two constraints on the sampling process of W. First, we set off-diagonal elements to zero if the cluster pairs do not express any complementary receptor-ligand pairs and second, we zero out the diagonals[1]. Formally, we achieve this by sampling $W(t)$ so that for $k, k' \in \{1, \ldots, K\}$.

$$W_{k,k'}(t) \sim \mathcal{GP}(0, K_{k,k'}^W(t, t)) \tag{2}$$

where

$$K_{k,k'}^W(t, t') = \begin{cases} v_W \exp\left(-\frac{(t-t')^2}{2\tau_W^2}\right) + \sigma_W^2 & \text{if } k \neq k' \\ 0 & \text{if } k = k' \text{ or } \Lambda_{k,k'} = 0 \end{cases} \tag{3}$$

and v_W, τ_W, and σ_W are shared hyper-parameters, retaining the same interpretations as before. To construct Λ, we scan for complementary expression of known RL pairs, i.e. when the sending cluster expresses a ligand at a defined threshold and the receiving cluster expresses the complementary receptor at a similarly defined threshold.

3 Results

DIISCO was applied to in vitro scRNA-seq data from an experiment involving co-culturing GFP-transduced Chimeric Antigen Receptor (CAR) T cells and MEC1 cells, a chronic lymphocytic leukemia cell line, across 10 time points in a 24 h span. Major cell types were defined through clustering and gene expression analysis, resulting in four metaclusters: cancer cells, exhausted CD8+ T cells, activated CD8+ T cells, and other CD8+ T cells. Omnipath was used to construct a binary interaction prior matrix Λ based on differentially expressed ligands and receptors across cell types.

Applied to CAR-T and MEC1 data, DIISCO revealed dynamic proportions of cell types, highlighting the decrease in cancer cells and the increase in exhausted T cells over time. The model predicted time-resolved interactions, such as the strengthening of interactions between exhausted T cells and MEC1 cells. We then calculated the correlations between different receptor-ligand gene pairs and the learned dynamic interaction (Fig. 2a). For calibration, we first confirmed that *CD19*, the target of the engineered CAR protein, is highly correlated with the interaction from Exhausted to MEC1 cells, as expected (Fig. 2a). Examining the MEC1 → Exhausted interaction, *CD86-CTLA4*, *CD80-CTLA4*, and *ICAM1-IL2RA* are the top RL pairs predicted by DIISCO. *CTLA4* is an established marker of T cell exhaustion, and *CD80* and *CD86* are costimulatory molecules that are expressed in malignant lymphocytes (including B cells) in a number of hematologic diseases [11]. *ICAM1* is a known regulator of inflammamtory response and is elevated in B-cell CLL patients with more severe disease progression [4].

Finally, we benchmarked the predicted DIISCO R-L interactions against other methods including CellChat [6] and CellphoneDB [5] by comparing the correlation of RL pairs predicted over time. We observe a significantly higher

---

[1] In the case when we are dealing with proportions and not raw counts this also ensures that we avoid a trivial solution due to the $\sum_k y_k(t) = 1$.

Pearson correlation and Spearman correlation for RLs in DIISCO-predicted interactions than those predicted by other methods (Fig. 2b). Our results thus confirm the ability of DIISCO to identify a monotonic increase in the expression of RL pairs underlying cell-cell interactions.

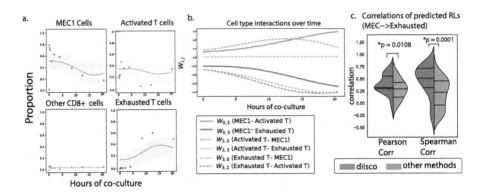

Fig. 2. DIISCO performance on CAR-T data. a. Temporal dynamics of cell types. Data points represent the measured proportion of cell types over time, and DIISCO output is shown as inferred mean (solid line) and 95% confidence intervals (shaded area) of y for each cell type. **b** Inferred W interaction matrix over the entire co-culture time window. **c.** Comparison of DIISCO predicted RL pairs with those predicted using Cellchat (cc) or CellphoneDB (cdb). Correlations between paired RLs shown for the $W_{MEC \rightarrow ExhaustedTcell}$ link. p-values calculated with MWU test.

4   Conclusion

DIISCO offers a robust framework for characterizing cell-cell communication and temporal variability in longitudinal single-cell datasets, aiding in understanding disease progression and complex biological systems. We demonstrate its performance on cancer-immune cell interaction data. A preprint of the full paper is available at https://www.biorxiv.org/content/10.1101/2023.11.14.566956v1.

Acknowledgements and Conflicts. We are thankful to David Blei and Dana Pe'er for helpful feedback and discussions. This work was made possible by support from the National Institute of Health (NIH) NCI grants R00CA230195, P01CA229092, Leukemia & Lymohoma Society grant SCOR-22937-22, and the MacMillan Family and the MacMillan Center for the Study of the Non-Coding Cancer Genome at the New York Genome Center. C.P. was supported by the Columbia University Kaganov Fellowship. K.M. was supported by the Richard K. Lubin Family Foundation Fellowship. C.J.W. is an equity holder of BioNTech and receives research funding from Pharmacyclics.

References

1. Azizi, E., et al.: Single-cell map of diverse immune phenotypes in the breast tumor microenvironment. Cell **174**(5), 1293–1308 (2018)
2. Bachireddy, P., et al.: Mapping the evolution of t cell states during response and resistance to adoptive cellular therapy. Cell Rep. **37**(6) (2021)
3. Browaeys, R., Saelens, W., Saeys, Y.: Nichenet: modeling intercellular communication by linking ligands to target genes. Nat. Methods **17**(2), 159–162 (2020)
4. Bui, T.M., Wiesolek, H.L., Sumagin, R.: ICAM-1: a master regulator of cellular responses in inflammation, injury resolution, and tumorigenesis. J. Leucocyte Biol. **108**(3), 787–799 (2020)
5. Efremova, M., Vento-Tormo, M., Teichmann, S.A., Vento-Tormo, R.: Cellphonedb: inferring cell-cell communication from combined expression of multi-subunit ligand-receptor complexes. Nat. Protoc. **15**(4), 1484–1506 (2020)
6. Jin, S., et al.: Inference and analysis of cell-cell communication using cellchat. Nat. Commun. **12**(1), 1088 (2021)
7. Kumar, M.P., et al.: Analysis of single-cell rna-seq identifies cell-cell communication associated with tumor characteristics. Cell Rep. **25**(6), 1458–1468 (2018)
8. Lönnberg, T., et al.: Single-cell rna-seq and computational analysis using temporal mixture modeling resolves th1/tfh fate bifurcation in malaria. Sci. Immunol. **2**(9), eaal2192 (2017)
9. Sievers, C., et al.: Phenotypic plasticity and reduced tissue retention of exhausted tumor-infiltrating t cells following neoadjuvant immunotherapy in head and neck cancer. Cancer Cell **41**(5), 887–902 (2023)
10. Tirosh, I., et al.: Dissecting the multicellular ecosystem of metastatic melanoma by single-cell rna-seq. Science **352**(6282), 189–196 (2016)
11. Vyth-Dreese, F.A., et al.: Localization in situ of costimulatory molecules and cytokines in b-cell non-hodgkin's lymphoma. Immunology **94**(4), 580–586 (1998)
12. Wilson, A.G., Knowles, D.A., Ghahramani, Z.: Gaussian process regression networks. arXiv preprint arXiv:1110.4411 (2011)
13. Yofe, I., Dahan, R., Amit, I.: Single-cell genomic approaches for developing the next generation of immunotherapies. Nat. Med. **26**(2), 171–177 (2020)

Enhancing Gene Set Analysis in Embedding Spaces: A Novel Best-Match Approach

Lechuan Li, Ruth Dannenfelser, Charlie Cruz, and Vicky Yao[✉]

Department of Computer Science, Rice University, Houston, USA
vy@rice.edu

Abstract. Embedding techniques have become valuable strategies for extracting crucial information from high-dimensional data and transforming it into more interpretable lower-dimensional spaces. In biology, embeddings are frequently used to capture a variety of functional relationships between genes to encode individual genes in a compact latent space. Genes, however, do not function in isolation but in coordinated gene sets where groups of proteins form complexes, function in pathways, or, more simply, have a localized set of possible interactions. Gene embeddings have been used mostly for downstream machine learning tasks, or, at best, comparisons between pairs of genes. There has been limited methodological development towards comparing gene sets in embedding spaces. Here, we propose a new method, ANDES, that compares how two gene sets are related in gene embedding spaces. ANDES uses a novel best-match approach that considers gene similarity while reconciling gene set diversity. ANDES is a flexible framework that has wide-ranging potential, especially when combined with different types of embeddings.

1 Introduction

The availability and abundance of genomic assays has increased with the development, improved efficiency, and cost effectiveness of recent high throughput technologies. There is now more demand for dimensionality reduction and other summarization techniques to make sense of the data deluge and model biological phenomena across diverse environments and states. Gene embeddings, in particular, allow for compact representations that can be used to predict gene function [1–3], disease associations [4,5], drug-targets [6], among other applications [7–10]. The gene embedding space is well characterized for these tasks, as well as analyzing a single gene in relation to other genes in the embedding, however little attention has been given to analyzing two or more gene sets in the context of a gene embedding.

By modeling the collective behavior of genes, gene sets provide a way to understand complex biological processes beyond what can be observed with single genes alone. Furthermore, the diverse nature of what constitutes a gene

J. Ma (Ed.): RECOMB 2024, LNCS 14758, pp. 396–399, 2024.
https://doi.org/10.1007/978-1-0716-3989-4_39

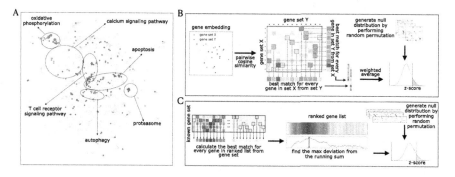

Fig. 1. Overview and motivation for ANDES. (A) node2vec gene embeddings of a human protein-protein interaction (PPI) network with colored genes depicting Alzheimer's disease genes from KEGG. These genes cover a diverse set of biological functions and sub-cluster within the embedding space. ANDES considers this sub-structure when estimating relationships between gene sets. **(B)** Overview of ANDES framework for gene set similarity. Given two gene sets, ANDES computes pairwise cosine similarities for genes in two sets, identifies the best matches in both directions, and calculates a weighted average to generate a unified score. Significance is estimated using a null distribution that considers set cardinality. **(C)** Depiction of ANDES rank-based gene set enrichment method. Given a curated gene set, such as a Gene Ontology term, and a gene list ranked by experimental results, ANDES determines the best-match similarity for each gene in the ranked list to calculate an enrichment score. The final score is corrected for set cardinality using a permuted background.

set such as: biological pathways, co-expression in response to certain conditions, reported GWAS genes, or protein complex membership, allows for unique insights into multiple facets of complex mammalian biology. Systematic analysis using gene sets has become a crucial part of routine analyses helping to disentangle disease processes [11–13], detecting phenotypically relevant drug targets [14,15], and analyzing functional relationships across-species [16–18]. Despite this importance, there appears to be limited to no research about how to best leverage gene embeddings for gene set comparisons revealing an untapped potential with far reaching applications.

Previous methods for set comparison with embeddings exist almost exclusively outside of biological use cases, and involve variations of averaging embedding information across set members. Typically the averaging is done by taking the centroid of all relevant set members in the embedding space [19,20], ultimately ignoring substructure within the set. Such methods can work well when set membership is localized to one region of the embedding space, but will fail when there are multiple distinct sub-functional groups in the set. This effect is especially salient in gene sets, even more so in those related to complex processes, because they typically contain a mixture of signals, as seen in the example of an Alzheimer's disease set shown in Fig. 1A. Thus, effectively leveraging embeddings to analyze gene sets necessitates a better method for gene set comparison.

While not typically applied to embedding spaces, network-based methods for comparing gene sets can also be used to measure functional similarity across gene sets. An example of such a method [21] frames the gene set comparison task as a t-test between the two sets, incorporating a permutation-based background correction to account for each set's size. However, despite the inclusion of a correction for gene set variability, this approach remains fundamentally centered on comparing means.

2   Results

Here, we present a new method, Algorithm for Network Data Embedding and Similarity analysis (ANDES), which takes a best match approach to analyze the similarity between a pair of gene sets given a gene embedding (Fig. 1B). To reconcile the functional diversity inherent in gene sets, ANDES identifies the reciprocal best match genes between two sets and calculates a weighted sum of the embedding distances between these similarities. Since gene set sizes can vary widely, ANDES also incorporates a significance estimation procedure that approximates a null distribution using Monte Carlo sampling to make comparable similarity estimates for different pairs of sets.

ANDES is a generic framework that can be used for various tasks that involve gene set comparisons and with custom gene embedding spaces to answer targeted biological questions. We adapt ANDES to perform the most common gene set comparison problem, gene set enrichment analysis, and show how it can be used in the overrepresentation-based case and be extended as a novel rank-based embedding-aware gene set enrichment analysis method (Fig. 1C). In both cases, ANDES achieves state-of-the-art enrichment performance on established baselines [22] when combined with an embedding space encoding protein-protein interactions. Additional benchmarking results, as well as additional use cases illustrating how ANDES can be extended for cross-organism knowledge transfer and drug repurposing, as well as methodological details, can be found in the full version of the research manuscript available on bioRxiv https://www.biorxiv.org/content/10.1101/2023.11.21.568145.

References

1. Kulmanov, M., Khan, M.A., Hoehndorf, R.: DeepGO: predicting protein functions from sequence and interactions using a deep ontology-aware classifier. Bioinformatics **34**, 660–668 (2018)
2. Kulmanov, M., Hoehndorf, R.: DeepGOPlus: improved protein function prediction from sequence. Bioinformatics **36**, 422–429 (2020)
3. Gligorijević, V., et al.: Structure-based protein function prediction using graph convolutional networks. Nat. Commun. **12**, 3168 (2021)
4. Xiong, Y., et al.: Heterogeneous network embedding enabling accurate disease association predictions. BMC Med. Genomics **12**, 1–17 (2019)

5. Yu, Z., Huang, F., Zhao, X., Xiao, W., Zhang, W.: Predicting drug-disease associations through layer attention graph convolutional network. Brief. Bioinf. **22**, bbaa243 (2021)
6. Gao, K.Y., et al.: Interpretable drug target prediction using deep neural representation. IJCAI **2018**, 3371–3377 (2018)
7. Mostavi, M., Chiu, Y.-C., Huang, Y., Chen, Y.: Convolutional neural network models for cancer type prediction based on gene expression. BMC Med. Genomics **13**, 1–13 (2020)
8. Kim, S., Lee, H., Kim, K., Kang, J.: Mut2Vec: distributed representation of cancerous mutations. BMC Med. Genomics **11**, 57–69 (2018)
9. Bryant, P., Pozzati, G., Elofsson, A.: Improved prediction of proteinprotein interactions using AlphaFold2. Nat. Commun. **13**, 1265 (2022)
10. Li, L., et al.: Joint embedding of biological networks for cross-species functional alignment. Bioinformatics **39**, btad529 (2023)
11. Subramanian, A., et al.: Gene set enrichment analysis: a knowledge-based approach for interpreting genome-wide expression profiles. Proc. Natl. Acad. Sci. **102**, 15545–15550 (2005)
12. Yao, V., Wong, A.K., Troyanskaya, O.G.: Enabling precision medicine through integrative network models. J. Mol. Biol. **430**, 2913–2923 (2018)
13. Maleki, F., Ovens, K., Hogan, D.J., Kusalik, A.J.: Gene set analysis: challenges, opportunities, and future research. Front. Genet. **11**, 654 (2020)
14. Fang, M., Richardson, B., Cameron, C.M., Dazard, J.-E., Cameron, M.J.: Drug perturbation gene set enrichment analysis (dpGSEA): a new transcriptomic drug screening approach. BMC Bioinf. **22**, 1–14 (2021)
15. Bateman, A.R., El-Hachem, N., Beck, A.H., Aerts, H.J., Haibe-Kains, B.: Importance of collection in gene set enrichment analysis of drug response in cancer cell lines. Sci. Rep. **4**, 4092 (2014)
16. Cardoso-Moreira, M., et al.: Gene expression across mammalian organ development. Nature **571**, 505–509 (2019)
17. Yao, V., et al.: An integrative tissue-network approach to identify and test human disease genes. Nat. Biotechnol. **36**, 1091–1099 (2018)
18. Djordjevic, D., Kusumi, K., Ho, J.: XGSA: a statistical method for crossspecies gene set analysis. Bioinformatics **32**, i620–i628 (2016)
19. Wieting, J., Bansal, M., Gimpel, K., Livescu, K.: Towards universal paraphrastic sentence embeddings. arXiv preprint arXiv:1511.08198 (2015)
20. Lin, Z., et al.: Evolutionary-scale prediction of atomic-level protein structure with a language model. Science **379**, 1123–1130 (2023)
21. Greene, C.S., et al.: Understanding multicellular function and disease with human tissue-specific networks. Nat. Genet. **47**, 569–576 (2015)
22. Tarca, A.L., Bhatti, G., Romero, R.: A comparison of gene set analysis methods in terms of sensitivity, prioritization and specificity. PLoS ONE **8**, e79217 (2013)

Prompt-Based Learning on Large Protein Language Models Improves Signal Peptide Prediction

Shuai Zeng🆔, Duolin Wang🆔, Lei Jiang, and Dong Xu(✉)🆔

Department of Electrical Engineer and Computer Science, Christopher S. Bond Life Sciences Center, University of Missouri, Columbia, MO 65211, USA
zengs@umsystem.edu, {wangdu,leijiang,xudong}@missouri.edu

Abstract. Signal peptides (SP) play a crucial role in protein localization in cells. The development of large protein language models (PLMs) provides a new opportunity for SP prediction. We applied a prompt-based learning framework, Parameter-Efficient Fine-Tuning (PEFT) for SP prediction, PEFT-SP, to effectively utilize pre-trained PLMs. We integrated low-rank adaptation (LoRA) into ESM-2 models to better leverage the protein sequence evolutionary knowledge of PLMs. Experiments show that PEFT-SP using LoRA enhances state-of-the-art results, leading to a maximum MCC gain of 0.372 for SPs with small training samples and an overall MCC gain of 0.048. Furthermore, we also employed two other prompt-based learning methods, i.e., Prompt Tuning and Adapter Tuning, into ESM-2 for SP prediction. More elaborate experiments show that PEFT-SP using Adapter Tuning can also improve the state-of-the-art results with up to 0.202 MCC gain for SPs with small training samples and an overall MCC gain of 0.030. LoRA requires fewer computing resources and less memory than the Adapter during the training stage, making it possible to adapt larger and more powerful protein models for SP prediction. The PEFT-SP framework is available at https://github.com/shuaizengMU/PEFT-SP. The web server for SP predic-tion leveraging the PEFT-SP framework is publicly available at https://www.mu-loc.org/peftsp/.

Keywords: Signal peptide · Large protein language model · ESM · Prompt-based learning · Parameter-Efficient Fine-Tuning · Low-rank adaptation

1 Introduction

Signal Peptides (SPs), short amino acid sequences typically located in the N-terminals of nascent polypeptides, play a crucial role in directing proteins through various translocation pathways. These pathways, such as the secretory (Sec) and the twin-arginine translocation (Tat) pathways, differ in their handling of protein conformation during translocation, with the Sec pathway transporting unfolded proteins and the Tat pathway translocating fully folded proteins. Upon

J. Ma (Ed.): RECOMB 2024, LNCS 14758, pp. 400–405, 2024.
https://doi.org/10.1007/978-1-0716-3989-4_40

successful translocation across the membrane, signal peptidase (SPase) precisely cleaves the SP, releasing the mature protein. SPases are categorized into three groups (SPase I, II, III), each dedicated to specific types of signal peptides. Precisely, SPase I (Sec/SPI) is responsible for cleaving general secretory signal peptides, while SPase II (Sec/SPII) and SPase III (Sec/SPIII) specialize in the cleavage of lipoprotein and prepilin signal peptides, respectively. Tat substrates are exclusively processed by SPase I (Tat/SPI) or SPase II (Tat/SPII).

Although these SP regions are recognizable, the absence of clearly defined consensus motifs presents a significant challenge to SP prediction. Advances in machine learning and deep learning have led to the development of various SP prediction tools, such as SignalP versions, SPEPlip, Deep-Sig, and SignalP 6.0. Large protein language models (PLMs), such as ProTrans and ESM-1 [4], have become foundational tools for various biological modeling tasks related to proteins. However, there is room for improvement. This paper presents a novel SP prediction framework, PEFT-SP, designed to harness the capabilities of PLM for signal peptide and cleavage site prediction. PEFT-SP consists of the ESM-2 model, a linear Conditional Random Fields (CRF) model, and PEFT modules, including Adapter Tuning [1], Prompt Tuning [3], and Low-Rank adaptation (LoRA) [2]. Our end-to-end solution performs better than SignalP 6.0, especially in SP types with limited training data. We evaluate different PEFT methods, including LoRA, and highlight the efficiency of our framework in utilizing PLMs for SP prediction. This study contributes to the exploration of PEFT on PLMs for SP prediction, emphasizing the importance of efficient PLM utilization in advancing prediction performance.

2   Methods

2.1   Pre-trained Large Protein Language Models

The recent surge in Protein Language Models (PLMs) has brought notable examples like ProtTrans, ESM-1, and the ESM-2 family. Among these models, the ESM-2 model family stands out, offering varying model sizes ranging from 8 million parameters to a substantial 15 billion parameters. The ESM-2 model family, encompassing ESM2-150M, ESM2-650M, and ESM2-3B, has showcased outstanding performance in structure prediction, surpassing many counterparts from ProtTrans and the ESM-1 model family in protein sequence-related tasks.

Unlike existing signal peptide prediction models that necessitate appending an organism identifier to the protein sequence, PEFT-SP with ESM-2 backbone streamlines the process by taking only the protein sequence as input. It encodes the sequence into token embeddings, which are then fed into a stack of multiple Transformer layers designed to capture contextual relationships between amino acids. These layers incorporate a self-attention mechanism and Position-wise Feed-Forward Networks (FFN) surrounded by separate residual connections.

The linear chain Conditional Random Field (CRF) is commonly employed in sequence labeling tasks, capturing relationships between labels and observed data. Viterbi decoding computes the most probable state sequence, including SP regions (n, h, c, twin-arginine). Cleavage site (CS) prediction identifies CS based on the last SP class state. The forward-backward algorithm calculates marginal probabilities per sequence position. Predicting signal peptide type sums marginal probabilities of states and divides by sequence length.

2.2   Parameter-Efficient Fine-Tuning Methods for ESM-2

PEFT methods for ESM-2 can enhance the model's performance in various downstream tasks. PEFT introduces tunable parameters while freezing the original parameters in the backbone model, enabling the model to be tailored to new tasks with reduced computational overhead and fewer labeled examples. Unlike the original configuration of Adapter Tuning and LoRA, which integrates related modules into all Transformer layers, they are specifically inserted into the bottommost Transformer layers within the ESM-2 model, inspired from LLaMA-Adapter. Adapter Tuning involves incorporating adapter modules with a bottleneck architecture within the Transformer layer of the ESM-2 model. These modules compress the input data into a bottleneck layer with reduced dimensionality and reconstruct it to match the original input size. Prompt Tuning adds trainable embeddings, referred to as soft prompts, into the sequence embeddings, serving as inputs to the ESM-2 model. Soft prompts are continuously updated using gradients, while all parameters within the ESM-2 model remain fixed throughout the training process. LoRA enhances the fine-tuning of ESM-2 by introducing trainable rank decomposition matrices into the Transformer architecture. This reparameterization is applied to the projection matrices of the Query, Key, Value, and FFN modules within the Transformer.

2.3   Model Evaluation and Experiment Setting

We utilized the Matthews correlation coefficient (MCC), standard in SP prediction methods, for a fair assessment. Since most methods involve binary SP classification, we computed MCC1 using samples of transmembrane and soluble proteins. Additionally, MCC2 was calculated using a dataset where a specific SP type was the positive sample, and all other SPs and non-SPs as negatives. Our CS prediction depends on the last SP class region, outputting the cleavage site position rather than probabilities. Precision and recall evaluate CS prediction within a 3-position window. Precision is the correct CS ratio to predicted CSs, while recall is the correct CS ratio to true CSs. Accurate CS predictions must align with SP labels.

Our SP dataset is sourced from SignalP 6.0, comprising diverse protein sequences: 3,352 Sec/SPI, 2,261 Sec/SPII, 113 Sec/SPIII, 595 Tat/SPI, 36 Tat/SPII, 16,421 intracellular, and 2,615 transmembrane sequences. Sec/SPIII and Tat/SPII have limited samples. Each sequence is labeled with SP type and region details, with the final label indicating the CS. Initially obtained from Archaea, Eukarya, Gram-positive, and Gram-negative bacteria, the dataset is partitioned into three subsets for fairness and robustness. We used a nested three-fold cross-validation, resulting in six distinct test sets.

3   Results

3.1   Comparisons with State-of-the-Art

We employed PEFT-SP using LoRA for each model from the ESM-2 model family and trained them independently. We evaluated the MCC1 and MCC2 scores for each SP type within each organism group across test sets. Additionally, we calculated the mean MCC scores for MCC1 and MCC2 across all SP types and organisms.

PEFT-SP using LoRA with ESM2-3B backbone achieves the best performance (as shown in Fig. 1). It consistently outperforms SignalP 6.0 in the SP types (Sec/SPIII and Tat/SPII) with limited training samples, except for Tat/SPII in Gram-positive bacteria. It achieves a maximum MCC1 gain of 79.8% and an MCC2 gain of 87.3% in Sec/SPIII for Archaea. It attains a mean MCC1 improvement of 5.6% and a mean MCC2 improvement of 6.1%. It performs slightly worse than SignalP 6.0, with MCC1 differences ranging between 0.3%

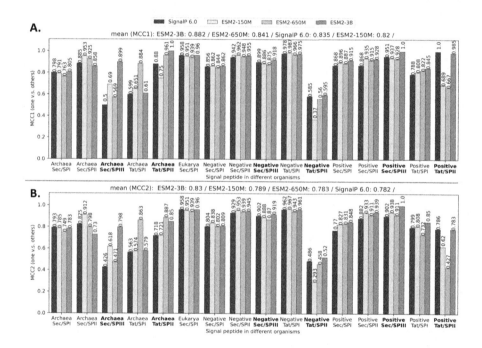

Fig. 1. PEFT-SP using LoRA and SignalP 6.0 performance in terms of MCC score for each SP type across different organisms. The bold text in the x-axis represents the SP type with small training samples. The MCC1 and MCC2 scores are shown along with the bars. The sorted mean for MCC1 and MCC2 are listed at the top. (A) MCC1 scores performance on the negative class composed of soluble and transmembrane proteins. (B) MCC2 scores performance on the negative class comprising soluble and transmembrane proteins and other SP types.

and 3.0% and MCC2 differences ranging between 0.4% and 11.5% in Sec/SPI and Sec/SPII for Archaea, and Tat/SPII for both Gram-negative and Gram-positive bacteria. For SP types (Sec/SPI, Sec/SPII, and Tat/SPII) with sufficient training data, PEFT-SP using LoRA with ESM2-3B demonstrates superior or closely comparable performance to SignalP 6.0.

3.2 Comparisons with Fine-Tuning and Other PEFT Methods

We compared PEFT-SP using different PEFT methods with ESM-3B, as well as SignalP 6.0 and finetuned ESM2-3B model. We trained all models independently with the same datasets generated from nest cross-validation. The performance of each model was measured using MCC2 across cross-validation.

Table 1 shows that the fine-tuning approach outperforms SignalP 6. This suggests that the ESM2-3B model holds promise as a potential candidate for other PEFT methods. The PEFT-SP using LoRA performs better than PEFT-SP using Prompt Tuning and Adapter Tuning regarding the mean MCC2. Moreover, the PEFT-SP using LoRA has fewer trainable parameters than fine-tuning and other PEFT methods during the training stage, dramatically reducing the computing resource and memory storage.

Table 1. Benchmark results of MCC2 for SignalP 6.0, Fine-tuning ESM2-3B, and PEFT-SP using different PEFT methods with ESM2-3B backbone. The SP type indicated with the symbol † represents SP types with limited training samples. The bold value indicates the highest value for each SP type among all methods.

Method/Backbone	-	Fine-tuning	Prompt Tuning	Adapter Tuning	LoRA
SP types	SignalP 6.0	ESM2-3B	ESM2-3B	ESM2-3B	ESM2-3B
Archaea Sec/SPI	0.793	0.771	0.777	**0.825**	0.783
Archaea Sec/SPII	0.825	**0.864**	0.509	0.783	0.730
Archaea Sec/SPIII †	0.426	0.724	0.500	0.351	**0.798**
Archaea Tat/SPI	0.563	0.564	**0.653**	0.538	0.579
Archaea Tat/SPII †	0.718	0.792	0.182	0.660	**0.850**
Eukarya Sec/SPI	0.958	0.948	0.954	0.954	**0.960**
Negative Sec/SPI	0.804	**0.813**	0.723	0.820	0.809
Negative Sec/SPII	0.929	0.946	0.886	0.950	**0.945**
Negative Sec/SPIII †	0.902	**0.982**	0.970	0.899	0.919
Negative Tat/SPI	**0.962**	0.902	0.853	0.899	0.961
Negative Tat/SPII †	0.486	0.358	0.325	0.405	**0.520**
Positive Sec/SPI	0.770	0.810	0.746	0.814	**0.848**
Positive Sec/SPII	0.882	0.908	0.833	0.911	**0.939**
Positive Sec/SPIII †	0.902	**1.000**	0.951	0.969	**1.000**
Positive Tat/SPI	0.799	0.746	0.590	0.752	**0.850**
Positive Tat/SPII †	**0.786**	0.603	0.148	0.669	0.783
Mean (MCC2)	0.781	0.796	0.663	0.762	**0.830**

4   Results

Our study introduced PEFT-SP, a new signal peptide prediction framework that operates without organism identifiers. Using LoRA with ESM2-3B, PEFT-SP effectively handles SP types with limited training data and matches or surpasses the baseline performance of the model across all SP types. The success of PEFT-SP with LoRA stems from two key factors: (1) leveraging the evolutionary insights of the ESM2-3B backbone model, and (2) implementing LoRA, a lightweight fine-tuning method, to adapt PLMs for SP prediction while maintaining their high quality. To our best knowledge, this is the first study to explore the effectiveness of PLM using the PEFT approach for SP prediction tasks.

Acknowledgments and Funding. We wish to thank Fei He and Yuexu Jiang for their useful discussions. This work was funded by the National Institutes of Health [R35-GM126985] and the National Science Foundation [DBI-2145226]. Funding for open access charge: National Science Foundation.

Availability of Data and Materials. The source code of PEFT-SP and trained models are publicly available at https://github.com/shuaizengMU/PEFT-SP. The web server is available at https://www.mu-loc.org/peftsp/.

Preprint. A detailed description of our methodology and results can be found in the preprint at https://www.biorxiv.org/content/10.1101/2023.11.04.565642v1.

References

1. Houlsby, N., et al.: Parameter-efficient transfer learning for nlp. In: International Conference on Machine Learning, pp. 2790–2799. PMLR (2019)
2. Hu, E.J., et al.: Lora: low-rank adaptation of large language models. arXiv preprint arXiv:2106.09685 (2021)
3. Lester, B., Al-Rfou, R., Constant, N.: The power of scale for parameter-efficient prompt tuning. arXiv preprint arXiv:2104.08691 (2021)
4. Rives, A., et al.: Biological structure and function emerge from scaling unsupervised learning to 250 million protein sequences. Proc. Natl. Acad. Sci. **118**(15), e2016239118 (2021)

Decoil: Reconstructing Extrachromosomal DNA Structural Heterogeneity from Long-Read Sequencing Data

Mădălina Giurgiu[1,2,3], Nadine Wittstruck[1,2], Elias Rodriguez-Fos[1,2], Rocío Chamorro González[1,2], Lotte Brückner[1,2,4], Annabell Krienelke-Szymansky[1,2], Konstantin Helmsauer[1,2], Anne Hartebrodt[5], Philipp Euskirchen[1,6,7], Richard P. Koche[8], Kerstin Haase[1,2], Knut Reinert[3], and Anton G. Henssen[1,2,4(✉)]

[1] Charité - Universitätsmedizin Berlin, Berlin, Germany
Anton.Henssen@charite.de
[2] Experimental and Clinical Research Center of the MDC and Charité Berlin, Berlin, Germany
[3] Freie Universität Berlin, Berlin, Germany
[4] Max-Delbrück-Centrum für Molekulare Medizin, Berlin, Germany
[5] Friedrich-Alexander-Universität Erlangen-Nürnberg, Erlangen, Germany
[6] German Cancer Consortium (DKTK), partner site Berlin, a partnership between DKFZ and Charité, Universitätsmedizin Berlin, Berlin, Germany
[7] Department of Neuropathology, Charité – Universitätsmedizin Berlin, corporate member of Freie Universität Berlin and Humboldt-Universität zu Berlin, Berlin, Germany
[8] Center for Epigenetics Research, Memorial Sloan Kettering Cancer Center, New York, USA

Abstract. Circular extrachromosomal DNA (ecDNA) is a form of oncogene amplification found across cancer types and associated with poor outcome in patients. EcDNA can be structurally complex and contain rearranged DNA sequences derived from multiple chromosome locations. As the structure of ecDNA can impact oncogene regulation and may indicate mechanisms of its formation, disentangling it at high resolution from sequencing data is essential. Even though methods have been developed to identify and reconstruct ecDNA in cancer genome sequencing, it remains challenging to resolve complex ecDNA structures, in particular amplicons with shared genomic footprints. We here introduce Decoil, a computational method which combines a breakpoint-graph approach with *LASSO* regression to reconstruct complex ecDNA and deconvolve co-occurring ecDNA elements with overlapping genomic footprints from long-read nanopore sequencing. Decoil outperforms *de-novo* assembly and alignment-based methods in simulated long-read sequencing data for both simple and complex ecDNAs. Applying Decoil on whole genome sequencing data uncovered different ecDNA topologies and explored ecDNA structure heterogeneity in neuroblastoma tumors and cell lines, indicating that this method may improve ecDNA structural analyzes in cancer.

K. Haase, K. Reinert, A. G. Henssen—These authors contributed equally.

J. Ma (Ed.): RECOMB 2024, LNCS 14758, pp. 406–411, 2024.
https://doi.org/10.1007/978-1-0716-3989-4_41

Keywords: long-read · ecDNA · nanopore · reconstruction · heterogeneity

1 Introduction

Circular extrachromosomal DNA (ecDNA) is an important form of oncogene amplification in cancer [5], which can be formed through multiple mechanisms [12,13,16] and have a large size (up to several MB [10]). As a result, ecDNA can be structurally diverse, with different functional outcomes. The structure of ecDNA can impact gene regulation through the rearrangement of regulatory elements as well as topologically associated domain (TAD) boundaries [3]. To explore ecDNA diversity and complexity, high-resolution computational methods to reconstruct ecDNA with high accuracy from genome sequencing data are required. The reconstruction of ecDNA from sequencing data remains challenging due to the variable complexity and intratumor heterogeneity of these circular elements. On the one hand, a single ecDNA can be heavily rearranged and contain low-complexity sequence regions (e.g. repeats), which pose a challenge to mapping and *de-novo* assembly based methods. On the other hand, one tumor can contain different ecDNA elements [1,4], which can either originate from different or shared genomic locations [14]. The latter scenario may be very challenging for ecDNA reconstruction, as different co-occurring ecDNA elements have overlapping genomic footprints, making it difficult to attribute the overlapping features to each of the different circular elements. In the past years, several computational tools have been developed to reconstruct ecDNA from different input data. Some methods were developed to detect circularized DNA regions by identifying the breakpoints leading to circularization (circle-enrich-filter [6], Circle-Map [11], ecc_finder [17]). These approaches are suitable for detecting simple circular amplicons, but overlook complex ecDNA structures. To overcome these limitations, more recently, methods focused on reconstructing complex ecDNA based on different technologies, e.g. short-read whole-genome sequencing (AmpliconArchitect [2]), optical-mapping combined with short-read sequencing (AmpliconReconstructor [7]), and long-read sequencing were developed (CReSIL [15]). Lastly, methods have been developed to delineate ecDNA structural heterogeneity [4], by isolating and reconstructing individual ecDNA elements, leveraging *a priori* knowledge about the ecDNA present in the sample of interest. However, a method that reconstructs complex ecDNA structures and captures heterogeneity by distinguishing between ecDNA elements with overlapping genomic footprints from whole-genome sequencing (WGS) data without such *a priori* knowledge is still largely missing to date. We here present Decoil, a computational method to reconstruct genome-wide complex ecDNA elements and deconvolve individiual ecDNAs with shared genomic sequences from bulk whole-genome long-read sequencing using Nanopore technology. Decoil is a graph-based approach integrating the structural variant (SV) and coverage profiles to deconvolve and reconstruct complex ecDNAs. It uses *LASSO* regression to infer likely ecDNA structures and estimate their relative proportions, by accounting for circular elements with overlapping genomic footprints. The model can separate individual ecDNA elements with shared genomic regions. This may improve the resolution to study ecDNA structural intratumor and intertumor heterogeneity from bulk sequencing data.

2 Methods

An Overview of the Decoil Algorithm. Decoil is a graph-based method to reconstruct circular DNA variants from shallow long-read WGS data. This uses (1) structural variants (SV) and (2) focal amplification information to reconstruct circular ecDNA elements (Fig. 1a). The algorithm consists of six modules: genome fragmentation, graph encoding, search simple circles, circle quantification, candidate selection, output, and visualization. The genome is initially fragmented using a clean breakpoint set (Fig. 1a #1). A weighted undirected multigraph is built to encode the structural rearrangements, where nodes are defined as genomic non-overlapping segments and edges represent the structural variants (Fig. 1a #2). Next, the graph is explored using a depth-first search approach to discover genome-wide simple circular paths (Fig. 1a #3). These can represent a unique circular element or be a sub-component of a more complex circular structure. Subsequently, to account for circular elements containing nested circles, simple circular paths with at least one overlapping genomic fragment are merged into a derived larger circular structure. In order to identify the likely ecDNA elements present in the sample, all simple and derived circle candidates are leveraged as features to fit a *LASSO* regression against the read-alignment mean coverage profile. This model will (1) select the likely circles explaining the amplification and (2) estimate their proportions within the sample (Fig. 1a #4). Using this approach, Decoil can account for ecDNA structures with overlapping genomic footprints (Fig. 1b). Lastly, a filtered confident set of circular paths is generated (Fig. 1a #5), together with the annotated topology (as defined below), proportion estimates and reconstruction thread visualization (Fig. 1a (#6+#7)). The full methods description is available in the full paper.

3 Results

Ranking and Simulating ecDNA Topologies to Capture ecDNA Structure Diversity. Currently, no guidelines exist for the assessment of ecDNA reconstruction performance from long-read data, nor do benchmarks exist like those for single nucleotide variant (SNV), insertion-deletion (INDEL) and structural variant (SV) detection [8,9]. The lack of gold standard datasets for assessing ecDNA reconstruction makes the evaluation of Decoil contingent on high-quality simulated data. Thus, to systematically evaluate ecDNA structure reconstruction, we propose seven ecDNA topologies with increased computational complexity: i. Simple circularization, ii. Simple SV's, iii. Mixed SV's, iv. Multi-region, v. Multi-chromosomal, vi. Duplications and vii. Foldbacks. This collection of more than 2000 simulations serves as a benchmark dataset for evaluating Decoil's reconstruction performance. The full description of ecDNA ranking as well as Decoil's benchmark results are available in the full paper.

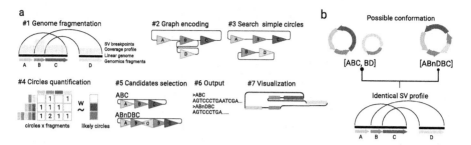

Fig. 1. Decoil algorithm overview. (a) Schematic of the Decoil algorithm depicting the major steps (#1 - Genome fragmentation, #2 - Graph encoding, #3 - Search simple circles, #4 - Circles quantification, #5 - Candidates selection, #6 - Output and #7 - Visualization). (b) The overlapping cycles challenge. The left panel displays a heterogeneity scenario, where two different ecDNA elements share a genomic footprint (B fragment), the right panel displays a large structure containing interspersed duplication rearrangement. Both scenarios lead to the same SV breakpoint profile.

Decoil Can Recover ecDNA Structure Heterogeneity. To demonstrate that structurally distinct ecDNA elements with overlapping genomic footprint can be resolved by Decoil, we generated 33 *in-silico* mixtures, by pair-wise combination of three neuroblastoma cell lines at different ratios. The breakpoint junctions of the individual ecDNA elements were recovered in the different mixtures with a recall of 93% and suggests that Decoil can distinguish between different co-occurring ecDNA elements with overlapping genomic footprints. These results enable a higher resolution for reconstructing intratumor ecDNA structure heterogeneity. Detailed results are available in the full paper.

4   Discussion

The structural complexity and heterogeneity of ecDNA make its reconstruction from sequencing data a challenging computational problem. We here presented Decoil, a method to reconstruct co-occurring complex ecDNA elements.

Due to their random mitotic segregation, many ecDNA elements, which may structurally differ, co-occur in the same cancer cells [1]. Disentangling ecDNA with shared genomic regions has not yet been addressed by other methods, and it cannot be resolved by *de-novo* assemblers (e.g. Shasta) when sequencing reads are smaller than the size of genomic fragments (mean length > 125 kb in our cohort). Decoil uses *LASSO* regression to reconstruct distinct ecDNA elements with overlapping genomic footprints, which enables the exploration of ecDNA structural heterogeneity. We have chosen this approach as it performed reasonably in our hands compared to other linear regression models. Ultra-long read sequencing (> 100 kb) at high coverage, or other sequencing technologies, may improve the SV detection and structural resolution of ecDNA using Decoil, but the aforementioned scenarios will remain difficult to resolve. In summary, we envision that Decoil will advance the exploration of ecDNA structural heterogeneity in cancer and beyond, which is essential to better understand the mechanisms of ecDNA formation and its structural evolution.

Acknowledgments. We would like to acknowledge Roland F. Schwarz, Julia Markowski, and Svenja Mehringer for their input and thoughtful suggestions during the development of this paper. We thank the Berlin Institute of Health (BIH) team for the support and providing the necessary infrastructure. Computation was performed on the HPC-for-Research cluster of the BIH. We thank the patients and their parents for granting access to the tumor specimens and clinical information that were analyzed in this study. We thank the Neuroblastoma Biobank and Neuroblastoma Trial Registry (University Children's Hospital Cologne) of the GPOH for providing samples. This project has received funding from the European Research Council under the European Union's Horizon 2020 Research and Innovation Programme (grant no. 949172). A.G.H. is supported by the Deutsche Forschungsgemeinschaft (DFG) (grant no. 398299703). A.G.H. is supported by the Deutsche Forschungsgemeinschaft (DFG, German Research Foundation, 398299703). A.G.H. is supported by the Deutsche Krebshilfe (German Cancer Aid) Mildred Scheel Professorship program - 70114107. This project received funding from the NIH/CRUK (398299703, the eDynamic Cancer Grand Challenge).

Manuscript and code availability. The manuscript is available as pre-print under https://www.biorxiv.org/content/10.1101/2023.11.15.567169v1.full.pdf and Decoil software is accessible on github https://github.com/madagiurgiu25/decoil-pre.

Disclosure of Interests. A.G.H. and R.P.K. are founders of Econic Biosciences Ltd.

References

1. Chamorro González, R., et al.: Parallel sequencing of extrachromosomal circular DNAs and transcriptomes in single cancer cells. Nat. Genet. (2023). https://doi.org/10.1038/s41588-023-01386-y
2. Deshpande, V., et al.: Exploring the landscape of focal amplifications in cancer using AmpliconArchitect. Nat. Commun. **10**(1) (12 2019) https://doi.org/10.1038/s41467-018-08200-y
3. Helmsauer, K., et al.: Enhancer hijacking determines intra- and extrachromosomal circular MYCN amplicon architecture in neuroblastoma (2019). https://doi.org/10.1101/2019.12.20.875807
4. Hung, K.L., et al.: Targeted profiling of human extrachromosomal DNA by CRISPR-CATCH. Nat. Genet. (2022) https://doi.org/10.1038/s41588-022-01190-0
5. Kim, H., et al.: Extrachromosomal DNA is associated with oncogene amplification and poor outcome across multiple cancers. Nat. Genet. **52**(9) (2020) https://doi.org/10.1038/s41588-020-0678-2
6. Koche, R.P., et al.: Extrachromosomal circular DNA drives oncogenic genome remodeling in neuroblastoma (2020). https://doi.org/10.1038/s41588-019-0547-z
7. Luebeck, J., et al.: AmpliconReconstructor integrates NGS and optical mapping to resolve the complex structures of focal amplifications. Nat. Commun. **11**(1) (2020) https://doi.org/10.1038/s41467-020-18099-z

8. Olsen, N.D., et al.: precisionFDA Truth Challenge V2: Calling variants from short- and long-reads in difficult-to-map Regions. bioRxiv (2020). https://www.cell.com/cell-genomics/pdf/S2666-979X(22)00058-1.pdf

9. Olson, N.D., et al.: Variant calling and benchmarking in an era of complete human genome sequences. Nat. Rev. Genet. (2023).https://doi.org/10.1038/s41576-023-00590-0

10. Pecorino, L.T., Verhaak, R.G., Henssen, A., Mischel, P.S.: Extrachromosomal DNA (ecDNA): an origin of tumor heterogeneity, genomic remodeling, and drug resistance (2022) https://doi.org/10.1042/BST20221045

11. Prada-Luengo, I., Krogh, A., Maretty, L., Regenberg, B.: Sensitive detection of circular DNAs at single-nucleotide resolution using guided realignment of partially aligned reads. BMC Bioinform. **20**(1) (2019).https://doi.org/10.1186/s12859-019-3160-3

12. Shoshani, O., et al.: Chromothripsis drives the evolution of gene amplification in cancer. Nature **591**(7848) (2021) https://doi.org/10.1038/s41586-020-03064-z

13. Storlazzi, C.T., et al.: MYC-containing double minutes in hematologic malignancies: Evidence in favor of the episome model and exclusion of MYC as the target gene. Hum. Mol. Genet. **15**(6) (2006) https://doi.org/10.1093/hmg/ddl010

14. Verhaak, R.G., Bafna, V., Mischel, P.S.: Extrachromosomal oncogene amplification in tumour pathogenesis and evolution (2019). https://doi.org/10.1038/s41568-019-0128-6

15. Wanchai, V., et al.: CReSIL: accurate identification of extrachromosomal circular DNA from long-read sequences. Briefings Bioinform. **23**(6) (2022).https://doi.org/10.1093/bib/bbac422

16. Yi, E., Chamorro González, R., Henssen, A.G., Verhaak, R.G.: Extrachromosomal DNA amplifications in cancer (2022). https://doi.org/10.1038/s41576-022-00521-5

17. Zhang, P., Peng, H., Llauro, C., Bucher, E., Mirouze, M.: ecc_finder: a robust and accurate tool for detecting extrachromosomal circular DNA from sequencing data. Front. Plant Sci. **12** (2021).https://doi.org/10.3389/fpls.2021.743742

Privacy Preserving Epigenetic PaceMaker: Stronger Privacy and Improved Efficiency

Meir Goldenberg[✉], Loay Mualem, Amit Shahar, Sagi Snir, and Adi Akavia

University of Haifa, Haifa, Israel
meirgold@hotmail.com, loaymua@gmail.com, ashaha16@campus.haifa.ac.il,
ssagi@research.haifa.ac.il, akavia@cs.haifa.ac.il

Abstract. DNA methylation data plays a crucial role in estimating chronological age in mammals, offering real-time insights into an individual's aging process. The Epigenetic Pacemaker (EPM) model allows inference of the epigenetic age as deviations from the population trend. Given the sensitivity of this data, it is essential to safeguard both inputs and outputs of the EPM model. In a recent study by Goldenberg et al., a privacy-preserving approach for EPM computation was introduced, utilizing Fully Homomorphic Encryption (FHE). However, their method had limitations, including having high communication complexity and being impractical for large datasets. Our work presents a new privacy preserving protocol for EPM computation, improving both privacy and complexity. Notably, we employ a single server for the secure computation phase while ensuring privacy even in the event of server corruption (compared to requiring two non-colluding servers in Goldenberg et al.). Using techniques from symbolic algebra and number theory, the new protocol eliminates the need for communication during the secure computing phase, significantly improves asymptotic runtime, and offers better compatibility to parallel computing for further time complexity reduction. We have implemented our protocol, demonstrating its ability to produce results similar to the standard (insecure) EPM model with substantial performance improvement compared to Goldenberg et al. These findings hold promise for enhancing data security in medical applications where personal privacy is paramount. The generality of both the new approach and the EPM, suggests that this protocol may be useful to other uses employing similar expectation maximization techniques.

Full version. This is a short abstract of our work; the full version appears in [9].

Background. Privacy regulations like GDPR [14], CCPA [13], and GIPA [6] pose constraints on the collection of extensive genomic data needed for training powerful machine learning models. A promising approach to address this challenge is to execute *privacy preserving genome analysis* i.e., to utilize cryptographic

© The Author(s), under exclusive license to Springer Nature Switzerland AG 2024
J. Ma (Ed.): RECOMB 2024, LNCS 14758, pp. 412–416, 2024.
https://doi.org/10.1007/978-1-0716-3989-4_42

techniques such as fully homomorphic encryption (FHE) [8,16].[1] Prior work focused on privacy-preserving genome analysis using homomorphic encryption, particularly in Genome Wide Association (GWAS) [3,4,7,12,18] and classification of DNA/RNA sequences in tumor tissues [5,11] and viral strains [1,22] respectively. Recently, privacy-preserving epigenetics, studying how behavior and environmental factors affect genome changes, was explored in gene expression [2] and DNA methylation data [10]. Elaborating on the latter, DNA methylation are chemical changes in the genome that are linked to numerous developmental, physiologic, and pathologic processes including malignancy, infections, and aging. Snir et al. suggested a flexible probabilistic framework [21] and expectation maximization (EM) algorithm [20] –the *Epigenetic PaceMaker (EPM)*– deducing the *epigenetic age (e-age)* of individuals from their methylation values on multiple CpG sites. The EPM algorithm yields a point on the likelihood surface that optimizes the probability of the entire system while explaining intrinsic key features in aging for both humans and animals [15,17]. The sensitivity of the EPM's input and output motivates a privacy preserving EPM computation as was proposed in Goldenberg et al. [10], using FHE as a central tool. The protocol in [10] requires two non-colluding servers throughout the entire computation, resulting in two main drawbacks: first, their protocol is insecure if an adversary corrupts both servers; second, their protocol suffers from a high communication and computational toll, making it impractical to real data volumes.

Our Contribution. In this work we propose a new privacy-preserving protocol for the EPM, improving over the prior work [10] in the following aspects:

1. **Improved complexity:** Unlike in [10], no communication is needed between the servers during the secure computation phase in our protocol.
2. **Stronger privacy:** Unlike [10], only a single server is needed for our secure computing phase (whereas the other server's role is minimized to key generation and output decryption in pre- and post-processing phases) thus making the non-collusion assumption more plausible. In addition, we propose extensions that hide the EPM output on top of its input. The threat model is as in [10]: security against any passive computationally-bounded adversary controlling any number of the individuals and up to one of the two servers.

Methods. Our starting point is the EM algorithm in [20] that searches the likelihood surface via several iterations consisting of two step –a *site step* and a *time step*– each increasing the likelihood function, where we employ the closed form solutions to both these steps as was formulated in [19]. In our privacy preserving protocol, each individual (or, data owner) encrypts her methylation data using an FHE scheme (where the public encryption key is provided to them from the key management server), and upload the ciphertexts to the machine

---

[1] FHE is an encryption scheme that supports processing ciphertexts –without knowledge of the underlying messages or the decryption key– to obtain ciphertexts for the result of mathematical computations on these underlying messages.

learning server (MLE). The MLE then employs homomorphic evaluation to produce ciphertexts encrypting the estimated e-ages – this is what we refer to as the secure computing phase. These ciphertexts can then be decrypted by any entity authorized to access the secret decryption key. Importantly, the homomorphic evaluation executed by the MLE includes critical modifications of the EPM algorithm as to produce the same output as the EPM but while bypassing complexity bottlenecks associated with homomorphic evaluation. In particular, the closed-form formulas provided in [19] to the site-step and time- step involve computing division, which is a complexity bottleneck for homomorphic evaluation. Following [2], we avoid homomorphic division by representing each rational number as a pair of integers: its numerator and denominator, and homomorphically updating these values throughout the computation. E.g., we homomorphically evaluate the division $\frac{a}{b} : \frac{c}{d}$ while using homomorphic multiplications only to produce the corresponding numerator and denominator: (ad, bc). We note that keeping track of the growing numerator and denominator, rather than computing division, leads to high magnitude numbers throughout the computation, which we reduce to a manageable scale using the Chinese Remainder Theorem.

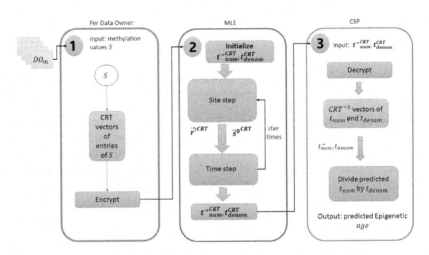

Fig. 1. System flow: (1) Each Data Owner (DO) employs the Chinese Remainder Theorem (CRT) on her methylation values (S) and encrypts the resulting CRT representation (CRT vector). (2) MLE initializes the CRT vectors for the numerator and denominator of the e-ages ($\overrightarrow{t_{num}^{CRT}}$ and $\overrightarrow{t_{denom}^{CRT}}$), and executes iter iterations of the site and time steps. (3) The final output is the predicted e-ages after decryption by the crypto service provide (CSP) and CRT decoding.

References

1. Akavia, A., Galili, B., Shaul, H., Weiss, M., Yakhini, Z.: Efficient privacy-preserving viral strain classification via k-mer signatures and FHE. In: IEEE 36th Computer Security Foundations Symposium (CSF), pp. 178–193. IEEE Computer Society (2023)
2. Akavia, A., Galili, B., Shaul, H., Weiss, M., Yakhini, Z.: Privacy preserving feature selection for sparse linear regression. Proc. Priv. Enhancing Technol. **2024**(1), 300–313 (2024)
3. Blatt, M., Gusev, A., Polyakov, Y., Goldwasser, S.: Secure large-scale genome-wide association studies using homomorphic encryption. Proc. Natl. Acad. Sci. **117**(21), 11608–11613 (2020)
4. Bonte, C., Makri, E., Ardeshirdavani, A., Simm, J., Moreau, Y., Vercauteren, F.: Towards practical privacy-preserving genome-wide association study. BMC Bioinform. **19**(1), 1–12 (2018)
5. Carpov, S., Gama, N., Georgieva, M., Jetchev, D.: Genoppml - a framework for genomic privacy-preserving machine learning. In: 2022 IEEE 15th International Conference on Cloud Computing (CLOUD), pp. 532–542 (2022)
6. C.clarity in privacy. The genetic information privacy act (2021)
7. Dong, C., et al.: Maliciously secure and efficient large-scale genome-wide association study with multi-party computation. IEEE Trans. Dependable Sec. Comput. **22**, 33 (2022)
8. Gentry, C.: A fully homomorphic encryption scheme. PhD thesis, Stanford University (2009). https://crypto.stanford.edu/craig
9. Goldenberg, M., Mualem, L., Shahar, A., Snir, S., Akavia, A.: Privacy preserving epigenetic pacemaker stronger privacy and improved efficiency. bioRxiv, 2024.02.15.580590 (2024)
10. Goldenberg, M., Snir, S., Akavia, A.L.: Private epigenetic pacemaker detector using homomorphic encryption. In: International Symposium on Bioinformatics Research and Applications, pp. 52–61. Springer (2022). https://doi.org/10.1007/978-3-031-23198-8_6
11. Hong, S., Park, J.H., Cho, W., Choe, H., Cheon, J.H.: Secure tumor classification by shallow neural network using homomorphic encryption. BMC Genomics **23**(1), 1–19 (2022)
12. Lu, W.-J., Yamada, Y., Sakuma, J.: Privacy-preserving genome-wide association studies on cloud environment using fully homomorphic encryption. In: BMC Medical Informatics and Decision Making, vol. 15, pp. 1–8. Springer (2015). https://doi.org/10.1186/1472-6947-15-S5-S1
13. S. of California Department of Justice. California consumer privacy act (ccpa) (2018)
14. J. of the European Union. Regulation (EU) 2016/679 of the european parliament (2016)
15. Pinho, G.M., et al.: Hibernation slows epigenetic ageing in yellow-bellied marmots. Nat. Ecol. Evolut. **6**(4), 418–426 (2022)
16. Rivest, R.L., Adleman, L., Dertouzos, M.L.: On data banks and privacy homomorphisms, pp. 169–179. Foundations of Secure Computation, Academia Press (1978)
17. Sagi Snir, C.F., Pellegrini, M.: Human epigenetic ageing is logarithmic with time across the entire lifespan. Epigenetics **14**(9), 912–926 (2019)
18. Simmons, S., Berger, B.: Realizing privacy preserving genome-wide association studies. Bioinformatics **32**(9), 1293–1300 (2016)

19. Snir, S.: Epigenetic pacemaker: closed form algebraic solutions. BMC Genomics **21**(2), 1–11 (2020)
20. Snir, S., Pellegrini, M.: An epigenetic pacemaker is detected via a fast conditional expectation maximization algorithm. Epigenomics **10**(6), 695–706 (2018)
21. Snir, S., vonHoldt, B.M., Pellegrini, M.: A statistical framework to identify deviation from time linearity in epigenetic aging. PLoS Comput. Biol. **12**(11), e1005183 (2016)
22. Zhou, J., Lei, B., Lang, H.: Homomorphic multi-label classification of virus strains. In: 2022 IEEE International Symposium on Software Reliability Engineering Workshops (ISSREW), pp. 289–294. IEEE (2022)

Mapping Cell Fate Transition in Space and Time

Yichen Gu[1], Jialin Liu[2], Chen Li[2], and Joshua D. Welch[2,3]($\boxtimes$)

[1] Department of Electrical and Computer Engineering, University of Michigan, Ann Arbor, MI, USA
`gyichen@umich.edu`
[2] Department of Computational Medicine and Bioinformatics, University of Michigan, Ann Arbor, MI, USA
`{alanliu,welchjd}@umich.edu`
[3] Department of Computer Science and Engineering, University of Michigan, Ann Arbor, MI, USA

Abstract. Cell fate transition is fundamentally a spatiotemporal process, but previous work has largely neglected the spatial dimension. Incorporating both space and time into models of cell fate transition would be a key step toward characterizing how interactions among neighboring cells, the presence of local niche factors, and physical migration of cells contribute to tissue development. To realize this potential, we propose a model for jointly inferring spatial and temporal dynamics of cell fate transition from spatial transcriptomic data. Our approach extends the RNA velocity framework to model single-cell gene expression dynamics of an entire tissue with spatially coupled differential equations. Our principled probabilistic approach enables the incorporation of time point labels and multiple slices. We further introduce the idea of cell velocity, which is defined as the physical direction of cell maturation and migration. Simulated data analysis indicates that incorporating spatial coordinates significantly improves the accuracy of velocity and time inference. Our work introduces a new dimension into the study of cell fate transitions and lays a foundation for modeling the collective dynamics of cells comprising an entire tissue. The full paper is at https://www.biorxiv.org/content/10.1101/2024.02.12.579941v1.

Keywords: Spatial Transcriptomics · Single-Cell Gene Expression · RNA Velocity · Graph Neural Network

1 Introduction

Cell fate transitions are fundamentally spatiotemporal processes regulated by factors that vary over space. Clonal relationships between progenitor and descendant cells are also spatial relationships: As cells divide over time, daughter cells arise in locations spatially adjacent to the mother cell. Such relationships are ubiquitous in different tissues as reported in previous studies [1,3,10,12].

Y. Gu and J. Liu—Equal Contribution.

© The Author(s), under exclusive license to Springer Nature Switzerland AG 2024
J. Ma (Ed.): RECOMB 2024, LNCS 14758, pp. 417–420, 2024.
https://doi.org/10.1007/978-1-0716-3989-4_43

Spatial transcriptomics [4,13,14] enables whole-transcriptome or targeted measurement of gene expression and spatial position at cellular or sub-cellular resolution. This novel technology provides the data we need to address a fundamental biological question - how are time and space linked during cell fate transition? However, no existing computational approaches can directly address this question. Here, we present Topological Velocity Inference (TopoVelo), a model for jointly inferring the dynamics of cell fate transition over time and space. Additionally, we can infer the physical directions and rates of cell maturation and migration–a quantity we term "cell velocity". Our results show that modeling spatial coupling improves cell velocity inference and brings a new dimension to the modeling of cell fate transition.

2   Methods

Problem Statement. Each sample (cell or spot), indexed by i, is represented by a vector of gene expression values $X_i(t) \in \mathbb{R}^d$ and spatial coordinates (x, y), both parametrized by developmental stage (time) t. The trajectory $X_i(t)$ is governed by some differential equation plus random noise. For each i, only the vector $x_i := X_i(t_i)$ is observed at some unknown time t_i. Furthermore, the parameters of the differential equations are spatially coupled in an unknown way, forming a random field. Our goal is two-fold: recover the latent times t_i for each sample and predict future gene expression values and spatial positions.

Key Modeling Assumptions. First, we describe the system using two differential equations: $\frac{du}{dt} = \rho(z) - \beta u$, $\frac{ds}{dt} = \beta u - \gamma s$ where ρ, β and γ are transcription, splicing and degradation rates. They reflect the biochemical steps required for gene expression: a gene is transcribed as unspliced pre-mRNA before being converted into spliced mature mRNA. This builds on previous work on RNA velocity [2,6,9,11]. Second, we represent the population of cells as a graph $\mathcal{G} = (V, E)$, where $V = [n]$ is a set of nodes representing cells and E contains the neighboring relations between any two cells. We denote the set of neighboring cells of i, including i, by $nbr(i)$. For each node (cell) i, we take its unspliced and spliced mRNA read counts as its node features, denoted as o_i. Importantly, we assume that this graph captures spatial dependence among the mRNA counts, and ρ parameters of the cells.

Probabilistic Modeling. We build a probabilistic model for the generative process of unspliced and spliced mRNA counts. Given the time, $\mathbf{T} = \{t_i : i \in [n]\}$, and low-dimensional latent representations, $\mathbf{Z} = \{z_i : i \in [n]\}$, of the whole cell population, the node features are generated from $\mathbf{Z}$ and $\mathbf{T}$ via a spatially-coupled dynamical system: $P(\mathbf{O}|\mathbf{Z}, \mathbf{T}) = \prod_{i=1}^{n} P(o_i|\{z_j, t_j : j \in nbr(i)\})$. We further assume $P(o_i|\{z_j, t_j : j \in nbr(i)\})$ is a factorized Gaussian distribution over all genes, i.e., $P(o_i|\{z_j, t_j : j \in nbr(i)\}) = \prod_{g=1}^{G} \mathcal{N}(\mu_{u,g}^{(i)}, \sigma_{u,g}^2) \mathcal{N}(\mu_{s,g}^{(i)}, \sigma_{s,g}^2)$ where $\mathcal{N}(\cdot)$ denotes a Gaussian distribution.

Variational Bayeisan Inference. Exact inference of the latent variables $\mathcal{T}$ and $\mathcal{Z}$ from the probabilistic model is intractable. We thus pursue a variational Bayesian approximation, specifically autoencoding variational Bayes [7]. This approach optimizes the evidence lower bound (ELBO) to jointly train an inference model (encoder network) and generative model (decoder network). To derive the ELBO in our setting, we use a variational posterior over all cell states and time, $q(\mathcal{Z}, \mathcal{T}|\mathcal{O})$, to approximate the true posterior. As is standard with autoencoding variational Bayes, we use a factorized Gaussian as our variational distribution, i.e. $q(\mathcal{Z}, \mathcal{T}|\mathcal{O}) = \prod_{i=1}^{n} \mathcal{N}(GNN(t_i|\mathcal{O})) \cdot \mathcal{N}(GNN(z_i|\mathcal{O}))$. To account for spatial correlation in the generative model, we use a GNN to map latent cell states to cell-wise transcription rates ρ_i.

We implement TopoVelo using an encoder-decoder neural network framework. The network takes a graph as input, with nodes representing cells or spots and node features indicating spliced and unspliced counts. The encoder neural network uses graph convolutional layers to estimate the cell state and time of each cell. The decoder network uses graph convolution to estimate the transcription rate of each gene in each cell. The node features are then reconstructed using the ODE solution given time and ODE parameters. In our approach, we consider two popular graph convolution approaches, spectral graph convolution(GCN) [8] and graph attention(GAT) [15].

Predicting Cell Velocity. Because we know the spatial coordinates (x, y) of cells in our spatial transcriptomic data, we can use our modeling framework to quantify temporal changes in cell position. In particular, we can infer $(\frac{dx}{dt}, \frac{dy}{dt})$, the time derivative of each cell's spatial coordinates. We refer to the quantity $(\frac{dx}{dt}, \frac{dy}{dt})$ simply as "cell velocity", because it is a change of physical position over time–a velocity in the traditional sense. There are at least two possible methods for inferring cell velocity: (1) use the heuristic method popularized by scVelo to project RNA velocity onto spatial coordinates and obtain an implicit estimate of cell velocity or (2) train a graph neural network to obtain an explicit parametric form for cell velocity as a function of cell state and time.

3 Results

We investigated the performance of TopoVelo using simulated data. To simulate cells from an entire tissue, we (1) sampled random starting positions for an initial set of cells at $t = 0$, (2) simulated their future locations using a defined tissue growth pattern, (3) defined a spatial correlation pattern for the transcription rates ρ, (4) calculated u and s using the analytical ODE solution and (5) added noise and simulated sparsity to match the properties of the real spatial transcriptomic data. We simulated two datasets with simple types of tissue growth patterns, layered growth and radial growth. These mimic two different types of biologically plausible patterns–the brain cortex grows layer by layer, while other structures grow from the inside to the outside.

To quantitatively evaluate our method, we computed several metrics and compared our performance with those from previous RNA velocity methods, scVelo [2] and VeloVAE [6]. Evaluation metrics include data reconstruction, cross-boundary direction correctness (CBDir) [5], velocity accuracy, time correlation, spatial velocity consistency and spatial time consistency. Our results show that TopoVelo achieves significantly better performance in terms of CBDir, velocity accuracy, time correlation, spatial velocity consistency, and spatial time consistency. This indicates that incorporating spatial coordinates can substantially improve the estimation of cell times and velocities.

References

1. Angevine, J., Sidman, R.L.: Autoradiographic study of cell migration during histogenesis of cerebral cortex in the mouse. Nature **192**(4804), 766–768 (1961)
2. Bergen, V., Lange, M., Peidli, S., Wolf, F.A., Theis, F.J.: Generalizing rna velocity to transient cell states through dynamical modeling. Nat. Biotechnol. **38**(12), 1408–1414 (2020)
3. Butt, S.J., et al.: The temporal and spatial origins of cortical interneurons predict their physiological subtype. Neuron **48**(4), 591–604 (2005)
4. Cho, C.S., et al.: Microscopic examination of spatial transcriptome using seq-scope. Cell **184**(13), 3559-3572.e22 (2021)
5. Gao, M., Qiao, C., Huang, Y.: Unitvelo: temporally unified rna velocity reinforces single-cell trajectory inference. Nat. Commun. **13**(1), 6586 (2022)
6. Gu, Y., Blaauw, D.T., Welch, J.: Variational mixtures of ODEs for inferring cellular gene expression dynamics. In: Chaudhuri, K., Jegelka, S., Song, L., Szepesvari, C., Niu, G., Sabato, S. (eds.) Proceedings of the 39th International Conference on Machine Learning. Proceedings of Machine Learning Research, 17–23 Jul, vol. 162, pp. 7887–7901. PMLR (2022)
7. Kingma, D.P., Welling, M.: Auto-encoding variational bayes. In: Bengio, Y., LeCun, Y. (eds.) 2nd International Conference on Learning Representations, ICLR 2014, Banff, AB, Canada, 14-16 April 2014, Conference Track Proceedings (2014)
8. Kipf, T.N., Welling, M.: Semi-supervised classification with graph convolutional networks. In: International Conference on Learning Representations (2017)
9. La Manno, G., et al.: Rna velocity of single cells. Nature **560**(7719), 494–498 (2018)
10. Lane, S.W., Williams, D.A., Watt, F.M.: Modulating the stem cell niche for tissue regeneration. Nat. Biotechnol. **32**(8), 795–803 (2014)
11. Li, C., Virgilio, M., Collins, K.L., Welch, J.D.: Multi-omic single-cell velocity models epigenome-transcriptome interactions and improves cell fate prediction. Nat. Biotechnol. **41**, 387–398 (2023)
12. Pleasure, S.J., et al.: Cell migration from the ganglionic eminences is required for the development of hippocampal gabaergic interneurons. Neuron **28**(3), 727–740 (2000)
13. Rodriques, S.G., et al.: Slide-seq: a scalable technology for measuring genome-wide expression at high spatial resolution. Science **363**(6434), 1463–1467 (2019)
14. Russell, A.J.C., et al.: Slide-tags: scalable, single-nucleus barcoding for multi-modal spatial genomics. bioRxiv (2023)
15. Veličković, P., Cucurull, G., Casanova, A., Romero, A., Liò, P., Bengio, Y.: Graph attention networks. In: International Conference on Learning Representations (2018)

Protein Domain Embeddings for Fast and Accurate Similarity Search

Benjamin Giovanni Iovino, Haixu Tang⬤, and Yuzhen Ye$^{(\boxtimes)}$⬤

Luddy School of Informatics, Computing and Engineering, Indiana University,
700 N. Woodlawn Avenue, Bloomington, IN 47408, USA
{biovino,hatang,yye}@iu.edu

Abstract. Recently developed protein language models have enabled a variety of applications of the protein contextual embeddings. Per-protein representations (each protein is represented as a vector of fixed dimension) can be derived via averaging the embeddings of individual residues, or applying matrix transformation techniques such as the discrete cosine transformation to matrices of residue embeddings. Such protein-level embeddings have been applied to enable fast searches of similar proteins, however limitations have been found; for example, PROST is good at detecting global homologs but not local homologs, and knnProtT5 excels for proteins of single domains but not multi-domain proteins. Here we propose a novel approach that first segments proteins into domains and then applies discrete cosine transformation to the vectorized embeddings of residues in each domain to infer domain-level contextual vectors. Our approach called DCTdomain utilizes predicted contact maps from ESM-2 for domain segmentation, which is formulated as a *domain segmentation* problem and can be solved using a *recursive cut* algorithm (RecCut in short) in quadratic time to the protein length. We showed such domain-level contextual vectors (termed as *DCT fingerprints*) enable fast and accurate detection of similarity between proteins that share global similarities but with undefined extended regions between shared domains, and those that only share local similarities.

Keywords: protein language model (PLM) · ESM-2 · Domain segmentation · Recursive Cut (RecCut) · Discrete Cosine Transformation (DCT) · DCT fingerprint · Homology detection

1 Introduction

Homology detection is a fundamental computation in biology due to it's role in protein annotation. Despite the simplicity of this task in its conception, it can be incredibly difficult in practice to detect remote homologs. Many methods have been developed, ranging from simple sequence-sequence comparisons to profile methods. Recent methods have been developed using contextualized embeddings generated by neural networks, such as neural protein language models (pLMs), for homology detection. pLMs are trained for the purpose of learning about the

ⓒ The Author(s), under exclusive license to Springer Nature Switzerland AG 2024
J. Ma (Ed.): RECOMB 2024, LNCS 14758, pp. 421–424, 2024.
https://doi.org/10.1007/978-0-1716-3989-4_44

nature of proteins beyond their sequence representation [1]. One of the most recent methods is ESM-2 [2], which was trained with the purpose of producing embeddings that ESMFold could use to predict the 3D structure of a sequence. Embeddings from both models have been successfully applied to many tasks, including homology detection, such as knnProtT5 [3] and PROST [4].

One tradeoff with using pLM embeddings to represent protein sequences is the increase in dimensionality compared to the original character representation. Protein-level embeddings can offset this increase. A typical approach of deriving protein-level embedding for a protein is to use the mean of the embeddings of all its residues, as in knnProtT5 [3]. However, knnProtT5 was found not competitive for comparing multi-domain proteins [3]. Another successful technique is the DCT quantization of embeddings as in PROST [4]. PROST has been shown to be effective for global homolog detection where the entirety of two proteins correspond to one another. However, it performed worse for the cases where two proteins share all of their domains, but with extended undefined regions between the domains, and for proteins that only share some of their domains.

To remedy the issues presented by existing protein-level embedding approaches, we developed a new method called DCTdomain for predicting domains using the predicted contact maps from ESM-2, and for deriving domain-level fingerprints based on DCT quantization. We proposed an improved solution to the domain segmentation problem proposed in FUpred by using the contact map prediction from ESM-2 and a new method we proposed called RecCut for domain segmentation. Predicted domains can then be used for generating domain-level fingerprints to facilitate fast and accurate similarity detection.

2   Methods

A brief overview of our method, DCTdomain is given in Fig. 1. Our domain segmentation approach called ESM2-RecCut uses contact map prediction from ESM-2, taking advantage of its capability of generating contextual embeddings without using multiple sequence alignment so there are no time-consuming iterative searches of similar sequences. In addition, we developed a quadratic time algorithm, RecCut, for domain segmentation given contact map predictions.

The domain segmentation problem is to partition a given single-chain protein into multiple contiguous or non-contiguous domains, given its contact map (predicted) as the input. To account for discontinuous domains, proteins are represented as circular strings. Formally, given a circular string $S[1, \ldots, n]$ of length n, we define a *segmentation* of the string as a sequence of k indices $(c_1, c_2, \ldots, c_k)$, where $1 \leq c_i \leq n$ represents the indices dividing the string into a set of k segments $S[c_i + 1, \ldots, c_{i+1}]$ for $i = 1, 2, \ldots, k$, and $c_{k+1} = c_1 + n$ to handle the circular nature of the string. We further define a *domain segmentation* of the string as an annotation of each segment by one of its d domains, i.e., $l[i] \in \{1, 2, ..., d\}$ so that all residues in a segment are all assigned to the same domain. So, given a contact map $C[i, j]$ representing if there is a contact between residues i and j (based on ESM-2 contact map predictions), our goal is to find

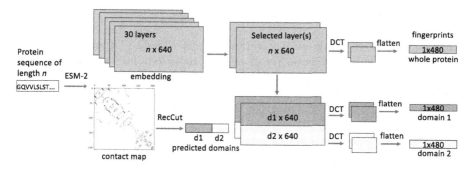

Fig. 1. A diagram showing the inference of domain-based embeddings (DCT fingerprints). For the example protein with two domains, a total of three DCT fingerprints will be derived, one representing the whole protein, and the other two are the representations of the domains. This diagram uses two-domain protein, ESM-2 t30 model, and DCT fingerprints of size 480 for demonstration purpose without loss of generality.

a maximum domain segmentation in which the number of contacts between any two domains is smaller than a threshold. FUpred [5] uses a dynamic programming algorithm to solve the problem in $O(dn^3)$ time (where d is the number of domains in the protein, and n is the length of the protein). We further improved the algorithm by introducing a few matrices, and our new algorithm RecCut runs in $O(dn^2)$.

Given an embedding matrix of a protein (also from ESM-2), 2d-DCT is first applied to the input embedding matrix to compute frequency coefficients, and then an inverse DCT (iDCT) is applied to only low frequency coefficients (discarding the high frequency ones) to produce a dimension reduced matrix. The compressed matrix is then flattened to produce 1D vector (referred as a *DCT fingerprint*), which represents a protein allowing for the usage of simple vector operations. For multi-domain proteins, DCT quantization is applied to each domain to generate a DCT fingerprint for the domain. By doing this, each protein is presented as a DCT fingerprint for single-domain proteins, or $(d+1)$ DCT fingerprints for proteins with d domains. Given two DCT fingerprints DCT_i and DCT_j, their similarity score is defined as $S(DCT_i, DCT_j) = 1 - L1(DCT_i, DCT_j)/c$, where $L1$ is the L1-distance between two vectors and c is a normalization constant such that the similarity score is transformed to the range of $[0, 1]$. Accordingly, given two proteins i and j each represented as one (for single-domain proteins) or multiple DCT fingerprints (for multi-domain proteins), their global similarity (DCTglobal) is computed as the similarity of the DCT fingerprints of the whole proteins, and their local similarity (DCTdomain) is computed as the maximum similarity of any pairs of DCTs (including those for the whole protein and those for individual domains) from the two proteins.

Our programs, benchmarks and results are available as open source on github at https://github.com/mgtools/DCTdomain.

3   Results

Table 1 shows that using ESM-2 contact maps (ESM2-FUpred, and ESM2-RecCut) resulted in very good recall of the predictions for multi-domain proteins and precision for single-domain proteins. RecCut significantly reduced the runtime especially for long proteins; it reduced runtime from 32 h by FUpred to 18 mins on a collection of 13k proteins. Table 2 shows that DCTdomain achieved fast and accurate homolog detection. All the results reported here were based on contact maps and embeddings generated by ESM-2's t30-150M checkpoint.

Table 1. Single- and multi-domain classification results on 2549 test proteins from the FUpred benchmark.

Method	Multi-domain		Single-domain		All	
	Precision	Recall	Precision	Recall	ACC	MCC
ResPRE-FUpred*	0.860	0.873	0.936	0.929	0.910	0.799
ESM2-FUpred	0.631	0.974	0.982	0.716	0.802	0.651
ESM2-RecCut	0.663	0.941	0.963	0.761	0.821	0.663

*ResPRE-FUpred results are taken from [5]. 'ACC' and 'MCC' are the accuracy and Matthew's correlation coefficient, respectively.

Table 2. AUC and total runtime for each method (listed from the least to most accurate) on pfam-local benchmark with 15273 pairs of proteins.

	UBLAST	USEARCH	FASTA	phmmer	BLAST	CS-BLAST	HHsearch	DCTdomain*
AUC	0.840	0.906	0.906	0.924	0.951	0.952	0.971	0.972
time	237 s	156 s	749 s	993 s	468 s	50 m	5.7 hr	6.6 s/47 m

*: 6.6 s for similarity calculation given DCT fingerprints; 47 min includes the time for computing DCT fingerprints of all proteins. AUC: Area Under Curve. Not included in this table: PROST (AUC=0.699) and DCTglobal (AUC=0.665).

Full Paper: A complete manuscript describing this work can be accessed at: https://www.biorxiv.org/content/10.1101/2023.11.27.567555.

References

1. Elnaggar, A., et al.: ProtTrans: toward understanding the language of life through self-supervised learning. IEEE Trans. Pattern Anal. Mach. Intell. **44**(10), 7112–7127 (2022). https://doi.org/10.1109/tpami.2021.3095381
2. Lin, Z., et al.: Evolutionary-scale prediction of atomic-level protein structure with a language model. Science **379**(6637), 1123–1130 (2023). https://doi.org/10.1126/science.ade2574
3. Schütze, K., et al.: Nearest neighbor search on embeddings rapidly identifies distant protein relations. Front. Bioinform. **2**, 1033775 (2022)
4. Kilinc, M., Jia, K., Jernigan, R.L.: Improved global protein homolog detection with major gains in function identification. PNAS **120**(9), e2211823120 (2023)
5. Zheng, W., et al.: FUpred: detecting protein domains through deep-learning-based contact map prediction. Bioinformatics **36**(12), 3749–3757 (2020)

Processing-Bias Correction with DEBIAS-M Improves Cross-Study Generalization of Microbiome-Based Prediction Models

George I. Austin[1,2] ⓘD, Aya Brown Kav[2] ⓘD, Heekuk Park[3] ⓘD, Jana Biermann[2,4,5] ⓘD, Anne-Catrin Uhlemann[3] ⓘD, and Tal Korem[2,6(✉)] ⓘD

[1] Department of Biomedical Informatics, Columbia University Irving Medical Center, New York, NY 10032, USA
[2] Program for Mathematical Genomics, Department of Systems Biology, Columbia University Irving Medical Center, New York, NY 10032, USA
tal.korem@columbia.edu
[3] Division of Infectious Diseases, Columbia University Irving Medical Center, New York, NY 10032, USA
[4] Department of Medicine, Division of Hematology/Oncology, Columbia University Irving Medical Center, New York, NY 10032, USA
[5] Herbert Irving Comprehensive Cancer Center, Columbia University Irving Medical Center, New York, NY 10032, USA
[6] Department of Obstetrics and Gynecology, Columbia University Irving Medical Center, New York, NY 10032, USA

Abstract. Microbiome profiling exhibits strong study- and batch-specific effects, impeding the identification of signals that are reproducible across studies and the development of generalizable prediction models. Prior work has attributed this to biases introduced during experimental protocols [1], with factors such as the type of DNA extraction kit affecting the efficiency of extracting and sequencing different microbes [2, 3]. While existing batch-correction methods show benefit in microbiome analysis [4–7], many make strong parametric assumptions, which do not necessarily apply in this data, or require the use of the outcome variable, which risks overfitting [8]. Lastly and importantly, the transformations performed to the data are largely non-interpretable, e.g., introducing counts to features that were initially very sparse. Here, we present DEBIAS-M (**D**omain adaptation with phenotype **E**stimation and **B**atch **I**ntegration **A**cross **S**tudies of the **M**icrobiome), an interpretable framework for processing-bias inference, batch correction, and domain adaptation in microbiome studies. DEBIAS-M learns bias-correction factors for each microbe in each batch that simultaneously minimize batch effects and maximize cross-study associations with phenotypes. Using benchmarks, including HIV classification from gut microbiome data, we demonstrate that DEBIAS-M outperforms alternative batch-correction methods commonly used in the field. Overall, we show that DEBIAS-M facilitates better modeling of microbiome data and identification of signals that are reproducible across studies.

Keywords: Microbiome · machine learning · batch correction · domain adaptation

© The Author(s), under exclusive license to Springer Nature Switzerland AG 2024
J. Ma (Ed.): RECOMB 2024, LNCS 14758, pp. 425–428, 2024.
https://doi.org/10.1007/978-1-0716-3989-4_45

1 Introduction

The conclusions of robust scientific analyses are expected to generalize beyond a specific dataset or study batch, lowering the risk of spurious findings. For prediction models, external validation in an independent dataset is imperative for robust assessment of generalizability to new populations [9]. Training models that use multiple datasets also increases sample size and power, especially in settings where data from many smaller studies is available, such as the gut microbiome in colorectal cancer [10].

Variability between microbiome profiling protocols, facilities, and bioinformatic analysis pipelines substantially affects the replicability of microbiome data [2, 3]. In a recent study, McLaren et al. [1] provide a mathematical framework for consideration of such variability, in which every experimental and analytic stage have a different efficiency for each taxon. Together, these form multiplicative taxon-specific biases that distort the observed abundances in a compositional manner [1]. McLaren et al. show that even standardization of experimental factors would not address the effects of this bias, highlighting the need for post-hoc computational correction [1].

Many approaches have been developed or applied to address experimental and other variability in microbiome studies, under the general term of "batch-correction" [4–7]. While methods of this type show some benefit in microbiome analysis, many make strong parametric assumptions, are suitable only for testing associations, or require the use of the outcome variable, which limits evaluation of generalization. Additionally, the changes these methods make to the data typically lack a biological interpretation. To address this gap, we present DEBIAS-M, a method for correction of processing bias in microbiome data, which is designed to operate in the context of multiple processing biases within a phenotypic prediction framework.

2 Methods

DEBIAS-M is a method for in silico detection and correction of processing bias. It takes as input a representation (e.g., read count or relative abundances of taxa) of microbiome samples from multiple processing protocols, studies or batches (hereafter collectively termed "batches"), and learns one multiplicative coefficient for each taxon in every batch, which is used to correct for the processing bias of that batch. Every sample is then renormalized before a downstream prediction model – identical across all batches – learns an association to a phenotype of interest.

DEBIAS-M simultaneously minimizes the cross-batch differences in the processing-bias-corrected samples and the prediction loss from predictive models utilizing the corrected data, using stochastic gradient descent. Samples for which the phenotype is unavailable or hidden, such as those with missing data or samples in a test set, are not included in the calculation of the prediction loss, and they are only considered when minimizing cross-batch differences. We further construct variations of DEBIAS-M that: (a) operates in logspace, which takes advantage of multiplicative biases becoming additive; and (b) are multi-task, and consider multiple prediction losses while inferring a single set of bias-correction factors.

Additionally, we develop a modification of DEBIAS-M that can adapt to previously unseen microbiome samples, which enables a complete separation between training and testing sets during bias correction and model training. This contrasts with traditional batch correction implementations, which require observing all input data from the test sets before running batch correction and subsequent model training, limiting the potential for downstream applications of trained models. In this "adaptation" implementation, DEBIAS-M first learns bias-correction factors and prediction model weights for the batches in the train sets, and freezes all parameters before incorporating any information from held-out samples. Then, when evaluating predictions on a test set, DEBIAS-M first corrects for the processing bias on the test set, followed by calculating all predictions using the trained predictive layer.

DEBIAS-M, as well as all analyses and results, are available on github: https://git hub.com/korem-lab/DEBIAS-M.

3   Results

We evaluated DEBIAS-M in extensive benchmarks across more than 30 different studies. Comparing DEBIAS-M to batch-correction methods commonly used in the field [4–7], we demonstrated that it consistently improved the ability of microbiome-based prediction models to predict phenotypes on held-out studies in a diverse range of clinical settings, including cervical neoplasia and HIV. We additionally show that the adaption version of DEBIAS-M, which does not observe any test set inputs before model training, performs similarly to the standard implementation. Using a simulation framework, we demonstrate the robustness of DEBIAS-M to a variety of study properties. Additionally, we find that bias-correction factors learned by DEBIAS-M are associated with experimental processing and design parameters, previously shown to be relevant for technical variation in microbiome data [1], such as choice of extraction kit and bacterial Gram status [1, 2]. Overall, we show that DEBIAS-M allows for better modeling of microbiome data and identification of interpretable signals that are reproducible across studies.

Full Paper: A complete manuscript describing this work can be accessed at: https://www.biorxiv.org/content/10.1101/2024.02.09.579716v1.

Acknowledgments. This work was supported by the Program for Mathematical Genomics at Columbia University (T.K.), R01HD106017 (T.K.), and T15LM007079 (G.I.A.).

Disclosure of Interests.   The authors have no competing interests to declare that are relevant to the content of this article.

References

1. McLaren, M.R., Willis, A.D., Callahan, B.J.: Consistent and correctable bias in metagenomic sequencing experiments. Elife. 8 (2019). https://doi.org/10.7554/eLife.46923
2. Costea, P.I., et al.: Towards standards for human fecal sample processing in metagenomic studies. Nat. Biotechnol. **35**, 1069–1076 (2017). https://doi.org/10.1038/nbt.3960

3. McOrist, A.L., Jackson, M., Bird, A.R.: A comparison of five methods for extraction of bacterial DNA from human faecal samples. J. Microbiol. Methods **50**, 131–139 (2002). https://doi.org/10.1016/s0167-7012(02)00018-0

4. Law, C.W., Chen, Y., Shi, W., Smyth, G.K.: Voom: precision weights unlock linear model analysis tools for RNA-seq read counts. Genome Biol. **15**, 1–17 (2014). https://doi.org/10.1186/gb-2014-15-2-r29

5. Ling, W., et al.: Batch effects removal for microbiome data via conditional quantile regression. Nat. Commun. **13**, 5418 (2022). https://doi.org/10.1038/s41467-022-33071-9

6. Johnson, W.E., Li, C., Rabinovic, A.: Adjusting batch effects in microarray expression data using empirical Bayes methods. Biostatistics **8**, 118–127 (2006). https://doi.org/10.1093/biostatistics/kxj037

7. Mecham, B.H., Nelson, P.S., Storey, J.D.: Supervised normalization of microarrays. Bioinformatics **26**, 1308–1315 (2010). https://doi.org/10.1093/bioinformatics/btq118

8. Whalen, S., Schreiber, J., Noble, W.S., Pollard, K.S.: Navigating the pitfalls of applying machine learning in genomics. Nat. Rev. Genet. **23**, 169–181 (2022). https://doi.org/10.1038/s41576-021-00434-9

9. Siontis, G.C.M., Tzoulaki, I., Castaldi, P.J., Ioannidis, J.P.A.: External validation of new risk prediction models is infrequent and reveals worse prognostic discrimination. J. Clin. Epidemiol. **68**, 25–34 (2015). https://doi.org/10.1016/j.jclinepi.2014.09.007

10. Wirbel, J., et al.: Meta-analysis of fecal metagenomes reveals global microbial signatures that are specific for colorectal cancer. Nat. Med. **25**, 679–689 (2019). https://doi.org/10.1038/s41591-019-0406-6

VICTree - A Variational Inference Method for Clonal Tree Reconstruction

Harald Melin[1]($\boxtimes$), Vittorio Zampinetti[1,2]($\boxtimes$), Andrew McPherson[3], and Jens Lagergren[1]

[1] School of EECS, KTH Royal Institute of Technology, Stockholm, Sweden
haraldme@kth.se
[2] Department of Mathematical Sciences, Politecnico di Torino, Turin, Italy
vittorio.zampinetti@polito.it
[3] Computational Oncology, Memorial Sloan Kettering Cancer Center, New York, NY, USA

Abstract. Clonal tree inference brings crucial insights to the analysis of tumor heterogeneity and cancer evolution. Recent progress in single cell sequencing has prompted a demand for more advanced probabilistic models of copy number evolution, coupled with inference methods which can account for the noisy nature of the data along with dependencies between adjacent sites in copy number profiles. We present VIC-Tree, a variational inference based algorithm for joint Bayesian inference of clonal trees, together with a novel Tree-structured Mixture Hidden Markov Model (TSMHMM) which combines HMMs related through a tree with a mixture model. For the tree inference, we introduce a new algorithm, LARS, for sampling directed labeled multifurcating trees. To evaluate our proposed method, we conduct experiments on simulated data and on samples of multiple myeloma and breast cancer. We demonstrate VICTree's capacity for reliable clustering, clonal tree reconstruction, copy number evolution and the utility of the ELBO for model selection. Lastly, VICTree's results are compared in terms of quality and speed of inference to other state-of-the-art methods. The code for VIC-Tree is available on GitHub: github.com/Lagergren-Lab/victree and the full paper on bioRxiv.

Keywords: Clone tree reconstruction · copy number evolution · scDNA-seq · Bayesian inference · Variational inference

1 Introduction

The well-established clonal theory of cancer [7] describes cancer development as a process of phenotypically distinct cell sub-populations, referred to as clones, undergoing Darwinian evolution driven by somatic genetic mutations. The resulting tumor heterogeneity is a substantial barrier for successful treatment [1]. To analyze the genetic content of a tumor, the recent single cell whole genome

---

H. Melin and V. Zampinetti—Equal contribution.

J. Ma (Ed.): RECOMB 2024, LNCS 14758, pp. 429–433, 2024.
https://doi.org/10.1007/978-1-0716-3989-4_46

sequencing (scWGS) technology Direct Library Preparation (DLP) [13], has shown proficiency in producing data of thousands of single cells suitable for copy number (CN) analysis [9,13]. Yet, the data exhibits imperfections and the experimental process is inherently noisy.

CN deletion and duplication events may effect multiple genomic sites. This has sparked recent surge in research of models able to accommodate for dependencies within the CN profile (CNP) [3,6,8,9,11,12]. Despite their demonstrated strengths, the phylogenetic methods either rely on heuristic approaches [3,11,12] which lack the rigor of probabilistic modeling, or on simplifying assumptions and pre-processing steps that break the full Bayesian aspiration [6,9].

We present *VICTree*, the first framework for fully automated joint Bayesian inference of site-dependent CN evolution, clonal tree reconstruction, cell-to-clone clustering and cell specific read baselines, using only GC-correction and normalization as data pre-processing. VICTree utilizes coordinate ascent Variational Inference (CAVI) [2] to avoid simplifying assumptions of the model required by Markov chain Monte-Carlo (MCMC) approaches [6,9] and draws inspiration from both the tumor [8] and classical phylogenetic literature [4,10]. The resulting VI framework contains three further novelties: the *Tree-Structured Mixture-HMM* (TSMHMM), a novel type of HMM, suitable for the tumor clonal tree context, *LARS*, an algorithm for sampling labeled multifurcating rooted trees (also known as *arborescences*) induced by a weighted graph and a novel *Split-and-merge algorithm*, tailored to the context of clonal trees, taking VI based clonal analysis from the theoretically interesting to the practically applicable.

2 Generative Model

The TSMHMM consists of two modules: a tree-structured Markov model, named CopyTree, that generates CNPs with horizontal and hierarchical dependencies, and a mixture emission model which associates the observations (corrected reads) to the hidden states (CNs) of the TSMHMM by a mixture over the tree nodes (clones). CopyTree models CN evolution by parent-child clone CN states of consecutive sites, $C_m^u, C_{m-1}^u, C_m^v, C_{m-1}^v$ with a CN transition function, which we name the *CN coherence function* (1):

$$h_{\varepsilon_{uv}}(C_m^v | C_m^u, C_{m-1}^v, C_{m-1}^u) = \begin{cases} 1 - \varepsilon_{uv}, & \text{if } C_m^v - C_{m-1}^v = C_m^u - C_{m-1}^u \\ \varepsilon_{uv}/(A-1), & \text{if } C_m^v - C_{m-1}^v \neq C_m^u - C_{m-1}^u, \end{cases} \tag{1}$$

where A is the maximum CN and ε_{uv} an arc specific transition probability. If ε_{uv} is small, the CN coherence function formalizes the intuition that if we observe a breakpoint in the CNP of u, then we are likely to observe the same breakpoint in a child, v, of u. We then relate our observations, $\mathbf{Y}$, to these hidden CN states by a Mixture Hidden Markov Model (MHMM), with Gaussian emissions $Y_{mn} | Z_n = k, \mu_n, \tau_n, C_m^k \sim \mathcal{N}(\mu_n \cdot C_m^k, \tau_n^{-1})$, cell-to-clone assignments $\mathbf{Z}$, clonal concentration parameter $\boldsymbol{\pi}$, cell reads baseline $\boldsymbol{\mu}$ and precision $\boldsymbol{\tau}$. The combined statistical model is the TSMHMM for a fixed tree T. Together with a uniform

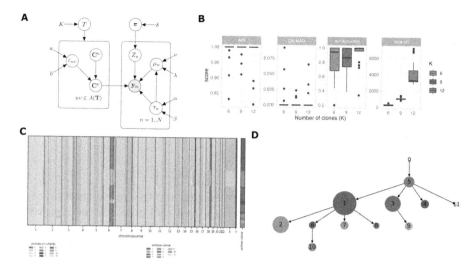

Fig. 1. A Bayesian network for VICTree model: the TSMHMM model with tree topology T. The M-plate over bins is left out for a more uncluttered view of the graphical model. **B** Scores against ground truth over 20 synthetic datasets for three values of K (number of clones). Clustering performance is quantified by the Adjusted-Rand index while CN calling performance by mean absolute deviation. Arc accuracy is the proportion of arcs in the ground truth tree that are included in the MAP estimate tree. Dots represent outliers. **C-D** Inferred clonal copy number profile and MAP estimate of the clonal tree of the xenograft breast cancer dataset SA501X3F with $K = 12$. Nodes size is proportional to the amount of cells to them attached.

prior distribution over the finite set of all possible tree topologies $\mathcal{T}_K$ for a fixed number of nodes K, this completes our generative model, which is summarized in Fig. 1.

3   Inference

We adopt a fully Bayesian approach by approximating the posterior with a variational distribution q under the widely-used mean-field assumption. Its factorization is

$$q(\mathbf{C}, \mathbf{Z}, T, \boldsymbol{\pi}, \boldsymbol{\mu}, \boldsymbol{\tau}) = q(T)q(\boldsymbol{\pi}) \prod_{uv \in A(\mathcal{G})} q(\varepsilon_{uv}) \prod_{n=1}^{N} q(\mu_n, \tau_n)q(Z_n) \prod_{u=1}^{K} q(\mathbf{C}^u) , \quad (2)$$

where $\mathcal{G}$ is the fully connected directed graph with K nodes and $A(\mathcal{G})$ is the set of arcs which does not contain self connections. We explicitly derive the CAVI updates for all the variational parameters. While updating the parameters related to $\mathbf{Z}, \boldsymbol{\pi}, \boldsymbol{\varepsilon}, \boldsymbol{\mu}, \boldsymbol{\tau}$ is relatively straightforward, the CAVI updates of $q(\mathbf{C})$ and $q(T)$ require elaborate procedures. Appealingly, we show that the optimal $q(\mathbf{C})$ for the TSMHMM corresponds to distinct non-homogeneous Markov chains for each clone. The full update asks for the expectation w.r.t. $q(T)$, however, the normalizing constant of $q(T)$ is not known, nor can we sample from $q(T)$. Therefore, we introduce a novel labeled arborescence sampler, LARS, to use for Importance sampling, a procedure similar to that in [4]. Optimization is susceptible to component degeneracy as a result of similarity between the underlying clones, motivating a subroutine for escaping these local optima. We develop a novel Split-and-merge algorithm which reassigns cells to clusters based on the evidence lower bound.

4   Results

Inference with VICTree shows good cells clustering and tree reconstruction capability. We test our method on both synthetic and real data. In the context of simulated cell reads and CN evolution, our method achieves near perfect accuracy against the ground-truth and it is robust to high rates of CN events, proving that VI strategy is not just faster than regular MCMC, but also effective. As for real data, we run experiments on a DLP+ dataset from a breast cancer [13] and three 10X multiple myeloma datasets [5]. In absence of ground truth for such datasets, we compare the former in terms of CN inference and tree reconstruction with CONET output, observing similar CNP estimates and more condensed tree reconstruction, even though CONET relies on additional input beyond the corrected reads. Time-wise, convergence on the real dataset executions (~ 1000 cells in some cases) is reached in less than two hours, which is a competitive running time considering the complexity of the model. This level of efficiency is achieved thanks to the adoption of VI and the custom mathematical CAVI derivations, which should be considered as part of the results of this work. The main limitation is due to the tree sampler's poor scalability w.r.t. the number of distinct clones K, a hyperparameter of the model to be fixed in advance, for which we only test values below 20. Although this seems not to affect inference substantially on the real datasets considered for evaluation, a more efficient method for tree sampling is a desirable improvement. Future works may also involve changes in the model so to explicitly model whole-genome duplication events and exchanging the observational model. The modular framework of VIC-Tree facilitates such improvements.

References

1. Greaves, M., Maley, C.C.: Clonal evolution in cancer. Nature **481**(7381), 306–313 (2012)
2. Jordan, M.I., Ghahramani, Z., Jaakkola, T.S., Saul, L.K.: An introduction to variational methods for graphical models. Mach. Learn. **37**(2), 183–233 (1999)
3. Kaufmann, T.L., et al.: MEDICC2: whole-genome doubling aware copy-number phylogenies for cancer evolution. Genome Biol. **23**(1), 241 (2022)
4. Koptagel, H., Kviman, O., Melin, H., Safinianaini, N., Lagergren, J.: VaiPhy: a variational inference based algorithm for phylogeny. In: Koyejo, S., Mohamed, S., Agarwal, A., Belgrave, D., Cho, K., Oh, A. (eds.) Advances in Neural Information Processing Systems, vol.35, pp. 14758–14770. Curran Associates, Inc. (2022)

5. Lee, H., et al.: Mechanisms of antigen escape from BCMA-or GPRC5D-targeted immunotherapies in multiple myeloma. Nat. Med. **29**(9), 1–12 (2023)
6. Markowska, M., et al.: CONET: copy number event tree model of evolutionary tumor history for single-cell data. Genome Biol. **23**(1), 128 (2022)
7. Nowell, P.C.: The clonal evolution of tumor cell populations. Science **194**(4260), 23–28 (1976)
8. Safinianaini, N., de Souza, C.P.E., Roth, A., Koptagel, H., Toosi, H., Lagergren, J.: CopyMix: mixture model based single-cell clustering and copy number profiling using variational inference. bioRxiv (2023). https://doi.org/10.1101/2020.01.29.926022, preprint
9. Salehi, S., et al.: Cancer phylogenetic tree inference at scale from 1000s of single cell genomes. Peer Commun. J. **3**, e63 (2023).https://doi.org/10.24072/pcjournal.292, https://peercommunityjournal.org/articles/10.24072/pcjournal.292/
10. Siepel, A., Haussler, D.: Combining phylogenetic and hidden Markov models in biosequence analysis. In: Proceedings of the Seventh Annual International Conference on Research in Computational Molecular Biology, pp. 277–286. RECOMB 2003, Association for Computing Machinery, New York, NY, USA (2003)
11. Wang, F., et al.: MEDALT: single-cell copy number lineage tracing enabling gene discovery. Genome Biol. **22**(1), 70 (2021)
12. Zaccaria, S., Raphael, B.J.: Characterizing allele- and haplotype-specific copy numbers in single cells with CHISEL. Nat. Biotechnol. **39**(2), 207–214 (2021)
13. Zahn, H., et al.: Scalable whole-genome single-cell library preparation without preamplification. Nat. Methods **14**(2), 167–173 (2017)

DeST-OT: Alignment of Spatiotemporal Transcriptomics Data

Peter Halmos[1], Xinhao Liu[1], Julian Gold[2], Feng Chen[3], Li Ding[3,4],
and Benjamin J. Raphael[1(✉)]

[1] Department of Computer Science, Princeton University,
35 Olden St., Princeton, NJ 08544, USA
braphael@princeton.edu
[2] Center for Statistics and Machine Learning, Princeton University,
26 Prospect Ave., Princeton, NJ 08544, USA
[3] Departments of Medicine and Genetics, Siteman Cancer Center,
Washington University in St. Louis, St. Louis, MO 63110, USA
[4] McDonnell Genome Institute, Washington University in St. Louis,
St. Louis, MO 63108, USA

Abstract. Spatially resolved transcriptomics (SRT) measures mRNA transcripts at thousands of locations within a tissue slice, revealing spatial variations in gene expression as well as the spatial distribution of cell types. In recent studies, SRT has been applied to tissue slices from multiple timepoints during the development of an organism. Alignment of this *spatiotemporal* transcriptomics data can provide insights into the gene expression programs governing the growth and differentiation of cells over space and time. We introduce DeST-OT (**De**velopmental **S**patio**T**emporal **O**ptimal **T**ransport), a method to align SRT slices from pairs of developmental timepoints using the framework of optimal transport (OT). DeST-OT uses *semi-relaxed* optimal transport to precisely model cellular growth, death, and differentiation processes that are not well-modeled by existing alignment methods. We further introduce two metrics to quantify the plausibility of a spatiotemporal alignment: a *growth distortion metric* which quantifies the discrepancy between the inferred and the true cell type growth rates, and a *migration metric* which quantifies the distance traveled between ancestor and descendant cells.

1 Formulation

A spatially resolved transcriptomics slice is represented by a tuple $\mathcal{S} = (\mathbf{X}, \mathbf{S})$. $\mathbf{X} \in \mathbb{N}^{n \times p}$ is the transcript count matrix, with n the number of spots and p the number of genes measured. Rows of $\mathbf{X}$ are the gene expression vectors at each spot. $\mathbf{S} \in \mathbb{R}^{n \times 2}$ is the spatial position matrix, whose rows are the (x, y) coordinates of each spot. Given two *spatiotemporal* slices $\mathcal{S}_1 = (\mathbf{X}^{(1)}, \mathbf{S}^{(1)})$ and $\mathcal{S}_2 = (\mathbf{X}^{(2)}, \mathbf{S}^{(2)})$, measured on the same set of genes at timepoints t_1 and t_2, we derive an alignment matrix $\mathbf{\Pi} \in \mathbb{R}_+^{n_1 \times n_2}$, whose entry $\mathbf{\Pi}_{ij}$ gives the probability

---

P. Halmos and X. Liu—These authors contributed equally to this work.

J. Ma (Ed.): RECOMB 2024, LNCS 14758, pp. 434–437, 2024.
https://doi.org/10.1007/978-1-0716-3989-4_47

that cells in spot i of $\mathcal{S}_1$ are the progenitors of cells in spot j of $\mathcal{S}_2$. The probabilities in the alignment matrix $\mathbf{\Pi}$ minimize a cost based on the gene expression at each spot and the spatial locations of aligned spots. We use the mathematical tool of optimal transport (OT) to solve for $\mathbf{\Pi}$. PASTE [3] uses OT to solve a related problem of static (non-temporal) spatial alignment, in which $\mathcal{S}_1$ and $\mathcal{S}_2$ are adjacent slices of the same tissue from the same timepoint, and minimizes the following objective function:

$$\mathcal{E}_{\text{PASTE}}(\mathbf{\Pi}) = (1 - \alpha) \sum_{i,j'} \mathbf{C}_{ij'} \mathbf{\Pi}_{ij'} + \alpha \sum_{i,j',k,l'} \left(\mathbf{D}_{ik}^{(1)} - \mathbf{D}_{j'l'}^{(2)} \right)^2 \mathbf{\Pi}_{ij'} \mathbf{\Pi}_{kl'}. \quad (1)$$

subject to the standard optimal transport constraints:

$$\mathbf{\Pi} \mathbf{1}_{n_2} = \mathbf{g}_1, \quad \mathbf{\Pi}^T \mathbf{1}_{n_1} = \mathbf{g}_2, \quad \mathbf{\Pi} \geq 0 \quad (2)$$

Matrix $\mathbf{C} \in \mathbb{R}^{n_1 \times n_2}$ stores the distance in gene expression between spots in $\mathcal{S}_1$ and spots in $\mathcal{S}_2$, while $\mathbf{D}^{(1)}$ and $\mathbf{D}^{(2)}$ come from intra-slice spatial distances. $\mathbf{g}_1 \in \mathbb{R}^{n_1}, \mathbf{g}_2 \in \mathbb{R}^{n_2}$ are uniform probability measures. PASTE is *balanced* OT, requiring the constraints on $\mathbf{g}_1, \mathbf{g}_2$ to be satisfied strictly. A recent preprint, moscot[2], considered the PASTE objective with a relaxation of both marginals $\mathbf{g}_1, \mathbf{g}_2$, where growth is informed by predefined marker genes in a supervised manner. These two methods are not amenable to tissue expansion because the term $(\mathbf{D}_{ik}^{(1)} - \mathbf{D}_{j'l'}^{(2)})^2 \mathbf{\Pi}_{ij'} \mathbf{\Pi}_{kl'}$ prefers to align identical or isometric shapes: it is minimized when the distances inside the square are the same.

We introduce DeST-OT for aligning spatiotemporal data with unsupervised inference of cell growth and death using *semi-relaxed* optimal transport. We relax only the constraint $\mathbf{\Pi} \mathbf{1}_{n_2} = \mathbf{g}_1$ in (2), allowing $\mathbf{\Pi} \mathbf{1}_{n_2}$ to represent an arbitrary posterior over the first slice, while the other constraint $\mathbf{\Pi}^T \mathbf{1}_{n_1} = \mathbf{g}_2$ is kept. We set both $\mathbf{g}_1, \mathbf{g}_2$ to assign equal weight $\frac{1}{n_1}$ to each spot. This leads to an interpretable *growth* $\boldsymbol{\xi} = \mathbf{\Pi} \mathbf{1}_{n_2} - \mathbf{g}_1$, the change in mass relative to a uniform prior $\mathbf{g}_1$ at each spot. For a spot i at time t_1, $\boldsymbol{\xi}_i > 0$ means that spot i has > 1 descendant, and correspondingly, $\boldsymbol{\xi}_i < 0$ implies spot i has < 1 descendant. To find a growth rate J_i for each spot i, one can take $J_i = \log(1 + n_1 \boldsymbol{\xi}_i)/(t_2 - t_1)$.

Under the semi-relaxed framework, DeST-OT optimizes a development-aware objective function. The objective cost of DeST-OT for finding an optimal spatiotemporal alignment matrix $\mathbf{\Pi}$ consists of three terms: a doublet term, a triplet term, and a quartet term. The doublet term, $\sum_{i,j'} \mathbf{C}_{ij'} \mathbf{\Pi}_{ij'}$, is the same as in PASTE. The term compares the expression of two spots, one from each slice, hence we call it the *doublet* term of our objective. The quartet term is defined as $\sum_{i,j',k,l'} (\mathbf{M}_{ik}^{(1)} - \mathbf{M}_{j'l'}^{(2)})^2 \mathbf{\Pi}_{ij'} \mathbf{\Pi}_{kl'}$. We define the matrix $\mathbf{M}^{(1)}$ as the entrywise product of the square matrices $\mathbf{C}^{(1)}$ and $\mathbf{D}^{(1)}$, and correspondingly for $\mathbf{M}^{(2)}$. $\mathbf{C}^{(1)} \in \mathbb{R}^{n_1 \times n_1}$ is the distance in the expression space between each pair of spots on $\mathbf{S}^{(1)}$. $\mathbf{C}^{(2)}$ is defined analogously. $\mathbf{D}^{(1)}, \mathbf{D}^{(2)}$ are the intra-slice spatial distance matrices as in PASTE. That is, DeST-OT aims to match transcriptomics and spatial information jointly in one matrix. While the spatial distance matrices $(\mathbf{D}^{(1)}, \mathbf{D}^{(2)})$ are appropriate for static alignment, they encode a rigid geometry that does not account for spatial deformations accompanying growth. DeST-OT matches an expression-smoothed geometry between the two slices, accounting for expansion or shrinkage. We refer to this term as the *quartet term* of our objective function since it compares spot-pairs, with one pair from each slice.

While the doublet terms matches pairs of spots and the quartet term matches pairs of pairs of spots, in growing tissues it is essential to model the ancestor-descendant relationship between spots. Specifically, when an ancestor spot differentiates into multiple descendant spots, these descendant spots should be close to each other in both physical space and expression space. Correspondingly, multiple ancestors should also be close. We make this notion precise by adding a *triplet* term to our objective: $\mathcal{E}_{\text{triplet}}(\mathbf{\Pi}) = \sum_{ij'k'} \mathbf{\Pi}_{ij'}\mathbf{\Pi}_{ik'}\mathbf{M}^{(2)2}_{j'k'} + \sum_{ijk'} \mathbf{\Pi}_{ik'}\mathbf{\Pi}_{jk'}\mathbf{M}^{(1)2}_{ij}$. The squares on the $\mathbf{M}$ matrices match the form of the quartet term, upweighting the triplet summands which enforce the similarity of descendants and ancestors. Adding these terms to our objective function has a regularizing effect: $\mathbf{\Pi}$ is penalized for predicting distant descendants j', k' of the same spot i in the first slice, or for predicting distant ancestors i, j of the same spot k' in the second slice. Distance is interpreted to be both spatial and transcriptomic due to the definition of $\mathbf{M}$. The DeST-OT objective is a sum of the doublet, triplet, and quartet energies:

$$\mathcal{E}_{\text{DeST-OT}} = (1-\alpha)\mathcal{E}_{\text{doublet}}(\mathbf{\Pi}) + \frac{\alpha}{2}\left(\mathcal{E}_{\text{triplet}}(\mathbf{\Pi}) + \mathcal{E}_{\text{quartet}}(\mathbf{\Pi})\right) \qquad (3)$$

The combination of these terms captures lower to higher order of interactions between spots in a growing tissue. The DeST-OT optimization problem, with entropic regularization and the semi-relaxed constraints is

$$\begin{aligned} \min \quad & \mathcal{E}_{\text{DeST-OT}}(\mathbf{\Pi}) + \gamma \text{KL}(\mathbf{\Pi}\mathbf{1}_{n_2} \parallel \mathbf{g}_1) - \eta\text{H}(\mathbf{\Pi}) \\ s.t. \quad & \mathbf{\Pi}^T\mathbf{1}_{n_1} = \mathbf{g}_2, \quad \mathbf{\Pi} \geq 0 \end{aligned} \qquad (4)$$

The parameter α balances the contribution of the doublet term and the triplet and quartet terms to the alignment. γ governs the compliance of the semi-relaxed constraint, and η governs the strength of entropic regularization in the Sinkhorn algorithm [1] which is adapted for the semi-relaxed case.

2   Assessing Alignment Quality by Cellular Growth and Migration

We introduce the *growth distortion metric* to quantify how well the growth-rates implied by an alignment match the observed change of cell type labels. The cell type labels are a partition of spots for each slice, denoted $\mathcal{P}_1 = (\mathcal{P}_1(p))_{p=1}^P$ and $\mathcal{P}_2 = (\mathcal{P}_2(p))_{p=1}^P$ for timepoints t_1 and t_2. The mass $m_1(p)$ of cell type p at time t_1 is $m_1(p) = \#\mathcal{P}_1(p)$, the number of t_1-spots with the label p. Likewise for time t_2. The change-in-mass for cell type p across these two timepoints is then $m_2(p) - m_1(p)$. Our metric makes two assumptions: first, that there are no cell type transitions between distinct cell types (we discuss how to relax this assumption shortly), and that the burden of accomplishing the change in mass is shared equally across cells of the same type. Under these two assumptions, the "true" growth $\gamma(p)$ at any $i \in \mathcal{P}_1(p)$ is

$$\gamma(p) = \frac{1}{m_1(p)} \left(\frac{m_2(p) - m_1(p)}{n_1} \right) \tag{5}$$

Summing these values over all t_1-spots yields the total (normalized) change in mass across the two slices, $\frac{n_2 - n_1}{n_1}$. The *growth distortion metric* $\mathcal{J}_{growth}$ of an alignment matrix $\mathbf{\Pi}$ measures the total distortion between the inferred growth $\boldsymbol{\xi}$ and the true growth $\boldsymbol{\gamma}$ at each spot:

$$\mathcal{J}_{growth} = \sum_{p=1}^{P} \sum_{i \in \mathcal{P}_1(p)} \| \boldsymbol{\xi}_i - \gamma(p) \|_2^2. \tag{6}$$

We generalize the growth distortion metric to the case when cell type transitions are present (but unknown) using a reverse-time transition matrix $\mathbf{T} \in \mathbb{R}^{P \times P}$. When the true cell type transitions are not given, we compute the growth distortion of an alignment as the lowest distortion achieved under any transition which we prove is achieved by $\mathbf{T}_{pq} = \left(\frac{n_1}{m_2(q)} \right) \sum_{i \in \mathcal{P}_1(p)} \sum_{j' \in \mathcal{P}_2(q)} \mathbf{\Pi}_{ij'}$.

We also introduce a migration metric $\mathcal{J}_{migration}$ between two slices that quantifies the distance cells move under an alignment $\mathbf{\Pi}$, formalizing the intuition that the descendants of a cell tend to be close to their parent over short time intervals. Given an alignment $\mathbf{\Pi}$ and function $\varphi : \mathbb{R}^2 \to \mathbb{R}^2$ placing slice $\mathcal{S}_2$ into a common-coordinate frame with slice $\mathcal{S}_1$, we define the *migration metric* as:

$$\mathcal{J}_{migration} = \mathbb{E}_{(i,j') \sim \mathbf{\Pi}} \left[\| \mathbf{s}_i - \varphi(\mathbf{s}_{j'}) \|_2^2 \right], \tag{7}$$

We use the function $\varphi(\mathbf{z}) = \mathbf{Q}(\mathbf{z} - \mathbf{h})$ for rotation $\mathbf{Q}$ and translation $\mathbf{h}$ that solve a generalized Procrustes' problem. This describes a rigid-body transformation relating the coordinate frames of slice $\mathcal{S}_1$ and $\mathcal{S}_2$.

Acknowledgements. This research was supported by NIH/NCI grant U24CA248453 to B.J.R. J.G. is supported by the Schmidt DataX Fund at Princeton University made possible through a major gift from the Schmidt Futures Foundation.

Data Availabilty Statement. The software and preprint are available at:
https://github.com/raphael-group/DeST_OT.
https://www.biorxiv.org/content/10.1101/2024.03.05.583575v1.

References

1. Cuturi, M.: Sinkhorn distances: lightspeed computation of optimal transport. Adv. Neural Inf. Proc. Syst. **26** , 2292–2300 (2013)
2. Klein, D., et al.: Mapping cells through time and space with moscot. bioRxiv (2023)
3. Zeira, R., Land, M., Strzalkowski, A., Raphael, B.J.: Alignment and integration of spatial transcriptomics data. Nat. Methods **19**(5), 567–575 (2022)

Determining Optimal Placement of Copy Number Aberration Impacted Single Nucleotide Variants in a Tumor Progression History

Chih Hao Wu[1,2], Suraj Joshi[1], Welles Robinson[3,4], Paul F. Robbins[3], Russell Schwartz[5,6], S. Cenk Sahinalp[1], and Salem Malikić[1(✉)]

[1] Cancer Data Science Laboratory, Center for Cancer Research, National Cancer Institute, National Institutes of Health, Bethesda, MD, USA
salem.malikic@nih.gov
[2] Department of Cell Biology and Molecular Genetics, University of Maryland, College Park, MD, USA
[3] Surgery Branch, Center for Cancer Research, National Cancer Institute, National Institutes of Health, Bethesda, MD, USA
[4] Tumour Immunogenomics and Immunosurveillance Laboratory, University College London Cancer Institute, London, UK
[5] Computational Biology Department, Carnegie Mellon University, Pittsburgh, PA, USA
[6] Department of Biological Sciences, Carnegie Mellon University, Pittsburgh, PA, USA

Abstract. Intratumoral heterogeneity arises as a result of genetically distinct subclones emerging during tumor progression. These subclones are characterized by various types of somatic genomic aberrations, with single nucleotide variants (SNVs) and copy number aberrations (CNAs) being the most prominent. In this paper, we introduce DETOPT, a combinatorial optimization method for accurate tumor progression tree inference that places SNVs impacted by CNAs on trees of tumor progression with minimal distortion on their variant allele frequencies observed across available samples of a tumor. We show that on simulated data DETOPT provides more accurate tree placement of SNVs impacted by CNAs than the available alternatives. When applied to a set of multi-sample bulk exome-sequenced tumor metastases from a treatment-refractory, triple-positive metastatic breast cancer, DETOPT reports biologically plausible trees of tumor progression, identifying the tree placement of copy number state gains and losses impacting SNVs, including those in clinically significant genes.

Full Text Preprint. https://www.biorxiv.org/content/10.1101/2024.03.10.584318v1.

C. H. Wu and S. Joshi—Joint first authors.
S. C. Sahinalp and S. Malikić—Joint last authors.

J. Ma (Ed.): RECOMB 2024, LNCS 14758, pp. 438–443, 2024.
https://doi.org/10.1007/978-1-0716-3989-4_48

1   Introduction

Cancer progression is a product of an evolutionary process through which the concomitant accumulation and selection of genomic aberrations in somatic cells promote their survival and unregulated proliferation [11]. Tumors typically develop into genetically heterogeneous subpopulations of cells (subclones), and those with more diverse intratumoral compositions may have an increased likelihood of acquiring treatment resistance and metastatic potential. Reconstructing the evolutionary progression history of heterogeneous tumors not only could inform risk stratification for targeted therapies, but may also reveal mutational mechanisms of resistance, as these would correspond to the positive selection and continual evolution of particular subclones over others [8].

While single-cell DNA sequencing has advanced studies of tumor progression substantially [10], most newly generated DNA sequencing datasets are still obtained through conventional and more cost-effective bulk DNA sequencing. The existing computational methods for inferring tumor progression trees (also known as trees of tumor evolution) aim to integrate multiple bulk-sequenced samples in a number of ways. However, most of these methods are primarily designed for somatic single nucleotide variants (SNVs) located in genomic loci not impacted by copy number aberrations (CNAs) [2,5,7,9,12,14,17]. Although there have been some developments in the design of computational methods that account for SNVs from copy number altered mutational loci, these methods either operate on a small set of variants and/or (sub)clones [3,4] or make restrictive assumptions about the possible relationships between SNVs and copy number gains and losses [1]. More recently, PACTION [13], a method for integration of trees independently derived by the use of CNAs (CNA-tree) and SNVs (SNV-tree) was proposed. While there is a history of methods for bulk sequencing data that focus specifically on CNA-trees [6,16], inference of CNA-trees is still a largely unsolved problem. In the original study [13] the authors performed exhaustive search over all possible CNA-trees, which limits practical applications of this method to tumors characterized by low numbers of CNA clones. DeCiFer [15] is another recent method, which clusters SNVs based on their read counts while accounting for the impact of CNAs. While descendant cell fractions of SNVs reported by this method can in principle be used as the input to several of the available tree inference methods (e.g., CITUP or AncesTree), DeCiFer does not impose a joint tree of tumor progression shared by all variants, which can result in decreased accuracy of the inferred trees.

There are several challenging problems encountered in the computational integration of SNVs and CNAs for tree inference. One particular limiting factor to the development of methods capable of handling CNA-impacted SNVs was the lack of scalable approaches for detailed copy number profiling of tumors with multiple bulk-sequenced samples. One notable recent development in this direction is HATCHet [18] which successfully leverages complementary signals from multiple bulk samples to provide a comprehensive subclonal architecture of a tumor with respect to CNAs.

In this work we introduce a combinatorial optimization method, DETOPT, for determining optimal placement in tumor progression history of SNVs from the genomic regions impacted by CNAs. DETOPT utilizes disjoint genomic segments, each with a consistent CNA profile across all subclones of the tumor, to simultaneously place CNAs and SNVs from regions impacted by CNAs onto a tree of tumor progression inferred by the use of SNVs from diploid regions. DETOPT is based on a time-efficient Integer Linear Programming formulation and is freely available at https://github.com/algo-cancer/DETOPT.

2 Methods

The progression history of a tumor can be represented as a rooted tree in which the root represents the population of normal cells and each of the remaining nodes represents a subclone, i.e. genetically uniform (sub)population of tumor cells (Fig. 1a). A subclone represented by node v differs from its parent, represented by node $p(v)$, by the set of genomic aberrations on the edge connecting v and $p(v)$.

We assume that we are given bulk DNA sequencing data of h tumor samples from the same cancer patient, denoted $\mathcal{B}_1, \mathcal{B}_2, \ldots, \mathcal{B}_h$ (Fig. 1b), from which the set $M = \{M_1, M_2, \ldots, M_m\}$ of somatic SNVs present in at least one of these samples were detected (Fig. 1c). Next, we infer subclonal architecture of samples $\mathcal{B}_1, \mathcal{B}_2, \ldots, \mathcal{B}_h$ with respect to copy number states (Fig. 1d). Using the SNVs that belong to the genomic segments not impacted by CNAs we infer a tree of tumor progression together with cellular prevalence of each subclone in each sample (Fig. 1e). We assume that the outputs of the above steps are given as the input to DETOPT.

For an arbitrary segment C_j impacted by CNAs, let $\mathcal{M}(C_j)$ denote the set of all SNVs located in C_j and let $\mathcal{S}(C_j)$ denote the set of all distinct copy number states of segment C_j reported during the data preprocessing. For example, in the example shown in Fig. 1, we have $\mathcal{S}(C_2) = \{(1,1), (1,0), (2,1)\}$. In DETOPT, our goal is to: (i) assign a copy number state from $\mathcal{S}(C_j)$ to each node of T, (ii) assign each SNV M_i from $\mathcal{M}(C_j)$ to one edge in T, and (iii) assign each SNV $M_i \in \mathcal{M}(C_j)$ to one of the alleles A and B of C_j, together with, for each node of T, the number of the allelic copies that harbor M_i at that node (see Fig. 1f). In addition, we also require that several biologically motivated constraints are fulfilled. Our objective is to find assignment that satisfies all the constraints and minimizes the weighted sum across all samples of: (i) absolute difference between the observed and inferred variant allele frequencies across all SNVs from $\mathcal{M}(C_j)$, and (ii) absolute difference between the input total fractional copy numbers of segment C_j and those implied by DETOPT-assignment. We formulate this as an instance of Integer Linear Programming (ILP) and solve it by the use of an ILP solver (in this work we used Gurobi). This procedure is then repeated for all segments C_j to obtain a complete tree of tumor progression involving all SNVs and segmental copy number changes.

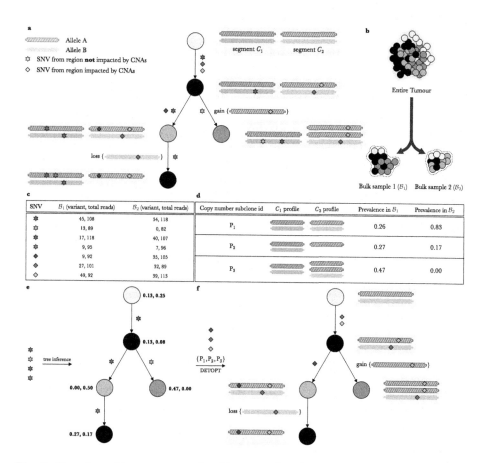

Fig. 1. Overview of tumor progression history and its reconstruction using our method DETOPT. **a.** A tree of tumor progression. In this figure we show only two genomic segments, one that is not impacted by CNAs (orange) and another that undergoes copy number gains and losses (blue). Next to each node, copy number profile of the corresponding subclone is shown in a shaded rounded rectangle. **b.** An example of the input to a bulk sequencing experiment consisting of two tumor samples, denoted $\mathcal{B}_1$ and $\mathcal{B}_2$, obtained from different regions of the same tumor biopsy. **c.** Read count data obtained for each SNV in each bulk sample. **d.** Subclonal architecture of the sequenced tumor samples inferred with respect to CNAs. **e.** A tree of tumor progression inferred using some of the well established methods designed for SNVs from genomic regions not impacted by CNAs. The first and the second number shown next to each node represent cellular prevalence of the corresponding subclone in samples $\mathcal{B}_1$ and $\mathcal{B}_2$, respectively. **f.** Placement in the tree of tumor progression of copy number gains and losses of genomic segments and SNVs that they harbor using DETOPT. In this panel we only show the placements that are inferred by DETOPT. Taking the union of trees in panels (e) and (f) yields complete tumor progression history on the entire set of SNVs and CNAs, together with cellular prevalence values of all subclones across both sequenced samples. (Color figure online)

3   Results

We first assessed the performance of DETOPT on simulated data. In order to compare its performance against the available alternatives, in addition to running DETOPT, we also ran PhyloWGS [1], as well as combination of DeCiFer [15] and CITUP [7]. We demonstrate that on these data DETOPT outperforms both alternatives achieving a better accuracy in capturing lineage relationships among SNVs across a wide range of simulation parameters.

We then applied DETOPT on a previously published multi-region longitudinal bulk whole-exome sequencing dataset obtained from multiple tumor metastases in a breast cancer patient (patient 4355 from [19]) which was not only refractory to previous lines of endocrine therapy and immunotherapy, but whose cancer subsequently progressed after partial response to adoptive cell therapy. DETOPT inferred that several clinically relevant neoantigenic and treatment resistance-mediating mutations have been subject to allele-specific CNAs, corroborating the hypothesis that SNVs can work in tandem with allele-specific CNAs to direct tumor progression.

References

1. Deshwar, A.G., Vembu, S., Yung, C.K., Jang, G.H., Stein, L., Morris, Q.: PhyloWGS: reconstructing subclonal composition and evolution from whole-genome sequencing of tumors. Genome Biol. **16**(1), 1–20 (2015)
2. El-Kebir, M., Oesper, L., Acheson-Field, H., Raphael, B.J.: Reconstruction of clonal trees and tumor composition from multi-sample sequencing data. Bioinformatics **31**(12), i62–i70 (2015)
3. El-Kebir, M., Satas, G., Oesper, L., Raphael, B.J.: Inferring the mutational history of a tumor using multi-state perfect phylogeny mixtures. Cell Syst. **3**(1), 43–53 (2016)
4. Fu, X., Lei, H., Tao, Y., Schwartz, R.: Reconstructing tumor clonal lineage trees incorporating single-nucleotide variants, copy number alterations and structural variations. Bioinformatics **38**(Supplement_1), i125–i133 (2022)
5. Jiao, W., Vembu, S., Deshwar, A.G., Stein, L., Morris, Q.: Inferring clonal evolution of tumors from single nucleotide somatic mutations. BMC Bioinform. **15**(1), 1–16 (2014)
6. Kaufmann, T.L., et al.: MEDICC2: whole-genome doubling aware copy-number phylogenies for cancer evolution. Genome Biol. **23**(1), 241 (2022)
7. Malikic, S., McPherson, A.W., Donmez, N., Sahinalp, C.S.: Clonality inference in multiple tumor samples using phylogeny. Bioinformatics **31**(9), 1349–1356 (2015)
8. McGranahan, N., Swanton, C.: Clonal heterogeneity and tumor evolution: past, present, and the future. Cell **168**(4), 613–628 (2017)
9. Myers, M.A., Satas, G., Raphael, B.J.: Calder: inferring phylogenetic trees from longitudinal tumor samples. Cell Syst. **8**(6), 514–522 (2019)
10. Navin, N.E.: The first five years of single-cell cancer genomics and beyond. Genome Res. **25**(10), 1499–1507 (2015)
11. Nowell, P.: The clonal evolution of tumor cell populations. Science **194**(4260), 23–28 (1976)

12. Popic, V., Salari, R., Hajirasouliha, I., Kashef-Haghighi, D., West, R.B., Batzoglou, S.: Fast and scalable inference of multi-sample cancer lineages. Genome Biol. **16**(1), 1–17 (2015)

13. Sashittal, P., Zaccaria, S., El-Kebir, M.: Parsimonious clone tree integration in cancer. Algorithms Mol. Biol. **17**(1), 1–14 (2022)

14. Satas, G., Raphael, B.J.: Tumor phylogeny inference using tree-constrained importance sampling. Bioinformatics **33**(14), i152–i160 (2017)

15. Satas, G., Zaccaria, S., El-Kebir, M., Raphael, B.J.: Decifering the elusive cancer cell fraction in tumor heterogeneity and evolution. Cell Syst. **12**(10), 1004–1018 (2021)

16. Schwarz, R.F., Trinh, A., Sipos, B., Brenton, J.D., Goldman, N., Markowetz, F.: Phylogenetic quantification of intra-tumour heterogeneity. PLoS Comput. Biol. **10**(4), e1003535 (2014)

17. Wintersinger, J.A., Dobson, S.M., Kulman, E., Stein, L.D., Dick, J.E., Morris, Q.: Reconstructing complex cancer evolutionary histories from multiple bulk DNA samples using Pairtree. Blood Cancer Discov. **3**(3), 208–219 (2022)

18. Zaccaria, S., Raphael, B.J.: Accurate quantification of copy-number aberrations and whole-genome duplications in multi-sample tumor sequencing data. Nat. Commun. **11**(1), 1–13 (2020)

19. Zacharakis, N., et al.: Breast cancers are immunogenic: immunologic analyses and a phase ii pilot clinical trial using mutation-reactive autologous lymphocytes. J. Clin. Oncol. **40**(16), 1741–1754 (2022)

Accurate Assembly of Circular RNAs with TERRACE

Tasfia Zahin[1], Qian Shi[1], Xiaofei Carl Zang[2], and Mingfu Shao[1,2(✉)]

[1] Department of Computer Science and Engineering,
The Pennsylvania State University, University Park, PA 16802, USA
`mxs2589@psu.edu`
[2] Huck Institutes of the Life Sciences, The Pennsylvania State University,
University Park, PA 16802, USA

Abstract. Circular RNA (circRNA) is a class of RNA molecules that forms a closed loop with its 5' and 3' ends covalently bonded. CircRNAs were severely overlooked previously owing to the biases in the RNA-seq protocols and in the detection algorithms, but recently gained tremendous attentions in both aspects. Most existing methods for assembling circRNAs heavily rely on the annotated transcriptomes, and hence exhibit unsatisfactory accuracy when a high-quality annotation is unavailable. Here we present TERRACE, a new algorithm for full-length assembly of circRNAs from paired-end total RNA-seq data. TERRACE is compared with leading circRNA detection methods on both simulations and biological datasets. Our method consistently outperforms by a large margin in sensitivity while maintaining better or comparable precision. In particular, when the annotations are not provided, TERRACE can assemble 123%–412% more correct circRNAs than state-of-the-art methods on human tissues. TERRACE presents a major leap on assembling full-length circRNAs from RNA-seq data, and we expect it to be widely used in the downstream research on circRNAs. TERRACE is freely available at https://github.com/Shao-Group/TERRACE. The full version of this manuscript is available at https://doi.org/10.1101/2024.02.09.579380.

1 Introduction

Splicing is a ubiquitous and essential post-transcriptional modification of precursor mRNAs. A class of noncanonical splicing, known as back-splicing, stitches the 3' end of a downstream exon to the 5' end of an upstream exon via a back-splicing junction (BSJ), forming a closed circular structure called circular RNA (circRNA). Due to this specific structure, circRNAs are more stable than linear RNAs, admit distinct biological properties and functions, and have been proven to be promising biomarkers. Numerous methods to detect circRNAs from total RNA-seq data were published lately (see [1] for a review). However, many of them require a fully annotated transcriptome, which significantly limits their capability to detect novel circRNAs and their applicability to non-model species. Other

---

Q. Shi and X. C. Zang—Contributed equally to this work.

J. Ma (Ed.): RECOMB 2024, LNCS 14758, pp. 444–447, 2024.
https://doi.org/10.1007/978-1-0716-3989-4_49

tools can be operated annotation-free, but the functionality of many of them are constrained to identifying BSJ only, resulting in a deficiency of assembling full-length circRNAs. Due to the complexity of alternative splicing and low circRNA abundance, current methods unfortunately fail to accurately detect BSJs while also producing exceedingly unsatisfying full-length assemblies. Here we present TERRACE (accura**T**e ass**E**mbly of circ**R**NAs using b**R**idging and m**AC**hine l**E**arning), a new tool for assembling full-length circRNAs from paired-end total RNA-seq data. TERRACE stands out by its high accuracy without relying on annotations, a feature absent in most existing tools.

2   Methods

TERRACE takes the alignment of paired-end total RNA-seq reads and, option-ally, a reference annotation as input. TERRACE first identifies back-spliced reads each of which will be assembled into a set of candidate, full-length circu-lar paths. These paths, optionally augmented by the annotated transcripts, are subjected to a selection process followed by a merging procedure to produce the resultant circRNAs. A score function is learned to assign a confidence score to each circRNA. TERRACE is outlined in Fig. 1.

Identification of Back-Spliced Reads. TERRACE identifies back-spliced reads from two sources: *chimerically aligned* reads in the input alignment, and by a new, light-weight, junction-targeted mapping algorithm. A chimerically aligned read is a special class of reads where different portions of it are aligned to different locations of the reference genome. A pattern often exists in the CIGAR strings if a chimerically aligned read contains a BSJ, for example, 30H70M and 30M70S. TERRACE collects reads satisfying this numerical relationship as back-spliced reads. In the mapping algorithm, TERRACE first extracts splicing positions from both reads alignment and reference transcriptome (if provided). Next, the reads that have soft clips at either end greater than a threshold (a parameter of TERRACE with a default value of 15) are considered candidates for back-spliced reads. The sequence of the soft clipped region will be remapped to the reference genome at a splicing position to identify a significant match. A Jaccard index of the two sets of kmers ($k = 10$ by default) will be calculated. If the Jaccard is greater than a threshold (0.9 by default) and such significant match is unique, TERRACE will identify it as a new BSJ.

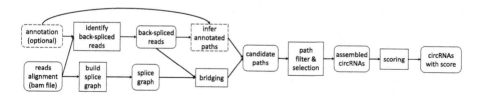

Fig. 1. Outline of TERRACE. Rounded boxes represent data and data structures. Rectangles represent procedures. Dashed boxes indicate optional.

Transforming Assembly to Bridging. A back-spliced read R is presumably expressed from a circRNA. It consists of three segments: $R1.primary$, $R2$, and $R1.supple$, assuming $R1$ contains the BSJ. Although the three segments are known to be part of the original circRNA, their connection within the circRNA remains unclear—a problem we refer to as "bridging". We formalize the bridging task using the underlying data structure: splice graph. A splice graph, denoted as $G = (V, E, w)$, is a weighted directed graph that organizes the splicing and coverage information and can be constructed using information in the read alignment. The three fragments of a back-spliced read can be represented as three paths in the splice graph G. Bridging now involves finding two paths connecting these known paths, resulting in a unified path threading the three fragments to form the circRNA with the BSJ. Multiple potential bridging paths exist due to alternative splicing and sequencing/alignment errors, necessitating a characterization for better bridging paths and an efficient algorithm to calculate them.

Formulation and Algorithm for Bridging. Let $A = (a_1, a_2, \cdots, a_i)$, $B = (b_1, b_2, \cdots, b_j)$, and $C = (c_1, c_2, \cdots, c_k)$ be the 3 paths in G corresponding to the 3 fragments of a back-spliced read. We aim to find the "best" paths in G from a_i to b_1 and from b_j to c_1. We adopt a definition we proposed in reconstructing the entire fragment of paired-end RNA-seq reads [2]. The idea was to seek a path whose "bottleneck weight" is maximized, which is effective for selecting the path with the strongest support and for excluding false paths due to errors which often contain edges with a small weight. An efficient dynamic programming algorithm can be designed to find optimal p_1 and p_2 (see [2] for details). The algorithm can be extended to produce suboptimal paths as candidates (by default TERRACE calculates top 10 optimal paths for each back-spliced read), which will be combined with additional information for selection.

Selection of Candidate Paths. Let P be the set of candidate full-length circular paths for a back-spliced read. We first apply some heuristic procedures to filter false-positive paths such as those with unsupported regions, intron retentions and low scores. We use P_1 to denote the set of survived paths. If a reference annotation is provided, TERRACE will then identify more paths that are "compatible" with a back-spliced read R, denoted as P_2. If $P_1 \cap P_2 \neq \emptyset$, the path in $P_1 \cap P_2$ with maximized bottleneck weight will be picked; if $P_1 \cap P_2 = \emptyset$ and $P_1 \neq \emptyset$, we pick the path in P_1 with maximized bottleneck weight regardless of P_2 (i.e., we give higher priority to paths inferred from the read alignment rather than from reference annotation); otherwise, we will pick one path from P_2 randomly if $P_2 \neq \emptyset$. The selected full-length circular path is then transformed to a fully annotated circRNA by borrowing genomic coordinates from the reference genome. Identical circRNAs or those with slightly different BSJs but same intron chain are merged to a single instance. The number of back-spliced reads generating this circRNA is recorded as its *abundance*.

Scoring Assembled Circular RNAs. Assigning a confidence score to assembled circRNAs is desirable to ensure that those with higher scores are more reliable. We investigate whether a machine-learning approach could yield a more accurate scoring function. We extract 13 features to characterize each assembled circRNA, ranging from its abundance to the (average) length of the soft clips of back-spliced reads. A random forest model is trained on one tissue sample (brain) and tested on other samples such that the model is generalized across tissues. CircRNAs assembled by TERRACE are used as training data for the model, with and without reference annotations.

3 Results and Conclusion

Table 1 summarizes the adjusted precision of TERRACE when its recall is matched against CIRI-full and CIRCexplorer2 on 8 biological RNA-seq samples. TERRACE substantially outperforms: the average adjusted precision of TERRACE is 75% compared to CIRI-full at 40% without annotation, 50% compared to CIRCexplorer2 at 40% with annotation (using the random-forest curve). TERRACE makes a significant advancement towards accurate assembly of circular RNAs. We anticipate widespread adoption of TERRACE, particularly in studies involving species lacking well-annotated transcriptomes.

Table 1. Adjusted precision (%) of TERRACE against CIRI-full and CIRCexplorer2 on real data samples.

sample	w/o annotation			with annotation		
	matched recall	TERRACE adjusted precision	CIRI-full precision	matched recall	TERRACE adjusted precision	CIRCexplorer2 precision
lung	0.88	75.94	26.07	4.80	60.63	54.23
brain	15.51	81.05	46.18	30.14	53.98	35.13
skeletal	1.01	74.49	28.72	3.98	50.69	44.15
heart	4.16	83.54	44.19	14.19	49.71	42.20
testis	9.81	76.97	46.25	21.66	53.09	42.26
liver	6.52	69.11	50.49	14.66	44.58	34.96
kidney	6.65	71.24	53.53	15.62	49.62	40.63
prostate	6.05	67.63	24.45	21.93	35.62	27.73
average	6.32	75.00	39.99	15.87	49.74	40.16

References

1. Vromman, M., et al.: Large-scale benchmarking of circRNA detection tools reveals large differences in sensitivity but not in precision. Nat. Methods **20**(8), 1159–1169 (2023)
2. Zhang, Q., Shi, Q., Shao, M.: Accurate assembly of multi-end RNA-Seq data with Scallop2. Nat. Comput. Sci. **2**(3), 148–152 (2022)

Semi-supervised Learning While Controlling the FDR with an Application to Tandem Mass Spectrometry Analysis

Jack Freestone[1], Lukas Käll[2] , William Stafford Noble[3,4] ,
and Uri Keich[1(✉)]

[1] School of Mathematics and Statistics F07, University of Sydney, Camperdown,
Australia
uri.keich@sydney.edu.au
[2] Science for Life Laboratory, KTH Royal Institute of Technology, Stockholm,
Sweden
[3] Department of Genome Sciences, University of Washington, Seattle, USA
[4] Paul G. Allen School of Computer Science and Engineering,
University of Washington, Seattle, USA

Abstract. Canonical procedures to control the false discovery rate (FDR) among the list of putative discoveries rely on our ability to compute informative p-values. Competition-based approach offers a fairly novel and increasingly popular alternative when computing such p-values is impractical. The popularity of this approach stems from its wide applicability: instead of computing p-values, which requires knowing the entire null distribution for each null hypothesis, a competition-based approach only requires a single draw from each such null distribution. This drawn example is known as a "decoy" in the mass spectrometry community (which was the first to adopt the competition approach) or as a "knockoff" in the statistics community. The decoy is competed with the original observation so that only the higher scoring of the two is retained. The number of decoy wins is subsequently used to estimate and control the FDR among the target wins.

In this paper we offer a novel method to extend the competition-based approach to control the FDR while taking advantage of side information, i.e., additional features that can help us distinguish between correct and incorrect discoveries. Our motivation comes from the problem of peptide detection in tandem mass spectrometry proteomics data. Specifically, we recently showed that a popular mass spectrometry analysis software tool, Percolator, can apparently fail to control the FDR. We address this problem here by developing a general protocol called "RESET" that can take advantage of the additional features, such as the ones Percolator uses, while still theoretically and empirically controlling the FDR.

Keywords: proteomics · false discovery rate control · tandem mass spectrometry

J. Ma (Ed.): RECOMB 2024, LNCS 14758, pp. 448–453, 2024.
https://doi.org/10.1007/978-1-0716-3989-4_50

1   Introduction

In the multiple testing problem we consider m null hypotheses $H_1, \ldots, H_m$, and our goal is to maximize the number of discoveries (rejections), subject to some control of the type I error (false discoveries). When m is large we typically control the false discovery rate (FDR), which is the expected value of the false discovery proportion (FDP) [2]. Canonically, we associate a test statistic T_i with each hypothesis H_i and compute p_i, the p-value of the observed value T_i. These p-values are then analyzed to determine the list of rejected hypotheses, so that the FDR is no more than the preselected threshold α.

Determining a p-value for each hypothesis can be challenging because (a) it requires the exact or approximate knowledge of the null distribution and (b) it can be computationally intensive. The *target-decoy competition* (TDC) approach allows us to control the FDR when computing informative p-values is impractical. Specifically, TDC only requires, in addition to the putative discovery score assigned to each null hypothesis (called the target score), at least one draw from the null distribution of the same hypothesis (called a decoy score). TDC then competes the score of each target and its associated decoy, keeping only the higher of the two, along with a label indicating whether the winning score corresponds to a target (target win) or a decoy (decoy win). For a true null hypothesis, there is an equal chance that a target or decoy will win each competition. TDC takes advantage of this equality, using the number of decoys wins as an estimate of the number of false discoveries among the target wins, which subsequently allows TDC to estimate and control the FDR.

Subsequent to the development of TDC, it was recognized that if the hypotheses can be rescored using additional information so that the target wins are generally ranked higher, then TDC will report more discoveries. This idea was implemented, for example, in the widely used Percolator tool, which is a semi-supervised machine learning algorithm used to improve the discovery of peptides in a biological sample. However, despite the popularity of Percolator, we have recently shown that in practice Percolator can fail to control the FDR [4].

Motivated by this problem, we offer a new approach for training a semi-supervised machine learning model in a way that does not break the FDR control in the general competition setting. We achieve this goal by randomly placing each decoy win into one of two sets, where the first set is used for training the model and the second is reserved for estimating the number of false target discoveries. Accordingly, we refer to our new approach as **RESET** (REScoring via Estimating and Training).

More generally, the problem of multiple hypothesis testing with additional information has been studied recently in the statistics community, with tools such as ZAP [6], AdaPT [5] and Adaptive Knockoffs [7] offering finite sample FDR control. However, none of these tools are applicable to the peptide detection problem. ZAP assumes a parametric model where p-values can be computed. AdaPT addresses both the p-value and the competition-based contexts, but only provides a meta scheme in the latter case. As for Adaptive Knockoffs, it is forbiddingly slow for a typical peptide detection problem and moreover, when run to completion on a small dataset it offers significantly fewer discoveries than RESET does when combined with the Percolator algorithm.

2   The RESET (REScoring via Estimating and Training) Procedure

The following section outlines the RESET procedure, with further details and experimental results available at https://www.biorxiv.org/content/10.1101/2023.10.26.564068v3. RESET was developed to take advantage of the additional features to rescore the discoveries so that correct discoveries will generally rank higher. While originally developed to integrate with the Percolator algorithm in the detection of peptides, RESET is generally compatible with any semi-supervised machine learning approach that takes advantage of the competition framework in a similar fashion. RESET is described through the following main steps, with further details given in Algorithm 1. In addition, Fig. 1 graphically illustrates RESET combined with the Percolator algorithm, which uses a support vector machine (SVM) in its inner loop.

1. RESET begins with a TDC-like competition step: from each pair of target and decoy discoveries we record the maximal score W, together with a label L indicating whether this was a target or a decoy win. RESET also records the vector of features $\mathbf{x}$ associated with the winning discovery. As an aside, note that there is some flexibility in how the winning score is defined—for example, it can be the absolute value of the difference in the scores [1]—but here we focus on the maximum.
2. RESET then defines the **training** decoy set by independently randomly assigning to it each winning decoy with probability s (we used $s = 1/2$ throughout). We refer to the remaining set of winning discoveries (targets, as well as non-training decoys) as **pseudo** targets.
3. Next, RESET applies a user-selected semi-supervised machine learning model whose input includes the following:
   - a negative set containing the scores and features of the training decoys, and
   - a set containing the winning scores and features of the pseudo targets but *without* the labels distinguishing between targets and decoys.

   The output of this step is a rescoring of the training decoys and pseudo targets, ideally ranking many of the correct pseudo target discoveries higher than they were ranked originally.
4. Once the training is complete, the training decoys are thrown out, and the pseudo targets are ordered according to the learned scores, with their corresponding original target/decoy winning labels revealed. Some of the revealed labels will correspond to decoy wins—we refer to those as **estimating** decoys—and the others correspond to target wins. RESET applies SeqStep+ ([1] and Algorithm S1 of the extended manuscript), as in TDC, but uses the number of estimating decoys in the top k pseudo target scores

to estimate the number of false discoveries among the targets in the same top k scores. The key difference with TDC is that because in RESET we use approximately half of the decoys for training purposes, each estimating decoy estimates more than one false target discovery. To adjust for that difference, we multiply the number of decoys (plus 1) by 2. The rest of SeqStep+ works exactly as in TDC.

2.1 Using an Extra Decoy: An Enhancement of RESET

We introduce an enhancement of RESET that makes use of an extra decoy for each target. It goes through the same steps as RESET with the following modifications:

- In step 1, the competition now takes place between all sets of triplets: the target and its two decoys. We record a target/decoy label L indicating whether the target or one of its two associated decoys is equal to the maximum of the three scores W, corresponding to a target or decoy win, respectively (again ties are broken randomly). In addition to the winning score and a target/decoy win label, we keep the vector of features $\mathbf{x}$ of the winning discovery. This multiple competition method is essentially the same as the *max method* introduced by Emery et al. [3].
- When applying SeqStep+ [1], each estimating decoy now estimates a single false target discovery (as in TDC itself), so no adjustment is made to the observed number of decoy wins.

Notably, in this enhanced version of RESET, each target competes in step 1 with two associated decoys rather than a single one. The sets of of training and estimating decoys are roughly equal-sized for both RESET procedures, and therefore both sets are typically larger in the case of the two-decoy version. While these larger training and estimating sets come at a cost of a reduced number of target wins, keep in mind that these lost targets only win one of their two decoy competitions; hence, they are unlikely to be high scoring enough to eventually make it to the reported discoveries list. At the same time, those larger sets of training and estimating decoys allow us to better train our model, as well as to have a more stable final procedure when defining the discovery list using SeqStep+.

Algorithm 1. RESET

Require: • $\{(Z_i, \tilde{Z}_i, \mathbf{x}_i^T, \mathbf{x}_i^D) : i = 1, \ldots, m\}$ - each hypothesis' (target score, decoy score, target features, decoy features);
        • α - FDR threshold for the discovery list;
        • s - the probability of assigning a decoy to the training set (default: $s = 1/2$);
        • $S : \mathbb{R}^2 \to \mathbb{R}$ - a symmetric score function such that $S(x, y) = S(y, x)$;
        • f - a semi-supervised machine learning model;

Ensure: A discovery list R
1: **for** $i = 1, \ldots, m$ **do**   ▷ if $Z_i = \tilde{Z}_i$, randomly break ties
2:     **if** $Z_i > \tilde{Z}_i$ **then**
3:         $(W_i, \mathbf{x}_i, L_i) \leftarrow (S(Z_i, \tilde{Z}_i), \mathbf{x}_i^T, 1)$ ▷ e.g. $S(x, y) := x \vee y$ or $S(x, y) := |x - y|$
4:     **else**
5:         $(W_i, \mathbf{x}_i, L_i) \leftarrow (S(Z_i, \tilde{Z}_i), \mathbf{x}_i^D, -1)$
6:     **end if**
7: **end for**
8: $I \leftarrow$ a subset of the decoy win indices, $\{i : L_i = -1\}$, determined by randomly including each one with probability s
9: $\tilde{L}_i \leftarrow -1$ for $i \in I$ ▷ training decoys
10: $\tilde{L}_i \leftarrow 1$ for $i \in J := I^c$ ▷ pseudo-targets
11: $(\tilde{W}_i)_{i=1}^m \leftarrow f\left((W_i, \mathbf{x}_i, \tilde{L}_i)_{i=1}^m\right)$ ▷ where f is any machine learning model
12: $R \leftarrow$ SeqStep+$((\tilde{W}_i, L_i)_{i \in J}, c = \frac{1}{2-s}, \alpha)$
13: **return** R

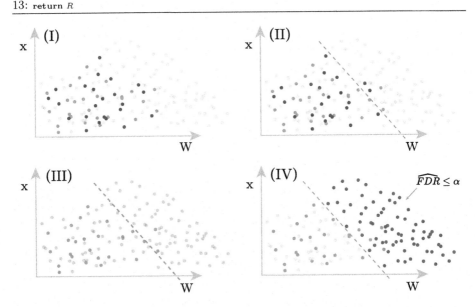

Fig. 1. Schematics of RESET using the SVM-like Percolator algorithm. Each point represents a different discovery described by its score W and associated feature information $\mathbf{x}$ (which for simplicity is one-dimensional here). Each discovery is colored according to a label L indicating whether it is a target (blue) or a decoy (red). In (I), approximately half of the decoys are selected as the negative set (the **training** decoys) and all other hypotheses are **pseudo** targets (opaque). In (II), the Percolator algorithm (similar to an SVM) is trained using the negative set and the pseudo targets as the unlabelled set (the dotted line represents the decision boundary). In (III), the training decoys are thrown out. In (IV), the remaining discoveries are ordered according to the learned Percolator scores (the direction perpendicular to the decision boundary) and the targets that exceed an FDR threshold of α are then reported (the dotted line here represents the cutoff for the targets that are reported). (Color figure online)

References

1. Barber, R.F., Candès, E.J.: Controlling the false discovery rate via knockoffs. Ann. Stat. **43**(5), 2055–2085 (2015)
2. Benjamini, Y., Hochberg, Y.: Controlling the false discovery rate: a practical and powerful approach to multiple testing. J. Roy. Stat. Soc. B **57**, 289–300 (1995)
3. Emery, K., Hasam, S., Noble, W.S., Keich, U.: Multiple competition-based FDR control and its application to peptide detection. In: Schwartz, R. (ed.) RECOMB 2020. LNCS, vol. 12074, pp. 54–71. Springer, Cham (2020). https://doi.org/10.1007/978-3-030-45257-5_4
4. Freestone, J., Noble, W.S., Keich, U.: Re-investigating the correctness of decoy-based false discovery rate control in proteomics tandem mass spectrometry. BioRxiv (2023). https://doi.org/10.1101/2023.06.21.546013
5. Lei, L., Fithian, W.: AdaPT: an interactive procedure for multiple testing with side information. J. R. Stat. Soc. Ser. B (Statistical Methodology) **80**(4), 649–679 (2018)
6. Leung, D., Sun, W.: Zap: Z-value adaptive procedures for false discovery rate control with side information. J. R. Stat. Soc. Ser. B Stat Methodol. **84**(5), 1886–1946 (2022)
7. Ren, Z., Candès, E.: Knockoffs with side information. Ann. Appl. Stat. **17**(2), 1152–1174 (2023)

CoRAL Accurately Resolves Extrachromosomal DNA Genome Structures with Long-Read Sequencing

Kaiyuan Zhu[1], Matthew G. Jones[2], Jens Luebeck[1], Xinxin Bu[3], Hyerim Yi[2], King L. Hung[2], Ivy Tsz-Lo Wong[4,5], Shu Zhang[2], Paul S. Mischel[4,5], Howard Y. Chang[2,6,7(✉)], and Vineet Bafna[1,8(✉)]

[1] Department of Computer Science and Engineering, UC San Diego, La Jolla, CA, USA
vbafna@ucsd.edu
[2] Center for Personal Dynamic Regulomes, Stanford University, Stanford, CA, USA
howchang@stanford.edu
[3] Bioinformatics Undergraduate Program, School of Biological Sciences, UC San Diego, La Jolla, CA, USA
[4] Department of Pathology, Stanford University School of Medicine, Stanford, CA, USA
[5] Sarafan ChEM-H, Stanford University, Stanford, CA, USA
[6] Department of Genetics, Stanford University, Stanford, CA, USA
[7] Howard Hughes Medical Institute, Stanford University, Stanford, CA, USA
[8] Halıcıoğlu Data Science Institute, UC San Diego, La Jolla, CA, USA

Abstract. Extrachromosomal DNA (ecDNA) is a central mechanism of focal oncogene amplification in cancer and can drive tumor formation, evolution, and drug resistance. Elucidating the genomic architecture of ecDNA amplifications is critical for understanding tumor pathology and developing more effective therapies. Current short-read based methods can predict the ecDNA presence in cancer samples, but are limited in resolving complex and heterogeneous ecDNA structures. Here, we propose CoRAL, an algorithm for identifying and reconstructing ecDNA amplicon structures from long-reads. CoRAL takes mapped long-reads as input, builds a breakpoint graph for each focally amplified region, and extracts cycles from the breakpoint graph representing the ecDNA structures. Through extensive benchmarks on simulated data and previously-characterized cell lines, we report that CoRAL substantially improves breakpoint detection and reconstruction of complex ecDNA structures over the existing short and long-read based methods.
Code Availability: https://github.com/AmpliconSuite/CoRAL.

Keywords: extrachromosomal DNA · focal amplification · long-read · structure · breakpoint graph · copy number

---

K. Zhu and M.G. Jones—These authors contributed equally to this work.

© The Author(s), under exclusive license to Springer Nature Switzerland AG 2024
J. Ma (Ed.): RECOMB 2024, LNCS 14758, pp. 454–457, 2024.
https://doi.org/10.1007/978-1-0716-3989-4_51

1   Introduction

Extrachromosomal DNA (ecDNA) is a central mechanism for focal oncogene amplification in cancer, occurring in approximately 15% of early stage cancers and 30% of late-stage cancers. EcDNAs drive tumor formation, evolution, and drug resistance by dynamically modulating oncogene copy-number and rewiring gene-regulatory networks [1–9]. Elucidating the genomic architecture of ecDNA amplifications is critical for understanding tumor pathology and developing more effective therapies.

Previously, paired-end short-read (Illumina) sequencing and mapping have been utilized to represent ecDNA amplifications using a *breakpoint graph*, where the inferred architecture of ecDNA is encoded as a cycle in the graph [10,11]. Traversals of breakpoint graph have been used to successfully predict ecDNA presence in cancer samples. However, short-read technologies are intrinsically limited in the identification of breakpoints, phasing together of complex rearrangements and internal duplications, and deconvolution of cell-to-cell heterogeneity of ecDNA structures. Long-read technologies, such as from Oxford Nanopore Technologies or PacBio, have the potential to improve inference as the longer reads are better at mapping structural variants and are more likely to span rearranged or duplicated regions.

Here, we propose CoRAL (Complete Reconstruction of Amplifications with Long reads), an algorithm for reconstructing ecDNA amplicon sequence and structure from long-reads. CoRAL takes mapped long-reads (in BAM format) as input, builds a distinct breakpoint graph for each focally amplified region, and extracts cycles (or walks) from the breakpoint graph representing ecDNA and the potential focally amplified genomes. In cases where the reads are not long enough to span the high multiplicity regions, CoRAL reconstructs cyclic architectures using quadratically constrained programming that simultaneously optimizes parsimony of reconstruction, explained copy number, and consistency of long-read mapping. Through extensive benchmarks on simulated data and previously-characterized cell lines, we report that CoRAL substantially improves breakpoint detection and the inference of complex ecDNA amplification structures over the long-read-based Decoil [12] and the short-read-based AmpliconArchitect (AA) [10] methods. As long-read usage becomes wide-spread, we anticipate that CoRAL will be a valuable tool for profiling the landscape and evolution of focal amplifications in tumors.

2   Methods

We provide a brief overview of the CoRAL method in this extended abstract. Details can be found in the full paper preprint. CoRAL takes mapped long-reads (in BAM format) as input, and begins by identifying focally amplified *seed intervals*. The seed intervals can be provided directly, or derived from whole genome CNV calls (e.g., with third party tools like CNVkit) of mapped long reads. From the CNV calls, CoRAL selects genomic segments with minimum thresholds on copy number and aggregate size as seed intervals. CoRAL uses these seed intervals to construct a copy-number-weighted breakpoint graph separately for each amplified region, as described below.

The graph construction starts with exploring all *amplified intervals* connected to the seed intervals through discordant edges (breakpoints connecting non-contiguous genomic sequences) given by chimeric long read mappings. Once all amplified intervals are identified for each focal amplification, a graph structure is organized by CoRAL to include the genome segments (sequence edges) from the amplified intervals, the concordant edges that join neighboring genome segments, and the discordant edges within the amplified intervals or those connecting different amplified intervals. Once the graph structure is fixed, CoRAL recomputes a *copy number* for each edge that best explains the long read coverage by balancing the copy number between concordant and discordant edges incident on nodes.

As its key step, CoRAL reconstructs potential ecDNA structures in the breakpoint graph by extracting a minimum number of *cycles and walks* from the graph, allowing duplication of nodes, where cycles represent the potential ecDNA species, and walks represent linearly amplified or rearranged genome. Each cycle or walk is associated with a positive weight – corresponding to the copy number – so that the sum of length-weighted edges of extracted walks explains a large fraction of the total copy number of the edges in the breakpoint graph. In addition, CoRAL takes advantage of the fact that long-reads may span several breakpoints and incorporates these reads as *subwalk constraints*. In its cycle extraction, CoRAL requires a majority of the subwalk constraints to be satisfied by the resulting cycles and walks, thus leveraging the power of long reads. CoRAL uses quadratic integer programming to solve a multi-objective optimization that minimizes the number of cycles or walks while maximizing the explained length-weighted copy number and the number of subwalk constraints. It finally outputs the reconstructed breakpoint graphs for each focal amplification in the sample, as well as the associated cycles or walks from the graph. It also optionally outputs stylistic visualizations of the breakpoint graphs and cycles.

3   Results

We first assessed the effectiveness of amplicon reconstruction algorithms using simulated Nanopore sequencing from 75 synthetic amplicon structures with varying numbers of breakpoints, and from one of three origins: *episomal*, *chromothripsis*, or *2-foldback*. Across the simulated datasets, we observed consistently improved performance of CoRAL over AA and Decoil in both breakpoint graph reconstruction, which indicates improved detection of structural variants (breakpoints) with long-reads, and cycle extraction, which suggests better algorithmic development by CoRAL. We also showed that CoRAL's reconstruction performance is robust to the complexity of amplicons (number of segments, or sequence edges), sequence coverage, their formation context, and the level of duplication (or multiplicity). However, we did observe examples where the interval ordering is incorrect despite near-perfect recovery of breakpoint graph and amplified intervals, reflecting the technological limitations of reads that were not long enough to resolve the true order of segments.

Next, we evaluated amplicon reconstruction using matched Nanopore sequencing and Illumina (short-read) sequencing in 10 previously characterized cell-lines spanning a range of cancer types and amplifications. We demonstrated that while CoRAL and AA both accurately predict the existence of ecDNA in cell lines, CoRAL's cycles give improved explanation of the copy numbers as well as the subwalk constraints in ecDNA amplicons. Reconstruction supported by long-read subwalk constraints additionally enabled the study of critical aspects of the amplicon structures, for example, a fusion transcript of the lncRNA *PVT1* to the second exon of the oncogene *MYC* in COLO320-DM [6]. Finally we showed that total running time and memory usage of CoRAL was comparable to AA for reconstructing the ecDNA amplicons in cell lines, and that most non-ecDNA focal amplifications are relatively easy to resolve, with the resulting breakpoint graphs being small.

Full Paper Preprint: https://www.biorxiv.org/content/10.1101/2024.02.15.580594v1.

References

1. Nathanson, D.A., et al.: Targeted therapy resistance mediated by dynamic regulation of extrachromosomal mutant EGFR DNA. Science **343**(6166), 72–76 (2014)
2. Turner, K.M., et al.: Extrachromosomal oncogene amplification drives tumour evolution and genetic heterogeneity. Nature **543**(7643), 122–125 (2017)
3. Wu, S., et al.: Circular ecDNA promotes accessible chromatin and high oncogene expression. Nature **575**(7784), 699–703 (2019)
4. Helmsauer, K., et al.: Enhancer hijacking determines extrachromosomal circular MYCN amplicon architecture in neuroblastoma. Nat. Commun. **11**(1), 5823 (2020)
5. Kim, H., et al.: Extrachromosomal DNA is associated with oncogene amplification and poor outcome across multiple cancers. Nat. Genet. **52**(9), 891–897 (2020)
6. Hung, K.L., et al.: ecDNA hubs drive cooperative intermolecular oncogene expression. Nature **600**(7890), 731–736 (2021)
7. Zhu, Y., et al.: Oncogenic extrachromosomal DNA functions as mobile enhancers to globally amplify chromosomal transcription. Cancer Cell **39**(5), 694–707 (2021)
8. Lange, J.T., et al.: The evolutionary dynamics of extrachromosomal DNA in human cancers. Nat. Genet. **54**(10), 1527–1533 (2022)
9. Luebeck, J., et al.: Extrachromosomal DNA in the cancerous transformation of Barrett's oesophagus. Nature **616**, 798–805 (2023)
10. Deshpande, V., et al.: Exploring the landscape of focal amplifications in cancer using AmpliconArchitect. Nat. Commun. **10**(1), 392 (2019)
11. Hung, K.L., et al.: Targeted profiling of human extrachromosomal DNA by CRISPR-CATCH. Nat. Genet. **54**(11), 1746–1754 (2022)
12. Giurgiu, M. et al.: Decoil: Reconstructing extrachromosomal DNA structural heterogeneity from long-read sequencing data. bioRxiv (2023)

A Scalable Adaptive Quadratic Kernel Method for Interpretable Epistasis Analysis in Complex Traits

Boyang Fu[1], Prateek Anand[1], Aakarsh Anand[1], Joel Mefford[2],
and Sriram Sankararaman[1,3,4(✉)]

[1] Department of Computer Science, UCLA, Los Angeles, CA, USA
`sriram@cs.ucla.edu`
[2] Semel Institute for Neuroscience and Human Behavior, UCLA, Los Angeles, CA, USA
[3] Department of Human Genetics, David Geffen School of Medicine, UCLA, Los Angeles, CA, USA
[4] Department of Computational Medicine, David Geffen School of Medicine, UCLA, Los Angeles, CA, USA

Abstract. Our knowledge of the contribution of genetic interactions (*epistasis*) to variation in human complex traits remains limited, partly due to the lack of efficient, powerful, and interpretable algorithms to detect interactions. Recently proposed approaches for set-based association tests show promise in improving power to detect epistasis by examining the aggregated effects of multiple variants. Nevertheless, these methods either do not scale to large numbers of individuals available in Biobank datasets or do not provide interpretable results. We, therefore, propose QuadKAST, a scalable algorithm focused on testing pairwise interaction effects (also termed as *quadratic effects*) of a set of genetic variants on a trait and quantifying the proportion of phenotypic variance explained by these effects. We performed comprehensive simulations and demonstrated that QuadKAST is well-calibrated with good statistical power. We applied QuadKAST to 53 quantitative phenotypes measured in $\approx 300,000$ unrelated white British individuals in the UK Biobank to test for quadratic effects within each of $9,515$ protein-coding genes (after accounting for linear additive effects). We detected 32 trait-gene pairs across 17 traits that demonstrate statistically significant signals of quadratic effects ($p \leq \frac{0.05}{9,515 \times 53}$ accounting for the number of genes and traits tested). Our method enables the detailed investigation of epistasis on a large scale, offering new insights into its role and importance.

1 Introduction

Genome-wide association studies (GWAS) have revolutionized the field of human genetics by providing valuable insights into the genetic basis of complex traits

B. Fu, P. Anand, A. Anand—Equal contribution.

© The Author(s), under exclusive license to Springer Nature Switzerland AG 2024
J. Ma (Ed.): RECOMB 2024, LNCS 14758, pp. 458–461, 2024.
https://doi.org/10.1007/978-1-0716-3989-4_52

and diseases. The primary goal of GWAS is to identify statistically significant associations between specific genetic variants and the phenotype being studied. During the past decades, models based on additive assumptions have been successfully applied to identify variants that impact complex traits and diseases due to their simplicity and interpretability. Recent studies indicate that interaction effects between genes or genetic variants that go beyond mere additivity can play an overlooked role in shaping complex traits [1]. Such interactions have been proposed as key factors in both human complex trait variation and disease susceptibility [2]. Epistasis also potentially accounts for some of the "missing heritability" not explained by additive genetic factors alone. Despite its likely importance, efficient methods for detecting, dissecting, and interpreting complex epistatic interactions remain largely undeveloped, and our knowledge of the epistasis remains limited. Having an efficient way of identifying and understanding epistasis could greatly advance our understanding of underlying biological pathways and can potentially increase the generalizability of polygenic scores within and across different ancestral populations.

Despite its importance, characterizing the role of epistasis in complex traits presents several challenges. The task of examining all potential interactive relationships among SNPs and genes necessitates navigating a large feature space that expands exponentially with the increasing order of interactions. Some methods have been developed to search for pairs of genetic variants that show evidence for epistatic effects from a large combinatorial space. However, such approaches have low statistical power due to the stringent thresholds needed to account for the number of tests performed. As a result, successful epistasis detection requires examining a large number of individuals to obtain adequate power.

An alternative powerful approach to identify trait-relevant genetic variants focuses on grouping variants into "sets" and jointly estimating the effects of all variants within each set. Existing set-based tests have shown their efficacy in detecting associations between complex traits and sets of rare and common variants [3,4]. However, these approaches, while largely scalable, focus primarily on testing the additive effect of variants within a set. None of the existing approaches can test epistatic effects in large-scale biobanks. Recent works, such as FastKAST [1], have ameliorated the computational challenge by employing advanced sampling strategies to approximate the kernel decomposition. However, these approaches can only approximate shift-invariant kernels, such as the radial basis function kernels, and hence lack the interpretability associated with testing for pairwise interactions among SNPs. The lack of flexibility in the kernel design makes it difficult to interpret the results. Overall, we lack efficient yet interpretable methods to identify and quantify the epistasis effects within sets of genetic variants.

We propose a novel algorithm, **Quad**ratic **K**ernel-based **AS**sociation **T**est (QuadKAST), to address the major limitations of existing set-based association test approaches. Unlike existing approaches, QuadKAST aims to test for the aggregate effect of pairwise genetic interactions across variants within a set on a trait. This approach offers several advantages. First, the pairwise effects offer an interpretable model of epistasis. Second, besides merely performing epistasis testing that yields a binary answer for statistical significance, QuadKAST estimates the proportion of phenotypic variance explained by non-linear effects.

2 Methods

QuadKAST takes genotypes measured at a set of genetic variants (single nucleotide polymorphisms or SNPs) as input, paired with a phenotype measured on each individual, and attempts to test whether pairwise interactions across this set of genetic variants are associated with the phenotype. The model underlying QuadKAST is a mixed model where the phenotype is modeled as a linear function of all pairwise interactions of the genotypes at the SNPs within a set and residual noise. The random effects associated with each pairwise interaction (termed *quadratic effects*) are assumed to be drawn independently from a normal distribution with mean zero and a variance parameter σ^2_{quad} that is the parameter of interest. To ensure that this model is sensitive to only non-additive genetic effects, we include additive genetic effects as fixed effects in the model. Overall, the model is specified as the following equation

$$y = X\alpha + \Phi\gamma + \epsilon, \quad \epsilon \sim \mathcal{N}(0, \sigma^2_\epsilon I_N), \quad \gamma \sim \mathcal{N}(0, \frac{\sigma^2_{quad}}{D}I_D) \qquad (1)$$

Here $\Phi = \begin{pmatrix} \phi(\boldsymbol{g}_1)^T \\ \vdots \\ \phi(\boldsymbol{g}_N)^T \end{pmatrix}$, with ϕ as a designed quadratic feature transformation.

$\gamma \in \mathbb{R}^D$ is a random vector of effects associated with each pairwise interaction. σ^2_{quad} represents the variance attributed to all pairwise effects or quadratic effects across the set of SNPs (*quadratic variance component*). To ensure that this model is sensitive to non-additive genetic effects, we include additive genetic effects (represented by the matrix G) within X (effectively regressing out their contribution to the phenotype).

Testing the aggregate effect of pairwise interactions is equivalent to a test of the hypothesis that the associated variance component is zero. A common approach to test this hypothesis is to use a score test. The score statistic in this model is a quadratic form whose sampling distribution is asymptotically distributed as a weighted sum of independent χ^2, 1-degree of freedom random variable where the weights are the eigenvalues of the kernel matrix $K = \Phi\Phi^T$ in the absence of covariates.

The challenge in testing this hypothesis is that computing the score statistic and its sampling distribution scale as $\mathcal{O}(N^3)$ where N is the number of individuals, rendering this algorithm impractical for large datasets. QuadKAST leverages the mathematical structure of the model with insights from numerical linear algebra to perform the hypothesis test in time $\mathcal{O}(ND^2)$ where D is the number of interactions in the test ($D = \mathcal{O}(M^2)$ where M is the number of SNPs in the set. Specifically, it uses the observation that the kernel matrix K is low-rank with rank substantially lower than its dimensionality N so that the score statistic and the eigenvalues needed to compute the sampling distribution can be obtained directly from the design matrix of pairwise features avoiding the need to explicitly form and operate on the kernel matrix. This algorithm is practical in our setting where the number of SNPs in a set ($M \leq 50$) is substantially smaller than the number of individuals ($N \approx 300,000$). QuadKAST uses similar insights to obtain an efficient algorithm to estimate the variance components (using a restricted maximum likelihood estimator). Further, Quad-KAST uses the resulting variance component estimates to efficiently compute the posterior probability of the effect size of each pairwise interaction using the insight that the joint posterior probability of the pairwise interaction effects is a multi-variate normal distribution. We convert the posterior probability of an interaction effect size into an importance score defined as $(1 - \Phi(\frac{|\mu|}{\sigma}))$ to rank and interpret the importance of epistasis signals, where μ and σ refer to the posterior mean and standard deviation of the effect and Φ refers to the cumulative distribution function of a standard normal.

3   Results

We performed comprehensive simulations and demonstrated that QuadKAST is well-calibrated and has adequate power. Compared to existing methods with similar functionality, QuadKAST is the only method that is feasible to run on large-scale data containing hundreds of thousands of individuals. For example, running QuadKAST on protein-encoded gene from UK-Biobank array data takes only a few minutes on average. To the best of our knowledge, QuadKAST is the first algorithm that offers scalable and calibrated epistatic effect testing and supports variance component estimation within the quadratic family.

We applied QuadKAST to the UK-Biobank dataset protein encoded genes on 53 quantitative traits. QuadKAST identified 32 trait-genes pairs across 17 traits demonstrating strong epistatic signals ($p \leq \frac{0.05}{9,515 \times 53}$ accounting for the number of traits and genes tested).

Full paper: A complete manuscript of this work can be accessed at: https://www.biorxiv.org/content/10.1101/2024.03.09.584250v1.

References

1. Boyang, F., Pazokitoroudi, A., Sudarshan, M., Liu, Z., Subramanian, L., Sankararaman, S.: Fast kernel-based association testing of non-linear genetic effects for biobank-scale data. Nat. Commun. **14**(1), 4936 (2023)
2. Thornton-Wells, T.A., Moore, J.H., Haines, J.L.: Dissecting trait heterogeneity: a comparison of three clustering methods applied to genotypic data. BMC Bioinf. **7**, 1–18 (2006)
3. Lunetta, K.L., et al.: Rare coding variants and X-linked loci associated with age at menarche. Nat. Commun. **6**(1), 7756 (2015)
4. Li, X., et al.: Dynamic incorporation of multiple in silico functional annotations empowers rare variant association analysis of large whole-genome sequencing studies at scale. Nat. Genet. **52**(9), 969–983 (2020)

Optimal Tree Metric Matching Enables Phylogenomic Branch Length Estimation

Shayesteh Arasti[1]($\boxtimes$) [ID], Puoya Tabaghi[2] [ID], Yasamin Tabatabaee[3] [ID], and Siavash Mirarab[4] [ID]

[1] Department of Computer Science and Engineering, UC San Diego, La Jolla, CA 92093, USA
sarasti@ucsd.edu
[2] Halıcıoğlu Data Science Institute, UC San Diego, La Jolla, CA 92093, USA
[3] Department of Computer Science, University of Illinois at Urbana-Champaign, Urbana, IL 61801, USA
[4] Department of Electrical and Computer Engineering, UC San Diego, La Jolla, CA 92093, USA

Abstract. Evolutionary histories are uncertain and heterogeneous across the genome. As a result, for any given set of species, we may obtain a large number of incongruent trees. The differences in these trees are not limited to topology as branch lengths are also uncertain and biologically heterogeneous. Yet, despite the biological significance of branch length differences, comparing and reconciling trees has predominantly focused on topology. To close this gap, we explore the problem of matching a query tree to a reference tree by assigning new branch lengths to the query tree. We formulate this objective as a least-squares optimization problem defined on the set of all pairwise distances. We prove that the problem is convex and thus can be solved optimally using standard tools. We also introduce dynamic programming algorithms to compute the required inputs to the optimization problem in quadratic time. We use this framework to estimate the branch lengths of a fixed species tree topology in the unit of the expected number of substitutions per site by matching it to gene trees that have branch lengths in the same unit.

Keywords: Phylogenomics · Convex Optimization · Phylogenetic Branch Length Estimation · Tree Comparison

1 Introduction

A great body of evidence now shows that evolutionary histories are heterogeneous across the genome, due to various biological processes such as incomplete lineage sorting [2]. In addition, for any given topology, we always have uncertainty regarding the true topology, leading many analyses to consider a set of possible trees. Crucially, differences among such trees are not restricted to the

S. Arasti and P. Tabaghi—These authors contributed equally to this work.

topology; even when different parts of the genome share the same topology, their true branch lengths are almost surely different due to the stochasticity of coalescent processes and changes in the rate of evolution. A great deal of effort has been devoted to comparing the topology of trees on the same set of leaves. However, there has been less attention directed to comparing and matching two trees considering both their topological and branch length differences.

Here, we introduce a linear algebraic approach for matching one tree to another, incorporating both topology and branch length. Given a reference tree and a query tree, we formulate the matching problem as follows: Make the pairwise distances of the query tree as similar as possible to the reference tree by only changing its branch lengths while keeping the topology fixed. We show that this problem can be solved optimally and efficiently. After solving the matching problem, we describe a particular application: assigning branch lengths to a species tree based on gene tree branch lengths.

2   TCMM Problem

Definitions: Let $T = (V_T, E_T)$ be an *unrooted* tree, L_T be the leaf set of T, and $p_T(u, v) \subseteq E_T$ be the set of edges in T that correspond to the path between u and $v \in V_T$. We define l_e as the length of the branch $e \in E_T$ and the vector $l_T \in \mathbb{R}^{|E_T|}$ as the vector of branch lengths for all the edges in E_T. The distance between two leaves $u, v \in L_T$ is $d_T(u, v) = \sum_{e \in p_T(u,v)} l_e$. The distance vector $d_T \in \mathbb{R}^{\binom{|L_T|}{2}}$ is the vector of all pairwise distances of the leaf set of T, i.e., L_T.

Definition 1. *The path matrix $A_T \in \mathbb{R}^{\binom{|L_T|}{2} \times |E_T|}$ is a zero-one matrix where each row corresponds to a pair of leaves in L_T and each column corresponds to an edge in E_T, that is, element $[(u, v), e]$ of A_T is one if and only if $e \in p_T(u, v)$.*

From this definition, the following equality readily follows: $d_T = A_T l_T$. Thus, for any branch length vector $x \in \mathbb{R}^{|E_T|}$, the vector $A_T x$ fully determines distances for a tree obtained by assigning weights of x to branches specified by A_T.

Problem Formulation: Given a query tree T and a reference tree R over the same leaf set ($L_T = L_R$), we define the Topology-Constrained Metric Matching (TCMM) problem to assign new branch lengths l_T^* to all edges of T such that:

$$l_T^* = \operatorname*{arg\,min}_{x \in \mathbb{R}^{|E_T|}, x \geq 0} \|d_R - A_T x\|_2^2 . \tag{1}$$

Expanding this objective function, we get

$$\operatorname{Obj}(x; R, T) = \|d_R - A_T x\|_2^2 = x^\top A_T^\top A_T x - 2(A_T^\top d_R)^\top x + \|d_R\|_2^2 . \tag{2}$$

The gradient of $\operatorname{Obj}(x; R, T)$ with respect to x can be computed as follows:

$$\nabla_x \operatorname{Obj}(x; R, T) = 2A_T^\top A_T x - 2A_T^\top d_R \tag{3}$$

It can easily be shown that the Hessian matrix of this objective function with respect to x is a positive semidefinite matrix ($\nabla_x^2 \operatorname{Obj}(x; R, T) = 2A_T^\top A_T \succeq 0$). Thus, $\operatorname{Obj}(x; R, T)$ is a convex function and a globally optimal solution can be attained using standard convex optimization techniques.

Scalability: Equation (3) depends on the two matrices $A_T^\top A_T$ and $A_T^\top d_R$. Naively computing these matrices from their building blocks A_T and d_R requires $O(n^4)$ and $O(n^3)$ time for $A_T^\top A_T$ and $A_T^\top d_R$, respectively, and $O(n^3)$ memory. However, a dynamic programming algorithm enables computing $A_T^\top A_T$ and $A_T^\top d_R$ in quadratic time and memory without forming A_T and d_R matrices.

Computing $A_T^\top A_T$. Every element $[e, e'] \in E_T \times E_T$ of $A_T^\top A_T$ corresponds to the number of pairs of leaves $u, v \in L_T$ such that $e, e' \in p_T(u, v)$. Let $|L_T(e)|$ be the number of leaves below the head of the edge $e \in E_T$. For any (e, e'), if e is a descendent of e', $A_T^\top A_T$ at $[e, e']$ is computed as:

$$A_T^\top A_{T[e,e']} = |L_T(e)| \times (|L_T| - |L_T(e')|) .$$

Ditto if e' is a descendent of e. If neither edge is a descendent of the other, then:

$$A_T^\top A_{T[e,e']} = |L_T(e)| \times |L_T(e')| .$$

Computing $A_T^\top d_R$. Each edge $e \in E_T$ divides the leaf set L_T into two parts $L_T(e)$ and $L_T \setminus L_T(e)$. The corresponding element of e, $A_T^\top d_{R[e]}$ can be written as

$$A_T^\top d_{R[e]} = \sum_{u \in L_T(e)} \sum_{v \in L_T \setminus L_T(e)} d_R(u, v) . \tag{4}$$

This sum can be computed in a single bottom-up traversal of R for every edge in the query tree. Thus, the matrix $A_T^\top d_R$ can be computed in quadratic time.

TCMM Variants: Here, we address the two challenges that we faced using TCMM in practice and for each challenge we introduce a variant of the TCMM problem that was specifically designed to address it. Note that all the variants of TCMM are still convex functions and therefore could be solved using the same approach as TCMM.

TCMM is agnostic to the query tree's initial branch lengths. The original TCMM problem was designed to require only the topology of the query tree T and not the initial branch lengths. However, in some applications, the query tree already contains branch lengths (perhaps only on some edges). In this case, the original TCMM problem assigns branch lengths to T by completely ignoring the initial branch lengths. To overcome this issue, we introduce the Regularized TCMM problem that incorporates the initial branch lengths l_T:

$$\text{Obj}_2(x; R, T) = \|d_R - A_T x\|_2^2 + \lambda \sigma^2(x/l_T) \tag{5}$$

where σ^2 computes the variance across a vector.

Multiple reference trees. We can easily generalize TCMM to multiple reference trees $\mathcal{R} = \{R_1, R_2, ..., R_k\}$ using:

$$\text{Obj}_3(x; \mathcal{R}, T) = \sum_{R \in \mathcal{R}} \alpha_R^2 \|d_R - A_T x\|_2^2 \tag{6}$$

where α_R is a weight assigned to each reference tree $R \in \mathcal{R}$.

3 Application: Species Tree Branch Length Estimation

Modern phylogenetic analyses often infer a set of gene trees across the genome and summarize them to obtain a species tree S [3]. The gene trees have branch lengths in the unit of the expected number of substitutions per site (SU), but standard summarization methods such as ASTRAL cannot infer SU branch lengths [3]. This shortcoming impedes downstream analyses such as dating. A recent attempt to solve this problem is the CASTLES method [4], which specifically uses coalescent theory to summarize gene tree branch lengths on the fixed species tree topology. Linear algebraic methods such as ERaBLE [1] have been proposed, but they allow limited branch length heterogeneity across the genes and thus were less accurate than CASTLES.

We propose that TCMM can be used to draw SU branch lengths on the species tree as follows: We use the species tree as the query and each gene tree as the reference. TCMM assigns a length to each branch per gene. The resulting distribution of potential branch lengths can be then aggregated using any summary statistic (e.g., geometric mean). In particular, when computing the summary, outliers can be detected and excluded. Alternatively, we can use the multiple reference tree formulation to directly assign a single branch length to each edge of S. Our experiments show that the former approach can produce accurate branch lengths, improving on CASTLES in some scenarios and coming close in others.

Acknowledgments. This research was supported by the National Science Foundation grant IIS 1845967 and the National Institutes of Health (NIH) grant 1R35GM142725.

Availability. Open source software is available at github.com/shayesteh99/TCMM. Data is availabile at github.com/shayesteh99/TCMM-Data.

Preprint. www.biorxiv.org/content/10.1101/2023.11.13.566962v1.

References

1. Binet, M., Gascuel, O., Scornavacca, C., Douzery, P.E.J., Pardi, F.: Fast and accurate branch lengths estimation for phylogenomic trees. BMC Bioinformatics **17**(1), 23 (2016). https://doi.org/10.1186/s12859-015-0821-8
2. Degnan, J.H., Rosenberg, N.A.: Gene tree discordance, phylogenetic inference and the multispecies coalescent. Trends Ecol. Evol. **24**(6), 332–340 (2009). https://doi.org/10.1016/j.tree.2009.01.009
3. Mirarab, S., Nakhleh, L., Warnow, T.: Multispecies coalescent: theory and applications in phylogenetics. Annu. Rev. Ecol. Evol. Syst. **52**(1), 247–268 (2021). https://doi.org/10.1146/annurev-ecolsys-012121-095340
4. Tabatabaee, Y., Zhang, C., Warnow, T., Mirarab, S.: Phylogenomic branch length estimation using quartets. Bioinformatics **39**(Supplement_1), i185–i193 (2023). https://doi.org/10.1093/bioinformatics/btad221

Inferring Allele-Specific Copy Number Aberrations and Tumor Phylogeography from Spatially Resolved Transcriptomics

Cong Ma[1], Metin Balaban[1], Jingxian Liu[2,3], Siqi Chen[2,3], Li Ding[2,3,4,5], and Benjamin J. Raphael[1(✉)]

[1] Department of Computer Science, Princeton University, Princeton, NJ, USA
braphael@cs.princeton.edu
[2] Department of Medicine, Washington University in St. Louis, St. Louis, MO, USA
[3] McDonnell Genome Institute, Washington University in St. Louis,
St. Louis, MO, USA
[4] Siteman Cancer Center, Washington University in St. Louis, St. Louis, MO, USA
[5] Department of Genetics, Washington University in St. Louis, St. Louis, MO, USA

Abstract. A key challenge in cancer research is to reconstruct the somatic evolution within a tumor over time and across space. Spatially resolved transcriptomics (SRT) measures gene expression at thousands of spatial locations in a tumor, but does not directly reveal genetic aberrations. We introduce CalicoST, an algorithm to simultaneously infer allele-specific copy number aberrations (CNAs) and a spatial model of tumor evolution from SRT of tumor slices. By modeling CNA-induced perturbations in both total and allele-specific gene expression, CalicoST identifies important types of CNAs - including copy-neutral loss of heterozygosity (CNLOH) and mirrored subclonal CNAs- that are invisible to total copy number analysis. CalicoST achieves high accuracy by modeling both correlations in space with a Hidden Markov Random Field and across genomic segments with a Hidden Markov Model.

Keywords: spatially resolved transcriptomics · cancer · copy number aberrations · evolution · phylogeography

1 Introduction

Tumors evolve through acquisition of somatic mutations—including single nucleotide variations (SNVs), copy number aberrations (CNAs), and large-scale structural variations (SVs). Sequencing of somatic mutations [7] enabled the reconstruction of a tumor's evolutionary history [13] Tumors also exhibit heterogeneity and undergo evolution within physical space. Incorporating the spatial perspective into somatic evolution studies [11] has been hampered by a lack of spatial data.

Recent technological advances in spatial sequencing provide a promising direction for studies of spatiotemporal tumor evolution. Spatially resolved transcriptomics (SRT) technologies that measure RNA from thousands of spatial

J. Ma (Ed.): RECOMB 2024, LNCS 14758, pp. 466–469, 2024.
https://doi.org/10.1007/978-1-0716-3989-4_54

locations in a tissue have found extensive applications in analyzing tumors [1,9]. However, somatic mutations occur in DNA and thus are not directly measured by SRT.

Large CNAs often perturb the transcriptome, but inferring CNAs from transcriptomic data is challenging. Gene expression is regulated by many factors and it is difficult to determine whether an observed expression change is due to CNAs or other causes. In addition, SRT, as well as single-cell RNA sequencing data (scRNA-seq) are sparse, generally having more than 75% zero counts across genes and cells/spots. Furthermore, SRT technologies (such as 10x Genomics Visium [6] and Slide-seqV2 [14]) measure a mixture of cells at each spatial spot, where normal cells can dilute the signals for CNAs. These challenges limit the performance of existing methods [2,4,12] to infer CNAs from scRNA-seq or SRT data without additional DNA sequencing data.

Importantly, a CNA in cancer alters one of the two parental chromosomes, and thus the identification of *allele-specific CNAs* is essential for accurately reconstructing tumor phylogenies. Particularly, copy number neutral loss of heterozygosity (CNLOH) [10] and mirrored-subclonal CNAs [8] can only be identified by allele-specific CNAs. A few methods for identification of allele-specific CNAs from scRNA-seq data have been recently been developed [5], but these methods are challenged by the sparse signals in scRNA-seq data.

2 Methods

We introduce a new algorithm, CalicoST, to infer allele-specific CNAs in SRT data and use these CNAs to reconstruct the phylogeographic evolution of a tumor. CalicoST identifies CNLOH and mirrored-subclonal CNAs. To reduce the sparsity, CalicoST models the correlation among adjacent spots using a Hidden Markov Random Field and the correlation of copy numbers between adjacent genomic regions using a Hidden Markov Model. Mathematically, the input to CalicoST is the transcript count matrix $\mathbf{X}$, the allele count matrix $\mathbf{Y}$ across genomic bins and across spots, and the spatial coordinates $\mathbf{S}$. CalicoST infers a clone label ℓ for each spot, a copy number state $\mathbf{Z}$ for each genomic bin with each clone, and a read depth ratio (RDR) parameter μ and a B allele frequency (BAF) parameter $\mathbf{p}$ for each copy number state by maximizing the likelihood of the observed data:

$$\max_{\ell,\mathbf{Z},\mu,\mathbf{p}} \mathbb{P}(\mathbf{X},\mathbf{Y} \mid \ell,\mathbf{Z},\mu,\mathbf{p})\mathbb{P}(\mathbf{Z})\mathbb{P}(\ell \mid \mathbf{S}). \tag{1}$$

We assume that the probability $\mathbb{P}(\mathbf{Z})$ follows a Markov model for each clone m along the genome with genomic bins indexed by g:

$$\mathbb{P}(\mathbf{Z}) = \prod_m \left(\mathbb{P}(\mathbf{Z}_{m,1}) \prod_g \mathbb{P}(\mathbf{Z}_{m,g+1} \mid \mathbf{Z}_{m,g})) \right). \tag{2}$$

We assume the probability $\mathbb{P}(\ell \mid \mathbf{S})$ follows a Markov Random Field, specifically, a Potts model that considers the abundance α_m of each clone m and the coherence between each pair of spatially adjacent spot (n,n'):

$$\log \mathbb{P}(\boldsymbol{\ell} \mid \mathbf{S}) \propto \sum_n \sum_m \alpha \mathbb{1}[\ell_n = m] + \sum_{n,n'} e_{n,n'} \mathbb{1}[\ell_n = \ell_{n'}] \tag{3}$$

To model the count data, CalicoST uses a Negative Binomial distribution for the emission probability of observed transcript counts $\mathbf{X}$, for which the expectation is parameterized by the RDR parameter of the corresponding copy number state:

$$\mathbb{E}(\mathbf{X}_{g,n} \mid \ell_n = m, \mathbf{Z}_{g,m} = k) \propto \boldsymbol{\mu}_k, \tag{4}$$

and uses a Beta-binomial distribution for the emission probability of the observed allele counts $\mathbf{Y}$, for which the expectation is parameterized by the BAF parameter:

$$\mathbb{E}(\mathbf{Y}_{g,n} \mid \ell_n = m, \mathbf{Z}_{g,m} = k) \propto \mathbf{p}_k, \tag{5}$$

CalicoST uses a coordinate ascend method to iteratively solve for copy number states $\mathbf{Z}, \boldsymbol{\mu}, \mathbf{p}$ and for clone labels $\boldsymbol{\ell}$.

Finally, CalicoST constructs a phylogeny of cancer clones and a phylogeographic model that describes the spread of the tumor across physical space using the inferred CNAs. CalicoST focuses on the inferred loss-of-heterozygosity (LOH) events, which is an irreversible phylogenetic character, to reconstruct a tumor phylogeny. Using the inferred phylogeny, CalicoST reconstructs the spatial tumor evolution, or a phylogeography, by inferring the spatial locations of each node in the phylogeny using a Gaussian diffusion model. Specifically, we assume the spatial distance between a node v and its parent $p(v)$ in the phylogenetic tree follows a Gaussian distribution with a variance proportional to the number of mutations $w_{v,p(v)}$ on the edge:

$$s_v \sim \mathcal{N}(s_{p(v)}, w_{v,p(v)}I).$$

3   Results

Applying CalicoST to SRT data from multiple slices of a prostate cancer patient [3], we identified mirrored subclonal CNAs and a phylogeography where two halves of the prostate coincide with the lineages.

Acknowledgements. This research is supported by NIH/NCI grants U24CA248453 and U24CA264027 to B.J.R and NIH grants U2CCA233303, U54AG075934, U24CA210972, R01HG009711 and R01CA260112 to L.D. C.M. is a Damon Runyon Fellow supported by the Damon Runyon Cancer Research Foundation (DRQ-15-22).

Availability. CalicoST software is available at https://github.com/raphael-group/CalicoST. A preprint is available at https://doi.org/10.1101/2024.03.09.584244.

References

1. Barkley, D., et al.: Cancer cell states recur across tumor types and form specific interactions with the tumor microenvironment. Nat. Genet. **54**(8), 1192–1201 (2022)

2. Elyanow, R., Zeira, R., Land, M., Raphael, B.J.: STARCH: copy number and clone inference from spatial transcriptomics data. Phys. Biol. **18**(3), 035001 (2021)

3. Erickson, A., et al.: Spatially resolved clonal copy number alterations in benign and malignant tissue. Nature **608**(7922), 360–367 (2022)

4. Gao, R., et al.: Delineating copy number and clonal substructure in human tumors from single-cell transcriptomes. Nat. Biotechnol. **39**(5), 599–608 (2021)

5. Gao, T., et al.: Haplotype-aware analysis of somatic copy number variations from single-cell transcriptomes. Nat. Biotechnol. **41**, 1–10 (2022)

6. 10x Genomics: Spatial transcriptomics (2021). https://www.10xgenomics.com/spatial-transcriptomics/

7. Gerlinger, M., et al.: Intratumor heterogeneity and branched evolution revealed by multiregion sequencing. N. Engl. J. Med. **366**(10), 883–892 (2012)

8. Jamal-Hanjani, M., et al.: Tracking the evolution of non-small-cell lung cancer. N. Engl. J. Med. **376**(22), 2109–2121 (2017)

9. Ji, A.L., et al.: Multimodal analysis of composition and spatial architecture in human squamous cell carcinoma. Cell **182**(2), 497–514 (2020)

10. Langdon, J.A., et al.: Combined genome-wide allelotyping and copy number analysis identify frequent genetic losses without copy number reduction in medulloblastoma. Genes Chromosom. Cancer **45**(1), 47–60 (2006)

11. Noble, R., et al.: Spatial structure governs the mode of tumour evolution. Nat. Ecol. Evol. **6**(2), 207–217 (2022)

12. Patel, A.P., et al.: Single-cell RNA-seq highlights intratumoral heterogeneity in primary glioblastoma. Science **344**(6190), 1396–1401 (2014)

13. Schwartz, R., Schäffer, A.A.: The evolution of tumour phylogenetics: principles and practice. Nat. Rev. Genet. **18**(4), 213–229 (2017)

14. Stickels, R.R., et al.: Highly sensitive spatial transcriptomics at near-cellular resolution with Slide-seqV2. Nat. Biotechnol. **39**(3), 313–319 (2021)

Contrastive Fitness Learning: Reprogramming Protein Language Models for Low-N Learning of Protein Fitness Landscape

Junming Zhao[1,2], Chao Zhang[1], and Yunan Luo[1(✉)]

[1] School of Computational Science and Engineering, Georgia Institute of Technology, Atlanta, GA, USA
{chaozhang,yunan}@gatech.edu
[2] School of Data Science, Fudan University, Shanghai, China
20307110324@fudan.edu.cn

Abstract. Machine learning (ML) is revolutionizing our ability to model the fitness landscape of protein sequences. Recently, the protein language model (pLM) has become the foundation of state-of-the-art ML solutions for many problems in protein biology. However, significant challenges remain in leveraging pLMs for protein fitness prediction, in part due to the disparity between the scarce number of sequences functionally characterized by high-throughput assays and the massive data samples required for training large pLMs. To bridge this gap, we introduce Contrastive Fitness Learning (ConFit), a pLM-based ML method for learning the protein fitness landscape with limited (low-N) experimental fitness measurements as training data (Fig. 1). We propose a novel contrastive learning strategy to fine-tune the pre-trained pLM, tailoring it to achieve protein-specific fitness prediction while avoiding overfitting.

Keywords: protein engineering · protein language models

1 Introduction

Protein engineering aims to expand the function capabilities of natural proteins. Machine learning (ML) has emerged as an effective approach to guide and accelerate protein engineering by predicting the sequence-fitness relationship, offering a faster and more cost-effective surrogate for experimental fitness screening in wet labs. However, while modern ML approaches such as neural networks often require $>10^5$ samples for training, screening variant fitness can be lab-intensive and require developing tailored assays for a specific function, with typical experiments yielding only 10^0–10^3 labeled variants. This discrepancy highlights a critical challenge in developing ML models capable of providing accurate fitness predictions with small-size ('low N') training data. Current strategies mitigate this issue by either fully fine-tuning pre-trained language models (pLMs), which leads to overfitting in low-N scenarios, or merely adjusting the pLM's top layer, preserving the remainder unchanged, which may sacrifice prediction accuracy [1,2].

J. Ma (Ed.): RECOMB 2024, LNCS 14758, pp. 470–474, 2024.
https://doi.org/10.1007/978-1-0716-3989-4_55

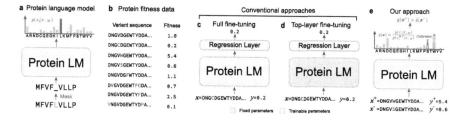

Fig. 1. Overview of ConFit. (a) pLM predicts the probability of amino acid at position given other unmasked positions. (b) Example of protein fitness data in which the variants of a wildtype (WT) sequence are experimentally characterized with fitness values. (c–d) Conventional approaches for fine-tuning pre-trained pLMs, including "full fine-tuning" which updates all parameters, and "top-layer fine-tuning" which trains the top-layer on the fitness data while fixing other parameters. (e) Our approach, ConFit, calibrates pre-trained pLM for low-N fitness prediction through contrastive learning.

2 Methods

In this work, we introduce ConFit (<u>Con</u>trastive <u>Fit</u>ness Learning), an ML algorithm that effectively reprograms a pre-trained pLM to high-accuracy, sample-efficient fitness prediction model under low-N settings. Our key idea is to calibrate the pre-trained pLM through contrastive learning such that its predicted sequence probability will correlate with the input protein's fitness.

From pLM to fitness prediction. Formally, we denote the amino acid (AA) sequence of a protein by $\boldsymbol{x} = (x_1, \ldots, x_L) \in \mathcal{X}^L$, where x_i is the i-th AA, L the sequence length, and $\mathcal{X}$ the alphabet of possible AAs. Masked pLMs [3,4] aims to learn the conditional probability $p(x_i|x_{-i})$ of an AA appearing at a given position, conditioned on the sequence excluding that position, i.e., $x_{-i} = (x_1, \ldots, x_{i-1}, x_{i+1}, \ldots, x_L)$ (Fig. 1a). We quantify the impact of a given mutation by comparing its pLM portability with the reference probability of the wild type. Specifically, let $\boldsymbol{x}^{\mathrm{MT}}$ and $\boldsymbol{x}^{\mathrm{WT}}$ denote the mutant and wild-type sequences, respectively, and M the mutated sites. The effect of a substitution $x_i^{\mathrm{WT}} \rightarrow x_i^{\mathrm{MT}}$ is quantified by the log probability ratio at the mutation sites:

$$\hat{y}_\theta(\boldsymbol{x}^{\mathrm{MT}}) = \sum_{i \in M} \log p_\theta(x_i^{\mathrm{MT}}|x_{-M}) - \log p_\theta(x_i^{\mathrm{WT}}|x_{-M}), \qquad (1)$$

Contrastive fine-tuning. Given a small (low-N) set of functionally characterized variants $\{\boldsymbol{x}^{(k)}, y^{(k)}\}_{k=1}^N$ of a particular protein, where $\boldsymbol{x}_k$'s are the variant sequences and y_k's are the experimentally measured fitness values, we sample pairs $(\boldsymbol{x}^+, y^+)$ and $(\boldsymbol{x}^-, y^-)$ such that $y^+ > y^-$ and use Bradley-Terry (BT) model [5] to encourage the model to rank predicted fitness scores in the correct order relative to the ground truth:

$$\mathcal{L}_{\mathrm{cal}} = \sum_{y^{(i)} > y^{(j)}} \log \left[1 + \exp\left(-[\hat{y}_\theta(\boldsymbol{x}^{(i)}) - \hat{y}_\theta(\boldsymbol{x}^{(j)})]\right)\right] \qquad (2)$$

Regularization. To better avoid catastrophic forgetting, we introduce a Kullback-Leibler (KL) divergence-based regularization to prevent the calibrated distribution p_θ deviating too far away from the pre-trained distribution p_{θ_0}:

$$\mathcal{L}_{\text{reg}} = \sum_i p_\theta(x_i^{\text{MT}}|x_{-i}^{\text{MT}}) \log \frac{p_\theta(x_i^{\text{MT}}|x_{-i})}{p_{\theta_0}(x_i^{\text{MT}}|x_{-i}^{\text{MT}})} \tag{3}$$

Our final loss function is a linear combination of the calibration loss and the KL regularizer: $\mathcal{L} = \mathcal{L}_{\text{cal}} + \lambda\mathcal{L}_{\text{reg}}$, where λ is a coefficient that balances the two losses.

Efficient Fine-Tuning with Low-Rank Reparameterization. We further employed Low-Rank Adaptation (LoRA) [6], a parameter-efficient fine-tuning (PEFT) method to reduce the number of updated parameters. By factorizing the weight updates in ESM1v, LoRA reduced the number of updated parameters to 1.35 million, a 99.79% reduction compared to the 650 million parameters in the full ESM-1v model.

Enhancing Fitness Prediction with MSA Context Retrieval. To reinforce the local evolutionary contexts specific to the input protein, we searched in the UniProt protein sequence database for its homology and built a multiple sequence alignment (MSA). Next, we fit DeepSequence [7] on the MSA to estimate sequence likelihood $p_{\text{MSA}}(\boldsymbol{x})$. DeepSequence used the log-odd ratio to predict the fitness of a variant: $\hat{y}_{\text{MSA}}(\boldsymbol{x}^{\text{MT}}) = \log p_{\text{MSA}}(\boldsymbol{x}^{\text{MT}}) - \log p_{\text{MSA}}(\boldsymbol{x}^{\text{WT}})$. We then refined the pLM-based fitness prediction $\hat{y}_\theta(\boldsymbol{x})$ by fusing it with the MSA-based prediction $\hat{y}_{\text{MSA}}(\boldsymbol{x})$: $\hat{y}(\boldsymbol{x}) = \alpha\hat{y}_\theta(\boldsymbol{x}) + (1 - \alpha)\hat{y}_{\text{MSA}}$.

3   Results

Evaluated across over 30 benchmark datasets of protein fitness, We systematically varied the size of the training set by randomly sampling $N = 48, 96, 168, 240$ variants from the non-test data. Compared to baseline methods, ConFit consistently outperformed existing supervised methods and unsupervised methods across various training data sizes (Fig. 2), which demonstrated the superior low-N fitness learning ability of ConFit.

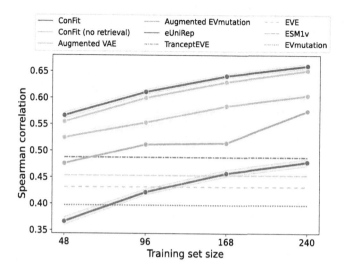

Fig. 2. Evaluations on low-N learning of protein fitness. Prediction performance of methods trained on $N = 48, 96, 168$, or 240 samples. Solid lines and error bands indicate the mean±SD of Spearman correlations achieved by supervised methods. Performances of unsupervised methods are shown in dashed lines.

Acknowledgements. Y.L. is supported in part by the NIH (R35GM150890), the Amazon Research Award, and the Seed Grant Program from the NSF AI Institute: Molecule Maker Lab Institute at the University of Illinois Urbana-Champaign (UIUC). This work used the Delta Supercomputer at NCSA of UIUC through allocation CIS230097 from the NSF ACCESS program and the computational resources provided by Microsoft Azure through the Cloud Hub program at GaTech IDEaS.

Code availability. The source code of ConFit is available at https://github.com/luo-group/ConFit.

Full manuscript: The full manuscript of this work is available at https://doi.org/10.1101/2024.02.11.579859.

References

1. Biswas, S., Khimulya, G., Alley, E.C., Esvelt, K.M., Church, G.M.: Low-n protein engineering with data-efficient deep learning. Nat. Methods **18**(4), 389–396 (2021)
2. Hsu, C., Nisonoff, H., Fannjiang, C., Listgarten, J.: Learning protein fitness models from evolutionary and assay-labeled data. Nat. Biotechnol. **40**(7), 1114–1122 (2022)
3. Rives, A., et al.: Biological structure and function emerge from scaling unsupervised learning to 250 million protein sequences. Proc. Natl. Acad. Sci. **118**(15), e2016239118 (2021)

4. Lin, Z., et al.: Evolutionary-scale prediction of atomic-level protein structure with a language model. Science **379**(6637), 1123–1130 (2023)
5. Bradley, R.A., Terry, M.E.: Rank analysis of incomplete block designs: I. the method of paired comparisons. Biometrika **39**(3/4), 324–345 (1952)
6. Hu, E.J., et al.: Lora: low-rank adaptation of large language models. In: International Conference on Learning Representations (2022)
7. Riesselman, A.J., Ingraham, J.B., Marks, D.S.: Deep generative models of genetic variation capture the effects of mutations. Nat. Methods **15**(10), 816–822 (2018)

Scalable Summary Statistics-Based Heritability Estimation Method with Individual Genotype Level Accuracy

Moonseong Jeong[1], Ali Pazokitoroudi[1,2], Zhengtong Liu[1], and Sriram Sankararaman[1,3,4,5(✉)]

[1] Department of Computer Science, UCLA, Los Angeles, CA, USA
[2] Department of Human Genetics, David Geffen School of Medicine, UCLA, Los Angeles, CA, USA
[3] Department of Computational Medicine, David Geffen School of Medicine, UCLA, Los Angeles, CA, USA
{bronsonj,sriram}@cs.ucla.edu
[4] Deparment of Epidemiology, Harvard School of Public Health, Boston, MA, USA
[5] Program in Medical and Population Genetics, Broad Institute of MIT and Harvard, Cambridge, MA, USA

Abstract. SNP heritability, the proportion of phenotypic variation explained by genotyped SNPs, is an important parameter in understanding the genetic architecture underlying various diseases and traits. Methods that aim to estimate SNP heritability from individual genotype and phenotype data are limited by their ability to scale to Biobank-scale datasets and by the restrictions in access to individual-level data. These limitations have motivated the development of methods that only require summary statistics. While the availability of publicly accessible summary statistics makes them widely applicable, these methods lack the accuracy of methods that utilize individual genotypes.

Here we present a SUMmary statistics-based Randomized Haseman-Elston regression (SUM-RHE), a method that can estimate the SNP heritability of complex phenotypes with accuracies comparable to approaches that require individual genotypes, while exclusively relying on summary statistics. SUM-RHE employs Genome-Wide Association Study (GWAS) summary statistics and statistics obtained on a reference population, which can be efficiently estimated and readily shared for public use. Our results demonstrate that SUM-RHE obtains estimates of SNP heritability that are substantially more accurate compared to other summary statistic methods and on par with methods that rely on individual-level data.

Keywords: Heritability · Summary statistics · Biobank · Scalability

1 Introduction

The exponentially decreasing cost of genotyping and sequencing technologies has led to an increase in the number and size of biobanks, covering a wide range

J. Ma (Ed.): RECOMB 2024, LNCS 14758, pp. 475–478, 2024.
https://doi.org/10.1007/978-1-0716-3989-4_56

of populations. One of the major analyses often performed with these large biobanks is estimating heritability, defined as the phenotypic variance explained by the variance in the genotype [1]. Heritability estimates in these large data sets have provided new insights into the underlying genetic architecture of complex traits. Most methods fit linear mixed models (LMMs) to map the variation in genotypes measured at single nucleotide polymorphisms (SNPs) to the variation in phenotypes and thereby estimate the SNP heritability, *i.e.*, the proportion of phenotypic variance explained by genotyped SNPs. Given the high dimensionality of the genotypes and the large sample sizes of biobanks, fitting or parameter estimation in LMMs is computationally prohibitive. Many methods have been proposed to reduce computational complexity while retaining statistical accuracy [2–6]. These methods, while highly accurate, generally take hours or days to run and require access to individual genotypes and phenotypes.

The rise of large-scale biobanks has also brought increased attention to the issue of genomic privacy due to a surge in security breaches. Nowadays there is a growing preference for summary statistics-based methods due to their portability and speed, even though they may sacrifice some statistical power compared to methods that use individual-level data [4,7,8]. Such a loss in statistical power is particularly pronounced in smaller sample sizes, and may result in inflated estimates of heritability due to underestimation of linkage disequilibrium (LD) [4], even if correct reference summary statistics were used.

To address these challenges of heritability estimation in large biobanks, we propose SUM-RHE (SUMmary-statistics Randomized Haseman-Elston regression), by extending our previous work, Randomized Haseman-Elston regression (RHE) [5,6], to work exclusively on summary statistics. This adaptation leverages the observation that the trace estimates of the squared genetic relatedness matrix (GRM), that are needed to compute the method-of-moments (MoM) estimator underlying RHE, can be related to population-level parameters. By combining these trace estimates from a reference sample with GWAS summary statistics from a target sample (consisting of individuals sampled from the same population as the reference sample), we can reconstruct the MoM estimates for the target sample without access to the individual data. In comprehensive simulations across various genetic architectures and scenarios, we show that SUM-RHE estimates are on par with methods that rely on individual-level data and substantially more accurate than summary statistic-based methods, all while exclusively utilizing summary statistics.

2   Method

For a standardized phenotype $\boldsymbol{y}$ and genotype $\boldsymbol{X}$ of M SNPs and N individuals, SUM-RHE fits a LMM under the model assumption that the linear SNP effect sizes $\boldsymbol{\beta}$ and the uniform noise $\boldsymbol{\epsilon}$ follow some arbitrary distribution $\mathcal{D}$:

$$ \boldsymbol{y} = \boldsymbol{X}\boldsymbol{\beta} + \boldsymbol{\epsilon}, \quad \boldsymbol{\beta} \sim \mathcal{D}\left(0, \frac{\sigma_g^2}{M}\mathbf{I}_M\right), \quad \boldsymbol{\epsilon} \sim \mathcal{D}\left(0, \sigma_e^2\mathbf{I}_N\right) \tag{1} $$

where σ_g^2 is the genetic variance component and σ_e^2 the noise. The SNP-heritability is then defined as the proportion of genetic variance over total phenotypic variance, $h_{SNP}^2 = \frac{\sigma_g^2}{\sigma_g^2 + \sigma_e^2}$. The Haseman-Elston regression minimizes the Frobenius norm of the difference between the population and the sample covariance matrices $\boldsymbol{y}\boldsymbol{y}^\top$, which results in the analytical solution for heritability:

$$\widehat{h^2} = \frac{\frac{1}{M}\left(\frac{\boldsymbol{X}^\top \boldsymbol{y}}{\sqrt{\boldsymbol{y}^\top \boldsymbol{y}}}\right)^\top \frac{\boldsymbol{X}^\top \boldsymbol{y}}{\sqrt{\boldsymbol{y}^\top \boldsymbol{y}}} - 1}{\frac{tr(\boldsymbol{K}^2)}{N} - 1} \tag{2}$$

where $\boldsymbol{K} = \frac{1}{M}\boldsymbol{X}\boldsymbol{X}^\top$ is defined as the GRM. The biggest bottleneck here is estimating the trace of $\boldsymbol{K}^2$ matrix, and the RHE framework addresses it by stochastically estimating the trace instead. SUMRHE further extends this framework by observing that the numerator of Eq. 2 can be expressed as the z-scores of (linear) GWAS effect sizes of the SNPs for phenotype $\boldsymbol{y}$, while the denominator only depends on the genotype matrix $\boldsymbol{X}$:

$$\widehat{h^2}_{MOM} = \frac{\frac{z^\top z}{M} - 1}{N\hat{\rho}} \tag{3}$$

Here $\hat{\rho} = \frac{1}{N}\left(\frac{tr(\boldsymbol{K}^2)}{N} - 1\right)$ is the stochastic population parameter, which can be efficiently calculated and readily shared, that we can reuse to estimate heritability for the given population. Our proposal is to release these $\hat{\rho}$ estimates as population summary statistics, so that in combination with GWAS summary statistics, researchers can easily perform heritability estimation with SUM-RHE.

A Python version of SUM-RHE, example scripts and documentation are available as open source on Github at https://github.com/sriramlab/SUMRHE.

3   Results

We performed a comprehensive benchmark of SUM-RHE against other widely used methods under various genetic architectures. We tested 3 individual data-based methods (BOLT-REML, GCTA-REML, and RHE) and 3 summary-based methods (LDSC, SumHer-GCTA, and SUM-RHE). Figure 1 shows the MSE of the five methods relative to RHE in 18 different settings of true $h^2 = 0.1, 0.25, 0.4$, sample sizes of $N = 10k, 50k$ and proportion of causal SNPs $p = 1.0, 0.1, 0.01$. We see that SUM-RHE, while relying exclusively on summary statistics, retains a performance comparable to methods that use individual data directly. Compared to other summary-based methods, SUM-RHE substantially improves accuracy: LDSC exhibits MSE ranging from 244% to 478% relative to that of SUM-RHE (mean 356%), while SumHer-GCTA has MSE ranging from 94% to 331% relative to that of SUM-RHE (mean 167%).

Full Paper: A complete manuscript with detailed derivations and results can be accessed at: https://www.biorxiv.org/content/10.1101/2024.03.09.584258v1.

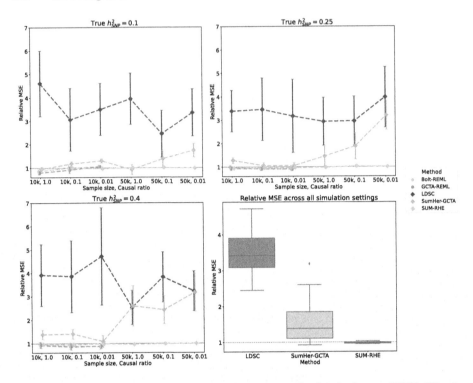

Fig. 1. MSE of heritability estimates of each method relative to RHE. The dot and errorbar denote the relative MSE and the 95% CI calculated based on bootstrap resampling, respectively.

References

1. Falconer, D.S.: Introduction to Quantitative Genetics. Pearson Education India (1996)
2. Yang, J., et al.: GCTA: a tool for genome-wide complex trait analysis. Am. J. Hum. Genet. **88**(1), 76–82 (2011)
3. Loh, P., et al.: Contrasting genetic architectures of Schizophrenia and other complex diseases using fast variance-components analysis. Nat. Genet. **47**(12), 1385–1392 (2015)
4. Zhou, X.: A unified framework for variance component estimation with summary statistics in genome-wide association studies. Ann. Appl. Biol. Stat. **11**(4), 2027 (2017)
5. Pazokitoroudi, A., et al.: Efficient variance components analysis across millions of genomes. Nat. Commun. **11**(1), 4020 (2020)
6. Wu, Y., et al.: A scalable estimator of SNP heritability for biobank-scale data. Bioinform. **34**(13), i187–i194 (2018)
7. Bulik-Sullivan, B., et al.: LD Score regression distinguishes confounding from polygenicity in genome-wide association studies. Nat. Genet. **47**(3), 291–295 (2015)
8. Speed, D., Balding, D.J.: SumHer better estimates the SNP heritability of complex traits from summary statistics. Nat. Genet. **51**(2), 277–284 (2019)

scMulan: A Multitask Generative Pre-Trained Language Model for Single-Cell Analysis

Haiyang Bian[1], Yixin Chen[1], Xiaomin Dong[1], Chen Li[1], Minsheng Hao[1], Sijie Chen[1], Jinyi Hu[2], Maosong Sun[2], Lei Wei[1(✉)], and Xuegong Zhang[1,3(✉)]

[1] MOE Key Laboratory of Bioinformatics and Bioinformatics Division of BNRIST, Department of Automation, Tsinghua University, Beijing, China
{weilei92,zhangxg}@tsinghua.edu.cn
[2] Department of Computer Science and Technology, Tsinghua University, Beijing, China
[3] Center for Synthetic and Systems Biology, School of Life Sciences and School of Medicine, Tsinghua University, Beijing, China

Abstract. Gene expression could be perceived as a form of "cell language", with underlying regulatory mechanisms akin to biological grammar. Decoding this language is critical in understanding cellular functions and behaviors. In this study, we proposed a new pre-training paradigm by integrating rich metadata and pre-training tasks, and developed scMulan, a multitask generative pre-trained language model for single-cell analyses. scMulan can accomplish multiple tasks in zero-shot manner such as cell-type annotation, batch integration, and conditional cell generation, guided by different task prompts. scMulan is also ready to be expanded for novel tasks through fine-tuning.

Keywords: Foundation Models · Single-cell Data · Pretraining

1 Introduction

Recently, a trend has emerged that well-designed task-specific models are being surpassed by foundation models with transformer architectures, also known as large language models (LLMs), in various tasks within the natural language processing (NLP) domain [1–4]. These models benefit from extensive pre-training on vast corpus, showcasing their prowess when fine-tuned for specific tasks or applied in a zero-shot manner. Inspired by those progress, some pre-trained models have been developed in the single-cell field [5–8], with typical pre-training tasks such as predicting masked gene expressions. These models demonstrated the feasibility of developing foundation models for single-cell data to improve performance on downstream tasks such as cell-type annotation and batch correction through fine-tuning. Yet, their zero-shot capabilities remain relatively underdeveloped [9]. Existing methods primarily focused on learning the information of gene regulations but underleveraged or even ignored the vast metadata information available in single-cell data in the pre-training stage.

H. Bian, Y. Chen, and X. Dong—Equal contribution.
Full-paper arvix: https://www.biorxiv.org/content/10.1101/2024.01.25.577152v1.

© The Author(s), under exclusive license to Springer Nature Switzerland AG 2024
J. Ma (Ed.): RECOMB 2024, LNCS 14758, pp. 479–482, 2024.
https://doi.org/10.1007/978-1-0716-3989-4_57

2 Methods

We developed scMulan, a **mu**ltitask generative pre-trained **lan**guage model for single-cell analyses, to fully exploit information in single-cell transcriptomic data and abundant metadata (Fig. 1). We proposed a formulation of "cell language" that transforms gene expressions and metadata terms into "cell sentences" (c-sentences), and developed a large generative pre-training model to learn the cell language. We designed multiple pre-training tasks that bridge the information in the transcriptomic data and metadata, and integrated these tasks within the unified generative framework of cell language modeling. We defined multiple natural-language-based terms as prompts for the cell language to make the model aware of the tasks it is expected to perform. In this way, scMulan can generate not only gene expressions, but also metadata and other terms according to the tasks.

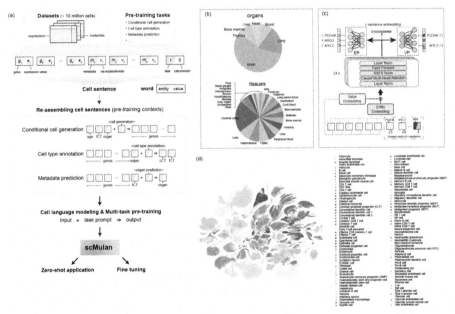

Fig. 1. The overview of scMulan. (a) The workflow of scMulan. We use cell sentences to represent scRNA-seq data into dense sentences and assemble the expressed genes and metadata to form multiple pre-training tasks. scMulan could conduct multiple tasks guided by predefined prompts by fine-tuning or in a zero-shot manner. (b) The proportion of organs and tissues in the pre-training dataset hECA-10M. (c) The detailed architecture of scMulan. (d) UMAP visualization of the cell embeddings from scMulan on a 10% validation set of hECA-10M, colored by all cell types. cCT = coarse-grained cell type, fCT = fine-grained cell type, EP = Entity prediction head, and VP = Value prediction head.

3   Results

We trained scMulan with dataset hECA-10M of more than 10 million manually annotated single-cell RNA-seq data we curated in the upgrade of hECA1.0 [10] and evaluated its effectiveness on multiple downstream tasks in zero-shot manner or through fine-tuning. The experiments validated scMulan's zero-shot capabilities in cell-type annotation and batch integration. Its zero-shot application results in cell-type annotation on the external datasets achieved a 10% of improvement over existing fine-tuned methods. On the hand, the fine-tuned scMulan model on just 40% of samples achieved competitive performance with the other models on 100% of training samples, and surpassed them when fine-tuned with 60% or more samples. In batch integration tasks, scMulan achieved competitive performance with fine-tuned models but worked much faster. We also applied scMulan to generate single-cell transcriptomic data conditioned on various metadata terms such as organs and cell types, and obtained synthetic cells with high similarity with real data.

4   Conclusion

We proposed a new strategy to represent the language of gene expression and metadata of single cells, and developed a new foundation model scMulan to facilitate multiple downstream single-cell analysis tasks using a single pre-trained model. It stands out as the first foundation model capable of performing multiple tasks without the need for additional fine-tuning or adding external layers upon the model. Experiments showed scMulan's superior zero-shot capabilities in cell-type annotation, batch integration and synthetic cell generation. scMulan can be well scaled up to larger foundation models and can serve as a unified model for various single-cell analysis tasks to empower biological research.

Acknowledgments. The work is supported in part of National Natural Science Foundation of China (grants 62373210, 62250005), and National Key R&D Program of China (grant 2021YFF1200900).

Availability. The pretrained model of scMulan can be found at https://github.com/SuperBianC/scMulan.

References

1. Bommasani, R., et al.: On the opportunities and risks of foundation models. arXiv preprint arXiv:2108.07258. (2021)
2. Radford, A., Wu, J., Child, R., Luan, D., Amodei, D., Sutskever, I.: Others: language models are unsupervised multitask learners. OpenAI Blog. **1**, 9 (2019)
3. Brown, T., et al.: Others: language models are few-shot learners. Adv. Neural. Inf. Process. Syst. **33**, 1877–1901 (2020)

4. Raffel, C., et al.: Exploring the limits of transfer learning with a unified text-to-text transformer. J. Mach. Learn. Res. **21**, 5485–5551 (2020)

5. Yang, F., et al.: ScBERT as a large-scale pretrained deep language model for cell type annotation of single-cell RNA-seq data. Nat. Mach. Intell. **4**, 852–866 (2022)

6. Cui, H., Wang, C., Maan, H., Pang, K., Luo, F., Wang, B.: scGPT: towards building a foundation model for single-cell multi-omics using generative AI (2023). https://www.biorxiv.org/content/10.1101/2023.04.30.538439v2

7. Hao, M., et al.: Large scale foundation model on single-cell transcriptomics (2023). https://www.biorxiv.org/content/10.1101/2023.05.29.542705v1

8. Theodoris, C.V., et al.: Transfer learning enables predictions in network biology. Nature **618**(7965), 616–624 (2023). https://doi.org/10.1038/s41586-023-06139-9

9. Kedzierska, K.Z., Crawford, L., Amini, A.P., Lu, A.X.: Assessing the limits of zero-shot foundation models in single-cell biology. Bioinformatics (2023). https://doi.org/10.1101/2023.10.16.561085

10. Chen, S., et al.: hECA: the cell-centric assembly of a cell atlas. Iscience 25 (2022)

Author Index

J. Ma (Ed.): RECOMB 2024, LNCS 14758, pp. 483–486, 2024.
https://doi.org/10.1007/978-1-0716-3989-4

Printed in the United States
by Baker & Taylor Publisher Services